W9-AKC-953

Industrial Marketing Management

Industrial Marketing Management

Michael D. Hutt
Miami University

Thomas W. Speh
Miami University

The Dryden Press
Chicago New York Philadelphia
San Francisco Montreal Toronto
London Sydney Tokyo Mexico City
Rio de Janeiro Madrid

Acquisitions Editor: Anita Constant
Project Editor: Kathy Richmond
Design Director: William Seabright
Production Manager: Peter Coveney

Cover design: William Seabright
Copy editing: Jeanne Berger
Indexing: Marlene Targ Brill
Cover photo: Arthur La Zar

Address orders to:
383 Madison Avenue
New York, New York 10017

Address editorial correspondence to:
901 North Elm Street
Hinsdale, Illinois 60521

Library of Congress Catalog Card Number: 80-65803
ISBN: 0-03-052656-6
Printed in the United States of America
2 3 4 144 9 8 7 6 5 4 3

CBS COLLEGE PUBLISHING
The Dryden Press
Holt, Rinehart and Winston
Saunders College Publishing

To Rita
and
To Donna, Scott and Michael

Preface

Special challenges and opportunities confront the marketer who intends to serve the needs of industrial or organizational customers. Commercial enterprises, institutions, and government at all levels constitute a lucrative and complex market worthy of a separate analysis. The past several years have witnessed a rich and growing body of literature and thought on this special marketing area. This work of the 1970s provides the proper environment for developing an integrated treatment of industrial marketing management for the 1980s. A comprehensive treatment of industrial marketing management appears to be particularly appropriate since over one-half of all business school graduates enter industrial product/service firms.

Three objectives guided the development of this volume:

1. *To highlight the similarities between consumer-goods and industrial-goods marketing and to explore the points of departure in depth.* Particular attention is given to industrial market analysis, organizational buying behavior, and the ensuing adjustments required in the marketing strategy elements to reach industrial customers.
2. *To present a managerial rather than a descriptive treatment of industrial marketing.* While some descriptive material is required to convey the dynamic nature of the industrial marketing environment, the relevance of the material is linked to industrial marketing management decision making.
3. *To integrate the growing body of literature into an operational treatment of industrial marketing management.* Here, relevant work is drawn from organizational buying behavior, procurement, organizational behavior, logistics, strategic planning, and the behavioral sciences, as well as specialized studies of industrial marketing strategy components.

The book is structured to provide a complete treatment of industrial marketing while minimizing the degree of overlap with other courses in the marketing curriculum. A basic marketing principles course or relevant managerial experience provides the needed background for this text.

Organization of the Text

The needs and interests of the reader provided the focus in the development of this volume. The authors' goal is to present a clear and interesting examination of industrial marketing management. To this end, each chapter provides an overview, highlights key concepts, and includes several carefully chosen examples of contemporary industrial marketing practices, a cogent summary, and a set of provocative discussion questions.

The book is divided into five parts, with a total of 16 chapters. Part one introduces the distinguishing features of the industrial marketing environment. Careful examination is given to each of the major types of customers that constitute the industrial market. Organizational buying behavior establishes the theme of part two. Here the many forces encircling the organizational buying process are explored in depth. Once this important background is established, part three examines techniques that can be employed in assessing market opportunities. Chapter-length attention is given to the topics of industrial market segmentation, measuring industrial market potential, sales forecasting, and industrial marketing planning. Part four centers on designing industrial marketing strategy. Each component of the marketing mix is examined from an industrial marketing perspective. The final section examines techniques for evaluating industrial marketing strategy and performance. Marketing profitability analysis and industrial marketing research are central themes of this final section. A number of cases, structured by a case planning guide, complete the volume.

Teaching Package

A comprehensive instructor's manual is available which includes suggestions for course design, supporting teaching materials for each chapter. Likewise, guidelines are provided for end-of-chapter discussion questions and suggestions provided for case use and analysis. A large bank of objective questions is also provided in the manual.

Acknowledgments

The development of a textbook draws upon the contributions of many individuals. First, we would like to thank our students and former students at Miami University, the University of Alabama, and the University of Vermont. They provided important input and feedback when selected concepts or chapters were class-tested. Second, we express our gratitude to several distinguished colleagues who carefully reviewed the manuscript at various stages of development and provided incisive comments and valuable suggestions that improved the volume. They include John J. Burnett, Texas Tech University; John A. Czepiel, New York University; Wesley J. Johnston, The Ohio State University; and Gary L. Lilien, Massachusetts Institute of Technology. We also wish to acknowledge the contribution of Paul

F. Anderson, Virginia Polytechnic Institute, who provided important suggestions.

A number of industrial marketing practitioners, including several participants at past management development seminars, provided valuable suggestions and interesting examples. We are especially indebted to Steven G. McCord, Dayco Corporation; Edward Sauer, Industrial Products Division, Proctor & Gamble; Patrick W. Fitzgerald, Cincinnati Electric Equipment Company; Mark F. Stachler, Applied Handling Equipment, Inc.; Gary H. Schmitt, Harding-Jones Paper Company; Jeffrey A. Coopersmith, Distribution Centers, Inc; and Leo Stevens, Tri-State Electric Supply Co., Inc.

The talented staff of The Dryden Press displayed a high level of enthusiasm and professionalism throughout the project. In particular, Anita Constant, Adrian Russert, and Kathy Richmond deserve special praise.

We would also like to thank Robert L. Thornton, chairman of the marketing department at Miami, who enthusiastically supported the project throughout its development. Our appreciation also extends to our departmental secretaries, Carol Muenchenbach and Sue Krause for typing and administrative support.

Finally, but most importantly, our overriding debt is to our wives, Rita and Donna, whose encouragement, understanding, and support were vital to the completion of the volume. Their involvement and dedication are deeply appreciated.

Contents

Part I

The Environment of Industrial Marketing

Chapter 1 An Industrial Marketing Perspective

The industrial market poses special challenges for the marketing manager. This chapter introduces the complex forces that are unique to the industrial marketing environment. After reading this chapter, you will understand:

1. *the basic similarities and differences between consumer and industrial marketing;*
2. *the types of customers in this important market;*
3. *the underlying factors that influence the demand for industrial goods;*
4. *the basic characteristics of industrial products and services;*
5. *some important dimensions of the processes that customers use in buying these industrial goods.*

All formal organizations, public or private, profit or not-for-profit, participate in the exchange of industrial products and services. Business firms purchase industrial goods that are used in forming or facilitating the production process or as component parts of other goods and services. Government agencies at all levels, as well as private institutions, secure industrial goods for the maintenance and delivery of services to their market—the public. Industrial marketing accounts for well over half of all the economic activity in the United States. The diverse nature of the industrial market poses unique challenges for the marketing manager.

The Industrial Marketing Environment

Insights into the nature of the industrial marketing environment can be gained by examining a familiar consumer product, the automobile, from the industrial marketer's perspective. The demand for a range of industrial products, such as steel, paint, and webbing for seat belts, is *derived* from the ultimate consumer demand for automobiles. To illustrate, automobile and truck manufacturers account for 24 percent of the country's steel consumption, 65 percent of its rubber consumption, and 30 percent of its aluminum consumption.[1]

If automakers forecast that sales will climb or fall next year, the industrial marketer must carefully scrutinize these projections and make corresponding changes in the forecast for this segment of the market. Any changes in the styling, design, or composition of the automobile dictated by potential car buyers, competitive pressure, or governmental agencies may create opportunities for some industrial marketers and problems for others. For example, federal law requires that the auto industry increase the average mileage of its models to 27.5 miles per gallon by 1985. To achieve this goal, the industry is moving ahead with plans to build smaller, lighter, more fuel-efficient cars.[2]

The automakers' search for lightweight materials has increased their demand for plastic products and machine tools. Since these industrial products will play a pivotal role in the creation of the models that the automakers will market for years, a particular machine tool is selected with great care. Specifications are carefully developed, and numerous alternatives are considered. Input into the decision may be provided by executives from engineering, production, quality control, marketing, purchasing, and other departments. Such *multiple buying influences,* which are common in the industrial market, pose a unique challenge for the marketer. The organization consumes the product, but many organizational members, often with different perspectives, jointly decide which product to consume. Organizational buying is a complex process rather than a single act. Throughout the evaluation process, the machine tool manufacturer works closely with the buying organization as specifications are revised and requirements changed. Once a decision is made, the product follows a direct channel of distribution to the automaker. Follow-up service and a close working relationship continue after the initial transaction.

Industrial Robots: Population Explosion in the 1980s?

Some analysts predict that robot machines are near the same threshold of growth as computers in the early 1950s. Robots—machine tools with movable arms—can be programmed to weld, paint, load machines, rivet, or perform other tasks. Robots can relieve workers of monotonous, uncomfortable, or dangerous tasks while contributing to improvements in productivity. To illustrate, the cost of labor in the automobile industry is more than $14 per hour. By contrast, the cost per robot-hour is $4.80, including installation, maintenance, depreciation, and energy. Although production managers are often reluctant to experiment with this relatively new technology, some forecasters predict that the present U.S. population of 5,000 will expand to 17,000 by 1985 and to 70,000 by 1990.

Source. "New Hand in the Workplace—The Robot," *U.S. News & World Report* (November 19, 1979), pp. 73–74.

Dynamic Forces

This illustration highlights some of the dynamic features of industrial marketing that are explored in depth throughout this volume. The industrial market is composed of diverse organizations that often require a unique blend of goods and services to further organizational objectives. To operate effectively in the industrial marketing environment, the marketer must carefully define a target market, isolate the factors that influence demand in that segment, and develop a responsive marketing program that serves the needs of that segment. Next, the industrial marketer must deal with a complex buying process that frequently includes not one but many decision makers. These and other complexities confront the marketer in the industrial environment.

What are the similarities and differences between the marketing of consumer products and the marketing of industrial products? How can the multitude of industrial goods be classified into manageable categories? Why do different types of industrial goods require entirely different marketing strategies? These questions lie at the heart of industrial marketing management and, thus, establish the theme of this first chapter.

Marketing Management: Industrial vs. Consumer

This volume centers on managing the marketing function within the industrial environment. The focus is on the *marketing of products and services to commercial enterprises, government, and not-for-profit institutions, either for resale to other industrial consumers or for use in the production of their own products or services.*[3] Simply put, these are goods used in producing consumer products or services, in producing other industrial goods or services, or in facilitating the operation of an enterprise. Many large industrial firms that produce products such as steel, copying machines, or computers cater exclusively to organizational customers and never come into direct contact with ultimate consumers.

Consumer-goods marketing, more visible by comparison, concerns the marketing of goods and services that are destined for the consumer for personal consumption. Note that some goods, such as calculators or typewriters, fall into both categories: consumer and industrial. Consumers as well as organizations purchase these items. The distinguishing characteristics between industrial and consumer-goods marketing are the intended use for the product and the intended consumer. Sometimes, the products are identical, but fundamentally different marketing approaches are needed to reach the industrial buyer.

Although the nature of the markets differ, the basic task of marketing management cuts across both consumer-goods and industrial-goods marketing. Marketers serving both sectors can benefit by forming the roots of their organizational plan with the *marketing concept*. This managerial orientation holds that the central aim of the organization is to define the needs of a target market and to adapt the organization's product or service to satisfy these needs more effectively than its competitors.[4] There is evidence that consumer-goods marketers have embraced this concept more completely than their industrial counterparts have.[5] Along with consumer-goods marketers, industrial marketers must define the needs of a target market segment and design a product/service offering, communication program, and pricing and distribution system that reaches and satisfies that segment's need. Philip Kotler's definition of marketing management captures the essence of this organizational task: *"Marketing management is the analysis, planning, implementation, and control of programs designed to create, build, and maintain mutually beneficial exchanges and relationships with target markets for the purpose of achieving organizational objectives."*[6]

There is a common body of knowledge, principles, and theory that applies to both consumer and industrial marketing, but their consumers and markets function quite differently and, therefore, merit separate attention. The hope of capturing a share of a large, but unfamiliar, market leads many consumer-goods companies into the industrial arena. Surprises often follow. Frequently, these firms are frustrated in their attempt to pinpoint specific target markets. They are also confused by the organizational buying process or disappointed that many of their traditional marketing approaches are irrelevant in the industrial market. Among other factors, they find differences in the nature of markets, market demand, buyer behavior, buyer-seller relationships, environmental influences (economic, political, legal), and marketing strategy. The potential payoffs are quite high for the firm that can successfully penetrate the industrial market. This market generates an annual national income of over *one trillion dollars* and employs over *87 million workers*.[7] Clearly, a market of this size and complexity is worthy of separate analysis.

Industrial and Consumer Marketing: A Contrast

The differences between consumer-goods marketing and industrial marketing can be highlighted by examining some familiar products. The J. M. Smucker Company operates successfully in both markets.[8] Jellies, preserves, and other products are marketed to ultimate consumers. Smucker also draws upon this product base and produces filling mixes used by manufacturers of yogurt and bakery items. The latter goods fall within our definition of an industrial product because they are used in producing other products, such as yogurt. The task of marketing strawberry preserves to ultimate consumers differs significantly from the job of marketing a related strawberry filling to a manufacturer of yogurt.

Smucker: A Consumer Goods Marketer

Smucker reaches the consumer market with a line of products sold through a range of retail outlets. New products that are added to the line are carefully developed, tested, and targeted for particular segments of the market. Marketing decisions must also be made concerning the pricing, promotion, and distribution of these products. To secure distribution for their products, the firm employs food brokers who call on wholesale and retail buying units. The company's own sales force is used in reaching selected larger accounts. Achieving a desired degree of market exposure and shelf space in key retail food outlets is essential to any marketer of consumer food products. Promotional plans are developed for the line and include media advertising, coupons, special offers, and incentives for retailers. Pricing decisions must reflect the nature of demand as well as the behavior of costs and competitors. In sum, the marketer must manage each component of the marketing mix: product, price, promotion, distribution.

Smucker: An Industrial Marketer

The marketing mix takes on a different form in the industrial setting. The market consists of manufacturers that could potentially use Smucker products in the goods that they produce. In essence, the Smucker product loses its identity in the manufacturing process as it is blended into another form—yogurt, cakes, cookies. Once a potential organizational consumer is identified, the company's sales force calls directly on the account. The salesperson may begin by contacting the company president but generally spends a great deal of time initially with the research and development director or the product development group leader. If new products are in the works, the discussion will center on specifications for the texture and composition of the required goods.

The salesperson provides these specifications to the research and development department at Smucker which develops samples. After receiving the samples, the potential customer may request further modifications. Several months may pass before a mixture is finally approved. Next, attention turns to price, and the salesperson's contact point shifts to the purchasing department. Because large quantities (truckloads or drums rather than jars) are involved, a few cents per pound can be significant to both parties. Quality and service are also vitally important criteria to the organizational decision-makers.

Once a transaction is culminated, the product will be shipped directly from the Smucker warehouse to the manufacturer's plant. The salesperson will follow up frequently with the purchasing agent and the plant manager. How much business can Smucker expect from this account? Interestingly, the performance of the new consumer product in the marketplace will determine the volume of business that this industrial account will provide to Smucker. Remember that the demand for industrial goods is derived from ultimate consumer demand.

Distinguishing Characteristics

This illustration spotlights some of the features that differentiate industrial marketing from consumer-goods marketing. First, the industrial marketer's *promotional* mix emphasizes personal selling rather than advertising (TV, newspaper) to reach potential buyers. Frequently, only a small portion of the industrial marketer's promotional budget is invested in advertising most commonly, through trade journals or direct mail. This advertising, however, often establishes the foundation for a successful sales call. The industrial salesperson requires a technical understanding of the organization's requirements and how those requirements can be satisfied. Second, the industrial marketer's *product* includes an important service component. The organizational consumer evaluates the quality of the physical entity and the quality of the attached services. Third, *price* negotiation is frequently an important part of the industrial buying/selling process. Products made to particular quality or design specifications must be individually priced. List prices are usually used for more standard items. Fourth, industrial firms generally find it more economical to sell to large accounts directly; direct *distribution* to larger customers strengthens relationships between buyer and seller. Smaller accounts can be profitably served through intermediaries—manufacturer's representatives or industrial distributors.

While selected industrial product/market situations closely resemble those found in consumer-goods marketing, table 1.1 emphasizes the common distinguishing traits of consumer-goods versus industrial marketing. Clearly, industrial marketers can often benefit from using some of the creative approaches to marketing strategy found in consumer-goods marketing. Making sound industrial marketing management decisions, however, requires knowledge of the fundamental characteristics that typify the industrial marketing environment.

Organizational Customers

A diverse array of organizations make up the industrial market (also referred to as the organizational market). Any attempt by the marketing strategist to isolate the similarities and differences among groups of industrial customers must begin with a definition of the customer type. Industrial customers can be broadly classified into three categories: (1) commercial enterprises, (2) governmental organizations, and (3) institutions.

Table 1.1 / Industrial Marketing vs. Consumer Goods Marketing: Selected Distinguishing Characteristics

	Industrial Marketing	Consumer Goods Marketing
Product	More technical in nature; exact form often variable; accompanying services very important.	Standardized form; service important, but less so.
Price	Competitive bidding for unique items; list prices for standard items.	List prices.
Promotion	Emphasis on personal selling.	Emphasis on advertising.
Distribution	Shorter, more direct channels to market.	Passes through a number of intermediate links in route to consumer.
Customer Relations	More enduring and complex.	Less frequent contact; relationship of a shorter duration.
Consumer Decision-Making Process	Involvement of diverse group of organizational members in decision.	Individual or household unit makes decision.

Each customer type represents a sizable market with many diverse parts.

Commercial Enterprises

Commercial enterprises can be divided into three categories: (1) users, (2) original equipment manufacturers (OEMs), and (3) dealers and distributors. This classification scheme centers on the purpose that the product serves in the consuming organization.

Users. Users encompass those commercial enterprises that purchase industrial products or services used in producing other goods or services that are, in turn, sold in the industrial or consumer markets. User customers purchase goods to form the manufacturing process. To illustrate, user customers are manufacturing companies that purchase injection-molding machines, grinding wheels, lathes, and related items that are used in generating their output. When purchasing machine tools, an auto manufacturer fits into the user classification. These machine tools do not become part of the automobile but, instead, are used in producing it.

Original Equipment Manufacturers. The original equipment manufacturer (referred to as an OEM) purchases industrial goods for the purpose of infusing them directly into other products sold in the industrial or ultimate consumer market. Note that the purchased product is incorporated directly into the final customer's product. A stereo manufacturer who buys electronic components for the receivers that the firm manufactures would be classified as an OEM customer. This stereo manufacturer is a customer in the eyes of the electronics firm—the industrial marketer.

Dealers and Distributors. Dealers and distributors include those commercial enterprises that purchase industrial goods and resell them in basically the same form to users and OEMs. Industrial distributors, in contrast to users and OEMs, are resellers rather than consumers of industrial products. Many industrial marketers depend heavily on industrial distributors for reaching the market. The distributor assembles, stores, and sells a large assortment of goods to industrial users. These distributors take title to the goods that they purchase.

Overlap of Categories. The three categories of commercial enterprises are not mutually exclusive but often overlap. Recall that the classification of commercial enterprises rests upon the intended purpose that the product serves for the customer. An automobile manufacturer purchasing a machine tool for the manufacturing process is a user customer. The same automaker is an OEM when purchasing radios that are to be incorporated into the ultimate consumer product.

A marketer requires a good understanding of the diverse organizational consumers in the industrial market. Properly classifying commercial customers as users, OEMs, and dealers or distributors is an important first step. This allows the marketer to gain a sharper understanding of the buying criteria that a particular commercial customer will emphasize in evaluating an industrial product.

Understanding Buying Motivations. Figure 1.1 depicts the different types of commercial customers that purchase a particular industrial product—electrical timing mechanisms. Each class of commercial customers will view the product differently because each purchases the product for a different reason.

The food-processing firm, a user, buys the electrical timers for use in a high-speed canning system. Given the critical role that the timer assumes in the production process, this customer is interested in quality, reliability, and prompt and predictable delivery. The appliance manufacturer, an OEM, incorporates the industrial product directly into consumer appliances and, thus, is concerned with the impact of the timers on the quality and depend-

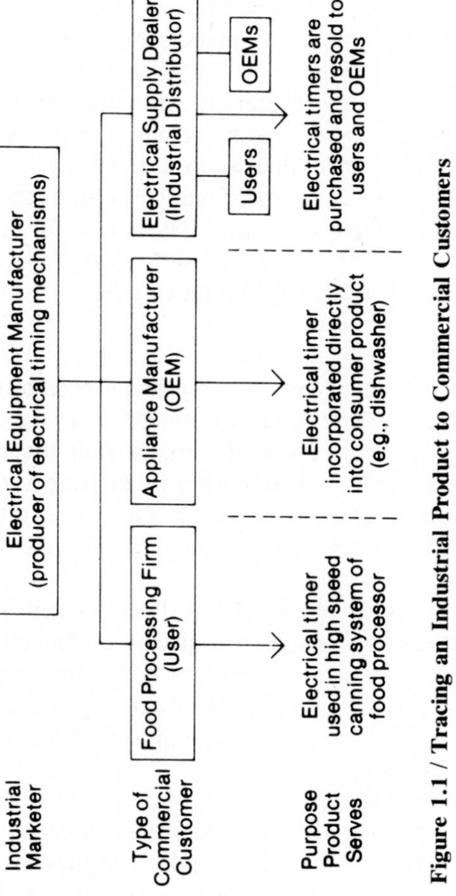

Figure 1.1 / Tracing an Industrial Product to Commercial Customers

ability of the final consumer product. Since the timers will be needed in large quantities, the appliance manufacturer will also evaluate the production capacity and delivery reliability of the industrial marketer. Finally, the electrical supply dealer, an industrial distributor, is most interested in assessing the capability of the timing mechanisms to match the needs of customers (users and OEMs) that are located within the geographical market served by the distributor.

Governmental Organizations as Consumers

The government is the largest consumer in the United States—purchasing over $350 billion of products and services annually.[9] Industrial goods and services are purchased by governmental units at the federal, state, and local levels in performing their functions. Governmental units purchase from virtually every category of goods—office supplies, missiles, fire engines, fuel, desks, lumber, grease, concrete, furniture, and so on. Governmental units, as consumers, comprise a lucrative market for the astute industrial marketer.

Governmental buying procedures are highly specialized and frustrate many marketers. Typically, the government carefully develops detailed specifications for a required good or service and invites bids from qualified suppliers. For more complex projects, the government agency may negotiate directly with the few suppliers that are known to have the knowledge or technical capability to handle the job. In both cases, the emphasis is on competitive procurement. While some consideration may be given to the supplier's reputation or past performance, the low bidder usually has the edge when contracts are awarded.

To reach this important class of organizational consumers, the marketer must understand these procurement procedures and locate the key individuals who make or influence decisions in the government market. This market is explored in detail in chapter 2.

Institutions as Consumers

Public and private institutions constitute another class of organizational customers that are included in the industrial market. Churches, hospitals, nursing homes, colleges, and universities all require goods and services in executing day-to-day tasks. Some of these institutional customers, such as public universities, have specific purchasing procedures and rules that are rigidly followed in securing needed items; others follow less standardized approaches. Industrial marketers often find it profitable to establish a separate division to respond to the unique needs and characteristics of institutional buyers.

A diverse group of organizational customers make up the industrial market. We broadly classify these consumers as commercial enterprises, governmental organizations, and institutions. The distinguishing feature of industrial consumers is that they buy products and services that are used, directly or indirectly, in their market offering. Each customer type offers profitable opportunities and special challenges for the marketer.

Industrial Demand

When target customers are organizations rather than ultimate consumers, market demand might be expected to behave differently, and it does.

Derived Demand

As illustrated earlier, *derived demand* is an important force in the industrial market. Industrial customers of all types are purchasing goods and services that they use in producing other goods and services; *their* customers determine the level of demand for industrial products and services. It is important to understand that demand is derived from the buying organization's customer, not the buying organization itself.

Aluminum is used in many different products: houses (for siding, wiring, piping), cars, appliances, beverage containers, and myriad other items. Any change in consumer demand for these items touches aluminum producers. In 1979, consumers purchased over 44 billion cans of beer and soft drinks, half of these containers were made of aluminum.[10] If consumer preference shifts away from cans to returnable glass containers, beverage producers adjust their purchasing plans, and shock waves are felt in the aluminum industry. Although never coming into direct contact with the aluminum producer, the ultimate consumer influences the demand for this industrial marketer's product by the choices made in the marketplace. Therefore, the industrial marketer can benefit by developing a marketing program that reaches the ultimate consumer. For this reason, aluminum producers develop television and magazine ads that point up the convenience and recycling opportunities aluminum containers offer to the consumer.

Wide Fluctuations: Up and Down

Because of its derived nature, market demand assumes a volatile personality in the industrial setting. The marketer confronts dramatic swings in levels of demand when basic economic conditions change or when consumer sentiments or preferences change.

The inconstant nature of demand for industrial goods and services is accentuated by the purchasing policies of organizational buyers. Purchasing managers are charged with the difficult task of insuring that an adequate supply of materials is on hand to support the production process. For each item, an inventory objective is developed that will satisfy operating needs for a certain time period, such as 90 days. The purchasing manager may, for example, base this inventory objective on forecasted sales for the firm's consumer products over the next three months. When consumer demand increases and optimism abounds, the purchasing manager will increase this inventory objective. In turn, the inventory objective may fall abruptly when projected demand in the consumer market is weak.

To recap, the derived nature of industrial demand coupled with the purchasing policies of organizational customers contribute to the volatility of demand for industrial goods and services. A small change in demand for a customer's product leads to changes of a greater magnitude in the demand for the industrial marketer's offering. The astute marketer recognizes the underlying forces that influence demand and anticipates fluctuations. The concept of derived demand is of critical importance in understanding the behavior of demand in the industrial market; however, it should be noted that organizations can and do make discretionary purchases that are not directly dictated by demand (e.g., corporate aircraft, office facilities).

Environmental Forces Influence Demand

In monitoring and forecasting demand, the industrial marketer must be alert to the factors in the competitive, economic, political, and legal environment that, directly or indirectly, influence demand. For example, a mild recession cuts deeply into some segments of the industrial market while leaving other segments unscathed. Rising interest rates alter the purchasing plans of home buyers and commercial enterprises contemplating expansion. Federal legislation targeted on higher gas mileage increases the demand for lightweight materials, such as aluminum. Ecological concerns render some industrial products and processes obsolete but also create challenging replacement opportunities. Foreign markets offer lucrative potential to some industrial marketers, while foreign competitors pose a serious challenge to other domestic producers, such as the steel industry. Constant surveillance of these and other environmental forces is fundamental to accurate demand analysis in the industrial setting.

Economic and Political Swings Mean Sales Fluctuations

Demand for industrial products is particularly subject to wide fluctuations as a result of environmental forces. A case in point is Boeing Vertol, the helicopter subsidiary of the Boeing Company. The company enjoyed boom years during the Viet Nam conflict in the late 1960s, as sales volume peaked at $350 million in 1968. However, inadequate planning for peacetime left the firm with annual sales volumes that were close to just 50 percent of their peak years, falling to a low of $180 million in 1972. Seeking to allay the impact of drastically reduced federal defense spending, Vertol diversified into the transit car industry in the mid 1970s with little success.

A return to former sales levels did not occur until 1979, when a major environmental shift took place—the cold war "heated up" and military spending experienced a significant resurgence. In 1979, sales approached the $300 million level and prospects appear bright for the 1980s. It is expected that the firm will further benefit from another environmental situation—a significant expansion of the commercial helicopter market to service the offshore oil business which is booming in response to worldwide demand for oil. The Vertol Boeing case convincingly demonstrates how the fortunes of industrial marketers ebb and flow with the dynamics of worldwide economic and political forces.

Source. "Boeing's Vertol: Revamping an Outmoded Helicopter Division," *Business Week* (February 25, 1980), p. 134.

The Organizational Buying Process

To create satisfied customers, the industrial marketer must respond to the needs of organizational buyers. Knowledge of organizational buying behavior is fundamental in developing each component of the marketing mix: product, price, promotion, and distribution strategy.

Organizational buying behavior is defined as "the decision-making process by which formal organizations establish the need for purchased products and services, and identify, evaluate, and choose among alternative brands and suppliers."[11] Key characteristics of organizational buying behavior are highlighted below.[12]

Multiple Buying Influences

The organizational buying process often involves not one but several organizational members who provide input into decision making. Buying responsibility may be delegated to a purchasing specialist within the organization (the purchasing agent), but other members also play an active role in determining the ultimate choices made by the organization. To illustrate, representatives from production, quality control, marketing, finance, and other areas are involved to varying degrees in the selection of machine tools required for a new product line. Each may play a different role and bring a different perspective to purchasing situations. Such multiple buying influences are a noteworthy characteristic of organizational buying behavior. The industrial marketer faces the complex task of identifying and reaching this diverse group of organizational members.

Buying Motives

Since norms, rules, and established procedures typify organizations, one might conclude that organizational buyers are more rational than ultimate consumers. This is *not* the case. Research indicates that organizational buyers are no more rational in making purchasing decisions than are their consumer counterparts.[13] Participants in the organizational buying process are influenced by both rational and emotional motivations. Rational motives include economic factors such as cost, quality, service. By contrast, emotional factors are more subjective in nature and might include, status, security, or fear. Organizational buyers are human, and their decisions are influenced by both rational and emotional considerations. As will be discussed in chapter 3, organizational buyers do, however, follow more formalized purchasing procedures than do consumers.

Technical Complexity

Major technical complexities influence many organizational buying decisions. The stakes can be quite high. The acquired products and services may influence the organization's performance for years. Specifications for needed equipment, materials, or services are meticulously developed, and alternative offerings are thoroughly examined. A large base of information is assembled and analyzed in making such decisions.

Time Lags

Another distinctive feature of organizational buying is that the decision process can span a considerable period of time. The technical complexity of many decisions, the large financial outlays involved, and the corresponding risks and uncertainties all contribute to an elaborate review process that can easily consume several months or more. For the industrial marketer, significant time periods can intervene between the application of marketing effort (e.g., personal sales calls) and a particular organizational customer's decision.

Organizations Vary

Each buying organization possesses characteristics that make it unique. Potential organizational customers are likely to vary significantly because of differing objectives, resource bases, abilities, and experience. The industrial marketing strategist is charged with the task of tailoring a marketing program to meet the special requirements of a particular organizational account.

To summarize, there are five characteristics of the organizational buying process that are of fundamental importance to the industrial marketer.

1. Many individuals are involved in the organizational decision-making process.
2. The organizational buyer is motivated by both rational and emotional factors in choosing industrial products and services.
3. Organizational buying decisions frequently involve a range of complex technical dimensions.
4. The organizational decision process frequently spans a considerable time period, thus creating a significant time lag between the marketer's initial contact with the customer and an ultimate decision.
5. Organizations cannot be grouped into precise categories. Each has a characteristic way of functioning and a personality that makes it different from other organizations.

These five characteristics provide some initial insights into the nature of the organizational buying process and the motivations of the participants in that process. Given the crucial importance of understanding industrial customers, these dimensions of organizational buying behavior are explored in more depth in subsequent chapters. Knowledge of organizational buying behavior provides the foundation for the formulation of responsive industrial marketing strategy.

Classifying Industrial Goods

The diverse organizations that make up the industrial market require a wide array of industrial goods and services in performing their functions. Having classified the type of customers that constitute the industrial market, attention now turns to examining the type of goods that these organizational customers require. Our task here is, first, to classify the myriad products and services into meaningful categories and, second, to examine how marketing programs differ by category.

A useful method of classifying industrial goods rests on this question: How does the industrial good or service enter the production process and the cost structure of the firm?[14] The answer allows the marketer to locate the organizational members who are influential in the buying process and to design a marketing program that responds to their specific needs. When put to this test, industrial goods can be divided into three broad categories, as shown in table 1.2.

Entering Goods

Entering goods become part of the finished product. This category of goods consists of raw materials and manufactured materials and parts. Importantly, the cost of both are treated as *expense items* which are assigned to the manufacturing process.

Raw Materials. Observe from table 1.2 that raw materials include both *farm* products and *natural* products. Raw materials are processed only to the level required for economical handling and transport. They enter the production process of the buying organization basically in their natural state.

Shortages or rapid changes in the price of raw materials can trigger a series of problems for producers that are heavily dependent on particular raw materials. To illustrate, silver is one of the largest components in Eastman Kodak's raw material costs. Each year Kodak purchases over 50 million ounces of silver on the open market to be used in the firm's photofinishing operations and industrial/medical X-ray film products.[15] Unexpected surges in the price of a particular raw material often require swift changes in pricing and product strategy by industrial and consumer-goods marketers.

Table 1.2 / Classification of Industrial Goods

I. *Entering Goods*
   A. Raw materials
      1. Farm products (examples: wheat, cotton, livestock, fruits, and vegetables)
      2. Natural products (examples: fish, lumber, crude petroleum, iron ore)
   B. Manufactured materials and parts
      1. Component materials (examples: steel, cement, wire, textiles)
      2. Component parts (examples: small motors, tires, castings)
II. *Foundation Goods*
   A. Installations
      1. Buildings and land rights (examples: factories, offices)
      2. Fixed equipment (examples: generators, drill presses, computers, elevators)
   B. Accessory equipment
      1. Portable or light factory equipment and tools (examples: hand tools, lift trucks)
      2. Office equipment (examples: typewriters, desks)
III. *Facilitating Goods*
   A. Supplies
      1. Operating supplies (examples: lubricants, coal, typing paper, pencils)
      2. Maintenance and repair items (examples: paint, nails, brooms)
   B. Business services
      1. Maintenance and repair services (examples: window cleaning, typewriter repair)
      2. Business advisory services (examples: legal, management consulting, advertising)

Source. Adapted from Philip Kotler, *Marketing Management: Analysis Planning and Control* (4th ed.; Englewood Cliffs, N.J.: Prentice-Hall, Inc., 1980), p. 172, with permission of Prentice-Hall, Inc.

Manufactured Materials and Parts. In contrast to raw materials, manufactured materials and parts undergo more initial processing before entering the manufacturing process. *Component materials,* such as textiles or sheet steel, have been processed before reaching the clothing manufacturer or automaker but must be processed further before becoming part of the finished product that you buy. *Component parts,* on the other hand, can be installed directly into another product with little or no additional processing. Examples of component parts include small motors, motorcycle tires, and automobile batteries.

Foundation Goods

The distinguishing characteristic of foundation goods is that they are *capital items*. As capital goods are used up or worn out, a portion of their original cost is assigned to the production process as a depreciation expense. The foundation goods category includes installations and accessory equipment.

Installations. Installations include the major long-term investment items that form the body of the manufacturing process, such as *buildings and land rights* and *fixed equipment.*

Accessory Equipment. These products are generally less expensive and shorter-lived capital items than installations, and they are not considered part of the fixed plant. Accessory equipment can be found in the plant as well as in the office. *Light factory equipment* and *office equipment* illustrate this point.

Facilitating Goods

Facilitating goods are the supplies and services that support organizational operations. These goods do not enter the production process or become part of the finished product but facilitate production and office activities. Thus, the costs of facilitating goods are handled as *expense items* in the period in which they are used. Note from table 1.2 that there are two categories of facilitating goods, supplies, and business services.

Supplies. Virtually every organization requires *operating supplies,* such as typing paper or staplers, and *maintenance and repair items,* such as paint and cleaning materials, to sustain day-to-day operations. These items are generally standardized and reach a broad cross-section of industrial users. In fact, they are very similar to the kinds of supplies that consumers might purchase at a hardware or discount store.

Services. An organization often turns to a specialist outside the firm to support operations through the performance of specific functions. This specialist possesses a level of expertise or efficiency that the organization can profitably tap. Business services include *maintenance and repair* support (e.g., machine repair) and *advisory* support (e.g., management consulting). Like supplies, services are considered expense items.

Industrial Marketing Strategy

The significance of an industrial goods classification system comes to light on examination of how marketing patterns differ by goods category. A marketing strategy appropriate for one category of goods may be entirely unsuitable for another. Often, entirely different promotional, pricing, and distribution strategies are required. The physical nature of the industrial good, coupled with its intended use by the organizational customer, dictate to an important degree the requirements of the marketing program. The following illustrations point up the diverse nature of industrial marketing strategy.

Illustration 1: Manufactured Materials and Parts

Recall that manufactured materials and parts enter the buying organization's own product. Some component parts are custom-made and, therefore, involve considerable interaction between the engineering departments of the buyer and the seller. Other component parts and materials are standardized and produced in larger quantities. Manufactured materials and parts are generally purchased in large quantities on a contractual basis. Smaller organizational customers may rely on industrial distributors or industrial wholesalers.

Salespersons call on purchasing agents, but organizational members from engineering or production develop the specifications. The basic appeals emphasized by the marketer in trade advertising, as well as on a personal sales call, center on price, quality, dependability, and service. Opportunities for product differentiation are stronger for component parts (e.g., tires) than component materials (e.g., steel). Many parts have a lucrative consumer goods replacement market, as in the case of automobile tires and batteries. In such cases, consumer advertising can be profitably used. A parts manufacturer who is successful in building brand preference in the replacement market frequently finds a receptive industrial market.

Producers of manufactured materials and parts often serve diverse customer groups that have unique needs. The challenge for the marketer is to locate and accurately define these needs, uncover key buying influences, and adjust the marketing program to profitably serve these consumers. For example, observe in table 1.3 the special needs of the customers that make up part of the market for springs. As a manufacturer of component parts, the Conrad Spring Company develops springs that are incorporated into products ranging from telephone dials to surgical equipment.

Illustration 2: Installations

Installations were classified earlier as foundation goods because they are capital assets that affect the buyer's scale of operations. For installations, the product is the central force in marketing strategy. Direct manufacturer-

Table 1.3 / Conrad Spring Company: Serving Diverse Customers and Unique Needs

Selected Customers	Manufactured Part Required	Application
Ford Motor Company	Piston Spring	Automatic Transmission
Kenner Toys	Springs and Wire Forms	Star Wars Toys
International Telephone and Telegraph Corp.	Springs	Telephone Dials
Kees Surgical Specialty Company	Torsion Spring	Surgical Device Used by Brain Surgeons

Source. Tom Hayes, "Rising Costs Plague Plucky Spring Company," *The Cincinnati Enquirer* (June 4, 1978), p. D-1.

to-user channels of distribution are the norm in the marketing of major installations. Less costly, more standardized installations, such as lathes, may be sold through marketing middlemen.

Personal selling is the dominant promotional tool used by the marketer of major installations. The salesperson works closely with prospective organizational buyers. Negotiations can span several months and frequently involve the top executives in the buying organization, especially for buildings or custom-made equipment. As discussed earlier, these multiple buying influences often complicate the selling task. Each executive may be applying slightly different criteria to the decision process. Trade advertising and direct mail advertising are used to supplement and reinforce the personal selling effort.

Buying motives center on economic factors, such as the projected performance of the capital asset, and emotional factors, such as industry leadership. In terms of economic considerations, a buyer would be quite willing to select a higher-priced installation if the projected return on investment supported the decision. To illustrate, a packaging machine that saves the using organization one gram of plastic per-unit-produced would yield substantial cost savings over its productive life. This installation would be preferred over lower-priced alternatives that did not offer such savings.

Illustration 3: Supplies

The final illustration centers on a facilitating good—supplies. Again we find different marketing patterns. Most supply items reach a horizontal market that is composed of organizational customers from many different industries. Although some large users are serviced on a direct basis, a wide variety of marketing middlemen are required to adequately cover this broad and diverse market.

The purchasing agent plays the dominant role in the choice of suppliers and evaluates alternative suppliers on dependability, breadth of assortment, convenience, and price. While always searching for value, the purchasing agent lacks the time to carefully evaluate all available alternatives each time a purchase requirement surfaces. Dependable sources have the edge.

For supplies, the marketer's promotional mix includes catalog listings, advertising, and personal selling. Advertising is directed to resellers and final users. Personal selling is less important for supplies than it is for other categories of goods, such as installations, that have a high unit value. Thus, personal selling efforts are generally confined to resellers and large users of supplies.

These illustrations point up the varied nature of marketing strategy across the industrial goods classification scheme. The focus and direction of marketing strategy change from one category to another. While this classification system provides insights into marketing strategy requirements, the marketer's ultimate concern must be on how potential organizational customers view a particular product. The same product may be viewed quite differently by different organizational customers. These potential buyers have varying levels of experience with specific products in addition to having distinct organizational objectives and requirements. The successful industrial marketer recognizes these unique organizational needs and satisfies them.

A Look Ahead

The chief components of the industrial marketing management process are shown in figure 1.2. Industrial marketing strategy is formulated within the boundaries established by the corporate mission and the enterprise's objectives. The determination of the corporate mission involves a definition of the enterprise's business and purpose, an assessment of environmental trends, and an evaluation of the firm's strengths and weaknesses. Corporate objectives provide guidelines within which specific marketing objectives are formed.

The industrial marketing management framework delineated in figure 1.2 provides an overview of the five major parts of this volume. This first chapter introduced some of the special features that distinguish industrial marketing from consumer-goods marketing. The remaining chapter in part one builds upon this base and examines in more detail the nature of industrial market organizations. A close examination is given to each of the major types of industrial customers—commercial enterprises, governmental units, and institutions.

Organizational buying behavior constitutes the theme of part two. The organizational buying process and the myriad forces that affect the organizational decision maker will be examined. Once this groundwork is established, the discussion in part three turns to the measurement of industrial market opportunities. Attention will be given in part three to specific techniques that can be used in measuring the relative attractiveness of alternative sectors of the industrial market and in selecting specific target segments.

Part four centers on designing industrial marketing strategy. Each component of the marketing mix is treated from an industrial marketing perspective. Note from figure 1.2 that the formulation of the industrial marketing mix requires careful coordination with other functional areas in the firm, such as research and development and production. Monitoring and controlling the marketing program are key topics analyzed in part five. The control component of the industrial marketing management process seeks to minimize the discrepancy between planned results in target market segments and actual results. This is accomplished by planning for and acquiring relevant and timely marketing information—a central theme of the final section.

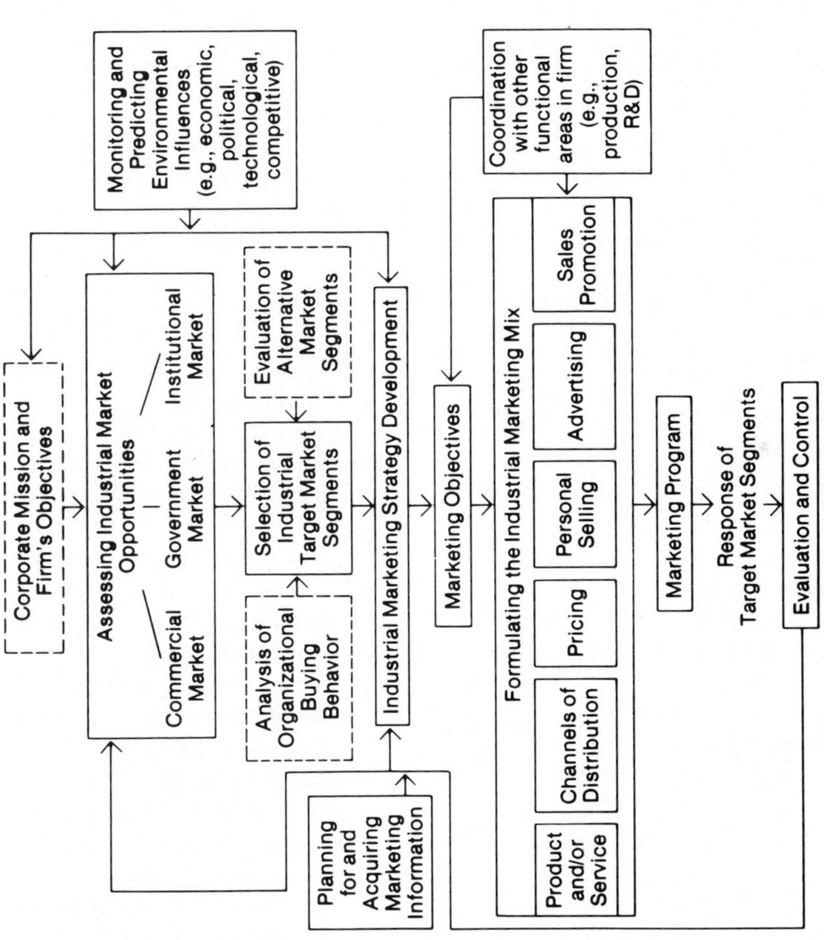

Figure 1.2 / A Framework for Industrial Marketing Management

Source. Adapted from David W. Cravens, Gerald E. Hills, and Robert B. Woodruff, *Marketing Decision Making: Concepts and Strategy* (Homewood, Ill.: Richard D. Irwin, Inc., 1976), p. 20.

Summary

Although there is a common body of knowledge and theory that spans all of marketing, important differences exist between consumer and industrial marketing. Among other distinctions, the industrial marketer confronts differences in the basic nature of markets, demand patterns, buyer behavior, and products.

A number of diverse organizations make up the industrial market. They can be broadly defined as: (1) commercial enterprises, (2) governmental organizations, and (3) institutions. Since purchases made by these industrial consumers are linked to goods and services that they, in turn, generate, derived demand is an important and often volatile force in the industrial market.

To penetrate the industrial market effectively, the marketer requires an understanding of the organizational buying process. Multiple buying influences, technical specifications, time lags, and complex buying motives surround the organizational decision process.

The exact form of the organizational decision process often varies with the type of industrial product under consideration. Industrial goods can be classified into three categories that are based on how the product enters the cost structure and production process of the buying organization. The three broad categories of industrial goods are: (1) entering goods, (2) foundation goods, and (3) facilitating goods. Specific categories of goods often require unique marketing programs.

Footnotes

[1]"A Troubled Auto Industry—Impact on U.S." *U.S. News & World Report* (August 27, 1979), p. 21.

[2]Ralph E. Winter, "Machine Tools Ordered in April at Record Pace," *Wall Street Journal* (May 30, 1978), p. 3.

[3]Industrial Marketing Committee Review Board, "Fundamental Differences Between Industrial and Consumer Marketing," *Journal of Marketing* 19 (October 1954), p. 153.

[4]Philip Kotler, *Marketing Management: Analysis, Planning, and Control* (4th ed.; Englewood Cliffs, N.J.: Prentice-Hall, Inc., 1980), p. 31.

[5]Frederick E. Webster, "Management Science in Industrial Marketing," *Journal of Marketing*, 42 (January 1978), p. 23; see also, Grandhi Balakrishna, "Better Use of the Industrial Marketing Concept," *Industrial Marketing Management* 7 (January 1978), pp. 71–76.

[6]Kotler, *Marketing Management*, p. 22.

[7]Ibid., p. 171.

[8]Material in this section is drawn from an interview with the industrial sales manager, The J. M. Smucker Company, May 1978.

[9]U.S. Department of Commerce, Bureau of the Census, *Government Finances in 1976–77*, Series GF77, No. 5 (November 1978), pp. 26–27.

[10]Amal Nag, "Recycling Ease Gives Aluminum an Edge over Steel in Beverage-Can Market Battle," *Wall Street Journal* (January 1, 1980), p. 28.

[11]Frederick E. Webster, Jr., and Yoram Wind, *Organizational Buying Behavior* (Englewood Cliffs, N.J.: Prentice-Hall, Inc., 1972), p. 2.

[12]The discussion of these characteristics is based on Webster and Wind, *Organizational Buying Behavior,* pp. 5–8.

[13]Jagdish N. Sheth, "Recent Developments in Organizational Buying Behavior," in A. Woodside, J. Sheth, and P. Bennett (eds.), *Consumer and Industrial Buying Behavior* (New York: Elsevier North-Holland, Inc., 1977), p. 30.

[14]Kotler, *Marketing Management,* p. 172.

[15]Charles J. Elia, "Profit Forecasts for Kodak, a Big User of Silver, Are Scaled Back as the Metal's Price Skyrockets," *Wall Street Journal* (September 21, 1979), p. 39.

Discussion Questions

1. What are the chief differences between consumer goods marketing and industrial goods marketing? Use the following matrix as a guide in organizing your response:

	Consumer Goods Marketing	Industrial Goods Marketing
Customers		
Buying Behavior		
Buyer/Seller Relationship		
Product		
Price		
Promotion		
Channels		

2. Explain how a company such as General Electric might be classified by some industrial marketers as a "user" customer but by others as an OEM.

3. Illustrate the concept of derived demand using a product with which you are familiar.

4. How do the inventory policies of purchasing managers influence changes in demand in the industrial market?

5. Consumer products are frequently classified as convenience, shopping, or specialty goods. This classification system is based upon how consumers shop for particular products. Would this classification scheme apply equally well in the industrial environment? Explain.

6. Compare and contrast the marketing program that would be required for an entering good versus a facilitating good. Focus your discussion on an example of each product type.

7. Evaluate this statement: "The buying decisions that an organizational buyer makes in the office are much more rational than those that the same individual makes in a supermarket or department store."

8. Evaluate this statement: "The demand for major equipment (foundation good) is likely to be less responsive to shifts in price than that for materials, supplies, and components." Agree or disagree? Support your position.

Chapter **2**

The Industrial Market: Perspectives on the Organizational Buyer

The industrial marketer requires an understanding of the needs of a diverse mix of organizational buyers drawn from three broad sectors of the industrial market. The three sectors include commercial enterprises, government (all levels), and institutions. After reading this chapter, you will understand:

1. *the nature and central characteristics of each of these market sectors;*
2. *how the purchasing function is organized in each of these sizable components of the industrial market;*
3. *the need to design a unique marketing program for each sector of the industrial market.*

The industrial market is vast and characterized by tremendous diversity. In fact, many goods that are commonly viewed as final consumer products claim a large industrial market. To illustrate, the industrial market for food is made up of *industrial companies* (Ford Motor Company serves over $6 million worth of food per year); *institutions*—schools, hospitals, colleges (Ohio State University was the 203rd largest food service organization in 1970); *retail food service firms* (the fastest growing part of the food service industry); *airlines* (United Airlines was the 40th largest food service organization in 1970); and the *government* (the army, the largest food service organization in the U.S., has an annual food sales volume exceeding $1 billion).

This brief institutional foods listing demonstrates the marketer's need to understand the variety of buyers that make up the industrial market. As introduced in chapter 1, these organizational consumers include commercial enterprises, governmental units, and institutions. A significant first step in creating successful marketing strategy is to isolate the unique dimensions of each of the major sectors of the industrial market. How much market potential does each sector of the industrial market represent? How is the buying function organized and administered in each case? Who makes the purchasing decision? Answers to these questions provide a foundation upon which the marketing manager can formulate industrial marketing programs that respond to the specific needs and characteristics of each sector of the industrial market.

Commercial Enterprises

Commercial enterprises include manufacturers, construction companies, service firms (e.g., hotels), transportation companies, selected professional groups (e.g., dentists), and resellers (wholesalers and retailers purchasing equipment and supplies for use in their operations). In terms of volume of purchases, manufacturers are the most important commercial customers.

Unique Characteristics: Distribution by Size

A startling fact about the study of industrial buyers (manufacturers) is that there are so few of them. In 1977 there were only 456,000 manufacturing firms in the United States.[1] An even more important statistic relates to the size of these industrial firms: roughly 13,500 firms employ more than 250 workers each, yet this handful of companies provides over 64 percent of all value added (i.e., economic value created) by manufacturing in the United States.[2] Clearly, these large buyers can be very important to the industrial marketer. Because each large firm represents such vast sales potential, the industrial marketer will often develop a tailor-made marketing strategy for each customer. Smaller manufacturing firms also constitute an important segment for the industrial marketer. Interestingly, over one-half of all manufacturers in the United States have fewer than 20 employees. Here the marketer will encounter an organizational buyer with different needs and, often, a different orientation. Again, the astute marketer has the opportunity to adjust the marketing program to the needs of this segment of the market.

Geographical Concentration. Concentration of industrial firms by size is not the only form of concentration important to the industrial supplier. Observe from figure 2.1 that manufacturers are also concentrated geographically. Primary areas of industrial concentration include the Midwest (Ohio, Indiana, Illinois, and Michigan) and Middle Atlantic states (New Jersey, Pennsylvania, and New York). The seven states of California, New York, Pennsylvania, Ohio, Illinois, New Jersey, and Michigan contain over 50 percent of all manufacturing firms in the United States. In addition, most large metropolitan areas are lucrative industrial markets.

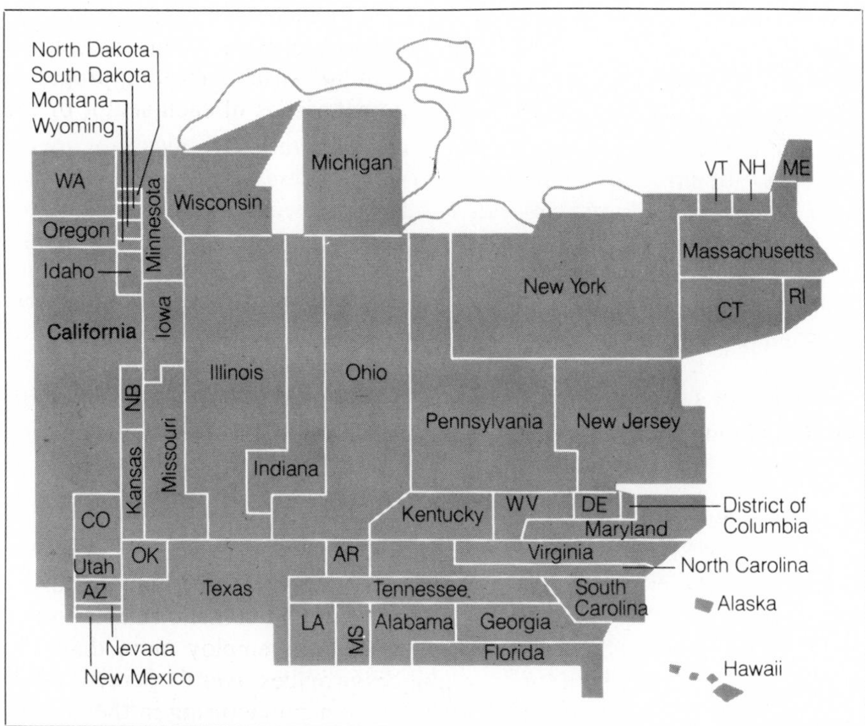

Figure 2.1 / The United States in Proportion to Value of Manufactured Products

Source: U.S. Department of Commerce, Bureau of the Census, *Census of Manufactures Area Statistics* (Washington, D.C.: Government Printing Office, 1971), p. 39.

Geographic concentration has some important implications for the formulation of marketing strategy. First, firms can concentrate their marketing efforts in areas of high market potential. Thus, the industrial marketer can make effective use of a full-time personal sales force in these markets. Second, distribution centers can be located in large volume areas to insure rapid delivery capability to a large proportion of the firm's customers. Finally, firms may not be able to tie their salespeople to specific geographic areas because many large industrial buyers entrust to one individual the responsibility for purchasing certain products and materials for the entire company. One buyer, located in Cincinnati, may buy industrial cleaning materials for all of the firm's plants, warehouses, and sales offices dispersed throughout the United States. A salesperson tied to one area could not be very effective against a competitor who maintains a sales office in Cincinnati. Thus, the marketer requires an understanding of how a potential buyer's purchasing organization is structured.

The Purchasing Organization

The way in which goods and services are purchased in the commercial firm depends upon such factors as the nature of the business, size of the firm, and the volume, variety, and technical complexity of items purchased. Every firm, regardless of its organizational characteristics, must procure the materials, supplies, equipment, and services necessary to successfully operate the business. Rarely do individual departments within a corporation do their own buying. In most instances, the procurement process is administered by an individual called the manager of purchasing, purchasing agent, or director of purchasing. The organization of the purchasing function will be examined next.

Purchasing in Large Firms. In large firms the purchasing function has become quite specialized, with the work divided into five homogeneous categories. The five classifications found in the purchasing operation are:

1. *Administrative*. Purchasing administration involves all the tasks associated with the management process with emphasis on the development of policies, procedures, controls, and mechanics for coordinating purchasing operations with those of other departments.
2. *Buying*. This includes a wide variety of activities such as reviewing requisitions, analyzing specifications, doing informal research, investigating vendors, interviewing salespeople, studying costs and prices, and negotiating.
3. *Expediting*. This order follow-up activity involves various types of vendor liaison work such as reviewing the status of orders, writing letters, telephoning and telegraphing vendors, and occasionally visiting vendors' plants.

4. *Special staff work.* Any well-developed purchasing operation has an unending number of special projects or studies requiring specialized knowledge and uninterrupted effort. Such projects are commonly found in the areas of economic and market studies, special cost studies, special vendor investigations, and systems studies.
5. *Clerical.* Every department must write orders, maintain working files, maintain catalog and library materials, and maintain records for commodities, vendors, and prices.[3]

The purchasing manager is responsible for administering the purchasing process and, on occasion, may be involved in the negotiations of a small number of important contracts.

Confessions of a Purchasing Agent

There is never enough time to do the things that I would like to do. With more time or a larger staff, I could save this company a lot of money. For example, I found out the other day that we were paying the highest rate in the city for lawn maintenance at our facilities. I learned this, not through my job, but as a volunteer member of our local parks and recreation board. Our company was being taken and I didn't know it.

Purchasing is a very complex function to manage, particularly with a small staff. Recently, I requested two additional staff positions from top management and guaranteed that I could pay their salaries with the savings we could generate. My request was turned down.

Source. Excerpts from an interview with the purchasing manager of a consumer products firm.

The day-to-day activity of the purchasing function is carried out by *buyers*. Each buyer is responsible for the procurement of a specific group of products. Organizing the purchasing function in this way permits the buyers to obtain a high level of technical expertise on a limited number of items. As products and materials become more sophisticated, buyers are finding it necessary to become more knowledgeable of the characteristics, manufacturing processes, and design specifications of those products and materials. The trend toward greater specialization in the purchasing process places increasing demands on the industrial salesperson who must match the expertise of potential buyers. In some cases the salesperson requires significant knowledge of competing products to effectively respond to a buyer's probing questions.

The typical purchasing department is organized on the basis of the type of product to be procured. If the firm is large, buyers will not report directly to the purchasing manager but to an intermediate level manager, usually with the title of purchasing agent or buying department manager.[4] Figure

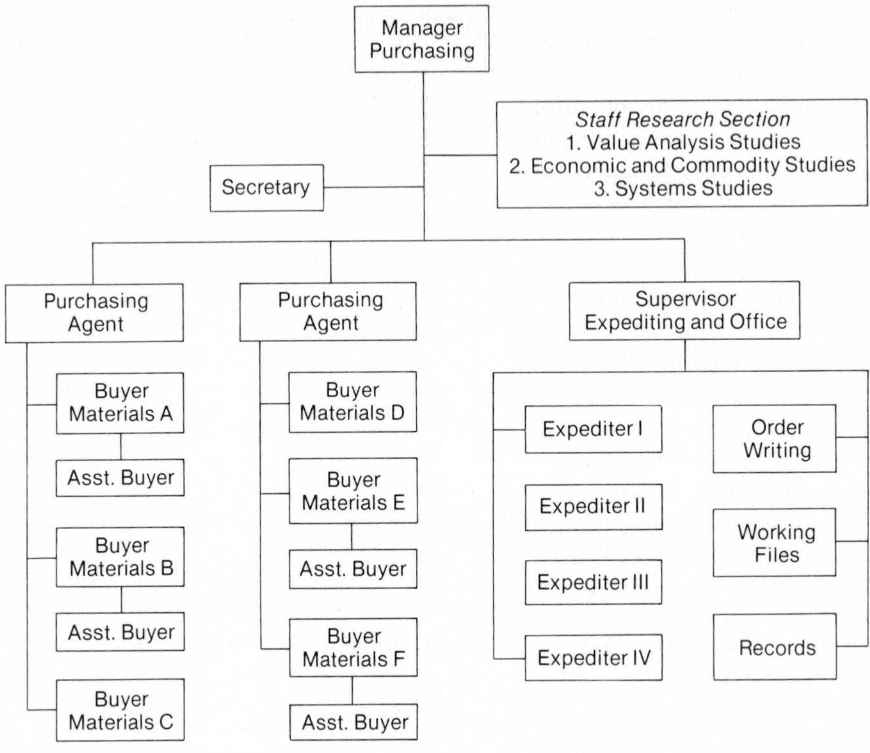

Figure 2.2 / Typical Purchasing Organization

Source. Lamar Lee, Jr., and Donald W. Dobler, *Purchasing and Materials Management, Text and Cases* (New York: McGraw-Hill Book Company, 1977), p. 442. Reprinted by permission of McGraw-Hill Book Company.

2.2 displays the typical organization structure for a medium-sized purchasing department.

Observe that the buyers, in this instance, are specialized by type of product. The expediters facilitate the processing of a customer's order and administer any follow-up work required to complete the delivery of the customer's order. In this organization's structure, each expediter works with a specific buyer. Being fairly large, this company can afford the luxury of a staff research section. (The influence of the staff research group on the purchase process can be substantial.) The function of this area is to conduct technical, in-depth research on complicated purchases and to administer the routine *value analysis* program.

Value Analysis. Value analysis is a method of weighing the comparative value of materials, components, and manufacturing processes from the standpoint of their purpose, relative merit, and cost. The goal of this analysis is to uncover ways of improving products, lowering costs, or both. Value analysis projects are usually sponsored or coordinated by the purchasing department, but the projects often include other departments of the enterprise. Purchasing organizations often find that a product can be value analyzed several times with savings realized each time. Why? Over the years, new components or materials become available, new manufacturing methods evolve, or new ways of looking at the product or the production process emerge.

A value analysis study by Black and Decker Manufacturing Company led to a change from using an off-the-shelf component in one of their products to using a component specifically designed and manufactured for the particular application.[5] The shift from a standard part to a special part resulted in material savings of 50 percent. The modification also led to improvements in the performance and service life of the product.

Some firms will assemble a value analysis team for a particular project. The team might consist of a purchasing specialist, a design engineer, a production engineer, and representatives from marketing and accounting. For other projects, a purchasing manager might work directly with a technical salesperson of a supplier in conducting a study. Clearly, the industrial salesperson can play an active role in value analysis studies by supplying technical assistance, relevant data, and valuable recommendations. In fact, the salesperson of the industrial marketer often plays a pivotal role in stimulating the purchasing organization to conduct a value analysis study. The salesperson must convince purchasing or other organizational members that the potential benefits derived from a particular study exceed the costs of performing the analysis.

The Marketer's Role. The nature and size of the purchasing department will have an important bearing on the formulation of marketing strategy. In smaller organizations, one person is often responsible for the entire range of buying activities. In fact, considering the large number of small companies in the United States, most purchasing departments are one- or two-person operations. The department head is usually called the purchasing agent, and he or she may report to the president, general manager, controller, production manager, or other official. The purchasing agent in the small firm lacks the detailed knowledge and expertise available to a purchasing department that employs many individuals with specialized skills. In this case, the industrial salesperson's role should be viewed as an extension of the customer's purchasing department. Here the salesperson acts as a consultant, providing assistance wherever required.

In dealing with the large corporation, where specialized buyers are assigned to limited product categories, the selling job takes on a different character. Because of specialization and sophistication in the act of purchasing, the salesperson must have detailed technical information in order to respond to very specific questions on product quality, performance, and costs.

While the structure and orientation of purchasing organizations vary, the astute marketer seeks to identify significant characteristics or needs that form the basis for classifying commercial accounts into meaningful market segments. Specific adjustments can then be made in industrial marketing strategy to respond to the particular needs of each segment. Sales personnel and marketing managers who can effectively adapt to the purchasing conditions in each market segment are generally the leading marketers in their industry.

Materials Management: Integrating Purchasing into the Business Operation

A relatively new idea in the organization of the purchasing function is the concept of *materials management.* A firm that adopts this concept places all activities included in bringing materials into and through the plant under one head called the materials manager.[6] By giving the materials manager overall authority, the activities of various departments can be coordinated to insure that the *total* cost of materials to the organization is minimized. Without this central authority, savings made in one function, such as purchasing, may be costly to another, such as inventory control. A recent study by Dean Ammer indicates that nearly 70 percent of all American industrial firms have adopted the materials management concept, and it is as common in small firms as in large ones.[7]

The materials management idea has made purchasing personnel aware of the need to evaluate the total flow of purchased materials—including net delivered price, inventory control, traffic, receiving, and production control. The result is to place an extremely heavy burden on the industrial marketer's program. Industrial marketing managers must coordinate all activities that affect the materials management function of their customers, including sales management, credit, traffic, expediting, warehousing, and production. In particular, industrial marketing managers must be able to secure the necessary distribution support from their logistics department. The advent of the materials management concept has stimulated a more systematic approach to the administration of industrial marketing strategy.

The Expanding Role of Materials Management. The materials management approach to purchasing will likely expand in scope and importance within the firm in the future. A 1977 study by Edward Bonfield and Thomas Speh reveals that both chief operating officers and purchasing managers of large industrial corporations expect purchasing's involvement in the following areas to increase dramatically in the coming years:

1. raw materials, components, and supplies inventory control;
2. planning and forecasting future supply needs;
3. maintaining supplier lists;
4. securing price quotations.

The study also concludes that sophistication in the administration of the purchasing job will continue to expand with an increase in the application of the computer and value analysis.[8] The implications for industrial marketers again point to the need to expand the level of sophistication in developing approaches which will appeal to purchasing personnel.

Governments: Unique Characteristics

Governmental units are an extremely important market segment for many industrial marketers and constitute the second major sector of the industrial market that will be examined. As chapter 1 indicated, the federal government is the largest consumer in the United States and, as a result of the huge buying volume, the buying procedures employed are highly specialized and often very confusing. The industrial marketer must develop a thorough comprehension of this complex buying process to compete effectively in the government market. A first step is to understand the variety of government units and their characteristics.

In 1972, there were 78,268 governmental units in the United States.[9] Table 2.1 indicates the number of each type of governmental unit. Note that a vast majority of the government units are local in nature, providing the industrial marketer with a widely dispersed market. The numbers in the table are somewhat misleading as they indicate a ratio of state and federal government units to local units of 1 to 1500. In reality, there are many functional areas within state government (education, state police, highway) and agencies within the federal government (defense, space, interior, transportation, postal service) that are responsible for a sizable procurement volume. Thus, federal and state governments literally have hundreds of people, agencies, and functional areas spread across the United States that that have direct and indirect impacts on the purchasing process.

Table 2.1 / Types of Governmental Units

Type of Unit		Number of Units
United States Government		1
State Government		50
Local Government		78,217
County	3,044	
Municipality	18,516	
Township	16,991	
School Districts	15,780	
Special Districts	23,886	
Total		78,268

Source. Government Units in 1972, U.S. Department of Commerce, Preliminary Report #1, December 1972, p. 1.

Influences on Government Buying

In addition to the large number of governmental purchasing units and their wide geographic dispersion, another level of complexity is added to the governmental purchasing process by the array of influences on this process. In large city, state, and federal procurement, buyers will be responsible to or influenced by dozens of other interested parties who specify, legislate, evaluate, and use the goods and services involved in the transaction.[10] Clearly, the range of outside influences extends far beyond the originating agency.

Understanding Government Contracts

Firms wishing to market to governments must often meet stringent legal requirements. Government contracts may contain provisions that have little to do with the product or service but relate to broader, social goals. Federal government contracts may require the contractor to give preference to small subcontractors, state that the contractor employ a certain proportion of minority employees, or require payment of the minimum wage.

Most government procurement, regardless of the level of government, is based on public law which establishes guidelines for the contractual arrangements.[11] For the federal government, all contractors must meet certain stated general contract provisions that are set forth by law and are published as part of the Federal Procurement Regulations. These general provisions include stipulations as to product inspection requirements, payment methods, actions as a result of default and disputes, and many other factors relative to the supplier's performance.

Vendors who plan to conduct a significant volume of business with the federal government must understand procurement laws and the many types of contracts that could be employed. Without a clear comprehension of the procurement laws the vendor is in an unfavorable position during the negotiation phase. The seller also needs to explore the advantages and disadvantages of the various types of contracts. There are two basic types of contracts: (1) *fixed-price contracts,* in which a firm price is agreed to before the contract is awarded, and full payment is made when the product or service is delivered in the agreed upon condition; and (2) *cost-reimbursement contracts,* where the vendor is reimbursed for allowable costs incurred in performance of the contract and is sometimes allowed a certain number of dollars above cost as profit. Each type of contract has many variations reflecting incentives that are built-in to control costs or cover future contingencies.

Generally, the fixed-price contract provides the greatest profit potential, but the risks are also greater if unforeseen expenses are incurred, inflation increases dramatically, or conditions change. Grumman Corporation lost $65 million on the first 20 "swing wing F-14 Mach 2 fighters" that it built for the navy as a result of inflation and certain developmental problems that were not anticipated.[12] However, if the seller is able to effect significant cost reducing actions during the contract, profits may be earned in excess of those estimated when the contract was negotiated. Cost-reimbursement contracts are carefully administered by the government because of the minimal incentives for the contractor to be efficient. They are usually employed for contracts involving considerable developmental work when it is difficult to estimate efforts and expenses.

Telling Vendors How to Sell: Useful Publications

Unlike most customers, governments often go to great lengths to explain to potential vendors exactly how to do business with the government. For example, such publications as *Selling to the Military* and *Selling to the U.S. Air Force* are made available by the federal government through the Department of Defense. These manuals offer the vendor a detailed description of the essentials of successfully selling to the military.

In addition to the wide array of manuals and publications, government agencies periodically hold seminars that provide businesses with an orientation to the buying processes and procedures used by the agency. The objective of these seminars is to encourage firms to seek government business and to inform them how to do it.

Purchasing Organizations and Procedures: Government

Government and commercial purchasing are similarly organized. However, in governmental purchases more emphasis is usually given to clerical functions because of the more detailed procedures demanded by statutory requirements.[13] Every government agency possesses some degree of buying influence or authority. Although government buying organizations are found on the federal, state, and local levels, the federal government is by far the largest and most complex buying unit. The most important aspects of how the federal government is organized to make its substantial volume of purchases will be examined.

Defense Procurement. Federal government procurement is divided into two categories: defense and nondefense. Defense procurement involves a many-faceted purchasing system in which each military department—army, navy, and air force—and the Defense Department are responsible for major purchases. However, the Defense Supply Agency (DSA) procures and distributes supplies used in common by all branches. The purpose of the DSA is to obtain favorable prices through volume purchasing and to reduce duplication of purchasing within the military. In addition to defense purchasing implemented by the DSA, military branches, and the Defense Department, defense-related items may be procured from other government agencies, such as the General Services Administration. Also, many supplies for military base operations are procured from local sources of supply.

Nondefense Procurement. Nondefense procurement is administered by a wide variety of agencies including cabinet departments (e.g., HEW, Commerce), commissions (e.g., Federal Trade Commission), the executive branch (e.g., Bureau of Budget), agencies (e.g., the Federal Aviation Agency), and administration (e.g., General Services Administration). Similar to the DSA for defense procurement, the General Services Administration (GSA) centralizes the procurement of many goods and services used by all nondefense segments of the government. The Federal Supply Service of the GSA has responsibility for purchasing many items in common use by other government agencies including office supplies, small tools, paint, paper, furniture, maintenance supplies, and duplicating equipment. The Federal Supply Service is like the purchasing department of a large diversified corporation because it provides a consolidated purchasing, storing, and distribution network for the federal government. The GSA should not be taken lightly—it has the market power to place orders for one item totaling over $500,000 at any one time! If the GSA has approved a supplier, departments within the government may purchase the particular item at specified retail outlets at the agreed upon price. However, securing the initial GSA contract is a difficult task indeed. To do so, the government marketer must first understand the government's buying process.

If You Build a Better Mousetrap, Should You Sell It to the Government?

Trying to untangle the maze of federal procurement specifications has, in the past, discouraged many firms from bidding for government business. Several years ago, Senator Lawton Chiles found that a firm attempting to sell mousetraps to the military would have to comply with almost 500 pages of specifications. One specification stated: "wire, steel, carbon (high carbon, round, for mechanical springs, general purpose)." Senator Chiles concluded that the detailed specifications were so stultifying that "if you build a better mousetrap, don't try to sell it to the federal government." However, all this may be changing as the government is moving to eliminate the lengthy and often unnecessary product specifications which all government bidders must meet. Legislation has been introduced into Congress to simplify all government purchase regulations and procedures. Generally, the new laws would require government agencies to buy standard commercial products whenever possible.

Source. Kenneth H. Bacon, "Military-Industrial Complex Becoming a Wee Bit Less So," *Wall Street Journal* (September 22, 1978), p. 1.

Federal Buying

The sources of federal needs for goods and services are many. The president may set the procurement process in motion when he signs a congressional appropriation bill, or an accountant in the General Accounting Office may initiate the process by requesting a new desk-top calculator. Once the need is known and documented, the government will follow one of two general procurement strategies: *formal advertising* (also known as open bid) or *negotiated contract.*

Formal Advertising. Formal advertising means the government will solicit bids from appropriate suppliers and, in most instances, the lowest bidder is awarded the contract. This type of purchase strategy is most frequently followed when the product in question is standardized and when the specifications for it are straightforward.

To participate in the bidding process, the interested supplier must gain a place on a bidder's list. Then, each time the government requests bids for a particular product, the supplier will receive an invitation to bid. The invitation to bid specifies the item and the quantity to be purchased, detailed technical specifications, delivery schedules, warranties required, packing requirements, and other relevant purchasing details. The bidding firm will then prepare its bid based on its cost structure and the anticipation of possible bid levels by competitors.

Each bid will be reviewed by procurement personnel in the agency making the purchase to assure its conformance to specifications. Bids that do not conform to government specifications will be automatically rejected. Contracts are generally awarded to the lowest bidder; however, the government agency may select the next to lowest bidder if it can document that the lowest bidder would not responsibly fulfill the contract.

The formal advertising approach to developing government contracts is expensive and time consuming for all parties. A rather substantial volume of paperwork is also generated. However, the process does allow free and open competition among any and all firms that desire to compete. In addition, the government has fairly good assurance that there is no collusion and that it obtained the lowest possible price.

Negotiated Contract Buying. This buying strategy is employed when nonstandard products are being purchased or when there are very few suppliers who have the capability to make the product. There may be some competition for contracts developed in this manner since the contracting office can carry on negotiations with several suppliers simultaneously.

Obviously, negotiation is a much more flexible procurement procedure. The government purchasing office has a wide range of personal judgment to exercise regarding the purchase. The military attempts to provide some uniformity to the negotiation process by setting up a uniform procedure to be followed by all military procurement organizations. This procedure specifies the manner in which purchase requirements are established, potential suppliers are identified, proposals are evaluated, and contracts are negotiated and awarded.[14]

As this brief discussion of the government's purchasing process has implied, selling to the government is a very involved, time-consuming, and paper-generating process. Government markets are some of the most sophisticated and complex environments within which the industrial marketer will be operating.

Negotiation: Working Out the Details

It is often assumed that the negotiation process is undertaken by government procurement personnel to persuade potential contractors to reduce their price. In reality, the purpose of negotiation is to provide a measure of flexibility to the bidding process so that *all* aspects of a contract can be arranged for the mutual benefit of both parties.

Negotiation may result in increasing the final contract price over the initial bid price! Such was the case with a recent International Telephone and Telegraph (ITT) contract in which the Air Force Electronics Systems Division contracted with ITT's Defense Communications division for the Strategic Air Command's Satin-4 communications network. Air Force officials revealed that the $36 million contract was almost $8 million higher than ITT's "best and final" bid price.

Why was the final contract $8 million higher than the original bid? The Air Force explained that the 22 percent increase over the original bid represented technical changes made during the final negotiating sessions with ITT.

Source. Based on information described by Jack Robertson, "Dealing in the Dark," *Electronic News*, May 2, 1977.

The Institutional Market: Unique Characteristics

To this point, we have examined two important sectors of the industrial market—commercial enterprises and government. The institutional market constitutes the third important market component.

Institutional buyers make up a sizable market—total expenditures on education exceeded $143 billion in 1977–78, and health care costs totaled over $178 billion in 1978.[15] Schools and health care facilities are important factors in the *institutional market,* which also includes penal institutions, colleges and universities, libraries, foundations, art galleries, clinics, and similar organizations. Institutional buyers fall somewhere between commercial enterprise and government buyers in terms of their characteristics, orientation, and purchasing process. In one sense institutional purchasers are similar to governments in that the purchasing process is constrained by political considerations and dictated by law. In fact, many institutions are administered by government units—schools, for example. Other institutions are privately operated and managed like corporations; they may even have a broader range of purchase requirements than their large corporate counterparts. Like the commercial enterprise, institutions are ever cognizant of the value of efficient purchasing. If a university can effect a savings of $100,000 due to purchasing efficiencies, and its endowment income generates a 10 percent earning rate, the $100,000 savings is equivalent to an endowment gift of $1,000,000! Because of the similarities of the institutional market to the previous markets, its characteristics will be presented very briefly.

Institutional Buyers: Purchasing Procedures

Diversity is the key element in the institutional market. The institutional marketing manager must be ready to respond to a school purchasing agent who buys in great quantity for an entire city's school system through a formal bid procedure. In the next case, the manager may have to develop an approach to satisfy the needs of a former pharmacist who has been elevated to purchasing agent for a small rural hospital.

Health care institutions provide a good example of the diversity of this market. In terms of food purchasing, some small hospitals delegate responsibility to the chief dietitian. Although many of these hospitals have purchasing agents, the agent cannot place an order unless approved by the dietitian. In other, larger hospitals, decisions are made by committees often composed of a business manager, purchasing agent, dietitian, and cook. In still other cases, hospitals may belong to buying groups consisting of many local hospitals, or its meal preparation may be contracted out to a company that specializes in institutional food preparation. Because of these varied purchasing environments, successful institutional marketers usually maintain a separate marketing manager, staff, and sales force to specifically tailor marketing efforts to each situation.

Multiple Buying Influences. Chapter 1 discussed the concept of the multiple buying influence; this simply means that several individuals with diverse backgrounds and goals have an influence on the organizational buying process. The institutional market offers some unique applications of the multiple buying influence concept.

Many institutions are staffed with expertly trained professionals—doctors, professors, researchers, and others. In most cases, depending upon size, the institution will employ a purchasing agent, and in large institutions, a sizable purchasing department. There is great potential for conflict between purchasing staff members, who are responsible for the purchasing function, and the professional staff, for whom the purchasing department is buying. The purchasing staff is in a logical position to be in constant contact with suppliers, challenge restrictive specifications, secure information on market availability, and arrange for product demonstrations from several major suppliers. The professional staff is quite knowledgeable about its professional activities, yet not so knowledgeable on the economics of purchasing. However, many professionals resent the usurping of their authority to buy from whom they wish. Industrial marketing and sales personnel, in formulating their marketing and personal selling approaches, must understand these conflicts and be able to respond to them. Often, the salesperson must carefully cultivate the professional staff in terms of product benefits and service while developing a delivery timetable, maintenance contract, and price schedule to satisfy the purchasing department.

Dealing with Diversity: A Market-Centered Organization

This detailed look at the broad sectors of the industrial market emphasizes the need for the marketer to adapt strategy to the specific characteristics of each sector. Because each sector of the industrial market is unique, many

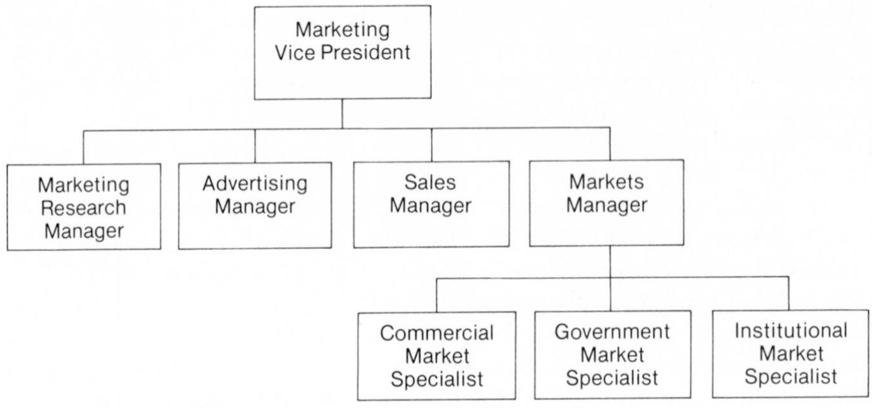

Figure 2.3 / A Market-Centered Organization

firms have built market specialization into the marketing organization. To illustrate, the industrial products area of the J. M. Smucker Company is organized around market sectors. The institutional, military, and industrial markets are each managed by different individuals who are thoroughly knowledgeable of their particular market. Mack Hanan refers to such a structure as a market-centered organization.[16] He contends that the most effective way to satisfy the needs of distinct customer groups is to structure the organization so that the firm's divisions are built around major customer markets.

One form of a market-centered organizational scheme is illustrated in figure 2.3. Observe that a markets manager supervises and coordinates the activities of three market specialists. Each market specialist examines the buying processes, product preferences, and similarities and differences among customers that fall within one sector of the industrial market. Such an analysis allows the market specialist to further partition customers in a particular sector into meaningful market segments. Specialized marketing programs can then be designed to fit the particular needs of each segment. A market-centered organization provides the industrial marketer with a structure for effectively dealing with the diversity in the industrial market.

Summary

A large market awaits the industrial marketing manager. The market can be divided into three major components: commercial enterprises, government (federal, state, and local), and institutions. To successfully reach one of these sectors, the marketer requires an understanding of its unique characteristics and the structure of the purchasing function.

Commercial enterprises include manufacturers, construction companies, service firms, transportation companies, selected professional groups, and resellers. Of these commercial customers, manufacturers account for the largest dollar volume of purchases. Furthermore, although the majority of these manufacturing firms are small, buying power is concentrated in the hands of relatively few large buyers. These manufacturing establishments are also concentrated geographically. Other commercial enterprises, such as service establishments and transportation and utility companies, are more widely dispersed. Every commercial enterprise must procure materials, supplies, and equipment to attain its organizational objectives. Often, the purchasing process is administered by a purchasing manager or purchasing agent. In larger firms, the purchasing function has become quite specialized, placing heavy demands on the industrial salesperson who must match the expertise of potential buyers. In smaller organizations, one person may be responsible for all buying activities.

Many marketers encounter frustration when dealing with the government sector of the industrial market. As we have seen, however, government is the largest consumer in the United States. The diligent marketer, who acquires an understanding of the procurement laws and different types of contracts employed by the government, can find a lucrative market on the federal, state, or local level. Federal buying follows two general procurement strategies: formal advertising or negotiated contract. The formal advertising approach is frequently followed for standardized products and involves the solicitation of bids from appropriate suppliers. Negotiated contract buying is employed for unique requirements and is typified by discussion and bargaining throughout all phases of the contract.

Diversity is the characteristic that best describes the institutional market. Institutional buyers are somewhere between commercial enterprise and government buyers in terms of their characteristics, orientations, and purchasing processes.

The industrial marketer must be prepared to encounter a wide range of purchasing approaches. Many industrial firms have found that a market-centered organization provides the specialization required to meet the needs of each sector of the industrial market.

Footnotes

[1]*Statistical Abstracts of the United States,* U.S. Department of the Census, 1977, p. 550.

[2]U.S. Department of Commerce, Bureau of Census, *Census of Manufacturers Area Statistics* (Washington, D.C.: Government Printing Office, 1971), p. 39.

[3]Lamar Lee, Jr., and Donald W. Dobler, *Purchasing and Materials Management* (New York: McGraw-Hill Book Company, 1977), p. 440.

[4]Ibid., p. 443.

[5]Charles F. Carpenter, *The Purchasing Role: A View from the Top* (New York: AMACOM, 1977), p. 23.

[6]J. H. Westing, I. V. Fine, and Gary J. Zenz, *Purchasing Management, Materials in Motion* (New York: John Wiley and Sons, Inc., 1976), pp. 4–5.

[7]*Guide to Purchasing* (New York: National Association of Purchasing Management, 1974), pp. 3, 6, 22.

[8]Edward H. Bonfield and Thomas W. Speh, "Dimensions of Purchasing's Role in Industry," *Journal of Purchasing and Materials Management* 13 (Summer 1977), p. 15.

[9]*Government Units in 1972*, U.S. Department of Commerce, Preliminary Report #1, December 1972, p. 1.

[10]Cecil Hynes and Noel Zabriskie, *Marketing to Governments* (Columbus, Ohio: Grid, Inc., 1974), p. 1.

[11]Ibid., p. 67.

[12]"Congressional Dogfight over the F-14," *Business Week* (December 16, 1972), pp. 58–62.

[13]Richard M. Hill, Ralph S. Alexander, and James S. Cross, *Industrial Marketing* (4th ed.; Homewood, Ill.: Richard D. Irwin, Inc., 1975), p. 74.

[14]Hynes and Zabriskie, *Marketing to Governments,* p. 58.

[15]*1978 United States Industrial Outlook,* U.S. Department of Commerce, Washington, D.C., January 1978, pp. 438, 452.

[16]Mack Hanan, "Reorganize Your Company around Its Markets," *Harvard Business Review* 52 (November–December 1974), pp. 63–74.

Discussion Questions

1. Research suggests that an increasing number of buying organizations have adopted the "materials management" concept. Describe this concept and outline the managerial implications that it raises for the industrial marketer.

2. Compare and contrast the two general procurement strategies employed by the federal government: (1) formal advertising and (2) negotiated contract.

3. Institutional buyers fall somewhere between commercial enterprise and government buyers in terms of their characteristics, orientation, and purchasing process. Explain.

4. Evaluate the wisdom of this personal selling strategy: the approach that is appropriate for large purchasing departments is equally effective in small purchasing departments.

5. Describe the role of value analysis in the contemporary purchasing organization. What steps can the industrial marketer take to benefit from such a value analysis?

6. Explain how the decision-making process that a university might employ in selecting a new computer would differ from that followed by a commercial enterprise. Who would be the key participants in the process in each setting?

7. Fearing red tape and mounds of paperwork, Tom Bronson, President of B&E Electric, has always avoided the government market. A recent discussion with a colleague, however, has rekindled Tom's interest in this industrial market sector. What steps should B&E Electric take to learn more about this market?

8. Why have some industrial firms moved away from product-centered organizations and toward market-centered organizations?

Part II

The Organizational Buying Process

Chapter 3 Dimensions of Organizational Buying

An understanding of the organizational buying process is fundamental to the development of sound industrial marketing strategy. After reading this chapter, you will understand:

1. *the decision process that organizational buyers apply as they confront different buying situations;*
2. *the specific strategy implications that different types of buying situations present for the industrial marketer;*
3. *the rational and emotional factors that influence organizational members in choosing among the offerings of competing industrial marketers;*
4. *the formal evaluation systems that organizational buyers employ in evaluating supplier performance.*

The organizational market, comprised of diverse customers with special needs, provides a challenging target for marketers. These organizations have differing objectives and orientations and vary in size and structure. Despite these differences, certain common elements are found in the purchasing systems of many organizations. What process do these organizational customers follow in selecting needed products and services? How do they evaluate the offerings of competing marketers? Clearly, a knowledge of the mechanics of the purchasing system is an important first step in successfully reaching these organizational customers.

The buying procedures of organizations, although more formalized, resemble the approach to buying that final consumers follow. The purchasing agent may automatically order an item in the same way that a shopper routinely selects a preferred brand from the retailer's shelf. Little time, effort, or deliberation goes into the decision. Other decisions, however, involve an elaborate search for information and a careful consideration of alternatives. In such cases, many members of the organization provide input during the lengthy decision-making process. Interestingly, some might consider the household a group decision-making unit that becomes operative in a similar fashion when major family purchases (e.g., a new car, television) are being considered.

To be effective, the marketer must understand the decision-making process that the organizational customers follow, the key participants in this process, and the criteria used by these decision makers. Importantly, the sensitivity and receptivity of organizational buyers to marketing communications varies significantly throughout the decision-making process. Thus, knowledge of the purchasing process provides the marketer with a firm base for building responsive industrial marketing strategy.

The Industrial Buying Process

Tracing the history of a procurement decision in an organization uncovers critical decision points and evolving information requirements. The following eight-stage model describes the sequence of activities that are performed in the organizational buying process.[1]

Stage 1. Anticipation or Recognition of a Problem (Need)

Recognition of a problem or of a potential opportunity triggers the purchasing process within the buying organization. Numerous situations can stimulate problem recognition; the firm's products become outmoded, equipment breaks down, or existing materials are of an unsatisfactory quality. A marketer can precipitate the need for a product by displaying potential opportunities for improving the organization's performance. Early involvement in the buying process provides the marketer with a clear understanding of the organization's needs and information requirements, and, therefore, a greater probability of success in securing the account.

Stage 2. Determination of the Characteristics and Quantity of the Needed Item

Here, organizational members must determine specifically how the problem can be solved. These decisions generally are made within the using department, where such needs invariably emerge. For example, members of the production department (using department) would play an active role in determining the characteristics needed in a new high-speed packaging system. In the case of technical products, performance specifications for the proposed product or service are prepared by the using department. For more standard goods, the using department may do no more than determine that the problem could be solved with items available on the market.

Stage 3. Description of the Characteristics and Quantity of the Needed Item

An extension of the second phase, this step involves the development of a detailed and precise description of the needed item which can be readily communicated to others. This can be a critical stage for the marketer because key buying influences emerge in the development of the specifications. A knowledge of these buying influentials and their relative roles and importance can place the marketer at a distinct advantage. It is important to note that a marketer who triggers the initial need may have the benefit of a close working relationship with organizational members throughout these formative stages in the procurement process.

Stage 4. Search for and Qualification of Potential Sources

Once the organization has determined the nature of the product that will satisfy its requirements, the search turns to available sources of supply. The objective in this stage is to determine which of the many possible suppliers are worthy of consideration as potential vendors. Potential sources of supply are screened and evaluated. The intensity of this evaluation procedure varies by organization and the particular buying situation. For example, the organization invests more time and energy in the evaluation process when the proposed product or service will have a strong bearing on organizational performance. (The approach used by organizational buyers in evaluating potential vendors is treated in more detail later in the chapter.)

Stage 5. Acquisition and Analysis of Proposals

When the information needs of the buying organization are low, stages four and five occur simultaneously. This is especially true when standardized items are under consideration. In that case the buying organization may merely check a catalog or contact a supplier to obtain up-to-date price information. For more complex goods, such as machine tools, many months may be consumed as proposals and counterproposals are exchanged. Note that stage five emerges as a distinct component of the buying process when the information needs of the buying organization are high.

Stage 6. Evaluation of Proposals and Selection of Suppliers

The alternative proposals are analyzed with one or more of the offers being accepted and others rejected. Negotiations may continue with the selected suppliers concerning the terms of the transaction.

Stage 7. Selection of an Order Routine

A marketer that survives the review process and is selected as a source of supply faces further tests. The using department, where the need originated, will not view its problem as resolved until the specified product is received and available for use. In terms of the order routine, a purchase order is forwarded to the vendor, status reports are forwarded to the using department, and inventory levels are planned. Thus, this stage centers on establishing procurement procedures for the particular item (e.g., the size and frequency of orders).

Stage 8. Performance Feedback and Evaluation

Did the purchased item solve the original problem of the buying organization? This constitutes the final stage in the procurement process. Feedback may flow through formal or informal channels in the organization. If the product fails to meet the needs of the using department, other vendors that were screened earlier in the procurement process may be given further consideration. Feedback critical of the chosen supplier and supportive of rejected alternatives can lead members of the decision-making unit to reexamine their position. Under such conditions, research indicates that their attitude toward rejected alternatives becomes more positive.[2] To retain a new account, the marketer must insure that the needs of the buying organization have been completely satisfied. Failure to follow through at this critical stage can place the marketer in a vulnerable position.

An Initial Structure

This eight-stage model provides important initial insights to the organizational buying process. The activities follow a logical sequence, take place sequentially, and involve continually changing interactions of organizational members. As noted, certain stages may be completed concurrently. The process may be reoriented at any point by a redefinition of the basic problem; it may be discontinued by a change in the external environment or in upper-management thinking.

Many small or incremental decisions are made during the procurement process that ultimately translate into the final selection of a supplier. For example, a quality control engineer might unknowingly establish specifications for a new production system that only supplier A can meet. Essentially, then, this incremental decision made in the early phases of the buying process dramatically influenced the favorable evaluation and ultimate selection of supplier A.

The marketer can play an active role in defining and meeting the buying organization's information requirements at critical decision points. The importance of these decision points varies with the specific buying situation confronting the organization.

Buying Situations Analyzed

Organizations have different levels of experience and information to call upon in purchasing certain products. The same product may elicit markedly different purchasing patterns in different organizations; therefore, attention must center on "buying situations" rather than on "products."

Three types of buying situations have been delineated: (1) new task, (2) modified rebuy, and (3) straight rebuy.[3] As illustrated in table 3.1, each type of buying situation must be related to the eight-stage buying process discussed earlier.

New Task

The problem or need in the new task buying situation is perceived by organizational decision makers to be totally different from experiences that

Table 3.1 / The Buygrid Framework for Industrial Buying Situations

Buyphases	Buyclasses		
	New Task	Modified Rebuy	Straight Rebuy
1. Anticipation or recognition of a problem (need) and a general solution.			
2. Determination of characteristics and quantity of needed item.			
3. Description of characteristics and quantity of needed item.			
4. Search for and qualification of potential sources.			
5. Acquisition and analysis of proposals.			
6. Evaluation of proposals and selection of supplier(s).			
7. Selection of an order routine.			
8. Performance feedback and evaluation.			

Source. From the Marketing Science Institute Series, *Industrial Buying and Creative Marketing*, by Patrick J. Robinson, Charles W. Faris, and Yoram Wind. Copyright © 1967 by Allyn and Bacon, Inc., Boston. Reprinted with permission.

have emerged in the past. For this reason a significant amount of information is required by the buying influentials. Alternative ways of solving the problem must be explored, and a search for alternative suppliers must be undertaken.

When confronting a new task buying situation, organizational buyers operate in a stage of decision making referred to as *extensive problem solving*.[4] The buying influentials and decision makers lack well-defined criteria that can be used in comparing alternative products and suppliers. They also lack strong predispositions toward a particular alternative solution.

The Direction of Marketing Effort. The industrial marketer, confronting a new task buying situation, can gain a differential advantage over competitors by participating actively in the initial stages of the procurement process. Here the marketer should gather information on the problems facing the buying organization, isolate specific requirements, and offer proposals that meet these requirements. Frequently, ideas that lead to new products originate not with the marketer but with the customer.[5]

Marketers who are presently supplying other items to the buying organization ("in" suppliers) have an edge over other firms because they see problems unfolding and are familiar with the "personality" and behavior patterns of the organization. The successful industrial marketer carefully monitors the changing needs of organizations and is prepared to respond to the needs of new task buyers.

Straight Rebuy

This buying situation centers on a continuing or recurring requirement. The buyers have substantial experience in dealing with the need and require little or no new information. Evaluation of new alternative solutions is considered unnecessary and unlikely to yield appreciable improvements.

Routinized response behavior is the decision process approach that organizational buyers employ when confronting the straight rebuy.[6] Here, organizational buyers have well-developed choice criteria that can be applied to the purchase decision. These criteria have been tested and refined over time as the organizational buyers have developed strong predispositions toward the offerings of one or a few carefully screened suppliers.

The Direction of Marketing Effort. The purchasing department handles straight rebuy situations by routinely selecting a supplier from a list (formal or informal) of acceptable vendors and placing an order. The marketing task appropriate in this situation depends on whether the marketer is an "in" supplier (on the list) or an "out" supplier (not among the chosen few). An "in" supplier must reinforce the buyer-seller relationship, meet the buying organization's expectations, and be alert and responsive to the changing needs of the organization.

The "out" supplier faces a number of challenging obstacles in efforts to penetrate this account. The goal of the nonsupplier is to convince the organization that significant benefits can be derived from breaking the routine. This can be a difficult task because organizational buyers perceive risk in shifting from the known to the unknown. The organizational spotlight shines directly on them if a new and untested supplier falters. Testing, evaluations, and approvals may be viewed by buyers as costly, time consuming, and unnecessary.[7]

The marketing effort of the "out" supplier rests on an understanding of the basic buying needs of the organization. Again, information gathering is essential to effective performance. The marketer must convince organizational buyers that their purchasing requirements have changed or that the requirements should be interpreted differently. The objective is to persuade decision makers that a reexamination of alternative solutions would be beneficial. Such a reassessment may lead to a revision of the preferred list to include the new supplier.

Modified Rebuy

The distinguishing characteristic of the modified rebuy situation is that organizational decision makers feel that significant benefits could be derived from a reevaluation of alternatives. The buyers have relevant experience in satisfying the continuing or recurring requirement, but they believe it may be worthwhile to seek additional information before a decision is made. Often, new alternative solutions are considered as buyers assess the additional information.

Several factors may trigger an organization to engage in such a reassessment. Internal forces include the search for quality improvements or cost reductions. A marketer offering cost, quality, or service improvements can be an external precipitating force. The modified rebuy situation is most likely to occur when the firm is displeased with the performance of present suppliers (e.g., poor delivery service).

Limited problem solving best describes the decision-making process that is consistent with the modified rebuy. Decision makers have well-defined criteria that can be applied to the procurement problem but are uncertain concerning which suppliers can most precisely fit their needs.[8] Additional information is needed.

The Direction of Marketing Effort. In the case of the modified rebuy, the direction of the marketing effort depends on whether the marketer is an "in" or an "out" supplier. An "in" supplier should make every effort to understand and satisfy the procurement need and, ideally, move decision makers into a straight rebuy situation. The buying organization perceives that some potential payoffs could be derived from a reexamination of alternatives. Why? The "in" supplier should examine this question and act immediately to remedy any customer problems. The marketer may be out of touch with the buying organization's requirements.

A modified rebuy provides the opportunity for the "out" supplier to enter the buyer's set of feasible suppliers. The goal of the marketer should be to

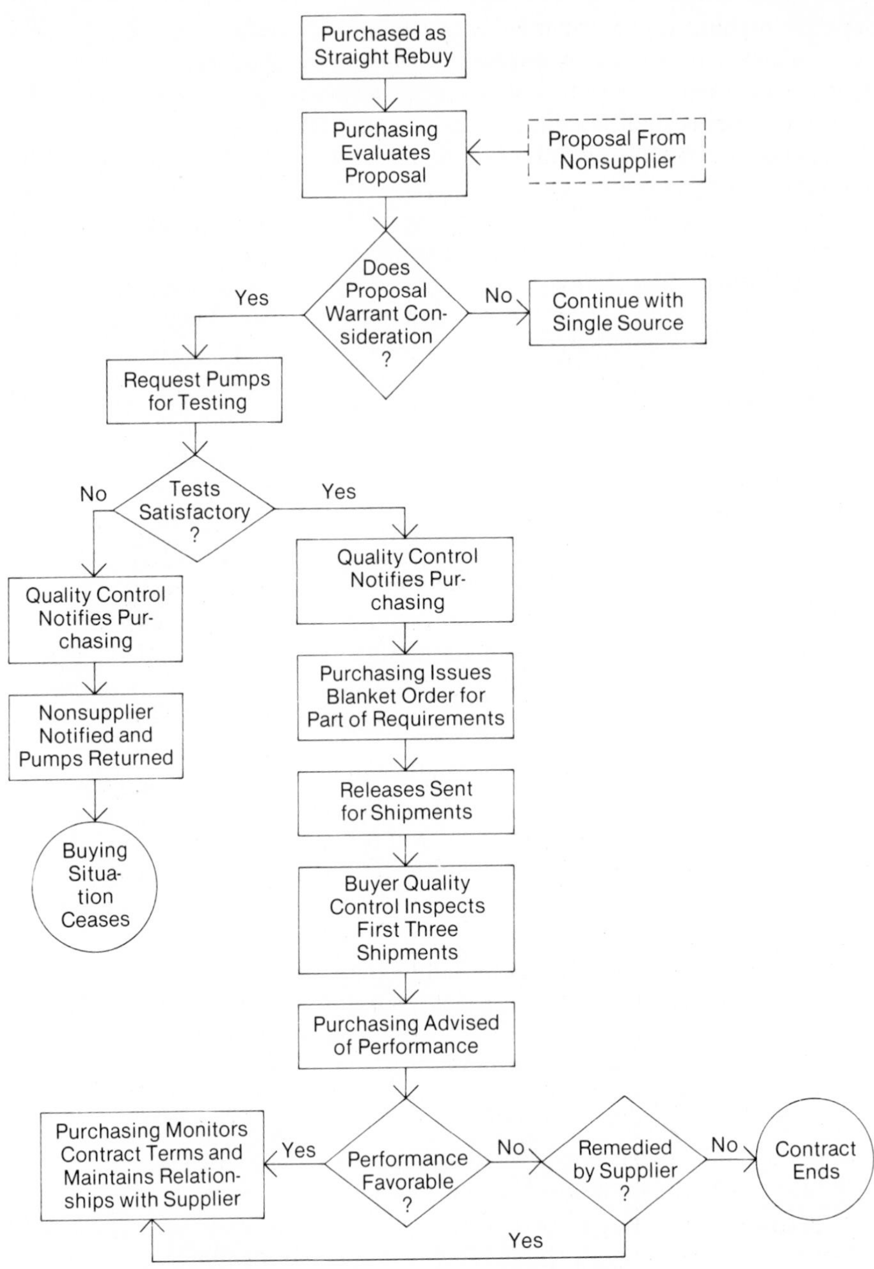

Figure 3.1 / Example of a Modified Rebuy: Hydraulic Pump

Hydraulic pumps were purchased as routine rebuys until an "out" supplier offered a substantially lower price which stimulated a reconsideration of sources. The resulting chain of events in the purchasing process is graphically outlined above.

Source. From the Marketing Science Institute Series. Patrick J. Robinson, Charles W. Faris, and Yoram Wind, *Industrial Buying and Creative Marketing*, p. 75. Copyright © 1967 by Allyn and Bacon, Inc., Boston. Reprinted by permission.

hold the organization in the modified rebuy status long enough for the buyer to evaluate and sample an alternative offering. Knowledge of the factors that led decision makers to reexamine alternatives could be pivotal to the marketer's penetration effort.

Each type of buying situation requires a unique response by the industrial marketer. Strategies appropriate for each of the three buying situations are summarized in table 3.2.

Buying Influentials and the Purchasing Task

Buying decisions typically involve not one but several members of the organization. This holds true for buying decisions made by commercial enterprises, institutions, and governmental organizations. Thus, the relevant

Table 3.2 / Responding to Different Buying Situations: A Profile of Required Marketing Strategies

	Supplier Status	
Buying Situation	In Supplier	Out Supplier
New Task	Monitor changing or emerging purchasing needs in organization.	
	Isolate specific needs.	Isolate specific needs.
	If possible, participate actively in early phases of buying process by supplying information and technical advice.	If possible, participate actively in early phases of buying process by supplying information and technical advice.
Straight Rebuy	Reinforce buyer-seller relationship by meeting organization's expectations.	Convince organization that the potential benefits of reexamining requirements and suppliers exceed the costs.
	Be alert and responsive to changing needs of customer.	Attempt to gain a position on organization's preferred list of suppliers even as a second or third choice.
Modified Rebuy	Act immediately to remedy problems with customer.	Define and respond to the organization's problem with existing supplier.
	Reexamine and respond to customer needs.	Encourage organization to sample alternative offerings.

Source. From the Marketing Science Institute Series. Patrick J. Robinson, Charles W. Faris, and Yoram Wind. *Industrial Buying and Creative Marketing* (Boston: Allyn and Bacon, Inc., 1967), pp. 183–210.

unit of analysis for the industrial marketer is the group decision-making unit or the buying center. The *buying center* includes all those individuals and groups that participate in the purchasing decision-making process and share some common goals and risks arising from the decision.[9] The composition and relative importance of organizational members in the buying center changes at a rapid pace as a firm moves from phase to phase in the decision process.

The role of buying influences also varies with the buying task. For example, buyers have differing levels of experience and follow different problem-solving approaches as they move along the learning curve from extended problem solving to routinized problem solving. To illustrate, the decision to purchase a lathe may be a new task buying situation in one organization while it is a modified or straight rebuy in another. As emphasized earlier, each type of buying situation could represent a different market segment that requires a specialized marketing strategy. The industrial marketer, therefore, must view the procurement problem or need from the perspective of the buying organization. How far has the organization progressed with the specific purchasing problem? How does the organization define the buying task at hand? Answers to these questions dictate, to an important degree, the direction and form of the industrial marketer's response and also provide insight to the composition of the relevant decision-making unit.

To this point in the chapter, the purchasing process as well as the various types of purchases or buying situations have been discussed. Table 3.3 highlights this discussion and illustrates the changing composition of the decision-making unit in different phases of the buying process for the three buying situations. The intent here is to outline "typical" influence patterns.

New Task: Buying Influentials. For the new task buying situation, note the involvement of top or general management in the early phases of the buying process. Of course, the involvement of top management will be greatest in those situations "where the results of the purchasing decision could substantially reduce the company's flexibility or ability to act in the future."[10] (For example, the addition of new fixed production facilities for selected products may limit the firm's ability to respond to changing market conditions for other products.) Once a policy decision has been made, the details of the procurement process can be delegated to others. Technical personnel play an important and active role in virtually all phases of the purchasing process in the new task buying situation. The purchasing agent is involved in later stages.

Modified Rebuy: Buying Influentials. The purchasing agent's involvement in the decision-making process expands in the case of the modified rebuy. Several factors can trigger the search for a new supplier—unfavorable feedback, quest for quality improvements, search for cost savings. When a change in suppliers comes under consideration, the buyer emerges as the

Table 3.3 / Decision-Making Unit Members Involved by Type of Purchase

Purchasing Stages	New Task	Modified Rebuy	Straight Rebuy
Recognition of Need to Purchase	Top Management, General Management	Buyer	Stock Control System
Determination of Product Characteristics	Technical Personnel	As specified when new purchase	As specified
Description of Product Characteristics	Technical Personnel	As specified	As specified
Search for Suppliers	Technical Personnel	Buyer	Approved Suppliers
Assessing Qualifications of Suppliers	Technical Personnel	Technical Personnel and Buyer	Approved Suppliers
Acquisition of Proposals	Buyer and Technical Personnel	Buyer	Purchasing Staff
Evaluation of Proposals	Technical Personnel	Buyer	Purchasing Staff
Selection of Supplier	Technical Personnel, General Management, Buyer	Buyer	Purchasing Staff
Selection of Order Routine	Buyer	Buyer	Purchasing Staff
Performance Feedback and Evaluation	Technical Personnel and Buyer (informal)	Buyer (informal) System (formal)	Buyer (informal) System (formal)

Source. Adapted from Gordon T. Brand, *The Industrial Buying Decision*, p. 71. Copyright © 1972 by Institute of Marketing and Industrial Market Research Ltd., London.

dominant influence in identifying, qualifying, and selecting the new source of supply.

Straight Rebuy: Buying Influentials. The purchasing staff, following relatively routine procedures, handles the straight rebuy transactions. Observe from table 3.3 that the stock control system alerts the purchasing department of the need to purchase. Senior buyers devote their attention to special problems or situations. While these senior buyers exert substantial influence concerning which companies become regular suppliers, junior buyers or clerks actually place the repeat orders and determine which of the listed suppliers gets the orders.

Buying Motivations of Organizational Buyers

The evaluation of potential suppliers constitutes a key phase in the industrial buying process. Here the fate of the industrial marketer is determined. The buying organization assesses the merits of alternative suppliers, selects the vendor that most precisely meets the organization's needs, and, pending favorable performance, may become routinized in future buying decisions. As discussed earlier, suppliers that were screened out during this evaluation process may find it difficult to again get the firm's attention. To respond effectively to customer needs, the industrial marketer requires an understanding of the criteria used by organizational buyers in evaluating potential suppliers.

Organizational members are influenced by both rational and emotional factors in choosing among the offerings of competing industrial marketers. Rational motives center on economic considerations such as price, quality, and service; emotional motives are concerned with noneconomic or human factors such as job security or organizational status. The industrial marketer faces the difficult task of defining the buying motives of the organizational members who will ultimately pass judgment on a product. This is a particularly difficult task because generalizations about the importance of selected buying motives cannot be made across all types of industrial buying decisions. Research indicates that members of the buying center often use different criteria in evaluating suppliers.[11] For example, the purchasing agent may value maximum price economy, but engineers are primarily concerned with product quality. Also, the importance of such criteria varies with the type of product being considered.[12]

The challenge for the marketer is to view the purchasing decision from the buying organization's perspective, to ascertain the roles of various members of the buying center, and to determine the factors that motivate each member.

Rational Motives

Since commercial enterprises are guided by profit objectives and governmental units, and not-for-profit organizations are encircled with budgetary constraints, rational or economic buying motives are often significant. Several of these buying motivations are considered below.

Price. The professional buyer evaluates a quoted price from many perspectives. To illustrate, a buyer considering a new piece of capital equipment will analyze potential savings (return) in manpower, energy, and material and relate these factors to the price (investment). Thus, a return on investment (ROI) calculation would be used by the buyer in comparing the offerings of competing equipment firms. In another case, such as in the purchase of a component part, the buyer might consider the price in relation to the ease of installation. A higher priced component that was easier and less costly to install would have an edge over a less expensive model that posed cumbersome installation problems. Marketers often overestimate the importance of offering the lowest price. Frequently, the low bidder fails other tests that are important to the buying organization.[13]

Quality. An industrial customer seeks a level of quality that is consistent with defined specifications and intended use. Organizational buyers do not want to pay for more quality than they need, and they are unwilling to compromise specifications for a reduced price. Uniformity or consistency of product quality is often the crucial factor to the industrial customer. Such consistency can: (1) guarantee uniformity in the end product that the buying organization markets, (2) reduce the need for careful and costly inspections of each incoming shipment, and (3) insure that the purchased material will mesh smoothly with the production process. A low degree of consistency in the quality of incoming materials and components creates costly problems for the buying organization.

Service. All sectors of the industrial market (commercial enterprises, government, and institutions) require a broad range of services to achieve organizational objectives. These services include technical assistance, information, delivery, repair capability, spare parts availability, and even financing. Service can be an important means of differentiation for the marketer and often plays a central role in organizational buying decisions. A marketer that offers sound technical advice, reliable and speedy delivery, and an available supply of replacement parts has an edge over a competing supplier offering a somewhat weaker service package.

To illustrate, the buying organization must make a larger investment in inventory if the supplier's delivery service is slow or unpredictable, rather than fast and reliable. The importance of physical distribution service to organizational buyers is vividly illustrated in a study by William Perreault and Frederick Russ.[14] Their survey of industrial purchasing managers reveals that physical distribution service ranks second only to product quality in influencing industrial purchase decisions.

Continuity of Supply. Continuity of supply can be a critical concern to the purchasing manager. Any interruption in the flow of key materials or components into the organization can bring the production process to an abrupt halt—costly delays and lost sales result. To guard against contingencies, such as an unanticipated strike in a supplier's plant, professional buyers are extremely reluctant to rely on a single source of supply. Instead, they choose to spread their business among two or more suppliers whenever possible. Continuity of supply is important to the buyer not only during periods of shortages, but also during times of plenty when shortages are anticipated. Concern with continuity of supply is greatest when the number of alternative suppliers is limited.[15]

Reciprocity. Buyers and sellers often have close and enduring relationships in the industrial market. Thus, reciprocal trade possibilities often emerge: "If you buy from me, I'll buy from you." Reciprocity can occur when two or more firms buy from and sell to each other. The motivation for buying from each other is the key to whether an arrangement involves reciprocity. A relationship involves reciprocity when the *buyer-seller arrangement,* rather than economic or performance factors, influences the purchase decision.

Reciprocal trade relations can be based on friendly or highly coercive pressure. The latter might involve the threat: "If you don't buy X percent more from me, I'll reduce my purchases from you by Y percent!" Reciprocity is legal as long as the arrangement is not enforced through coercive power by one or more parties, and if the reciprocal agreement does not serve to substantially lessen competition. One authority, F. Robert Finney, contends that anticompetitive and coercive reciprocity have been successfully checked by the government in recent years.[16] However, he concludes that friendship reciprocity continues to be a force in the industrial market. "Innocent reciprocity continues and will continue—not illegal, not injurious to competition, and of no consequence in antitrust."[17]

Emotional Motives

A marketer that centers exclusively on the rational motives of buyers has an incomplete picture of the organizational buyer. Emotional motives play a key role in many industrial buying decisions. These motives include the desire for status within the organization as well as a desire for promotion, salary increases, and increased job security.[18] Buyers "often get caught up in tradition, fight change, and exhibit a high degree of fear in resisting the new."[19]

Delicate Buyer-Seller Relationships

Many marketers take steps to insure that they buy, display, and support the products of their customers.

- U.S. Steel salesmen often go to great lengths to drive GM cars when calling on GM plants.
- A GM visitor at PPG Industries, Inc., (autoglass producer) is likely to be picked up at the airport in a GM car.
- N.W. Ayer ABH International, an ad agency, promptly removed Pepsi machines from its offices when the Seven-Up account was secured.

Source. "If Calling on GM, Should One Avoid Arriving in a Ford?" *Wall Street Journal* (September 21, 1979), p. 1.

Organizational buyers are motivated by a strong need to reduce uncertainty.[20] The buyer may be uncertain concerning: (1) the number of buying alternatives that are available, (2) the specific level of performance that can be expected from each alternative, and (3) how other organizational members (that may have other goals) will evaluate the buying decision. The buyer will often reduce uncertainty by relying on familiar suppliers that have been used in the past or by favoring suppliers with the best reputation.

Emotional motives often influence buying decisions in subtle ways. A purchasing manager may be known to select suppliers on the basis of a competitive bid process, but may work diligently with a friend "to get him competitive" on price level and product specifications.[21] Emotional motives cannot be overlooked. To effectively reach a particular buying organization, the marketer requires an understanding of the buying motives (rational and nonrational) that are salient to the members of the buying center. This knowledge is vital in designing responsive marketing strategy.

How Organizational Buyers Evaluate Potential Suppliers

The rational and emotional buying motives of individual organizational buyers are ultimately reflected in the buying organization's formal evaluation of suppliers. The specific type of evaluation followed by the organizational buyers in assessing an industrial marketer's capability varies with the type of buying situation as well as with the complexity and dollar value of the purchases to be made. The buyer's knowledge of the suppliers under consideration, coupled with the organization's perception of the value and importance of the purchase, determine the problem-solving approach followed. When purchasing a standardized product, deemed to be uncomplicated and of minor significance to organizational performance, the buyer may limit the examination to information already available in the purchasing department: catalogs, brochures, data on current suppliers drawn from files. However, if the procurement need is unique or the functional significance of the product in the organization is high, a more elaborate evaluation is required. Here the firm is purchasing the *supplier's technical and managerial capability*.

Evaluating Supplier Capability

A buying organization facing an important purchasing decision must carefully analyze the total capability of suppliers. Observe from table 3.4 that this assessment covers the technical, managerial, financial, and service capabilities of potential suppliers. Each provides a measure of the potential supplier's ability to comply with promises made to the buying organization.

After the list of potential suppliers has been screened and narrowed, the buying organization generally conducts an on-site inspection of vendor facilities. For such plant visits, the buying organization may send representatives from purchasing, engineering, and, on occasion, production and finance. The trained observer can quickly appraise the production capability of a supplier through discussions with technical and managerial staffs and by conducting a firsthand review of manufacturing operations. Is the equip-

Table 3.4 / Supplier Capability: Key Attributes Evaluated by Buyers

Attribute	Measure
Technical/Production Capability	Adequacy of equipment, production control, quality control, cost control.
Managerial Capability	The ability of supplier to plan, organize, and control operations.
Financial Condition	The financial stability of the supplier—profit record, cash flow, equity, working capital, credit rating.
Service Capacity	Supplier's ability to comply with promised product specifications, delivery dates, and technical assistance.

ment modern and up-to-date? Are scheduling and production control properly organized to allow promised delivery dates to be met? The industrial marketer must be prepared to encounter and pass such technical and managerial tests.

The financial condition of potential suppliers is also evaluated by buyers. A solid financial position usually points to a well-managed operation. Financial stability is a critical attribute of a potential vendor to assure continuity of supply and uniformity of product quality. A buyer consults such sources as Dun and Bradstreet (D&B) Reports, Moody's Industrials, or corporate annual reports in assessing the financial condition of a supplier.

The exact meaning of the term *service* varies with the nature of the product and the specific requirements of the buying organization. Service encompasses reliable delivery, technical assistance, innovative suggestions, credit arrangements, rapid support for special needs, and advance notice of impending price changes or shortages of supply. Buyers carefully assess the capacity of potential suppliers to provide the required level of service. The marketer with strong service capabilities will be in a favorable position when the final buying decision is made.

Evaluating Supplier Performance

Once a contract is awarded to a supplier, the evaluation process does not end but merely takes a different form. Actual performance must be evaluated. Objective ratings of supplier performance are used by buyers in assessing the quality of past decisions and in making future vendor selections. The National Association of Purchasing Management has examined the area of supplier evaluation in some depth and offers a variety of methods.[22] The specific method employed, as well as the scope of the rating system, varies by industry and firm.[23] Three are briefly described below: the categorical plan, the weighted-point plan, and the cost-ratio plan.[24]

Categorical Plan. Under this plan, supplier performance is evaluated by several departments in the organization that maintain informal records on each major vendor. Personnel from purchasing, engineering, quality control, receiving, and inspection may be involved in the evaluative effort. For every major supplier, each individual develops a list of the performance factors which are significant to him or her. At a regularly scheduled meeting (usually monthly), each major supplier is aligned against each evaluator's list of criteria and given an overall group evaluation. Suppliers are then placed into such categories as "preferred," "neutral," or "unsatisfactory." Ease of administration is the chief advantage of this highly subjective method.

The Weighted-Point Plan. Here the buying organization assigns weights to each performance factor. These weights represent the relative importance of the performance factors to the buyer. To illustrate, quality might be given a weight of 40, service 30, and price 30. This system alerts the industrial marketer to the nature and importance of the evaluative criteria used by a particular organization. The marketer's total offering can then be adjusted to more precisely fit the organization's needs.

A weighted-point plan that is currently in operation will be examined. A consumer products manufacturer "grades" suppliers on three criteria that are assigned the following weights:

- Delivery 40
- Quality 30
- Buyer Evaluation 30

A performance score is developed for each factor and, in turn, the three factor scores are totaled to give the supplier's overall rating for the period. For example, the performance score for quality is determined as follows:

Factor Weight × Percentage of material received that passes inspection

If 10 percent of supplier X's goods failed inspection, the quality performance score would be:

Factor	Weight	Actual Performance	Performance Score
Quality	30	10 percent rejects	30 × (1.00 − .10) = 27.0

Related performance measures and scores are developed for *delivery* and *buyer evaluation* and summed to give supplier X's overall evaluation. The performance of competing suppliers can then be compared quantitatively. The weighted-point plan has the advantages of being more objective and flexible than the categorical method. The buying organization can adjust the weights of various performance factors to meet its particular needs. Likewise, the method forces the organizational buyer to define the key attributes of a supplier and to objectively measure the supplier's performance on those attributes.

Some industrial customers send a report card to each of their suppliers on a regular basis. Such feedback reports serve to isolate supplier problems, stimulate improved performance, and strengthen buyer-seller relationships.

Cost-Ratio Plan. This method draws upon standard cost analysis in evaluating supplier performance. Under this plan, the buying organization evaluates quality, delivery, and service, assigning a minus (−) weight for favorable performance on a factor and a plus (+) weight for unfavorable performance. (That's right—a minus for good performance, a plus for bad performance. You will soon see why.) The weights for each performance factor are derived from standard cost calculations. For the delivery rating, the standard cost base might include the expense of factory downtime and rescheduling caused by a delinquent shipment as well as telephone follow-ups and associated costs. A penalty rating of +.02 might be assigned for a shipment received one week late and +.05 for a shipment delayed three weeks. Similar weights, based on standard costs, are made for quality and service and then combined into a final composite rating for each supplier. This composite rating is used in calculating an "adjusted price" for each major supplier. Supplier X will be evaluated using this approach.

An illustration: Assume that supplier X offers a bid price of $80.00 and has a quality cost ratio of +1 percent, a delivery cost ratio of +5 percent, and a service cost ratio of −1 percent. The three cost ratios sum to +5 percent. Thus, the adjusted price for supplier X is [$80.00 + (.05 × 80.00)] = $84.00. The organizational buyer would select the vendor offering the most economical total package rather than the supplier with the lowest bid price. Poor delivery performance clearly damaged the position of supplier X in relation to other suppliers. A competing supplier that offered solid delivery performance and competitive quality and service would be selected even at a slightly higher bid price.

A computerized cost accounting system is needed to provide the cost estimates that form the core of the cost-ratio plan. While this method has generated widespread interest, many firms prefer the weighted-point plan because of its simplicity and flexibility. The quality of each of the methods discussed—categorical, weighted-point, and cost-ratio—is determined by the accuracy and appropriateness of the underlying assumptions made by the evaluator.

Vendor Analysis: Implications for the Marketer

Industrial marketers must be sensitive to the criteria that organizational buyers employ in evaluating their offerings. Many criteria may be factored into a buyer's ultimate decision: quality, service, price, company image, capability, etc. Organizations have varying needs, objectives, and levels of experience. Buyers' perceptions are also critical. When products are perceived as highly standardized, price assumes more importance. On the other hand, if products are perceived as unique, other criteria may dominate. As we have seen, the price of a product cannot be separated from the attached bundle of services and other intangible values. The marketer must view his or her product-service offering from the perspective of the buying organization—only then can needs be defined and satisfied.

Organizational buyers employ a range of methods in formally evaluating the performance of suppliers. The marketer who secures a new account must be prepared to pass frequent performance tests in order to maintain that account. Research suggests that as purchasing departments increase their use of the computer, purchasing becomes more centralized, the number of suppliers declines, and the performance of suppliers is subjected to increased quantitative scrutiny.[25]

Summary

Knowledge of the process that organizational buyers follow in making purchasing decisions is fundamental to the design of responsive marketing strategy. As a buying organization moves from the problem recognition phase, where a procurement need is defined, to later phases, where suppliers are screened and ultimately chosen, the marketer can play an active role. In fact, the astute marketer often triggers the initial awareness of the problem and aids the organization in effectively solving that problem. Incremental decisions made throughout the buying process narrow the field of acceptable suppliers and dramatically influence the ultimate outcome.

The nature of the buying process depends upon the organization's level of experience with similar procurement problems. For that reason, attention centers on how the organization defines the buying situation: new task, modified rebuy, straight rebuy. Each buying situation elicits a different problem-solving approach and involves different buying influentials. In turn, each purchase situation requires a different type of marketing response.

Organizational buyers apply a wide range of rational and emotional buying motives to the purchasing decision process. After a purchasing decision is made, the buying organization evaluates and monitors the performance of the marketer, often through the use of a formal vendor rating system. These systems center on key supplier attributes that are deemed important to the buying organization, such as quality, service, delivery, and price. Specific vendor rating systems range from the easily administered categorical plan to the more complex cost-ratio method. Many firms have devised weighted-point plans to meet their individualized needs. Vendor rating systems define the requirements that the industrial marketer must meet.

The discussion of the purchasing process delineated in this chapter establishes the groundwork for an in-depth look at organizational buying behavior.

Footnotes

[1]The discussion in this section is based on Patrick J. Robinson, Charles W. Faris, and Yoram Wind, *Industrial Buying and Creative Marketing* (Boston: Allyn and Bacon, Inc., 1967), pp. 12–18.

[2]David R. Lambert, Ronald J. Dornoff, and Jerome B. Kernan, "The Industrial Buyer and the Postchoice Evaluation Process," *Journal of Marketing Research* 14 (May 1977), pp. 246–51.

[3]Robinson, Faris, and Wind, *Industrial Buying and Creative Marketing,* chapter 1.

[4]John A. Howard and Jagdish N. Sheth, *The Theory of Buyer Behavior* (New York: John Wiley and Sons, Inc., 1969), chapter 2.

[5]Eric Von Hippel, "Successful Industrial Products from Customer Ideas," *Journal of Marketing* 42 (January 1978), pp. 39–49.

[6]Howard and Sheth, *Theory of Buyer Behavior,* chapter 2.

[7]Robinson, Faris, and Wind, *Industrial Buying and Creative Marketing,* pp. 201–4.

[8]Howard and Sheth, *Theory of Buyer Behavior,* chapter 2.

[9]Frederick E. Webster, Jr., and Yoram Wind, *Organizational Buying Behavior* (Englewood Cliffs, N.J.: Prentice-Hall, Inc., 1972), p. 6.

[10]Robinson, Faris, and Wind, *Industrial Buying and Creative Marketing,* p. 135.

[11]For example, see Jagdish N. Sheth, "A Model of Industrial Buyer Behavior," *Journal of Marketing* 37 (October 1973), pp. 50–56; see also J. Patrick Kelly and James W. Coaker, "Can We Generalize about Choice Criteria for Industrial Purchasing Decisions?" in Kenneth L. Bernhardt, ed., *Marketing: 1776–1976 and Beyond* (Chicago: American Marketing Association, 1976), pp. 330–33.

[12]Donald R. Lehmann and John O'Shaughnessy, "Difference in Attribute Importance for Different Industrial Products," *Journal of Marketing* 40 (April 1976), pp. 36–42.

[13]Kelly and Coaker, "Can We Generalize about Choice Criteria?" pp. 330–33.

[14]William D. Perreault, Jr., and Frederick A. Russ, "Physical Distribution Service in Industrial Purchase Decisions," *Journal of Marketing* 40 (April 1976), pp. 3–10.

[15]Thomas V. Bonoma and Gerald Zaltman, "Introduction," in Bonoma and Zaltman, eds., *Organizational Buying Behavior* (Chicago: American Marketing Association, 1978), p. 8.

[16]F. Robert Finney, "Reciprocity: Gone but Not Forgotten," *Journal of Marketing* 43 (January 1978), pp. 54–59; see also Reed Moyer, "Reciprocity: Retrospect and Prospect," *Journal of Marketing* 34 (October 1970), pp. 47–54.

[17]Finney, Ibid., p. 59.

[18]For example, see Delbert J. Duncan, "Purchasing Agents: Seekers of Status, Personal and Professional," *Journal of Purchasing* 2 (August 1966), pp. 17–26; see also George Strauss, "Tactics of Lateral Relationships: The Purchasing Agent," *Administrative Science Quarterly* 7 (September 1962), pp. 161–86.

[19]H. Lazo, "Emotional Aspects of Industrial Buying," in R. S. Hancock, ed., *Proceedings of the American Marketing Association* (Chicago: American Marketing Association, 1960), pp. 258–65, reported in Thomas Bonoma, Gerald Zaltman, and Wesley J. Johnston, *Industrial Buying Behavior* (Cambridge, Mass.: Marketing Science Institute, 1977), p. 98.

[20]Webster and Wind, *Organizational Buying Behavior,* p. 96.

[21]Bonoma and Zaltman, *Organizational Buying Behavior,* pp. 3–4.

[22]For example, see Douglas V. Smith, B. G. Lowe, D. H. Lyons, and William H. Old, *Evaluation of Supplier Performance* (New York: National Association of Purchasing Agents, 1963).

[23]C. David Wieters, "Influence in the Design and Use of Vendor Performance Ratings," *Journal of Purchasing and Material Management* (Winter 1976), pp. 31–35; see also Wieters, "The Design and Use of Supplier Performance Rating Systems in Selected Industries," unpublished D.B.A. dissertation (Arizona State University, 1976).

[24]The following discussion is based in part on Lamar Lee, Jr., and Donald W. Dobler, *Purchasing and Materials Management* (3d ed.; New York: McGraw-Hill, 1977), pp. 86–88.

[25]David T. Wilson and H. L. Mathews, "Impact of Management Information Systems upon Purchasing Decision-Making," *Journal of Purchasing* (February 1971), pp. 48–56, reported in Thomas V. Bonoma, Gerald Zaltman, and Wesley J. Johnston, *Industrial Buying Behavior* (Cambridge, Mass.: Marketing Science Institute, 1977), p. 114.

Discussion Questions

1. What strategic advantage does the marketer gain by interfacing with the buying organization at the early rather than the late stages of the purchase decision process?

2. Jim Jackson, an industrial salesperson for Pittsburgh Machine Tool, will call on two accounts this afternoon. The first sales call will be made on a buying organization that Jim has been servicing for the past three years. The second sales call, however, poses more of a challenge. This buying organization has been dealing with a prime competitor of Pittsburgh Machine Tool for five years. Jim, who has good rapport with the purchasing and engineering departments, feels that the time may be right to penetrate this account. Recently, Jim learned that the purchasing manager was extremely unhappy with the poor delivery service provided by the firm's existing supplier. Define each of the buying situations confronting Jim, and outline the appropriate strategy that he should follow in each case.

3. Compare and contrast the following methods used by organizational buyers in evaluating alternative suppliers: weighted-point plan and the cost-ratio method.

4. Organizational buying decisions can be classified as new task, modified rebuy, or straight rebuy. Each elicits a different problem solving approach and involves different buying influentials. Explain.

5. Describe how the industrial marketer can profit by understanding the type of vendor rating system that a particular buying organization employs.

6. Assume that your career path takes you into purchasing rather than marketing. You are assigned the responsibility for purchasing an important component part that will be embodied in your firm's final consumer product—calculators. Describe the criteria that you would apply in evaluating the offerings of different industrial suppliers.

7. Mike Weber, the purchasing agent for Smith Manufacturing, views the purchase of widgets as a routine buying decision. What factors might lead him to alter this position? More importantly, what factors will determine whether a particular competing supplier, such as Albany Widget, will be considered by Mike?

Chapter 4 Organizational Buying Behavior

The organizational buyer is influenced by a wide array of forces inside and outside of the organization. Knowledge of these forces provides the marketer with a foundation on which to build responsive industrial marketing strategies. After reading this chapter, you will have an understanding of:

1. *the specific individual, group, organizational, and environmental variables that influence organizational buying decisions*
2. *a model of organizational buying behavior that integrates these important influences*
3. *how a knowledge of organizational buying characteristics allows the marketer to make more informed product design, pricing, and promotional decisions.*

Since organizations rather than individual households provide the target for the industrial marketer, many questions must be addressed before marketing strategy can be developed. What factors influence the purchasing plans of an organization? How and why do organizations, as well as individual organizational members, differ in their approach to buying? Why are some buying decisions made by a group, while others are handled by an individual? These issues strike at the core of organizational buying behavior and raise significant managerial implications. Knowledge of the dynamics of organizational buyer behavior is crucial to the marketer in identifying profitable segments of the organizational market, locating buying influences within these segments, and reaching these organizational buyers efficiently and effectively with an offering that responds to their needs.

Each decision that the industrial marketer makes is based on a premise concerning the probable response of organizational buyers. A marketer who is sensitive to the forces that shape and influence organizational buying decisions is best equipped to make sound decisions concerning product, price, distribution, and promotional strategy.

In the last chapter, the discussion centered on an eight-stage model of the buying process and on the salient characteristics of different purchasing situations. Building upon that foundation, this chapter examines the myriad forces that influence organizational buyer behavior. These forces, depicted in figure 4.1, include environmental factors (e.g., health of the economy); organizational factors (e.g., size of buying organization); group factors (e.g., composition and roles of members); and individual factors (e.g., preference of individual organizational members).[1] Each of these areas constitutes a sphere of influence that encircles organizational buying decisions.

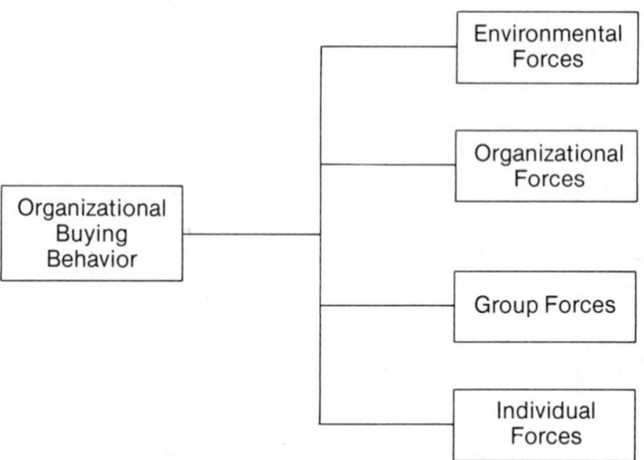

Figure 4.1 / Forces Influencing Organizational Buying Behavior

Environmental Forces

Organizational buyers do not make decisions in isolation, but instead are influenced by a broad range of forces in the external environment. These environmental forces embody a set of constraints and opportunities that can significantly influence the nature, direction, and timing of organizational buying decisions. A projected change in business conditions, a technological development, or a new piece of legislation can drastically alter organizational buying plans. Collectively, such environmental influences define the boundaries within which industrial buyers and sellers interact.

Types of Environmental Forces

Six types of environmental forces influence organizational buying behavior: economic, political, legal, cultural, physical, and technological.[2] Each is briefly illustrated below.

Economic Influences. The general condition of the economy is reflected in the level of economic growth, employment, price stability, and income, as well as the availability of resources, money, and credit. Because of the derived nature of demand in the industrial market, the marketer must also be sensitive to the strength of demand in the ultimate consumer market. As illustrated in chapter 1, the demand for many industrial products fluctuates more widely than the general economy.

The economic environment influences an organization's ability to buy and, to a degree, its willingness to buy. However, shifts in general economic conditions do not fall evenly on all sectors of the market. For example, a rise in interest rates, coupled with tight money, may damage the housing industry (lumber, cement, insulation) but have minimal effects on other industries such as paper, hospital supply, office products, and soft drinks. Marketers that serve broad sectors of the organizational market must be particularly sensitive to the differential impact that selective economic shifts have on buying behavior.

Different types of organizations—for-profit versus not-for-profit—approach purchasing decisions from a different economic perspective. Compared to for-profit organizations, such as commercial enterprises, research indicates that not-for-profit organizations are more likely to justify a purchase simply because funds were allocated for a particular item in their budget.[3] Often, the rationale in the not-for-profit organization is that if the funds are not spent this fiscal year, the budget will be cut next year.

Political and Legal Influences. The political environment includes tariffs and trade agreements with other countries, government funding of selected programs (discussed in chapter 2), and government attitudes toward business and social activities. By contrast, the legal environment includes legal and regulatory forces at the federal, state, and local levels that specify the boundaries of the buyer-seller relationship.[4]

The potential impact of these governmental influences on a particular sector of the industrial market can be illustrated by examining the sequence of events triggered by a change in federal fuel-economy standards. Each automobile manufacturer's 1985 model cars must average 27.5 miles per gallon. To achieve this goal, virtually every part of the automobile is being redesigned, thereby increasing the demand for machine tools, aluminum, lighter-weight steel, plastic, and related materials. Conceivably, the amount of aluminum used in the average car could triple by the mid-1980s.[5]

Culture. Human decision making is greatly affected by the culture in which it operates. Culture can be thought of as the means and methods of coping with the environment that are shared by people as members of society and are passed from one generation to another. "Culture as reflected in values, mores, customs, habits, norms, traditions and so on will influence the structure and functioning of the organization and the way members of the organization feel and act toward one another and various aspects of the environment."[6]

Physical Influences. The physical environment which also affects organizational buying decisions includes such factors as climate and geographical location of the organization. The availability of labor, selected raw materials, and transportation services often play dominant roles in the initial selection of a location by an organization. In turn, suppliers that are located in close proximity to the buying organization often have an advantage in the vendor selection process, particularly when procurement requirements necessitate a close buyer-seller relationship. Thus, the physical environment defines the constraints and options that surround the specific buying tasks of an organization.[7]

Technological Influences. Rapidly changing technology can restructure an industry and dramatically alter organizational buying plans. Existing and projected technological changes are given careful attention in the organizational buying process. The technological environment defines the availability of goods and services to the buying organization and, in turn, the quality of goods and services that the organization can provide to its consumers. Technology such as the computer can directly influence the nature of the organizational buying process. Computer-assisted buying is treated in more detail later in the chapter.

The rate of technological change in an industry influences the composition of the decision-making unit in the buying organization.[8] As the pace of technological change increases, the importance of the purchasing manager in the buying process declines. Technical and engineering personnel tend to play a more important role in the organizational buying process in industries where the rate of technological change is great.

In the face of rapidly changing technology, buying organizations often employ technological forecasting techniques to aid them in their buying decisions. The intent here is to forecast the time periods in which major changes in technology might occur. Given the pivotal role that these changes have on buying behavior, the marketer must also actively monitor signs of technological change and be prepared to adapt marketing strategy to deal with new technological environments.[9]

Environmental Influences: Boundaries of the Organizational Buying Process

Collectively, these environmental influences define the general business conditions, the political/legal setting, the availability of products and services, and the values and norms that encircle the specific buying actions of organizations. In addition, the environment provides a stream of information to the buying organization. Marketing communications directed toward the buying organization constitutes a particularly important information source.[10]

Organizational Forces

Significant insights to organizational buying behavior can be secured by examining the domain of the decision makers—the organization. Individual decision makers influence the functioning of organizations in several ways. A marketing strategist can benefit from an understanding of how organizational decision makers approach decisions, set priorities, search for information, resolve internal conflicts, and establish organizational goals. Likewise, the marketer must understand where the purchasing function is positioned in the executive hierarchy and the type of buying technology organizational buyers employ. Both the organizational status and the operating procedures of purchasing vary from firm to firm, thereby creating problems and opportunities for the marketer.

In an effort to unravel these complex organizational forces, attention will center first on key concepts, drawn from the behavioral theory of the firm, that are particularly significant to organizational buying behavior. Once this important groundwork is established, the influence of the organizational positioning of procurement on buying behavior will be analyzed. Finally, the discussion will center on how the buying technology employed by an organization influences the nature of the organizational buying process. Here, particular attention is given to understanding and reaching the computer-assisted buyer.

The Behavioral Theory of the Firm

The behavioral theory of the firm contributes to the understanding of organizational behavior by describing how organizations actually operate rather than prescribing how organizations should operate.[11] Drawn from empirical research on executive decision making, the important concepts in the behavioral theory of the firm serve to dispel many assumptions that have guided organizational thought for years. Four concepts form the foundation of the theory: (1) quasi-resolution of conflict, (2) uncertainty avoidance, (3) problemistic search, and (4) organizational learning.[12] Each provides rich insights to the nature of the organizational buying process.

Quasi-resolution of Conflict. Latent conflict exists among the goals of organizational members. To illustrate, purchasing agents may be concerned with economy, engineers with performance, and product users with prompt delivery.[13] The goals reflect the decision makers' specialized interests and responsibilities within the organization, as well as their background and personal needs. Given these competing goals, how do organizational members ever achieve a consensus? Richard Cyert and James March describe three mechanisms that are used to reduce goal conflict:

1. *local rationality*—complex problems are broken down into subproblems and handled by subunits in the organization, which in turn are motivated by only a part of broader organizational goals;
2. *acceptable level decision rules*—rather than seeking optimal decisions, organizational members search for solutions that are acceptable within the constraints of organizational goals and subgoals;
3. *sequential attention to goals*—conflicting goals are treated by approaching problems one at a time. (To illustrate, the purchasing manager might favor engineering's wishes this month and the goals of the production unit next month.)

Uncertainty Avoidance. Organizational members are motivated by a strong desire to reduce uncertainty. Thus, the decision maker centers attention on shorter range problems that offer more immediate feedback of results. Organizational members have a tendency to delay long-range problem solving and planning. Likewise, the desire to reduce uncertainty stimulates organizational members to seek a "negotiated environment," that is, a "set of relationships with the environment worked out through planning, procedures, contractual relationships with suppliers, and following traditional practices."[14]

Research suggests that organizational buyers attempt to avoid uncertainty by favoring known suppliers, avoiding the risks of innovation, and splitting orders between two or more vendors. The very nature of the organizational buying process illustrates an attempt to avoid risk by creating a negotiated environment.[15] The concept of perceived risk is examined in detail later in the chapter.

Problemistic Search. The search for information by organizational members is stimulated by the definition of a problem and directed toward solving that problem. This search process follows the simplest path and moves from the familiar to the less familiar until an acceptable alternative is found. There is a bias in the search process because the direction of the search reflects the decision maker's specialization, past experience, hopes and expectations, as well as the unresolved conflicts within the organization.

Studies of the organizational buying process offer support for the problemistic search concept.[16] Organizational buyers do not consider new vendors unless their requirements change or problems emerge with existing vendors. Often, there is no attempt to identify all of the possible alternatives to a particular problem. Generally, the buyer will consider new suppliers only after all of the familiar alternatives have been screened. As discussed in chapter 3, this search pattern poses a real challenge for the "out" supplier who is attempting to penetrate a straight rebuy situation.

Organizational Learning. The concept of organizational learning provides additional insight to the behavior of organizations. Cyert and March identify three significant types of adaptive behavior that are exhibited by organizations over time:[17]

1. *Adaptation of goals*—goals are shifted up or down to reflect success or failure in reaching goals in previous periods.
2. *Adaptation in attention rules*—organizations learn to pay attention to some parts of the environment while ignoring other parts. Organizations learn to pay attention to some comparable organizations and to selected components of performance and evaluative criteria within those organizations. For example, an organization may be particularly sensitive to product-line modifications made by well-known firms in their industry while being less cognizant of changes made by other competitors.
3. *Adaptation in search rules*—search rules are adjusted to reflect success and failure. Future search efforts generally begin in an area where a solution was found in the past.

Each of these adaptive mechanisms have been observed in organizational buying behavior.[18] First, if an acceptable alternative cannot be identified, purchasing managers will adjust their goals, thus rendering a previously identified alternative "acceptable." Second, organizational buyers devote their attention to the most urgent problems and rely on criteria in selecting alternatives that have yielded rewards in the past. Third, buyers consistently return to suppliers that provide satisfactory performance and turn to these suppliers first when new procurement requirements emerge.

Collectively, the four related dimensions of organizational decision making delineated in the behavioral theory of the firm advance our understanding of how and why organizational buying tasks occur.[19] Individual members of the organization influence organizational performance by using a set of mechanisms for partially resolving goal conflicts, avoiding uncertainty, employing a selective and narrow search for solutions to problems, and adapting their behavior in response to their experiences.

Organizational Positioning of Purchasing

The position of purchasing activities within the organizational structure strongly influences the nature and direction of buying behavior. To illustrate, an organization that centralizes procurement decisions at regional, division, or headquarters level will approach purchasing differently from a company that is decentralized with purchasing decisions made at individual user locations. A marketer who is sensitive to these organizational influences can more accurately map the decision-making process, isolate buying influentials, identify salient buying criteria, and target marketing strategy.

Centralization vs. Decentralization. Several important differences in buying behavior emerge when centralized and decentralized procurement functions are compared.[20] First, centralization leads to purchasing specialization. Purchasing specialists who concentrate their attention on selected items develop comprehensive knowledge of supply/demand conditions, vendor options, cost factors affecting the supply industry, and other relevant information concerning the supply environment. This knowledge, coupled with the significant volume of business that centralized procurement functions control, enhances their buying strength and supplier options.

Second, the priority given to selected buying criteria is also influenced by the organizational location of the purchasing function. By identifying the organizational domain that the buyer represents, the marketer can generally identify the purchasing manager's objectives. Centralized purchasing units place more weight on long-term supply availability and the development of a healthy supplier complex. At the local level, short-term cost efficiency and profit considerations may be assigned more weight in the decision-making process. Organizational buying behavior is influenced to an important degree by the *measures* and regulatory system that an organization employs in monitoring the performance of an organizational unit.

Third, the personal selling skills of the sales force and the brand preferences of users influence purchasing decisions to a greater degree at user locations than at centralized buying locations. At user locations, E. Raymond Corey notes that "engineers and other technical personnel, in particular, are prone to be specific in their preferences, while nonspecialized, nontechnical buyers have neither the technical expertise nor the status to challenge them."[21] By contrast, purchasing specialists at central locations possess the technical knowledge and power to challenge a particular request. The conflicting priorities that exist between central buyers and local users often lead to conflict in the buying organization. In stimulating demand at the user level, the marketer should assess the potential for such conflict and attempt to develop a strategy that can resolve the differences between the two organizational units.

The organization of the marketer's selling strategy should parallel the organization of the purchasing function of key accounts in the market. The marketer will interact with centralized purchasers that have plants in several different territories of the seller. Decisions made at a central level would involve and affect several organizational units in both the buying and selling firms. To avoid disjointed selling activities and internal conflict in the sales organization, well-conceived policies and a carefully coordinated marketing strategy are required.

Centralization of Procurement: Contributing Factors[22]

There is a trend toward centralizing purchasing at the headquarters, divisional, or regional level. For example, General Motors first established a vice president of procurement and production central in 1974. General Foods and PPG Industries likewise revamped and centralized the purchasing function in the early 1970s. The factors that strongly contribute to this trend are highlighted in table 4.1.

An organization that has multiple plant locations can often achieve cost savings by pooling common requirements. Before the centralization of the procurement function at General Motors, 106 G.M. buying locations invested over $10 million annually on nearly 24 million pairs of work gloves. Over 200 different styles were purchased from 90 different sources. The cost savings generated from pooling the requirements for this item alone are substantial.

The nature of the supply environment also can determine whether purchasing for a given item is centralized or decentralized.

Table 4.1 / Factors Contributing to the Centralization of Procurement

Commonality of Requirements	Two or more procuring units within the organization have common requirements (e.g., sugar and packaging material at General Foods).
Cost-Saving Potential	Opportunity to strengthen bargaining position, secure lower prices through the aggregation of a firm's total requirements, and achieve economies in inventory control.
Structure of Supply Industry	Opportunity to consolidate purchasing power and secure favorable terms and service when a few large sellers dominate the supply industry.
Involvement of Engineering in Purchasing	If high, purchasing group and engineering group must be in close organizational and physical proximity.

Source. Adapted from E. Raymond Corey, *The Organizational Context of Industrial Buying Behavior* (Cambridge, Mass.: Marketing Science Institute, 1978), pp. 9–12.

If the supply environment is dominated by a few large sellers, a centralized buying structure may be particularly useful in securing favorable terms and in insuring proper service to user locations. By contrast, if the supply industry consists of many small firms with each covering limited geographical areas, decentralized purchasing may be required to achieve proper support.

Finally, note from table 4.1 that the location of purchasing in the organization often hinges on the location of key buying influences. If engineering plays an active role in the purchasing process, the purchasing function must be in close organizational and physical proximity.

Marketing Implications. An industrial salesperson must be sensitive to the location and organizational positioning of procurement because of the impact that these factors have on buying behavior. Two organizations, with seemingly identical purchasing requirements, may have entirely different philosophies concerning the "proper" location of the purchasing function. Each may utilize different operating procedures and employ markedly different criteria in evaluating the marketer's offering. The marketer who recognizes such differences is best equipped to satisfy the needs of organizational buyers.

Buying Technology

The buying technology employed by an organization also influences the nature of the organizational decision-making process. One of the most important technological developments in organizational purchasing is the application of electronic data processing (EDP) to the procurement function. The objective of these computer-based purchasing systems is to improve the quality of managerial purchasing decisions by improving the decision maker's ability to handle and process information.[23] Essentially, the computer system expands the memory of the buying organization by storing relevant data that may be retrieved and profitably applied to future purchasing decisions. Computers often provide management with the following information:[24]

1. vendor price and address files
2. purchase history data
3. purchase usage data
4. receiving and invoicing information
5. inventory control data

Although such information provides a foundation for improved purchasing efficiency and performance, experts predict that significant advancements in computer applications to purchasing are still to come. Once considered a luxury, computer assistance is now a necessity for a manufacturing firm producing complex products with a significant amount of purchased material content. The number of buying organizations employing EDP in purchasing is expected to continue to increase.[25] What impact does computerization have on the purchasing function? Researchers have analyzed this question and uncovered some interesting results.[26]

First, the computer system is especially useful in highly repetitive buying tasks (straight rebuys). Such routine purchases can be handled faster and more economically by the computer than by the purchasing staff. A computer program can be written to simplify inventory management and the automatic reordering of selected items. The marketer of standardized products will frequently confront computer-assisted buyers. Researchers project, however, that the computerization of new task-buying situations is unlikely in the near future.

Second, computerized decision-making capability allows the purchasing agent to quickly dispense with routine purchases, thereby providing time for a more thorough evaluation of possible vendors in more complex buying situations. Likewise, the purchasing agent can devote more time to direct negotiation with potential suppliers and assume an expanded role in interdepartmental activities in the organization. Often, these new roles of the purchasing agent lead to an upgrading of the purchasing function in the organizational ranks.

Third, the introduction of the computer into purchasing influences the vendor selection decisions of buying organizations. The computer-assisted buyer engages in a more intensive search for potential suppliers but concentrates orders with fewer vendors.[27] Thus, the addition of the computer to the purchasing function leads to a reduction in the number of suppliers utilized by the buying organization.

Marketing Strategy: Reaching the Computer-Assisted Buyer. The industrial marketer must be prepared to match wits with the computer-assisted buyer. As the buying organization expands its ability to store, retrieve, and analyze significant data on alternative suppliers, corresponding changes are necessary in selling strategies. Since the computer is employed predominantly for repetitive buying tasks, marketers of supplies and maintenance items should attempt to build a long-term contractual relationship with buyers.[28] One contractual strategy that a marketer can solicit is *blanket ordering,* which might be encouraged by offering fast and reliable delivery service or lower prices for a range of selected items. Blanket ordering simplifies inventory control for the buyer and allows the marketer to strengthen customer loyalty while achieving economies of scale in the selling effort. Research suggests that blanket ordering increases the likelihood that a buying organization will remain with a single supplier.[29] Likewise, these buying organizations frequently prefer annual vendor contracts and review the vendor list at the end of each contract period.[30]

Group Forces

The organizational buying process typically involves a complex set of smaller decisions which are made or influenced by several individuals. Purchasing managers rarely make a buying decision independent of the influence of others in the organization.[31] Thus, multiple buying influences or group forces play a critical role in organizational buying decisions. As discussed in chapter 3, the degree of involvement of group members in the procurement process varies from routine rebuys, where the purchasing agent takes into account the preferences of others, to complex new task buying situations, where a group plays an active role throughout the decision process.

The industrial salesperson must address three questions. Who are the organizational members that will take part in the buying process? What is each member's relative influence in the decision? What criteria are important to each member of the group in evaluating prospective suppliers? These questions highlight the importance and complexity of group forces in organizational buying behavior.

Do Key Buying Influentials Know Us?

Important industrial customers of one of the country's largest corporations—DuPont—are a bit unclear about what the company produces. Design engineers, who specify the materials in the products that they design, were asked in a survey to identify the materials that DuPont markets. Interestingly, 42 percent of these buying influentials did not know that DuPont manufactures acetol resin or polymide resin. Conversely, 65 percent of the design engineers attributed epoxy resin to DuPont, although the company does not make it. The results challenge the assertion, frequently made by industrial marketers of all types, that "everybody knows us."

Source. "Customers Little Versed on DuPont, U.S. Steel," *Industrial Marketing* (September 1977), p. 1.

Buying Center

The concept of the buying center, briefly introduced in chapter 3, provides rich insights to the role of group forces in organizational buying behavior.[32] The buying center, which includes all the organizational members involved in the purchase decision, is an "informal, cross-departmental decision unit in which the primary objective is the acquisition, impartation, and processing of relevant purchasing-related information."[33] The size of the buying center varies, but on the average, buying centers will include more than four persons per purchase.[34] In some cases, the number of people involved in all stages of one purchase may be as many as 15 or 20.[35]

The composition of the buying center may change from one purchasing situation to another and is not prescribed by the organizational chart. Instead, membership in the buying group evolves during the purchasing process in response to the information requirements and specific type of purchase situation. An industrial salesperson must define the type of buying situation and the information requirements from the organization's perspective in order to anticipate the size and composition of the buying center. Important points to note are that the composition of the buying center: (1) evolves during the purchasing process, (2) varies from firm to firm, and (3) varies from one purchasing situation to another.

Composition. A central task for the marketer is to identify the organizational members that will constitute the buying center for a particular product. Such knowledge is crucial for well-targeted personal selling and marketing communications. As indicated, an important first step is to define the type of buying situation that the product will elicit in the buying organization and to determine whether the firm is in the early or later stages of the procurement decision-making process. To illustrate, the buying center for a new task-buying situation in the not-for-profit organizational market is presented in table 4.2. The product, intensive-care monitoring systems, involves a complex and costly purchase for hospitals. Note that buying center members are drawn from five functional areas, with each participating at varying degrees in the buying decision process. A marketer who centered attention exclusively on the purchasing function would be overlooking key buying influentials such as administrators and physicians.

The purchasing function, however, is generally a common identifiable element in buying centers in all sectors of the organizational market—commercial enterprises, government, and institutions. This often provides a convenient starting point for the industrial salesperson who is attempting to piece together the membership of the buying center. Often, company policy or organizational directives dictate that the industrial salesperson must first touch base with the purchasing department before meeting with other organizational members. Attempts to bypass purchasing and initiate contact at other points in the organization are viewed negatively by many purchasing managers. The purchasing manager often plays an important gatekeeping role—controlling the flow of information and the access of salespersons to other members of the buying center. Importantly, purchasing managers can readily identify the individuals of the buying center but are often inaccurate

Table 4.2 / The Involvement of Buying Center Participants at Different Stages of the Procurement Process

	Stages of Procurement Process for a Medical Equipment Purchase			
Buying Center	Identification of Need	Establishment of Objectives	Identification and Evaluation of Buying Alternatives	Selection of Suppliers
Physicians	High	High	High	High
Nursing	Low	High	High	Low
Administration	Moderate	Moderate	Moderate	High
Engineering	Low	Moderate	Moderate	Low
Purchasing	Low	Low	Low	Moderate

Source. Adapted from Gene R. Laczniak, "An Empirical Study of Hospital Buying," *Industrial Marketing Management*, 8 (January 1979), p. 61. Reprinted by permission.

in their estimation of the relative impact that each member has on the purchasing decision.[36]

A marketer can also predict the composition of the buying center by projecting the impact that the industrial product will have on different functional areas in the buying organization.[37] If the procurement decision will affect the marketability of a firm's product (e.g., product design, price), the marketing department will play an active role in the decision process. Engineering will be actively involved in procurement decisions involving new capital equipment as well as materials and components that differ from those purchased in the past. Engineering will establish specifications, define product performance requirements, and qualify potential vendors. Manufacturing executives will be included in the buying center in procurement decisions that affect the production mechanism (e.g., the acquisition of materials or parts used in the production process). When procurement decisions involve a substantial economic commitment or impinge on strategic or policy matters, top management will exercise a strong influence on buying decisions.

Rather than merely predicting which functional or organizational levels will be involved in a decision, the marketer can sometimes influence the composition of the buying center. To illustrate, the desirable attributes of a new material handling system can best be understood and appreciated by a warehouse supervisor. By directing marketing communications (advertising and personal selling) to receptive users of the product, the marketer can draw them into the buying center and stimulate their active involvement in the procurement process.

The Buying Committee. A more formalized buying center, the buying committee, is used by some organizations in the purchasing process. Universities, hospitals, and industrial firms may assemble a temporary buying committee to jointly decide which computer system can best meet the organization's needs. Other organizations, such as food retailers, utilize permanent buying committees that meet on a regular basis for multiple decisions, such as which new food products should be given shelf space.[38] The philosophy underlying the committee concept is: (1) different viewpoints and a wider range of experience is applied to the decision-making process, (2) decisions are made in a more scientific atmosphere, and (3) the level of pressure in the buyer-seller relationship is lowered.

The industrial salesperson may not be given the opportunity to make a presentation before the full committee; often, he or she must meet with the various committee members individually. Selected committee members may be inaccessible to the marketer. Here the salesperson must provide the accessible committee members with product-related information that may be salient to the inaccessible members of the committee. Potential questions and problems that may arise when the committee convenes should be anticipated and addressed. Also, the marketer should note that the members of the buying group have differing levels of influence and assign importance to different criteria in the purchasing decision. The most influential member of the buying group cannot be determined by comparing the organizational rank of committee members. Past product-related experience, technical expertise, personality traits, and other personal and organizational factors combine to determine the structure of the decision-making unit and the relative influence of individual participants.

Buying Center Influence

Members of the buying center assume several different roles throughout the procurement process. These roles, which are defined in table 4.3, include users, influencers, buyers, deciders, and gatekeepers.[39] It is important to remember that one person could assume all roles in a purchase situation,

Table 4.3 / Buying Center Roles Defined

Role	Description
Users	As the role name implies, these are the personnel who will be using the product in question. Users may have anywhere from inconsequential to an extremely important influence on the purchase decision. In some cases, the users initiate the purchase action by requesting the product. They may even develop the product specifications.
Gatekeepers	Gatekeepers control information to be reviewed by other members of the buying center. The control of information may be in terms of disseminating printed information or advertisements or through controlling which salesperson will speak to which individuals in the buying center. To illustrate, the purchasing agent might perform this screening role by opening the gate to the buying center for some sales personnel and closing it to others.
Influencers	These individuals affect the purchasing decision by supplying information for the evaluation of alternatives or by setting buying specifications. Typically, technical personnel, such as engineers, quality control personnel, and research and development personnel are significant influences to the purchase decision. Sometimes, individuals outside of the buying organization can assume this role (e.g., an engineering consultant or an architect who writes very tight building specifications).
Deciders	Deciders are the individuals who actually make the buying decision, whether or not they have the formal authority to do so. The identity of the decider is the most difficult role to determine: buyers may have formal authority to buy, but the president of the firm may actually make the decision. A decider could be a design engineer who develops a set of specifications that only one vendor can meet.
Buyers	The buyer has *formal* authority for selecting a supplier and implementing all procedures connected with securing the product. The power of the buyer is often usurped by more powerful members of the organization. Often the buyer's role is assumed by the purchasing agent, who executes the clerical functions associated with a purchase order.

Source. Adapted from Frederick E. Webster, Jr., and Yoram Wind, *Organizational Buying Behavior* (Englewood Cliffs, N.J.: Prentice-Hall, Inc., 1972), pp. 77–80.

or each individual could assume a different buying role. To illustrate, many users of a new computer might be involved in the decision process. As users, personnel from marketing, accounting, purchasing, and production all may have a stake in which computer is selected. Thus, the buying center can be a very complex organizational phenomenon to understand.

As the procurement process begins to unfold in an organization, the marketer faces the difficult task of defining the composition of the buying center and determining the *role* and *relative influence* that each member carries in the decision-making unit. While generalizations covering all types of products and buying situations cannot be made, research indicates that key influencers are frequently located outside of the purchasing department. James McMillan reports that the buying center for highly technical products includes the purchasing agent, scientists, engineers, and other managers—with the scientist having the greatest level of influence in the buying group.[40]

Another study, which centers on the purchasing process for component parts, indicates that only one-half of product or vendor selection decisions are made by the purchasing department.[41] Other functional areas, such as design and development engineering, research, and production engineering, play an active role in the buying center by dominating project initiation and the specification of requirements. Similar influence patterns emerge in the acquisition of materials and capital equipment by surveyed organizations.

The Right and Wrong Questions

An industrial salesperson often confronts the somewhat humorous but difficult situation where several members of the buying center each confess privately that they will have the most influence in the procurement decision. With such confusion, how can the key buying influentials be identified? Some salespersons screen potential buying influentials by noting the questions that they ask and, more importantly, questions that they fail to ask. The nature and quality of the questions provide a clue to the organizational buyer's product knowledge and to the type and degree of involvement that the individual will assume in the procurement process.

The Influence of Purchasing. The purchasing function exercises a high level of influence in the procurement process for selected types of purchases and also when certain environmental conditions are present. Purchasing assumes a position of power in the buying center in procurement decisions ". . . in a steady-state condition, that is, when the design of the purchased product is established and vendors have been qualified."[42] Likewise, purchasing becomes a dominant force in repetitive buying situations by building technical expertise, knowledge of the dynamics of the supplying industry, and close working relationships with individual suppliers. This cumulative experience leads to a level of expertise in purchasing that cannot be matched by any other functional area in the buying organization.[43]

Understanding the potential sources of strength from which the purchasing function derives its power in internal negotiations provides a key to understanding the stature and influence of purchasing in organizational buying decisions. Factors that contribute to purchasing's strength include: (1) its level of technical competence and credibility, (2) its base of relevant information, (3) its base of top management support, and (4) its organizational status as an authority in selected procurement areas.[44] Since different purchasing departments are endowed with varying levels of resources, expertise, information, and status, the marketer cannot make sweeping generalizations concerning the "typical" level of power that purchasing possesses in the buying center. Instead, attention should center on the relative importance of purchasing in a particular buying situation and in a particular organizational context.[45]

The nature of group deliberations and the relative importance of purchasing in the buying center is also influenced by the firm's external environment. Research by Robert Spekman and Louis Stern suggests that as the information needs of buying groups grow in response to conditions of higher environmental uncertainty (e.g., change in company leadership, change in economic conditions), there is greater participation in decision making in the buying groups.[46] Also, the research indicates that the *influence* of the purchasing agent increases as the level of environmental uncertainty rises. Why? The authors note that as a firm's external environment becomes more unstable, "the information processing function of boundary role persons (here, the purchasing agent) becomes central to a firm's ability to effectively gather, analyze, and act on relevant environmental information."[47] Such conditions provide an ideal setting for purchasing agents to advance their position of influence.[48] Research by George Strauss indicates that purchasing agents are motivated by a strong desire to enhance their status and position within the organization.[49]

Individual Forces

Because individuals, and not organizations, make buying decisions, attention must ultimately center on individual behavior within the organizational context. Each member of the buying center has a unique personality, a particular set of learned experiences, a specified organizational function to perform, and perceptions of how to best achieve both personal and organizational goals. Equipped with varying levels of information and expertise, these organizational members interact at different stages of the purchasing process and, often, hold widely differing perceptions of the same buying situation. To understand the organizational buyer, the marketer should be aware of these differing perceptions.

Different Evaluative Criteria

Evaluative criteria refer to the specifications that organizational buyers use in comparing alternative industrial products and services. Often, each member of the buying group considers different (and frequently conflicting) criteria to be salient in evaluating the merits of alternative suppliers or industrial brands. Industrial product users generally value prompt delivery and efficient servicing; engineering values product quality, standardization of the product, and pretesting of the product; while purchasing assigns the most importance to maximum price advantage and economy in shipping and forwarding.[50] Jagdish Sheth contends that product perceptions and evaluative criteria differ among organizational decision makers as a result of differences in educational backgrounds, the source and type of information exposure, the interpretation and retention of relevant information (perceptual distortion), and the level of satisfaction with past purchases.[51] Compared with plant managers or purchasing agents, engineers have a different educational background, are exposed to different journals, attend different conferences, and possess different professional goals and values. A sales presentation that is effective in the purchasing department may be entirely off the mark in the engineering department.

Responsive Marketing Strategy. A marketer who is sensitive to differences in the product perceptions and the evaluative criteria of individual buying center members is well equipped to prepare responsive marketing strategy. To illustrate, a research study examined the industrial adoption of solar air-conditioning systems and identified the criteria of importance to key decision makers.[52] Table 4.4 suggests that marketing communications directed at *production engineers* should center on the operating costs and energy savings, while *heating and air-conditioning consultants* (HVAC) should be addressed concerning the noise level and initial cost of the system. Knowledge of the criteria that key buying center participants employ is of significant operational value to the marketer in designing new products and in developing and targeting advertising and personal selling presentations.

Information Processing

Organizational buyers, like all consumers, must be very selective about the information they take in. Volumes of information flow into the organization through direct-mail advertising, journal advertising, trade news, word-of-mouth, personal sales presentations, and other sources. What an individual organizational buyer chooses to pay attention to (or not pay attention to), comprehend, and retain has an important bearing on procurement decisions.

Selective Processes. Information processing is generally encompassed in the broader term, cognition, which refers to "all the processes by which the sensory input is transformed, reduced, elaborated, stored, recovered, and used."[53] An important component of an individual's cognitive structure includes the processes of selective exposure, selective attention, selective perception, and selective retention. Each is discussed below and briefly illustrated in an organizational buying context.

Table 4.4 / Issues of Importance in the Formation of Individual Preferences

	Key Importance	Less Importance
Production Engineers	Operating Cost Energy Savings Reliability Complexity	First Cost Field Proven
Corporate Engineers	First Cost Field Proven Reliability Complexity	Energy Savings Up-to-Date
Plant Managers	Operating Cost Use of Unproductive Areas Up-to-Date Power Failure Protection	First Cost Complexity
Top Managers	Up-to-Date Energy Savings Operating Cost	Noise Level in Plant Reliability
HVAC Consultants	Noise Level in Plant First Cost Reliability	Up-to-Date Energy Savings Operating Cost

Source. Jean-Marie Choffray and Gary L. Lilien, "Assessing Response to Industrial Marketing Strategy," *Journal of Marketing*, 42 (April 1978), p. 30. Reprinted from the *Journal of Marketing*, published by the American Marketing Association.

1. Selective exposure is the tendency to attend to communication messages that are consistent with one's existing attitudes and beliefs. For example, a purchasing agent chooses to talk to some salespersons and not to others.
2. Selective attention concerns the filtering or screening of all incoming stimuli in order to admit into the individual's cognition only certain stimuli. To illustrate, an organizational buyer will be more likely to notice a trade advertisement if it is consistent with his or her needs and values.
3. Selective perception is the tendency to interpret stimuli in terms of one's existing attitudes and beliefs. To illustrate, organizational buyers may modify or distort a salesperson's message in order to make it more consistent with their predispositions toward the company.
4. Selective retention is the tendency to store in memory only the information that is pertinent to the individual's needs and dispositions. For example, an organizational buyer may retain product-related information concerning the attributes of a particular brand because they match the criteria he or she deems important.

Each of these selective processes influences the way in which an individual decision maker will respond to marketing stimuli. Since the procurement process often spans several months and the marketer's contact with the buying organization is infrequent, marketing communications must be carefully designed and targeted. Poorly conceived messages will be "tuned out" or immediately forgotten by key decision makers.

Memory. Some memory theorists hypothesize that individuals possess three different types of memory storage systems.[54] These include a set of sensory stores (SS), a short-term memory store (STS), and a long-term memory store (LTS). According to this multiple-store approach, information passes from the sense organs to a sensory store where information is lost in a fraction of a second unless attention is devoted to the stimulus. If, however, the information is processed, it moves into the STS, which has limited capacity. Here, information can be kept active by further processing. Active information in the STS can be retrieved quickly, and information in the LTS can be called upon as needed to interpret information. Thus, the STS is the center of current processing activity. Lastly, part of this information, if properly processed, is transferred to the LTS, which is hypothesized to have unlimited capacity. What information is likely to be stored? Information that is deemed important to achieving goals or can be easily stored is likely assigned the highest priority.[55] Also, the individual's expectation concerning how the information will be used determines what is to be stored and the form of the storage.

External Memory. It is important to note that the organizational buyer has an external memory which can hold vast amounts of information. Catalogs, technical reports, and on-line computer systems are potential parts of this external memory system. Thus, a purchasing agent may need to keep only a vendor's name in his or her memory because extensive product-related information can be retrieved from external memory when the need arises. The marketer must provide information that is relevant and in a form that can be assimilated into the buying organization's external memory. As indicated, the procurement process is often quite lengthy and requires the processing of large amounts of information. Often, pamphlets and technical reports provided by the industrial salesperson are retrieved from storage by organizational buyers weeks later at critical stages in the procurement process.

Perceived Risk

H. Lazo makes the provocative observation that "fear is one of the major influences in industrial buying. Fear of displeasing the boss. Fear of making a wrong decision . . . fear of losing status. Fear indeed, in extreme cases, of losing one's job."[56] Significant insights to buying behavior can be secured by examining the way in which individual organizational buyers perceive and handle risk.[57] They face the risk that the product will not perform satisfactorily (functional risk) or that others in the organization will view the decision negatively (psychological risk). There are two components of the perceived risk concept: (1) the *uncertainty* concerning the outcome of a decision and (2) the magnitude of the *consequences* associated with making the wrong choice.

Risk-Reduction Strategies. Individual decision makers are motivated by a strong desire to reduce the level of risk in purchase decisions. In analyzing the risk-reduction strategies of organizational buyers, researchers uncovered four categories of action:[58]

1. external uncertainty reduction (e.g., visit supplier's plant)
2. internal uncertainty reduction (e.g., consult with other buyers)
3. external consequences reduction (e.g., multiple sourcing)
4. internal consequences reduction (e.g., consult with company's top management).

Organizational buyers can also reduce the level of risk in a purchasing situation by relying on familiar suppliers.[59] Such source loyalty provides the organizational buyer with a convenient method of reducing risk and thus constitutes a significant barrier to entry for an "out" supplier. As discussed in chapter 3, this makes straight rebuy situations very hard for the new supplier to break. When an organizational buyer selects a particular supplier and, in turn, receives rewards for the decision, the probability of selecting the same supplier again in the future increases.

The reputation of the supplier also influences the level of risk that organizational buyers perceive in purchase decisions. Theodore Levitt reports that well-known companies, being viewed by organizational buyers as credible sources, tend to be favored by decision makers facing high-risk decisions.[60] The importance of source credibility appears to increase as the level of perceived risk increases. A first-time purchaser of a computer may feel "comfortable" in dealing with a large well-known manufacturer such as IBM.

Anticipating Perceived Risk Level. Industrial marketers should carefully consider the level of risk that their product will elicit for a particular buying organization and for specific decision makers within the buying center. When introducing new products, entering new markets, or approaching new customers, the marketing strategist should recognize the important influence of perceived risk in organizational decision making and evaluate the impact of alternative strategies on this risk.

Individual vs. Group Decision Making

On some occasions, procurement decisions are made jointly by a group, the buying center, while at other times the decision is delegated to one party (not necessarily the purchasing agent) who will decide on behalf of other organizational members. What factors determine whether a specific buying situation will be a group or individual decision?

Jagdish Sheth theorizes that the following factors influence the structure of the decision-making unit:[61]

Product Specific Factors

1. *Perceived risk*—the higher the level of perceived risk in a buying situation, the greater the likelihood that the decision will be made by a group.
2. *Type of purchase*—new task-buying situations are more likely to involve group decision making (e.g., a first-time purchase of a computer).
3. *Time pressure*—with minimal time constraints, a group decision-making format becomes more feasible.

Company Specific Factors

1. *Size*—large companies tend to utilize group decision making.
2. *Degree of centralization*—the more decentralized an organization, the more likely decisions will be made by a group.

Sheth notes that these factors are supported by research conducted in the organizational behavior area, but they are in need of further empirical verification in the industrial buying context.

The Organizational Buying Process: Major Elements

The behavior of organizational buyers is influenced by environmental, organizational, group, and individual factors. Each of these important spheres of influence has been discussed in an organizational buying context, with particular attention centering on how the industrial marketer should interpret these forces and, more importantly, factor them directly into marketing strategy planning. A model of the organizational buying process is presented in figure 4.2, which serves to reinforce and integrate the key areas discussed to this point in the chapter.[62]

This framework centers on the relationship between an organization's buying center and three major stages in the individual purchase decision process through:

1. the screening of alternatives which do not meet organizational requirements
2. the formation of decision participants' preferences
3. the formation of organizational preferences.

Observe from figure 4.2 that individual members of the buying center utilize different *evaluation criteria* and are exposed to different *sources of information*. The latter influences the industrial brands that are included in the buyer's *evoked set of alternatives*. The evoked set constitutes the alternative brands that a buyer calls to mind when a need arises and represents a few brands out of the many that may be available in the market.[63]

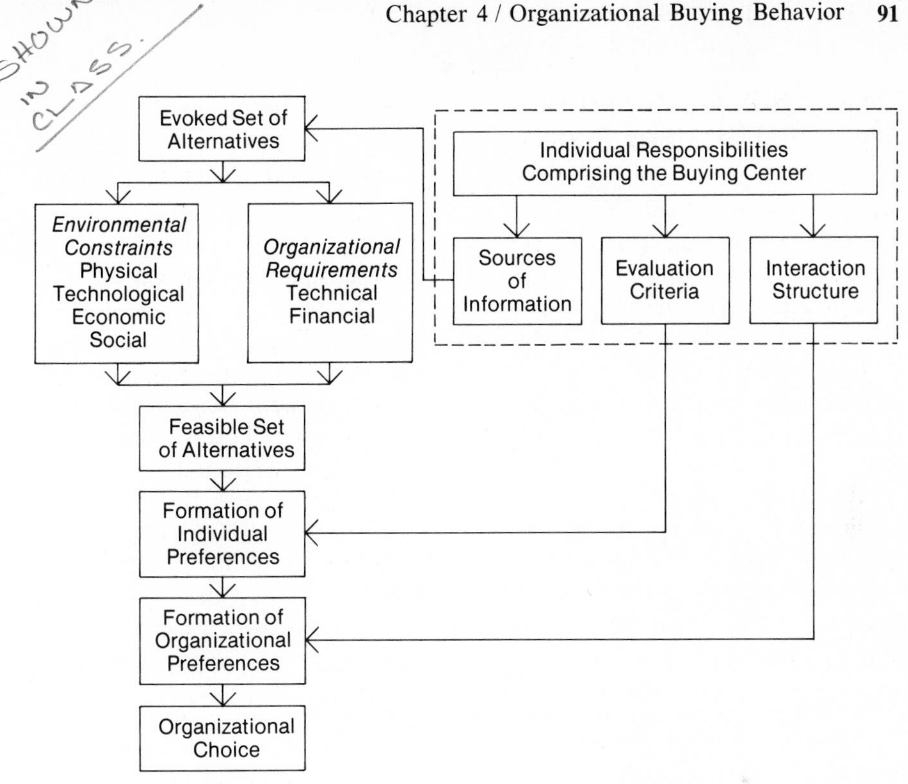

Figure 4.2 / Major Elements of Organizational Buying Behavior

Source. Jean-Marie Choffray and Gary L. Lilien, "Assessing Response to Industrial Marketing Strategy," *Journal of Marketing*, 42 (April 1978), p. 22. Reprinted from the *Journal of Marketing*, published by the American Marketing Association.

Environmental constraints and organizational requirements influence the procurement process by limiting the number of product alternatives that satisfy organizational needs. For example, capital equipment alternatives that exceed a particular cost (initial or operating) may be eliminated from further consideration. The resulting brands become the *feasible set of alternatives* for the organization over which individual preferences are defined. The *interaction structure* of the members of the buying center, who have differing criteria and responsibilities, leads to the formation of organizational preferences, and, ultimately, to organizational choice.

An understanding of the organizational buying process allows the marketer to play an active rather than a passive role in efforts to stimulate market response.[64] The marketer who identifies organizational screening requirements and the salient evaluative criteria of individual buying center members can make more informed product design, pricing, and promotional decisions.

Organizational Buying Behavior: Marketing Strategy Implications

Since the marketing manager confronts a wide array of organizations in the industrial market that often have different objectives, structures, and requirements, an understanding of organizational buying behavior is required to identify meaningful market segments and to design responsive strategies. In probing this complex behavioral process, the marketer must systematically gather relevant market information by asking the right questions.

Illustrative questions are presented in table 4.5. These questions draw together the material of part two, "The Organizational Buying Process." The industrial marketer can understand an individual decision maker only after examining the broader forces that form the decision-making process. The marketer must define the context of the buying situation, which includes environmental, organizational, product-specific, group, and individual forces. Such an analysis will allow the marketer to identify profitable segments of the organizational market and direct focused marketing strategy at these segments. As we will see in chapter 5, key dimensions of organizational buying behavior, which are highlighted in table 4.5, play a significant role in industrial market segmentation strategies.

Table 4.5 / Organizational Buying Behavior: Forming the Foundation of Marketing Strategy

	Level	Illustrative Questions
Marketing Strategy Planning	Environmental	How will present economic projections for the industry and the economy affect the purchasing plans of this organization?
	Organizational	What are the unique *company attributes* (e.g., size, orientation) and *procurement attributes* (e.g., structure and organization position of purchasing) that will influence buyer behavior?
	Product-Specific	How far has the firm progressed in the *buying process* (early or late phase)?
		What type of *buying situation* does this purchase represent for the organization (new task, straight rebuy)?
		To what degree will organizational buyers perceive risk in purchasing this product?
	Group	Will the decision be made by an individual or a group?
		Who are the members of the buying task group?
		What is each member's relative influence in the decision?
	Individual	What criteria are important to each member of the buying task group in evaluating prospective suppliers?
		How do the potential suppliers rate on these criteria?

Summary

To understand the behavior of organizational buyers, the industrial marketer must become sensitive to the environment within which buying decisions are made. Upon entering the organization, the marketer confronts a buyer who is constrained by several forces. These forces or spheres of influence can be classified as: environmental, organizational, group, and individual. First, environmental forces define the boundaries within which buyers and sellers interact. Second, each organization develops a personality that makes it unique. The marketer requires an understanding of how organizational buyers approach decisions, set priorities, gather information, resolve conflicts, and establish and revise organizational goals. Importantly, the location of the procurement function in the organizational hierarchy and the type of buying technology available to the purchasing staff directly influence marketing strategy requirements. Third, the relevant unit of analysis for the marketing strategist is the buying center. The composition of this group evolves during the buying process, varies from firm to firm, and changes from one purchasing situation to another. Fourth, the marketer's attention must ultimately center on individual members of the buying center. Each has a particular set of experiences and a unique personal and organizational frame of reference that is brought to bear on the buying decision. The marketer who is sensitive to such individual differences is best equipped to develop responsive marketing communications that will be processed and retained by the organizational buyer.

The task of unraveling the complex forces that encircle the organizational buying process is indeed difficult. The goal of this chapter has been to provide a framework which allows the marketing manager to begin this task by asking the right questions. The answers provide the base for effective and efficient industrial marketing strategy.

Footnotes

[1]Frederick E. Webster, Jr., and Yoram Wind, *Organizational Buying Behavior* (Englewood Cliffs, N.J.: Prentice-Hall, Inc., 1972), pp. 28–37.

[2]Ibid., pp. 40–46.

[3]Thomas V. Bonoma and Gerald Zaltman, "Introduction," in Bonoma and Zaltman (eds.), *Organizational Buying Behavior* (Chicago: American Marketing Association, 1978), p. 23.

[4]For an expanded treatment of this area, see Reed Moyer and Michael D. Hutt, *Macro Marketing* (New York: John Wiley and Sons, Inc., 1978), chapter 9.

[5]Leonard M. Apcar, "As Detroit Trims the Pounds Off its Cars, Suppliers Scramble to Get New Contracts," *Wall Street Journal* (October 17, 1978), p. 40.

[6]Webster and Wind, *Organizational Buying Behavior,* pp. 45–46.

[7]Ibid., pp. 42–43.

[8]Bonoma and Zaltman, "Introduction," p. 22.

[9]For example, see James R. Bright, "Evaluating Signals of Technological Change," *Harvard Business Review,* 48 (January-February, 1970), pp. 62–70.

[10]Webster and Wind, *Organizational Buying Behavior,* p. 41.

[11]Richard M. Cyert and James G. March, *A Behavioral Theory of the Firm* (Englewood Cliffs, N.J.: Prentice-Hall, Inc., 1963).

[12]Ibid., pp. 114–27.

[13]Jagdish N. Sheth, "A Model of Industrial Buyer Behavior," *Journal of Marketing,* 37 (October 1973), p. 53.

[14]Webster and Wind, *Organizational Buying Behavior,* p. 69.

[15]Yoram Wind, "Applying the Behavioral Theory of the Firm to Industrial Buying Decisions," *The Economic and Business Bulletin,* 20 (Spring 1968), pp. 22–28.

[16]Ibid.

[17]Cyert and March, *A Behavioral Theory of the Firm,* pp. 114–27.

[18]Wind, "Applying the Behavioral Theory," pp. 22–28.

[19]Webster and Wind, *Organizational Buying Behavior,* p. 73.

[20]The discussion in this section is based on E. Raymond Corey, *The Organizational Context of Industrial Buying Behavior,* (Cambridge, Mass.: Marketing Science Institute, 1978), pp. 6–12.

[21]Ibid., p. 13.

[22]Ibid., pp. 6–16.

[23]For example, see D. Larry Moore and Harold E. Fearon, "Computer Assisted Decision Making in Purchasing," *Journal of Purchasing,* 9 (November 1973), pp. 5–25.

[24]Michael J. Timbers, "Status of Computer Development Activity in Purchasing," *Journal of Purchasing,* 6 (November 1970), pp. 45–64.

[25]David T. Wilson and H. Lee Mathews, "Impact of Management Information Systems upon Purchasing," *Journal of Purchasing,* 7 (February 1971), pp. 48–56.

[26]H. Lee Mathews, David T. Wilson, and Klaus Backhaus, "Selling to the Computer Assisted Buyer," *Industrial Marketing Management,* 6, No. 4 (1977), pp. 307–15.

[27]H. Lee Mathews and David T. Wilson, "Industrial Marketing's New Challenge: A Computerized Buyer," Working Series in Marketing Research, Pennsylvania State University, No. 9 (October 1970), reported in Mathews, Wilson, and Backhaus, "Selling to the Computer Assisted Buyer," p. 308.

[28]Mathews, Wilson, and Backhaus, "Selling to the Computer Assisted Buyer," pp. 307–15.

[29]Leonard Groeneveld, "The Implications of Blanket Contracting for Industrial Purchasing and Marketing," *Journal of Purchasing,* 8 (November 1972), pp. 51–58.

[30]Mathews and Wilson, "Industrial Marketing's New Challenge," reported in Mathews, Wilson, and Backhaus, "Selling to the Computer Assisted Buyer," p. 309.

[31]Yoram Wind, "Preference of Relevant Others and Individual Choice Models," *Journal of Consumer Research,* 3 (August 1976), pp. 50–57.

[32]For example, see Yoram Wind, "The Organizational Buying Center: A Research Agenda," in Gerald Zaltman and Thomas Bonoma (eds.), *Organizational Buying Behavior* (Chicago: American Marketing Association, 1978), pp. 67–76; and Robert E. Spekman, "An Alternative Framework for Examining the Industrial Buying Process," in Zaltman and Bonoma (eds.), pp. 84–90.

[33]Robert E. Spekman and Louis W. Stern, "Environmental Uncertainty and Buying Group Structure: An Empirical Investigation," *Journal of Marketing,* 43 (Spring 1979), p. 56.

[34]"Industrial Sales People Report 4.1—Buying Influences in Average Company," *LAP Report 1042.2* (McGraw-Hill Research, October 1977).

[35]G. van der Most, "Purchasing Process: Researching Influences Is Basic to Marketing Plan," *Industrial Marketing* (October 1976), p. 120.

[36]See Yoram Wind, "The Organizational Buying Center: A Research Agenda," pp. 67–76; see also Robert E. Weigand, "Identifying Industrial Buying Responsibility," *Journal of Marketing Research,* 3 (February 1966), pp. 81–84.

[37]E. Raymond Corey, *The Organizational Context of Industrial Buying Behavior,* pp. 28–36.

[38]Michael D. Hutt, "The Retail Buying Committee: A Look at Cohesiveness and Leadership," *Journal of Retailing,* 55 (Winter 1979), pp. 87–97.

[39]Webster and Wind, *Organizational Buying Behavior,* p. 77.

[40]James R. McMillan, "Role Differentiation in Industrial Buying Decisions," in *Proceedings of the American Marketing Association* (Chicago: American Marketing Association, 1973), pp. 207–11; see also James R. Cooley, Donald W. Jackson, and Lonnie L. Ostrom, "Analyzing the Relative Power of Participants in Industrial Buying Decisions," in *Proceedings of the American Marketing Association* (Chicago: American Marketing Association, 1977), pp. 243–46.

[41]Scientific American, Inc., *How Industry Buys/1970* (New York: Scientific American, Inc., 1969), pp. 1–5.

[42]E. Raymond Corey, *The Organizational Context of Industrial Buying Behavior,* p. 34.

[43]Ibid.

[44]Ibid., pp. 34–35.

[45]For example, see Wesley J. Johnston, "Communication Networks and Influence Patterns in Industrial Buying Behavior," unpublished doctoral dissertation (University of Pittsburgh, 1979).

[46]Spekman and Stern, "Environmental Uncertainty and Buying Group Structure," p. 56.

[47]Ibid., p. 60.

[48]Robert E. Spekman, "Information and Influence: An Exploratory Investigation of the Boundary Role Person's Basis of Power," *Academy of Management Journal,* 22 (March 1979), pp. 104–17.

[49]George Strauss, "Tactics of Lateral Relationship," *Administrative Science Quarterly,* 7 (September 1962), pp. 161–86.

[50]Jagdish N. Sheth, "A Model of Industrial Buyer Behavior," p. 51.

[51]Ibid., pp. 52–54.

[52]Jean-Marie Choffray and Gary L. Lilien, "Assessing Response to Industrial Marketing Strategy," *Journal of Marketing,* 42 (April 1978), pp. 20–31.

[53]U. Neisser, *Cognitive Psychology* (New York: Appleton, 1966), p. 4, quoted in James F. Engle, David T. Kollat, and Roger D. Blackwell, *Consumer Behavior* (2 ed.: Chicago: Holt, Rinehart and Winston, Inc., 1973), p. 210.

[54]R. C. Atkinson and Richard M. Shiffrin, "Human Memory: A Proposed System and Its Control Processes," in K. W. Spence and J. T. Spence (eds.), *The Psychology of Learning and Motivation: Advances in Research and Theory, Vol. 2* (New York: Academic Press, 1968), pp. 89–195, discussed in James R. Bettman, "Memory Factors in Consumer Choice: A Review," *Journal of Marketing,* 43 (Spring 1979), pp. 37–53.

[55]Richard M. Shiffrin and R. C. Atkinson, "Storage and Retrieval Processes in Long-Term Memory," *Psychological Review,* 76 (1979), pp. 179–93, discussed in James Bettman, Ibid.

[56]H. Lazo, "Emotional Aspects of Industrial Buying," in R. S. Hancock (ed.), *Proceedings of the American Marketing Association* (Chicago: American Marketing Association, 1960), p. 265.

[57]Raymond A. Bauer, "Consumer Behavior as Risk Taking," in R. S. Hancock (ed.), *Proceedings of the American Marketing Association,* Ibid., pp. 389–400; see also, James R. McMillan, *The Role of Perceived Risk in Vendor Selection Decisions,* unpublished Ph.D. dissertation (Columbus: The Ohio State University, 1972).

[58]Timothy W. Sweeney, H. Lee Mathews, and David T. Wilson, "An Analysis of Industrial Buyers' Risk Reducing Behavior: Some Personality Correlates," *American Marketing Association Proceedings* (Chicago: American Marketing Association, 1973), pp. 217–21.

[59]For example, see Richard N. Cardozo and James W. Cagley, "An Experimental Study of Industrial Buyer Behavior," *Journal of Marketing Research,* 8 (August 1971), pp. 329–34.

[60]Theodore Levitt, *Industrial Purchasing Behavior: A Study of Communication Effects* (Boston: Division of Research, Graduate School of Business Administration, Harvard University, 1965).

[61]Sheth, "A Model of Industrial Buyer Behavior," p. 54.

[62]Choffray and Lilien, "Assessing the Response to Industrial Marketing Strategy," pp. 20–31. Other models of organizational buying behavior include Webster and Wind, *Organizational Buying Behavior,* pp. 28–37; Sheth, "A Model of Industrial Buyer Behavior," pp. 50–56; Thomas V. Bonoma, Gerald Zaltman, and Wesley J. Johnston, *Industrial Buying Behavior* (Cambridge: Marketing Science Institute, 1977), chapter 2; and Rowland T. Moriarty and Morton Galper, *Organizational Buying Behavior: A State-of-the-Art Review and Conceptualization* (Cambridge: Marketing Science Institute, 1978).

[63]John A. Howard and Jagdish N. Sheth, *The Theory of Buyer Behavior* (New York: John Wiley and Sons, Inc., 1969), p. 26.

[64]Choffray and Lilien, "Assessing the Response to Industrial Marketing Strategy," pp. 20–31.

Discussion Questions

1. Environmental influences define the boundaries within which industrial buyers and sellers interact. Select a recent legal, political, or economic development that will affect demand patterns in a particular industry.

2. How does the rate of technological change in an industry influence the composition of the decision-making unit in the buying organization?

3. Fuel-economy, exhaust-emission, and safety standards are creating changes in the purchasing requirements of automobile manufacturers. In what way will such changes influence the demand for aluminum, steel, rubber, and related materials?

4. Since the composition of the buying center is often made up of individuals who perform different organizational functions (e.g., production vs. purchasing) and value different product and supplier attributes, how are decisions ever made? How is conflict within the buying center resolved?

5. An organization that centralizes procurement decisions at regional, division, or headquarters level will approach purchasing differently from a company that is decentralized with purchasing decisions made at individual user locations. Explain.

6. How does the introduction of the computer into purchasing influence the vendor selection decisions of buying organizations?

7. Explain how the composition of the buying center evolves during the purchasing process and varies from one firm to another, as well as from one purchasing situation to another.

8. The Kraus Toy Company recently decided to begin development of a new electronic game. Can an electrical parts supplier *predict* the likely composition of the buying center at Kraus Toy? What steps could an industrial salesperson take to *influence* the composition of the buying center?

9. Why does the influence of the purchasing manager appear to increase as the level of environmental uncertainty rises?

10. Carol Brooks, purchasing manager for Apex Manufacturing Co., read the *Wall Street Journal* this morning and carefully read, clipped, and saved a full-page ad by the Allen-Bradley Company. Ralph Thornton, the production manager at Apex, read several articles from the same paper but could not recall seeing this or, for that matter, any ads. How could this occur?

11. What factors determine whether a particular buying situation will be a group or an individual decision?

12. The industrial marketer who identifies organizational screening requirements and the salient evaluative criteria of individual buying center members can make more informed product design and advertising decisions. Explain.

Part III

Assessing Market Opportunities

Chapter **5**

Segmenting the Organizational Market

The industrial seller faces a market made up of many different types of organizational customers with varying needs. Only when this aggregate market is broken down into meaningful categories can the industrial marketing strategist more readily and profitably respond to unique needs. After reading this chapter, you will have an understanding of:

1. *the benefits of and requirements for segmenting the organizational market*
2. *how to utilize key secondary sources of information for industrial market planning*
3. *potential bases for segmenting the organizational market*
4. *the role of market segmentation in the development of industrial marketing strategy.*

The task of industrial marketing management is complicated by the numerous options open to the manager. The organizational market consists of three broad sectors—commercial enterprises, institutions, and government. A marketer that elects to operate in one or all of these sectors will encounter diversity in organizations, purchasing structures, and decision-making styles. Each sector of the organizational market consists of many different parts or segments; each segment may have different needs and require a unique marketing strategy. The industrial marketer that recognizes the needs of the different segments of the market is best equipped to isolate market opportunities and respond with an effective marketing program.

The goal of this chapter is to provide an approach that will aid the manager in selecting and evaluating segments of the organizational market. The chapter is divided into three parts. First, the benefits of and requirements for successful market segmentation are delineated. Second, important secondary sources of information are examined that can be profitably used in segmenting the organizational market. Here, particular emphasis is given to the Standard Industrial Classification (SIC) system—a tool of significant value to the industrial marketer. Third, specific bases upon which the organizational market can be segmented are explored and evaluated.

Organizational Market Segmentation: Requirements and Benefits

A *market segment* is "a group of present or potential customers with some common characteristic which is relevant in explaining (and predicting) their response to a supplier's marketing stimuli."[1] Since virtually every market that is made up of more than one potential buying organization could conceivably be divided or segmented, the industrial marketer requires an understanding of the requisites for successful segmentation.

Requirements

Philip Kotler identifies three requirements that a marketer can use in evaluating the desirability of potential market segments:[2]

1. *measurability,* the degree to which information exists or is obtainable on the particular buyer characteristic;
2. *accessibility,* the degree to which the firm can effectively focus its marketing efforts on chosen segments;
3. *substantiality,* the degree to which the segments are large and/or profitable enough to be worth considering for separate marketing cultivation.

Thus, the art of market segmentation involves identifying groups of consumers that are sufficiently large, and sufficiently different, to justify separate attention in marketing strategy development. The core idea is to locate customer segments with differing needs and, thus, differing levels of responsiveness to marketing strategy.

Although the concept of market segmentation is widely acclaimed and applied, a segmented marketing strategy is not appropriate in selected cases. In addition to applying the criteria already outlined, the marketing manager must carefully examine the competitive environment of the specific product category in question. One group of researchers isolates three product/market situations where a segmented marketing strategy is not appropriate:[3]

1. heavy users account for such a large proportion of the sales volume that they are the only relevant target;
2. the market is so small that marketing to a portion of it is unprofitable (i.e., a brand must appeal to all segments);
3. the brand holds the dominant position in the market (i.e., it draws from all segments of the market).

Thus, a careful analysis of the competitive environment is required to determine the appropriateness of a particular segmentation approach.

Benefits

If the requirements for effective segmentation are met, several benefits accrue to the firm. First, segmentation provides the firm with an approach that operationalizes the marketing concept. The mere attempt at segmenting the organizational market forces the marketer to become more attuned to the unique needs of customer segments. Often, segments are identified that are being neglected or inadequately served by competitors. Second, segmentation provides guidelines that are useful in designing all phases of marketing strategy. To illustrate, marketing communications can be refined and more sharply focused to address the evaluative criteria of different customer segments. Third, market segmentation provides the industrial marketer with guidelines that are of significant value in allocating marketing resources. Ultimately, the costs, revenues, and profits accruing to the firm must be monitored and evaluated on a segment by segment basis. Thus, market segmentation provides the structure or basic unit of analysis for marketing planning and control.

The Industrial Market: Key Information Sources

To effectively segment the organizational market, a significant amount of market knowledge is required. Secondary sources of information provide a valuable and often inexpensive start in building this market knowledge. While the consumer-goods marketer is interested in identifying meaningful profiles of consumers (demographics, lifestyle, benefits sought), the industrial marketer centers on profiles of organizations (e.g., size, end use) and organizational buyers (decision style, salient criteria). This section explores important sources of information that can be used by the industrial marketer in developing organizational profiles. The Standard Industrial Classification (SIC) system is a vital source in beginning this task.

The Standard Industrial Classification System

In order to develop meaningful data on United States businesses, the federal government devised a system whereby all business activity could be segmented and categorized into homogeneous groups. The classification system, known as the Standard Industrial Classification (SIC), facilitates the collection, tabulation, and analysis of a wide variety of economic data related to United States business firms.[4] The complete description of the SIC is provided in the *Standard Industrial Classification Manual,* which is published by the Office of Management and Budget and distributed through the U.S. Government Printing Office.

The purpose of the SIC system is to classify and identify groups of business firms that produce the same type of product. Every plant and business establishment in the United States is assigned a code which reflects the primary product produced at that location. The SIC coding system works in the following way:

First, the nation's economic activity is divided into 10 *basic industries,* each of which is given a two-digit classification code. For example, codes 01–09 represent agriculture, 19–39 manufacturing, 70–89 services, and so on. Next, *major groups* are developed within each basic industry. Each major group has a specific two-digit code. Thus, manufacturing has 20 two-digit codes, each representing a major group such as SIC 34, which is fabricated metal products.

Major groups are then further subdivided into three-digit *industry groups.* There are 143 industry groups, including SIC 342, which represents hand tools and hardware. The next level of detail, four-digit codes, are referred to as *specific industries.* The SIC contains 454 specific industries, and SIC 3423, hand and edge tools, is an example of one of the four-digit specific industries.

The SIC system extends to additional levels of detail in some cases. *Product classes* are defined by five-digit codes, and the SIC contains 1,300 such categories. Finally, *products* are assigned seven-digit codes, and this subdivision contains 10,000 segments.[5]

Figure 5.1 illustrates the basic elements of the SIC system, with hand tools shown as a specific example. As figure 5.1 indicates, the more digits, the finer the classification. Generally, the most useful level of aggregation is the four-digit code, as there is little published data available for five- and seven-digit codes. The *Census of Manufacturers* does assemble data at the five- and seven-digit level, but the census is only published every 10 years—which often makes its information outdated.

The Design of the SIC System. To effectively use the SIC data, the industrial marketing manager must understand how the SIC codes are developed and, in turn, their major limitations. First, SIC codes are based on the product produced or the operation performed, with the final product as the major determining factor of classification. Second, codes are given to an "establishment," which refers to a single physical location such as a plant,

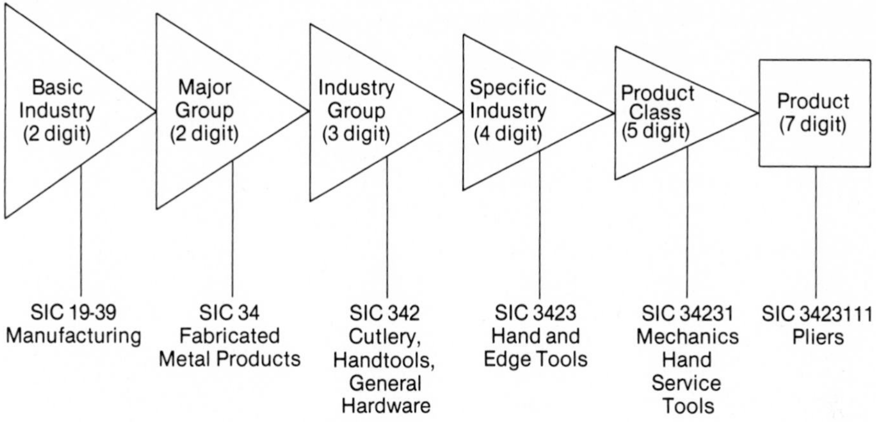

Figure 5.1 / **The Standard Industrial Classification**

factory, store, mine, farm, bank, office, or mill. Thus, a company may have many SIC codes, each applied to the separate plants in the corporate system. For example, Cincinnati Milacron, a billion-dollar producer of industrial manufacturing systems, operates a number of plants in the Cincinnati area which have the following diverse SIC codes:

2869 Industrial organic chemicals
2992 Lubricating oils and grease
3291 Abrasive products
3541 Screw machine products
3559 Special industry machinery
3622 Industrial controls
3679 Electronic components

The classification assigned to an individual establishment will depend on the "principal product" produced by the plant. If two or more products are made, the principal product is determined by the one with the largest "value added."[6] However, sales or shipments are often used because of the difficulty in determining value added for individual products. All statistics reported for a particular plant will reflect activity associated with both the primary product and all secondary products. For example, if an electronics plant in Chicago manufactured $2.6 million of transformers (SIC 3612) and $5.9 million of electronic resistors (SIC 3676) in 1979, an SIC code of 3676 would be assigned based on the procedure just described. In this case, all data relevant to employment, investment, and value added are assigned to SIC 3676 because it is the primary product.

Finally, many companies have production facilities that manufacture items to be incorporated into the final product of their parent companies. In this situation, the data for the captive plant is assigned to the SIC of the parent plant's final product. The problem with this method of assignment is that the output of the parent plant will be overstated, and the data for the industry to which the captive plant belongs will be understated.

Overcoming SIC Problems. In response to some of the difficulties associated with gathering data by "establishments" and assigning SIC by "primary product" produced, the *Census of Manufacturers* has developed two ratios which indicate the degree of error involved. The *primary product specialization ratio* indicates the percentage of total shipments of a given four-digit industry that is accounted for by its primary product. For example, SIC 3011, tires and inner tubes, has a specialization ratio of 97 percent, while SIC 2812, alkalies and chlorine, has a ratio of 65 percent. The specialization ratio for SIC 2812 suggests that many firms in this category produce a variety of secondary products that make up a sizable portion of their total output. The specialization ratio indicates just how much of the production activity in an industry (four-digit SIC) is associated with its primary product. The higher the ratio, the more homogeneous the industry; thus, the SIC code more accurately describes the firms in the industry. As a rough rule of thumb, when ratios exceed 90 percent, data for the industry are very reliable.[7]

The *coverage ratio* compares the shipments of a primary product by a four-digit industry to the total shipments of that product by all SICs. SIC 3452, nuts, bolts, and washers, has a coverage ratio of 90 percent; SIC 2873, nitrogenous fertilizers, has a ratio of 69 percent. Thus, 31 percent of the nitrogenous fertilizer is made by establishments in other SIC groups. The coverage ratio indicates the extent to which the primary product is produced by other industries. Obviously, if the manager is gathering data on a particular four-digit SIC industry with a low coverage ratio, it will be necessary to carefully investigate the total range of industries other than the SIC under scrutiny. As with the specialization ratio, a 90 percent coverage ratio indicates that the data are reliable.

The preceding discussion suggests that the industrial marketing manager must use a degree of caution when applying data based on the SIC for segmentation purposes. Reference should be made to the specialization and coverage ratios to assess the reliability of the information to be analyzed. Sometimes it will be necessary for the manager to conduct market surveys to develop original data to circumvent the problems associated with the classification system. However, the limitations of the SIC are in no way an indictment of the system. The process of classifying economic activity in an economy as vast and diverse as that in the United States is a tremendous undertaking. The SIC is an invaluable tool that industrial marketers can use to collect and analyze data about their markets from a variety of sources and know that the data are developed from a common base.

Using the SIC. The power of the SIC for industrial market analysis is demonstrated by the underlying basis of the classification itself. Industrial firms are segmented by the products that they produce and the production processes that they employ. If the coverage and specialization ratios are high, each SIC group should be relatively homogeneous in terms of the raw materials required, components used, manufacturing process employed, and the problems faced. If the manager understands the needs and requirements faced by a few firms within an SIC category, total requirements can be projected for all firms within that category. For example, most firms manufacturing truck trailers (SIC 3715) will need to purchase components such as wheels, tires, sheet steel, grease, oil, plastic parts, and electrical parts. The requirements of SIC 3715 firms will be similar, and potential suppliers can evaluate the total market available through a detailed analysis of a few SIC 3715 companies. Suppose a supplier of steel wheels determines through a sales analysis of present customers that SIC 3715 firms purchase $.08 of wheels per dollar of their final shipments. A total market estimate of wheel sales to SIC 3715 could be developed by reference to total shipments of that group. The *Annual Survey of Manufacturers* for 1977 reveals that SIC 3715 shipped $1,223.1 million of trailers, which suggests a potential wheel sales volume of $1,223.1 million × .08 = $97.85 million for SIC 3715.

Identifying New Customers. The SIC is useful for identifying new customers. The marketing manager can study four-digit industries to evaluate whether the firms making the kind of product indicated by the SIC code could potentially use the marketer's product or service. Although this analysis will only provide rough estimates, it is very helpful in eliminating industries that are not potential product users. Those SIC groups that show promise of possible use can be singled out for evaluation in depth. The resulting SIC categories become an important dimension for segmenting the market and developing individual marketing mixes tailored to them. Since each SIC is relatively homogeneous in terms of problems and processes, segmentation on the basis of SIC is often very effective.

Here, the primary application of the SIC system will be determining market and sales potentials. The federal government gathers and publishes a wealth of economic information on SIC industries that can be employed in this determination. Before we investigate the various techniques for segmenting industrial markets, we will briefly explore the nature and type of information available for use with SIC industry codes.

Information Sources for Industrial Marketing

Market segmentation and demand analysis are only as good as the underlying data used to generate them. It follows that a key step in the process of industrial market analysis is to locate and use the most appropriate sources of published data. The breadth of data available to the industrial marketing manager provides both an opportunity and a challenge. On the positive side, government at all levels, trade associations, trade publications, and private research companies gather and publish a great deal of

Table 5.1 / A Selection of Data Sources for Use in Industrial Market Analysis

Source	Title of Publication	Type of Data	Application	Frequency of Publication	Comments
Federal Government	*Census of Manufacturers* (U.S. Dept. of Commerce)	General data by 4-, 5-, 7-digit SIC on value added, employees, number of establishments, shipments, and materials consumed. Data shown by region, state, employment size, etc.	Provides comprehensive data to determine potential by area and for specific industries.	Every 5 years	Broadest array of industrial data; based on a census, may be dated.
	Annual Survey of Manufacturers (U.S. Dept. of Commerce)	Based on a sample of firms; yields current 4-digit SIC data similar to the *Census.*	Similar to the *Census.*	Annually	Less comprehensive and detailed than the *Census;* up to date.
	County Business Patterns (U.S. Dept. of Commerce)	Statistics on number of establishments and employment by 4-digit SIC for all counties in the U.S.	Used to estimate market potential by region; evaluate industry concentration by region.	Annually	Provides effective estimates of potential if number of employees is correlated to industry demand.
	Standard Industrial Classification Manual (U.S. Bureau of the Budget)	Complete description of the SIC system. Describes all 4-digit industries.	Used to evaluate possible industrial users based on products they produce.	Every 5 years	Lists each 4-digit SIC category and its primary products.
	U.S. Industrial Outlook (U.S. Dept. of Commerce)	Overall view of over 200 4-digit SIC industries with past and future growth rates in shipments and employment.	Project future market concentration and potential.	Annually	Reasonably current data; provides useful look at growth prospects in selected industries.
	Current Industrial Reports (U.S. Dept. of Commerce)	Series of over 100 reports covering 5000 products; usually based on 3-digit SIC, but may use 7-digit codes. Shipment and production data provided.	Provides in-depth analysis of potential by specific industry.	Monthly to Annually	Very timely data; published 4–8 weeks after data is collected.
	A Guide to Federal Data Sources on Manufacturing (U.S. Dept. of Commerce)	Describes nature and sources of all federal government data related to manufacturing.	A quick guide to locate appropriate government data.	Annually	Valuable source document for understanding government statistics.

State, Local Government	State and Local Industrial Directories	Type of data varies, but usually provides individual company data such as SIC code, sales, number of employees, products, and address.	Useful for defining specific potential customers by state and region.	Usually Annual	Provides data on firms of all sizes. Particularly useful when markets are concentrated in a few states.
Trade Associations	For example: National Machine Tool Builders Association, Glass Container Manufacturers Institute, Iron and Steel Institute, Rubber Manufacturers Association.	Sales history of the industry; industrial, financial, and operating data.	Provides an evaluation of past and present growth potentials by industry.	Usually Annual	May provide useful industry data not contained in other sources, i.e., average age of equipment, etc.
Trade Publications	For example: S&MM "Survey of Industrial Purchasing Power"	Number plants and shipments by SIC code by county; county percentage of total U.S. shipments by SIC category.	Provides a ballpark estimate of market potential by state and county.	Updated Annually	Very timely source for quickly assessing potential by county and state.
	Iron Age: "Basic Marketing Data on Metal-Working."	Census of metalworking industry. Data on plants and employees on a regional basis.	Quick estimate of potential for the metalworking industry.	Annual	Useful for easy estimation of potential for a particular industry.
Private Industrial Directories and Research (Fee) Companies	For example: *Predicasts* (Predicasts, Cleveland, Oh.)	Growth forecasts and market outlook for various industries by SIC.	Can be used to extrapolate potential estimates for the long run.	Quarterly	Up-to-date information on growth trends by 7-digit SIC.
	Dun's Market Identifiers (Dun & Bradstreet, N.Y.)	Data on 3.5 million corporations relative to company SIC, address, locations, sales, and employees.	Provides an evaluation of potential sales by individual company.	Continuous file	Timely information on specific firms can be obtained quickly.
	Standard & Poor's Industry Surveys' Basic Analysis (Standard & Poor's Corp., N.Y.)	Data on major industries and companies.	In-depth data on specific companies	Weekly	Timely, general data on major industries.

economic data on a national, state, and county basis. Most of this data is collected by SIC code, allowing the analysis of data on an industry by industry and, sometimes, product by product basis. The challenge issues from the need to develop familiarity with secondary data sources, to understand the nature of the data in these sources, and to comprehend how the data can be applied to organizational market segmentation and demand analysis. Table 5.1 provides a compact summary of key data sources available to the industrial marketing manager. These sources are valuable in defining target segments in the organizational market as well as in forecasting the market potential and sales expected from these segments.

Federal Government Data Sources. Understanding the abundance of industrial economic data published by the federal government is a difficult assignment. Some of the more important federal government sources are described in table 5.1. Federal data is oriented to industries; that is, the basic unit of analysis is a particular four-digit SIC category. In this regard, federal data sources are often the cornerstone for the determination of market and sales potentials by industry.

The most comprehensive set of federal data is published in the *Census of Manufacturers*. Every five years the Bureau of Census conducts a nationwide census of all manufacturing establishments in the United States. The information gathered includes statistics on the number of employees, value added, cost of materials, shipments, number of production workers, capital expenditures, etc. The data is summarized for four-digit SIC categories, geographic regions, and states. Thus, detailed economic statistics can be determined for every SIC category and for every SIC by state and region. Another aspect of the *Census* is that product shipments for five- and seven-digit SIC categories are presented, allowing the marketing manager to focus on very specific industries within regions and states.

As Table 5.1 suggests, data in the *Census of Manufacturers* make it possible to investigate, by geographic region, the size and scope of industries that have the potential to purchase the firm's products and services. The primary difficulty associated with the *Census* is the timeliness of the data—it is only published every five years. In addition, it takes from one to three years from the time the data is collected until it is published.

The problem of timeliness associated with the *Census* is partially circumvented by reference to the *Annual Survey of Manufacturers*. The *Annual Survey* is a probability sample of 70,000 manufacturers drawn from the *Census of Manufacturers* and supplemented by Social Security Administration lists of new establishments. All establishments with over 250 employees in the preceding *Census* are included in the sample.[8] The *Annual Survey* provides essentially the same data as the *Census*, but in less detail and to only the four-digit SIC code level. Survey data is usually published one to two years after the data has been collected.

County Business Patterns is an annual publication that provides employment statistics for all manufacturing establishments on a county-by-county basis. Statistics include taxable payrolls, number of employees, and the number of reporting units, and are reported for each four-digit SIC group in the county. *County Business Patterns* is an especially valuable data source in those instances when demand for a company's product is highly correlated with the size of potential establishments as indicated by the number of employees. In such cases, market potential can be calculated on a county, region, state, or territorial basis by reference to the total employment in each area in those industries deemed to be potential product users. A serious limitation of *County Business Patterns* is the nondisclosure rule, which prevents the Census Bureau from publishing data that could identify a specific firm. In such cases, the data for a particular county is not reported, which leads to underestimates of industrial activity for that area.

There are, of course, many additional federal data sources. Table 5.1 contains a short reference to some of them. A complete description of the remaining sources can be found by reference to *A Guide to Federal Data Sources on Manufacturing,* published by the Department of Commerce.

Other Data Sources. The federal government's data is primarily oriented to *industry* statistics; however, a variety of data provided by states, local governments, and private industrial directories is oriented to individual firms. State and local governments publish annual directories of businesses within their jurisdiction. The directories generally include company name, address, SIC code, products produced, sales volume, and number of employees. The directories enable the marketing manager to evaluate market potential on a specific firm-by-firm basis and by well-defined geographic areas.

Private industrial directories and research companies maintain up-to-date files on industrial firms which include a variety of SIC-related data. Dun and Bradstreet and Standard and Poors are some of the most active in this area. *Dun's Market Identifiers* provides current data, relative to sales volume, products, employees, and location, on over 3.5 million firms. The distinguishing feature of this source is the ability to quickly develop information on an individual company basis.

The remaining industrial data sources include both industry and individual company data. Trade associations often provide industry statistics that are not found in government sources (e.g., average age of capital equipment in the industry). Trade publications report data oriented to the industry to which their publication is directed. *Iron Age* annually develops a census of the metalworking industry, which includes information on plants and employees. On a broader scale, *Sales and Marketing Management* publishes an annual *Survey of Industrial Purchasing Power,* which provides a quick reference to shipments by SIC groups on a county basis. The *Survey* will be discussed in greater depth in the next chapter.

In summary, the scope of data for use by the industrial marketing manager is vast. Federal, state, and local governments, plus a host of private firms, publish statistical information which can be effectively used in segmenting the market and estimating market potential. Once available sources of information have been examined, the marketer can begin the task of organizational market segmentation. The remainder of the chapter draws upon these sources of information and explores alternative ways of segmenting the organizational market.

Bases for Segmenting Organizational Markets

The organizational market can be segmented on several bases. These bases for segmentation can be broadly classified into two major categories: macro and micro. *Macro* bases of segmentation center on the characteristics of the buying organization and the buying situation. By contrast, *micro* bases require a higher degree of market knowledge and focus on the characteristics of decision-making units within each of the various macrosegments.[9] In evaluating alternative bases for segmentation, the marketer is attempting to identify variables that are good predictors of differences in buyer behavior. Once the differences among buyers are recognized, the marketer can select target segments and respond with appropriate marketing strategy.

Macro Bases

Selected macro bases of segmentation are presented in table 5.2. Note that these bases center on general characteristics of the buying organization, the nature of the product application, and the characteristics of the buying situation.

Table 5.2 / Selected Macro Bases of Segmentation

Variables	Illustrative Breakdowns
Characteristics of Buying Organizations:	
Size	Small, Medium, Large—based on sales or number of employees
Geographical Location	New England, Middle Atlantic, South Atlantic, East North Central, etc.
Usage Rate	Nonuser, Light user, Moderate user, Heavy user
Structure of Procurement	Centralized, Decentralized
Product Application:	
SIC Category	Varies by product
End Market Served	Varies by product
Characteristics of Purchasing Situation:	
Type of Buying Situation	New Task, Modified Rebuy, Straight Rebuy
Stage in Purchase Decision Process	Early Stages, Late Stages

Characteristics of Buying Organizations. The marketer may find it useful to partition the market on the basis of the size of potential buying organizations. Large buying organizations may possess unique requirements and respond to marketing stimuli differently from smaller firms. Likewise, the marketer may recognize regional variations within the market and adopt geographical units as the bases for differentiated marketing strategies.

Usage rate constitutes another macro variable that is often useful in segmenting the organizational market. Here, buyers are classified on a continuum ranging from nonuser to heavy user. While this classification scheme may be more appropriate for industrial-goods rather than consumer-goods marketers, one authority notes that very limited attention has been given to this segmentation dimension in the industrial marketing literature.[10] Clearly, a great deal of market knowledge is required to effectively implement this classification system. However, the potential payoff for distinguishing heavy users from light users is indeed high.

The structure of the procurement function constitutes a final characteristic of buying organizations that the marketer can employ in segmentation. As discussed in chapter 4, firms that have a centralized purchasing function behave differently from those that operate with decentralized procurement. The structure of the purchasing function influences the degree of specialization of buyers, criteria emphasized, and the composition of the buying center. Thus, the position of procurement in the organizational hierarchy provides a base for categorizing organizations and isolating specific needs and marketing requirements.

Product Application. Because a specific industrial good often is purchased by many types of industries and used in several different ways, the marketer can divide the market on the basis of specific product applications.[11] To illustrate, the manufacturer of a component material, such as springs, may reach many industries, each utilizing the product in a different way and serving a different end market. This industrial good could be incorporated into machine tools, bicycles, surgical devices, office equipment, telephones, and missile systems. Often, each industry and each application represents a unique market environment. The SIC system and related information sources described earlier (see table 5.1) are especially valuable in segmenting the market on the basis of products produced. The marketer can divide the overall market into smaller homogeneous parts for the purpose of examining each separately.

Purchasing Situation. A final macro base for segmenting the organizational market centers on the purchasing situation.[12] First-time buyers have different perceptions and information needs from repeat buyers. Therefore, buying organizations can be classified as in the *early* or *late* stages of the procurement process, or alternatively, as *new task, straight rebuy,* or *modified rebuy* organizations. As discussed in chapter 3, the position of the firm in the procurement decision process or its location on the buying situation continuum dictates marketing strategy requirements.

The macro bases of segmentation outlined in this section are illustrative of the type that industrial marketers can apply to the organizational market. Clearly, other macro bases may be identified by the marketer that more precisely fit a specific product/market situation. A key benefit of the segmentation effort is that it forces the manager to search for bases that explain similarities and differences among buying organizations.

Micro Bases

While macro segmentation bases deal with the characteristics of organizations, micro bases focus on characteristics of decision-making units.[13] Having identified macro segments, the marketer often finds it necessary and useful to divide each macro segment into smaller micro segments on the basis of the similarities and differences among decision-making units. Often, several important micro segments—that each have unique requirements and, in turn, respond differently to marketing stimuli—are buried in macro segments. To effectively isolate them, the marketer generally must move beyond secondary sources of information by soliciting input from the sales force or conducting a special market segmentation study. Selected micro bases of segmentation appear in table 5.3. A brief description of each is provided next.

Table 5.3 / Selected Micro Bases of Segmentation

Variables	Illustrative Breakdowns
Key Criteria	Quality, Delivery, Supplier Reputation
Purchasing Strategies	Optimizer, Satisficer
Importance of Purchase	High Importance. . . . Low Importance
Attitude toward Vendors	Favorable. . . . Unfavorable
Personal Characteristics:	
Demographics	Age, Educational Background
Decision Style	Normative, Conservative, Mixed-Mode
Risk	Risk Taker, Risk Avoider
Confidence	High Confidence. . . . Low Confidence

Key Criteria. For some industrial goods, the marketer can divide the market according to which criteria are assigned the most importance in the purchase decision.[14] Criteria of varying degrees of importance include product quality, prompt and reliable delivery, technical support, low price, and supply continuity. The marketer might divide the market based on the predominant criterion of decision-making units or on broader supplier profiles that appear to be preferred by decision makers (e.g., high quality, prompt delivery, premium price vs. standard quality, less-prompt delivery, low price).

The marketer can benefit by examining the criteria employed by decision-making units in different sectors of the organizational market—commercial, governmental, and institutional. For example, the institutional market (hospitals, universities, etc.) represents a sector of growing significance in the United States economy. Given their divergent objectives, do these noncommercial buyers employ the same criteria as their commercial counterparts? In addressing this question, G. E. Kiser and C. P. Rao explore the similarities and differences that exist between industrial purchasing agents and hospital buyers.[15]

For standard product buying situations, reliability (e.g., quality, fairness) and efficiency (e.g., delivery with required follow-up) are the supplier attributes of most importance to both industrial and hospital buyers. Both buying groups identify "cost" as an important criterion. Compared to industrial purchasing managers, hospital buyers, however, assign *more* importance to service and *less* importance to technical capabilities, past experience with supplier, and direct source.[16] Thus, certain supplier attributes that are of considerable importance in the commercial sector are assigned little value in the noncommercial segment of the organizational market. Again, such knowledge guides the marketer in selecting desirable segments within the various sectors of the organizational market and facilitates the development of differentiated marketing strategies.

Purchasing Strategies. Research suggests that micro segments can be formed on the basis of the purchasing strategy employed by buying organizations. Organizational buyers often rely on a particular routine in purchasing. Two purchasing strategies, or profiles, that have been identified are often referred to as *satisficers* and *optimizers*.[17]

Satisficers approach a given purchasing requirement simply by contacting familiar suppliers and placing the order with the first one that satisfies product and delivery requirements. By contrast, optimizers would consider numerous suppliers, familiar and unfamiliar, solicit bids, examine all alternative proposals carefully, and select the preferred supplier.

These purchasing strategies raise numerous implications. To illustrate, a new supplier entering the market would have a higher probability of successfully penetrating a decision-making unit made up of optimizers rather than one that consisted of satisficers. The latter group would rely on familiar suppliers.

The identification of different purchasing patterns can aid the marketer in understanding differential responses to marketing stimuli. For example, an organizational marketer of deep-frying shortening encounters both satisficers and optimizers. Large universities review and test alternatives carefully, consult with student committees, and analyze the price per unit cooked before selecting a supplier (optimizers). Other organizational customers, such as restaurants and company cafeterias, follow a different pattern. Here the restaurant manager consults with the chef and selects a supplier that provides the required product quality and delivery (satisficer). Clearly, marketers of all types of industrial goods can benefit from an awareness of the similarities and differences in the purchasing strategies followed by their customers. Note that satisficing and optimizing are only two of many purchasing strategies that can be employed by organizational buyers.

Importance of Purchase. Organizational customers can be classified on the basis of the perceived importance of a particular product. Such a classification scheme is especially appropriate when the industrial product in question is applied in different ways by organizational customers. The nature of the application influences the degree of significance of the product to the functioning of the organization. Likewise, buyer perceptions vary according to the impact of the product on the total mission of the firm. A large commercial enterprise may consider the purchase of an office machine as routine, while the same purchase for a small manufacturing concern is "an event."

Attitudes toward Vendors. The attitudes of decision-making units toward the vendors that compete in a particular product class provide a means of micro segmentation. A marketer can profit from an understanding of how various clusters of buyers view alternative sources of supply. This analysis often uncovers opportunities in the form of vulnerable segments that are being neglected or are not fully satisfied by competing sellers.

Personal Characteristics. A number of micro segmentation possibilities deal with the personal characteristics of organizational decision makers: demographics (age, education), personality factors, decision styles, risk preference or risk avoidance, confidence, and related individual characteristics. Although some interesting studies have shown the viability of segmentation on the basis of individual characteristics, future research is needed to further explore the potential of this area as a firm base for micro segmentation.[18]

Micro Segmentation: Illustrated. A comprehensive analysis of the commercial air conditioning market led to the identification of four micro segments.[19] These segments are profiled in table 5.4. Note that micro segment 3, which represents 32 percent of the potential market, contains decision participants who perceive a high level of risk in purchasing an unreliable system and a low to medium level of satisfaction with their current system. Such an analysis allows the marketer to identify meaningful micro segments and respond with finely tuned marketing communications.

Table 5.4 / Micro Segments for Industrial Air Conditioning Systems

Characteristics	Micro Segment 1	Micro Segment 2	Micro Segment 3	Micro Segment 4
Major Decision Participants	Plant Managers and HVAC Consultants	Production Engineers and Plant Managers	Production Engineers and HVAC Consultants	Top Management and HVAC Consultants
Satisfaction with Current System	Medium to High	Low	Low to Medium	High
Perceived Risk of Purchasing an Uneconomical System	Medium to High	Low	Low to Medium	High
Perceived Risk of Purchasing an Unreliable System	Medium to High	Low	High	Low to Medium
Percentage of Plant Area Requiring A/C	Medium to Large	Small	Large	Medium
Number of Separate Plants	Medium to Large	Small	Large	Small to Medium
Company Size	Medium	Large	Large	Small
Percentage of Potential Market	12%	31%	32%	25%

Source. Adapted from Jean-Marie Choffray and Gary L. Lilien, "A New Approach to Industrial Market Segmentation," *Sloan Management Review*, 19 (Spring 1978), pp. 23–24. Reprinted by permission of the publisher.

A Model for Segmenting the Organizational Market

To this point, selected macro and micro bases of segmentation have been discussed. A model appears in figure 5.2 that combines these bases and outlines the specific steps required for effective segmentation. This approach to organizational market segmentation, developed by Yoram Wind and Richard Cardozo, begins with an analysis of potential buying organizations on the basis of key characteristics of the organization and of the buying situation (macro dimensions). The initial goal of the marketer is to identify, evaluate, and select meaningful macro segments. Note that the segmentation task is complete at this stage if *each* of the selected macro segments exhibits a distinct response to the firm's marketing stimuli. Since the information needed for macro basis segmentation can often be drawn from available secondary sources, the research investment is low.

The cost of the research effort increases, however, if a micro level of segmentation is required. At this level, chosen macro segments are divided into micro segments on the basis of similarities and differences among the decision-making units. The goal is to identify small groups of buying organizations that each exhibit a distinct response to the firm's marketing strategy. Observe from figure 5.2 that the desirability of a particular target segment depends upon the costs and benefits of reaching that segment. The costs are associated with marketing strategy adjustments that are needed to reach the segment. Such costs might include expenditures for modifying the product, altering personal selling or advertising strategies, or entering new channels of distribution. The benefits include the short- and long-term opportunities that would accrue to the firm for tapping this segment. Thus, the marketer must evaluate the potential profitability of alternative segments before investing in a number of separate marketing strategies.

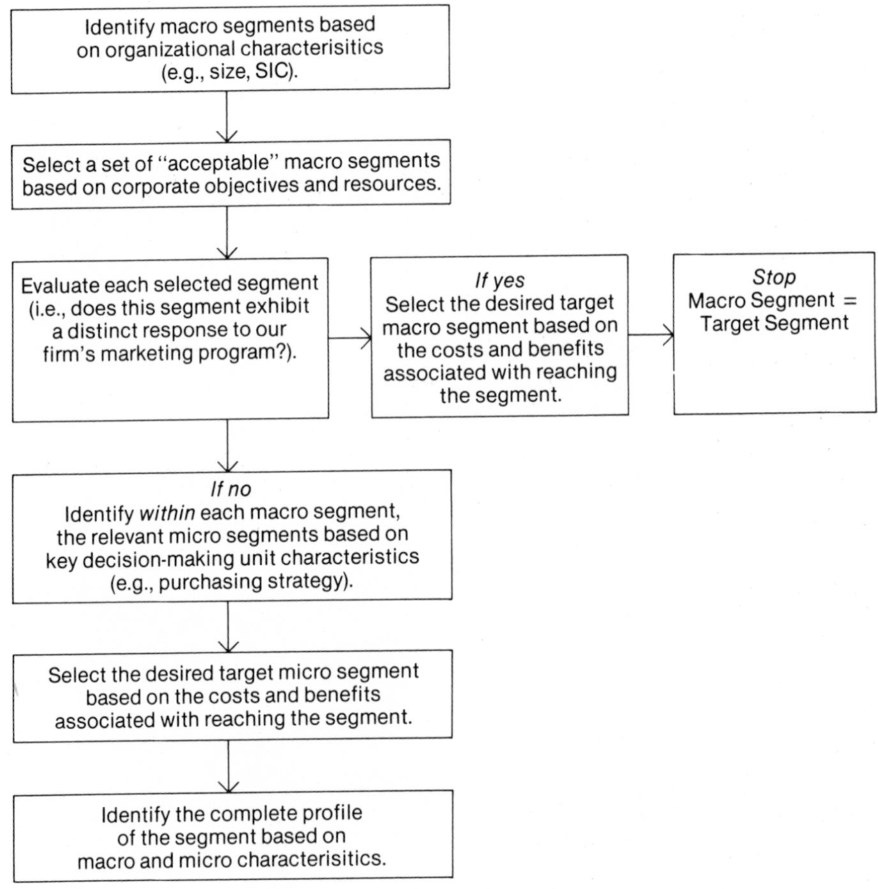

Figure 5.2 / An Approach to Segmentation of Organizational Markets

Source. Adapted from Yoram Wind and Richard Cardozo, "Industrial Market Segmentation," *Industrial Marketing Management*, 3 (March 1974), pp. 153–66. Reprinted by permission.

Segmenting the Organizational Market: A Final Note

The concept of market segmentation has had a major impact on the marketing discipline for over two decades. Unfortunately, research suggests that industrial marketers have failed to apply the concept as profitably as their counterparts in consumer-goods marketing. Rather than utilizing segmentation as a base for marketing planning and control, industrial marketers often have used it after the fact to explain why a particular marketing strategy succeeded or failed.[20] Likewise, research indicates that industrial firms tend to rely on macro bases of segmentation, giving little attention to potentially useful micro bases. Clearly, the rewards are great for the marketer who creatively utilizes segmentation in the organizational market.

Summary

The organizational market contains a complex mix of customers that have diverse needs and objectives. The marketing strategist that analyzes the aggregate market and identifies neglected or inadequately served groups of buyers (segments) is ideally prepared for a market assault. Specific marketing strategy adjustments can be made to fit the unique needs of each target segment. Of course, such differentiated marketing strategies are feasible only if the target segments are measurable, accessible, and large enough to justify separate attention.

Procedurally, industrial market segmentation involves categorizing actual or potential buying organizations into mutually exclusive clusters (segments) which each exhibit a relatively homogeneous response to marketing strategy variables. To accomplish this task, the market analyst must identify characteristics that provide a basis for categorizing buying organizations into distinct groups. The industrial marketer can draw upon two types of segmentation bases: macro and micro. Macro dimensions center on key characteristics of buying organizations and of the purchasing situation. The SIC system, together with other secondary sources of information, is a valuable tool that can be applied in macro level segmentation. Micro bases of segmentation center on key characteristics of the decision-making unit and require a higher level of market knowledge.

This chapter outlined a systematic approach that can be applied by the organizational marketer in identifying and selecting possible target segments. Before a final decision is made, the marketer must weigh the costs and benefits of a segmented marketing strategy. Here, the market potential of possible target segments is calculated. Specific techniques for measuring market potential (opportunity) provide the theme of the next chapter.

Footnotes

[1]Yoram Wind and Richard N. Cardozo, "Industrial Market Segmentation," *Industrial Marketing Management,* 3 (March 1974), p. 155.

[2]Philip Kotler, *Marketing Management* (Englewood Cliffs, N.J.: Prentice-Hall, Inc., 1976), p. 143.

[3]Shirley Young, Leland Ott, and Barbara Feigin, "Some Practical Considerations in Market Segmentation," *Journal of Marketing Research,* 15 (August 1978), p. 405.

[4]*Standard Industrial Classification Manual,* 1972 (Washington, D.C.: U.S. Government Printing Office).

[5]Adapted from "Survey of Industrial Purchasing Power," *Sales and Marketing Management,* 120 (April 24, 1978), p. 32.

[6]*Standard Industrial Classification Manual,* 1972, p. 646.

[7]Francis E. Hummel, *Market and Sales Potentials* (New York: The Ronald Press Company, 1961), p. 77.

[8]U.S. Department of Commerce, "A Guide to Federal Data Sources on Manufacturing" (September 1977), p. 45.

[9]Wind and Cardozo, "Industrial Market Segmentation," p. 155; see also, Richard N. Cardozo, "Segmenting the Industrial Market," in Robert L. King, ed., *Marketing and the New Science of Planning* (Chicago: American Marketing Association, 1968), pp. 433–40, and Ronald E. Frank, William F. Massy, and Yoram Wind, *Market Segmentation* (Englewood Cliffs, N.J.: Prentice-Hall, Inc., 1971), chapter 4.

[10]Jagdish N. Sheth, "Recent Developments in Organizational Buying Behavior," in Arch Woodside, Jagdish N. Sheth, and Peter D. Bennett, eds., *Consumer and Industrial Buying Behavior* (New York: Elsevier-North Holland, Inc., 1977), p. 31.

[11]For example, see Joel J. Barr, "SIC: A Basic Tool for the Marketer," in Donald E. Vinson and Donald Sciglimpaglia, eds., *The Environment of Industrial Marketing* (Columbus, Ohio: Grid, Inc., 1975), pp. 114–19.

[12]Patrick J. Robinson, Charles W. Faris, and Yoram Wind, *Industrial Buying and Creative Marketing* (Boston: Allyn and Bacon, Inc., 1967), chapter 1.

[13]Wind and Cardozo, "Industrial Market Segmentation," p. 155.

[14]Cardozo, "Segmenting the Industrial Market," pp. 433–40; see also, Donald R. Lehmann and John O'Shaughnessy, "Differences in Attribute Importance for Different Industrial Products," *Journal of Marketing,* 38 (April 1974), pp. 36–42.

[15]G. E. Kiser and C. P. Rao, "Important Vendor Factors in Industrial and Hospital Organizations: A Comparison," *Industrial Marketing Management,* 6 (August 1977), pp. 289–96; see also, Kjell Gronhaugh, "Exploring Environmental Influences in Organizational Buying," *Journal of Marketing Research,* 13 (August 1976), pp. 225–29.

[16]Kiser and Rao, "Important Vendor Factors," pp. 289–96.

[17]Cardozo, "Segmenting the Industrial Market," pp. 433–40.

[18]For example, see David T. Wilson, "Industrial Buyers' Decision-Making Styles," *Journal of Marketing Research,* 8 (November 1971), p. 433; David T. Wilson, H. Lee Mathews, and Timothy W. Sweeney, "Industrial Buyer Segmentation: A Psychographic Approach," *AMA Proceedings* (Chicago: American Marketing Association, 1971), pp. 327–31; and Timothy W. Sweeney, H. Lee Mathews, and David T. Wilson, "An Analysis of Industrial Buyers' Risk Reducing Behavior: Some Personality Correlates," *AMA Proceedings* (Chicago: American Marketing Association, 1973), pp. 217–21.

[19]For a complete discussion of the methodology used in the research, see Jean-Marie Choffray and Gary L. Lilien, "A New Approach to Industrial Market Segmentation," *Sloan Management Review,* 19 (Spring 1978), pp. 23–24.

[20]Wind and Cardozo, "Industrial Market Segmentation," pp. 153–66.

Discussion Questions

1. Two years ago, Jackson Machine Tool selected four SIC categories as the key market segments for the firm's marketing program. A unique marketing strategy was then developed for each segment. In retrospect, they wonder if they are appealing to the right segments of the market. Again this year, sales were up slightly, profits were down rather sharply. They need your help. Outline the approach that you would follow in evaluating the appropriateness of their segmentation approach.

2. Critique this statement: "As an industrial-goods product manager, I am most concerned with sales and profits from the *total* market. I don't have time to worry about the advantages and disadvantages of little subcomponents in this overall market."

3. To overcome some of the problems that arise in using SIC data for market planning, two ratios are particularly valuable: the primary product specialization ratio and the coverage ratio. Describe how an industrial marketer can improve the quality of segmentation decisions by applying these ratios.

4. The Tarlton Varnish Company would like to locate furniture manufacturers in Michigan that may be potential users of their product line. What sources of information could they consult in evaluating the potential demand for their products in Michigan? What sources could be used in identifying potential customers by name and address?

5. What information can the industrial marketer draw from: (1) *Census of Manufacturers*, (2) *Annual Survey of Manufacturers*, and (3) *County Business Patterns?* How is the SIC system used in each?

6. List some potential macro and micro bases of segmentation that a small manufacturer of printed packaging materials might employ.

7. Can the concept of market segmentation be applied to all sectors of the industrial market: commercial enterprises, institutions, government (state, federal, local)? Support your position.

8. What personal selling strategy would be most appropriate in dealing with an organizational buyer that is an optimizer? A satisficer?

9. How can the marketing strategist determine whether a particular basis of segmentation (e.g., SIC, company size) is appropriate and meaningful for the firm's product/market situation?

10. Some industrial firms follow a single-stage segmentation approach, using macro dimensions, while others follow a two-stage segmentation approach, using both macro and micro dimensions. As an industrial marketing manager, what factors would you consider in making a choice between the two methods?

Chapter 6

Organizational Demand Analysis: Measuring Market Potential

The industrial marketer confronts the difficult task of predicting the market response of organizational customers. The efficiency and effectiveness of the marketing program rests on the manager's ability to isolate and measure organizational demand patterns. Developing accurate projections of market potential and future sales are two of the most significant and challenging dimensions of organizational demand analysis. After reading this chapter, you will have an understanding of:

1. *the importance of organizational demand analysis to industrial marketing management*
2. *the role of market potential analysis and sales forecasting in the planning and control process*
3. *specific techniques that can be effectively applied in measuring market potential.*

To successfully implement an organizational segmentation strategy, the industrial marketing manager must develop an estimate of the market potential that exists for the firm's products. Accurate estimates of the potential business available enable the manager to allocate scarce resources to the customer segments, products, and territories that offer the greatest return. Estimates of market potential also provide the manager with a standard that can be used to assess just how well the firm performed in the various product and market situations to which they focused their attention. Thus, the accurate assessment of market potential is required to effectively plan and control industrial marketing strategy.

Sales forecasting likewise assumes a vital role in marketing management. The sales forecast reflects management's estimate of the probable level of company sales, taking into account the potential business available *and* the level and type of marketing effort to be employed. Virtually every decision made by the marketer is based on a formal or informal forecast.

Because projections of market potential and sales forecasts assume such importance in the industrial marketing process, the marketer must be familiar with the techniques that can be applied in generating these estimates. This chapter explores the role of organizational demand analysis in the industrial marketing planning and control process. First, the nature and purpose of the market potential estimate and the sales forecast are contrasted. Once this important groundwork is established, several methods that can be used in measuring market potential are described, illustrated, and evaluated. This discussion provides a base for understanding and applying sales forecasting techniques—the theme of the next chapter.

Organizational Demand Analysis

The industrial marketing manager must analyze organizational demand from two perspectives and address the following questions. First, what is the highest possible level of market demand that may accrue to all producers in this industry during a particular time period? This constitutes the *market potential* for a product and is influenced by the level of *industry* marketing effort and the assumed conditions in the external environment. Second, what is the expected level of sales that the firm can reasonably expect to achieve, given a particular level and type of marketing effort and a particular set of environmental conditions? This constitutes the firm's *sales forecast*. Note that the forecast is dependent upon the level of the *firm's* marketing effort. Thus, the marketing plan must be developed before the sales forecast. This section examines the significance of both components of organizational demand analysis to industrial marketing management.

The Role of Market Potential in Planning and Control

Market potential refers to "the maximum possible sales of all sellers of a given product in a defined market during a specified time period."[1] In some cases, the manager wishes to determine the maximum sales opportunities for a product for an individual company. This type of available business is referred to as *sales potential.* Sales potentials indicate the maximum share of market potential an individual company might expect to receive for a specific product or product line.[2]

An example will clarify the nature of potentials. In 1977, manufacturers of aircraft engines and parts generated sales of $8.1 billion. What level of market potential would be expected for the industry during 1978? Based upon commercial and government contracts awarded for 1978, estimates of general economic growth, and commercial airline activity, total volume for the industry in 1978 was projected to increase by 20 percent. Thus, the aircraft industry has a market potential of $9.7 billion in 1978 ($8.1B × 1.20). The aircraft engine division of General Electric in Cincinnati might expect to obtain a 16 percent market share of that industry based on current market share, anticipated marketing efforts, production capacity, and other factors. General Electric's sales potential is therefore $1.55 billion for 1978 ($9.7B × .16).

Potential Represents Opportunity. In most instances, market potentials exceed total market demand and sales potentials exceed actual company sales volume. Market potential is just that—it represents an *opportunity* to sell. In the aircraft engine and parts example, market potential may not be converted to demand for a number of reasons: the government may reduce aircraft defense spending; commercial airlines may postpone aircraft orders if passenger airline travel declines; the major aircraft manufacturers could experience a labor strike which would reduce their orders for jet engines. In similar fashion, sales potentials are based upon an ideal set of circumstances: past market performance, a certain level of competitive activity, and a variety of events both favorable and unfavorable to the firm. Clearly, a change in competitive actions, a decline in the general economy, or a reduction in the level and effectiveness of marketing efforts may cause actual sales to fall short of sales potential.

Absolute vs. Relative Potential. Potentials may be developed in a variety of ways, but generally the most common expressions are in terms of *absolute* potential and *relative* potential. Absolute potentials are measured in dollar or unit terms and indicate the total business available in the entire United States or within a certain market segment. Thus, the absolute potential for aircraft engines and parts is $9.7 billion for the United States market. A marketer of aircraft engines would be interested in analyzing the regional pattern of potential demand for the firm's products, and thus would determine the important geographic locations for aircraft production. Analysis might reveal that the absolute market potential for engines and parts is $970 million in Seattle, Washington (home base for the Boeing Corporation). The relative market potential, that portion of potential business in a given market segment or region as compared with the total market, would be 10 percent

(970 million/9.7 billion) for Seattle. Relative potentials facilitate the comparison of market segments on the basis of business available, as the absolute potentials are expressed as a ratio to total potential.

Potentials: Planning and Control by Segment. The primary application of market and sales potential information is clearly in the planning and control of marketing strategy by market segment. Recall from chapter 5 that *segments* refer to homogeneous units, such as customers, products, territories, or channels, to which marketing efforts are specifically tailored. When sales potentials are determined for each segment, the manager is then able to allocate expenditures on the basis of potential sales volume. There is little benefit to spending huge sums of money on advertising and personal selling in segments where the market opportunity is low. Similarly, sales that are achieved in each segment can be compared with potential sales to evaluate the effectiveness of the marketing program. Figure 6.1 illustrates the role of potentials in the planning and control system.

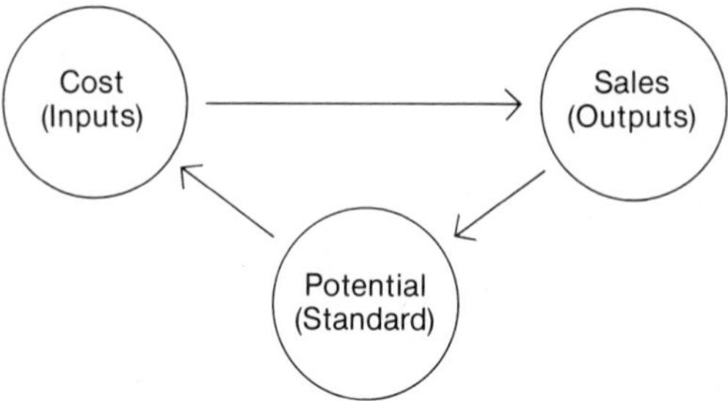

Figure 6.1 / The Role of Potential in Marketing Planning and Control

Source. Adapted from Richard J. Lewis and Leo G. Erickson, "Distribution System Costing: An Overview," in *Distribution Systems Costing: Concepts and Procedures.* Proceedings of the Fourth Annual James R. Riley Symposium on Business Logistics; Transportation and Logistics Foundation; The Ohio State University; 1972.

A Systems View. If the marketing planning and control process is conceptualized as a system, the inputs are the expenses allocated to various efforts and the outputs are the sales achieved in each segment. The key role of potential is to serve as a *standard* for both the input and the output. Those segments with the largest potential are the ones in which the corresponding marketing effort should be the greatest. The segments which achieve the highest sales level relative to potential are the ones which are the most successful. Of course, the level of effort must also be considered if competition is intense in a segment. The marketing expenditures required to generate a certain share of the market may be so high as to negate the advantage of high potential. For this reason, the profitability (sales minus required marketing expenses) must also be considered.

An example of the value of market and sales potentials is the experience of a Cleveland manufacturer of quick-connective couplings for power transmission systems.[3] For over 20 years, one of their large distributors had been increasing its sales volume of the firm's products. In fact, this distributor was considered one of the firm's top producers. The firm then conducted a study of the sales potentials for each of their 31 distributors. The large distributor ranked thirty-first in terms of sales volume relative to sales potential, achieving only 15.4 percent of available potential! A later evaluation revealed that the distributor's sales personnel did not know how to sell the couplings to their large accounts.

A further example demonstrates how a manufacturer of paper might allocate the sales budget. Assume that a company produces quality paper to be used in the greeting card industry. The firm would obviously concentrate its selling efforts in those areas where greeting card production is located. Table 6.1 shows the percentage of United States shipments of greeting cards for a selected number of counties. In this case, the firm would allocate 27.5 percent of their sales budget to the Jackson County area in Missouri and 5.6 percent to Hamilton County in Ohio. Adjustments are often needed to reflect different levels of competitive activity across the counties.

As this discussion demonstrates, market and sales potentials play a pivotal role in the marketing planning and control process. Therefore, great care must be taken in determining market and sales potential estimates. It is the responsibility of the industrial marketing manager to fully understand the various techniques for developing accurate potentials.

Table 6.1 / Percentage of Total United States Shipments (Production) of Greeting Cards

County	Percent
Cuyahoga (Ohio)	11.7
Hamilton (Ohio)	5.6
Jackson (Missouri)	27.5
Cook (Illinois)	5.4

Source. "Survey of Industrial Buying Power," *Sales & Marketing Management* (April 24, 1978).

The Role of the Sales Forecast

A second component of organizational demand analysis, sales forecasting, likewise poses a significant challenge for the marketer. The role of the sales forecast is slightly different from the role of market potential estimates. It answers the question: "What level of sales do we expect next year, given a particular level and type of marketing effort?" Once potentials have been determined, the industrial marketing manager is in a position to allocate resources to the various elements of the marketing mix. After the marketing strategy is developed, expected sales can be forecasted. Note that a sales forecast can be developed only after the strategy has been specified. The proper sequence is crucial because many firms are tempted to use the forecast as a tool to decide on the level of marketing expenditures. Clearly,

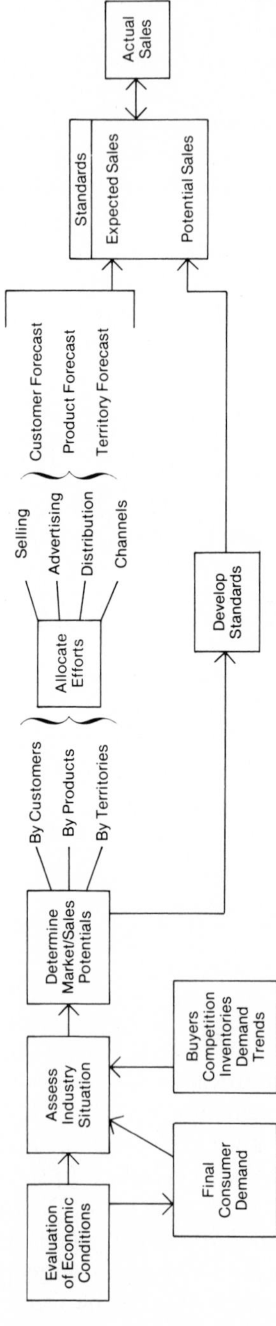

Figure 6.2 / The Relationship of Potentials and Forecasts: A Planning Framework

marketing strategy is a determinant of the level of sales and not vice versa! Figure 6.2 illustrates the position of market potential estimates and the sales forecast in the marketing planning process.

The sales forecast represents the firm's best estimate of the sales revenue expected to be generated by a given marketing strategy. In most cases, the forecast will be less than sales potential. Sales potential represents the sales *available* to the firm and there are numerous reasons why the sales potential would not be realized. The firm may find that it is uneconomical to try and capture the total available business. Strong competitors within certain segments may preclude the achievement of total potential sales. Similar to sales potential data, the sales forecast is an aid in the allocation of resources and the measurement of performance.

Observe from figure 6.2 that a sales forecast may be made for the entire company or for individual product, territory, or customer segments. The time period covered may be short (weekly forecasts up to 12 months) or the forecast may be long-range (extending as far as 5 years into the future). The time period of the forecast is one of the most important criteria in selecting a forecasting technique. The length of the forecast period also determines how the forecast will be used. Short-range forecasts are typically employed to plan production schedules, determine inventory commitments, determine purchasing requirements, and plan working capital needs for the fiscal year. Long-range forecasts are used to plan the development and location of plant and warehouse facilities, estimate long-run capital requirements, and set long-term channel strategies.

Having discussed the role of organizational demand analysis in the marketing planning and control process, attention now turns to the specific tools that the manager can utilize in developing accurate estimates of market potential. Here available techniques will be described, illustrated, and evaluated. The industrial marketer requires an understanding of the purpose of alternative techniques as well as their value and limitations.

Determining Market and Sales Potentials

Selection of a technique for determining potentials is influenced by many factors. Availability of relevant secondary data, whether the product is new or established, the number of potential customers, and the extent of internal company information all play a role in deciding on the appropriate approach to estimating potentials. Regardless of the specific approach, market potential is based on an analysis of variables which relate to, or cause, aggregate demand for the product. The important issue is finding the best measure of the underlying variables so that potential can be accurately measured. Each method of potential estimation takes a different approach to assessing these variables. The methods of estimating potentials can be classified into three categories: (1) statistical series methods, (2) surveys, and (3) input/output analysis.

Statistical Series Methods

Statistical series methods presume that a close correlation exists between the level of product demand and some statistical series, such as the number of production workers or the value added by manufacturing. It is important to understand the basic logic of this approach to market potential estimation because the technique is not effective in those cases where the logic does not hold. First, the manager must identify specific industries that presently use the firm's product or could possibly use it. Second, a measure of economic activity is determined for each of these actual and potential consuming industries. The measure of economic activity is assumed to represent the relative sales volume of each industry. For example, the number of production workers is most frequently used as the statistical series representing potential demand. Presumably, the larger the work force in an industry, the greater the potential need for a given industrial product, whether it is a component part or a capital equipment item. Additional statistical series are also employed, including value added, capital equipment expenditures, materials consumed, total value of shipments, and total employees and payrolls.

Clearly, statistical series methods are most effective when a good correlation or relationship exists between the series and demand. If the relationship between a single series and demand is not strong, multiple series can be employed.[4] In one case, an industrial firm used eight statistical series to determine market potential for its power transmission equipment. Almost 80 percent of the variation in sales of their equipment was related to variations in the eight variables.

Obviously, a key dimension to the statistical series technique is to incorporate those specific factors which have the greatest influence on the sales of a given product. Thus, new industrial products pose special problems for the market analyst because there is no way to assess the validity of the relationship between the statistical series and demand. Finally, the analyst must remember the critical assumptions that form the basis of statistical series methods. For example, when market potential among industries is being estimated by determining the value of a statistical series for each (e.g., number of production workers), the assumption is made that each and every industry is the same in terms of production requirements, the extent of components purchased versus components made, and their general manufacturing process. Certainly, no two industries are similar in all these respects, and the analyst must be cautious in applying the statistical series methods when extensive heterogeneity exists. Keeping these limitations in mind, the various statistical series methods will now be considered.

Sales and Marketing Management's Survey of Industrial Purchasing Power. *Sales and Marketing Management* (S&MM) magazine annually publishes the *Survey of Industrial Purchasing Power*. The *Survey* includes the following data which are reported for each county in the United States with more than 1000 employees:

1. the total number of plants with over 20 employees for each SIC group located in the county;
2. the total number of "large" plants, those with over 100 employees, for each SIC group in the county;
3. the dollar value of shipments by each SIC group in the county;
4. the percentage of county shipments for each SIC which are accounted for by "large plants."

Table 6.2 provides a sample of the type and format of the data contained in the *Survey*.

Two statistical series are provided by the *Survey:* the number of plants and the value of shipments. Separately or together, these data can be used to develop market potential. Consider the following example. An industrial manufacturer of meat analyzers and formulators has recently developed a particular type of machine that has application primarily in the meat packing industry. Studies by the firm's trade association reveal that this specific machine, if used by all meat packers, would cost each packer approximately one-half cent on each sales dollar. The machine maker desires an estimate of total market potential as well as a forecast of potential by geographic region. The *Survey* can be utilized to find both.

First, total shipments for four-digit manufacturing industries are provided in one section of the *Survey*. The relevant SIC groups for the manufacturer of meat formulators will include:

- SIC 2011 Meat packing plants
- SIC 2013 Sausages and prepared meats
- SIC 2017 Poultry and egg processing

The *Survey* shows the total shipments for each of the important SICs. With this information, an estimate of total market potential can be calculated as shown in table 6.3. Total dollar shipments of each four-digit industry SIC are multiplied by .005 (which represents a cost of one-half cent per sales dollar) to determine the market potential for each. In reality, each SIC may use more or less formulators per dollar of sales, and this fact can be accounted for by adjusting the percentage applied to each SIC's shipment volume. Total market potential is $217.5 million, the majority of which is accounted for by the meat packing industry—SIC 2011.

Potential for each geographic region may be determined by reference to the body of *S&MM*'s *Survey*. Here, shipments by SIC groups 2011 and 2013 (2017 is excluded) will be shown for each county in the United States in which these industries are located. Let us assume that the formulator manufacturer presently has sales offices in California, Iowa, Indiana, Illinois, and Texas, and desires an estimate of relative potential for these five states. Table 6.4 indicates how the *Survey* data would be used to calculate the relative market potential.

Table 6.2 / Example of the Data in the Survey of Industrial Purchasing Power

County SIC	Metro Area Industry	Number of Plants: Total Plants	Number of Plants: Large Plants	Total Shipments ($Mil.)	% of U.S. Shipments	% in Large Plants
New Jersey						
Atlantic	20 All mfg.	92	27	555.1	.0369	68
2311	Men's & boys' suits & coats	8	6	52.7	1.4792	91
3262	Vitreous china food utensils	1	1	27.9	10.4182	100
Bergen	194 All mfg.	1,122	301	8,830.4	.5869	75
2052	Cookies & crackers	2	2	68.3	2.8609	100
2253	Knit-outerwear mills	12	4	117.4	3.8784	85
2335	Women's & misses' dresses	23	3	61.4	1.2943	64
2641	Paper coating & glazing	11	2	344.2	7.1984	90
2653	Corrugated & solid fiber boxes	13	11	123.9	1.6527	91
2711	Newspapers	4	3	55.3	.4238	98
2721	Periodicals	6	4	138.6	2.2178	96
2731	Book publishing	13	8	255.1	4.1520	90
2732	Book printing	3	2	39.9	2.9067	97
2751	Letterpress commercial printing	22	2	43.8	.6197	29
2752	Lithographic commercial printing	19	3	89.1	1.1979	47
2833	Medicinals & botanicals	6	1	158.5	7.0579	81
2834	Pharmaceutical preparations	12	5	98.2	.7375	72
2842	Polishes & sanitation goods	10	4	104.8	2.4864	67
2844	Toilet preparations	13	10	440.6	6.8248	97
2865	Cyclic crudes & intermediates	10	4	160.6	3.3586	75
2869	Industrial organic chemicals n.e.c.	17	9	372.2	1.6904	84
3079	Miscellaneous plastics products	44	17	250.0	.9316	71
3324	Steel-investment foundries	1	1	45.3	14.4914	100
3429	Hardware n.e.c.	7	3	84.3	1.8154	89
3494	Valves & pipe fittings	8	5	62.7	1.2567	92
3572	Typewriters	1	1	147.7	8.1715	100
3599	Machinery, except electrical, n.e.c.	23	1	42.0	.7391	39
3621	Motors & generators	7	5	86.7	1.9166	94
3662	Radio & TV communication equipment	10	5	352.8	2.7070	98
3679	Electronic components n.e.c.	20	3	53.0	.6188	53

Table 6.2 / Example of the Data in the Survey of Industrial Purchasing Power (*Continued*)

County SIC	Metro Area Industry	Number of Plants: Total Plants	Number of Plants: Large Plants	Total Shipments ($Mil.)	% of U.S. Shipments	% in Large Plants
Bergen *(Continued)*						
3714	Motor-vehicle parts & accessories	7	3	778.2	1.7699	96
3841	Surgical & medical instruments	5	3	72.1	3.2270	97
3861	Photographic equipment & supplies	13	5	154.1	1.3737	71
Burlington	211 All mfg.	179	58	1,562.5	.1038	80
3511	Turbines & turbine-generator set units	1	1	171.3	3.6613	100
3573	Electronic computing equipment	2	2	130.1	.7425	100
3662	Radio & TV communication equipment	7	2	136.8	1.0497	91
3944	Games, toys, & children's vehicles	2	2	77.2	2.1504	100
Camden	211 All mfg.	277	80	2,095.9	.1393	74
2032	Canned food specialties	2	1	129.9	5.3040	95
3211	Flat glass	1	1	122.1	5.0199	100
3296	Mineral wool	3	3	160.7	8.4623	100
3554	Paper-industries machinery	2	2	27.0	2.5984	100
3662	Radio & TV communication equipment	7	4	95.5	.7328	91
Cape May	All mfg.	21	3	68.8	.0046	31
Cumberland	285 All mfg.	117	45	872.7	.0580	73
2033	Canned fruits & vegetables	5	3	65.8	.7711	84
2037	Frozen fruits & vegetables	2	2	72.1	1.8308	100
2311	Men's & boys' suits & coats	10	9	59.9	1.6813	96
3221	Glass containers	5	4	118.8	5.9323	99
3229	Pressed & blown glass n.e.c.	3	1	51.4	3.0115	98
3231	Products of purchased glass	15	4	101.3	3.4906	54
Essex	185 All mfg.	917	188	5,903.9	.3924	66
2051	Bread, cake, & related products	9	5	58.0	.6597	90
2082	Malt beverages	2	2	259.6	4.1734	100
2337	Women's & misses' suits & coats	15	4	53.5	2.0705	44
2381	Fabric dress & work gloves	2	1	27.9	6.5187	94

Table continued on the following page

Table 6.2 / Example of the Data in the Survey of Industrial Purchasing Power (*Continued*)

County SIC	Metro Area Industry	Number of Plants: Total Plants	Number of Plants: Large Plants	Total Shipments ($Mil.)	% of U.S. Shipments	% in Large Plants
Essex *(Continued)*						
2751	Letterpress commercial printing	26	5	155.7	2.2029	80
2833	Medicinals & botanicals	3	2	639.0	28.4544	100
2834	Pharmaceutical preparations	5	5	147.6	1.1085	100
2851	Paints & allied products	21	5	161.4	2.5179	59

Source. Sales and Marketing Management, April 23, 1979, p. 71. Reprinted by permission from *Sales and Marketing Management* magazine, copyright 1979.

Table 6.3 / Market Potential for Meat Formulators

SIC	Total Dollar Shipments	Usage	Market Potential
2011	34.9 Billion	.005	174.5 Million
2013	5.6 Billion	.005	28.0 Million
2017	3.0 Billion	.005	15.0 Million
			217.5 Million

Table 6.4 / Relative Market Potential for Meat Formulators

State	County	Relative Potential: Percent of Total U.S. Shipments SIC 2011	SIC 2013
California	Los Angeles	2.8	3.0
Illinois	Cook	3.1	12.0
	St. Clair	1.0	—
	Vermillion	—	1.3
	ILLINOIS TOTAL	4.1	13.3
Indiana	Allen	—	2.6
	Geleson	1.1	—
	Marion	1.1	—
	INDIANA TOTAL	2.2	2.6
Iowa	Blackhawk	0.4	—
	Dubuque	1.3	—
	Linn	1.3	—
	Polk	1.0	—
	Pottawattami	1.0	—
	Scott	0.4	—
	Webster	1.0	—
	Woodbury	1.0	—
	IOWA TOTAL	7.4	—
Texas	Bexar	1.3	—
	Dallas	1.0	—
	Harris	1.0	—
	Potter	2.0	—
	TEXAS TOTAL	5.3	—

The county-by-county reporting of shipments for SIC 2011 and SIC 2013 provided by the *Survey* allows the manager to easily calculate relative potentials for the five states. Iowa (7.4 percent) has over three times the potential of Indiana (2.2 percent); Texas and Illinois are almost equal for SIC 2011, but Illinois has a significantly larger potential in SIC 2013 (13.3 percent). Dollar potential could be estimated for each state by multiplying the relative potential by the total dollar potential. Thus, the potential for SIC 2011 in California would be computed by multiplying $174.5 million times 2.8 percent, which equals $4.9 million.

S&MM's *Survey of Industrial Purchasing Power* is most useful in situations where the manager wants a quick estimate of potential by geographic region and by SIC category. To the extent that demand for a firm's product is well correlated to final shipments of consuming industries, the *Survey* will generate valid estimates of potential. In addition, the *Survey* offers an advantage over *County Business Patterns* in that the *Survey* is not bound by the nondisclosure rule; so, the data in the *Survey* are not distorted by deletion of a single large plant in a particular county. However, the *Survey* data is developed only for counties that have more than 1000 employees in the county and only includes plants that have at least 20 employees. As a result, not all industrial manufacturing activity is included in the *Survey* data. For example, shipments of *Survey*-listed counties represented 76 percent of the total output of SIC 3312 (blast furnaces and steel mills) and 87 percent of SIC 3573 (electronic computing equipment), but included only 45 percent of SIC 2033 (canned fruits and vegetables).[5] Generally, if a marketer's products are consumed by industries made up of many small and medium-sized firms which are geographically dispersed, the *Survey* will not provide accurate estimates of geographic and total potentials. If demand is related more closely to a different statistical series, reference will then have to be made to another source of data.

Single Series Method. Similar to the approach taken with *S&MM*'s *Survey,* the single series method calculates market potential on the basis of secondary data that reflects the relative buying power of industrial markets. The *number of production workers* is frequently utilized to measure potential business, although value added by manufacturing has been effective in this regard also. To employ this procedure, management must have adequate knowledge of the SIC groups that are potential users of their product. Once the relevant SIC groups are identified, an estimate must be made of their relative importance in terms of potential sales. One approach subjectively weights the value of the statistical series for each group based on management's judgment of the group's possible consumption. Potential is then determined on the basis of a weighted average of the statistical series. This approach to measuring market potential is illustrated below.

Assume that a manufacturer of industrial hand soap wishes to determine the *relative market potential* in the state of Illinois. Production workers will be used as the statistical series because product usage is directly related to the size of the production work force. Past experience indicates that demand will be concentrated in SIC groups involving a significant degree of hand labor, and where the operations involve oiled, greased, or "dirty" raw materials, components, and parts. Table 6.5 lists the SIC groups that management feels have the greatest potential use for the product. The SIC groups were determined by analyzing the full description of SICs contained in the *Standard Industrial Classification Manual.*

To calculate the relative potential for Illinois, management next refers to *County Business Patterns* to determine the number of production workers for each SIC group. The proportion of United States production workers is calculated in column five of table 6.5. Column six indicates the subjective weights that management applies to each SIC group; these weights reflect an estimate of the relative consumption strength for each group. Finally, column seven is the weighted proportion of United States production workers in Illinois. Column seven is then totaled and divided by the sum of the weights to show the relative market potential for Illinois. Similar analyses could be made for remaining states (or by region or city) to provide the necessary data on which to allocate sales efforts to various geographic areas.

Instead of relative potentials based on subjective weights, the industrial

Table 6.5 / Relative Market Potential for Illinois, 1976: Industrial Hand Soap Single Statistical Series Method

SIC (1)	Industry (2)	Number of Illinois Production Workers* (3)	Total Number of U.S. Production Workers* (4)	Proportion of U.S. Production Workers (5)	Subjective Weights (6)	Weighted Proportion of U.S. Workers (7)
2752	Commercial printing	20,818	194,315	0.107	3	.321
2893	Printing ink	1,732	9,720	0.178	2	.356
3312	Steel mills	38,798	452,306	0.086	1	.086
3317	Steel pipe	1,853	24,615	0.075	1	.075
3361	Aluminum foundries	3,212	45,912	0.070	1	.070
3411	Metal cans	7,685	60,743	0.127	2	.254
3462	Iron and steel forgings	5,884	36,470	0.161	2	.322
3537	Industrial trucks and tractors	3,008	26,244	0.115	1	.115
3541	Machine tools	6,391	59,762	0.107	3	.321
3561	Pumps and pumping equipment	5,768	66,003	0.087	2	.174
				TOTALS	18	2.094

$$\text{Market Potential for Illinois} = \frac{2.094}{18} = 11.63\%$$

Source. County Business Patterns, 1976.

marketer may want to determine *absolute market potential* (in dollars or units) for the entire United States, various geographic areas, or by specific SIC groups. In this situation, assuming employees will again be the statistical series, an estimate of potential sales per production worker will be required. In most instances a survey will be conducted to elicit information from respondent companies regarding past purchases of the product. A sample of firms from each SIC group would be used to estimate purchases of the product per production worker. For example, if the survey reveals that $2088 worth of hand soap was purchased last year by SIC 3541 companies, and the sample companies have a total of 1460 production workers; their purchases per worker were $1.43. Similar calculations are then made for each SIC group to be analyzed. A Cleveland manufacturer of couplings recently conducted a similar study and found that sales per employee ranged from $1.56 in SIC 33 to $3.48 for SIC 35.[6] This data was then used to project total potential by multiplying the sales per employee figures by the total number of employees in each SIC for each market area.

After using a survey to calculate usage rates per production worker, the potential for the national market can be estimated by multiplying the average purchases per worker in each SIC group by the number of total production workers reported by the *Census of Manufacturers* in that group. Similarly, total potential within a specific geographic area could be developed by following the same approach with data in *County Business Patterns*. Table 6.6 illustrates the hand soap market potential calculations for the entire United

Table 6.6 / Total Market Potential for Industrial Hand Soap Using Survey Data on Purchases Per Worker, 1976

SIC (1)	Industries (2)	Average Purchases Per Worker* (3)	×	Total Workers in U.S.** (4)	=	Total Market Potential (5)
2752	Commercial printing	$1.62		194,315		$314,790
2893	Printing ink	2.01		9,720		19,537
3312	Steel mills	1.28		452,306		578,952
3317	Steel pipe	1.32		24,615		32,492
3361	Aluminum foundries	1.41		45,912		64,736
3411	Metal cans	1.64		60,743		99,619
3462	Iron and steel forgings	1.58		36,470		57,623
3537	Industrial trucks and tractors	1.29		26,244		33,854
3541	Machine tools	1.91		59,672		113,974
3561	Pumps and pumping equipment	1.70		66,003		112,205
				Total Potential		$1,427,782

*Source. Survey of a sample of firms in each SIC industry.
**Source. County Business Patterns, 1976

States. Data in column three are based on a research survey of hand soap consumption. Note that total potential and potential by SIC group is developed with this procedure.

The critical aspect of the single series method of market potential estimation is *determining the appropriate statistical series*. The examples discussed previously used production workers, but variables such as value added, capital expenditures, materials consumed, or shipments may be more valid. Thus, before a statistical series is finally selected, management should attempt to measure the relationship between the series and either industry sales or company sales. Relationships between industry sales, company sales, and the statistical series can be evaluated through correlation techniques. The statistical series with the highest correlation will then be selected for the analysis of potential.

Value added is considered the best available measure of relative economic importance.[7] The drawback to using value added is that relevant figures are not always readily available. Detailed statistics in the *Annual Survey of Manufacturers* are not always present at the four-digit SIC level, and the more complete *Census of Manufacturers* may withhold publication of value added data if it might reveal data for any single establishment. In fact, most statistical series are affected by the "disclosure rule," timeliness of government census data, and lack of good correlation with demand. A study of the accuracy of estimating market potential by state using total employment as the statistical series revealed that none of the estimates for 10 different products fell within 50 percent of actual consumption.[8] However, the study suggested that even if the estimates are erroneous, a workable base for assessing potential is established which can be modified with additional information. For example, Allis-Chalmers developed potential estimates by weighting the SIC single series estimate by 0.5, past sales by 0.3, and district sales managers' estimates by 0.2.

In summary, the effectiveness of the single series method depends on the validity of the series in representing underlying demand. Modifications to the series and considerable managerial judgment may be required in applying the results of market potential studies. One way to develop better estimates of potential is to use more than one statistical series.

Multiple Statistical Series Methods. Frequently, more than one statistical series is required to effectively represent the demand for a product. The demand for a product depends on a host of factors and representation of it by one variable is frequently insufficient. To overcome the limitations of a single series, industrial marketers will often use sophisticated statistical techniques to measure the combined influence of a number of series on market potential. In this instance, those factors indicating the greatest association with industry demand are given the highest weight or relative influence.

For example, a manufacturer of industrial cranes believes that product sales are related to the number of production workers and to expenditures on new plant and equipment (P&E) by potential customers. Data for these variables are secured from relevant government sources. Analyzing this data using statistical regression techniques yields an equation which relates crane sales to the number of production workers and to plant and equipment expenditures.[9] The regression equation indicates the nature of the relationship between a dependent variable (industry sales) and the independent variables (expenditures = x_1 and workers = x_2). The resulting equation might look like:

$$\text{Potential Crane Sales} = 7920 + 0.2363\ (\text{P\&E expenditures}) - 1.024\ (\text{production workers})$$

In this case, crane sales increase directly with plant and equipment expenditures, but decrease as the size of the work force expands (probably resulting from less automation in plants with a large labor force).

Once the crane supplier determines the amount of P&E expenditures and production workers in any given market, total potential can be calculated with the equation. If Ohio has 9000 production workers in potential user industries, and expenditures on new P&E are estimated at $16 million, total potential crane sales in Ohio is:

$$\begin{aligned}\text{Potential} &= 7920 + 0.2363\ (\$16\text{ million}) - 1.024\ (9000)\\ &= \$3{,}779{,}504\end{aligned}$$

Similar to the single series method, great care must be taken in selecting the appropriate series to be included in the analysis. It may be necessary to experiment with a number of series to see which combinations produce the best estimates. Comparison of sales potential estimates for prior years can be compared to actual sales in those years to evaluate which combination of statistical series provides the best results.

Market Surveys

To avoid the problems inherent in historical statistical data, firms can use market surveys to gather primary information on future buyer intentions. Surveys are also used in conjunction with the statistical series method to generate data to be used with the statistical series. The techniques and procedures for conducting industrial market surveys will be treated in chapter 16. However, here it is important to note the use of the *results* of surveys for estimating market and sales potentials. The value of surveys is indicated in the industrial hand soap example, presented on page 136, where purchases per worker were used to estimate potential within various SIC groups. In that case, purchases per worker were determined by surveying a small sample of firms, and then the results were projected to the national market. Thus, a market research field study was used to provide the information used in weighting the statistical series data on production workers.

The survey method is particularly applicable to estimating market potential for new products. Surveys can provide information as to whether specific plants are in the market for a new product, the extent of their needs, and the likelihood of purchase. Surveys are useful in determining potential product use by specific SIC groups, the percentage of plants in each SIC which have the greatest potential, and the relative importance of each SIC group to the total sales of the product. In some cases, surveys have been utilized to evaluate the purchase potential of individual firms.

The National Lead Company conducted personal interviews with technical, marketing, and purchasing directors of major users to determine the usage factor of a new product. The company mailed questionnaires to small users, distributors, dealers, and jobbers who were too numerous for personal interviews.[10] In addition, National Lead annually surveys many customers to determine their purchase intentions for the coming year.

The survey method is particularly appropriate in developing a forecast of the market potential for new products and in providing estimates of potential which are based on objective facts and opinions rather than executive judgment. In addition, the data can be focused on specific industries that are the existing important customers or have the greatest potential for future use. The limitation of the method is the one associated with any survey—the research method used. Thus, nonrepresentative samples may bias the results, nonresponse bias may distort findings, the wrong person in the respondent companies may fill out the questionnaire, and a small sample size may make sophisticated statistical analysis impossible. It is the responsibility of the marketing manager to insure that the survey research design will generate valid and reliable results.

Input/Output Analysis

To this point, two major categories of techniques have been examined that can be used in measuring market potential: statistical series methods and surveys. Input/output (I/O) analysis constitutes a third approach that is available to the industrial marketer in evaluating market potential. Input/output analysis is based on the concept that the sales of one industry represents the purchases of another industry.[11]

The essence of I/O analysis is to provide an effective understanding of the transactions that take place between industries in the economy. Consider the plastics industry—plastics are used in thousands of products as well as being directly purchased by consumers. To develop effective estimates of total market demand, a plastics manufacturer must first comprehend all the potential applications of plastics to other products. Consider all of the products—automobiles, washing machines, clothing, furniture, packaging material, typewriters, and many more—that utilize plastics or plastic parts. For each application, the plastics supplier would want to know the expected sales volume for each product utilizing plastic and the amount of plastic used in producing each product. To undertake separate studies of each of several thousand product/market situations would be virtually impossible. In such cases, I/O analysis makes a significant contribution.

Simply stated, I/O data express the demand for one industry's output (plastics) in terms of the amount of that output (plastics) required to produce one unit of the using industry's output (automobiles). For example, an input/output table might indicate that $185 of plastic is required to produce one automobile.

The United States I/O Tables. The most comprehensive I/O analysis is that provided by the federal government in the United States Input/Output Tables. The I/O tables are developed by the Commerce Department's Office of Business Economics, and they are published in various issues of the *Survey of Current Business*.[12] These tables provide an aggregate view of the internal productive structure of the entire United States economy by showing the transactions among industries. The I/O accounting scheme is a systematic organization of each industry's purchases from and sales to every other industry. Every sale by a selling industry is a purchase from the point of view of the purchasing industry. Transactions among industries are organized into a flow matrix, where sales of each industry are shown along a horizontal row and purchases by each are found by reading down the column.

One of the many types of I/O tables developed by the government is the basic "input and output flow" table. The form of this table is illustrated with hypothetical data in table 6.7. Note that the row for an industry shows how its output was distributed to other industries. For example, mining sold 80 units of output to Mfg. A and 60 units to Mfg. B. The columns, on the other hand, show purchases by an industry from every other industry. Services purchased 30 units of input from mining and 120 units from Mfg. A.

Industrial demand can also be based on sales of final products. The industrial marketer can use U.S. I/O tables to examine the interrelationship between producing and consuming industries and, in turn, analyze how these relate to the demand for finished products by ultimate users and consumers. To estimate potential demand for plastics in the automobile industry, the plastics firm would estimate the amount of plastics required to

Table 6.7. / Example of a Hypothetical Input-Output Flow Table

		Purchases by:				Total Intermediate Output
		Mining	Mfg. A	Mfg. B	Services	
Sales by:	Mining	20	80	60	30	190
	Mfg. A	10	50	180	120	360
	Mfg. B	—	200	20	100	320
	Services	10	40	60	20	130
	Total Inputs	40	370	320	270	1000

produce one automobile. The "direct and indirect requirements coefficients" matrix in the U.S. Input/Output tables is designed for this purpose. Table 6.8 displays an example of a hypothetical coefficients matrix.

The entries in each cell of the matrix represent what each industry in a column would have to purchase from each industry in a row to deliver one dollar of its output to final users or consumers. Assume that industry Mfg. A produces only plastics and that industry Mfg. B produces automobiles. Table 6.8 shows the entry in the cell in row 2, column 3 is 0.1125. This means that for the automobile industry to deliver $1000 worth of automobiles to final users, plastics manufacturers must produce $112.50 worth of plastics.

Table 6.8 / Sample of a Hypothetical Direct and Indirect Requirements Coefficients Matrix

	Mining	Mfg. A	Mfg. B	Services
Mining	1.2801	0.3142	0.1965	0.1258
Mfg. A	0.0894	1.3871	**0.1125**	0.4215
Mfg. B	0.1075	0.3016	1.2419	0.5924
Services	0.0209	0.0840	0.1867	1.1104

This type of I/O coefficients table can be useful for estimating aggregate levels of market potential for a broadly defined industry. Industry by industry estimates of market potential can be determined by the following procedure. First, an estimate of total demand for automobiles could be determined from industry estimates, trade association studies, or government estimates. Then, the entries in the coefficients table would be multiplied by the expected final demand for automobiles. The result would show total plastics requirements for automobiles for the forthcoming year. In the present example, assume that automobile sales are estimated to be $7.5 billion next year. Reference to table 6.8 indicates the requirements coefficient for the plastics industry to produce one dollar of output in the automobile industry is 0.1125. Thus, total plastics requirements for the automobile industry for next year would be:

$$\$7.5 \text{ billion} \times 0.1125 = \$843{,}750{,}000$$

To build up estimates for the remaining plastics-using industries, similar procedures would be utilized.

Realistically, the application of U.S. Input/Output tables in this manner is very difficult because of the aggregate nature of the data. The level of analysis provided by the Commerce Department's I/O tables is at the industry level rather than the product level. As a result, the technique is most appropriate for developing potential estimates for very broad product categories that can be related to the industry categories in the I/O tables. Input/

output analysis may also be applied to the evaluation of performance across many market segments. Consider the plastics producer once again. Reference to the I/O tables will indicate the broad industry groups that require plastics in their production process and the amount required. The plastics producer can compare its sales in those segments to the total requirements for plastics as specified by the I/O tables. In this way, the firm is able to evaluate in rather general terms its relative performance among the various consuming industries. Such an analysis also provides a means of identifying new markets, as the I/O tables may reveal industries to which the firm is not presently directing any of its marketing efforts.

Because the government's I/O tables may be too broad to apply on a specific product or company basis, some firms have attempted to develop their own I/O models. However, applications in this area are limited as considerable effort and funds are required to develop a firm's own I/O model. In addition, private consulting firms have developed I/O tables for many industry segments with detailed data for much finer breakouts than those given by the U.S. government tables. Unfortunately, there are problems in applying the models developed by private consulting firms. Although the I/O models provided by consulting firms are similar, the outputs or forecasts are quite different.[13] Such discrepant results emerge because each firm uses different information sources and different methods of analysis. Thus, the industrial marketer who decides to use the I/O models provided by private firms must carefully scrutinize the methodologies employed and the assumptions underlying the results.

I/O Analysis: Extent of Utilization. Although the I/O technique has been publicized as an effective means for identifying and locating new markets, actual applications have been limited.[14] A poll of Fortune 500 companies shows that only one in ten firms utilizes I/O analysis.[15] Celanese Corporation, however, used I/O techniques to pinpoint future markets. American Metal Climax has also employed I/O to locate end users of metal in an attempt to improve projections of future demand.[16]

I/O Analysis: Limitations. There are several limitations of I/O analysis. First, I/O techniques are best suited for large firms that produce items which are relatively undifferentiated. Chemicals and similar bulk commodities are examples. A second problem relates to data: because data requirements are extensive, most published I/O tables are frequently out of date. Third, I/O analysis presumes that all firms within an industry have the same production requirements and technology. Clearly, such a situation is highly unlikely. Finally, I/O techniques cannot account for situations in which there are either increasing or decreasing returns to scale. If such returns to scale exist, application of the I/O technique will result in demand estimates that are too high or too low.[17] In estimating market potential, the marketing manager must carefully consider the strengths, weaknesses, and assumptions which underlie the various techniques. As noted above, the problems associated with I/O analysis must be clearly understood before the technique is used by the manager.

Summary

Estimating market potential and forecasting sales are the two most significant dimensions of organizational demand analysis. Each plays a fundamental role in the marketing planning and control process. Knowledge of market potential enables the marketer to isolate market opportunity and efficiently allocate the firm's marketing resources to those product and customer segments that offer the highest return. Importantly, measures of market potential provide a standard against which the manager can monitor performance. Similarly, the sales forecast, which represents the firm's best estimate of expected sales with a particular marketing plan, forces the manager to ask the right questions and to consider various strategies before allocating resources.

A number of methods are available to the manager in developing estimates of market potential. These methods fall into three categories: (1) statistical series methods, (2) market surveys, and (3) input/output analysis. The marketer requires an understanding of the strengths and weaknesses of the various techniques as well as knowledge of their appropriateness in the firm's particular marketing environment. While the task of measuring market potential is always challenging, accurate estimates facilitate the design of effective and efficient industrial marketing strategy.

Footnotes

[1]William E. Cox and George N. Havens, "Determination of Sales Potentials and Performance for an Industrial Goods Manufacturer," *Journal of Marketing Research,* 14 (November 1977), p. 574.

[2]Francis E. Hummel, *Market and Sales Potentials* (New York: The Ronald Press Company, 1961), p. 8.

[3]Cox and Havens, "Determination of Sales Potentials," p. 578.

[4]Joseph C. Seibert, *Concepts of Marketing Management* (New York: Harper & Row, Inc., 1973), p. 71.

[5]"Survey of Industrial Purchasing Power," *Sales & Marketing Management* (April 24, 1978), p. 18.

[6]Cox and Havens, "Determination of Sales Potentials," p. 575.

[7]Robert J. Piersol, "Accuracy of Estimating Markets for Industrial Products by Size of Consuming Industry," *Journal of Marketing Research,* 5 (May 1968), p. 150.

[8]Ibid., p. 153.

[9]For a discussion of regression analysis, see Morris Hamberg, *Statistical Analysis for Decision Making* (New York: Harcourt Brace Jovanovich, Inc., 1977), pp. 411 *ff.*

[10]M. C. MacDonald, Jr., "Appraising the Market for New Industrial Products," *Conference Board Studies in Business Policy, No. 123* (New York: The Conference Board, 1967), pp. 77–80.

[11]James Rothe, "The Reliability of Input-Output Analysis for Marketing," *California Management Review,* 14, No. 4 (1972), p. 75.

[12] "Input-Output Structure of the U.S. Economy," *Survey of Current Business* (February 1974).

[13] John C. Chambers, Satinder K. Mullick, and Donald D. Smith, *An Executive's Guide to Forecasting* (New York: John Wiley and Sons, Inc., 1974), p. 297.

[14] Rothe, "The Reliability of Input-Output Analysis," p. 77.

[15] "After Many a Year Comes the Matrix," *Sales Management* (January 15, 1970), p. 54.

[16] "How Input-Output Helped Map the Marketing Strategy of Glass Containers Corp.," *Industrial Marketing,* 55 (January 1970), pp. 21–25.

[17] G. David Hughes, *Marketing Management, A Planning Approach* (Reading, Mass.: Addison-Wesley Publishing Company, 1978), p. 198.

Discussion Questions

1. Market potential can be used as a standard for planning and controlling marketing inputs (costs) and outputs (sales). Explain.

2. What is the basic underlying logic of statistical series methods that are used in measuring market potential?

3. What statistical series are provided in the *Survey of Industrial Purchasing Power?*

4. Distinguish between single and multiple statistical series methods for estimating market potential.

5. Why are market surveys often favored over statistical series methods in measuring the market potential for new industrial products?

6. Before using input/output analysis, what limitations should be understood by the industrial market analyst?

7. Define the following terms/concepts
   a. absolute potential
   b. relative potential
   c. direct technical coefficients (I/O analysis)

8. If an industrial marketing manager wanted to determine the demand potential in the Boston market for the firm's products, how could the manager use SIC information? Be very specific—this manager is totally unfamiliar with the SIC system.

Exercises

1. The Thornton Company manufactures ink for use in all types of printing operations. The Midwest sales manager is confronted with the need to develop sales quotas for each of the five salespersons located in Pennsylvania, Ohio, Michigan, Indiana, and Illinois. The sales quotas are to be based on the market potential for printing ink in each of the five states, and preliminary analysis suggests that SIC 2711 (newspapers), SIC 2721 (periodicals), SIC 2732 (book printing), and SIC 2751 (letterpress commercial printing) are the primary ink-using industries. Historical sales records suggest that the cost of printing ink comprises about 0.1

percent of the sales dollar for the using industries. Using *Sales Management's 1979 Survey of Industrial Purchasing Power,* determine:

a. The total market potential for each SIC industry for the entire five-state area.
b. The total market potential for each state.
c. The relative market potential for each state.

2. What cautions should the sales manager in problem 1 be aware of in applying the market potential data to the formulation of sales quotas?

3. The Simpson Company manufactures electronic controls and sells them to a variety of industrial users. One of their primary markets is New York State, where past sales volumes have not been up to management expectations. Last year New York accounted for only 14 percent of total company sales volume, and in an effort to evaluate that performance, management seeks to determine the relative market potential available in New York. The market research department determines that the following SIC groups account for the vast majority of sales; and the value added for New York and the entire U.S. is shown for each.

SIC	Value added—New York*	Value added—U.S.*
2992	$21,100	$142,600
3291	5,600	52,600
3541	46,500	420,300
3559	28,400	112,000
3662	12,500	205,400
3679	17,000	158,100

*In 1000's of dollars

Management estimates that the relative consumption strength (subjective weights) for each SIC in New York is 3 for SIC 2992 and 3662; 2 for SIC 3291, 3541, and 3679; and 1 for SIC 3559.

a. Use the single statistical series method to determine relative potential in New York.
b. How did the company perform last year in light of this information?

4. The Simpson Company (from number 3 above) requires an estimate of the total dollar market potential for the purpose of allocating advertising expenditures to the New York market. A small-scale study of a sample of customers in each SIC group reveals the following data on "electronic control purchases per dollar of value added":

SIC	Electronic Control Purchases Per Dollar of Value Added
2992	$.11
3291	.08
3541	.07
3559	.05
3662	.12
3679	.10

Determine the total dollar market potential for New York.

Chapter **7**

Organizational Demand Analysis: Sales Forecasting

The sales forecast has a pervasive influence on all facets of the industrial marketing plan. While being inextricably linked to market potential analysis, sales forecasting represents a separate and distinct component of organizational demand analysis. After reading this chapter, you will have an understanding of:

1. *the role of the sales forecast in industrial marketing management*
2. *the general approaches to sales forecasting;*
3. *the purpose of different forecasting time frames*
4. *specific qualitative and quantitative techniques that can be effectively applied in developing a sales forecast.*

The sales forecast represents the manager's best estimate of the sales that will be generated if a particular marketing plan is adopted. Thus, a difficult challenge confronting the industrial marketer is to predict how organizational customers will respond to alternative marketing strategies or to differing levels of marketing effort. The marketer faces nearly unlimited options in blending the marketing mix and putting the final marketing budget together. Which products, customer segments, and territories should be given particular emphasis in the marketing plan? Knowledge of market potentials is a useful aid in addressing these critical questions, but organizational demand analysis must be extended a step further to include an actual forecast of sales.

This chapter examines the salient dimensions of sales forecasting. Particular attention is given to describing, illustrating, and evaluating selected sales forecasting techniques that can be effectively applied by the industrial marketer.

The Essential Dimensions of Sales Forecasting

Selection of a sales forecasting technique is dependent on many factors, including: the period of time for which the forecast is desired; the purpose of the forecast; the availability of data; the level of technical expertise possessed by the company; the nature of the product; the accuracy desired; and the extent of the product line. Evaluations of each of the factors will suggest the limits within which the firm must work in terms of forecasting methods.

The industrial marketer is confronted with a unique situation, because forecasts often must be prepared for various levels of the market and for various channels of distribution. Because industrial demand is derived from final consumer demand, the industrial marketer frequently must forecast final consumer sales of products for which his or her goods become a part. To provide a complete picture of the possible demand requirements, the marketer may also have to develop estimates of distributor and wholesaler sales volumes. Violent swings in inventory positions by these middlemen will affect the manufacturer's ability to satisfy their requirements. For example, Owens-Illinois containers are used to package foods and beverages whose sales are not very sensitive to changes in business conditions. Container sales, however, have definite cyclical swings because of inventory adjustments. Thus, market analysts at Owens-Illinois feel that they must track inventory conditions at all levels of distribution.[1] Finally, the industrial firm will develop forecasts for direct sales to industrial customers. Each of these forecasts may require a different approach, and the manager needs to be familiar with the basic purpose of each forecast.

General Approaches to Forecasting

Sales forecasts have a pervasive influence on the industrial marketer's entire operation. A forecast determines company-wide commitments for everything from raw materials and labor to capital equipment and advertising.[2] In the marketing area alone, forecasts are applied to setting sales quotas, evaluating advertising budgets, assessing long-range product strategy, setting inventory levels, determining transportation requirements, estimating sales personnel requirements, setting sales compensation plans, evaluating distribution channel alternatives, and other significant decision areas. Because estimates of future sales are applied to so many activities, different types of forecasts are often required.

A forecast to determine inventory commitments for the next month has to be more precise than one used to set sales quotas, which may differ from expected sales due to their motivational value. A five-year forecast of machine tool industry growth will require a very detailed and sophisticated model which incorporates a multitude of economic variables, while a six-month projection of no. 28 ball bearing sales may simply require the extrapolation of a trend line. The forecasting process may be administered from a *top-down* or *bottom-up* approach, or a combination of the two.

Top-Down. In the top-down approach, estimates of the general economy and the industry are developed first to give management members a picture of the environmental conditions under which they will be operating. These estimates include an evaluation of all the key economic and industry variables that would influence sales of their products. The data base necessary to develop these forecasts might include economic indicators such as GNP, unemployment, capital expenditures, price indices, industrial production, and housing starts. A model (i.e., a mathematical equation) would be created which links the economic indicators to either industry sales or sales of a company's product line. For example, Interroyal, a major supplier of commercial and institutional furniture, utilizes a forecasting model in which current GNP, construction starts 18 months earlier, and current plant and equipment expenditures are linked to expected sales of metal office furniture.[3] Eaton Corporation, a manufacturer of forklift trucks, used an overall economic forecast to build a five-year plan; then, an industry forecast of unit volume is created from which upper management sets market share targets.[4]

The top-down approach often will include *econometrics,* which refers to large, multivariable, computer-based models of the United States economy. Such models attempt to forecast changes in the United States economic activity in total or for specific industries by the use of complex equations which may number over 1000 for any particular model. The equations mathematically represent the historical interworkings of the economy.

Econometric models are developed by a variety of commerical, university, and bank sources. Chase Manhattan Bank, the University of Michigan, Wharton School of Finance, Harris Trust, and Data Resources, Inc., are some of the organizations providing econometric models. Econometric forecasts and other industry estimates can be purchased from these sources. Chase Econometric Associates, for example, provides clients with a monthly report on over 200 economic indicators and also includes current quarter data and data for the next 10 quarters. In addition, Chase has supplemented its macroeconomic model with 80 industry models that make 10-year forecasts.[5] Some firms, such as General Electric, develop their own econometric models that can be adapted to their particular situation. General Electric's model is used to provide a long-range economic forecast that is employed by group and division managers as a starting point for their own industry projections.

Bottom-Up. While the top-down approach begins with a macro view of the economy and industry and is initiated by upper management, the bottom-up method of sales forecasting originates with the sales force and marketing personnel. The underlying logic behind the bottom-up approach is that sales personnel possess a good understanding of the market in terms of customer requirements, channel member activities and needs, inventory situations, and general market trends. Salespersons can also be supplied economic data by corporate staff so that their projections will be based not only on historical sales data and customer needs, but also on economic and industry data. The bottom-up approach works well in situations where a firm's or division's sales are limited to a well-defined industry. Jet aircraft is a good example. A firm supplying gaskets to this industry knows that there are long lead times in the production of engines and a very limited number of producers. Thus, salespersons know almost exactly what will be built in the next one to three years, and who will build them. Very specific estimates can then be made as to the gaskets required by all manufacturers. There is little need for a broad, all-encompassing macroeconomic forecast.

It is rare that either the top-down or bottom-up procedure will be used exclusively. The more common approach is to use both, with the marketing executive having responsibility for coordinating the estimates provided by each method. For example, at Interroyal, the national sales manager uses both estimates to project product line sales for the year. TRW used a combination of top-down/bottom-up approaches, which included economic projections for specific SIC codes made by Chase Econometric Associates and input from the field sales organization.[6] In the Rockwell Division of TRW, managers integrate the tailored econometric projections for each of their customer industries with the forecasts they receive from their 42 salespersons.[7] Moreover, to insure that all division managers and field personnel base their forecasts on the same assumptions, TRW's internal economic monitoring service supplies them with an evaluation of the economic outlook for the next three years. In summary, the marketing manager will be responsible for reconciling the various types of forecasts and developing the appropriate sales estimates. A decision must also be made as to the time frame of the forecast.

The Forecasting Time Frame

Sales forecasts may be prepared on a day-by-day basis for inventory control purposes. At the same time, an estimate of sales 10 years into the future may be needed to plan for the construction of additional plant and warehouse capacity. The methodologies selected to develop each of these forecasts would probably be different; each forecasting method is particularly suited for a specific forecasting time frame. In fact, the time horizon for which forecasts are being prepared can often serve as a substitute for most of the criteria used to evaluate forecasting techniques.[8] Time horizons reflect such characteristics as the value of accuracy in forecasting, the cost of various methodologies, the timeliness of their results, and the types of data patterns involved in the sales data.[9]

Although the forecast time frame may range from a yearly forecast to a 10- to 15-year forecast, four basic time frames are commonly considered:[10]

1. *Immediate term.* Forecasts for this period range from daily to monthly sales estimates. The purpose is to provide data to make operating decisions on such things as delivery scheduling and inventory.
2. *Short-term.* Short-term forecasts range from one month to six months. The time frame is somewhat arbitrary and may overlap with the immediate and intermediate terms. Short-term forecasts are necessary for planning merchandising and promotion tactics, production scheduling, and cash requirements. The seasonal pattern of sales is generally the data pattern of interest.
3. *Intermediate term.* Again, the length of this time frame is arbitrary, but generally ranges from six months to two years. Forecasts over the intermediate term are generally employed in setting promotional levels, assessing sales personnel needs, and setting short-term capital requirements. Seasonal, cyclical, and turning points in the sales data are of interest here.
4. *Long-term.* Long-term forecasts are made for periods extending beyond two years. The focus is on estimating the trend and rate of sales growth for broad product lines. The results are used to plan product line changes, capital requirements, distribution channels, and plant expansion.

As the various forecasting techniques are discussed, reference will be made to their application to the appropriate time frame.

Forecasting Methods

As discussed, the sales forecast may be developed on the basis of a highly complex mathematical model or, more informally, on the basis of sales force estimates. Generally, two primary approaches to sales forecasting are recognized: (1) qualitative and (2) quantitative, which includes time series and causal. Within each of these categories, a variety of specific techniques are available; effective utilization of forecasting requires the matching of the characteristics of the marketing situation with the characteristics of an appropriate methodology.[11]

Qualitative Techniques

Qualitative techniques rely on informed judgment and rating schemes to develop estimates of future sales. Thus, the sales force, a group of top-level executives, or a group of distributors may be called upon to use their knowledge of the economy, the market, and the customers to create quantitative estimates of demand. The techniques included in this category are *executive panels, sales force composite,* and the *delphi method.*

Industrial firms are more likely to employ qualitative techniques than are consumer-goods producers.[12] The effectiveness of these techniques depends a great deal on a close relationship between customers and suppliers, and these relationships are typical in the industrial market. Qualitative techniques work well for items such as heavy capital equipment, where the nature of the forecast does not lend itself to mathematical analysis. These techniques are also particularly suitable for new product forecasts or in new technology areas where historical data are nonexistent or scarce.[13] An important advantage of these qualitative approaches is that users of the forecast are brought into the entire forecasting process. The effect is usually increased understanding of the forecast procedure and a higher level of commitment to the resultant forecast.

Executive Panels. A recent study of sales forecasting methods reports that the executive panel method and the sales force composite method have significantly greater usage than other forecasting procedures among a large sample of business firms.[14] The popularity of the panel method results from its ease of application and understandability. This method consists of combining and averaging top executives' estimates of future sales. Typically, executives from a variety of departments, such as sales, marketing, production, finance, and purchasing, are brought together to collectively apply their expertise, experience, and opinions to the forecast.

The primary limitation of the panel approach is that it does not involve a systematic analysis of cause and effect relationships. The resulting forecasts are only as good as the opinions of the panel members involved. Likewise, the accuracy of the executive panel approach is difficult to assess in a way that allows meaningful comparison with alternative forecasting techniques.[15]

The panel method is useful in providing "ballpark" estimates for the intermediate and long run. The estimates are often used in conjunction with forecasts developed from quantitative methods. Where historical data are limited or unavailable, the panel approach can be most effective, and it may be the only approach available.

Sales Force Composite This method is similar to the executive panel approach except that salespersons and sales managers are queried concerning their sales estimates for individual product, territory, or total sales. The rationale behind the approach is that salespersons can effectively estimate future sales volume because they possess the required knowledge about customers, the market, and competition. In addition, the opportunity for participating in the forecasting process gives sales personnel an understanding of the way forecasts are derived and a heightened involvement in achieving that level of sales. For example, in the Industrial Abrasives Division of 3M:

. . . (they) rely on their sales force quite heavily. Forecasting starts with the assets the salesman is responsible for. Forecasts are made from the "bottom-up" and then top management forecasts down. The salesman just tells management how many units he will sell this year compared to last, taking into account the inventory levels of each customer. Information about promotions, new products, pricing and industry models are studied by management, then sales are forecast downward to give the salesman his quota, which is based on his input and top management's.[16]

Very few companies rely solely on sales force estimates, but usually adjust or combine the estimates with forecasts developed by top management or additional quantitative methods.

The advantage of the sales force composite method is the ability to draw on the market and customer knowledge of the sales force. This advantage is particularly important in the industrial market because buyer-seller relationships are close and enduring. The salesperson often is the best source of information concerning customer purchasing plans and inventory levels. In addition, the method can be executed relatively easily at a minimal cost.

The problems with this approach are similar to those associated with the panel approach: it is not statistical, and it relies on informed judgment and opinions. There are also problems that stem from sales personnel overestimating sales to "look good" or underestimating them to generate a lower quota. In either case, the estimates must be carefully reviewed by management.

Despite the limitations, salespersons can provide extremely valuable information for forecasting. In cases where a good historical data base is not available, the salesperson's experience and judgment become the primary input for forecasting. Sales force estimates are relatively accurate for immediate and short-term projections, but are not very effective for long-range sales estimates.

Delphi Method. In this approach to forecasting, a panel of experts is used, and their opinions on future sales are converted into an informed consensus by means of highly structured multistage polling.[17] Similar to the executive panel technique, a group of management officials is used as the panel, but complete anonymity of each estimator is maintained. On the first round, opinions are sought concerning the likelihood of some future event (e.g., sales volume, competitive reaction, or technological breakthroughs). The responses to this first questionnaire are used to produce the second questionnaire. The objective is to provide feedback to the group so that first-round estimates and information available to some of the experts are made available to the entire group.

After each round of questioning, the analyst who administers the process will assemble, clarify, and consolidate information to be disseminated in the succeeding round. Throughout the entire process, panel members are asked to reevaluate their estimates based on the new information from the group. Opinions are kept anonymous, eliminating "me-too" estimates and the need to defend a position. After continued reevaluation, the final goal is to have some experts modify their estimates so that a consensus results. The number of experts will vary from six to hundreds, depending on how the process is organized and its purpose. The number of rounds of questionnaires will depend on how rapidly the group reaches a consensus.

The Delphi technique is usually applied to long-range forecasting. The technique is particularly well suited to: (1) new product forecasts, (2) estimation of future events for which little historical data is available, or (3) situations which are not suited to quantitative analysis. The Delphi method has found application in technological forecasting. The objective is to predict areas where new product breakthroughs might occur as a result of new technology in the industry. Such estimates are very important to demand forecasting in high technology industrial markets. In areas where the market for a new product is not well-defined and the product concept is unique, the Delphi technique can produce some broad-gauged estimates. Corning Glass Works has used the procedure to estimate demand for unique industrial products like gas turbines, pollution measurement devices, and time-shared computer terminals.[18]

The Delphi technique suffers from the same problems as any of the qualitative approaches to forecasting, but importantly, it may be the only way to develop certain types of estimates. However, there are some shortcomings specific to the approach. The task of assembling a panel of truly independent experts is extremely difficult. Officials in the same firm or individuals in the same profession tend to read the same literature and have similar training and backgrounds. Thus, they tend to share the same attitudes on the phenomena under study. In addition, some experts refuse to modify their views in light of feedback, thereby negating the consensus-forming process.

In summary, the qualitative forecasting techniques play an important role in the forecasting process: they can be applied to developing ballpark estimates in situations where product uniqueness, data unavailability, and the nature of the situation preclude the application of quantitative techniques. The accuracy of qualitative forecasts is difficult to measure on a meaningful basis due to a lack of standardization in approach. Typically, qualitative estimates will be merged with those developed through quantitative ap-

Table 7.1 / Summary of Qualitative Forecasting Techniques

Technique	Approach	Application
Executive Panels	Combining and averaging top executives' estimates of future sales.	"Ballpark" estimates. New product sales estimates. Intermediate and long term.
Sales Force Composite	Combining and averaging of individual salesperson's estimates of future sales.	Effective when intimate knowledge of customer plans is important. Useful for short and intermediate term.
Delphi Method	Consensus of opinion on expected future sales volume is obtained by providing each panelist with the projections of all other panelists on preceding "rounds." Panelists modify estimates until a consensus results.	Appropriate for longer-term forecasting. Effective for projecting sales of new products or forecasting technological advances.

proaches. Table 7.1 provides a brief summary of the qualitative approaches. The quantitative approaches to forecasting will be evaluated next.

Quantitative Techniques

Quantitative forecasting methods include two approaches: (1) time series and (2) regression or causal methods. Time series techniques use historical data ordered in time to project the future trend and growth rate of sales. The rationale behind time series analysis is that the past pattern of sales will apply to the future. However, to discover the underlying pattern of sales, the analyst must first understand all of the possible patterns that may be affecting the sales series. Thus, a time series of sales may include trend, seasonal, cyclical, and irregular patterns. Once the impact of each of these has been isolated, the analyst can then project the expected future nature of each pattern. Time series methods are well suited to short-range forecasting because the assumption that the future will be like the past is more reasonable over the short run than over the long run.[19] With the time series approach, the analyst is basically interested in understanding the pattern that sales have taken or will take through time.

Regression or causal analysis, on the other hand, takes an opposite view. Causal methods involve establishing the factors that have affected sales in the past and fitting them together into some form of mathematical model.[20] The important aspect of such a model is that sales are expressed mathematically as a function of the items which affect it. Recall the earlier discussion of market potential in chapter 6 (p. 139) where an equation was used to project potential based on production workers and on new equipment expenditures. Such an equation is referred to as a regression equation. A forecast is derived by determining expected values for each of the factors in the model, inserting these values into the regression equation and solving for expected sales. Typically, causal models have better reliability for intermediate as opposed to the long-range forecast. The reason is that the magnitude of each of the factors affecting sales must first be estimated for some future time, which becomes difficult when estimating for periods far into the future.

An important value associated with causal or regression models is the ability to predict turning points in sales. If the regression equation embodies the critical factors affecting sales, then management is in a position to predict the up- or downswing in the sales series. However, the problem of estimating the values of factors arises here again. Probably the greatest benefit associated with causal models is that the process of creating them forces the manager to think very carefully about the factors that are likely to influence sales and to estimate the nature of those influences.

The remainder of the chapter will focus on providing an understanding of these quantitative forecasting procedures.

Time Series Analysis. A time series is nothing more than a set of chronologically ordered data points. Company sales reported on a monthly basis for the past five years is an example. As indicated earlier, a time series is composed of measurable patterns, and the objective of the analysis is to identify these so that they may be projected into the future. A time series is composed of four components:

T = Trend
C = Cycle
S = Seasonal
I = Irregular

Figure 7.1 displays the nature of the T, C, and S components.

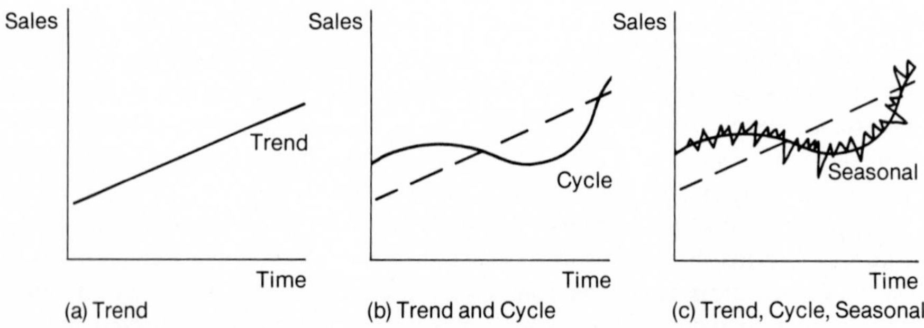

Figure 7.1 / Trend, Cycle, and Seasonal Components of Time Series

The *time series components* will be examined in detail. The *trend* indicates the long-term general movement in the data in one direction. The trend may be a straight line of the form $y = a + bx$; or a curve, $y = ab^x$; or $y = a + bx + cx^2$. A straight line trend is displayed in figure 7.1(a). The *cycle* component represents intermediate-term, regularly recurring, upswings and downswings of the data around the trend. For example, the industrial chemical industry in England shows a fairly regular rise and fall in demand over four- or five-year periods. The cycle variations are shown in figure 7.1(b). The cycle may originate from business cycle movements in the economy as a whole, from inventory swings in industry, or from a succession of new product introductions.[21] The cycle is extremely difficult to estimate because reversals need not occur at fixed intervals of time and, as a result, there may be no regularity to the pattern.

The seasonal pattern is depicted in figure 7.1(c). These patterns represent regular, recurring movements in a series that take place within the year. Data expressed daily, weekly, monthly, and quarterly may show seasonal patterns. Seasonal patterns depend on such factors as seasonality of final consumption, end of period inventory adjustments, tax dates, business vacations, pipeline inventory adjustments, and the scheduling of special promotions.

The *irregular* component in a time series reflects short-term random movements in the data that do not conform to a pattern which is regularly related to the calendar. Many factors contribute to such random swings in the sales patterns (e.g., strikes, competitive actions). Generally, the assumption is made that these short-term random effects will average out over a year.

One way to forecast future sales volumes is to consider that actual sales can be expressed as the combination of the four elements of the time series model. Thus:

$$\text{actual sales} = \text{trend} \times \text{seasonal} \times \text{cycle} \times \text{irregular}$$

Developing a forecast requires that the analyst determine each of the four patterns and then extrapolate them into the future. To accomplish this goal, a significant amount of historical sales information is required. The following illustration considers each element of the time series and demonstrates how a forecast would be derived.

1. Trend. Deriving a trend forecast requires fitting the most appropriate line to a series of historical sales observations and projecting the line one or more time periods into the future. Consider the data in figure 7.2. A relatively simple method for determining the trend line for this data is to draw a straight line through the data in order to describe the underlying, long-term movement in sales. This is referred to as a "freehand" trend line. The straight line shown in figure 7.2 seems to approximate the general trend pattern in sales.

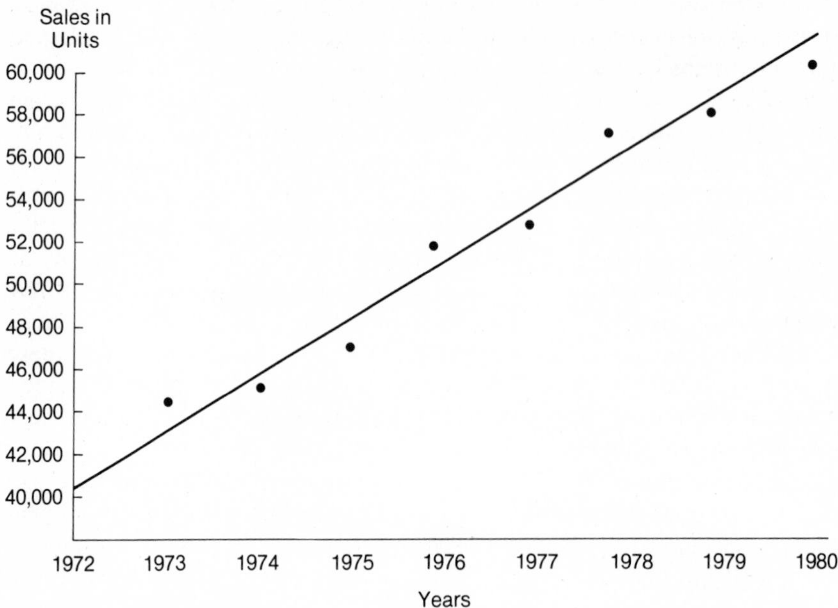

Figure 7.2 / "Freehand" Trend Line of Annual Sales

A straight line equation that describes the trend takes the form $y = a + bx$, where a refers to the y intercept (value of sales at the origin or where $x = 0$), and b represents the slope of the line, or the annual change in sales volume. To determine a and b, reference to figure 7.2 indicates $a = 41{,}000$ units at the origin (1972 in this case, i.e., at the y intercept), and b can be approximated by looking at the total change in the trend over the eight-year period. Thus, the trend line reflects sales of 41,000 units in 1972 and 60,000 units in 1980—or an increase of 19,000 units over an eight-year period. The average yearly change is therefore 19,000/8 or 2375. This means that $b = 2375$. With this information, the equation of the trend line can be summarized as:

$$\begin{aligned} \text{sales } (y) &= 41{,}000 + 2375x \\ \text{origin} &= 1972 \\ x &= 1 \text{ year} \\ y &= \text{unit sales} \end{aligned}$$

To forecast sales for any year in the future, simply substitute the x value representing the year for which the trend is desired. For example, a forecast of sales for 1983 would be:

$$\begin{aligned} \text{x} &= 11 \text{ in } 1983 \\ \text{forecasted sales} &= 41{,}000 + 2375\,(11) \\ &= 67{,}125 \end{aligned}$$

The freehand method is the simplest method of determining trend lines. There are many cases in which a good trend line can be located in this manner, particularly when there is little fluctuation around the trend line. However, a more precise method for calculating trend lines is often required, and the method of "least squares" is the most widely used approach. The *least squares method* mathematically derives the trend line that provides a straight line that "best fits the data." Mathematically, the approach develops an equation $y = a + bx$, so that the squared deviations of the actual values from the trend values are a minimum. Hence the term, *least squares*. The actual procedures for developing the least squares trend line are comprehensively treated in many sources and, therefore, will not be repeated here.[22]

If, however, the least squares method were applied to the above example, the trend line would be:

$$\begin{aligned} \text{sales } (y) &= 41{,}290 + 2483x \\ \text{origin} &= 1972 \\ x &= 1 \text{ year} \\ y &= \text{unit sales} \end{aligned}$$

Although there is not much difference between this trend line (least squares) and that computed by the freehand approach, the least squares line will provide the best fit to the data and the most accurate estimates. The greater the variability of the sales data around the trend, the more accurate the least squares line will be in estimating future sales values.

Of course, sales data do not always conform to straight line trends. In many cases the trend may approximate a curve. Here a curvilinear trend line will be required to develop accurate forecasts of future sales trends. Frequently, the analyst will need to experiment with several types of trend lines (straight line, parabola, logarithmic, for example) to determine which model best fits the data.[23]

2. *Seasonal.* Whenever sales data are expressed in time intervals less than one year (e.g., quarterly, monthly, weekly), the effect of seasonal patterns is intermixed with the trend and cycle influences. Thus, seasonal influences must be examined carefully in developing sales forecasts.[24] Typically, seasonal patterns are expressed as index numbers. The index represents how far above or below "average" the sales are in a particular time period as a result of seasonal influence. Assume the seasonal index for quarterly sales of five horsepower gasoline engines is as follows:

	Seasonal index
1st Quarter	85
2nd Quarter	115
3rd Quarter	90
4th Quarter	110

The value of 85 in the first quarter means that engine sales are only 85 percent of what they would have been (average level) had there been no seasonal influence. Similarly, sales in the second quarter are 15 percent higher than normal as a result of seasonal influences. The pattern depicted above probably would result from increased production—of lawnmowers in the winter and snowblowers in the summer—as manufacturers gear up to provide inventory to their distribution channel in anticipation of the sales season.

Predictable seasonal patterns do not emerge in every industrial product/market situation. If the seasonal factors are reasonably constant from year to year, an average seasonal pattern can be computed. However, if seasonal patterns fluctuate widely from year to year, computations of an average seasonal pattern are much less reliable.

The seasonal pattern, if reasonably constant, can be merged with the trend estimation to produce sales forecasts for periods of time less than one year. For example, assume the quarterly trend equation for gasoline engines is:

$$\begin{aligned} \text{sales } (y) &= 400{,}000 + 22{,}000x \\ \text{origin} &= 1976, \text{ 1st quarter} \\ x &= 1 \text{ quarter} \\ y &= \text{unit sales} \end{aligned}$$

The trend forecast for third quarter, 1984 (34 quarters from origin) is:

$$\begin{aligned} \text{sales } (y) &= 400{,}000 + 22{,}000\ (34) \\ &= 1{,}148{,}000 \text{ units} \end{aligned}$$

Recall that the seasonal index is 90 for the third quarter, and actual sales would be only 90 percent of "normal" sales because of seasonal influences. Thus, a forecast which considers the seasonal element would be: trend × seasonal, or

$$\begin{aligned} \text{sales} &= 1{,}148{,}000 \times .90 \\ &= 1{,}033{,}200 \text{ units} \end{aligned}$$

As the example demonstrates, seasonal patterns must be considered for short-term forecasts. If the forecast above had been based solely on trend projections, a rather substantial error would have resulted (i.e., 1,148,000 vs. 1,033,200). An important aspect of infusing seasonal elements into forecasting is to constantly monitor the patterns to detect any gradual or abrupt changes. Because business practices constantly change, seasonal patterns can be expected to shift over the years, and reformulation of the seasonal indices may be required.

3. *Cycle and Irregular.* The sales history of a company is not only affected by long-term trends and short-term seasonal fluctuations, but also by inter-

mediate-term variations in the business cycle and by random influences. Cyclical sales fluctuations arise from cycles in a particular industry or in the total economy, and result in successive waves of expansion and contraction in the firm's sales volume. Such fluctuations represent the most damaging effects on forecasting of all time series components because they are less predictable than the other type of patterns. The length of a complete business cycle may vary from one year to almost 12 years. The irregular component of time series is usually merged with the cycle as a result of its basic inconsistency.

Unfortunately, no completely satisfactory method of directly measuring the cyclical swings in a time series has been developed.[25] Cycles show a wide variation in the length of the cycle as well as the amplitude of the variations. Because of the cycle's inherently irregular nature, it is extremely difficult to find an average cycle to represent the long-term cycle pattern.

The most effective way to estimate the cycle pattern has been a "backdoor" approach. That is, a sales series which includes trend, seasonal, cycle and irregular forces is "decomposed"—first by removing the seasonal variations and second by removing the trend influences. The remaining variations are considered to be the cycle and irregular movements.

Consider sales data that have no seasonal variation, such as the yearly sales of electric motors. To estimate the cyclical variation, all that must be done is to divide the actual sales by the trend value of sales. The effect is to express the cycle as a ratio of actual sales to trend sales. In this case, variations around the trend line are assumed to be the result of business cycle forces.

Table 7.2 shows hypothetical data for electric motors, in which actual sales are expressed as a percentage of trend. Obviously, the actual cyclical pattern would not be as consistent. However, in this hypothetical case, a fairly regular cyclical pattern is evidenced by the percentage of trend figures. Similar to the seasonal index, it is possible to develop some average index of cyclical variation. Such a procedure would be risky, though, as cycle

Table 7.2 / Hypothetical Sales Data for Electric Motors: Actual Sales as a Percentage of Trend

	Actual Sales	Trend Sales	Actual/Trend (%)
1970	130	100	130
1971	99	110	90
1972	132	120	110
1973	104	130	80
1974	168	140	120
1975	150	150	100
1976	184	160	115
1977	179	170	105
1978	216	180	120
1979	171	190	90
1980	250	200	125

patterns are not consistent. Thus, the analysis of "percentage of trend" data does provide some, although limited, insight into cyclical patterns. The reason for analyzing cyclical variations is to be able to accurately project the cyclical patterns forward. If the forecaster knew, for example, that the cycle (percentage of trend) would be 125 in 1985, a sales forecast could be derived by multiplying the trend projection for 1985 by 125. Unfortunately, the forecaster is never that confident of an estimate of cycle behavior very far into the future. Because the causes of cyclical fluctuations are complex, it is doubtful that any method of statistical forecasting can be effectively used to forecast cycles. The analyst must rely on knowledge of historical cyclical measurements, forecasts of experts, government estimates, and intuitive judgment in projecting cyclical patterns.

In summary, time series analysis provides a means of evaluating past patterns in sales data and projecting these patterns to the future. Future estimates of each time series component can then be combined to develop the sales forecast.

Regression or Causal Techniques. Causal techniques have as their objective the determination of a relationship between sales and a variable, presumed to be related to sales; thus, knowledge of the "causal" variable can be used to determine expected future sales volumes. A causal model requires a significant amount of historical data so that a valid relationship can be determined between sales and the causal variable. The model mathematically expresses the causal relationship, and the mathematical formula is usually referred to as a *regression equation*.

Forecasting with causal analysis involves two important steps: (1) determining the mathematical relationship of sales and some causal variable and (2) determining how "good" the relationship is, that is, the degree of association among the variables. The first step, estimating the regression equation, involves determining the appropriate values for the coefficients in the equation. Although there are many different functional forms that the regression equation may take, this treatment will deal with two-variable straight line relationships. Hence, the regression equation is of the form:

$$Y_c = a + bX.$$

Where Y_c is the dependent variable, or the variable to be estimated (sales), and X is the independent, or causal variable, from which estimates are made. Where sales are related to more than one independent variable, a multiple regression equation would be utilized ($Y_c = a + bX + cX_2$). For example, to estimate glass container sales, Owens-Illinois used the following multiple regression equation to forecast package beer consumption:[26]

$$\text{Beer} = 8959 + 70\,(\text{Yd}) + 1963\,(\text{Pop}) - 23839\,(\text{Price})$$

where

Beer = Beer consumption (1000 barrels)
Yd = Real disposable personal income
Pop = Population, ages 21 to 34

$$\text{Price} = \frac{\text{Consumer price index for beer}}{\text{Consumer price index for food}}$$

To simplify the discussion, we will focus on simple straight line regression.

Determining the regression equation involves the same type of analysis applied in estimating the linear trend line: finding a line that best describes the relationship between sales and another variable. In this case, as opposed to trend analysis, the *X* variable represents the causal variable, instead of representing time.

To illustrate, consider the data shown in figure 7.3. The scatter diagram shows a plot of the investment in office telephone equipment in the United

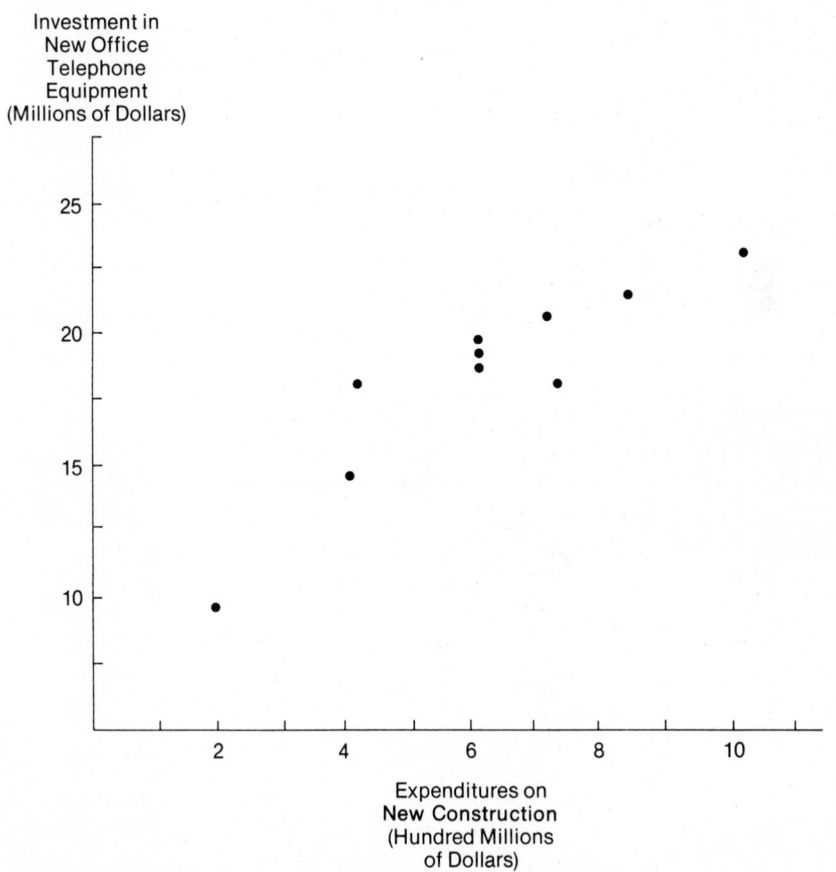

Figure 7.3 / Scatter Diagram of Investment in New Telephone Equipment and New Construction Expenditures

States against expenditures on new construction for the past 10 years. Suppose the telephone company desires to forecast sales of new equipment for the next five years using regression analysis. Management assumes that knowledge of new construction expenditures can be used to predict new telephone equipment sales.

Examination of figure 7.3 suggests that there may be a good relationship, as the two series appear to move in the same direction. To determine the precise relationship, the regression equation must be determined. The least squares approach is used to develop a regression line that minimizes the squared deviations of the actual data points from the regression line. The mathematical equations necessary to determine the regression line are:

$$a = \overline{Y} - b\overline{X}$$

$$b = \frac{\Sigma XY - N\overline{X}\,\overline{Y}}{\Sigma X^2 - N\overline{X}^2}$$

Table 7.3 provides the data required to solve the equations for the telephone equipment example.

Substituting the appropriate values into the equation we get:

$$\overline{X} = \frac{\Sigma X}{N} = \frac{60}{10} = 6 \text{ (hundred million)}$$

$$\overline{Y} = \frac{\Sigma Y}{N} = \frac{180}{10} = 18 \text{ (million)}$$

$$b = \frac{1159 - 10(6)(18)}{406 - 10(6)^2} = \frac{79}{46} = 1.717$$

$$a = 18 - 1.717(6) = 18 - 10.302 = 7.698$$

Table 7.3 / Data to Calculate the Regression Equation

Year	Investment in Office Telephone Equipment (millions)	New Construction Expenditures (hundred millions)			
	Y	X	XY	X^2	Y^2
1970	22	8	176	64	484
1971	23	10	230	100	529
1972	18	7	126	49	324
1973	9	2	18	4	81
1974	14	4	56	16	196
1975	20	6	120	36	400
1976	21	7	147	49	441
1977	18	6	108	36	324
1978	16	4	64	16	256
1979	19	6	114	36	361
	180	60	1159	406	3396

The least squares regression line is:

$$Y_c = 7.698 + 1.717X$$

and figure 7.4 shows a plot of the line against the original data points. The b term in the regression equation indicates the slope of the line. In this case it is positive; this means that if construction expenditures increase, telephone equipment investment increases. Secondly, for each $1000 increase in new construction expenditure, telephone equipment investment will increase by $17.17.

How "good" is the relationship? Before the regression equation is employed to produce a forecast, the second phase of the analysis, measuring the degree of association, should be completed. If the association between X and Y is high, the analyst will be more confident in predicting future sales with the equation. If the association is weak, then further research should

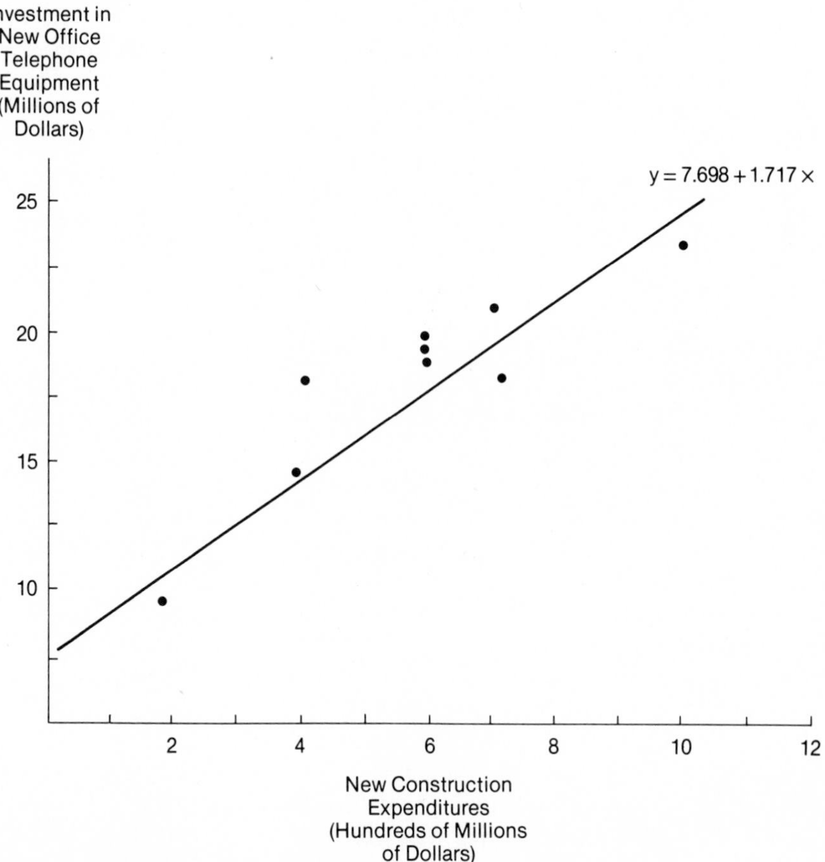

Figure 7.4 / Regression Line Plotted against the Original Data Points

be undertaken to find causal variables that are more closely associated with sales, or the forecaster should investigate the applicability of multiple regression.

To measure the degree of association, variation in the actual Y (sales) values around the regression line ($Y - Y_c$) is compared to the total variation of the values around the mean of Y (i.e., $Y - \overline{Y}$). The smaller the variation of the Y values around the regression line ($Y - Y_c$), the better the regression line "fits" the data, and the better $Y_c = 7.698 + 1.717X$ is at predicting sales volume. A measure of the degree of association, the coefficient of determination, r^2, may be calculated from the above quantities:

$$r^2 = 1 - \frac{\Sigma(Y - Y_c)^2}{\Sigma(Y - \overline{Y})^2}$$

This indicates that as $(Y - Y_c)^2$ approaches zero (i.e., all Y values fall on the regression line), the value of r^2 approaches 1. If there were no association between X and Y, r^2 would equal 0. Since r^2 is interpreted as the percentage of the variation in Y that is associated with variation in X, then if $r^2 = 1$, *all* of the variation in Y is associated with variation in X. A computational formula to determine r^2, based on the quantities used to determine the regression line is:

$$r^2 = \frac{a\Sigma Y + b\Sigma XY - N\overline{Y}^2}{\Sigma Y^2 - N\overline{Y}^2}$$

for our example:

$$r^2 = \frac{7.698(180) + 1.717(1159) - 10(18)^2}{3396 - 10(18)^2}$$

$$r^2 = .87$$

Thus, an interpretation of r^2 suggests that 87 percent of the variation in telephone equipment investment is associated with variations in new construction expenditures. A general rule for r^2 in such cases is that it should be equal to .66, that is, at least two-thirds of the variation in sales are associated with variations in the causal variable. However, this is only a very rough rule of thumb.

Continuing with our telephone equipment illustration, a good relationship exists, and the regression equation should produce relatively accurate estimates of sales. A forecast of 1984 sales of telephone equipment can now be made. The critical aspect of the entire process is that a reliable estimate of the causal variable for 1984 must be determined! The federal government frequently projects variables like new construction 1 to 10 years into the future and reference to such sources as *U.S. Industrial Outlook* may provide the necessary estimate of new construction expenditures. Regression analysis, however, will allow the analyst to create a variety of scenarios as to future construction levels and then insert these values into the regression equation, thus producing a variety of estimates of future telephone equipment volume.

Assume that federal sources indicate new construction at $1.1 billion in 1984. The regression forecast of sales would be:

$$\begin{aligned} Y_c &= 7.698 + 1.717(11) \\ &= 7.698 + 18.89 \\ &= 26.585 \end{aligned}$$

or $26.585 million. Again, various estimates of new construction could be employed to produce a range of estimates. Regression estimates are rarely applied by themselves, but are tempered with qualitative estimates developed by management.

Causal models are the most sophisticated forecasting tools; and, typically, they are applied to intermediate and long-term forecasting if meaningful long-range estimates of the independent variable are available. A recent study of forecasting found that regression techniques were used more frequently by firms for long-range forecasting than for short-range forecasts.[27] As an indication of the complexity of regression techniques, that same study showed that only 17 percent of the firms regularly use regression techniques for forecasting, and 24 percent have never tried them. Regression models are useful to industrial firms in projecting final consumer demand for items for which their products become a part. This was illustrated in the Owens-Illinois forecast of beer consumption presented earlier. Similarly, American Can's projections of motor oil sales are based on a regression model that includes auto registrations, average miles driven per car, average crank case size, and average interval between oil changes as the causal variables. Further, an important dimension in forecasting is the ability to predict a turning point in the sales series. To the extent that turning points in the causal variables can be foreseen, turns in company sales can be predicted.

Although causal methods provide a quantitative estimate of sales based on sophisticated mathematical techniques with levels of accuracy that can be measured, there are some important caveats and limitations associated with their application. First, the fact that sales and some causal variable are correlated (associated) does not imply that the X or independent variable "caused" sales. Although the relationship may yield a high r^2, the high association may be due to: chance, the high autocorrelation (both Y and X have the same time series trend pattern) in each series, and the fact that both X and Y are highly correlated to some other causative series. Even though a high correlation exists, management must examine the underlying logic of the relationship: that is, the relationship should "make sense."

Second, because of the autocorrelation in each series, one may be, in effect, correlating the trends of each series, when the other components (for example, cyclical and seasonal) are not highly correlated.[28] Thus, reliance on regression equations with high r^2's may be unsuitable for short-range projections, where cyclical and seasonal factors are important. Third, regression methods require a good deal of historical data to develop valid and reliable equations, and the required data may not be available to establish stable relationships. In addition, caution must always be used in extrapolating such relationships into the future. The equation relates what happened in the past, and a variety of economic and industry factors may be altered in the future—making past relationships invalid.

The last, and probably the most crucial of the limitations associated with causal methods, is the problem of determining future values of the independent or causal variables. Before the regression equation can be applied to projecting future sales levels, future values of the independent variables must be determined. Thus, "what is actually done is to shift the burden of forecasting from that of directly predicting some factor of interest (sales) to another one which attempts to estimate several independent variables before it can forecast."[29] In the final analysis, the quality of the sales forecast generated by regression models will depend on the forecaster's ability to generate valid and reliable estimates of the independent variables. It is true that some excellent projections of a variety of economic series are provided by government sources, but in some instances, management must face the fact that a direct estimate of sales is more reliable than a regression model estimate.

Time Series vs. Causal Methods. An important issue faced by the forecaster is the extent to which each of the methods should be applied and the situations to which they are best suited. The answers depend upon the basic criteria associated with forecast technique selection: time frame, accuracy, data requirements, cost, available expertise, and purpose of the forecast. Table 7.4 provides a brief summary of the two approaches. Time series models are better suited for immediate-, short-, and, on occasion, long-term projections, while regression models are more effective in the intermediate term.[30] Of course, these are general guidelines and are not meant to be totally definitive. Although time series analysis does not always have a high accuracy for long-term forecasting, it may be the only viable approach. It is often impossible to accurately estimate long-run future values of the independent variables required by the regression approach.

In general, research on the performance of a variety of time series and regression models suggests that the time series models have done as well as, or better than, both the simple and complex regression models in terms of accuracy.[31] The limitations associated with causal models do not necessarily negate their value but, instead, indicate that management must carefully consider their application. A significant benefit associated with these models is the knowledge that management gains in attempting to quantitatively link sales volumes to underlying causative factors. The understanding that is gained in the causal procedure compared to the purely mechanistic time series approach of extending past data patterns may outweigh the associated limitations.

Table 7.4 / Summary of Quantitative Forecasting Techniques

Technique	Approach	Application
Time Series	Determination of past sales patterns and projection of these patterns to the future. Estimated patterns are combined to develop the sales forecast.	Provides reasonable estimates of short- and immediate-term sales. Assumes past sales patterns will hold in the future. May be the only available technique for long-term forecasts.
Causal	Past sales levels are correlated to another variable, which is presumed to be related to sales. A mathematical model of the relationship is determined. Forecasts are made by inserting reliable future estimates of the independent variable into the model to predict sales for any given future year.	Are effective for intermediate-term sales forecasts if reliable future estimates of the independent variables can be developed. Valuable in other respects as management is forced to consider all factors that have some effect on sales.

A key aspect of forecasting, noted at the outset of the chapter, is that a forecast can be developed only after the marketing plan has been devised. Both time series and causal methods of forecasting seek to project sales into the future based on knowledge of past or current relationships. Thus, the marketing manager must be cautioned that the forecast derived from these quantitative approaches has to be adjusted to reflect marketing plans and strategy.

A Final Note on Forecasting

According to the study of forecasting methods mentioned earlier, industrial firms experience an average error of 7.6 percent in forecasting; this compares to an average error of 6.9 percent for all firms and 6.7 percent for consumer-goods firms.[32] The study concluded that demand for industrial goods is more difficult to predict because of the separation from the final consumer. In fact, the study suggests that the qualitative approaches to forecasting are more frequently used by industrial firms than consumer firms. This result, when coupled with a research study comparing qualitative and quantitative techniques (which indicated that quantitative techniques outperformed qualitative methods), suggests that industrial forecasting performance could be improved through the application of more sophisticated techniques.[33]

The industrial marketer is faced with a difficult forecasting situation; therefore, an understanding of the available approaches and their characteristics is certainly paramount. In general, the qualitative approaches to forecasting will continue to be of considerable importance in industrial marketing because of the close buyer-seller relationships, well-defined markets, the importance of high unit-value sales, and sales force knowledge of customer product and inventory requirements. However, application of time series and causal approaches should be merged with the qualitative estimates. John Chambers and his colleagues predict that quantitative and qualitative methods will be combined in future forecasting systems.

> At the present time, most short-term forecasting uses only statistical methods, with little qualitative information. Where qualitative information is used, it is only used in an external way and is not directly incorporated into the computational routine. We predict a change to total forecasting systems, where several techniques are tied together, along with a systematic handling of qualitative information.[34]

Summary

The sales forecast is a projection of what the firm actually expects to sell if a particular marketing plan is followed. Forecasts are developed for different time periods ranging from the immediate term (e.g., daily or weekly) to the long-term (e.g., two or more years), depending on their purpose.

The forecasting techniques that are available to the industrial marketer can be divided into two categories: (1) qualitative and (2) quantitative. Qualitative techniques rely on informed judgments of future sales and include executive panels, the sales force composite, and the Delphi method. By contrast, quantitative techniques rely on more complex data requirements and include time series and causal approaches. The time series method uses historical data ordered in time to project the future trend and growth rate of sales. Causal methods, on the other hand, seek to identify the factors which have affected sales in the past and to incorporate these factors into a mathematical model.

Each technique is suited for certain situations and forecast time intervals; however, the essence of good forecasting is to effectively combine the forecasts provided by the variety of methods. The processes of market potential estimating and sales forecasting are challenging ones, requiring the industrial marketing manager to have a good working knowledge of the available alternatives. This chapter has been structured to provide that opportunity.

Footnotes

[1]Elmer Lotshaw, "All the Economics You Need for Industrial Market Planning—And No More," *Industrial Marketing Management* 7 (1978), p. 6.

[2]"Doing a Number on Forecasting," *Sales and Marketing Management, Special Report* (November 1975), p. 4.

[3]Ibid., p. 11.

[4]Ibid., p. 14.

[5]Ibid., p. 34.

[6]Ibid., p. 30.

[7]Ibid., p. 31.

[8]Spyros Makridakis and Steven Wheelwright, "Forecasting: Issues and Challenges for Marketing Management," *Journal of Marketing* 41 (October 1977), p. 30.

[9]Ibid., p. 30.

[10]Adapted from R. A. Lomas and G. A. Lancaster, "Sales Forecasting for the Smaller Organization," *Industrial Management* 20 (February 1978), p. 37.

[11]Makridakis and Wheelwright, "Forecasting: Issues and Challenges," p. 25.

[12]Douglas J. Dalrymple, "Sales Forecasting Methods and Accuracy," *Business Horizons* 18 (December 1975), p. 70.

[13]John C. Chambers, Satinder K. Mullick, and Donald D. Smith, "How to Choose the Right Forecasting Technique," *Harvard Business Review* 49 (July–August 1971), p. 46.

[14]Dalrymple, "Sales Forecasting Methods and Accuracy," p. 70.

[15]Makridakis and Wheelwright, "Forecasting: Issues and Challenges," p. 31.

[16]"Doing a Number on Forecasting," p. 4.

[17]David J. Luck and O. C. Farrell, *Marketing Strategy and Plans* (Englewood Cliffs, N.J.: Prentice-Hall, Inc., 1979), p. 113.

[18]Chambers, Mullick, and Smith, "How to Choose the Right Forecasting Techniques," p. 53.

[19]Spyros Makridakis, "A Survey of Time Series," *International Statistics Review* 44, No. 1 (1976), p. 63.

[20]K. J. Rosier, "Sales Forecasts," *The Accountant* 175 (December 9, 1976), p. 675.

[21]Vernon G. Lippitt, *Statistical Sales Forecasting* (New York: Financial Executives Research Foundation, 1969), p. 167.

[22]For example, see John R. Stockton, *Introduction to Business and Economic Statistics* (Cincinnati: Southwestern Publishing Co., 1966), pp. 354–62.

[23]For example, see Frank H. Eby, Jr., and William J. O'Neill, *The Management of Sales Forecasting* (Lexington, Mass.: Lexington Books, 1977), chapter 5.

[24]For a more detailed discussion of procedures for estimating seasonal influences, see John C. Chambers, Satinder Mullick, and Donald D. Smith, *An Executive's Guide to Forecasting* (New York: John Wiley and Sons, Inc., 1974), chapter 10.

[25]Stockton, *Introduction to Business*, p. 436.

[26]Lotshaw, "All the Economics You Need," p. 4.

[27]Dalrymple, "Sales Forecasting Methods and Accuracy," p. 70.

[28]Paul E. Green and Donald S. Tull, *Research for Marketing Decisions*, 3d ed. (Englewood Cliffs, N.J.: Prentice-Hall, Inc., 1975), p. 669.

[29]Makridakis, "A Survey of Time Series," p. 62.

[30]Ibid., p. 63.

[31]Makridakis and Wheelwright, "Forecasting: Issues and Challenges," p. 31.

[32]Dalrymple, "Sales Forecasting Methods," p. 70.

[33]V. A. Mabert, "Statistical Versus Sales Force—Executive Opinion Short Range Forecasts: A Time Series Analysis Case Study," working paper, Krannert Graduate School, Purdue University, 1975.

[34]Chambers, Mullick, and Smith, "How to Choose the Right Forecasting Technique," p. 73.

Discussion Questions

1. The industrial marketing manager must develop not one but many forecasts over several time frames. Explain.

2. Compare and contrast the sales force composite and the Delphi method of developing a sales forecast.

3. As alternative methods for sales forecasting, what is the underlying logic of: (1) time series and (2) regression or causal methods?

4. Briefly define the four components of a time series: (1) trend, (2) cycle, (3) seasonal, and (4) irregular.

5. What are the key limitations that must be understood before applying and interpreting the sales forecasting results generated by causal methods?

Exercises

1. The Seibert Company manufactures V-belts and distributes them nationally through industrial distributors. The company requires a sales forecast for V-belts for 1985. The following information has been obtained from the market research department:

$$\begin{aligned} \text{Sales trend} &= 1250 + 95X \\ X &= \text{quarters} \\ \text{origin} &= 1975\text{, 1st quarter} \\ Y &= \text{unit sales (hundreds)} \end{aligned}$$

Seasonal Index:

Quarter	
Quarter 1	75
2	150
3	110
4	65

a. Develop a forecast of trend sales for the third quarter, 1985.
b. Develop a sales forecast for the fourth quarter, 1985, showing the effect of trend and seasonal influences.
c. If actual unit sales in the first quarter 1985 are 380,000, what would they have been if there had been no seasonal influence?

2. A manufacturer of bearings wishes to estimate future sales over the next five years. The marketing manager is presented with the following historical data for the past 10 years as well as data on the sales of heavy industrial equipment. The manager believes there is a good relationship between bearing sales and sales of heavy industrial equipment. In addition, future estimates of heavy industrial equipment sales are readily available from secondary sources.

Bearing Sales (Millions)	*Heavy Equipment Sales (Billions)*
12	30
19	45
10	10
12	24
8	10
8	9
17	41
13	30
12	27
10	20

a. Calculate the regression equation.
b. Determine whether there is a good relationship between bearing sales and sales of heavy industrial equipment.
c. Determine a sales forecast for 1985 if heavy equipment sales are projected to be $35 billion.

3. The following information on sales of electrical cable (*Y*) and an index industrial supply prices (*X*) has been developed in preparation for determining a sales forecast for 1987. The data is based on 100 observations. (*Y* in millions of dollars)

$$
\begin{aligned}
EX &= 2{,}300 \\
EY &= 38{,}000 \\
EXY &= 850{,}000 \\
EX^2 &= 64{,}000 \\
EY^2 &= 14{,}500{,}000
\end{aligned}
$$

a. Calculate the regression equation. Explain how cable sales vary with the price index.
b. Determine how good the relationship is. Interpret the measure you have calculated.
c. If the price index is forecasted to be 1.10 by 1987, develop a sales forecast of electrical cable for 1987.
d. In evaluating the 1987 forecast, what limitations of this technique should the manager consider?

Chapter 8 Industrial Marketing Planning

To this point, the text has examined the techniques available to the industrial marketing manager for segmenting the organizational market, forecasting market potential, and forecasting sales. Likewise, you have developed an understanding of organizational buying behavior and the unique characteristics of the industrial marketing environment. This aggregate background provides a perspective that is of fundamental importance to the industrial marketing planner.

After reading this chapter, you will have an understanding of:

1. *the special challenges that surround marketing planning in industrial organizations*
2. *the role of strategic planning in corporate strategy development*
3. *the essential components of the industrial marketing planning process*
4. *the specific role of market segmentation and forecasting in the marketing planning process.*

To meet the challenges brought on by rising material costs, growing competition, reduced profit margins, and limited cash reserves, marketers are increasingly recognizing the importance of formal approaches to marketing planning.[1] Key product and market decisions made by the industrial marketer can influence the direction and fate of the firm for years to come. Which segment or segments of the organizational market should be served? Which customer needs should be satisfied? What are the best means available to the company to satisfy these unique needs? Successful marketing planning involves an analysis of market opportunity and an assessment of the firm's ability to take advantage of that opportunity.

Planning encourages managers to think creatively about the future, to sharpen objectives, and to develop, coordinate, and control company efforts.[2] While few would question the benefits that accrue to the planner, industrial marketing managers are often sadly disappointed with results of formal planning efforts. This chapter examines the nature and critical importance of planning in industrial marketing management.

First, attention centers on the special requirements and problems that surround planning in the industrial marketing environment. Second, consideration is given to the role that strategic planning assumes in designing long-run corporate strategies. Here the discussion will center on properly matching the strengths of the corporation to attractive market opportunities. Third, the key components of the marketing planning process are examined. Particular emphasis is given to developing industrial marketing strategy. Thus, this chapter serves as a conceptual bridge to succeeding chapters where each component of the marketing mix is isolated and examined in depth.

Planning in the Industrial Marketing Environment

If marketing planning can be profitably applied by manufacturers of consumer goods, such as cake mixes and toothpaste, similar success should result when producers of office equipment, chemicals, machine tools, and similar industrial products and services utilize marketing planning. Industrial practitioners report, however, that this is often not the case. Why? Several unique problems in industrial market planning are reported in a survey of 50 large industrial companies.[3]

Functional Interdependence

First, marketing success in the industrial world depends, to a large degree, on other functional areas in the firm, such as engineering, research and development, manufacturing, and technical service.[4] Planning in the industrial setting thus involves a higher degree of functional interdependence and a closer relationship to total corporate strategy than planning in the consumer-goods sector.[5] ". . . Changes in marketing strategy are more likely to involve capital commitments for new equipment, shifts in development activities, or departures from traditional engineering and manufacturing approaches, any one of which would have companywide implications."[6] Some industrial companies have made the mistake of concentrating all planning efforts in the marketing department, thereby failing to recognize the need for an integrated effort across several functional areas.

Table 8.1 highlights eight areas in which there is a strong probability of conflict in managing the marketing/manufacturing interface in the industrial firm. Observe that the seeds for internal conflict or potential friction between manufacturing and marketing touch such fundamental areas as sales forecasting, production scheduling, distribution, and product planning. To increase the level of cooperation and decrease conflict between marketing and manufacturing, management must first understand the basic causes of that conflict.

Table 8.1 / Marketing/Manufacturing
Areas of Necessary Cooperation but Potential Conflict

Problem area	Typical marketing comment	Typical manufacturing comment
1. Capacity planning and long-range sales forecasting.	"Why don't we have enough capacity?"	"Why didn't we have accurate sales forecasts?"
2. Production scheduling and short-range sales forecasting.	"We need faster response. Our lead times are ridiculous."	"We need realistic customer commitments and sales forecasts that don't change like wind direction."
3. Delivery and physical distribution.	"Why don't we ever have the right merchandise in inventory?"	"We can't keep everything in inventory."
4. Quality assurance.	"Why can't we have reasonable quality at reasonable cost?"	"Why must we always offer options that are too hard to manufacture and that offer little customer utility?"
5. Breadth of product line.	"Our customers demand variety."	"The product line is too broad—all we get are short, uneconomical runs."
6. Cost control.	"Our costs are so high that we are not competitive in the marketplace."	"We can't provide fast delivery, broad variety, rapid response to change, and high quality at low cost."
7. New product introduction.	"New products are our life blood."	"Unnecessary design changes are prohibitively expensive."
8. Adjunct services such as spare parts inventory support, installation, and repair.	"Field service costs are too high."	"Products are being used in ways for which they weren't designed."

Source. Benson P. Shapiro, "Can Marketing and Manufacturing Coexist?" *Harvard Business Review* 55 (September–October 1977), p. 105.

Causes of Conflict. One researcher, who has explored the marketing/manufacturing interface in depth, identifies three prime reasons for the conflict.[7] First, the two functional areas, marketing and production, are evaluated and rewarded on the basis of different criteria. Marketing managers are evaluated on the basis of sales, profits, or market share, while production managers are evaluated on the basis of the efficiency and cost-effectiveness of the manufacturing process. Second, the inherent complexity of the two functions engender conflict. The difficulty of accurately forecasting sales in marketing is matched by complexities that emerge from frequent changes in the production schedule. A third basic cause of conflict between marketing managers and production managers centers on differences in orientation, experience, and lifestyle. Each often has a different educational background, a different career history, and a different orientation from the other. Other factors that further complicate the marketing/manufacturing interface include budget constraints, a rapid pace of technological change, and the rapid growth of the enterprise.

Managing the Conflict. The task for top management is to create an atmosphere that fosters cooperation and a proper balance between manufacturing and marketing. Clearly, a constructive amount of tension is healthy and promotes effectiveness and efficiency. Severe problems emerge when this conflict becomes dysfunctional and evolves into open warfare. An atmosphere of cooperation can be promoted by clear corporate policies, an evaluation and reward system that stresses interfunctional cooperation, and company activities that encourage interfunctional contact (e.g., inviting manufacturing managers to sales meetings). Likewise, marketers should analyze not only their customer needs, but also the operational strengths of the manufacturing unit.[8] The marketing program can then be adjusted to better meet the needs of specific target markets by capitalizing on the strengths of the manufacturing unit.

Diversity of Markets

In addition to dealing with interfunctional conflict, a second problem that frustrates industrial marketing planners concerns the multitude and diversity of markets and channels.[9] Industrial products often reach many different markets and pass through several distinct channels. A manufacturer of insulation will distinguish among such market segments as commercial contractors, small residential builders, large residential builders, and government agencies. Each may require a unique marketing strategy. Market segments must be selected with care because of the close working relationship that must be fostered between buyer and seller after the sale.

Production Orientation

Marketing planning often goes awry in the industrial setting because managers frequently make the mistake of adopting a production rather than a consumer orientation.[10] Because of the technical perspective that prevails in industrial companies, marketers often become preoccupied with the product and its technical capabilities. Consumer needs—the central focus of marketing—are somehow forgotten. The industrial marketer often requires an understanding of the cost characteristics of the customer's operations, the specific role that the product will assume in that operation, as well as the competitive structure of the industry within which the customer operates. Both industrial and consumer-goods companies have been found guilty of adopting a production rather than a marketing orientation. However, because industrial marketers are serving technically complex customer needs, a perceptive and knowledgeable response is of particular importance.

In summary, the basic theory of marketing planning applies to both consumer-goods and industrial companies. However, successful implementation of marketing planning by the industrial marketer requires a sensitivity to the problems that are particularly salient to industrial markets. First, a functionally integrated planning effort is required. Second, the unique needs and special marketing requirements of different market segments must be addressed. Third, the trappings of a production orientation must be avoided.

Strategic Planning

Many industrial firms have many divisions, product lines, products, and brands. Systematic steps must be taken at the corporate and divisional levels to formulate long-term master strategies that insure survival and growth of the enterprise. Policies established at the corporate level provide the framework for strategy development in each business division. In turn, corporate and divisional policies ultimately establish the boundaries and constraints within which individual product or market managers develop strategy.

Assessing Opportunities

Strategic marketing management is the process that integrates "broadly defined sets of strategic and operating marketing decisions together for the purpose of directing resources toward opportunities consistent with enterprise capabilities to achieve predetermined outcomes."[11] One researcher emphasizes that there are only limited periods during which the match between the key requirements of a market and the particular capabilities of a supplier competing in that market are at an optimum.[12] Thus, resources should be invested in a product or market to coincide with periods in which the "strategic window" is open. Likewise, resources should be withdrawn (i.e., disinvestment should be considered) when the product/market fit erodes.

Large industrial firms compete in many industries and are, in essence, a portfolio of different businesses. Organizations must actively manage this portfolio by deciding which businesses should be expanded, which businesses should be maintained, and which businesses should be phased out.

Likewise, management should always be seeking to identify new businesses that would strengthen the portfolio. Such portfolio candidates are generally businesses that capitalize on the organization's present or developing strengths.

Defining Strategic Business Units

A first step in assessing the quality of the industrial firm's portfolio of businesses is to define the *strategic business units* (SBUs) making up the company. An SBU is a single business or collection of businesses that has a distinct mission, a responsible manager, its own competitors, and is independent of other business units.[13] An SBU could be one or more divisions of the industrial firm, a product line within one division, or, on occasion, a single product. Eaton Corporation, a large automotive and industrial parts producer, created 400 "product market segments" within its 26 divisions. Along with the corporation, each division and market segment unit develops a five-year plan. Also, Mead Corporation defined 24 SBUs and assigned 24 top executives to the new slots on the basis of a match between their expertise and the business requirements.[14]

General Electric's Business Screen

The industrial marketer must manage the dual tasks of resource generation and resource allocation. Some SBUs are well-positioned in attractive industries and possess the potential to generate significant resources in the future; others are poorly situated and do not provide much promise. Thus, some SBUs merit additional resources while others do not. To properly

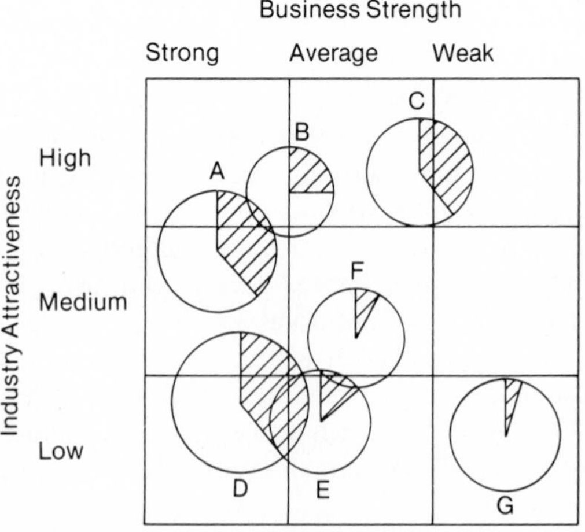

Figure 8.1 / General Electric's Business Screen

Source. Adapted from Charles W. Hofer and Dan Schendel, *Strategy Formulation: Analytical Concepts* (St. Paul: West Publishing Company, 1978), p. 32.

classify SBUs, General Electric pioneered the development of a nine-cell strategic business screen.

Business Strength/Industry Strength. The business screen, illustrated in figure 8.1, matches the level of strength of the business under analysis to the level of attractiveness of the industry in which it operates. *Business strength* is based on a rating of market share, product quality, technological position, price competitiveness, distribution effectiveness, and other criteria deemed important by management. *Industry attractiveness* is based on a rating of market size, market growth rate, inflation vulnerability, industry profitability, and related dimensions.[15] The area of the circles in figure 8.1 corresponds to the size of the industries in which the various businesses compete. The pie-shaped slices within the circles reflect a particular SBU's market share. Observe, then, that G represents an SBU with a small market share in an industry of average size. Likewise, note that G lacks business strength and competes in an unattractive industry.

Projecting Future Positions. Once SBUs are classified, management should plot the projected positions of these businesses, assuming no changes in basic strategies. A comparison of the current and projected position of the SBUs allows management to isolate problems and identify strategic alternatives. Through strategic planning efforts, the Olin Corporation identified and sold a number of poorly performing businesses—a polyester film plant, a tent business, a propane camping equipment business. In turn, strategy planning suggested that investments should be made in businesses that better matched corporate expertise. Thus, Olin expanded the capacity of its chlorine-caustic soda, hydrazine chemical, and copper-based alloy operations. These and other businesses are divided into over 30 SBUs.[16]

The Industrial Marketing Planning Process

The industrial marketing planning process is inextricably linked to planning in other functional areas and to overall corporate strategy. Here, attention centers on the industrial marketing planning process that takes place *within* the larger strategic marketing management process of the corporation. To survive and prosper, the industrial marketer must properly diagnose the existing environment and balance the firm's resources with its objectives and opportunities. Every organization requires clearly defined goals and a carefully conceived course of action to achieve these goals. Thus, marketing planning is a continuous process.

A model for the industrial marketing planning process is presented in figure 8.2. Observe that the model consists of five central components: (1) situation analysis, (2) problems and opportunities, (3) master marketing strategy, (4) integrated marketing plan, and (5) measurement and evaluation of results. Note that the marketing plan is the output of the planning process.

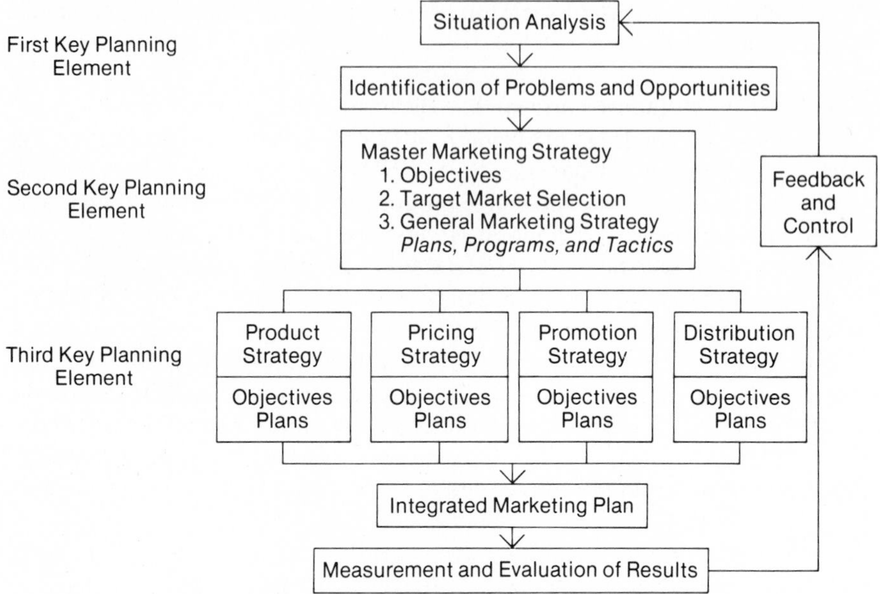

Figure 8.2 / A Marketing Planning Model

Source. Leonard L. Berry and James H. Donnelly, Jr., *Marketing for Bankers* (American Institute of Banking, American Bankers Association, 1975), p. 232. Reprinted by permission.

Situation Analysis

The marketing planning process begins with the situation analysis. The intent here is to gain an understanding of the environment in which marketing effort will be expended. Here the industrial marketer assesses the external environment in an effort to: (1) identify the forces that surround the present market situation and (2) project the forces that will shape the market situation during the planning period. Thus, the situation analysis outlines the facts and assumptions on which the plan is based. Key components of the situation analysis are outlined in table 8.2. Observe that the situation analysis includes an assessment of environmental, competitive, and company conditions; a profile of past performance; and a forecast of future performance.

Problems and Opportunities

The searching questions that arise in the situation analysis inevitably uncover problems and opportunities. For example, a firm may find that one of their products enjoys a dominant market share, but in an unprofitable market (problem). In turn, the same company may discover that it possesses the unique production and marketing skills to meet the needs of profitable and growing market segments (opportunity). To illustrate, Crown Cork & Seal, a large producer of metal cans and other items, captured a large share of the sizable motor oil can business by introducing in 1958 the first one-quart aluminum oil can.[17] However, the firm elected *not* to continue to aggressively pursue this market because of the trend toward other packaging materials and the incidence of self-manufacture of such containers by large users. Instead, Crown Cork decided to concentrate on the beer, soft drink, and aerosol can markets. These markets displayed a high growth rate, offered a low risk of self-manufacture by users, and were more consistent with its corporate capabilities.

Problems represent constraints that the industrial marketer must recognize, while opportunities provide possible directions for growth. By ranking problems and opportunities in order of importance, the market planner is better prepared for the task of defining specific marketing objectives and designing specific marketing strategies.

Table 8.2 / Selected Components of the Situation Analysis

Areas of Analysis	Illustrative Questions
Environmental Climate	What are the relevant political, social, economic, and technological trends that will influence our product(s), industry, or customers?
Competitive Climate	What is the present and future structure and form of competition (e.g., number, aggressiveness, and anticipated retaliatory actions of competitors)?
Company Resources	What are the unique human skills and experience that qualify our organization to be in this business (e.g., marketing, research and development, production expertise)?
	Does our firm possess sufficient financial resources to support an effective marketing program?
Performance Profile	What level of sales, market share, and profitability did each of our products achieve in each of the last five years?
Market Potentials/ Market Description	What is the growth rate and market potential of each market?
	Describe the customer profiles of relevant market segments.
Performance Forecast	Assuming no changes in marketing strategy, what level of sales, market share, and profitability is anticipated?
	What are the key assumptions that underlie this forecast?

Master Marketing Strategy

This component of the planning process involves: (1) the establishment of marketing objectives, (2) the selection of market targets, and (3) the development of the general marketing strategy required to achieve the established objectives. Here the industrial marketer makes decisions concerning how the controllable marketing mix variables will be blended to achieve predetermined goals.

NCR: A Strategy Profile

NCR's hold on the market for cash registers and accounting machines faced stiff challenges in the early 1970s. These mechanical or key-driven products were becoming obsolete because of the movement toward electronic information handling systems. To adapt to this changing environment, NCR initiated dramatic changes in strategy. This strategy centers on electronics and builds on the company's traditional strengths in banking and retailing. Drastic changes were made in the product line as well as the technical marketing and manufacturing functions. NCR customers are encouraged to start on a small scale in data processing and gradually upgrade to more sophisticated NCR equipment. The firm became a complete line supplier of electronic data processing systems and terminals. Also, specialized electronic products were developed to fit the needs of bankers and retailers.

(R&D) To effect these changes, NCR substantially increased its research and development expenditures. These expenditures are geared to projects which will yield marketable products within one or two years. *(Marketing Organization)* The marketing organization was realigned into four groups and matched with important sectors of the market: (1) retail, (2) financial, (3) commercial industrial, and (4) medicine, education and government. *(Personal Selling)* Salespersons assigned to a particular group were educated concerning the needs of that market sector and their role changed from a salesperson to that of a consultant for their customers. *(Technical Service)* The company's technical service function that was heretofore independent of the marketing organization was reorganized to fit the new marketing structure. Training programs were initiated to improve the understanding of electronics. Nearly 7000 field engineers were retrained.

Collectively, these changes strengthened the firm's market position and facilitated a complete turnaround.

Source. "NCR's New Strategy Puts It in Computers to Stay," *Business Week* (September 26, 1977), pp. 100–102.

Objectives. Planning for marketing activities must be consistent with the overall objectives of the corporation. Marketing objectives are the results or ends that are sought. These objectives should be expressed in qualitative and quantitative terms. To be of operational value, objectives must be specific and the degree of success or failure in reaching them must be measurable. Marketing objectives are often expressed in terms of: (1) sales volume (dollars or units), (2) market share, and (3) profit, or alternatively, return on investment.

In addition to developing concrete standards of performance, the role of marketing objectives is to direct the organization toward a specific market level. To illustrate this: industrial marketers may have the option of concentrating on different levels of the manufacturing chain. For example, ". . . the aluminum producer serving the residential housing market may have a choice whether to sell raw materials, semifabricated materials, components, or end products."[18] This question assumes critical importance when the industrial marketing planner is selecting a target market.

Target Market Selection. A critical component of the master industrial marketing strategy is identifying and locating a need of a target segment of organizational buyers and then directing the firm's resources toward the satisfying of that need. Here the marketer can draw upon information gathered in the situation analysis. In selecting a target market, an objective assessment must be made of market potentials, competition, customer profiles, and company strengths and weaknesses. The concepts and techniques presented in the past three chapters are fundamental in evaluating the merits of alternative segments: industrial market segmentation approaches (chapter 5); market potential forecasting techniques (chapter 6); and sales forecasting techniques (chapter 7). Rather than merely describing and identifying possible target markets, the manager must carefully analyze the nature of the customer's need, the best means of satisfying that need, and the size and the growth trend of the market segment.

General Marketing Strategy. Once the planner defines the target market, specific decisions must be made concerning each of the controllable marketing variables: product, promotion, price, and distribution. Objectives, plans, and tactics for each marketing variable must be developed and coordinated into a total marketing program. *Strategy* prescribes what will be done; *tactics* concerns how it will be accomplished. Of course, the decisions made concerning the general marketing strategy must be consistent with budgetary constraints.

Formulating industrial marketing strategy is a difficult and complex task. The marketing planner must determine the function and relative weight that should be given to each marketing variable in order to maximize the impact of the total strategy. Clearly, unlimited variations and combinations exist. Jean-Marie Choffray and Gary Lilien provide a model that is valuable in dealing with such difficult decisions.[19]

Their approach, the industrial market response model, consists of four subcomponents.

1. *Awareness model*—relates the level of marketing effort invested in an industrial product to the probability that an individual organizational member will be aware of the product.
2. *Acceptance model*—relates product "design characteristics to the likelihood that an organization will find the product feasible."[20] To illustrate, 50 percent of the organizations surveyed concerning the purchase of industrial air conditioning systems require that the investment cost per ton be less than $988.

3. *Individual evaluation models*—"relate evaluation of product characteristics to the preferences of each category of decision participants."[21] For example, the criterion of key importance to buying center members evaluating industrial air conditioning systems varied by job category. Plant managers were most interested in operating costs, top managers in up-to-date technology, and heating and air conditioning consultants in noise level in the plant.
4. *Group decision model*—relates group choice to the preference of the members composing the group.

The contribution of the industrial market response model is that it links industrial marketing strategy to the buying center concept (group decision making) and offers a methodology for measuring the group's response to that strategy.[22] Clearly, this approach can be used to improve product design and pricing decisions and to develop and target advertising and sales presentations.

Integrated Marketing Plan

The master marketing strategy should be recorded as a written marketing plan. This constitutes the formal documentation of the marketing strategy and includes all supporting plans and tactics. This plan should reflect the coordinated components of the total marketing strategy—markets to be served, products/services to be marketed, price schedules, distribution methods, and so on. The plan delineates clearly defined objectives and the specific course of action that will be followed in achieving these goals.

Measurement and Evaluation of Results

The marketing plan covers only a specified time period, but marketing planning is a continuous process. A plan cannot be forgotten until the next period. A central mechanism is required to compare actual results to planned results and to insure that the firm's strategy and tactics are leading to the achievement of objectives. If there is a serious gap between actual results and key performance standards, a change in strategy or objectives is warranted. Thus, an important component of the marketing planning model, presented in figure 8.2, is the feedback and control mechanism. The industrial marketer relies upon such feedback to check on the various components of the marketing program, as well as to monitor the effectiveness of the program as a whole.

Summary

Special problems surround planning efforts in the industrial marketing environment. First, a high degree of functional interdependence is required and is often difficult to achieve. The interface between marketing and manufacturing requires a sensitive response by top management. Industrial marketing planning efforts are also often complicated by the diversity of markets in the industrial setting, and by a tendency of managers to follow a production rather than a marketing orientation.

Policies established at the corporate level provide the framework for strategy development in each of the strategic business units in the organization. Strategic marketing management provides the means by which the particular capabilities of the company can be matched with attractive market opportunities. The industrial marketer can benefit by examining the current and projected strategic position of each of its many business units.

The industrial marketing planning process takes place within the larger strategic marketing management process. It represents the means for the industrial marketer to develop an integrated marketing program targeted at carefully defined market segments for the purpose of achieving predetermined performance goals. To be successful, the industrial marketer must be attuned to the special internal as well as external requirements that must be reconciled in industrial marketing planning efforts. A continuous process, marketing planning involves the five successive stages: (1) situation analysis, (2) the evaluation of problems and opportunities, (3) formulation of a master marketing strategy, (4) the development of an integrated marketing plan, and (5) the measurement and evaluation of results. The marketing plan, an end result of the planning process, is the formal written description of the marketing strategy.

Having examined the overall marketing planning process, attention in succeeding chapters will turn to an analysis of each marketing mix variable.

Footnotes

[1]For example, see Derek F. Abell and John S. Hammond, *Strategic Market Planning: Problems and Analytical Approaches* (Englewood Cliffs, N.J.: Prentice-Hall, Inc., 1979), pp. 3–15.

[2]Melville C. Branch, *The Corporate Planning Process* (New York: American Management Association, 1962), pp. 48–49.

[3]B. Charles Ames, "Marketing Planning for Industrial Products," *Harvard Business Review* 46 (September–October 1968), pp. 100–111.

[4]Ibid, pp. 101–2.

[5]Frederick E. Webster, Jr., "Management Science in Industrial Marketing," *Journal of Marketing* 42 (January 1978), p. 22.

[6]B. Charles Ames, "Trappings vs. Substance in Industrial Marketing," *Harvard Business Review* 48 (July–August 1976), pp. 95–96.

[7]Benson P. Shapiro, "Can Marketing and Manufacturing Coexist?" *Harvard Business Review* 55 (September–October 1977), pp. 104–14.

[8]Ibid.

[9]Ames, "Marketing Planning," p. 101.

[10]Ames, "Trappings vs. Substance," pp. 93–102; see also, Webster, "Management Science," pp. 22–23.

[11]Roger A. Kerin and Robert A. Peterson, "The Strategic Marketing Management Process," in Kerin and Peterson (eds.), *Perspectives on Strategic Marketing Management* (Boston: Allyn and Bacon, Inc., 1980), p. 5.

[12]Derek F. Abell, "Strategic Windows," *Journal of Marketing* 42 (July 1978), pp. 21–25.

[13]Philip Kotler, *Marketing Management: Analysis, Planning, and Control* (4th ed.; Englewood Cliffs, N.J.: Prentice-Hall, Inc., 1980), p. 76.

[14]"Olin Shifts to Strategic Planning," *Business Week* (March 27, 1978), pp. 102–5.

[15]For a discussion of selecting criteria, see Charles W. Hofer and Dan Schendel, *Strategy Formulation: Analytical Concepts* (St. Paul: West Publishing Company, 1978), pp. 72–74.

[16]"Olin Shifts to Strategic Planning," pp. 102–5.

[17]E. Raymond Corey, "Key Options in Market Selection and Product Planning," *Harvard Business Review* 47 (September–October 1975), pp. 119–28.

[18]Corey, "Key Options," p. 122.

[19]Jean-Marie Choffray and Gary L. Lilien, "Assessing Response to Industrial Marketing Strategy," *Journal of Marketing* 42 (April 1978), pp. 20–31.

[20]Ibid., p. 24.

[21]Ibid., p. 25.

[22]For a comprehensive discussion of this methodology, see Choffray and Lilien, pp. 20–31.

Discussion Questions

1. While the need for careful planning and coordination cuts across both consumer-goods and industrial-goods companies, special requirements encircle marketing planning in the industrial environment. Explain.

2. What are the underlying factors that contribute to the conflict that often exists between marketing and manufacturing in the industrial firm? Describe the steps management can take to foster an atmosphere of cooperation between these two functional areas.

3. Explain how an industrial firm that is organized around four product lines might benefit by redesigning the organization around 19 strategic business units.

4. An industrial marketer is considering entry into one of four alternative industries. What specific procedures could the industrial marketer follow in measuring the relative attractiveness of these industries?

5. What is the basic role of the situation analysis in the marketing planning process?

6. John S. Painter, president of Eagle-Pitcher, a Fortune 500 industrial firm, stated: "Unless we see that we are now No.1 or have a strong chance of becoming No. 1 in a short period of time, it is not a product line we want to be in." How will this clear statement of corporate objectives influence marketing objectives and, in turn, master marketing strategy?

7. Describe how an industrial firm could apply the industrial market response model in formulating a marketing strategy for a new packaging machine.

8. Once a master marketing strategy is developed and implemented, when should the industrial marketer first begin to compare actual versus planned results? At the end of the first quarter? At the end of the year?

Part IV

Formulating Industrial Marketing Strategy

Chapter 9

Managing the Industrial Product Line

The industrial product constitutes the central force in the marketing mix. The ability of the firm to put together a line of products and services that respond to the needs of customers lies at the heart of industrial marketing management. After reading this chapter, you will have an understanding of:

1. *the concept of the "total product"*
2. *the different types of industrial product lines*
3. *a strategic approach for managing the existing product line*
4. *the process of developing and managing new industrial products.*

An industrial marketer's identity in the marketplace is established through the products and services offered. Decisions concerning the product/service mix stand at the heart of corporate strategy. Without careful product planning and control, marketers often are guilty of introducing new products that are inconsistent with market needs, of arbitrarily adding new items that contribute little to existing product lines, and of maintaining weak products that could be profitably eliminated.

Industrial product management is directly linked to market analysis and market selection, as discussed in part three. As figure 9.1 illustrates, product policy is a circular process that centers on the needs of the market. Products are developed to fit the needs of the market and modified as those needs change. Drawing upon the tools of demand analysis, such as organizational market segmentation and market potential forecasting techniques, the marketer evaluates opportunity and selects viable market segments which determine the direction of product policy. Clearly, product policy cannot be separated from market selection decisions.[1] In evaluating potential product market fits, the firm must evaluate market opportunities and the number and aggressiveness of competitors. The corporate strengths and weaknesses, in such areas as marketing, production, and research and development, must also be gauged.

This chapter examines the product management function in the industrial marketing environment. First, an important perspective concerning the definition of an "industrial product" is delineated. Second, industrial goods can assume several different forms; therefore, attention is devoted to describing these industrial product line options. Third, particular emphasis will be given to managing existing product lines. The final section of the chapter centers on managing the new industrial product development process.

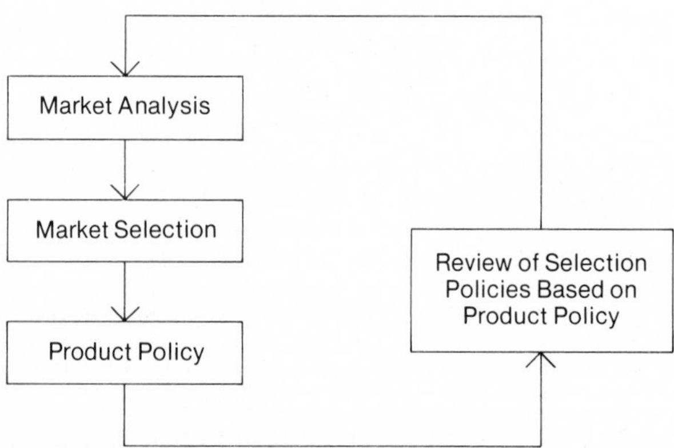

Figure 9.1 / The Role of Product Policy in Market Analysis

Source. Benson P. Shapiro, *Industrial Product Policy: Managing the Existing Product Line* (Cambridge, Mass.: Marketing Science Institute, 1977), p. 30. Reprinted by permission.

The Industrial "Product"

What is a product? A marketer can only answer this question through the viewpoint of a consumer. Thus, a product encompasses all of the value satisfactions that a customer derives from the industrial marketer at both an organizational and a personal level.[2] To illustrate, the purchaser of cold rolled steel is buying physical specifications (thickness, chemical composition, for example), a particular form of package, technical advice, and delivery reliability.[3] In addition, the seller may satisfy more personal needs of the buyer by reducing risk, improving the buyer's organizational status, or merely by breaking the monotony of a day with a pleasant discussion concerning outside interests. Thus, the physical attributes of the product can be augmented in many ways which add extra value to the product. The seller's identity in the market is established not only by the product or service, but also by the value satisfactions that surround that product or service in the eyes of the buyer.

Integrated Effort

The development of marketing strategy in general, and product policy in particular, requires a high degree of functional coordination within the enterprise. Manufacturing, research and development, engineering, inventory control, technical service, and marketing are involved in creating and delivering the total product and the related customer value satisfactions.[4] If perceived benefits, such as strong technical support, are not provided to the buyer, the marketer's reputation could be irreparably damaged.

Decisions concerning modifications or extensions in the product line are often a source of conflict in the industrial firm. Manufacturing personnel are interested in short product lines that facilitate long and smooth production runs. By contrast, marketers are often interested in extending rather than cutting product lines in the face of competition or changing market requirements.[5] The discussion of organizational buying behavior, presented in chapter 4, described the nature of interfunctional conflict that often emerges in the buying organization. Such conflict also encircles product planning in the selling organization and stems from the same root causes: differing backgrounds, perspectives, and departmental objectives.

Organizing the Industrial Product Management Function

To implement corporate strategy for industrial or consumer goods, a coordinated effort is required. The need for interfunctional coordination is particularly acute in the industrial marketing setting. The industrial product management function cannot assume an isolated position within the organization, but instead, must interface with other key functional areas. The firm's technical service and research and development groups constitute an important part of the product offering. The capability of manufacturing (low cost or high quality) may become a key marketing weapon. The cost accounting function likewise assumes an important role in product management by providing accurate data on the profitability of the product mix.

A key requirement in organizing the product management function is to link product plans to overall corporate objectives and planning. Firms that overlook this requirement and place product planning in a vacuum are often disappointed with the results. The resulting plans clash with corporate goals and capabilities.

The specific organizational design of the product management function depends upon company and market characteristics. Some industrial firms are organized around products, while others are organized in relation to markets. The *product manager form* of organization might be followed by an industrial firm that offers several products to the same general market. By contrast, a *market-centered form* of organization might be appropriate for a firm that offers the same product in a number of different industry or market segments. Regardless of the specific organizational arrangement adopted, the responsibilities of the product management function are the same: to plan, coordinate, and control the firm's product mix. Top management must insure that the proper environment for product planning is fostered.[6]

Industrial vs. Consumer Goods Product Managers: A Comparative Profile

Compared to their consumer goods counterparts, industrial product managers:

1. have more experience and also are responsible for more products;
2. report greater levels of contact with distribution, sales and final consumers, but interface less with marketing research, advertising and advertising agencies;
3. have greater involvement with decisions involving pricing and distribution and somewhat less involvement in promotion and marketing research decisions.

Industrial goods product managers did not differ from consumer goods product managers on role conflict, job tension, and job satisfaction. Product managers with industrial goods responsibilities do, however, report a lower level of role clarity—the extent to which they receive and understand information needed to perform their assigned function.

J. Patrick Kelly and Richard T. Hise suggest that the role clarity for these managers may be enhanced by increasing the level of contact with marketing research and reducing the number of products that the typical manager handles.

Source. J. Patrick Kelly and Richard T. Hise, "Industrial and Consumer Goods Product Managers Are Different," *Industrial Marketing Management* 8 (November 1979), pp. 325–32.

Industrial Product Policy

Product policy involves ". . . the collection of decisions concerning the products and services which the company offers."[7] Three levels of decisions fall into the product policy area: (1) item, a specific version of the product; (2) product line, a group of closely related items; and (3) product mix, a collection of items and product lines marketed by the company.[8] Thus, product policy involves decisions concerning the items, the product lines, and the associated services offered by the marketer.

This section centers on managing the existing industrial product line. First, the different types of industrial product lines are described. Second, specific decisions concerning the management of the existing product line are examined. Particular attention is given to determining the length of the product line and the strategic position of specific items in the line.

Types of Product Lines Defined

Since product lines of industrial firms differ from those found in the consumer-goods sector, a classification scheme is useful. Four types of product lines are found in industrial marketing:[9]

1. *Proprietary or catalog items*—items that are offered only in certain configurations and produced in anticipation of orders. Product line decisions concern the selection of products to be added, deleted, or repositioned within the line.
2. *Custom-built items*—items that are offered as a standard set of basic units, including numerous accessories and options. To illustrate, a lathe manufacturer may offer several basic sizes, including a range of options (such as different motor sizes) and a complement of accessories for different applications. Here the marketer is offering the organizational buyer a set of building blocks that can assume many configurations. Product line decisions center on offering the proper mix of options and accessories.
3. *Custom-designed items*—items created to meet the needs of one or a small group of customers. These may include a unique, singly produced unit, such as a power plant or a specific machine tool. Selected items produced in relatively large quantities, such as a specific aircraft model, may fall into this category. The product line is described in terms of the company's capability, and the consumer buys that capability. Ultimately, this capability is transformed into a finished good.
4. *Industrial services*—a physical product does not exist. The buyer is purchasing a company's capability in a particular area, such as maintenance, technical service, or management consulting.

Each of these product situations presents unique problems and opportunities for the marketer; each draws upon a different type of capability. The core of industrial product strategy rests on the intelligent utilization of corporate capability.[10] All types of industrial firms confront product policy decisions. This holds true even though some firms offer pure services (no physical product) while others offer a product/service combination.

Services: Marketing Requirements. Services, as noted above, provide a special case in the deployment of the marketer's capability. The marketer must not only stimulate demand for the service, but also manage the buyer-seller interaction. Often, the services are rendered by personnel not directly assigned to the marketing function. The interactions between buyer and seller that take place during the consumption process are often critical in influencing the client's perception of the quality of the service rendered as well as the service company. Thus, the marketing of services in the industrial setting includes an interactive marketing function.[11] Such buyer-seller interactions are of equal importance to marketers who augment their product offering with services (e.g., technical support). The nature of the relationship between representatives of the buyer and seller will influence the client's image of the total "product."

Managing the Existing Product Line[12]

Two important questions challenge the manager of the existing product line: (1) How many items should be included in the line? and (2) How should the products be positioned? The general concept of a product space is particularly valuable in dealing with these questions. Figure 9.2 is a map of such a product space. Product attributes of importance to buyers form the boundaries of the space. Thus, once the most important attributes are identified, a product space can be formed in which the positions of the company's and competitors' items in the product lines can be exhibited. The product map for a paper product, illustrated in figure 9.2, centers on two dimensions (product attributes): weight and finish quality. Benson Shapiro offers a model for managing the existing product line that draws on the concepts of "product space" and "product positioning."

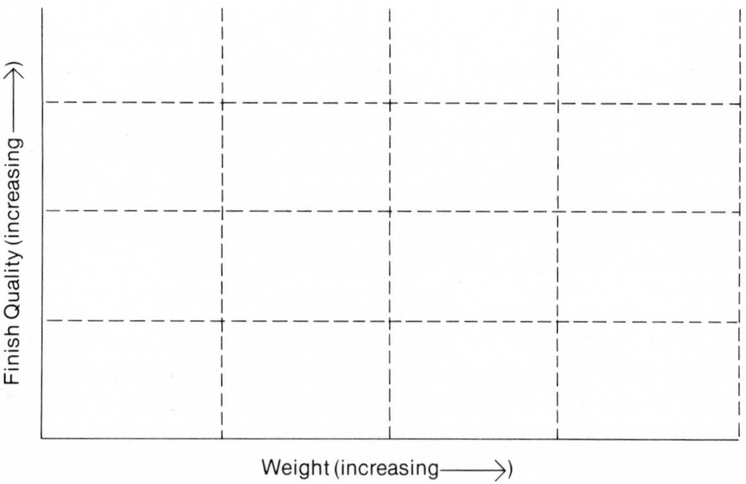

Figure 9.2 / Product Map for a Paper Product

Source. Benson P. Shapiro, *Industrial Product Policy: Managing the Existing Product Line* (Cambridge, Mass.: Marketing Science Institute, 1977), p. 99. Reprinted by permission.

The product-space map concept forces the manager of the existing product line to identify the product attributes of central importance to consumers and to evaluate the position of individual items in the line relative to competitors. This deepens the manager's understanding of the firm's existing product market position. Figure 9.3 presents a more detailed product map that delineates: (1) existing items in the product line, (2) the specific items in competitors' product lines, and (3) particular market segments or prospects.

Product Line Length. The question of product line length can be addressed by reference to the product map. Does an opportunity exist to add an item at a particular point in the product space or, alternatively, should a particular item be deleted? Benson Shapiro notes that "the line is, in essence, viewed as a collection of separate items, with the length determined intuitively on an item-by-item basis."[13] The industrial product manager seeks a group of items that capitalizes on the firm's capability and has meaning in the marketplace.

To facilitate the analysis of individual items, the product manager should gather the data on the price, direct cost, output per unit time, and place in the production cycle.[14] In addition, the manager may gather other relevant data on production, marketing costs, and demand patterns. By entering such data into a computer, the profit implications of various product line decisions can be calculated. By assigning subjective estimates of the impact of a new line item or the effect of the elimination of an existing item on the

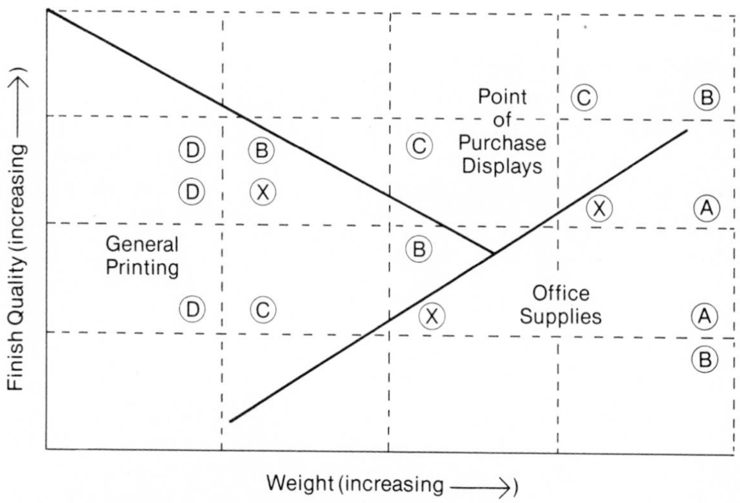

Figure 9.3 / Product Map for a Paper Product

Source. Benson P. Shapiro, *Industrial Product Policy: Managing the Existing Product Line* (Cambridge, Mass.: Marketing Science Institute, 1977), p. 101. Reprinted by permission.

rest of the product line, the computer can be used as a decision support system to simulate the profit results of product line changes.[15]

Once such a model is developed and refined, further extensions can be made. For example, the relationships between the product line and other components of the marketing mix can be analyzed. Thus, the model begins with simple, but important, building blocks and, through testing and refinement, can evolve in stages to a model of high operational value to the product planner. In addition to its conceptual appeal, the model is also of political value by dealing with issues that often create conflict between manufacturing and marketing.[16]

To recap, the concepts of product space and product positioning are of significant operational value to the industrial marketer in determining the composition and length of the product line.

Planning Industrial Product Strategy

Formulating a strategic marketing plan for the firm's existing product line is the most vital part of the company's marketing planning efforts. Having identified product attributes of critical importance to organizational buyers, and having compared the firm's product offerings to those of competitors, attention must now turn to the current and projected performance of the firm's product mix. This evaluation can center on four performance measures: (1) cash flow, (2) market share, (3) sales, and (4) profitability.

The product manager must view product decisions from more than one perspective. To illustrate, current profit and sales figures considered alone do not provide a clear picture of the firm's cash position. The cash needed to support one item in a product line must come from another item. Likewise, available cash is needed to develop and launch promising new product candidates.[17]

Two strategic planning tools available to the manager for planning product line strategy are: (1) portfolio analysis and (2) a matrix approach. Each approach is of value to the industrial marketer in illuminating the firm's current product market position as well as in establishing a clear direction for future industrial product strategy.

Product Portfolio Analysis

The product portfolio approach seeks ". . . to achieve a balanced mix of products that will produce the maximum long run effects from scarce cash and managerial resources."[18] Each item in the firm's product line is classified on the basis of market growth and a measure of market share dominance. The rationale for using market share rests on the growing body of research indicating that market share is positively and strongly related to product profitability.[19] The close linkage between market share and profitability results from several factors. Research suggests that increases in market share are accompanied by a decline in marketing costs as a percentage of sales, a higher profit margin, and higher quality products that demand a higher price. Research indicates that market share is even more significant for industrial products than for consumer products. This is especially true for infrequently purchased industrial goods, such as capital equipment.[20]

Market growth is incorporated into portfolio analysis because it represents the product's position in the product life cycle. The product life cycle is often described in four stages: introduction, growth, maturity, and decline.[21] The product life cycle provides an indication of the trend in primary demand and the patterns of competition. The benefits and costs of gaining and holding market share vary throughout the product life cycle. For example, a firm may be able to increase market share during the growth stage at a much lower cost than during the maturity stage. At some points, improvements in the market share position are extremely valuable to the firm in the long run, while on other occasions, the best decision may be to disinvest in a product.[22]

The goal of product portfolio analysis is to define the strategic role of each of the firm's products on the basis of the product's market growth rate and market share relative to competition. What is each product's growth potential, relative market share, and, hence, cash flow potential? The answer to this question serves to identify: (1) products that supply cash funds; (2) products that appear to be opportunities for investment; and (3) products that are candidates for deletion from the portfolio. The Boston Consulting Group assigned illustrative titles to categories of products on the basis of their cash flow attributes. Figure 9.4 illustrates the four categories which result.

1. *Stars*. These are products with a high market growth rate and a high market share. Reported profits may be high, but a substantial amount of cash is needed to finance rapid growth. These products often use more cash than they generate.
2. *Problem children*. These are products that possess a low market share of a rapidly growing market. The low market share often translates into low profits and a poor cash flow from operations. Because the markets are growing rapidly, a substantial amount of cash is needed to maintain market share and even more substantial amounts to gain market share.
3. *Cash cows*. These are products that generate substantial amounts of cash—far more than is required to maintain market share. Cash cows provide the cash needed to support the research and growth of other products in the enterprise.
4. *Dogs*. These are products that have a low market share of slow-growth mature markets. They require little cash and they generate little cash. Limited opportunities exist for reasonable or profitable growth.[23]

For an industrial firm to grow and prosper, some products must generate cash and acceptable profit levels. In turn, other products that use cash are needed to support continued growth. Thus, the industrial firm's product mix

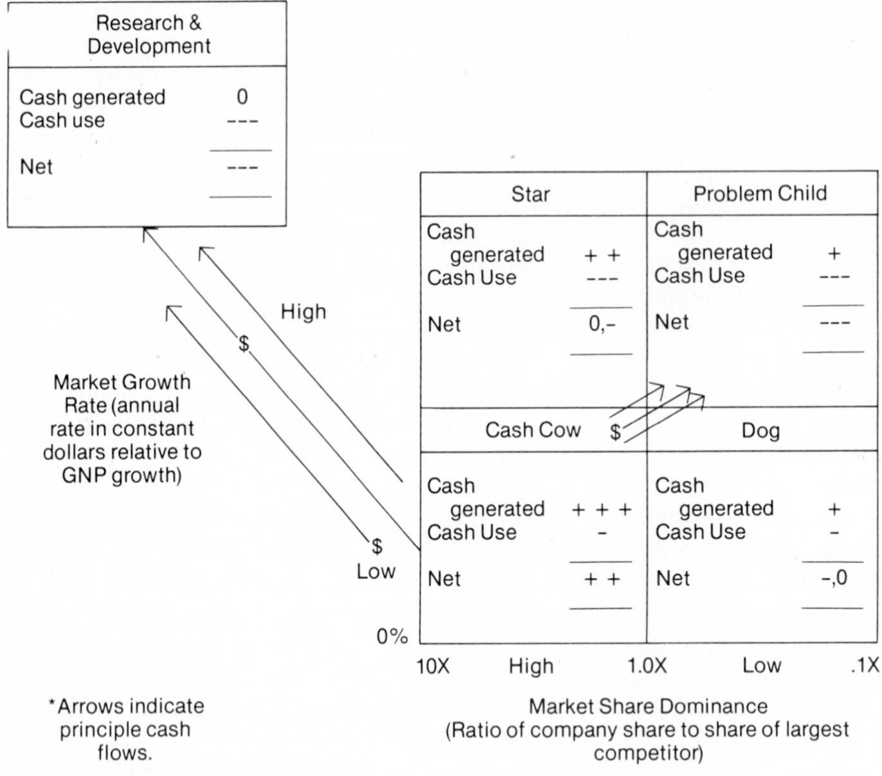

Figure 9.4 / The Cash Quadrant Approach to Describing the Product Portfolio*

Source. George S. Day, "Diagnosing the Product Portfolio," *Journal of Marketing* 41 (April 1977), p. 32. Reprinted from the *Journal of Marketing*, published by the American Marketing Association.

should be viewed as an interdependent group with each product performing a clearly defined and supportive role. For example, note in figure 9.4 that the firm is utilizing the cash generated by "cash cows" for new product research and development and to improve the position of a "problem child." The direction of this cash flow is represented by the arrows.

An industrial marketer can draw upon the cash quadrant approach and illustrate the distinctive role of each of the firm's products. Once the current position has been isolated in such a diagram, decisions can be made concerning the forecasted position of each product. Appropriate strategies for each of the four portfolio positions are outlined in table 9.1.

Product Evaluation Matrix

The product portfolio approach allows the marketer to examine the balance of items in the firm's product line from a cash flow perspective. Once this is accomplished, a second planning aid—a matrix approach developed by

Table 9.1 / Basic Strategies Appropriate for Components of the Product Portfolio

Product Type	Recommended Strategy
Stars	Protect existing market share by product improvements, price reductions, increased production efficiency, and improved market coverage.
Problem Children	*Options:* 1. Invest substantially in the product in order to achieve a large share of new sales. 2. Purchase existing market shares by acquiring competitors. 3. Withdraw support through: a. harvesting (a cutback of all supporting costs to some minimum level); b. divestment of the business; or c. deletion of item from the product line.
Cash Cows	Maintain market dominance and the strong cash flow position through product, technological, and price leadership. Guard against over-investment that may come through product proliferation and unattractive market expansion. Excess cash should support research and growth in other areas.
Dogs	*Options:* 1. Focus on a specialized market segment that can be dominated. 2. Harvest. 3. Divestment of the business. 4. Deletion of item from the product line.

Source. Adapted from George S. Day, "Diagnosing the Product Portfolio," *Journal of Marketing* 41 (April 1977), p. 30.

Yoram Wind and Henry Claycamp—can be utilized effectively by the manager in formulating marketing strategy for the firm's existing product line.[24] This is a comprehensive planning tool that centers on three product performance measures: sales, market share, and profitability. As with any strategic planning tool, a strong market focus is needed; each product must be examined in relation to the important market segment that it serves.

This approach to product line planning includes five levels. Each level provides increasingly specific guidance to product management decisions. The levels of analysis are presented in table 9.2. Note that the first step in the analysis encompasses a profile of the product in terms of industry sales, company sales, market share, and profitability. At succeeding levels, the product's performance is projected for alternative marketing strategies based on key assumptions about competition and other external influences (e.g., business conditions). Thus, the analysis begins with a determination of the strategic position of each product, and it proceeds through an evaluation of alternative product strategies under different competitive and external conditions. Thus, a key contribution of the approach is that it forces a manager to ask the right questions about the product's current and future position.[25]

Table 9.2 / Levels of Analysis and Specificity of Guidance

Specificity of Guidance	Nature of Analytical Operation
Lowest	1. Current product position on industry sales, company sales, market share, and profitability.
↓	2. Projected product position on sales, market share, and profitability, assuming no major changes in the firm's marketing activities, competitive action, and environmental conditions.
↓	3. Projected product position on sales, market share, and profitability under alternative marketing strategies (conditional forecast), assuming no major changes in competitive action and environmental conditions.
↓	4. The above plus diagnostic insights into the competitive structure and the effectiveness of the firm's marketing activities.
Highest	5. Projected product position on sales, market share, and profitability under alternative marketing strategies, anticipated competitive action, and alternative environmental conditions (based on computer simulation).

Source. Yoram Wind and Henry J. Claycamp, "Planning Product Line Strategy: A Matrix Approach," *Journal of Marketing* 40 (January 1976), p. 8. Reprinted from the *Journal of Marketing*, published by the American Marketing Association.

Paper Mate: A Changing Product Portfolio

Paper Mate, a division of Gillette Co., assessed market opportunities in the sizable office supplies market ($7 billion-a-year market) and decided to strengthen its product portfolio. In 1979, over one-half of the sales of its writing instruments and ancillary office products came from the commercial and governmental sectors. To enhance Paper Mate's position in the 1980s, the parent company—Gillette—acquired Liquid Paper Corporation, a producer of typewriter correction fluid and ribbons. These products have been experiencing a 25 percent growth rate and are projected to maintain that pace into the 1980s. The correctable typewriter ribbon is compatible with several systems and serves a large replacement market. Through new product development and a blending of existing sales forces and product lines, Paper Mate hopes to expand growth in the office supply market, where a dominant supplier has yet to emerge.

Source. "Paper Mate's Broader Outlook," *Business Week* (January 28, 1980), p. 69.

The approach is operationalized using the product evaluation matrix illustrated in figure 9.5. First, observe that company sales are illustrated on the horizontal scale and industry sales on the vertical scale. Each is divided into three categories: growth, stable, or decline. Second, profitability is classified as below-target, target, or above-target, and market share as either dominant, average, or marginal. The number of categories for sales, market share, and profitability is merely illustrative and can be varied to meet specific company and industry situations. The manager also must define the

Industry Sales	Company Sales / Profitability / Market Share	Decline			Stable			Growth		
		Below Target	Target	Above Target	Below Target	Target	Above Target	Below Target	Target	Above Target
Growth	Dominant								A	
	Average									
	Marginal									
Stable	Dominant									
	Average					B_1				
	Marginal				B					
Decline	Dominant									
	Average									
	Marginal									

Figure 9.5 / The Product Evaluation Matrix

Source. Structure provided by Yoram Wind and Henry J. Claycamp, "Planning Product Line Strategy: A Matrix Approach," *Journal of Marketing* 40 (January 1976), pp. 2–9. Reprinted from the *Journal of Marketing*, published by the American Marketing Association.

intervals for each category. For example, market share might be assigned these intervals: less than 10 percent—*marginal;* 10–24 percent—*average;* over 25 percent—*leading*. Again, the appropriate intervals are heavily dependent upon the standards relevant to the firm and the industry.[26]

Two products are positioned in the evaluation matrix displayed in figure 9.5. Product *A* enjoys a solid performance position, possessing a dominant market share, growing company sales, and target profitability in a growing industry. Product *B,* on the other hand, occupies a place in a stable industry and possesses marginal market share, stable company sales, but profits below target. The marketing strategy appropriate for product *A* would be to gear the strategy to the maintenance of the favorable market position. For product *B,* however, several alternative strategies must be considered by the product manager. The performance of product *B* should be considered under a number of different marketing strategy scenarios. The sales, market share, and profitability of product *B* next year are conditional upon the strategy decisions that are made. Thus, a conditional forecast of the product's performance should be made for each alternative marketing strategy. In search of the most desirable marketing strategy, the industrial marketer would also consider potential competitive behavior and projected external conditions.[27] This comprehensive analysis of strategy options and likely external events may lead to a strategy that improves the market position of product *B*. This improved profit and market share position is illustrated as product B_1 in figure 9.5.

Wind and Claycamp identify five strategy options that might be appropriate for a particular item in a product line or for an entire product line.

1. Maintain the product and its marketing strategy in the present form.
2. Maintain the present form of the product but change its marketing strategy.
3. Change the product and alter the marketing strategy.
4. Drop the product or the entire product line.
5. Add one or more new items into the line or add new product lines.[28]

To summarize, two planning tools are of particular value to the industrial marketer in planning strategy. These are: (1) product portfolio analysis, which examines the firm's product mix from a cash flow perspective; and (2) the product evaluation matrix, which provides a vehicle for examining the current and projected positions of the firm's products on three measures—sales, market share, and profitability. To this point in the chapter, attention has centered on managing the firm's existing product line. Often, this analysis uncovers market opportunities that could be profitably tapped with new products.

The New Product Development Process

The high expectations ascribed to new products are often never fulfilled. Worse yet, many new industrial products fail.[29] While the definitions of "failure" are somewhat illusive, research suggests that 30 to 40 percent of industrial products fail. While there may be some debate over the number of failures, there is no debate over the fact that a new product rejected by the market constitutes a substantial waste to the firm and to society.

Attaining Success with Low Market Share

While research indicates that profitability and market share are closely correlated, this does not necessarily indicate that a firm with low market share faces imminent extinction. Low market share companies (those with half of the industry leader's share) are often quite successful—possess an average return on equity above the industry median. Burroughs Corporation, Crown Cork & Seal Co., Inc., and the Union Camp Corporation fit this profile.

Four characteristics are important to the success of each of these low market share industrial firms.

1. Each follows a market segmentation approach that capitalizes on the company's strengths, rather than attempting to compete in broad markets. (E.g., Burroughs is strong in the banking segment of the computer market.)
2. Each channels limited research and development expenditures to areas that are most promising to their situation.
3. Each is specialized rather than diversified and concentrates on profits rather than sales, growth, or market share.
4. Each possesses a chief executive who takes an active involvement in almost all dimensions of company operations.

Source. R. G. Hamermesh, M. J. Anderson, Jr., and J. E. Harris, "Strategies for Low Market Share Businesses," *Harvard Business Review* 56 (May–June 1978), pp. 95–102.

Since new product ventures can represent a significant risk or, alternatively, an important opportunity, the new product development process requires careful and systematic thought by the marketer. This section examines key components of that process: (1) organization of the new product development effort, (2) sources of new product ideas, (3) new product review and evaluation, and (4) determinants of new product success and failure.

New Product Organizational Arrangements

The strong need for integrated effort in developing industrial marketing strategy has been emphasized throughout this volume. Close coordination is needed between marketing, production, engineering, and other functional areas. This need is particularly strong in bringing a new product to fruition. While the specific organizational design of the new product function is dependent on many factors, such as company size and structure, three are worthy of some consideration.[30]

1. *New product committee*—a top management committee consisting of representatives from marketing, production, accounting, engineering, and other areas who review new product proposals. While not being involved in the actual development process, the committee's main function is evaluating new product plans.
2. *New product department*—a department created in many large firms to generate and evaluate new ideas, to direct and coordinate development work, and to implement field testing and precommercialization of the new product. The department head generally has substantial authority and access to top management.
3. *New product venture team*—"a group specifically brought together from various operating departments and charged with the responsibility of bringing a specific product to market or a specific new business into being."[31] The composition of the venture team changes as the venture passes through various stages of development. The venture team may be dissolved once a product is established.

Regardless of the particular organizational scheme adopted, careful coordination and control are needed during and after the development process.

Sources of New Product Ideas

The industrial marketer should be alert to new product ideas that may originate from several sources within and outside of the company. Internally, new product ideas may flow from salespersons who are closest to customer needs, from research and development specialists who are closest to new technological developments, and from top management who may have the best knowledge of overall company strengths and weaknesses. Externally, ideas may come from channel members, such as distributors, or from an assessment of competitive moves.

Eric von Hippel challenges the traditional view that marketers typically introduce new products to a passive market.[32] His research suggests that industrial customers often develop the idea for a new product and even select the supplier capable of making that product. Thus, a product request from a customer often spawns a new industrial product. The customer is responding to the perceived *capability* of the industrial marketer, rather than to a specific physical product. This points up the need for involving the customers in new product development efforts and promoting corporate capability to consumers (idea generators).

Screening New Product Ideas

Before committing resources to the costly process of transforming an idea into a finished industrial product, close scrutiny must be given to the proposed item. Firms that fail to properly assess market needs, the level of demand potential, the nature of production requirements, the nature of the buying process, the aggressiveness of competitors, the extent of technical service requirements, and related factors are doomed to failure in the new product development game. To guard against such omissions, many industrial marketers have developed elaborate screening procedures that evaluate new products from several perspectives.

New Product Innovation: Key to Success in Industrial Markets

How important is new product innovation in the industrial market? The experience of Xerox in the decade of the 1970s suggests that it is very important. Between 1972 and 1978, Xerox pursued a strategy of cost cutting at the expense of product innovation. As one market researcher put it, "Xerox developed constipation in product development," virtually ignoring the threat of new competition. The results were not pleasing—Xerox's market share in plain paper copiers fell from 85 percent in 1973 to 55 percent in 1978! The lesson has not gone unheeded, however.

The president of Xerox during those critical years has since assumed the role of chairman to International Harvester. In the new position, he has embarked on a $2.5 billion capital expansion plan, primarily focused on plant modernization and new product development. Already, market share gains have been evidenced in the farm group as the result of the introduction of a new rotary combine and a small, highly maneuverable four-wheel-drive tractor.

Source. "International Harvester: When Cost-Cutting Threatens the Future," *Business Week* (February 11, 1980), pp. 98–100.

New Product Profile Chart. A new product profile chart that has been adopted by Monsanto Corporation is presented in table 9.3. The major points of analysis include: (1) financial aspects, (2) marketing and product aspects, (3) production and engineering aspects, (4) research and development.[33] Such a chart analyzes the profit, sales, and cash requirements of a venture, and it examines the degree to which the potential product converges on the production, research and development, and marketing capabilities of the firm. The quality of this review effort often rests squarely on the firm's knowledge of market needs. Many products have numerous applications among diverse groups of buying organizations; therefore, it is often necessary to examine each potential application separately.[34] Thus, each application may represent a distinct market segment with special requirements.

To implement the new product profile chart, firms often rate each dimension on a scale. For example, the dimension of "marketability to present customers" might be rated in this manner:

−2 entirely different customers
−1 some present customers
+1 mostly present customers
+2 all present customers

Table 9.3 / A New Product Profile Chart

Financial Aspects	Return on investment (before taxes) Estimated annual sales New fixed capital payout time Time to reach estimated sales volume
Marketing and Product Aspects	Similarity to present product lines Effect on present products Marketability to present customers Number of potential customers Suitability of present sales force Market stability Market trend Technical service
Production and Engineering Aspects	Required corporate size Raw materials Equipment Process familiarity
Research and Development Aspects	Research investment payout time Development investment payout time Research know-how Patent status

Source. John S. Harris, "New Product Profile Chart," *CHEMTECH* (September 1976), p. 559. Reprinted by permission from *CHEMTECH*. Copyright © 1976 the American Chemical Society.

Comparable measures could be developed for each dimension deemed important by the firm. The assignment of such numerical values provides a *visual* indication of the level of desirability of the venture on each criterion. This analysis provides management with a means of evaluating the merits and drawbacks of alternative new product ideas. Since the selected criteria are not equally important and vary by project, this weighing system does not replace the need for managerial judgment. Management must weigh the relative importance of each criterion to a specific project before evaluating the project on that dimension.

Determinants of New Product Success and Failure

A prime limitation of the new product checklist approach is that neither the screening criteria nor their relative importance is empirically derived. Many factors must be screened by the industrial marketer, but which factors are most important in determining the success or failure of the new product offering? Robert Cooper examines this complex research question.[35]

A Good Idea—But?

A large supplier of industrial grease developed a novel approach for delivery, storage, and use by customers. Manufacturers typically purchase grease in 400 pound drums, and in order quantities 10 times that large. The drums are bulky to handle and are nonreturnable, thus creating a disposal problem. When used on the production line, a significant amount of grease is wasted because supervisors like to begin each shift with a full drum. This alleviates the need to stop a production line in mid-shift to replace an empty.

The supplier's functional innovation involved the delivery of grease in bulk by a specially designed delivery truck capable of pumping grease directly into the customer's plant. The customer would have to install some relatively inexpensive equipment to use the system—several 5,000 pound capacity tanks, plus piping from the reservoirs to greasing stations on the production line. Substantial savings would accrue to adopters of the system—lower purchase cost, reduced drum handling and waste, and reduced production line shut-downs. The new system failed! Why? Salespersons were poorly trained in describing the advantages and cost savings of the system. Customers were uneasy about making the low cost plant alterations required by the system. Here, the industrial marketer failed to understand the buying motives and potential objections of buyers. The delivery truck remains idle.

Source. Peter M. Bunting, "Unsuccessful Innovation in the Industrial Market," *Journal of Marketing* 42 (January 1978), pp. 99–100.

The Determinants of Success. Three factors appear to be of utmost importance to new product success. First, the *level of product uniqueness and superiority* is the most important dimension contributing to new product success. Thus, highly innovative products that improve on competing offerings in satisfying customer needs gain a strong differential advantage. Such products offer clear benefits, such as reducing customer costs, and are of a higher quality (e.g., more durable) than the products of competitors.

Second, *market knowledge and marketing proficiency* are pivotal in new product outcomes. As might be expected, industrial marketers that have a solid understanding of market needs, buyer behavior, and market potential, and combine this with a well-conceived launch effort, derive success in the marketplace. *Technical and production synergy and proficiency* emerge as the third most important new product dimension. New product success results in industrial firms that can draw upon a compatible technical and production resource base and proficiently pass through the stages of the new product development process (e.g., product development, prototype testing, pilot production, and production start-up).

Barriers to Success. Three barriers to success, uncovered by Cooper, are likewise worthy of emphasis. "These are:

1. having a high-priced product, relative to competition (with no economic advantage to the customer);
2. being in a dynamic market (with many new product introductions);
3. being in a competitive market, where customers are already well satisfied."[36]

Overall, this research points up the critical importance of the *product* in industrial marketing strategy. Likewise, new industrial product success is heavily dependent upon a strong market orientation that is smoothly blended with strong technical/production capability.

The New Industrial Product Adoption Process

Because a strong consumer focus is instrumental to the success of a new product, the industrial marketer can benefit by examining the industrial product adoption process. This process has been conceptualized to include two basic stages: (1) the initiation stage and (2) the implementation stage.[37] Each has important substages that are briefly described in table 9.4.

Table 9.4 / Stages of Innovation-Adoption Process in Organizations

Stage	Description
I. Initiation Stage	
1. Knowledge-awareness substage	Organizational decision makers perceive that there is a discrepancy between desired and actual performance.
2. Formation of attitudes toward the innovation substage.	Important attitudinal dimensions include the openness of organizational decision makers to the innovation and their perception of the potential for innovation.
3. Decision substage	Information concerning the potential innovation is evaluated. If organizational members are highly motivated to innovate or their attitudes are highly favorable toward innovation, implementation is likely.
II. Implementation Stage	
1. Initial implementation substage	Organization makes first attempt to utilize the specific innovation.
2. Continued-sustained implementation substage	A successful and relatively trouble-free initial implementation increases the likelihood that the innovation will be further utilized by the organization.

Source. Adapted from Gerald Zaltman, Robert Duncan, and Jonny Holbek, *Innovations and Organizations* (New York: Wiley Interscience, 1973), p. 158.

In the industrial setting, research efforts have sought to identify the relative importance of various information sources throughout this adoption process. In general, trade journals or mass communication tends to be the most significant information sources in triggering awareness of a new industrial product. Salespersons, along with proposals provided by them, play a dominant role in the remaining phases of the adoption process.[38] The organizational buyer's requirement for information of all types increases as the product moves from the initiation stage to the implementation stage. Information needs are particularly high when organizational buyers perceive a great amount of risk in the adoption decision.

As informal information sources, opinion leaders within the organization also play an important role in the adoption process, especially in the later stages.[39] In contrast to other organizational members, opinion leaders tend to have more exposure to trade journals.

In designing promotional support for a new industrial product, the marketer must recognize the specific roles performed by advertising and personal selling. Technical and trade journals stimulate awareness, while the personal selling effort is crucial in identifying key buying influences and satisfying significant information needs. Both are fundamental to the successful launching of a new product.

Summary

The product often constitutes the most important component of the industrial marketing mix. Conceptualizations of a "product" must go beyond a mere description of physical characteristics and must include all of the attached benefits and services that provide consumer satisfaction. Industrial product lines can be broadly classified into four major categories: (1) proprietary or catalog items, (2) custom-built items, (3) custom-designed items, and (4) industrial services. Generally, industrial product management can best be described as the management of capability.

Managing the existing industrial product line involves two important questions. (1) How many items should be included in the line? (2) How should they be positioned in the market? The concepts of *product space* and *product positioning* facilitate the analysis of these strategic questions. In monitoring the performance of specific products and formulating marketing strategy, the industrial marketer can profitably utilize two planning aids: portfolio analysis and the product evaluation matrix.

Sustained growth in the industrial enterprise is dependent upon the development of innovative products that respond to existing or emerging consumer needs. Before committing substantial resources to a new product idea, the proposed venture must be carefully screened on many important dimensions. An idea that successfully passes this screening test must progress through a well-organized and integrated development process. In turn, marketers must understand that innovative products are carefully evaluated by consumers before they are adopted.

Footnotes

[1]E. Raymond Corey, "Key Options in Market Selection and Product Planning," *Harvard Business Review* 53 (September–October 1975), pp. 119–28.

[2]Theodore Levitt, *The Marketing Mode: Pathways to Corporate Growth* (New York: McGraw-Hill, Inc., 1969), pp. 2–3.

[3]Benson P. Shapiro, *Industrial Product Policy: Managing the Existing Product Line* (Cambridge, Mass.: Marketing Science Institute, 1977), pp. 37–39.

[4]B. Charles Ames, "Marketing Planning for Industrial Products," *Harvard Business Review* 46 (September–October 1968), pp. 100–111.

[5]Benson P. Shapiro, "Can Marketing and Manufacturing Coexist?" *Harvard Business Review* 55 (September–October 1977), pp. 107–14.

[6]For a comprehensive discussion of this organizational design issue, see B. Charles Ames, "Dilemma of Product/Market Management," *Harvard Business Review* 49 (March–April 1971), pp. 66–74.

[7]Shapiro, *Industrial Product Policy,* p. 17.

[8]Philip Kotler, *Marketing Management: Analysis, Planning and Control* (2nd ed.; Englewood Cliffs, N.J.: Prentice-Hall, Inc., 1972), p. 439, reported in Shapiro, ibid., p. 1.

[9]Shapiro, ibid., pp. 17–21.

[10]Ibid., pp. 18–20.

[11]Christian Grönroos, "An Applied Theory for Marketing Industrial Services," *Industrial Marketing Management* 8 (January 1979), pp. 45–50.

[12]Shapiro, *Industrial Product Policy,* pp. 5–10.

[13]Ibid., p. 102.

[14]Ibid., pp. 102–3.

[15]For a comprehensive discussion of decision support systems, see John D. C. Little, "Decision Support Systems for Marketing Managers," *Journal of Marketing* 43 (Summer 1979), pp. 9–25; see also, Little, "Models and Managers: The Concept of a Decision Calculus," *Management Science* 18 (April 1970), pp. 466–85; and David A. Aaker and Charles B. Weinberg, "Interactive Marketing Models," *Journal of Marketing* 39 (October 1975), pp. 16–23.

[16]Shapiro, *Industrial Product Policy,* p. 103.

[17]For example, see Derek F. Abell, "Using PIMS and Portfolio Analysis in Strategic Market Planning: A Comparative Analysis" (Boston, Harvard Business School: Intercollegiate Case Clearing House, 1977).

[18]George S. Day, "Diagnosing the Product Portfolio," *Journal of Marketing* 41 (April 1977), p. 29.

[19]Robert D. Buzzell, Bradley T. Gale, and Ralph G. M. Sultan, "Market Share—A Key to Profitability," *Harvard Business Review* 53 (January–February 1975), pp. 97–106.

[20]Ibid., pp. 97–106.

[21]For a more comprehensive discussion of the product life cycle concept, see Chester R. Wasson, "The Importance of the Product Life Cycle to the Industrial Marketer," *Industrial Marketing Management* 5 (1976), pp. 299–308.

[22]Bernard Catry and Michel Chevalier, "Market Share Strategy and the Product Life Cycle," *Journal of Marketing* 38 (October 1974), pp. 29–34.

[23]Bruce D. Henderson, *The Experience Curve Reviewed: The Growth-Share Matrix or the Product Portfolio* (Boston Consulting Group, 1973); see also, George S. Day, "Diagnosing the Product Portfolio," pp. 29–38.

[24]Yoram Wind and Henry J. Claycamp, "Planning Product Line Strategy: A Matrix Approach," *Journal of Marketing* 40 (January 1976), pp. 2–9.

[25]Ibid., pp. 3–4.

[26]Ibid., p. 4.

[27]Such an analysis can be greatly facilitated by the use of a computer simulation. For an example, see Wind and Claycamp, ibid., and John D. C. Little, "Decision Support Systems," pp. 9–12.

[28]Wind and Claycamp, ibid., p. 8.

[29]*Management of New Products* (Chicago: Booz, Allen and Hamilton, 1968), pp. 11–12.

[30]Philip Kotler, *Marketing Management: Analysis, Planning and Control* (3rd. ed.; Englewood Cliffs, N.J.: Prentice-Hall, Inc., 1976), pp. 199–201.

[31]Ibid., p. 200.

[32]Eric von Hippel, "Successful Industrial Products from Customer Ideas," *Journal of Marketing* 42 (January 1978), pp. 39–49; see also, von Hippel, "Has Your Customer Already Developed Your Next Product?" *Sloan Management Review* 18 (Winter 1977), pp. 63–74.

[33]John S. Harris, "New Product Profile Chart," *CHEMTECH* (September 1976), pp. 554–62.

[34]For example, see Pierre Chenu and David L. Wilemon, "A Decision Process for New Product Selection," *Industrial Marketing Management* 3 (1973), pp. 33–46.

[35]Robert G. Cooper, "The Dimensions of Industrial New Product Success and Failure," *Journal of Marketing* 43 (Summer 1979), pp. 93–103; see also, Cooper, "Identifying Industrial New Product Success: Project NewProd," *Industrial Marketing Management* 8 (April 1979), pp. 124–35; and Cooper, "Why New Industrial Products Fail," *Industrial Marketing Management* 4 (1975), pp. 315–26.

[36]Cooper, "The Dimensions of Industrial New Product Success and Failure," p. 101.

[37]Gerald Zaltman, Robert Duncan, and Jonny Holbek, *Innovations and Organizations* (New York: Wiley-Interscience, 1973), p. 158; see also, Urban B. Ozanne and Gilbert A. Churchill, "Adoption Research: Information Sources in the Industrial Purchasing Decision," in Robert L. King, ed., *Marketing and the New Science of Planning* (Chicago: American Marketing Association, 1968), pp. 352–59.

[38]Frederick E. Webster, Jr., "Informal Communication in Industrial Markets," *Journal of Marketing Research* 7 (May 1970), pp. 186–89; see also, Ozanne and Churchill, ibid., pp. 352–59.

[39]John A. Martilla, "Word-of-Mouth Communications in the Industrial Adoption Process," *Journal of Marketing Research* 8 (May 1971), pp. 173–78. For related research, see John A. Czepiel, "Word-of-Mouth Processes in the Diffusion of a Major Technological Innovation," *Journal of Marketing Research* 11 (May 1974), pp. 172–80.

Discussion Questions

1. Robots, with programmed mechanical arms, can be used to perform monotonous, uncomfortable, or dangerous tasks in the production process. Robots can pour hot molten aluminum, load and unload heavy stacks of laminated parts for motors, paint refrigerators as they move down the assembly line, and perform other related functions. Yet acceptance of these machine tools has been slow. As a new industrial product, what steps could the industrial marketer take in speeding the rate of adoption of this technology? What barriers would the marketer of robots face in your view?

2. Distinguish among catalog items, custom-built items, custom-designed items, and services. Explain how marketing requirements vary across this product line classification scheme.

3. Illustrate how the concept of product space can be used by the industrial marketer in determining the composition and length of the product line.

4. Compare and contrast the marketing strategy that might be appropriate for "stars" versus "cash cows."

5. Valves play an important role in American industry. For example, they are used to control the flow of liquids in refineries, chemical plants, and electric power facilities. Thus, valve manufacturers serve many users, including chemical-petrochemical complexes, refineries, pipelines, and electric power plants. These producers face a fundamental problem: how much effort should be invested in the development of special valves for the nuclear power market? Given the political, legal, and general uncertainties that surround this potentially large market, what steps should the product planner take?

6. In your position as product manager for the Bronson Machine Tool Company, you have to develop a marketing program for product X, an existing product in the company's line. In determining how much to spend and where to spend it, you are given information on the sales, profitability, and market share of product X for the past five years. You are also provided with a forecast of general economic conditions. Describe the approach that you would follow in developing a strategy for product X.

7. The Los Angeles Motor Works Company has experienced numerous new product failures in the industrial market. As a marketing consultant, you have been asked to develop a new product review guide that they can use in screening new product ideas. To be useful to them, this evaluation checklist or guide should be relatively concise and highlight priority areas in order of their importance. Present your recommendations.

8. The ultimate criterion in adding a new item to an industrial firm's existing product line should be that product's contribution to overall company profits. Agree or disagree? Support your position.

9. Critique this statement: "Industrial products and consumer products fail for the same basic reasons."

10. Some industrial product managers argue that their prime function is to market the "capability" of their firm, rather than physical products. Do you agree or disagree with this philosophy of product management? Explain.

Chapter 10 Industrial Marketing Channels: Channel Participants

The channel of distribution constitutes the marketing manager's bridge to the market. In managing the industrial channel, many decisions must be made that directly influence the effectiveness and efficiency of marketing strategy. The appropriateness and quality of these decisions often hinge on an understanding of the role and function of various industrial channel participants.

After reading this chapter, you will have an understanding of:

1. *the alternative forms of industrial channels of distribution*
2. *the nature and function of industrial distributors*
3. *the role of manufacturer's representatives*
4. *the special problems and opportunities that these and other types of channel members present for the industrial marketer.*

A good industrial marketing manager follows the dictum that marketing channels focus the firm's marketing strategy and deliver the product to all customer segments. The marketing channel is the primary means through which the industrial firm finds new prospects for its products, communicates with existing customers, and physically delivers the product to the industrial user. The selection of the best channel system to accomplish these ends is a challenging task because: (1) the alternatives are numerous; (2) marketing goals differ; and (3) a variety of customer market segments often require that a number of separate channels be employed concurrently.

To illustrate, Motorola, a supplier of semiconductors, recently added an additional channel—manufacturer's representatives—to their distribution network.[1] The company already utilized two distinct channels: (1) its own sales force that calls on large accounts where the sales volume justifies the selling expense; and (2) a vast system of franchised distributors that provide local market inventories, service repeat orders, and provide credit. The manufacturer's reps were added in an attempt to penetrate the market consisting of small and medium sized accounts. The rep, who works on a fixed commission and can spread costs over a broad range of complementary products, allows Motorola to effectively reach certain markets where the market potential would not justify the use of its own direct sales force.

The number of different channels required is just one of the many decisions to be made about the channel aspect of industrial marketing strategy. Additional considerations include whether to use middlemen, the types and number of middlemen, the methods required to effectively administer the channel, and approaches to designing an efficient physical distribution network. This chapter will focus on the key channel participants. The role of middlemen in industrial channels, the nature of their operations, and some of the relevant trends expected to develop with these middlemen will be explored. The discussion will concentrate on industrial distributors and manufacturer's representatives, because they are the primary middlemen employed by industrial marketers. Chapter 11 will examine the design of industrial channels and the nature of the management process required to achieve channel objectives. Chapter 12 concentrates on the physical distribution aspects of industrial marketing channels. Collectively, these chapters will provide a comprehensive treatment of the distribution management function.

The Industrial Channel

The link between a manufacturer and customers is the channel of distribution. The channel exists to accomplish all the tasks necessary to effect a sale and to physically deliver products to the customer. The tasks are considerable and include making *contact* with potential buyers, *negotiating,* establishing *contractual* arrangements, *transferring* title, *communications,* providing required *financial* arrangements, *servicing* the product, providing local *inventory, transportation,* and *storage*. These tasks may be performed entirely by the manufacturer, entirely by specified middlemen, or the manufacturer and the middlemen may each perform selected tasks. One of the most challenging aspects of industrial marketing is to allocate the tasks among the middlemen and the manufacturer in a way that insures efficient and effective channel performance. The tasks listed above cannot be eliminated but must always *be performed* as the product moves from manufacturer to customer. The key issue in channel management is, therefore, focused on how to best structure the channel so that the tasks are performed in the optimal manner. One alternative is for the manufacturer to perform all of the channel tasks.

Direct Distribution

Direct distribution is very common in industrial marketing. It is a channel strategy that does not utilize middlemen, but instead, the manufacturer's own sales force deals directly with the customer. In this situation, the manufacturer has full responsibility for performing all the necessary channel tasks. Direct distribution is often required in the industrial marketing environment because of the nature of the selling situation. A case in point is Rockwell International's Municipal and Utility (M&U) Division.[2] The M&U Division markets a line of water, gas, and parking meters to local municipalities and gas utilities through a direct sales organization. The direct sales approach is viable for Rockwell's M&U Division as its customers are large and well defined; the customers often insist upon direct sales; and extensive negotiations with high level utility management are required. Also, control of the selling job is necessary to insure proper implementation of the total product package and to guarantee a quick response to market conditions. In the last regard, employment of the direct sales force allowed the company to change its price schedule five times in a six-month period as well as negotiate all important contracts as required by those price changes.

Indirect Distribution

Indirect distribution involves the utilization of one or more types of middlemen in the channel. Industrial channels typically include fewer types of middlemen than do consumer-goods channels. A study of 156 industrial manufacturers in 220 product lines revealed that six types of channels accounted for 100 percent of the sales for those firms.[3]

Figure 10.1 shows the six possible channel arrangements. *Manufacturer's representatives* and *industrial distributors* account for the majority of the business that is handled through indirect industrial channels. The discussion of these two types of middlemen in the remainder of the chapter will clarify the need for, and importance of, indirect distribution channels in industrial marketing.

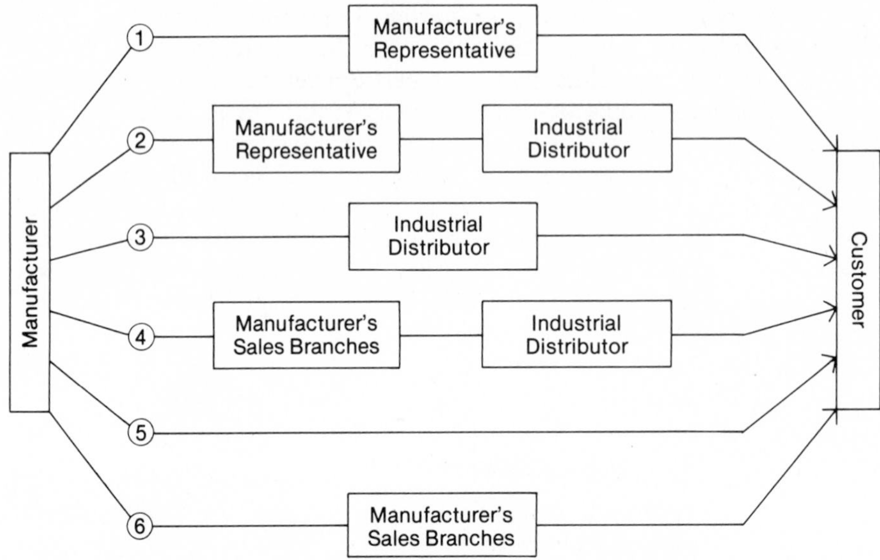

Figure 10.1 / Channel Alternatives in the Industrial Market

Source. Adapted from William M. Diamond, *Distribution Channels for Industrial Products* (Columbus, Ohio: Bureau of Business Research, College of Commerce and Administration, The Ohio State University, 1963), p. 56.

Many Channels Often Required

As figure 10.1 indicates, various combinations of middlemen and direct selling may be employed in the industrial channel. In fact, a number of separate combinations of channels may be utilized by the same manufacturer. The need to employ more than one channel arises as a result of different marketing tasks for the variety of products produced by a given manufacturer or the different target markets sought by the firm.

Timeplex, a manufacturer of time division multiplexes, sells through manufacturer's reps.[4] Reps offer low cost distribution, expertise in the data communication field, and carry a complementary product line that facilitates the sale of Timeplex's products. The key buying influence in the end-user firm, to which reps direct their attention, is the data communications manager. As Timeplex commercializes new products already on the drawing board, the key buying influence for the newer products will be the electronic data processing manager. The president of Timeplex indicates that "there is an iron wall between the data communications manager and the electronic data processing manager. Because our reps may be unable or reluctant to call on the EDP manager, we'll probably have to consider building a parallel direct sales organization." A careful analysis of the buying process in customer and potential user firms is a prerequisite to the determination of the most effective channels to be employed.

The utilization of indirect channels of distribution is common to a wide variety of industrial products. The quality and performance of the middlemen employed in an indirect channel have a critical impact on whether the industrial marketer's strategy will achieve its goals. An important first step in designing and managing industrial marketing channels is to fully comprehend the nature and role of the types of industrial middlemen who function in the channel.

Participants in the Industrial Channel

The types of industrial middlemen are confined to distributors, manufacturer's agents (reps), jobbers, brokers, and commission merchants. By a very wide margin, distributors and reps handle the preponderance of sales made through industrial middlemen. This section of the chapter will focus primarily on these two important intermediaries. Emphasis will center on the role that each plays in the industrial channel, the nature of their operations, and some of the trends and future directions expected to occur in both these industries.

Distributors

Industrial distributors are the most important and pervasive single force in industrial distribution channels. They number close to 12,000 and accounted for almost $38 billion in total sales volume in 1979.[5] A recent study of purchasing patterns among plant purchasing agents and other buying influences revealed that few, if any, of the plants deal with less than five different industrial distributors and over 50 percent buy from between 30 and 100 different distributors.[6] What accounts for the unparalleled position of the industrial distributor in the industrial market? What role do they play in the industrial distribution process? These questions merit examination.

Industrial Distributor Profile

Table 10.1 provides a concise view of the "typical" industrial distributor. Distributors are generally small, independent business firms serving narrow geographic markets. Sales average about $3.4 million, although some distributors top $200 million in sales. Net profits are relatively low as a percentage of sales (4.5 percent), yet return on investments averages an impressive 19.2 percent. The typical order is small—$150—and these orders are generated by a sales force of four "outside" salespersons and four or five "inside" salespersons. Outside salespersons make regular calls on customers and handle normal account servicing and technical assistance. Inside salespersons complement the efforts of the outside sales force, handling customer order processing and scheduling delivery. Their primary activities

Table 10.1 / Profile of an Industrial Distributor

Annual Sales:	$3,400,000
Gross Profit:	18 percent
Net Profit:	4.5 percent
ROI:	19.2 percent
Average Inventory:	$400,000–500,000
Average Order:	$150
Sales per Employee:	$115,000
Number of Employees:	17
Number of Outside Salespersons:	4
Number of Inside Salespersons:	4–5
Warehouse Square Feet:	11,700
Number of Branch Locations:	1–2
Ownership:	Independent
Geographic Market:	
Urban Areas:	25-mile-wide radius
Rural Areas:	125-mile-wide radius

Source. "'78 Sales Up 13%, Profits Down," *Industrial Distribution*, March 1979, pp. 39–49; "ID's 1978 Census of Industrial Distributors," *Industrial Distribution*, September 1978, pp. 57–63.

involve order taking over the telephone. Most distributors operate from a single location, but some approach the "supermarket" status with as many as 50 different branch locations.

The Distributor's Responsibilities

Contact and Product Availability. The industrial distributor's primary responsibility to the manufacturers he or she represents is to contact present and potential customers and to make the product available—with all the required supporting activities like delivery, credit, order processing, and technical advice—as quickly as economically feasible.[7] The products distributors sell—cutting tools, power tools, pipe, bearings, handling equipment, fasteners, electric equipment, welding equipment, maintenance, repair and operating supplies, and contractor supplies—are generally those that buyers need quickly (to avoid production disruptions). Thus, the distributor serves the vital roles of informing potential customers of the availability of these products and making sure that the products are readily available when a need arises. Table 10.2 indicates the importance of the distributor in the sale of such items. For the majority of the products listed, distributors supply over 50 percent of products purchased and almost four times as much as are bought direct from the manufacturer.

Industrial users/purchasers who buy through distributors, like the manufacturers who sell through distributors, look on the distributor as playing a key role in their businesses. In a recent article, *Purchasing* magazine notes that "the 'middlemen' image that for years haunted industrial distributors is vanishing—at least in the eyes of professional buyers. Purchasing execs now view distributors more as extensions of their buying arms than as con-

Table 10.2 / Maintenance Repair and Operating Supply Purchases: Direct vs. Distributor

	Percentage of Total Purchases:	
	Purchased from Distributors	Purchased from Factory-Direct
Cutting tools and accessories	63	9
Mechanics and power tools and accessories	57	14
Powered equipment and quality control	52	18
Pipe, tubing, valves, fittings	45	5
Fluid power (air and hydraulic) products	49	8
Mechanical power transmission equipment	40	10
Bearings	52	4
Material handling (and storage) equipment	62	9
Industrial rubber and plastic products	37	7
Fasteners	40	7
Electric and electronic equipment	37	7
Safety supplies	75	5
Contractors' supplies and accessories	72	2
Maintenance-repair-operating items (lubes, coatings, tapes, etc.)	57	12
Welding equipment and supplies	60	10
Facility maintenance and sanitation supplies	73	5

Source. "Distributor Image: '79—How the Buyer Sees It," *Industrial Distribution,* February 1979, p. 53. Reprinted by permission.

duits from prime manufacturers."[8] An effective distributor can provide the user firm with valuable technical advice, suggest substitute products, promote standardization of basic operating and maintenance supplies, and aid the user in negotiating price and credit terms with the manufacturer.

Repair Service. With complex equipment like construction and mining machines, repair is a crucial aspect of the customer-supplier relationship. The local distributor is in the best position to provide this type of service. Because of the cost of extensive repair facilities and the distance from manufacturer to customer, the local industrial distributor can economically and effectively supply the vital repair service required for many industrial products.

Distributors Do Some Assembly and Light Manufacturing. Bulk transportation of sheet steel, tubing, or pipe is much less expensive than the shipment of finished products made from these materials. In addition, inventory costs can be reduced substantially by maintaining inventory in the bulk, unfinished state rather than in individual inventories of each finished product. As a result, many distributors buy products of this nature in bulk, and perform the necessary assembly and manufacturing as orders for individual products are received. For example, a saw manufacturer now ships rolled band saw stock which a distributor cuts, welds, and finishes to customer specifications for each order.[9] The assembly and manufacturing processes offered by an industrial distributor provide an important means for reducing overall distribution costs and for more careful tailoring of the final product to customer requirements.

In summary, the industrial distributor is a full-service middleman who takes title to the products sold, maintains inventories, provides credit, delivery, wide product assortment, technical assistance, and may even do some assembly and manufacturing. Although the distributor is primarily responsible for contacting and supplying present customers, industrial distributors also actively engage in new account solicitation and market expansion. The products handled by the industrial distributor are generally established products—typically used in manufacturing operations, repair and maintenance—that have a broad and large demand.

Classification of Distributors

To select the most appropriate distributor for a particular channel, the marketing manager must understand that there is considerable diversity in distributor operations. There is a wide variety of industrial distributors based on the nature of the product line handled and the user markets served. Firms range from the ultra-specialized (e.g., distributors selling only to municipal water works) to those carrying a broad line of industrial products of all kinds. Generally, however, three primary distributor classifications are recognized.

General Line Distributors. General line distributors cater to a broad array of needs of their industrial customers. They stock an extensive variety of industrial products and could be likened to the supermarket in the consumer-goods markets. Some general line distributors maintain separate departments, such as abrasives and power tools, to meet very specific needs for certain important accounts.

Specialists. Specialists focus their operations on one or a few related lines. For example, a distributor may handle only power transmission equipment—belts, pulleys, and bearings. The most prevalent specialty today is fasteners, with more than 2900 distributors specializing in this product group.[10] Other important product specialization occurs in cutting tools, power transmission equipment, pipe, valves, and fittings. There is a trend toward increased specialization as a result of the increasing technical complexity of products and the need for higher levels of precision and quality control.

Combination House. A combination house operates in two markets: industrial and consumer. Thus, a combination house might carry electric motors to be used by industrial customers as well as hardware and automotive parts that will be sold through retailers to final consumers.

The selection of the type of distributor will depend upon the manufacturer's requirements. The general line distributor offers the advantage of "one-stop" purchasing to the manufacturer's potential customers. If a high level of service and technical expertise is not required, the general line distributor is an effective alternative. The specialist, on the other hand, provides the manufacturer with a high level of technical capability and a well-developed understanding of user requirements. Fasteners are handled by specialists because of the strict quality control standards imposed by users. The specialist is able to effectively meet this challenge.

The Distributor as a Valuable Asset

The preceding discussion on distributor operations provides insights into the considerable advantages afforded by an effective distributor. The quality of an industrial firm's distributors often is the difference between a highly successful marketing strategy and a rather lackluster one. Good distributors are recognized and prized by the manufacturer's customers, making it all the more necessary to continually strive to engage the best ones in any given market. Importantly, there are many cases where distributors provide the only economically feasible way of obtaining comprehensive market coverage.

Industrial Distributors: Selected Problems

Although industrial distributors are a vital part of the channel for many industrial products and offer significant benefits to their suppliers, important problems still remain in the process of marketing through them. Many distributors are small—a great many have sales volumes under $2 million. Because they are small, distributors often do not possess the highest levels of management expertise; a lack of management professionalism is often evidenced. This tends to frustrate the manufacturer and makes it difficult to maintain a workable partnership between supplier and distributor.

Some manufacturers have found their distributors to be overly committed to their end-user customers. A result could be that the manufacturer's brand is substituted by the distributor for a less expensive competitive brand. The problem is that distributors view themselves as *independent* entrepreneurs with their main obligation being to respond to their customers' needs (regardless of whether such actions suit a particular manufacturer).[11] Manufacturers, on the other hand, view the end-user/customer as *their* customer, and distributors as only a facilitating link.

Sources of Conflict. These different perceptions are manifested in a number of other problem areas. A constant source of controversy involves competing lines carried by the distributor. Another source of conflict is large accounts, which the manufacturer often prefers to serve through a direct channel. However, distributors feel cheated if they are not given an opportunity to reap the economic rewards associated with these large accounts. Inventory commitments are still another area of friction. The manufacturer views inventory as essential to good customer service, while the distributor is sensitive to the impact of inventory requirements on profitability.

Toward a Manufacturer-Distributor Partnership

Thus, the manufacturer-distributor relationship is not always a smooth one. The potential for conflict and dispute is sometimes high. From the manufacturer's vantage point, there is no single solution to the problem. First, the manufacturer-distributor relationship should be viewed as a partnership. Such a perspective suggests that the manufacturer provide all the assistance that is economically feasible to enhance the distributor's performance. Increased margins or financial assistance may be required to stimulate the distributor to increase inventory levels. Some manufacturers allow distributors a percentage commission on sales to large accounts in their territory—easing the "large account" conflict. Second, manufacturers must be sensitized to the role their sales force can play in aiding distributors' performance. The supplier's salespeople can be used to strengthen the distributor through joint sales calls or supplemental technical support. Third, training programs for distributor personnel may not only improve distributor effectiveness, but also strengthen the bond between distributor and manufacturer. The partnership will be made more effective through the coordinated efforts of the manufacturer to strengthen and support distributors in their weak areas.

Distributor Dynamics: The Future

One of the great challenges of industrial marketing is to develop the ability to understand the dynamics of a market and forecast its future directions. This is particularly meaningful in the case of industrial distributors as a result of important changes unfolding in that industry. A gradual evolution in distributor operations has begun to take place. Table 10.3 provides insights into some of the more significant trends. The key distributor developments from the manufacturer's perspective—size, chain operations, and specialization—pose important questions for future channel management strategies. Each trend suggests that a higher level of distributor sophistication, market power, and customer loyalty will result. The effect on the manufacturers will be to make careful distributor selection even more important.

To this point, the discussion has centered on the nature, functions, and trends in the industrial distributor field. Industrial distributors are a powerful

Table 10.3 / New Directions in Distributor Operations

Changes in Distributor Operations	Impacts on the Manufacturer
Increased Size	Average distributor sales volume has increased from $2.1 million in 1974 to $3.4 million in 1978.* Larger, more sophisticated distributors are emerging. By utilizing only a few, well-managed distributors, a manufacturer can reduce logistics costs and enhance effectiveness of dollars spent on training and support. However, fewer effective uncommitted distributors will be available.
Distributor "Supermarkets"	A growing force in the industrial field is the distributor chain operation—a chain of distributor outlets with regional or nationwide coverage, owned and managed by a single corporation.** Chains may carry multiple brands as opposed to exclusive brand coverage; offer private labels in some product categories; use price discounting; provide wide and deep inventories. The net result will probably be a shift of market power to the chain.
Specialization	The tendency to concentrate efforts in restricted product lines appears to be growing. Specialist distributors offer buyers expert knowledge, effective service and a variety of brands in a narrow line. From the manufacturer's view, these factors may serve to link the end user/customer more closely to the distributor. Again, a shift of market power and control to the specialist distributor is a likely result. Since the manufacturer's brand may be only one of several carried by the specialist, the industrial marketer may be forced to provide price concessions, heavy advertising, or direct sales controls to the end user to maintain a viable market position.

*"29th Annual Survey of Distributor Operations," *Industrial Distribution* 65 (March 1975), pp. 31–39; and "33rd Annual Survey of Distributor Operations," *Industrial Distribution* 69 (March 1979), pp. 39–49.

**J. G. Main, "The Chain Reaction That's Rocking Industrial Distribution," *Sales and Marketing Management* 114 (February 23, 1976), pp. 41–45.

force in the industrial channel arena and all indications point to an expanded role in the future. The manufacturer's representative is an equally viable force in the industrial channel.

Manufacturer's Representative

For many industrial marketers who need a strong selling job with a technically complex product, manufacturer's representatives, or reps, provide the only cost-effective way to meet these requirements. Reps are salespersons who work independently, representing several different companies in the same geographic area, selling noncompeting but complementary products. Table 10.4 provides a concise sketch of a typical rep.

The Rep's Responsibilities

A rep is a knowledgeable salesperson who works independently (or for a manufacturer's rep company) and neither takes title nor holds inventory of the products handled. (Some reps do, however, keep a limited inventory of repair and maintenance parts.) The rep's forte is expert product knowledge coupled with a keen understanding of the market and customers covered. Reps are usually restricted to limited geographical areas; thus, a manufacturer desiring nationwide distribution will usually work through a number of different rep companies.

The Rep-Customer Relationship. Reps are the selling arm for the manufacturers that they represent—making contact with existing and potential customers, writing orders, following up the orders, and providing the link between manufacturer and the final industrial end-users. While paid by the

Table 10.4 / Profile of a Manufacturer's Representative

Company:	Alcon Company
Location:	Middle Village, N.Y.
End-User Market:	Bottling and Brewery Industry
Estimated Average Commission:	10–14 percent
Geographic Market Coverage:	New England States, New York, New Jersey, Pennsylvania, Maryland, Delaware, eastern Virginia
Products Handled:	Bottle filler replacement parts: conveyors, case packers, uncasers, warmers and reusers, empty bottle inspectors, plastic cases, packer girds, decappers
Companies Represented:	P. T. Barkmann & Sons, Hamrich Manufacturing, McQueen Technology Corp., Bacmis Volckening, Inc., Kyowa America Corp.

manufacturer, the rep is also an important figure for the customers served. Often, the efforts made by a rep during a customer emergency (e.g., an equipment failure) mean the difference between continuing or stopping production. Most reps are thoroughly experienced in the industries that they serve, and they can offer technical advice while enhancing the customer's leverage with suppliers in securing parts, and repair and delivery services. In addition, the rep provides customers with a continuing flow of information on innovations and trends in equipment applications, as well as in the overall industry.

Operate on a Commission Basis. Reps are paid a commission on all sales that they make, and the commission varies by industry and by the nature of the selling job. Table 10.5 provides a sample of average rep commission percentages for various industries in 1978. Note that commissions range from a low of 4.9 percent for rubber and plastics to 14.1 percent for the printing and publishing industry. Percentage commission compensation is very attractive to manufacturers because their sales costs are totally a variable expense. Reps are paid only when orders are generated—thus, avoiding the overhead costs associated with a firm's own direct sales force. Because reps are paid on a commission, they are motivated to generate high sales levels, another fact appreciated by the manufacturer.

Experience and an Expanding Role. Reps possess sophisticated product knowledge and typically have extensive experience in the markets to which they sell. Most reps develop their field experience while working as a salesperson for a manufacturer. The incentives to become a rep relate to the

Table 10.5 / Manufacturer's Representative's Commissions

Industry	Average 1978 Commissions
Automotive parts	9.5 percent
Chemicals	8.3
Containers and packaging material	7.3
Electrical materials	5.8
Electronics	10.5
Fabricated metals	6.8
Fabrics	12.5
Instruments	10.0
Machinery (heavy)	8.6
Machinery (light)	13.4
Printing and publishing	14.1
Rubber, plastics, leather	4.9
Tools and hardware	9.0

Source. "S&MM's 1979 Survey of Selling Costs," *Sales and Marketing Management* (February 26, 1979), p. 60.

desire to be independent combined with the substantial monetary rewards that are possible under a commission compensation arrangement. The number of reps appears to be growing. Based on trade association membership, the number of manufacturer's representatives has grown from 2000 members in 1970 to 5000 in 1978.[12]

When Reps Are Used

Large and Small Firms. Small- and medium-sized firms generally have the greatest need for a rep, although many large firms—for example, Dow Chemical and W. R. Grace—utilize reps. Why are reps so important for smaller firms? The reason is primarily economic: these firms could not justify the expense of maintaining their own sales force. The rep provides a very effective and efficient means to obtain total market coverage, with costs incurred only as sales are made. The quality of the selling job is often very good as a result of the rep's prior experience and market knowledge.

Limited Market Potential. The rep also plays a vital role in markets where the manufacturer's market potential is limited. A manufacturer may utilize a direct sales force in heavily concentrated industrial markets where the demand is sufficient to support the expenses associated with a direct sales force. However, less dense markets will be covered by reps. In this instance, because the rep carries several lines, expenses can be allocated over a much larger sales volume, thereby providing an economically viable alternative for the manufacturer.

Servicing Distributors. Reps may also be employed by a firm that markets through distributors. When a manufacturer sells through hundreds of distributors across the United States, reps may be employed to sell and service these distributor accounts. Here, the use of reps eliminates the need for a direct sales force whose sole function would be to contact and service distributors.

Reducing Overhead Costs. There are instances where the commission rate paid to reps exceeds the cost of a firm's own direct sales force, yet the supplier continues to utilize reps. This policy is not as irrational as it appears on the surface. Assume, for example, that costs for a direct sales force approximate 8 percent of sales, while a rep's commission rate is 11 percent. The use of reps in this case is often justified because of additional, hidden costs associated with a sales force. First, the manufacturer does not provide fringe benefits or a fixed salary to reps. Second, the costs of training a rep are usually limited to those required to provide product information. Thus, reps present an opportunity to eliminate rather significant overhead costs. Of course, the employment of reps in place of a direct sales force is not without pitfalls and problems.

Sources of Conflict

Degree of Effort. The employment of any middleman by a manufacturer involves a loss of *control* over the marketing of the product. Reps are independent businessmen and businesswomen with a line of products which they carry to satisfy their customers. Their allegiance is to their customers and to those products in their line that are most lucrative to them. Quite obviously, the overall sales effectiveness achieved through reps does not usually approximate that generated by a direct sales force. Thus, a constant source of friction between the manufacturer and the rep centers on the amount of attention the rep is devoting to the firm's product. Frequently the rep carries products that are easier to sell or involve a higher commission rate than a particular manufacturer's product. In such cases, the marketer will have little control over the rep's effort.

Commission Rate. The commission rate itself is a source of conflict between manufacturers and reps. In 1978, manufacturer's reps in the electronic field argued for an increase on the 5 percent commission paid on sales to distributors as a result of increased operating costs.[13] The commission rate is a critical issue because it influences the quality of the rep's performance. In the case of the electronic industry reps, the low commission rate to distributors influenced reps to accept small orders from end-users (higher commission rate) that should have been processed through distributors. The net result is that the small orders must be processed by the manufacturer, and these orders are extremely expensive. Thus, an increase in rep commissions for distributor sales would focus the rep's attention on serving distributors rather than soliciting small end-user orders.

Manufacturer's Attitudes. A final area of concern is the manufacturer's attitude toward the rep's function. Unfortunately, some firms will use a rep to develop a new territory, and as soon as sales volume is sufficient the territory is assigned to a direct salesperson. Such a policy does not develop long-term goodwill between a manufacturer and rep organizations. Although this situation may be inevitable, the long-term policy issues should be agreed upon in advance by the manufacturer and the rep. This dialogue strengthens the relationship between the parties and serves to reduce the level of uncertainty that often surrounds such channel arrangements.

As with distributor relationships, the manufacturer-rep association should be viewed as a partnership. Whatever the manufacturer can do to increase the effectiveness of reps will be reflected in the long-term sales and profits of the company. In some cases, the manufacturer may have to compromise on the commission rate issue and be willing to accept the level of sales effort the rep can devote to the firm's products. After all, the rep may be the only viable selling alternative available to the manufacturer.

Other Industrial Middlemen

The importance of distributors and reps far outshadows the other types of industrial intermediaries. Jobbers, brokers, and commission merchants each play a selected role in industrial channels and may be a vital cog in the distribution network for certain manufacturers.

Jobbers

Jobbers typically obtain orders from industrial customers and pass them along to the manufacturers that they represent. The distinguishing feature of jobbers is that they take title to the products that they sell but do not physically handle, stock, or deliver them. The jobber's niche in the industrial marketplace is in the marketing of products that are so bulky that additional handling would be prohibitively expensive and only add to the risk of damaging the product. Thus, jobbers function in markets dealing with products like coal, iron ore, lumber, and chemicals where bulk shipments in carload quantities do not necessitate any grouping and assorting by the middleman.

Commission Merchants

Commission merchants function in market situations dealing with bulk commodities—usually raw materials. Typically, these industrial middlemen do not operate on a permanent basis with their suppliers, rather they perform a one-time selling function. An industrial company involved in mining might ship its output to a large central market where buyers inspect the material before purchase. In this case, the commission merchant handles the product, making it available for inspection as well as performing the selling function. Although commission merchants do not take title, they can negotiate prices and execute the sale for the supplier. The primary services provided by commission merchants to sellers include: representation in the marketplace, physical handling of goods, and completion of a transaction.

Brokers

Brokers facilitate transactions between buyers and sellers by providing information on what is demanded and what is available. Similar to the commission merchant, the broker operates on a more-or-less irregular basis. A firm desiring to sell used machinery might employ a broker to seek out potential buyers and to complete negotiations leading to the eventual sale of the machinery. The party that engages the broker pays the commission. The broker's role is particularly important where product and market information is nonexistent or inadequate.

Summary

Industrial middlemen play a vital role in the success of the marketing strategies for many industrial products. A clear understanding of their functions, operating characteristics, and limitations is necessary to make effective decisions regarding the employment of these middlemen. Distributors and reps are the key middlemen in most industrial channels.

Distributors provide the full range of marketing services for their suppliers, although customer contact and product availability are the functions of particular value to industrial manufacturers. The trend in industrial distributors points to the growth of large distributors with multiple branch locations. Likewise, there is a trend toward growing specialization in distributor lines and toward the use of marketing techniques that were previously confined to consumer-goods marketing.

Reps specialize in the selling side of marketing—providing their suppliers with quality representation in the market and extensive product and market knowledge. The rep is not involved with the physical distribution aspects of marketing, leaving that burden to the manufacturers that they represent.

The relationship between the manufacturers and their middlemen often determines the success or failure of the marketing program, but conflict often surfaces in the relationship. The treatment of large accounts, the emphasis given to the supplier's products, and the termination of the relationship are often the major points of friction. An enlightened view of the channel—one of supplier-middleman partnership—is required for success. Brokers, commission merchants, and jobbers complete the group of industrial middlemen. These channel intermediaries are usually employed in special situations on an infrequent basis.

Comprehension of the industrial middleman's role in the industrial channel sets the stage for the development of industrial channel strategy. Chapter 11 will examine the channel design and management process.

Footnotes

[1]Denny Mosier and Richard Bombrick, "Distributors Evaluate Motorola Rep Network," *Electronic News* 22 (December 9, 1977), p. 26.

[2]P. H. Luckett, "Industrial Marketing Channels: Direct or Indirect?" in Bruce J. Walker and Joel B. Haynes, ed., *Marketing Channels and Institutions, Selected Readings* (Columbus, Ohio: Grid Publishing, Inc., 1978), p. 53.

[3]Robert J. Haas, *Industrial Marketing Management* (New York: Petrocelli/Charter Publishers, Inc., 1976), p. 141.

[4]Thayer C. Taylor, "A Line Turn for Timeplex," *Sales & Marketing Management* 117 (February 5, 1979), p. 5.

[5]"33rd Annual Survey of Distributor Operations," *Industrial Distribution* 69 (March 1979), p. 39.

[6]"Distributor Image: '79—How the Buyer Sees It," *Industrial Distribution* 69 (February 1979), p. 54.

[7]Frederick E. Webster, Jr., "The Role of the Industrial Distributor in Marketing Strategy," *Journal of Marketing* 40 (July 1976), p. 13.

[8]"Middlemen Are Out, Problem Solvers Are In," *Purchasing* 78 (September 13, 1978), p. 62.

[9]Webster, "Perceptions of the Industrial Distributor," *Industrial Marketing Management* 4 (1975), p. 260.

[10]"1978 Census of Industrial Distributors," *Industrial Distribution,* 68 (September 1978), p. 63.

[11]Webster, "Perceptions of the Industrial Distributor," p. 261.

[12]Loel Kuzela, "How to Work with a Manufacturer's Rep," *Industry Week* 197 (April 17, 1978), p. 40.

[13]James Alkon, "Reps Seek Higher Distribution Rates," *Electronic News* 24 (October 2, 1978), p. 74.

Discussion Questions

1. Explain how a direct channel of distribution may be the lowest cost channel alternative for one industrial marketer and the highest cost alternative for another marketer that competes in the same industry.

2. Why do some industrial firms find it necessary to put together a number of separate channels, utilizing direct distribution for some sectors of the market and indirect distribution for other sectors?

3. Compare and contrast the functions performed by industrial distributors versus manufacturer's representatives.

4. Since both industrial marketers and distributors are interested in achieving profit goals, why are manufacturer-distributor relationships characterized by conflict? What steps can the marketer take to reduce the level of conflict and, thus, improve channel performance?

5. What product/market factors lend themselves to the use of manufacturer's representatives by industrial firms?

6. Manufacturer's representatives often offer this complaint. "If I do an excellent job in building demand for the manufacturer's products in my market area, I will be replaced by a company salesperson. This umbrella of uncertainty makes it difficult for me to commit too much time to any one industrial firm." What steps can the industrial marketer take to remove this uncertainty and strengthen the relationship with reps?

7. Describe the functions performed by: (a) jobbers, (b) commission merchants, and (c) brokers in the industrial channel of distribution.

Chapter 11

Industrial Marketing Channels: Design and Management

Designing and managing the industrial channel is a challenging and ongoing task. The industrial marketer must insure that the firm's channel is properly aligned to respond to the needs of important market segments. Parallel attention must also be given to satisfying the needs of channel members, whose support is crucial to the success of industrial marketing strategy.

After reading this chapter, you will have an understanding of:

1. *the central components of the channel design process*
2. *managerial aids that can be employed in evaluating alternative channel structures*
3. *the key requirements for managing the existing channel*
4. *methods for monitoring channel performance.*

In the process of designing marketing strategy, the industrial marketing manager's primary objective is to maximize the chance that customers will respond favorably to the firm's product offerings. The way to maximize that opportunity is to effectively make contact with those buyers, insure that the product is readily available when needed, and effectively provide all the required services before and after the sale. The channel of distribution utilized by the industrial manufacturer is probably the single most important component to providing the services noted above. It is the industrial channel that creates the communication and physical supply linkages with existing and potential customers.

The channel component of industrial marketing strategy involves two related and important dimensions. First, a channel structure must be designed to accomplish desired marketing objectives. The design of a distribution channel includes a number of interesting challenges which involve specifying channel goals, evaluating constraints on the design, analyzing channel activities, and specifying channel alternatives. Each of these areas requires evaluation in designing the channel of distribution. Once the channel structure has been specified, the industrial marketer faces the requirement of managing the channel to achieve prescribed goals. To effectively administer channel activities, the manager must develop procedures for selecting middlemen, motivating them to achieve desired performance, mediating conflict among channel members, and evaluating performance.

A high priority must be placed on the design and management of industrial channels as a result of the pivotal role of channels in the overall scheme of industrial marketing. The purpose of this chapter is to provide a structure for designing and administering the industrial channel.

The Channel Design Process

Channel design is a dynamic process involving the development of new channels where none existed previously and the modification of existing channels.[1] In most cases, the industrial marketer deals with modification of existing channel structures. The development of new products and customer segments may require an entirely different channel structure from those currently utilized. Regardless of whether the manager is dealing with a new channel or modification of existing channels, channel design is an *active* rather than a *passive* task. Effective distribution channels do not simply evolve: they are developed by management action on the basis of a well-conceived plan which reflects overall marketing goals.

The channel design process is best conceptualized as a series of steps or stages that must be completed. In this manner, the industrial marketing manager is assured that all important channel dimensions have been evaluated during the design process. The channel design process includes the important steps shown in figure 11.1.

The end result of the channel design process is to specify the channel

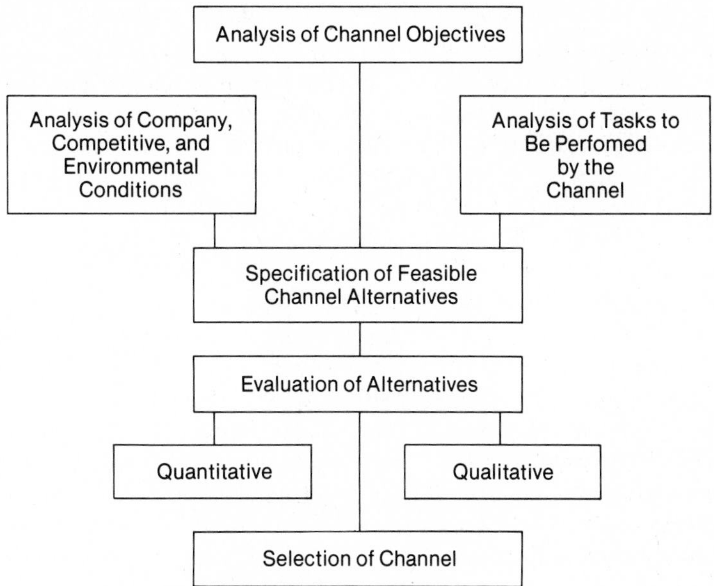

Figure 11.1 / The Channel Design Process

structure that will provide the highest probability of achieving the firm's objectives. Note that the process focuses on *channel structure* and not on individual channel participants. Channel structure refers to the underlying framework of the channel: the number of middlemen, the number of channel levels, the types of middlemen, and the linkages between channel members. Selection of individual middlemen also constitutes an important aspect of channel management and will be examined later in the chapter.

Stage 1. Channel Objectives

Industrial firms formulate their marketing strategies to appeal to selected market segments, to earn targeted levels of profits, to maintain or increase sales and market share growth rates, and to achieve these goals within specified resource constraints. In addition, each element of the marketing strategy is designed with a specific purpose in mind. Thus, the initial phase of channel design is to fully comprehend these marketing goals and formulate a set of channel objectives based on them. The objective formulation phase is required whether the industrial marketer is designing a totally new channel or redesigning an existing one.

Structure Based on Profits and Strategy Integration. Profit considerations and asset utilization must be reflected in channel objectives and the resultant design. For example, the costs of maintaining a salesperson in the field, including lodging, meals, and auto rental expense, increased by 71 percent from 1971 to 1978, and averaged $423 per week for 1978.[2] For the manufacturer, these costs are somewhat "fixed," at least in the short run. Working capital committed to these "semi-fixed" costs might be eliminated by switching from a direct sales force to manufacturer's reps, whose compensation is totally variable (a certain percentage of sales). Of course, many other factors, such as quality of the selling job, must also be evaluated. Likewise, channel structure must be compatible with all marketing strategy elements.

Channel Objectives Reflect Marketing Goals. Specific distribution objectives are established on the basis of the broad marketing objectives. Distribution objectives prescribe the role of the marketing channel in accomplishing the overall marketing goals. Thus, distribution objectives act as guidelines which force the manager to relate channel design decisions to broader marketing goals. A manufacturer of industrial cleaning products might have a distribution objective to "provide product availability in every county in the Midwest with over $5 million in market potential." In turn, a supplier of air conditioning units might follow this distribution objective: "to make contact with industrial plant architects once every month and industrial contractors once every two months."

In each case, the distribution objective reflects fundamental marketing goals and provides guidance on what the channel structure must accomplish. In summary, marketing and distribution objectives guide the channel design process and actually limit the range of feasible channel structures. However, before the alternative channel structures can be evaluated, the industrial marketing manager must evaluate several additional factors that also limit and constrain the choice of channel structures.

Stage 2. Channel Design Constraints

Frequently, the manager has very little flexibility in the selection of channel structures because of a variety of trade, competitive, company, and environmental factors. In fact, the decision on channel design may be *imposed* on the manager as a result of these conditions. The variety of such constraining factors is almost limitless.[3] Figure 11.2 provides a summary of those factors most relevant to the industrial marketer.

Stage 3. Pervasive Channel Tasks

Clearly, each alternative channel structure will be evaluated on the basis of its ability to effectively and efficiently perform the required channel activities. The conception of a channel as a sequence of activities to be performed, rather than as a set of channel institutions, is essential to the channel design process. Such a perspective focuses the industrial marketing manager's attention on creatively structuring the necessary tasks to meet

Figure 11.2 / Factors Limiting Industrial Channel Choice

1. *Availability of Good Middlemen*
   Competitors often "lock-up" the better middlemen
   Established middlemen not always receptive to new products
2. *Traditional Channel Patterns*
   Established patterns of distribution are difficult to violate
   Large customers may demand direct sales
3. *Product Characteristics*
   Technical complexity dictates direct distribution
   Extensive repair requirements may call for local distributors to service the product line
4. *Company Financial Resources*
   Capital requirements often preclude direct distribution
5. *Competitive Strategies*
   Direct service by competitors may force all firms to sell direct
6. *Geographic Dispersion of Customers*
   A widely dispersed market of small customers often requires low-cost representation afforded by middlemen

customer requirements and company goals rather than being overly committed to existing channel structures or traditional distribution patterns.

As an example, manufacturer's reps typically carry no inventory of their supplier's products as they are generally restricted to the process of selling. A manufacturer of semiconductors and microcircuits, upon a careful analysis of required channel activities, may decide that—although reps can provide the level of sales service needed—large accounts require local inventory availability of a few selected microcircuits for emergency situations. The solution in this case would not be to abandon the rep as a viable channel, but to negotiate a compensation scheme that would perhaps induce the rep to carry the limited inventory of the emergency circuits. Thus, the analysis of required tasks and the view of the channel as a sequence of activities would lead the firm to a creative and effective solution to the channel problem.

The backbone of the channel design process rests with the careful analysis of objectives, constraints, and channel activities. With each of these aspects clearly delineated, channel alternatives can be evaluated.

Stage 4. Channel Alternatives

Four primary issues must be evaluated in regard to the specification of channel alternatives. These issues include:

1. the number of steps or levels to be included in the channel (i.e., the degree of "directness");
2. the number of channel intermediaries to employ in each level of the channel;
3. the types of intermediaries to employ;
4. the number of distinct channels to be employed.

Each of these issues will now be considered, with the understanding that the decisions made for each are predicated upon the objectives, constraints, and activities previously specified in the analysis.

Degree of "Directness." Industrial channels may range from *one-step* distribution, in which the manufacturer sells direct to the industrial customer, to elaborate systems which involve various levels of different types of industrial middlemen. *Level,* in the channel context, refers to each separate type of marketing institution employed by the manufacturer to successfully bring about a sale and deliver product to the customer. A multilevel industrial channel might include a manufacturer, sales rep, distributor, and the customer. This type of channel structure prevails for a product like abrasives where as many as 1000 general line distributors might be needed to secure adequate market coverage and product availability for the industrial marketer. The reps would be utilized to sell to distributor accounts and to coordinate relations between manufacturer and distributors.

There is a greater tendency in industrial marketing to sell directly to the customer than exists in consumer-goods marketing. However, there are many situations where direct selling is not feasible. For products such as tools, abrasives, fasteners, pipes, valves, materials handling equipment, and wire rope, as much as 97 percent of the annual volume moves only through industrial distributors.[4] Clearly, these products are typically bought repetitively (straight rebuy), frequently, and in small quantities. Wide and instantaneous availability is fundamental to the effective marketing of these products. Industrial distributors efficiently provide these functions.

The decision on the number of channel levels depends on a host of company, product, and market variables. Gary Lilien reports the results of a study aimed at developing an understanding of marketing mix decisions for industrial products.[5] Table 11.1 displays the results of the study in terms of the channel component of the marketing mix. Analysis of these variables for an individual firm provides the industrial marketing manager with valuable insights to the feasibility of direct distribution.

The Number of Middlemen. The question to be answered in terms of the number of middlemen is: how many middlemen of each type are required to effectively cover a particular market area? In certain situations, the question is easy to answer—for example, when a firm distributes through reps. Since reps act as the firm's sales force, there would be no point to using more than one rep to call on a specific customer. (Unless, of course, each rep specialized in a different part of the company's product line.) Thus, the number of reps is determined by the geographic territory covered by the rep's organization. The industrial marketer would select the best rep organization in each of the geographical areas to be covered.

In the case of distribution through industrial distributors, the company may require two, three, or even more carefully selected distributors in a geographic market to ensure adequate market coverage.[6] The policy of care-

Table 11.1 / Factors Determining the Feasibility of Direct Distribution

1. *Size of Firm*

   The size of the firm is the most important variable associated with direct distribution. As firms grow larger, they are better able to support a company-owned distribution channel.
2. *Size of Average Order*

   Direct distribution is more economical (ratio of sales costs to sales volume) with larger orders.
3. *Technical-Purchase Complexity*

   The greater the degree of analysis required by the buyer prior to purchase and the greater the importance of technical service in the purchase decision, the greater the likelihood of direct distribution.
4. *Stage in Product Life Cycle*

   As a product moves from growth to maturity, direct distribution is more appropriate.
5. *Degree of Standardization*

   Products that are complex, unique and made-to-order are more frequently sold through direct means.
6. *Purchase Frequency*

   As a product becomes more of a commonly purchased item, it becomes advantageous to sell through distributors.

Source. Reprinted by permission from Gary L. Lilien, "Advisor 2: Modeling the Marketing Mix Decision for Industrial Products," *Management Science* 25 (February 1979), pp. 190–99. Copyright 1979, The Institute of Management Sciences.

fully evaluating and choosing channel members in a particular geographical area is referred to as *selective distribution.* The nature of the product and the purchasing process usually dictate a selective policy. Products like materials handling equipment, electric motors, power transmission equipment, and tools typically fall into the category of straight or modified rebuy situations. The time spent in evaluating sources for these products is not great, yet it is not always a simple repetitive purchase either. The buyer needs some advice about applications, maintenance, and repair, and the buyer usually demands rapid product delivery, repair, and service. Thus, the manufacturer wants to be represented by a distributor organization that can satisfy these customer requirements. To ensure that distributors will perform the job required and provide proper emphasis to the manufacturer's line, the number of distributors will be limited to a select few in a given market.

Generally, the more standardized the products, the more frequently that they are purchased; and the smaller their unit value, the greater will be the number of distributors in a given market. Recall the earlier example where an abrasives manufacturer might require up to 1000 general-line distributors. Here the firm is following an *intensive* rather than a selective distribution policy. An intensive distribution policy is especially appropriate when availability is a key requirement of organizational buyers. Customers must be able to readily secure the product from a source in close proximity to their plants.[7]

As this discussion has indicated, the number of middlemen to employ depends on the types of middlemen to be included in the channel. The decision to use a particular type of channel institution must also be examined.

Type of Middlemen. A particular type of middleman is selected on the basis of the tasks or activities that they perform. Middlemen may be classified in the following ways:

1. whether they take title;
2. whether they take physical possession;
3. the type of products they sell;
4. the breadth of product line;
5. the markets they serve.

Although the various middlemen types were discussed in depth in chapter 10, a brief review of middlemen and the activities that they perform will be useful here to understand the nature of the decision to be made. *Industrial distributors* take title, hold inventory, and usually perform the full range of marketing tasks. One step removed from the distributor are *jobbers,* who may or may not take possession, although they do take title to goods that they sell. *Manufacturer's agents,* or *reps,* usually do not take title or possession of the goods that they sell, but handle the selling job for a limited number of suppliers.

The decision process regarding the levels, number, and types of middlemen often suggests that more than one channel structure will be needed to satisfy all target markets. The company must carefully evaluate alternate structures to reach all segments.

The number of distinct channels is important to determine. The primary reason for utilizing more than one distribution channel for the same product is that different market segments require different channel structures. An important segment characteristic in this regard is the size of prospective accounts. Recall the example cited in chapter 10 regarding Motorola: the company works through three distinct channels. Large accounts are called on by the firm's own sales force, distributors handle small repeat orders, and manufacturer's reps were added to the firm's network to develop the market made up of medium-sized firms. In addition to the size of accounts, differences in purchase behavior may also dictate the need for more than one channel system. If a firm produces a wide line of industrial products, some of these may require high caliber selling efforts to a multitude of buying influences within the potential buyer's firm. In this case, the firm's own sales force would focus on the more complex buying situations, while distributors sell and deliver standardized products from local stocks.

Companies seeking to expand marketing efforts to new customers or different geographic areas frequently need to use more than one channel. A midwestern supplier of cranes and other handling equipment, whose sales force operates only east of the Mississippi River, would be likely to use reps to initially expand its marketing efforts to the western sections of the United States.

The maintenance of more than one channel is not without problems. There is the potential that some accounts will be double-covered, or that the different channel members will find themselves competing for business among a significant number of accounts. As indicated earlier, industrial marketers often want to reserve large accounts for their own sales force. However, it is a violation of the Sherman Act for a manufacturer to restrict the territory of distributors when those distributors take title to the goods.[8] Thus, industrial marketers cannot prevent distributors from calling on large accounts, although they can try to reach an acceptable agreement with distributors on general channel policy on the treatment of large accounts. Distributors may even force a manufacturer to distribute through them. In a recent case, the courts ruled that a supplier could not refuse to sell to a qualified distributor, even though the supplier had an acceptable exclusive agreement with another distributor. The manufacturer is not so confined in dealings with reps because reps do not take title to the products. This gives the manufacturer the right to impose territorial restrictions.[9] As this discussion suggests, a dual channel policy may be dictated by customer and market conditions, but its implementation can be fraught with considerable behavioral and legal difficulties.

To recap, the careful analysis of company objectives, channel goals, design constraints, and required channel tasks and activities are the basic input to the evaluation of industrial channel structure alternatives. An almost endless number of channel alternatives are possible in terms of channel levels, number of middlemen, types of middlemen, and the number of distinct channel systems. Obviously, company objectives, financial commitments, middlemen availability, and the channel tasks required will eliminate many of the possible alternative channel structures. In addition, most channel design decisions are of the channel modification variety—where the structure is to be slightly altered, rather than totally redesigned. Here the feasible alternatives are much more limited in scope. The task now before the industrial marketing manager is to select the most efficient and effective channel structure from among the feasible set of alternatives.

Stage 5. Channel Selection

Most channel design decisions center on slight modifications in the channel structure, for example, in response to changing markets, expanding geographic coverage, new customer requirements, and new product developments. In these cases, selection of the appropriate modification in channel structure might be rather straightforward. In fact, the range of choice may be quite limited.

Complex Channel Selection Decisions. The total redesign of an existing channel system or the initiation of a totally new company or channel system generally requires a more thorough analysis of the possible channel alternatives. There are usually more alternatives to consider, and the number of influencing variables is quite extensive. Although the manager seeks to design the "optimal channel" in terms of maximum long-run profit, such results are nearly impossible to achieve. Why?

First, the cost and revenue data necessary to make such a decision may not be available. So many factors influence the channel decision that it is often impossible to assess their future impact on channel costs and revenues. Second, channels exist in a dynamic setting, while the design decision is made at a point in time. Thus, the optimal channel today may not be optimal in five years or even in one year. This accounts for the point made earlier that channel design is a continuing process rather than a one-time decision. Lastly, the chance of effectively specifying all the relevant channel alternatives is slim.

Techniques for Evaluating Alternative Channels

Recognizing these constraints, the industrial marketer must approach the channel structure decision systematically in an attempt to come as close as possible to achieving the optimal channel structure. A number of approaches are available for structuring the process of selecting the best channel system. We will examine two of the approaches which have relevance to industrial channels: (1) the weighted factor approach and (2) cost/revenue approaches.

Weighted Factor Approach

The essence of this approach is to utilize the analysis of company objectives, distribution tasks, and constraints to evaluate each alternative channel structure.[10] An example of this approach is displayed in table 11.2. In this case, a manufacturer of materials handling equipment seeks to expand distribution to the New England states. Prior analysis reveals the following variables to be important:

1. higher level personal selling;
2. maintenance of local repair and spare parts inventories;
3. intensive market coverage;
4. control of marketing tactics by the manufacturer;
5. relatively low selling costs;
6. knowledge of user/customer requirements;
7. low investment by the manufacturer.

The feasible alternatives include selling through distributors versus manufacturer's reps.

The weighted factor approach, illustrated in table 11.2, involves five steps. First, the factors that are important in achieving channel objectives are defined. Observe the seven factors that were identified by management

Table 11.2 / Weighted Factor Method of Channel Selection

Factor (1)	Factor Weight (2)	Factor Score* .0	.1	.2	.3	.4	.5 (3)	.6	.7	.8	.9	1.0	Distributor Rating (x) (2 × 3)	Rep Rating (y) (2 × 3)
1. Selling Ability	0.10				x						y		0.03	0.09
2. Inventory	0.15	y									x		0.135	0.00
3. Market Coverage	0.20							y			x		0.18	0.12
4. Control	0.05		x					y					0.005	0.03
5. Selling Costs	0.05							x				y	0.03	0.05
6. Customer Knowledge	0.25							x		y			0.15	0.20
7. Investment	0.20	y								x			0.16	0.00
	1.00											Total Score =	0.690	0.490

*x = Distributor's Rating
y = Rep's Rating

as being important in the channel selection decision. Second, each of these factors is assigned a weight to reflect its relative importance. (The sum of these factor weights should always equal 1.0.) Third, each factor is rated on a 0.0 to 1.0 scale for each channel alternative. To illustrate, distributors were assigned a factor score of 0.3 for the *selling ability* factor, and reps received a score of 0.9. Fourth, each factor weight is multiplied by each factor score. For example, distributors achieve a score for *selling ability* of 0.03 (0.10 × 0.3); reps = 0.09 (.10 × 0.9). Fifth, a total composite score for each channel alternative is calculated by summing the individual scores.

Table 11.2 indicates that the distributor alternative achieved the higher score and, in the absence of other data, should be selected. Distributors scored higher than the reps for two primary reasons: (1) superiority in maintaining inventory and (2) lower relative investment requirements. If more than two alternatives were under consideration, this approach would allow management to compare them all on the basis of a quantitative ranking.

The advantage of the weighted factor approach is that it forces management to consider explicitly the important variables in the channel decision and to evaluate quantitatively each alternative on the basis of these variables. Of course, there are limitations to the approach. The results are only as good as management's estimate of the relative importance of channel variables and of each alternative's likely performance on each variable. In addition, the approach provides no estimate of profit or risk associated with each alternative. An approach that evaluates expected costs and revenues associated with each channel alternative may be necessary in its own right or to complement the weighted factor method.

Cost/Revenue Approaches

Cost/revenue approaches focus on evaluating the profit and return on investment dimensions associated with the channel alternatives. Again, it must be reiterated that estimating future channel costs and revenues is tenuous at best. A recent study on the use of cost data in channel management decisions revealed that most internal cost information necessary for analysis was available from a firm's accounting system; however, the information was not generally available to managers making channel decisions.[11] This study also indicates that the contribution of individual channel members to corporate profitability is often not considered by marketing managers. Thus, systems for gathering extensive internal and external channel cost and revenue data will be required for management to effectively evaluate the profit and return-on-investment (ROI) consequences of channel alternatives.

A Capital Budgeting Approach

Eugene Lambert suggests a capital budgeting approach to channel evaluation.[12] To implement this approach, the industrial marketing manager evaluates the stream of earnings and investment requirements for each channel alternative under consideration. In this way, the ROI of each channel alternative could be compared to the firm's cost of capital. By comparing the ROI of various channel options to the expected returns that might accrue to other company projects, the firm can isolate the most profitable venture. For example, a firm might decide that funds saved by using intermediaries rather than a direct sales force could be more profitably invested in a new product.

The value of Lambert's approach is that it focuses management attention on important channel financial dimensions, such as capital investment requirements, future earning streams, and estimated future cost streams. Unfortunately, the approach is severely constrained by the state-of-the-art in forecasting investment requirements and future revenue/cost streams for something as dynamic as a distribution channel.

This discussion has centered on two approaches to evaluating channel structure alternatives, the weighted point method and the capital budgeting approach, but a range of other quantitative methods can also aid decision making. To illustrate, when data and cost requirements are met, computer simulations can be applied to distribution planning.[13]

Qualitative Dimensions

Besides the formal approaches to evaluating channel alternatives, the channel decision maker must consider a variety of qualitative factors. *Control* is a prominent dimension in channel choice. Given two channels with nearly similar economic performance, the critical factor may be the degree of control that the industrial marketer can exercise over the channels. In this regard, a rep channel, as opposed to a distributor channel, generally gives the manager a higher level of control because the manufacturer maintains title and possession of the goods when reps are used. In some cases, the manufacturer may be willing to trade off short-run economic benefits to gain long-term control over channel activities.

Adaptation by channel members may assume importance in the long run. Small, undercapitalized distributors may not be able to respond effectively to new competitive thrusts or to problems caused by economic downturns. If the manufacturer decides that distributors are incapable of adapting to changing situations, the viable solutions are to sell direct or use reps and provide product availability through a system of public warehouses.

There are, of course, many factors to be analyzed besides cost, revenue, control, and adaptation in the evaluation of channel alternatives. Such factors as middleman *image, financial capacity, sales,* and *merchandising ability* are only a few of the additional factors. Now that the channel design process has been analyzed, attention turns to the day-to-day administration of the channel.

Channel Administration

Channel administration is concerned with the procedures necessary to make the channel structure work effectively and efficiently. Once a particular industrial channel structure is selected, specific channel participants must be selected, and appropriate arrangements made to ensure that all obligations are unilaterally established. Next, channel members must be motivated to perform the necessary tasks to achieve channel objectives. Third, steps must be taken to ensure that conflict within the channel is properly controlled. Lastly, devices must be created for controlling and evaluating channel performance. Channel member selection is the first consideration.

Selection of Middlemen

Why is the selection of specific channel members considered part of channel management rather than an aspect of channel design? The primary reason is that middleman selection is an ongoing process—some middlemen choose to leave the channel and others are terminated by the supplier. Thus, selection of middlemen takes place on a more or less continuous basis. In addition, the performance of individual channel members should be evaluated continuously. The manufacturer should be prepared to quickly replace poor performers with potentially better ones. Thus, including the selection process in the domain of ongoing channel management is a matter of putting the process in its proper perspective.

Selection Criteria. Channel objectives and the tasks to be accomplished by the distribution channel provide the general guidelines for selecting individual middlemen. Although some firms find it impossible to reduce the selection of middlemen to a rigid procedure, some means for objectively comparing potential channel members is required. Ideally, the industrial marketing manager wants to examine objective factors concerning the channel situation and sensibly temper evaluations of these factors with personal impressions, opinions, and judgment.

Because all firms do not have the same channel objective or activities to be performed, there is no single set of criteria that have universal application. Each industrial marketer will have to develop criteria that are relevant to the firm's product/market situation. Many companies develop checklists as an aid in comparing prospective distributors or reps on a common basis. The form used by the McGraw-Edison Company is shown in figure 11.3. Note the criteria that McGraw-Edison feels are important: market coverage, product lines, personnel, growth, and financial standings.

Securing Good Middlemen. The marketer can identify prospective middlemen through discussions with company salespersons and existing or potential customers. Likewise, candidates can be identified through trade sources, such as *Industrial Distribution* magazine or the *Verified Directory of Manufacturer's Representatives*. Once the list of potential middlemen is reduced

LINE MATERIALS INDUSTRIES
A Division of MC GRAW-EDISON COMPANY

Distributor Evaluation Form

In any business arrangement, the parties must know each other well. We have told you all about ourselves and would, in return, like to know about you. Please furnish the requested information so we can judge each other on an equal basis. Thank you.

Company Name ____________________
Address ____________________
City and State ____________________
Telephone Number ____________________

1. Geographic and Market Coverage
   a. What is present geographic coverage (list counties)? ____________________
   b. Is geographic expansion planned in near future? Yes _____ No _____.
      If yes, please list additional counties to be covered. ____________________
   c. What is present market coverage and how frequently are calls made in these markets?

MARKET	CALL FREQUENCY	APPROXIMATE SALES VOLUME – DOLLARS

2. Present Product Lines
   What major product lines (competitive as well as compatible) are presently handled?

PRODUCT OR PRODUCT LINE	MANUFACTURER

3. Products and Markets – Historical Performance
   a. What, if any, major products were previously carried, but have been dropped? Why?

PRODUCT LINE	WHY DISCONTINUED?

   b. What markets, if any, were covered, but are no longer contacted? Why?

MARKET	REASON

4. Personnel
   Total number of employees? ____________________
   Number of inside sales personnel? ____________________
   Number of outside salesmen? ____________________

   Do you have a lighting engineer? Yes _____ No _____.
   Do you have technically trained employees familiar with electrical power apparatus? Yes _____ No _____.
   If yes, how many? _____

5. Financial Information
   a. Sales volume last year? ____________________
   b. Sales volume this year to date? ____________________
   c. Financial Statements: Please attach balance sheets and profit and loss statements for past two years. In addition, please include any information showing financial soundness and growth that you desire.
   d. Comments: ____________________

6. Current Dun & Bradstreet rating? ____________________

7. Growth Outlook
   a. What are your plans for future growth? ____________________
   b. Do you plan any building expansions in the near future? Yes _____ No _____. If yes, please indicate plans.
   ____

8. Do you feel that the addition of L-M products will appreciably increase your sales volume? Yes _____.
   No _____. If yes, what annual sales increase would you feel acceptable? $ _____

9. Additional Comments: ____________________

Signed ____________________
Title ____________________
Date ____________________

Figure 11.3 / Distribution Evaluation Form

Source. Roger Pegram, *Selecting and Evaluating Distributors,* Business Policy Study No. 116 (New York: The National Industrial Conference Board, 1965), p. 51. Reprinted by permission of The Conference Board.

to a select group, the manufacturer will proceed to evaluate the prospective middlemen on the basis of the selection criteria.

The formation of the channel is not at all a one-way street. The manufacturer now must provide the proper inducements to convince the middlemen to become part of the firm's channel system. Some distributors evaluate potential suppliers just as rigorously, and on many of the same dimensions, as the manufacturer rates them. Manufacturers often must demonstrate the sales and profit potential associated with their product and be willing to grant the middleman a degree of territorial exclusivity for their products. Massey-Ferguson, a large industrial equipment concern, provides prospective distributors with a six-page analysis of the distributor's potential sales and profit opportunities, personnel requirements, estimated expenses, market potentials by product and market, and the estimated operating expenses.[14]

Motivating Channel Members

Distributors and reps are independent and profit-oriented. Their general orientation is toward their customers and the means necessary to satisfy customer needs for industrial products and services. Their perceptions and outlook may be at substantial variance from those of the manufacturers that they represent. As a consequence, marketing strategies can fail because managers at the manufacturer's level do not tailor their programs to the capabilities and orientation of their middlemen.[15] A prerequisite for the marketer's effective management of the industrial channel is to understand the middleman's perspective and devise methods for motivating the middleman to perform in ways which enhance the manufacturer's long-term success. The manufacturer will be continually involved in seeking support from the middleman, and the quality of that support will depend on the nature of the motivational techniques employed.

A Partnership. Designing channel member motivational techniques begins with the understanding that the channel relationship is one of *partnership*. Manufacturers and middlemen are in business together, and whatever expertise and assistance the manufacturer can provide to the middlemen will be a step toward improving total channel effectiveness. Some industrial firms formally recognize the partnership concept in specially prepared documents that they distribute to channel members. Figure 11.4 shows a "Statement of Policy" of Rustoleum. The statement is provided to prospective distributors and is intended to outline the nature of their partnership. The more effective techniques for motivating industrial channel members and operationalizing the partnership concept are examined below.

Management Aids. Manufacturers often possess the size and skill to develop sophisticated management techniques. Sound business practices in the areas of purchasing, inventory, order processing, and the like can be developed and provided to channel members. The Norton Company, an industrial abrasives manufacturer, provides a cost accounting and profitability measurement system for their suppliers, many of whom have adopted it.[16]

Dealer Advisory Councils. Distributors or reps may be brought together with management personnel of the manufacturer on a periodic basis to review distribution policies. Middlemen are able to voice their opinions on various policy matters and are brought directly into the decision-making process regarding channel operations. To be effective, dealer councils must be

RUST-OLEUM STATEMENT

We're in Business Together . . .

Just as you and your organization follow a creed in your business, so we at Rust-Oleum follow ours. We call it doing business by the Golden Rule . . . doing business together with sincerity, honesty, and cooperation.

We Are Mindful . . .

. . . that the Rust-Oleum distributor has played a major role in the successful introduction and growing sales of Rust-Oleum coatings. Down through the years, as we have continued to expand our facilities to meet the demand, we have become increasingly aware of the many and varied contributions made by Rust-Oleum distributors—contributions that are vital to our mutual success.

. . . that the Rust-Oleum distributor has provided local warehousing, invested in the stock necessary for effective service. Distributor salesmen have effectively pioneered Rust-Oleum, introducing it—demonstrating it—to their prized customers. Distributors have supplied the credit necessary to broad coverage selling.

. . . that Rust-Oleum's suggested resale prices have been well observed, to protect the profit structure necessary for effective distributor services, and to provide everyone a fair reward for stock investment and specialized sales effort.

. . . that the Rust-Oleum distributor has lent the prestige and acceptance of his firm name, imprinted on Rust-Oleum advertising and direct mail, sent to thousands of carefully selected accounts. Distributors have presented the Rust-Oleum line in their individually sponsored trade shows, carrying the customer benefits of Rust-Oleum still deeper into their markets.

. . . that these and the many other contributions of our distributors have been of inestimable value in the sound and continuous growth of the Rust-Oleum Corporation.

We Are Resolved . . .

. . . that we shall sell through the distributor, not just to him.

. . . that Rust-Oleum distributors shall be selectively limited to the fewest possible number needed to provide effective coverage of each market.

. . . that constant consideration be given to the distributor's costs of doing business, with profit margins planned accordingly.

. . . that no Rust-Oleum products for industry, farm or home be sold direct, irrespective of the purchaser's size or buying power.

. . . that Rust-Oleum shall provide well-trained and cooperative factory representatives, indoctrinated in this sales philosophy.

. . . that communications between Rust-Oleum management and distributor management be frank, constructive and objective.

. . . that complete stocks of all standard Rust-Oleum products be kept in factory stocks for immediate shipment.

. . . that catalogs, application data, sales help, and direct mail be carefully developed and regularly furnished to distributors.

. . . that Rust-Oleum industrial advertising shall feature the benefits of "buying through your industrial distributor."

. . . that we shall seek to win the distributor's friendship, as well as his effective sales performance.

Figure 11.4 / The Supplier-Distributor Partnership

Source. Roger Pegram, *Selecting and Evaluating Distributors,* Business Policy Study No. 116 (The National Industrial Conference Board, 1965), p. 98. Reprinted by permission of The Conference Board.

formed with the purpose of providing meaningful input to channel policy decisions.

Margins and Commissions. In the final analysis, the primary motivating device will be the compensation that the middlemen receive for their selling efforts. The surest way to lose middleman support is to develop compensation policies which do not meet industry and competitive standards. Reps or distributors that feel cheated on commissions or margins will focus their selling attention on those products that generate the highest profit. The manufacturer must stay attuned to the prevailing compensation rates in the industry and be willing to adjust its rates as conditions change. The recent inflation in travel, lodging, and entertainment expenses have forced many reps and distributors to seek higher commissions and margins. Although such increases are painful to the manufacturer, if rates are not adjusted fairly, suppliers can expect to witness a marked reduction in the sales efforts given to their products.

The compensation provided to middlemen should reflect the nature of the marketing tasks performed. If the manufacturer desires that special attention be given to a new industrial product, then most reps will require higher commission rates. Conversely, requiring distributors to hold excess inventories in selected product lines will entail higher gross margins for those items. Ingersol-Rand's program for pneumatic tools provides distributors with an extra 10 percent discount if they maintain inventory at one-third of the dollar volume of their previous year's sales of I-R products.[17] Thus, compensation must always be geared to the objectives to be achieved by the channel participants.

Market Protection. Most middlemen want some form of territorial protection from excessive competition among distributors of a supplier's product. Often, selective distribution will benefit both the manufacturer and the distributors. The manufacturer receives loyal commitment from the distributor, and the distributor enjoys limited product competition and a relatively large market potential.

Additionally, a wide array of other tools may be used to motivate industrial channel members. However, the success of the motivational program hinges on the overall quality of the firm's channel strategy *and* management's attitude toward channel members. An attitude of assistance, cooperation, and partnership is foremost; this attitude should be reinforced by a well-conceived plan that provides support, training, and communication to the channel participants.

Conflict: The Need for Interorganizational Management

The very nature of the distribution channel—where each member is dependent upon another member for the successful realization of goals—provides the seeds for conflict among the members. Although channel members realize the need for cooperation, individual members seek to maximize their autonomy and, hence, their individual profitability.[18] *Channel conflict* is a situation in which one channel member (A) perceives another channel member (B) to be engaged in behavior that is preventing or impeding A from achieving important goals.[19] The opportunities for conflict in industrial channels are limitless—a manufacturer's refusal to increase reps' commissions, a distributor's refusal to maintain required inventory levels, a manufacturer's insistence on a nonexclusive distribution policy, and so on. Thus, because channel participants have different goals, different perceptions of their roles in the channel and different evaluations of their spheres of influence, tensions develop between them, which may cause them to perform in ways which damage the performance of the channel.[20] The industrial marketer must focus on managing conflict by employing interorganizational management approaches.[21] Interorganizational management seeks to improve overall channel performance through a careful coordination of the relationships among the organizations that comprise the channel.

Does Conflict Exist? Quite frequently, managers do not realize a conflict situation exists until after the fact—at which time it may be too late to respond to the causes. Clearly, a device is needed to recognize a potential conflict situation before it occurs. Surveys of distributors and reps at periodic intervals can uncover potential conflict areas by evaluating their perceptions of the basic workings of the channel. Open communication between the company's sales force and channel members is an informal method for assessing potential conflict areas. Whether following a formal or an informal approach, the key factor is that management must be alert to present or emerging areas of conflict.

Reducing Conflict. Larry Rosenberg suggests three interorganizational approaches for dealing with conflict.

1. A *channel-wide committee* could be established to periodically evaluate emerging problems related to conflict. This provides a forum which considers the diverse viewpoints of the various channel members.
2. *Joint-goal setting* by the committee (or an advisory council) can help mitigate the effects of conflict. Although a consensus on goals may not always be possible, the attendant dialogue is beneficial in reducing conflict.
3. A *distribution executive* position could be established in each major organization in the channel to coordinate internal and external issues that often start conflict in the channel.[22]

The industrial marketer can draw upon these approaches in establishing a distribution council.

The results of conflict management are improved channel performance and enhanced channel solidarity.[23] In some cases, the reduction of conflict may be the only means of preserving the channel system. The discussion will now turn to the final aspect of channel management—evaluation.

Evaluating Channel Performance

An essential aspect of the channel management process is the evaluation of middleman performance on the basis of the manufacturer's channel objectives. The extent and frequency of performance evaluation depends to a great degree on the scope of the firm's channel, the power of the manufacturer, the relative importance of middlemen, and the type of product. Firms selling through thousands of distributors could not afford the time or expense of frequent, comprehensive distributor reviews. The manufacturer with extensive market power and a sought-after product can usually demand detailed information on the performance of channel members. By the same token, firms that depend on middlemen for only a small portion of their total volume would have little need for frequent and comprehensive evaluation. Firms producing repetitively purchased, low unit-value industrial products generally require limited evaluation. Each situation will differ, and the nature of the review and evaluation process will be expanded or contracted on the basis of the above factors.

Criteria

The specific criteria used to evaluate distributor and rep performance should be similar to those used in selecting the middlemen. The criteria must center on the channel objectives specified by the manufacturer. Although the types of evaluative criteria are vast, there are a number of factors that have broad applications. Possible criteria include total sales compared to market potential, inventory turnover rate, selling ability (e.g., new accounts developed), financial performance, and end user/customer evaluation.

Taking Action

The industrial marketing manager must now make the evaluation data actionable, that is, use it to make adjustments in channel operations. As a result of this performance evaluation, some intermediaries may be terminated and replaced by stronger ones. In other cases, corrective steps will be taken to improve performance in weak areas. Importantly, the performance evaluation also provides the opportunity for the industrial marketer to identify excellent channel members. Such performance should be reinforced.

On occasion, the annual evaluation may even suggest that a change in channel structure is required. Reps may be replaced by a direct sales force in areas where potential appears to be far outstripping sales. Thus, middleman performance evaluation enables the manufacturer to continually adjust the channel to changing market conditions.

Summary

Industrial channel strategy is an exciting and challenging aspect of industrial marketing. The challenge comes from the numerous alternatives available to the manufacturer in distributing industrial products. The channel area is exciting because markets, user needs, and competitors are always changing—requiring the industrial marketer to be continually attuned to the dynamics involved.

Channel strategy concerns two primary management tasks: designing the overall channel structure and managing the operation of the channel. The channel design process includes the evaluation of distribution goals, activities, and available middlemen. Channel structure includes the number, types, and levels of middlemen to be utilized in the channel. The primary participants in industrial channels include distributors and reps; both perform key marketing functions for their suppliers.

Channel management is an ongoing activity concerned with administering the channel structure to achieve distribution objectives. The selection and motivation of middlemen are two management tasks vital to channel success. In addition, the industrial marketing manager may need to apply interorganizational management techniques in order to resolve channel conflict. The final phase of channel management is the evaluation of industrial middlemen. Evaluation provides the necessary feedback to effectively adjust channel operations to accomplish prescribed goals.

Logistical or physical distribution performance is a key variable in determining the success or failure of industrial marketing strategy. This constitutes the theme of the next chapter—Industrial Marketing Channels: The Logistical Interface.

Footnotes

[1]Bert Rosenbloom, *Marketing Channels, A Management View* (Hinsdale, Ill.: The Dryden Press, 1978), p. 105.

[2]Thayer C. Taylor, "1979 Survey of Selling Costs," *Sales & Marketing Management* 117 (February 26, 1979), p. 9.

[3]For example, see Bert Rosenbloom, *Marketing Channels,* pp. 119–27; Louis W. Stern and Adel I. El-Ansary, *Marketing Channels* (Englewood Cliffs, N.J.: Prentice-Hall, Inc., 1977), pp. 351–53; and Philip Kotler, *Marketing Management, Analysis, Planning and Control,* 3rd ed., (Englewood Cliffs, N.J.: Prentice-Hall, Inc., 1976), pp. 287–89.

[4]Frederick E. Webster, Jr., "Perceptions of the Industrial Distributor," *Industrial Marketing Management* 4 (1975), p. 259.

[5]Gary L. Lilien, "Advisor 2: Modeling the Marketing Mix Decision for Industrial Products," *Management Science* 25 (February 1979), pp. 191–204.

[6]Roger M. Pegram, *Selecting and Evaluating Distributors* (New York: The National Industrial Conference Board, Inc., 1965), p. 5.

[7]For a comprehensive discussion of distributor/market coverage issues, see Frederick E. Webster, Jr., "The Role of the Industrial Distributor in Marketing Strategy," *Journal of Marketing* 40 (July 1976), pp. 10–16.

[8]U.S. *vs.* Arnold Schwinn Co., et al., 388 U.S. 365 (1967); see also, "Never Say No to a Distributor," *Sales and Marketing Management* 117 (February 5, 1979), pp. 16–17.

[9]"Clemmer Moving and Storage *vs.* North American Van Lines and Louderback Transportation Co.," *Journal of Marketing* 34 (April 1970), p. 84.

[10]Philip Kotler, *Marketing Decision Making: A Model Building Approach* (New York: Holt, Rinehart and Winston, 1971), p. 293.

[11]Douglas M. Lambert, "The Distribution Channels Decision: A Problem of Performance Measurement," *Management Accounting* 60 (June 1978), p. 63.

[12]Eugene A. Lambert, Jr., "Financial Considerations in Choosing a Marketing Channel," *MSU Business Topics* 14 (Winter 1966), pp. 17–26.

[13]For example, see Kotler, *Marketing Decision Making,* p. 296.

[14]Pegram, *Selecting and Evaluating Distributors,* p. 95.

[15]Stern and El-Ansary, *Marketing Channels,* p. 374.

[16]Pegram, *Selecting and Evaluating Distributors,* p. 96.

[17]Somerby Dowst, "Manufacturers Turn More to Distributor Sales," *Purchasing* 77 (February 22, 1977), p. 49.

[18]Stern and El-Ansary, *Marketing Channels,* pp. 276–317.

[19]Ibid., p. 283.

[20]Louis W. Stern and James L. Heskett, "Conflict Management in Interorganizational Relations: A Conceptual Framework," in Louis Stern (ed.), *Distribution Channels: Behavioral Dimensions* (Boston: Houghton-Mifflin Company, 1969), pp. 293–94.

[21]For example, see Robert F. Lusch, "Sources of Power: Their Impact on Intrachannel Conflict," *Journal of Marketing Research* 13 (November 1976), p. 384; Stern and Heskett, "Conflict Management in Interorganizational Relations," p. 293; Larry J. Rosenberg and Louis Stern, "Conflict Measurement in the Distribution Channel," *Journal of Marketing Research* 8 (November 1971), pp. 437–42; Louis Stern and Ronald H. Gorman, "Conflict in Distribution Channels: An Exploration," in Stern (ed.), *Distribution Channels: Behavioral Dimensions,* p. 156; Larry J. Rosenberg, "A New Approach to Distribution Conflict Management," *Business Horizons* 16 (October 1974), pp. 67–74; and Louis P. Bucklin, "A Theory of Channel Control," *Journal of Marketing* 37 (January 1973), pp. 39–47.

[22]Larry J. Rosenberg, "A New Approach to Distribution Conflict Management," *Business Horizons* 17 (October 1974), pp. 67–74.

[23]Stern and El-Ansary, *Marketing Channels,* Chapter 7.

Discussion Questions

1. For many years, critics have charged that middlemen contribute strongly to the rising prices of goods of all types in the American economy. Would industrial marketers improve the level of efficiency and effectiveness in the channel by reducing as far as possible the number of intermediate links in the channel? Support your position.

2. Describe specific product, market, and competitive conditions that lend themselves to: (a) a direct channel of distribution, (b) an indirect channel of distribution.

3. Often, the industrial marketer may have very little latitude in selecting the number of channel *levels*. Explain.

4. The trend in industrial channels of distribution is toward an increased reliance on few, but larger, distributors. Why?

5. Explain how a change in segmentation policy (i.e., entering new markets) may trigger the need for drastic changes in the industrial channel of distribution.

6. Assume perfect information. What specific information would you desire in comparing channel alternatives? How would you use this information in making channel decisions?

7. The opportunities for conflict in the channel of distribution are limitless. What steps can the industrial marketer take to reduce the chances of conflict emerging in the channel?

8. Explain how two industrial distributors that generate identical sales results for the industrial marketer might receive markedly different performance appraisals: one favorable, the other unfavorable.

Chapter 12 Industrial Marketing Channels: The Logistical Interface

If the delivery performance provided by the marketer breaks down, buyers will search for a new supplier. Organizational buyers assign a high degree of importance to responsive physical distribution, or logistical, systems. Therefore, substantial resources are invested in the servicing of demand through the logistical system.

After reading this chapter, you will have an understanding of:

1. *the role of logistical management in industrial marketing strategy*
2. *the importance of achieving the desired interface between logistics and the channel of distribution*
3. *the importance of cost and service tradeoffs in creating effective and efficient logistical systems.*

Industrial marketers frequently choose to delegate selling and other demand stimulation tasks to middlemen. Other functions of equal importance, however, must be performed to successfully implement marketing strategies and to satisfy customer needs. Products must be delivered to industrial customers *when* they are required, *where* they are required, and in *usable condition*. Unfortunately, an industrial marketer cannot totally shift the burden of these logistical functions to middlemen. Even if distributors are employed in the channel, manufacturers must possess the capability of efficiently delivering products to the distributor. The industrial marketer's effectiveness in performing this function will dramatically influence the distributor's ability to satisfy delivery requirements of the end user/customer. Even when middlemen are utilized, *logistical* responsibilities still must be assumed by the marketer. Direct channels place even greater logistical burdens on the manufacturer.

This chapter will impart a clear comprehension of the role of logistical management in industrial marketing strategy in general and in industrial channel performance in particular.[1] Several key questions concerning the logistical function establish the direction of the discussion. How do logistical activities of an industrial marketer interface with the channel of distribution? What are the key logistical variables that must be managed to create an effective interface with the channel? What role does logistics play in the purchase decision of an industrial buyer? What types of logistical services are sought by buyers? How can these services be designed and implemented most effectively and efficiently? As a starting point, let us first examine the nature of logistical management.

Logistical Management

Logistics is an imposing and sometimes mysterious term which originated in the military. In business usage, *logistics* refers to the design and management of all activities (basically transportation, inventory, and warehousing) necessary to make supplies and materials available for manufacturing and, in turn, to make finished products available to customers when and where they are needed in the condition required. As the definition suggests, logistics embodies two primary product flows: (1) *physical supply,* or those flows dealing with developing the assortment of raw materials, component parts and supplies necessary to undertake the production process; and (2) *physical distribution,* or those flows concerned with delivering the completed product to customers and channel intermediaries. Figure 12.1 depicts the nature of the business logistics system. The physical supply and physical distribution flows must be coordinated to successfully meet delivery requirements of industrial customers. If raw materials are not available to meet the production schedule, the chance of fulfilling customer orders on time is substantially reduced. Although the physical supply dimension of logistics is an important one, the focus in this chapter will be on the physical

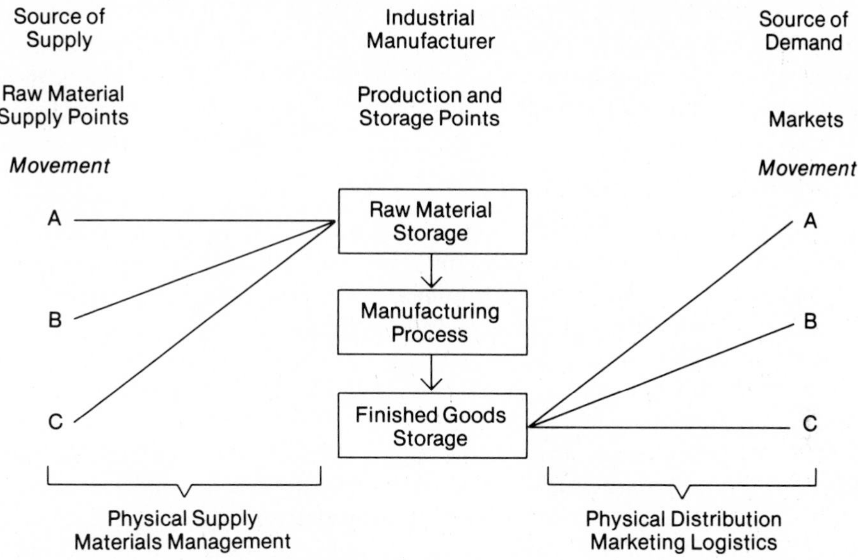

Figure 12.1 / The Industrial Logistics System

Source. Adapted from John J. Coyle and Edward J. Bardi, *The Management of Business Logistics* (New York: West Publishing Co., 1976), p. 6.

distribution component of logistics. From an industrial marketing perspective, the development of a system to deliver finished products efficiently to middlemen and industrial users is the key dimension of logistics.

The definition of logistics underscores the importance of logistical performance in the industrial setting. Recall that the physical supply side of logistics deals with making production inputs available to the manufacturing process. It is here that an industrial supplier's logistics system interacts with the customer's logistics and manufacturing process. Suppliers must develop the logistical capability to respond to the manufacturing requirements of their customers. A repair part that is delivered only five hours late may cost a manufacturer thousands of dollars in lost production time!

An example of how precisely a supplier must tailor its logistics system to customer needs is the case of Owens-Illinois, a major supplier of glass containers. Owens-Illinois is a primary supplier to the J. M. Smucker Company, the jam and jelly manufacturer. Because of the vast container requirements in the production process, Smucker must carefully manage its inventory and delivery of glass containers. In an effort to reduce container inventory, Smucker follows the policy of maintaining only enough glass containers to run the production line for a *few hours!* The burden of this policy falls directly on the shoulders of the Owens-Illinois logistics system. First, Owens-Illinois must schedule the production process at its Toledo plant to provide required inventories in the container sizes desired by Smucker. Then, warehouse systems and reliable motor carriers are utilized to assure that deliveries are made to match Smucker's inventory policy and to avoid production interruptions. Consistent delivery performance to Smucker standards is surely one of the essential ingredients to a long-term supplier-customer relationship in this case.

Elements of a Logistics System

The controllable variables of a logistics system are described in table 12.1. Each of these elements plays an important role in the overall performance of the logistics system, and each interacts with the others. Almost no decision on a particular logistics activity can be made without evaluating its impact on the other areas.

The influence of logistics on business and marketing strategies is particularly important in the industrial market. The system of warehouse facilities, inventory commitments, and transportation linkages will determine the supplier's ability to provide timely product availability to industrial users. Poor logistical performance as evidenced by long delivery times and less than adequate inventory levels can produce a number of results—none of which are favorable. As a result of poor performance, customers may have to bear the extra cost of higher inventories, institute expensive priority order expediting systems, develop secondary supply sources, or, in the worst case, shift patronage to another supplier. The impact of logistics, then, is reflected in cost and service performance. Examination of the value of logistical cost management will be considered first.

Total Cost Approach

The management of logistical activities is focused upon two essential performance variables: (1) total distribution costs and (2) the level of logistical service provided to customers. The logistics system is designed and administered to achieve a combination of cost and service levels that yield maximum profits to the firm and the channel. A first step in achieving maximum profitability is to understand the scope and behavior of logistical costs.

Management concern with logistics results from the overall magnitude of logistics costs. Industrial marketers have wide-ranging logistical costs depending on the nature of their product and the salience of logistics service to the buyer. However, research suggests that logistics costs approximate 13.6 percent of the sales dollar for the average manufacturing firm.[2]

The need to manage logistics efficiently arises as a result of the magnitude of logistics costs and the potential for substantial cost reduction. It is generally felt that productivity gains in production, selling, and promotion have been exploited, and logistics can be considered ". . . the last frontier of cost reduction in American business."[3] How, then, must the manager approach this important area of logistical cost management?

The *total-cost or tradeoff* approach to logistical management provides the means to guarantee that total logistics costs in the firm and within the channel are minimized. The essence of the total cost approach is that the

Table 12.1 / Controllable Elements in a Logistics System

Elements	Key Aspects
Transportation	Represents the single most important activity in the creation of place-values and time-values; is the means of moving goods from the end of the production line to consumers in the marketplace.
Warehousing	Creates place-values and time-values by making goods available in the marketplace when needed.
Inventory Management	Insures that the right mix of products is available at the right place and at the right time, in sufficient quantity to meet demands; balances the risks of stockouts and lost sales against the risks of overstocks and obsolescence; facilitates production planning.
Protective Packaging	Protective packaging insures good condition of products when they arrive in the marketplace, and maximizes use of warehouse space and transport equipment cube.
Materials Handling	Maximizes speed and minimizes cost of: order-picking, moving to and from storage, loading of transportation equipment, and unloading at destination; relates to product protection.
Order Processing	Assists in creation of place-time values by communicating requirements to appropriate locations. Relates to inventory management by reflecting demands on current stocks and changes in inventory position.
Production Planning	Insures realization of place-time values by making goods available for inventory. Permits planning of warehouse facility utilization, transportation requirements.
Customer Service	Relates place-time values as seen by the company to place-time values as seen by its customers. Establishes levels of customer service consistent with marketing objectives as well as with cost limitations.
Plant Location: *Warehouse Location, Facilities Planning*	Maximizes place-time values by relating plant and warehouse location to transportation services and costs in terms of markets to be served. Facilities planning insures that capacity, configuration, and throughput of warehouse and shipping facilities are compatible with product flow.

Source. Adapted from: "The Many Faces of PDM," (*Japan Airlines* 1969), p. 10.

costs associated with individual logistics activities are interactive. That is, the decision made for one logistical variable affects all or some of the other logistics variables. Management attention is therefore focused on the efficiency of the *entire* logistics system rather than on minimizing the cost associated with any one logistics activity. The term used to describe the interactions among logistics activities (i.e., transportation, inventory, warehousing) is *cost tradeoffs*. In effect, the manager is willing to trade off a cost *increase* in one activity for a larger cost *decrease* in another activity, with the net result that total logistics costs are reduced.

Figure 12.2 shows the patterns of costs associated with a change in the number of warehouses maintained by an industrial firm. As additional warehouses are added to the system, *transportation costs* decline as a result of high volume shipments at low rates into the warehouses and, with small volume, high cost shipments moved shorter distances to the customers. The total transportation costs (inbound and outbound) decline with more warehouses as the high cost, small volume shipments are moved over shorter and shorter distances. Conversely, *inventory costs* rise as more warehouses are added to the system because more stock is required to maintain the same level of product availability than with fewer warehouses. Combining inventory and transportation costs, the least cost solution, where the tradeoff of inventory for transportation is optimized, is to maintain 10 warehouses. Thus, as figure 12.2 suggests, a warehouse decision made on the basis of inventory costs or transportation costs alone would not result in the least total cost system.

Cost tradeoffs are not limited to any specific activity, but occur among all logistics activities. Xerox at one time maintained a large inventory of supplies, chemicals, and parts for its machines at 40 different warehouses. Analysis of product volume revealed that 80 percent of the items were "slow movers." These slow movers were then consolidated at one central warehouse location and transported by air freight when needed. The tradeoff of higher transportation costs for lower inventory costs was estimated to have saved Xerox millions of dollars annually.

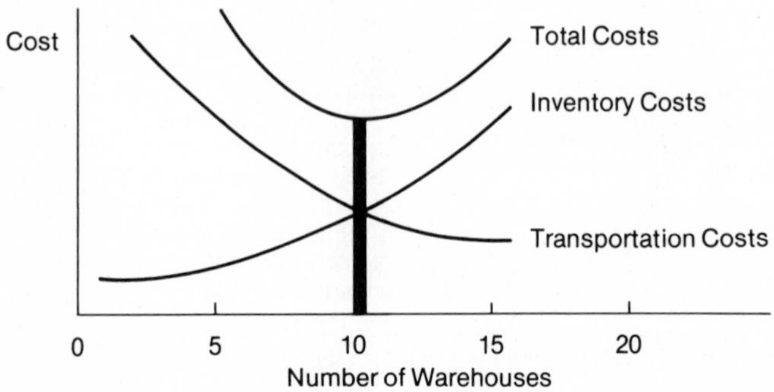

Figure 12.2 / Cost Tradeoffs

Service-Cost Tradeoffs

The other half of the logistics equation is the service aspect. For many industrial products, the ability to deliver customer orders rapidly is more important than the logistics costs involved. More will be said about logistical service later in the chapter, but the essential point here is that different levels of service are capable of producing different demand responses from the firm's customers.[4] However, each aspect and level of logistics service has a cost, and the cost must be evaluated in light of the revenue generated from the service level. Profitability, measured by the difference between revenue and cost of logistics, is the important control variable, and this approach requires management to evaluate the tradeoff of cost and service.

Total Channel System Orientation

A channel-wide orientation to logistical management suggests that the industrial marketer evaluate the impact of logistical decisions on the channel members' operations. Manufacturer shifts in inventory policy, transportation modes, and warehouse locations directly affect channel members and end users. The reduction of field warehouses from ten to two may require distributors to hold more inventory to assure end users/customers of product availability. Although the manufacturer's warehousing and inventory costs are diminished, distributor costs will rise, and customer service may be substantially curtailed. The net result may dramatically reduce the overall performance of the channel system.

In summary, the total cost, total system, tradeoff framework is a necessary point of departure for the management of industrial logistics strategy. The interaction of logistics costs and the interface of channel member logistics activities suggests that channel-wide performance can only be optimized through the systematic evaluation of logistical tradeoffs. The discussion will now turn to an evaluation of the customer service dimension of industrial logistics.

Industrial Logistics Service

Studies of the purchasing process in the forgings industry revealed that purchasing managers begin the vendor selection process by first calling suppliers with the *best delivery service* to assess whether they are willing to negotiate their prices.[5] Buyers with known low prices were *not* contacted first to see if they would improve delivery service! Similar approaches to vendor selection are evidenced in numerous industries as a result of the importance of logistics service to the industrial buyer. As a consequence, the industrial marketing manager needs a keen insight to the role of logistical service in the purchase process and the techniques for creating the required service level. The first step is to understand the nature of logistical customer service.

Definition of Customer Service

Logistics service relates to anything involved with the availability of products and/or the delivery of products to the customer. An expert in the customer service field defines it as "the series of sales-satisfying activities which begin when the customer places the order and ends with the delivery of product to customers."[6] Clearly, logistics service includes all of the supplier logistical performances that are important to the industrial *customer.* A description of the more frequently cited logistics service elements is shown in table 12.2. Observe that these service elements encompass areas of vital importance to organizational buyers and touch such areas as order cycle time, order accuracy, and expediting. Each one of these elements assumes importance for industrial purchasers because each has the potential for affecting their production processes, final product output, or costs, or all three.

Impacts of Supplier Logistical Service on Industrial Customers

In general terms, many of these customer service elements translate into product *availability*. For a manufacturer to produce or a distributor to resell, industrial products have to be available at the right time, at the right place,

Table 12.2 / Elements of Logistics Service

Element	Description
1. Order cycle time	The elapsed time from placement of the order to receipt of the order.
2. Consistency of order cycle time	The variation of order cycle lengths from average or expected order cycle times.
3. Percent of stockouts	Percentage of total items ordered from a supplier's warehouse which are unavailable from existing supplier inventory.
4. Order accuracy	The degree to which items received conform to the specification of the order.
5. Percentage fill rate	The proportion of orders which are filled completely at the time of order placement.
6. Order condition	The physical condition of the goods when received by the buyer.
7. Order size and frequency constraint	Minimum order size requirements; maximum frequency of order placement limitations.
8. Billing accuracy	The agreement of billing with the actual order received.
9. Back orders, expediting	Supplier's ability for handling back orders and expediting the delivery of products back ordered.

Source. Adapted from P. Ronald Stephenson and Ronald P. Willett, "Selling with Physical Distribution Service," *Business Horizons* 11 (December 1968), p. 78. Copyright, 1968, by the Foundation for the School of Business at Indiana University. Reprinted by permission.

and in usable condition: the longer the supplier's order delivery time, the less available the product; the more inconsistent the delivery time, the less available the product. Each aspect of logistical service directly affects the industrial customer's manufacturing activity, and each has important cost implications.

For example, a reduction in the supplier's order cycle time period permits a buyer to hold less inventory because its needs can be met rapidly. The net result for the customer is a reduction in inventory carrying cost and a diminished probability of interrupting the production process. The same is true for order cycle consistency. Consistent delivery performance allows the buyer to program more effectively or routinize the purchasing process, thus lowering the costs associated with this function. A dramatic impact of consistent order cycle performance is the opportunity for the buyer to cut the level of buffer or safety stock maintained. If a supplier's order cycle time varied between 10 and 40 days, the buyer, in order to meet production schedules, would need a relatively large safety stock in case the delivery time was toward the 40-day end of the scale. Contrast this to a situation where order cycles range between 10 and 14 days—here the buyer need only be concerned with a 4-day variance in delivery time, resulting in much lower safety stocks. However, for many industrial products, most of which are low unit value and relatively standardized, the overriding concern is not inventory cost, but simply *having* the products! A malfunctioning $.95 bearing could shut down a whole production line if a replacement was not immediately available. For such reasons, logistical service performance is of great importance to industrial buyers when evaluating potential suppliers.

The Role of Logistics Service in the Industrial Buying Decision

Because the cost and production process impacts of logistics service are so dramatic, it is not surprising to learn that buyers rank logistics service above many other important supplier characteristics. William Perreault and Frederick Russ report in a recent study that logistics service rates are second only to product quality in influencing industrial purchasing decisions.[7] The key results of their study of 216 purchasing managers are displayed in table 12.3. These findings corroborate those obtained in an earlier study that "on-time delivery performance" was rated second only to maintenance of product quality within specifications.[8] Table 12.3 shows that a sizable group of purchasing managers indicate that the first time a supplier fails to respond to a rush order request, they would find a different supplier. The conclusion is clear: industrial marketing managers can not afford to lose sight of the need to create effective systems to provide product availability to their industrial customers. A brief discussion of how the manager determines the appropriate logistical service level is next.

Determining the Level of Service

Obviously, not all products or all customers require the same level of logistical service. Many industrial products that are made to order—such as

Table 12.3 / Summary: A Study of How Industrial Purchasing Managers Evaluate Logistics Service

I. The importance of logistics service:

Supplier Characteristics	Mean Index of the Relative Importance of Supplier Characteristics in the Purchase Decision
Product Quality	0.176
Distribution Service	0.171
Price	0.161
Supplier Manager	0.152
Distance to Supplier	0.114
Required Order Size	0.108
Minority/Small Business	0.078
Reciprocity	0.046

II. What happens when you receive a stockout notice for a product?

32 percent of the time, purchasing managers switch to another supplier.

Over a prior two-year period, 50 percent of the purchasing managers stopped using a supplier because of slow or inconsistent service.

III. What would you do if the request for a rush order was not acted upon by the supplier?

42 percent of the purchasing managers would change suppliers after only *one* such inaction on a rush order.

54 percent would change suppliers if the problem occurred several times.

Source. William D. Perreault, Jr., and Frederick A. Russ, "Physical Distribution in Industrial Purchase Decisions," *Journal of Marketing* 40 (April 1976), pp. 5, 6. Reprinted from the *Journal of Marketing*, published by the American Marketing Association.

heavy machinery—have relatively low logistical service requirements. Others, such as replacement parts, components, and subassemblies, require extremely demanding logistical performance. Similarly, each customer will be more or less responsive to varying levels of logistical service. The Perreault and Russ study indicated that some purchasing agents are far more sensitive to *poor* service than the majority of purchasing managers.[9] The identification of market segments on the basis of logistical service sensitivity would enable management to develop logistics programs tailored to the needs of each segment.

Profitability is the major criterion for evaluating the appropriate customer service levels. Information on the alternative service levels and their associated sales results must be evaluated in relation to the cost of providing those service levels.[10] Figure 12.3 demonstrates the cost-service relationship, which indicates that profit contribution varies with the service level. In this case, the optimal service level is at point x, where profits are maximized.

To reiterate, service level standards are developed by assessing customer service requirements. The sales and cost impacts of various service levels are analyzed to find the service level generating the highest profits. The

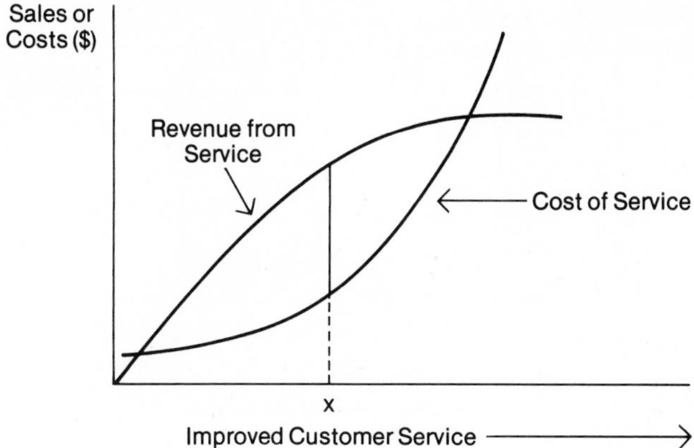

Figure 12.3 / Cost-Service Relationship

nature of this procedure implies that the needs of different customer segments will dictate different logistics system configurations. For those customers where logistics service is critical, industrial distributors may be utilized to provide the vital product availability. In other cases, customers with less rigorous service demands can be served from factory inventories. The following section deals with understanding the interface of logistics in the overall channel.

The Interface of Logistics in the Channel

The importance of logistical coordination in the channel of distribution can not be overemphasized. Logistical activities—whether manufacturer or middleman induced—touch every phase of channel performance and are inherently linked to the success or failure of most industrial channel systems. The task of the industrial marketer is to first understand the impacts of supplier logistical performance on the middleman's operations, and then to effect programs that will enhance middleman performance and overall channel coordination.

Logistical Impacts on Industrial Middlemen

A supplier's logistics system directly affects the middleman's ability to control cost and service to end users/customers. Just as the order cycle time between the manufacturer and customer influences the customer's inventory requirements, order cycle performance also affects the operations of channel members. If a supplier provides erratic delivery service to distributors, the distributor is forced to carry higher inventory in order to provide a satisfactory level of product availability to end users. The result of inefficient logistics service to the distributors is to increase their costs (larger inventories) or to create stockouts of the supplier's products at the distributor level. Neither result is beneficial: in the first instance, distributor loyalty and marketing efforts will surely suffer; in the second case, end users will eventually change suppliers.

Impact on Customer Service

Poor logistical performance is a double-edged sword. It constricts sales possibilities and antagonizes middlemen. In a study of customer service, industrial middlemen indicated that a 5 percent reduction in customer service would result in an expected sales decrease of 20 percent.[11] Thus, an industrial distributor will not long remain loyal to a manufacturer whose logistical performance causes service levels to end users to diminish. Because inventories typically represent the single largest item among distributor assets and also the largest distribution expense, distributors are becoming increasingly aware of the impact of supplier logistical service. The length and consistency of supplier delivery time is highly correlated to the level of those distributor inventories. Because distributors often pass freight charges along to their customers, abnormally high transportation costs can place the manufacturer's product at a price disadvantage in the marketplace. Clearly, an effective and efficient logistics system has considerable channel-wide ramifications.

Improving Logistical Performance in the Channel

The industrial marketer can take a number of steps to improve channel-wide logistical performance. First, information systems can be developed to provide realistic sales forecasts for individual channel members. Similarly, inventory control systems can be developed for channel members and linked to the manufacturer's information system. Second, coordination of logistical activities can be facilitated by the industrial supplier. The standardization of packaging, handling, and palletization systems is effective in this regard. Third, in some cases, the manufacturer may perform certain functions (e.g., warehousing) that contribute to improved efficiency for the entire channel. Finally, shipment consolidation programs are often effective in reducing channel-wide transportation costs. Here, distributors in a particular area might be encouraged to "pool" shipments into a truckload quantity, or they might be advised to place all of their orders on the same day. In summary, channel-wide logistical integration is required to effectively implement marketing strategy.

Industrial Logistics Management

Logistics management involves the integration of transportation, inventory, facilities, and communications to provide a level of logistics service desired

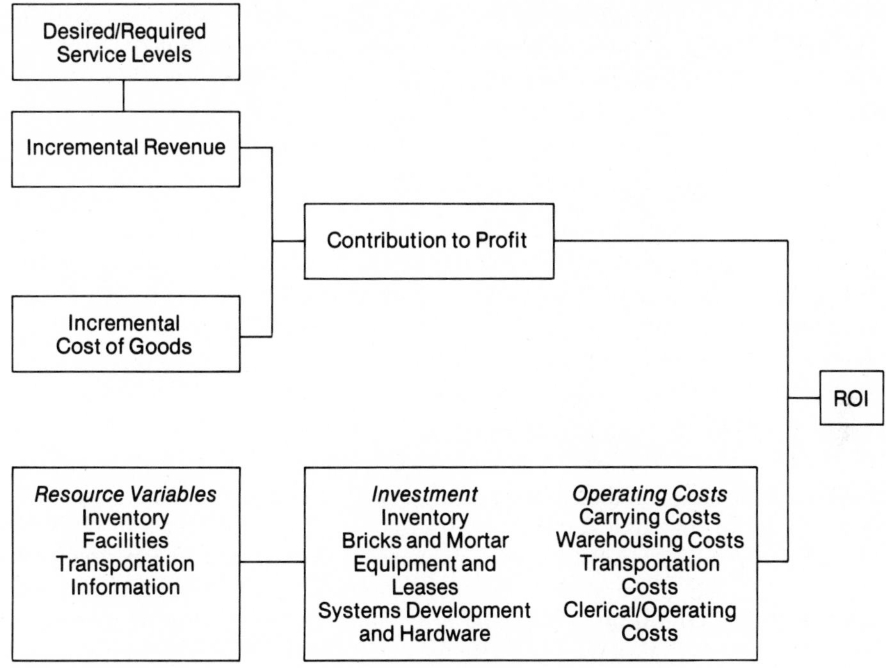

Figure 12.4 / Framework for Selecting the Optimum Logistics System

Source. Adapted from "A Logistics Hotseat: Customer Service Redefined," Cleveland Consulting Associates, Cleveland, Ohio, 1978. Reprinted by permission.

by customers and middlemen at the lowest possible cost. Figure 12.4 provides a framework for understanding the nature of the logistical decision. The upper portion of figure 12.4 focuses on determining customer service levels and their impact on revenues and profits as treated earlier in the chapter. The remainder of the figure highlights the integration of the major logistical variables necessary to create the desired level of service. Particularly noteworthy is the need to consider both the operating costs and investment levels associated with the logistics system. In this manner, the impact of logistics on the company's return on investment is viewed in terms of revenue (customer service levels) minus the logistics operating costs and the required capital investments in the logistics system. Importantly, such a framework cues the industrial marketing manager to evaluate logistics system alternatives on the basis of all three aspects—revenue, cost, and capital investments. Thus, a modification in the logistics system that increases operating costs, yet leaves the capital investment unchanged while more than proportionately expanding sales, would be viewed as highly favorable. A logistics alternative where sales are unchanged, operating costs increase, and the investment base is substantially reduced would also be viewed favorably.

An examination of important aspects of the industrial logistics resource variables in light of their operating cost and investment considerations is necessary. While the basic approach is to discuss each area separately, these decisions (facility, transportation, and inventory) are so intertwined that it is impossible to evaluate one of them without considering the other two. Thus, the salient dimensions of each of these logistical variables will be examined along with an analysis of their interaction with the remaining variables.

Logistics Facilities

The key aspect of the logistical facilities decision centers on warehousing requirements in the channel of distribution. The strategic deployment of a warehouse provides the industrial marketer with the opportunity to increase the level of delivery service to buyers, or reduce transportation costs, or both. Industrial firms distributing many repair, maintenance, and operating supplies often find that the only way to achieve desired levels of delivery service is to maintain inventories in warehouses located in key markets. The warehouse circumvents the need for premium transportation (air freight) and costly order processing procedures by making products readily available in local markets.

Servicing Channel Members. The nature of the industrial channel affects the warehousing requirements of an industrial supplier. In the case where manufacturer's reps are utilized, the industrial supplier will often require a significant number of strategically located warehouses to provide the delivery service required by customers. The deployment of such warehousing facilities often dictates the level of satisfaction of industrial customers with this type of system. On the other hand, a channel system involving distributors will offset the overriding need for warehousing associated with the rep channel. Obviously, a key service provided by the distributor is the local warehousing function. Nevertheless, a few, well-located supplier warehouses may be required to effectively distribute to the distributors.

Private or Public. Operating costs, service levels, and investment requirements are essential aspects in the decision on the type of warehouse to employ. The industrial firm may either own, rent, or lease warehousing space. A *public warehouse* provides storage space to manufacturers on a fee basis. Space may be rented on a monthly basis or leased for a longer time frame. The advantage to the user of public warehousing is flexibility—the firm can increase or decrease its use of space in a given market or move into or out of any market in a short time frame. Public warehousing involves no fixed investment; the costs are totally variable to the user. In cases where sales volume is seasonal, erratic, or generally low in a given market, the public warehouse is an economical means of providing excellent product availability.

In some cases, public warehousing may supplement or replace distributors in a market. Many public warehouses provide a variety of logistical services for their clients, including packaging, labeling, order processing, and some light assembly. Distribution Centers, Inc. (DCI), a public warehouse based in Columbus, Ohio, maintains warehouse facilities in eight major markets. Clients are able to position inventories in all these markets while dealing with only one firm. DCI is also able to link its computer with the suppliers' to facilitate order processing and inventory updating. In addition, they will repackage products to the end user's order, label, and arrange for local delivery. In this case, an industrial marketer could ship standard products in bulk to the DCI warehouse, gaining transportation economies, and still enjoy excellent customer delivery service. The public warehouse is a feasible alternative to the distributor channel when the sales function can be economically executed with a direct sales force or reps.

The alternative to renting or leasing warehouse space is *private warehousing*. Here, the manufacturer has a capital investment in the facility. Although the investment is substantial, private facilities can provide operating cost advantages when the facility is utilized close to its capacity on a regular basis. Often, more important than the cost and investment aspects, is the enhancement of customer service. For example, National Trust Drill and Tool Company's private warehouse in Rochester, Michigan, uses a computerized inventory location system that enables the company to ship all orders within 24 hours.[12] Thus, the private warehouse offers more control over the warehousing operation, permitting efficient levels of operation and delivery service.

Transportation

Transportation is usually the largest single logistics expense, and the impact of continually rising fuel costs suggests that its importance will probably increase. Typically, the transportation decision involves the evaluation and selection of the mode, the legal form, and the individual carrier(s) that will ensure the best performance at the lowest cost. *Mode* refers to the type of carrier—rail, truck, air—while *legal form* refers to the extent to which the carrier's operation is regulated by the federal government. The evaluation of *individual carriers* is based on rates and delivery performance. In-depth treatment of each of these three areas is beyond the scope of this text, and the reader is referred to a number of sources that discuss them in detail.[13] Therefore, the focus in this section will be on: (1) the role of transportation in industrial channels; (2) key performance criteria for evaluating transportation options; (3) the purpose of expedited logistics systems; and (4) the private carrier alternative.

Transportation and Logistics Service. An industrial marketer must establish the capability to effectively move finished inventory between facilities, to channel middlemen, and to customers. The transportation system utilized by the supplier is the link that binds the logistical network together and ultimately results in timely delivery of products to middlemen and customers. Unfortunately, efficient warehousing has little impact on order cycle performance when transportation delivery performance is inconsistent or inadequate.

Effective transportation service may be used in combination with warehouse facilities and inventory levels to generate the required customer service level or it may be used *in place* of them. The tradeoff principle suggests that inventory maintained in a variety of market positioned warehouses can be pulled back to one centralized warehouse location if rapid transportation service can be secured from the central location to industrial customers. The Xerox situation cited earlier is an example of using premium air freight service to offset the need for high inventories and extensive warehouse locations. Again, decisions of this type hinge on careful evaluation of the tradeoffs between transportation, warehouse, and inventory costs. Importantly, then, the decision on transportation modes and particular carriers will depend on the cost tradeoffs and service capabilities of each.

Transportation Performance Criteria. *Cost of service* is the variable cost associated with moving products from origin to destination, plus any additional terminal or accessory charges. The cost of service varies between modes of transportation, ranging from 2.07 cents per ton-mile for rail, 4.59 cents per ton-mile for motor carrier, to 45.8 cents per ton-mile for air freights.[14] Although these figures are averages, they represent the relative structure of costs among the modes. The important aspect of selecting the mode of transportation is not the cost per se, but the cost relative to the objective to be achieved. Bulk raw materials generally do not require rapid delivery service, so the cost of anything other than rail transportation could not be justified on the basis of service objectives. On the other hand, air freight may be almost 10 times more expensive than motor freight, yet when a customer needs an emergency shipment of spare parts, the cost is inconsequential. Additionally, the cost of premium (fast) transportation modes may be justified in terms of the resulting inventory reductions.

Speed of service refers to the elapsed time to move products from one facility (plant or warehouse) to another facility (warehouse or customer plant). Again, speed of service often overrides the cost of service in many industrial situations. The key dimension of speed of service is the impact on inventories. Rail, a relatively slow mode used for bulk shipments, requires inventory buildups at the supplier's factory and the middleman's or customer's warehouse. The longer the delivery time, the more inventory customers must maintain to service their needs while the shipment is in transit. Again, the tradeoff of cost, service, and investment comes into play. The slower modes involve lower variable costs associated with product movement, yet result in lower service levels and higher investments in inventory. The faster modes produce just the opposite effect. Not only must an intermodal comparison be made in terms of service, but different carriers within a mode must be evaluated on their "door-to-door" delivery time.

As indicated earlier in the discussion of total order cycle time, *service consistency* is usually more important than average delivery time. Table 12.4 shows the results of an extensive study which investigated performance consistency by various transportation modes. Note that air and truckload provide the best average delivery performance over short distances, while the superiority of air increases dramatically for longer hauls. Also noteworthy is the fact that although air provides the fastest average delivery time, it also has the highest variability in transit time *relative* to average delivery time. The data in the table also suggest that rail shipments become relatively consistent (compared to average time) over long distances.

Consideration of the wide variation in modal service consistency is particularly critical in industrial marketing planning. The choice of transportation mode cannot be made on the basis of cost or average transit time if effective customer service is to be achieved. In situations where rush orders are required, the obvious choice of mode is not so obvious (e.g., the relative inconsistency of air freight). In routine replenishment situations—for example, rail—may offer the most consistent service if the shipments are to be made over long distances.

In summary, industrial buyers often place a premium on effective and consistent delivery service. Because of this fact, the choice of transportation mode is an important one—one in which cost of service is often secondary. However, the best decision on transportation carriers will result from a careful evaluation of service, variable costs, and investment requirements. The manager must also consider the transportation requirements associated with everyday shipments versus those of expedited or rush-order shipments.

Normal vs. Expedited Systems. A fact of life of many logistics systems in industrial marketing channels is that they are often *two-tier*. The routine logistical requirements are satisfied through one system, while the rush order needs are met through a different system. The normal system is designed

Table 12.4 / Average Transit Time and Time Range for 95 Percent of Shipments in Days, by Various Transport Modes and Distances

	300–400 Miles		2500–2600 Miles	
	Average	95% Range	Average	95% Range
Rail Carload	8.3	1.4–15.2	12.4	8.3–16.6
Truckload	1.9	0.0–4.7	8.8	3.3–14.3
Less than Truckload	5.0	0.4–9.6	12.3	6.7–17.9
Air Freight	1.8	0.0–5.9	4.4	0.0–10.1
Air Express	2.1	0.0–5.7	3.4	0.0–9.6

Source. James Piercy, "A Performance Profile of Several Transportation Freight Services," unpublished PhD dissertation, Case-Western Reserve University, 1977, p. 89. Reprinted by permission of the author.

to provide low-cost delivery at required service levels. In this case the transportation modes and carriers are selected on the basis of efficiency—lowest rates and average delivery performance. Thus, a manufacturer of brake shoes may find that rail shipments from factory to distributor or to customer warehouses provide very low cost transportation at a service level that is adequate for most customer orders. However, brake shoes may be rush ordered perhaps 5 percent of the time as a result of increased customer production requirements or abnormally high breakdowns in a customer's truck fleet. In this case, the brake shoe supplier requires a transportation carrier which can rapidly expedite delivery. The backup system might entail air express shipments from a special warehouse or any of a number of small package express services.

Reliance Electric encourages distributors to order in fewer, but larger, orders to economize on freight rates. However, to handle distributor rush orders, United Parcel Service is utilized when shipment sizes total under 50 pounds per package.[15] Often such carriers form the backbone of the second-tier, priority logistics system.

The decision to use a premium transportation mode depends on the unit cost of the item, how predictable the demand, inventory carrying costs, cost of the premium mode, savings in transit time, and the importance of priority delivery to the customer. The alternative to premium transportation is, of course, the maintenance of inventories close to customers. David Herron proposes a model which explicitly evaluates the variables listed above.[16] The model suggests that for items with high unit value, low sales, and unpredictable demand, low inventories should be maintained at the destination, and premium transportation modes should be utilized to expedite orders. In addition, faster transportation modes are profitable for high cost items when delivery time by the normal carrier is inconsistent and demand is unpredictable. Herron concludes that,

> . . . a two-tier combination of normal and expedited operations is the most profitable. The cheaper mode is used to ship products whose demand is predictable; the faster mode for expedited items whose inventories at the destination has been reduced. This arrangement results in savings in the sum of transportation and inventory-carrying costs compared with costs of using either transportation mode alone.[17]

Private Carriers. Sometimes the only way for a supplier to achieve the consistent delivery performance required by customers is to utilize its own fleet of trucks. Importantly, service improvement is the primary justification for utilizing a company fleet, because the private fleet often may be more expensive than for-hire transportation. In addition, the investment requirements are significant—vehicles, maintenance facilities, and the like. In some cases, the heavy investment can be reduced by leasing equipment. The decision to enter the private fleet business is a complex one and must be made with care.[18] However, private ownership and management of transportation service may provide a feasible method of effectively balancing the cost, investment, and service aspects of transportation. Inventory, the third leg of logistics management, is very much interrelated with the transportation decision.

Inventory Management

Inventory management is the "buffer" in the logistics system. Inventories are needed in industrial channels because: (1) production and demand for industrial products are not perfectly matched; (2) operating deficiencies in the logistics system often would result in product unavailability (e.g., delayed shipments, carrier's performance is inconsistent); and (3) industrial customers cannot predict their product needs with certainty (e.g., a machine breakdown or a sudden need to expand production). Inventory may be viewed in the same light as warehouse facilities and transportation: it is an alternative method for providing the level of service required by industrial users, and the level of inventory is determined on the basis of cost, investment, and service (revenue). The first aspect of effective inventory management is to understand the costs associated with inventory.

Inventory Costs. Inventory costs are subtle and difficult to comprehend because they are often not recorded in a specific account, but are found throughout a firm's system of accounts. Inventory costs include four basic cost categories: (1) capital costs; (2) inventory service costs (e.g., taxes and insurance); (3) storage space costs; and (4) inventory risk costs (e.g., damage and pilferage).[19]

The sum of these four cost categories make up what is known as *inventory carrying costs*. The typical way of stating carrying costs is as a percentage of the value of the products held in inventory. (Thus, a carrying charge of 20 percent means that the cost of holding one unit in inventory for one year is 20 percent of the value of the product.) Estimates of inventory carrying costs have typically ranged from 12 to 35 percent; yet a recent study indicates that these percentages may be much higher if all relevant inventory-related costs are considered.[20] A detailed case study of two firms revealed that one company historically applied a 19 percent carrying charge for making inventory decisions, while detailed analysis revealed the true carrying charge to be 38 percent![21]

The implications are clear. To make sound inventory decisions, industrial managers must develop workable systems for capturing the true cost associated with holding inventories. Because inventory costs are not always obvious, methodologies that accurately capture the four inventory cost categories are a necessity. Only after the true costs of inventory are developed can management begin evaluating important cost/service and inventory cost/transportation cost tradeoffs. Effective inventory policy also demands that a product-by-product analysis be made.

The 80/20 Rule. Most industrial marketers with extensive product lines are aware of the fact that a great bulk of their product line does not turn over very rapidly. This is the essence of the 80/20 principle: 80 percent of the sales are generated by 20 percent of the product line.

The major implication of the 80/20 principle is that industrial marketers must manage their inventory selectively, that is, treat fast and slow moving items differently. If a company has half of its inventory committed to products that produce only 20 percent of the unit sales volume, significant gains can be made by reduction of inventories of the slow-sellers to the point where their turnover rate approximates that of the fast sellers.[22] For example, the company just described could reduce total inventories by 25 percent if it reduced inventory in the slow moving items by 50 percent. Obviously, if inventory carrying costs are approaching 30 percent for an industrial supplier, an overall reduction of inventory by 25 percent could produce savings in the hundreds of thousands of dollars. These rules apply regardless of how the inventory function is handled in the channel. Thus, suppliers can develop more efficient channels and substantially reduce distributor inventory costs by allowing the distributor to cut back inventory on slow turnover items. Not only will distributor cost performance improve, but enhanced channel goodwill should result.

Selective Inventory Strategies. Selective inventory strategies can be achieved in a number of ways, and the evaluation of each will depend on the cost and service tradeoffs involved. First, inventory of slow movers can be reduced at all locations; the result, however, may be a rather marked reduction in customer service levels. The discussion in the transportation section provided a workable alternative: centralize the slow moving items at a single location, thereby reducing total inventories. The result is a higher sales volume per unit of product maintained at a given location. In turn, inventories of the fast moving items can be expanded, enhancing the service levels associated with these items.

The application of a selective inventory policy must be made cautiously. Typically, fast moving items are standardized items that customers expect to be readily available; slow movers often are nonstandardized, and customers expect to wait a significant length of time to receive them.[23] However, there is no rule that all slow moving items require low service levels. If a slow moving item is critical in the production process or is needed to repair a machine, an extremely high level of service is required. Thus, a selective inventory policy mandates that turnover rates and the critical nature of the product to the customer be evaluated in determining the inventory-transportation system.

The Critical Role of Forecasting. Estimates of future sales levels are the primary variable in determining inventory levels throughout the industrial logistics system. Short-term sales forecasts for weekly, monthly, quarterly, or yearly sales are the heart of any inventory planning system. Inventories throughout the channel will be based on the expected demand over the next planning interval. The approaches to forecasting developed in chapter 7 are relevant to the inventory decision. However, it is often necessary to adjust the broad sales forecasts to logistical purposes. A general forecast that is used to plan sales and promotional efforts is usually not specific enough for logistical inventory planning. Product-by-product estimates for short intervals need to be defined so that inventories can be adjusted. These estimates are often not contained in general marketing-sales forecasts. Finally, forecasting must be integrated within the channel to adjust inventory levels properly. Distributors and suppliers must work from the same sales estimates so that order timing and quantities can be accurately determined for the channel.

In summary, inventory decisions are based on the important cost-service and transportation-inventory tradeoffs. Inventory costs must be accurately calculated through accounting systems designed to capture all relevant inventory expenses. Often, the true costs are higher than expected. Analysis of product turnover and customer product usage will dictate the selectivity of the inventory policy and specify the type of transportation service required. Finally, short interval sales forecasting developed on a common basis for all channel members is essential to create channel-wide inventory policy.

The System: Focal Point of Logistics Planning

This chapter has provided an overview of some of the more important dimensions of logistics as it relates to industrial marketing. The "systems" perspective in logistical management cannot be stressed enough—it is the only way that management can be assured that the logistical function will meet prescribed goals. Not only must each logistics variable be analyzed in terms of its impact on every other variable, but the sum of the variables must be evaluated in light of the service level provided to customers. Logistics elements throughout the channel must be integrated so that smooth product flow is assured.

The burden on management is to plan the system to meet desired objectives *and* monitor the system's performance relative to those objectives. Management must be cognizant of the signs of *maldistribution*. Maldistribution is the undesirable state where a firm provides *poorer* service than its competitors at *higher* costs than its competitors.[24] Signs of maldistribution include slow inventory turnover, poor customer service, and excessive premium freight charges. Louis Stern and Adel El-Ansary suggest that one reason for maldistribution is that management is "technique-" or "equipment-" oriented rather than system-oriented in the approach to logistics management.[25]

Summary

Logistics service is a critical dimension in the evaluation of suppliers in the industrial purchasing decision process. Most evidence indicates that logistics service ranks second only to product quality in terms of supplier characteristics. Because of the salience of logistics service to industrial buyers, industrial marketing managers are faced with a stern challenge to develop cost-efficient logistics systems which provide the necessary service levels.

Decisions in the logistics area are approached from the basis of cost tradeoffs among the logistics variables. In addition, it is necessary to evaluate the cost of logistics relative to the revenue associated with alternative levels of service. The optimal system is one that produces the highest profitability relative to the capital investments required.

The major logistics variables include facilities, transportation, and inventory. Each can be utilized to some extent as a substitute for the other in terms of the level of customer service provided. Decisions are required on the number of warehouses, whether they are owned or rented, the transportation mode and specific carrier, the level and deployment of inventory, and the selectivity of inventory levels. The systems approach is adopted to structure effectively these three variables. Management must continually evaluate system performance, watching for signals of maldistribution. Finally, the industrial supplier must pay close attention to the impact of logistics on channel members and to the role logistics plays in overall channel performance.

Footnotes

[1]For a comprehensive discussion of all facets of business logistics, see Ronald H. Ballou, *Business Logistics Management* (Englewood Cliffs, N.J.: Prentice-Hall, Inc., 1973); Donald J. Bowersox, *Logistical Management* (2nd ed.; New York: Macmillan Publishing Company, 1978); James L. Heskett, Nicholas A. Glaskowsky, Jr., and Robert M. Ivie, *Business Logistics* (New York: The Ronald Press Company, 1973).

[2]Bernard J. LaLonde and Paul H. Zinszer, *Customer Service: Meaning and Measurement* (Chicago: National Council of Physical Distribution Management, 1976), p. 170.

[3]Wendell M. Stewart, "Physical Distribution: Key to Improved Volume and Profits," *Journal of Marketing* 39 (January 1965), pp. 65–70; see also, Thomas W. Speh and Michael D. Hutt, "The Other Half of Marketing: Lost or Found," in Robert S. Franz, Robert M. Hopkins, and Al Toma (eds.), *Proceedings: Southern Marketing Association* (University of Southwestern Louisiana: Southern Marketing Association, 1978), pp. 332–35.

[4]P. Ronald Stephenson and Ronald P. Willett, "Selling with Physical Distribution Service," *Business Horizons* 11 (December 1968) p. 76.

[5]Patrick J. Robinson, Charles W. Faris, and Yoram Wind, *Industrial Buying and Creative Marketing* (Boston: Allyn and Bacon, Inc., 1967), pp. 170, 173–74.

[6]Warren Blanding, *11 Hidden Costs of Customer Service Management* (Washington, D.C.: Marketing Publications, Inc., 1974), p. 3.

[7]William D. Perreault and Frederick A. Russ, "Physical Distribution in Industrial Purchase Decisions," *Journal of Marketing* 40 (April 1976), p. 3.

[8]Bernard Klass, "What Factors Affect Industrial Buying Decisions," *Industrial Marketing* 46 (May 1961), p. 34.

[9]Perreault and Russ, "Physical Distribution in Industrial Purchase Decisions," p. 10.

[10]For example, see David P. Herron, "Managing Physical Distribution for Profit," *Harvard Business Review* 57 (May-June 1979), pp. 121–32; Harvey N. Shycon and Christopher Sprague, "Put a Price Tag on Your Customer Servicing Levels," *Harvard Business Review* 53 (July-August 1975), pp. 71–78.

[11]LaLonde and Zinszer, *Customer Service: Meaning and Measurement,* p. 77.

[12]"The Nation's Newest Private Distribution Centers," *Handling and Shipping* 13 (July 1972), pp. 71–75.

[13]For example, see Marvin L. Fair and Ernest W. Williams, *Economics of Transportation and Logistics* (Dallas: Business Publications Inc., 1975); Robert C. Lieb, *Transportation: The Domestic System* (Reston, Virginia: Reston Publishing, Inc., 1978); and Donald V. Harper, *Transportation in America* (Englewood Cliffs, N.J.: Prentice-Hall, Inc., 1978).

[14]Ronald H. Ballou, *Basic Business Logistics* (Englewood Cliffs, N.J.: Prentice-Hall, Inc., 1978), p. 134.

[15]"Closing the Transportation/Delivery Gap," *Industrial Distribution* 68 (April 1978), p. 46.

[16]David P. Herron, "Managing Physical Distribution for Profit," *Harvard Business Review* 57 (May-June 1979), p. 128.

[17]Ibid.

[18]For example, see "The Elements of Private Carriage," booklet, reprinted from *Transportation and Distribution Management* magazine (Washington, D.C.: The Traffic Service Corporation, 1970); H. G. Becker, Jr., "Private Carriage: Facts and Trends. Some Reasons Why," *Handling and Shipping* 17 (July 1976), p. 42.

[19]Bernard J. LaLonde and Douglas M. Lambert, "A Methodology for Determining Inventory Carrying Costs: Two Case Studies," in James Robeson and John Grabner (eds.), *Proceedings of the Fifth Annual Transportation and Logistics Educators Conference* (October 1975), p. 47.

[20]Ibid., p. 47.

[21]Ibid., p. 39.

[22]James L. Heskett, "Logistics—Essential to Strategy," *Harvard Business Review* 56 (November-December 1977), p. 89.

[23]Ibid., p. 29.

[24]Stephen B. Oresman and Charles D. Scudder, "A Remedy for Maldistribution," *Business Horizons* 17 (June 1974), p. 72.

[25]Louis W. Stern and Adel I. El-Ansary, *Marketing Channels* (Englewood Cliffs, N.J.: Prentice-Hall, Inc., 1977), p. 193.

Discussion Questions

1. Adopting the perspective of an organizational buyer, carefully illustrate how the most economical source of supply might be the firm that offers the highest price, but also the fastest and most reliable delivery system.

2. Why is the logistical function often singled out as "the last frontier of cost reduction in American business"?

3. Describe a situation where *total* logistics costs might be reduced by doubling transportation costs.

4. A key goal in logistical management is to find the optimum balance of logistical cost and customer service which yields optimal profits. Explain.

5. Explain how consistent order cycle performance gives the organizational buyer the opportunity to cut the level of safety stock maintained.

6. Explain how the use of reps versus distributors influences the number of warehouses that the industrial marketer will need to employ in the logistics system.

7. Why is it often necessary for industrial marketers to have a *two-tier* logistical system: one for routine orders, one for rush orders?

8. Inventory decisions for the industrial marketer are based on important cost-service and transportation-inventory tradeoffs. Illustrate the nature of these tradeoffs.

9. Frequent interwarehouse shipments and slow inventory turnover are two signs of maldistribution. If these danger signals appear, what steps should the industrial marketer take?

Chapter 13 Managing the Industrial Pricing Function

The price that an industrial marketer assigns to a product or service is one of many factors that will be placed under close scrutiny by the organizational buyer in evaluating alternative offerings. Thus, pricing decisions cannot be made in a vacuum, but rather must be in concert with other marketing strategy decisions. The diverse nature of the industrial market presents unique problems and opportunities for the price-setter.

After reading this chapter, you will have an understanding of:

1. *the role of price in the cost/benefit calculations of organizational buyers*
2. *the central elements of the industrial pricing process*
3. *the requirements for establishing effective new product prices and the need for periodic adjustment of the prices of existing product line items*
4. *strategic approaches that can be employed in competitive bidding*
5. *the strategic role of lease marketing.*

The industrial marketing manager faces the difficult task of blending the various components of the marketing mix into a total offering that responds to the needs of the market and provides a return consistent with the firm's objectives. Price must be carefully meshed with the product, distribution, and communication strategies of the firm. To illustrate, organizational customers view price as one attribute of a product; thus, close coordination of product and pricing policies is required. In turn, price decisions can also influence channel relationships by altering the profit margins that distributor's or manufacturer's representatives receive for promoting the firm's products. Thus, the pricing objectives of the industrial firm are linked to the objectives of the marketing program as well as overall corporate objectives.

The interdependency of price and other strategy components must be recognized before the pricing function can be isolated for analysis. With this point of view, this chapter examines pricing in the industrial marketing environment. Clearly, there is no one best way for establishing the price of a new industrial product or making the decision to modify the price of existing products. The price-setter requires an understanding of the firm's objectives, market, costs, competition, and customer demand patterns. A clear assessment of each of these areas is often difficult because of a lack of time, incomplete information, and a rapidly changing competitive and business climate. Rising inflation, material shortages, growing competition (foreign and domestic), new technology, changing consumer requirements, and the changing fortunes of different business sectors—these forces challenge the industrial marketer and call for an active rather than a passive approach to the pricing function.

This chapter is divided into five parts. First, the special meaning of price is defined in an industrial marketing context. Second, key determinants of the industrial pricing process are analyzed. Likewise, an operational approach to the pricing decision process will be provided. Third, the pricing policies for new and existing products will be examined. Here, attention will be given to the need for actively managing a product throughout its life cycle. The fourth component of the chapter centers on price administration (i.e., various types of price adjustments). Last, attention is given to two areas of particular importance to the industrial marketer—competitive bidding and leasing.

An Industrial Pricing Perspective

Organizational buyers evaluate the offerings of competing industrial firms on many dimensions. Their assessment centers on the costs and benefits that a particular supplier's total offering provides to them. When organizational decision makers select a particular firm, they are "buying" a given level of product quality, technical service, and delivery reliability. This offering may also include other elements of importance to the buyer—the reputation of the supplier, a feeling of security, friendship, and other personal benefits that may flow from a particular buyer-seller relationship. Thus, the total product (as discussed in chapter 9) includes much more than mere physical attributes. Likewise, the *cost* of an industrial good includes much more than the seller's *price*. An understanding of how organizational buyers weigh these costs and benefits is essential in determining the role of price in the marketing mix. Pricing decisions and product policy decisions are inseparable and must be balanced with the firm's market segmentation plan.[1]

Benefits

Different market segments, possessing unique needs, base their evaluation of a firm's product on dimensions of particular value to them. The benefits of a particular product can be functional, operational, financial, or personal.[2] These benefits are of varying degrees of importance to different market segments as well as to different individuals within the buying center of an organization. Functional benefits center on design characteristics that might be deemed attractive by technical personnel; operational attributes focus on the durability and reliability of the product, qualities that are salient to production managers. Financial benefits include favorable terms and opportunities for cost savings of importance to purchasing managers and controllers. Organizational status, reduced risk, and personal satisfaction are among the personal benefits that might accrue to an individual from a particular supplier choice.

Costs

A broad perspective is likewise needed in examining the costs that a particular supplier alternative presents for the buyer. These costs include not only the seller's price, but also transportation, installation, order handling, and inventory carrying costs. Less obvious, but no less important, costs are the risk of product failure and poor technical and delivery support.[3] A view of costs from a total perspective has assumed great importance to the contemporary organizational buyer of industrial goods.

These costs are made especially vivid in buying organizations that employ formal supplier evaluation programs. These rating systems were discussed in chapter 3. Recall that the systems, such as the cost-ratio and the weighted-point methods, seek to provide a tool to the buyer for measuring the total cost of dealing with alternative suppliers on important dimensions (e.g., product quality, delivery service, and price).[4]

An organizational buyer may find that a supplier that offers the lowest price may, indeed, be the highest cost alternative in the long run! Clearly, the supplier with the lowest price is not guaranteed an account. This was reinforced in a study of purchasers of selected capital items (e.g., liquid transfer and control systems). In an analysis of over 100 purchase decisions, the low bidder was *not* selected in over 40 percent of the cases.[5]

The Industrial Pricing Process

An easy formula does not exist for pricing an industrial product or service. The price-setter faces a decision that is multidimensional rather than one-dimensional. Consideration must be given to the interactive variables of demand, cost, competition, profit relationships, and customer usage patterns. Each assumes significance as the marketer approaches the pricing decision and formulates the role that price will play in the firm's marketing strategy. Key dimensions of the industrial pricing process are examined in this section. These include (1) price objectives, (2) demand determinants, (3) cost determinants, and (4) competition.

Price Objectives

The pricing decision cannot be made in isolation, but must be based on objectives congruent with marketing objectives and overall corporate objectives. Often, the marketer develops principal, as well as collateral, pricing goals. These objectives often center on: (1) achieving a target return on investment; (2) achieving a market share goal; or (3) meeting competition. Clearly, there are many other potential pricing objectives that go beyond profit and market share goals, and include an emphasis on competition, channel relationships, and product line considerations.

An example of pricing objectives, drawn from a classic study by Robert Lanzillotti, illustrates the nature of principal and collateral pricing goals.[6] United States Steel's principal pricing goal was to achieve an 8 percent return on investment after taxes. Collateral pricing objectives were to achieve: (1) a target market share of 30 percent, (2) a stable price, and (3) a stable margin.

Pricing objectives must be established with care because they have far-reaching effects on marketing strategy and the overall goals of the firm. Each firm faces unique internal and external environmental forces. Contrasting the strategies of DuPont and the Dow Chemical Company illustrates the importance of a unified corporate direction.[7] Dow's strategy centers on low margin commodity goods that are priced low in an attempt to build a dominant market share. Once attained, emphasis turns to maintaining that dominant share. DuPont's strategy, on the other hand, emphasizes specialty products that carry a higher margin. Initially, these products are priced at a high level, and prices are reduced as the market expands and competition intensifies. Thus, each industrial firm requires explicit pricing objectives that are consistent with its corporate mission.

Demand Determinants

A strong market perspective is fundamental in the industrial pricing process. The marketer of an industrial product faces a diverse and complex market. Often, a single industrial product can be utilized in many different ways by potential buyers. Each segment may represent a unique application for the product and a particular usage level. The degree of importance that the industrial good assumes in the buyer's end product also varies by market segment. Therefore, the potential demand, the sensitivity to price, and the potential profitability can vary markedly across market segments. As emphasized in discussing each component of the marketing mix, a sound market segmentation strategy is pivotal in effective marketing strategy development. Price is clearly no exception.

A Customer Focus. A sound industrial pricing perspective, as noted earlier, involves an analysis of the benefits and costs of the product from the standpoint of the organizational customer. In making choices, organizational buyers carefully weigh the benefits and costs of alternatives.[8] In calculating the benefits of a product, the marketer can examine the physical attributes of a product (hard benefits) and the attached services (soft benefits). Often, an industrial marketer can define hard benefits with a price-performance ratio. For example, one performance variable for a piece of earth-moving equipment may center on dollars per horsepower or, better yet, in consumer-oriented terms—the yards of earth moved per hour. This approach forces the marketer to examine the product from the consumer's perspective and allows for a comparison of the firm's product offering with those of competitors. Soft benefits are more difficult to precisely define, but an effort should be made to determine their degree of importance to various market segments.

To the organizational customer, costs include more dimensions than the seller's price. To illustrate, the "costs" of a new packaging machine, purchased by a manufacturer, begin with the price but also include transportation, installation, repair and maintenance, energy usage, and many other facets. In calculating the customer costs of a product, the marketer can apply *life cycle costing*. This is a method of calculating the total cost of a purchase over its life span. Thus, maintenance, repair, operating costs, and useful product life are included in this analysis. Rising labor, energy, and material prices are among the factors that have stimulated renewed interest in life cycle costing by government agencies, commercial enterprises, and institutions.[9] Such an environment provides an ideal opportunity for a marketer to apply this concept creatively in analyzing customer needs.

Although the concept has generally been applied to capital items (e.g., computers, heavy industrial equipment, health facilities), it can also be applied to lighter industrial goods. To use life cycle costing as a marketing tool, the producer of a packaging machine may be able to justify a high initial price if clear savings in energy, material, labor, and maintenance costs can be illustrated over the life of the asset.

Other costs, more difficult to precisely quantify, may also be worthy of consideration by the marketer.[10] For example, the organizational buyer of packaging equipment might be very concerned about the possibility of a production stoppage due to a machine failure. Segments of the market that are sensitive to this risk will be interested in the benefit of reliability, and they may be willing to pay a higher price to reduce the risk of system failure. To recap, the industrial price-setter must examine the means by which organizational buyers balance the costs and benefits of alternative offerings. This approach is useful, not only in determining an appropriate price, but also in facilitating the development of responsive product, advertising, and personal selling strategies.

Elasticity Varies by Market Segment. Price elasticity of demand is a measure of the degree to which customers are sensitive to price changes. Specifically, price elasticity of demand refers to the rate of percentage change in quantity demanded attributable to the percentage change in price. Clearly, the industrial marketer is interested in determining the effect of changing prices on demand.

The price elasticity of demand is not the same at all prices. An industrial marketer who is contemplating an alteration in price policy requires an understanding of the elasticity of demand. For example, total revenue (price × quantity) will *increase* if price is decreased and demand is price elastic, whereas, revenues will *fall* if the price is decreased and demand is price inelastic. Many factors influence the price elasticity of demand—one of which may be the organizational buyers' perceptions of price/quality relationships. Research suggests that organizational buyers do *not* associate higher quality with higher price or lower quality with lower price.[11]

Efforts to measure the demand patterns of an individual firm or even an entire industry are extremely difficult and complex. One pricing expert notes that ". . . no one has yet developed a completely reliable method to measure the price elasticity of demand for a particular brand."[12] Since price is only one of many variables under the control of the marketing manager and only one component of the total product offering, other demand elasticities—promotion, distribution, service—also assume importance. However, recognition of the fact that measurement of price elasticity is difficult should not deter the marketer attempting to define buyer sensitivity to the price variable across market segments.

A cognizance of the end use of the product is of value to the marketer in understanding demand patterns and the buyer's sensitivity to price. Here, important insights can be secured by answering this question: how important is the industrial marketer's product as an input in the total cost of producing an end product? If the industrial marketer's product input assumes an insignificant role in the final product's total cost, demand is likely inelastic. This phenomenon can be best illustrated by the following example.

> A manufacturer of precision transistors was contemplating an across-the-board price decrease to increase sales. However, an item analysis of the product line revealed that some of its low volume transistors were used in exotic applications by the firm's customers. A technical customer used the component in an ultrasonic testing apparatus which was sold for $8,000 a unit. This fact prompted the transistor manufacturer to raise the price of the item. Ironically, the firm then experienced a temporary surge of demand for the item as purchasing agents stocked up in anticipation of future price increases.[13]

Of course, the marketer must temper this estimate with an analysis of the costs, availability, and suitability of substitutes. Generally, if the industrial product constitutes an important, but low cost, input in the total cost of the end product, price is less important than quality and delivery reliability.[14]

An analysis of other applications or market segments may indicate that the industrial product input assumes a more substantial portion of the final product's total cost. Here, changes in price may have an important effect on the demand of both the final product as well as the industrial product input. Assuming that demand in the final consumer market is price elastic, a reduction in price of the end item that is caused by a price reduction of an industrial product input would generate an increase in demand for the final product and, in turn, for the industrial product.

Because the demand for many industrial products is derived from the demand of the product of which they are a part, a strong end user focus is needed. In addition to analyzing the product's proportionate role in the total cost of producing end items, the marketer can benefit by examining the trends and changing fortunes of important final consumer markets. Different sectors of the market grow at different rates, confront different levels of competition, and face different short-run and long-run challenges. To illustrate, a downturn in the economy does not fall equally on all sectors, but affects some more severely than others. In making pricing decisions, a two-tier market focus—of organizational customers and final product customers—is required. For example, ". . . all things being equal, an industrial supplier will have more success in passing on a price increase to customers who are prospering than to customers who are hard-pressed."[15]

Methods of Estimating Demand. What tools are available to the industrial marketer in measuring the price elasticity of demand? Some of these techniques rely on objective statistical data, while others center on the intuition and judgment of managers. Three of these approaches are briefly described below: test marketing, surveys, and managerial judgment.

Test marketing, as a rule, is considered a tool only appropriate for the consumer-goods manufacturer.[16] However, this technique should not be eliminated from the industrial marketer's repertoire of tools. Industrial products that are sold to a large number of potential users have short usage cycles (which permit an analysis of repurchase patterns), and have feasible test market sites, lend themselves to test marketing. While most high priced capital items do not fit this profile, other products such as industrial paints and maintenance items often meet test market requirements.

The *survey approach* also provides a vehicle for measuring price elasticity. The survey approach will be treated in detail in chapter 16; however, in this instance, interviews would be conducted with existing or potential customers to ascertain their willingness to buy at various prices or price ranges. On occasion, a joint research approach with a consumer goods manufacturer could be followed and centered on final consumer demand. Since price is only one variable of concern to organizational buyers in making choices, the questionnaire must also contain queries concerning product and service perceptions. A key objective is to ascertain how organizational buyers view price in fundamental cost/benefit tradeoffs. This broader perspective is particularly useful in isolating market segments.

Since the price-setter often lacks the time and resources to utilize the more formal survey or field experimentation approaches, a more informal and subjective approach becomes practical. This technique draws upon the experience, intuition, and judgment of executives and permits an analysis of the relationship of price to other marketing mix variables. Thus, a particular pricing plan must include assumptions concerning product, promotion, and distribution strategies and a particular competitive setting.[17]

To recap, knowledge of the market constitutes the cornerstone in the industrial pricing process. A strong market focus, which examines how consumers tradeoff benefits and costs in their decision-making process, establishes a base for assigning a price for an industrial product or service. While a precarious task, the goal for the price-setter is to estimate as precisely as possible the probable demand curve for the firm's product. Knowledge of demand patterns must be augmented by knowledge of costs.

Cost Determinants

Industrial marketers often pursue a strong internal orientation, and they base prices on their own costs. Here, manufacturers calculate unit costs and add a percentage profit to yield the selling price. Strict adherence to a cost-plus philosophy of pricing results in a decision environment that overlooks customer perceptions of value, competition, and the interaction of volume and profit.

Costs do, however, establish the lower limit pricing point. Since costs fluctuate with volume and vary over time, costs must be considered in relation to demand, competition, and objectives in the industrial pricing process. The marketer requires an understanding of which costs are relevant to the pricing decision and knowledge of how these costs will fluctuate with volume and over various time intervals. Thus, the determinants and behavior of product costs are crucial in projecting the profitability of individual products as well as the entire product line. A first step is the proper classification of costs.

Classifying Costs.[18] Some costs are directly related to the rate of activity, while others are not. The goals of a cost classification system are to: (1) properly classify cost data into their fixed and variable components and (2) properly link them to the activity causing their cost. The manager can then analyze the effect of volume on these costs and, more importantly, identify sources of profit. The following cost concepts are instrumental in this analysis.

1. *Direct traceable or attributable costs*—those costs, fixed or variable, incurred by and solely for a particular product, customer, or sales territory (e.g., raw materials).

2. *Indirect traceable costs*—those costs, fixed or variable, that can be traced to a product, customer, or sales territory (e.g., general plant overhead may be indirectly assigned to a product).
3. Those *general costs* that support a number of activities and that cannot be objectively assigned to a product on the basis of a direct physical relationship (e.g., the administrative costs of a sales district).

Note that common costs, such as administrative costs, will not change if an item is added or deleted from the firm's product line. Marketing, production, and distribution costs are all relevant to this classification system. In developing a new product line or in deleting or adding an item to an existing line, the marketer requires a firm grasp of the cost implications. Properly identifying and classifying costs is an important starting point in making profitable pricing decisions.

Experience Effects. In addition to properly classifying costs, attention must be given to the behavior of costs over time. Here, the industrial marketer is concerned with forecasting costs and, in turn, prices. Two concepts of strategic importance to the industrial price-setter are: (1) the learning curve and (2) the experience effect.

The *learning curve,* also referred to as the progress function or start-up function, indicates that *manufacturing costs* decline as volume rises. To illustrate, the costs of computers were significantly reduced by a drop in the price of ferro-magnetic memory cores from five cents per bit (unit of memory) in 1965 to less than one-half cent in 1973.[19] Clearly, a manager who is contemplating a new contract or new extension to the product line must examine the degree to which the proposal will converge on the firm's past manufacturing experience. If the firm has successfully ascended the learning curve, the new product could be produced at lower costs and with a higher degree of confidence. Higher start-up costs, uncertainty, and a period of learning are obstacles confronting the first-time producer.

The *experience effect,* a related concept, shows that *total costs* of a product line decline over time as volume increases. In contrast to the learning curve, the experience effect encompasses a broader range of costs—administration, marketing, distribution, and manufacturing.[20] Specifically, the experience effect indicates that costs (measured in constant dollars) decline by a predictable and constant percentage each time *accumulated* experience (volume) is doubled. Thus, each time accumulated volume is doubled, the cost of many products falls by 10 to 30 percent. The usual decline is in the range of 20 to 30 percent. The experience effect also applies to suppliers. For example, an industrial firm that supplies components to a consumer-goods manufacturer—that has been gaining substantial experience and consistently expanding output—likewise benefits from the experience effect. The industrial supplier realizes a reduction in costs each time cumulative production doubles.

An experience curve that depicts the relationship between cost and experience is provided in figure 13.1. The curve illustrated is an 85 percent experience curve. This merely indicates that with every doubling of experience, costs per unit drop to 85 percent of their original level. Alternatively, this could be expressed as a 15 percent reduction in costs per unit for every doubling of cumulative production. Different products and industries experience different learning rates (75 percent, 80 percent, 85 percent, and so on).

To capitalize effectively on the experience effect, the industrial marketer must understand why costs decline with accumulated volume.[21] First, workers of all types become more adept at the job as they repeat the performance of their functions. Second, as volume expands, greater job specialization becomes possible. Specialization has traditionally been one of the most effective ways to increase labor productivity. Third, new production processes and technologies can be applied as volume grows, and this often results in important cost reductions. Fourth, experience with production equipment and systems often suggests methods for expanding output, thus lowering production costs per unit. Finally, changing the mixture of production inputs (automation for labor), input standardization, and product redesign are all related to the experience gained with a product and can bring about meaningful cost reductions.

Equally important is the fact that as experience is gained, costs do not perforce decline. In fact, costs that are not carefully managed will inevitably

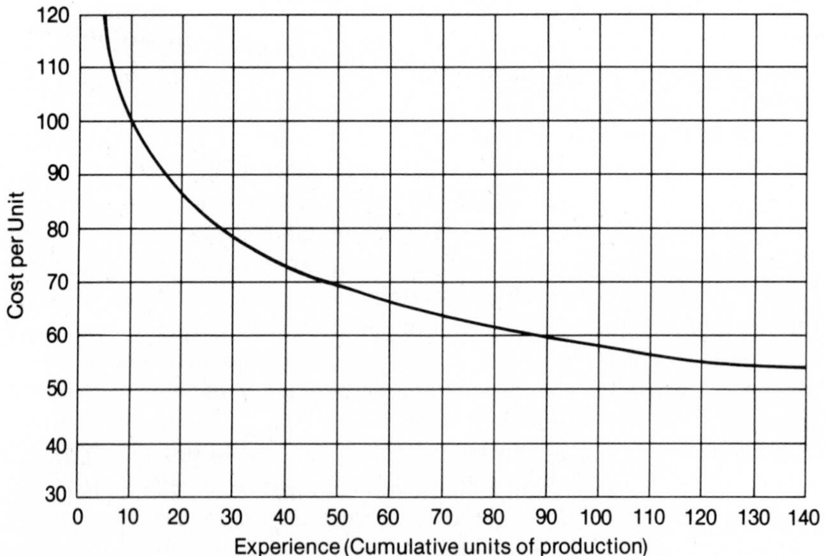

Figure 13.1 / A Typical Experience Curve (85 percent)

Source. Adapted from *Perspectives on Experience* (Boston: Boston Consulting Group, Inc., 1968), p. 13. Reprinted by permission.

rise. Experience merely gives management the opportunity to seek cost reductions and efficiency improvements. A conscious and thorough effort must be made to exploit the benefits of experience. Product standardization, new production processes, labor efficiency, work specialization—these are a few of many areas that must be examined to capitalize on the experience effect.

The experience effect can raise a strategic dilemma for the industrial marketer. Often, the aggressive pursuit of a cost minimization strategy leads to a reduced ability to make innovative product changes in the face of competition.[22] Clearly, any firm that is following an efficiency strategy must insure that its product remains in line with the needs of the market. A product that is efficiently produced and carries a low price can only survive if there are significant market segments that emphasize low price as a key choice criterion.

The experience effect provides the marketer with an approach that can be used in projecting costs and prices in an industry. The concept is also of value when product line modifications are being considered. Often, two or more products in the firm's line share a common resource or involve the same production or distribution activity. Such *shared experience* is significant because the costs of one item in the product line are reduced even more because of the accumulated experience with the other product line item.[23] The marketer that has costs carefully classified (as illustrated earlier) is best equipped to take advantage of shared experience opportunities.

Break Even Analysis. Break even point analysis, a basic financial tool, inevitably enters the pricing process. Break even point analysis allows the decision maker to determine the level of sales required to cover all relevant fixed and variable costs. The break even point quantity can be calculated as follows:

$$\text{BEQ} = \frac{\text{FC}}{\text{P} - \text{VC}}$$

where BEQ = break even sales quantity

FC = fixed costs

P = selling price

VC = direct variable costs

Assume that the industrial marketer is evaluating this situation: fixed costs are \$200,000; direct variable costs are \$15; and consideration is being given to a \$20 selling price. Thus,

$$\text{BEQ} = \frac{200{,}000}{20-15} = \frac{200{,}000}{5} = 40{,}000 \text{ units}$$

This relationship is illustrated graphically in figure 13.2. From the diagram, note that break even analysis assumes that: (1) fixed costs remain

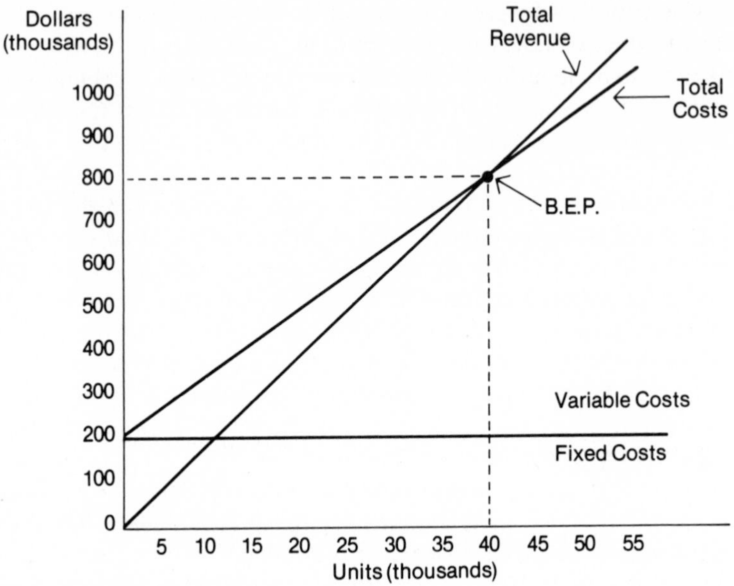

Figure 13.2 / Break Even Analysis

constant as the volume of production increases and (2) variable costs increase proportionately with increases in production. Break even point calculations are often based heavily on historical cost data when, in fact, projected costs and prices are more critical to the decision maker. Drawing upon the experience effect, the price-setter must make a concerted effort to project future cost patterns.

Competition

Competition establishes an upper limit on price and, therefore, must be given careful attention in the industrial pricing process. Research suggests that industrial marketers regard "competitive level pricing" as the most important pricing strategy.[24] The degree of latitude that the individual industrial firm has in its pricing decision depends heavily upon the level of differentiation that the product has in the perceptions of organizational buyers. As discussed earlier, price is only one component that enters the cost-benefit equation of buyers. Thus, the marketer can gain a differential advantage over competitors on many dimensions other than the physical product characteristics. Reputation, technical expertise, delivery reliability, and related factors may distinguish the firm's product in the minds of organizational customers.

In addition to assessing the degree of differentiation that the firm's product possesses among various market segments, an estimation must be made of the anticipated response of competitors to particular pricing decisions.

Gauging Competitive Response. To predict the response of competitors, several areas are worthy of analysis. First, the marketer can benefit from an examination of the cost structure of direct competitors and producers of potential substitutes. Here the marketer can draw upon public statements and records (e.g., annual reports) which may provide a base for rough estimates. Likewise, the experience effect can be used as a tool in assessing the cost structure of competition. Competitors that have ascended the learning curve have lower costs than those that have just entered the industry and are beginning the climb. An estimate of the cost structure is valuable in gauging the competitors' ability to respond to price reductions and in providing an estimate of the pattern that prices might follow in the future.

A second factor worthy of consideration in analyzing competition is the market strategy employed by competing sellers. Competitors will be more sensitive toward price reductions that threaten market segments that *they* deem important. Competitors are more likely to learn of such price reductions earlier when their market segments overlap with those of the price initiator. Of course, a competitor may choose not to follow a price decrease, especially if that firm feels that it enjoys a differentiated position in the market. A third area of importance in predicting the response of competitors to price changes centers on the structure of the industry in which the industrial marketer operates.

Industrial manufacturers are particularly sensitive to the reaction of competitors to price changes because they often operate in oligopolistic industries. An *oligopoly* refers to a market structure consisting of few sellers, where the actions of one seller produce reactions on the part of its competitors. Examples of oligopolistic industries include computers, aluminum, steel, automobiles, electrical equipment, and glass. In each case, a small number of manufacturers produce a dominant proportion of total output. Oligopolies can assume two forms—pure or differentiated. A pure oligopoly exists when competing firms offer homogeneous products (e.g., steel), while a differentiated oligopoly contains producers of differentiated products (e.g., computers). As the extent of product differentiation in an oligopoly increases, the degree of price differences among competing sellers also increases.

The *kinked demand curve* is an often-noted characteristic of oligopolistic markets. This describes a pattern of behavior in which competing sellers are assumed to follow any decrease in price in order to protect their existing market shares, but to refrain from following price increases, hence capturing part of the market share of the price-raiser. Thus, the individual firm's demand curve, as illustrated in figure 13.3, is kinked at the current price-quantity combination. Note that a price decrease results in a relatively small increase in sales. On the other hand, a price increase would lead to a significant reduction in quantity demanded and, in turn, total revenue, as customers shift to competing firms that choose not to follow the price increase.

A recognized price leader exists in many industries and is frequently found in the industrial market. *Price leadership* results when one firm es-

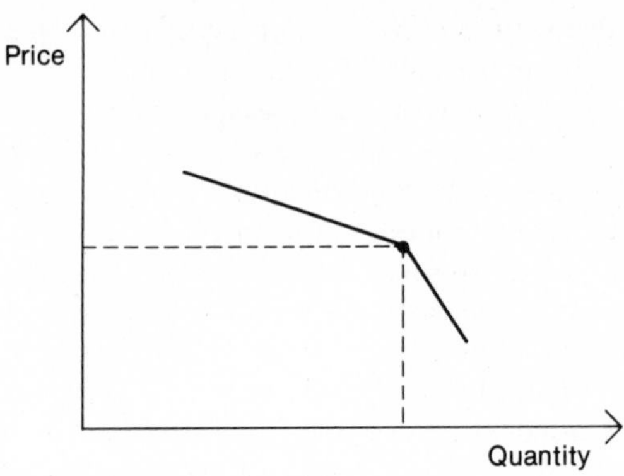

Figure 13.3 / Kinked Demand Curve

sentially serves as the industry spokesman and other sellers in the industry accept its pricing policy. This leadership position can result from one or more of the following: technical superiority, size and strength, cost efficiency, power in the channel of distribution, and market information. The industry leader is presumed to bring profitability and stability to an industry by establishing a price that produces satisfactory profits for all sellers. Thus, a price increase initiated by the leader and generally thought to be in the best interests of the industry will be followed by other sellers.

The discussion to this point has centered on key components of the industrial pricing process: objectives, demand, cost, and competition. Legal factors (discussed later in the chapter) must also be considered by the price-setter. The manager requires a grasp of each to approach the multidimensional pricing decision. Price-setting is not a single act but an ongoing process.

Pricing across the Product Life Cycle

The specific types of pricing decisions that the industrial marketer faces take many forms. What price should be assigned to a distinctly new industrial product or service? When an item is added to an existing product line, how should it be priced in relation to existing products in the line? While the discussion to this point in the chapter establishes a framework for dealing with these questions, each is worthy of some specific attention.

Pricing New Products

The strategic decision of pricing new products can be best understood by examining the policies that establish the boundaries of a continuum—from *skimming* (a high initial price) to *penetration* (a low initial price). Recall the earlier discussion of the contrasts between the pricing strategies of DuPont and Dow Chemical. DuPont assigns an initial high price to new products in order to generate immediate profits or to recover research and development expenditures, while Dow Chemical follows a low price strategy for new products with the objective of gaining market share.

Skimming vs. Penetration. In evaluating the merits of skimming compared to penetration, the marketer must again examine the price of the new product from the buyer's perspective. Such an approach ". . . recognizes that the upper limit is the price that will produce the minimum acceptable rate of return on the investment of a sufficiently large number of prospects."[25] This is especially important in pricing new products, because the potential profits accruing to buyers of a new machine tool, for example, will vary by market segment. Likewise, these market segments may differ in the minimum rate of return that will induce them to invest in the machine tool. In addition, selection of an appropriate new product pricing policy must involve a consideration of the cost structure of existing and potential competitors, as well as that of the new product initiator. The experience effect reasserts itself as a useful pricing tool.

Skimming. A skimming approach, appropriate for a distinctly new product, provides the firm with an opportunity to profitably reach market segments that are not sensitive to the high initial price. As a product ages, and as competitors enter and organizational buyers become accustomed to evaluating and purchasing the product, demand becomes more elastic with respect to price. The policy of using a skimming approach at the outset, followed by penetration pricing as the product matures, is referred to by Joel Dean as *time segmentation.*[26] Hence, a skimming policy allows the marketer to capture early profits, then reduce the price to reach segments that are more price sensitive. A final benefit of the skimming approach is that it provides a means for the innovator to recover more quickly high developmental costs.

Penetration. A penetration policy, by contrast, is appropriate when there is: (1) a high price elasticity of demand, (2) a strong threat of imminent competition and (3) an opportunity for a substantial reduction in production costs as volume expands. Drawing upon the experience effect, a firm that can quickly gain substantial market share and experience acquires a strategic advantage over competitors. The viability of this strategy increases with the size of the future market potential. By taking a large share of new sales, experience can be gained when there is a large market growth rate. Of course, investment requirements, the potential benefits of experience, and expected market trends must be given careful attention before embarking on this particular strategy.

Product Line Considerations. The contemporary industrial firm with a long product line faces the complex problem of achieving balance in pricing the firm's product mix. Firms extend their product lines because the demands for various products are interdependent, the costs of producing and marketing those items are interdependent, or both.[27] A firm may add to its product line—or even develop a new product line—to fit more precisely the needs of a particular market segment. If both the demand and costs of individual product line items are interrelated, production and marketing decisions concerning one product line item inevitably influence both the revenues and costs of the firm's other products.

Are specific product line items substitutes or complements? Will a change in the price of one item enhance or retard the usage rate of this or other products in key market segments? Should a new product be priced high at the outset to protect other product line items (e.g., potential substitutes) and give the firm time to revamp other items in the line? These questions point up the delicate challenge that confronts the marketer in making product line pricing decisions. As discussed earlier, such decisions require a knowledge of demand, costs, competition, and strategic marketing objectives.

Announcements of new product introductions are often accompanied by revisions in the price schedule for other product line items. To illustrate, technological advances have been bringing down the prices of computers for years. IBM's introduction of a less expensive, but more sophisticated, central processing unit was paralleled by a reduction in the price of older models.[28] Such product line pricing adjustments must be made with care and are common in the industrial market.

Organizational buyers often screen out product alternatives that fall outside of an acceptable price range, thereby centering attention on a feasible set of alternatives. Kent Monroe suggests that if all products in the firm's product line are priced within the acceptable price range, there is a higher probability that a buyer will purchase a product from that line.[29] Thus, success in penetrating a buying organization with one item often means success for other items in the firm's product line.

Price Administration

The industrial marketer deals with different types of customers (e.g., middlemen vs. original equipment manufacturers) who buy in different quantities and who are located in different geographical regions. Thus, there is a need to make adjustments to price based on these conditions which encircle transactions in the industrial market. This is the goal of price administration.

At the outset, it is important to understand a basic pricing tradition. Industrial sellers often provide a list price and a multiplier. The net price, which is the price of most importance to the organizational buyer, equals the list price times the multiplier. To illustrate, a product that has a list price of $100 and a multiplier of 82 percent has a net price of $82. Why do industrial price-setters send their customers on such a circuitous route in determining a net price? The key reason is that industrial manufacturers have many items in their product line and, often, many product lines that are presented and described in a catalog. Rather than printing a new catalog each time the price of one or more items is adjusted, the firm merely prints a new price schedule and conveys the changes in adjusted multipliers. (For example, for the above illustrated item, the multiplier might be changed to 80 percent, a two-dollar reduction in price.) Likewise, the list-price/multiplier system of pricing makes it a bit more difficult for competitors to detect price changes as they unfold.

Discounts

Price administration involves the development of a discount schedule. Decisions are required concerning trade, quantity, and cash discounts. Each is defined and illustrated in table 13.1.

Trade Discounts. Trade discounts, offered to middlemen or particular classifications of customers, allow the marketer to adjust the price based on the costs and benefits of dealing with different classifications of customers or middlemen. Trade discounts are offered to distributors because they are performing important services. Trade discounts for original equipment manufacturers could be justified on the basis of their high volume purchasing and low selling requirements. In establishing trade discounts, the marketer must recognize competitive norms and the relative importance of different channel members and customer types in their overall marketing objectives.

Quantity Discounts. Note that two types of quantity discounts—cumulative and noncumulative—are defined in table 13.1. The choice of the type and specific schedule for quantity discounts depends on an assessment of demand, costs, and competition. In determining break points in the discount schedule, a strong customer focus is valuable. Here, consideration is given to inventory carrying costs, order processing costs, transportation costs, and usage rates of different market segments. Likewise, as discussed in chapter 12, the marketer can benefit from an examination of important cost/service tradeoffs.

Cash Discounts. Cash discounts are offered to encourage prompt payment of invoices, thereby allowing the marketer to maintain a more favorable cash flow position. As illustrated in table 13.1, a 2 percent discount might be offered if the bill is paid within 10 days. Often, cash discounts present a delicate problem for marketers. Large buyers pay their bills well beyond the 10-day period and still deduct the cash discount. Such tactics are especially prevalent during periods of high interest rates. The marketer's success in correcting this problem often depends on the power that the industrial firm brings into the buyer-seller relationship. This dilemma is compounded by the fact that the Robinson/Patman Act requires sellers to offer the same terms to all competing buyers, large or small.

Table 13.1 / Types of Discounts

<table>
<tr><th>Types</th><th>Characteristics</th></tr>
<tr><td>Trade Discounts</td><td>Those offered to different types of customers and/or middlemen. Often consist of a chain of discounts, subtracted successively from each new net price.
Example: An item with a $10 list price might be offered to distributors with a discount of 25 + 10 percent:
$10.00 − .25(10.00) = $7.50, and
$7.50 − .10(7.50) = $6.75.</td></tr>
<tr><td>Quantity Discounts:</td><td></td></tr>
<tr><td>Noncumulative</td><td>Those granted on the basis of the size (measured in dollars or units) of a single purchase, with the purpose of encouraging large orders.
Example:
<table>
<tr><th>Size of Order</th><th>Percent Off</th></tr>
<tr><td>Less than 20 units</td><td>0</td></tr>
<tr><td>20–29 units</td><td>2</td></tr>
<tr><td>30 or more units</td><td>4</td></tr>
</table></td></tr>
<tr><td>Cumulative</td><td>Those granted on the basis of the size (measured in dollars or units) of orders over a specified period of time.
Example:
<table>
<tr><th>Annual Customer Purchases</th><th>Size of Discount</th></tr>
<tr><td>Less than $1,000</td><td>0%</td></tr>
<tr><td>1,000–1,999</td><td>3%</td></tr>
<tr><td>2,000–2,999</td><td>4%</td></tr>
<tr><td>3,000–3,999</td><td>5%</td></tr>
</table></td></tr>
<tr><td>Cash Discounts</td><td>Those offered for payment of an invoice within a specified period of time.
Example: 2/10, net 30 (i.e., a 2 percent discount may be taken by the buyer if paid within 10 days).</td></tr>
</table>

Legal Considerations

Since the industrial marketer deals with different classifications of customers and middlemen and different types of discounts, an awareness of legal considerations is vital in price administration. The Robinson/Patman Act holds that it is unlawful to:

> . . . discriminate in price between different purchasers of commodities of like grade and quality . . . where the effect of such discrimination may be substantially to lessen competition or tend to create a monopoly, or to injure, destroy, or prevent competition. . . .

Under this act, price differentials are permitted, but they must be based on cost differences or the need to "meet competition."[30] It should be noted that cost differentials are very difficult to justify, and clearly defined policies and procedures are needed in price administration. Such cost justification guidelines are useful to the marketer, not only in making pricing decisions, but also in providing a legal defense to price discrimination charges.

Geographical Pricing

An element in the ultimate price to the buyer is the transportation cost. Thus, geographical pricing decisions must play a role in overall price administration. Essentially, the alternate forms differ on the basis of the degree to which the buyer or seller assumes transportation costs. The specific type used by the industrial marketer depends upon the weight and bulk of the product, the nature and location of key market segments, the percentage of the total price represented by transportation costs, competitive conditions, and industry norms. As treated earlier in the chapter, buyers carefully analyze the total cost of dealing with a particular supplier. Transportation is one factor in the cost/benefit equation. Thus, attention must be given to organizational buyer sensitivity to different types of geographical price arrangements.

To recap, the industrial marketer cannot leave price administration to chance. Discounts must be carefully aligned with the firm's pricing policies and related to the requirements of key market segments. Pricing policies are often based on a defensive, or risk-aversive, perspective rather than a positive one.[31] For example, industrial firms might offer larger quantity discounts to buyers in order to partially offset price level increases. Likewise, opportunities for revising discount schedules may emerge as costs change. Tradition-bound firms can easily overlook such creative uses of pricing policies.

Competitive Bidding

A significant volume of business in the industrial market is transacted through the competitive bidding process. Rather than relying on a specific list price, the industrial marketer must develop a price, or bid, to meet particular product and/or service requirements of a customer.

The Buyer's Side of Bidding

Buying by government and other public agencies is done almost exclusively by competitive bidding. By contrast, the use of competitive bidding by private industry is a bit more limited and is most commonly applied to the purchasing of nonstandardized materials, complex fabricated products where design and manufacturing methods vary, and products made to the buyer's specification.[32] Industrial buyers, in these instances, use competitive bidding as a means of exploring and determining price levels. The types of items procured through competitive bidding are ones for which there is no generally established market price level. Competitive bids allow the purchaser to evaluate the appropriateness of the prices.[33] Competitive bidding may assume two forms: closed and open.

Closed Bidding

Closed bidding, often employed by industrial and governmental buyers, involves a formal invitation to potential suppliers to submit written, sealed bids for a particular business opportunity. All bids are opened and reviewed at a pre-established time, and the contract is generally awarded to the lowest bidder who meets desired specifications. It is important to recognize that the low bidder is not guaranteed of getting the contract because buyers often make such awards on the basis of "lowest responsible bidder." Thus, the ability of alternative buyers to perform may also be infused into the bidding process.

Open Bidding

Open bidding, by contrast, is conducted more informally and allows suppliers to make offers (oral or written) up to a certain date. Here the buyer may continue deliberations with several suppliers throughout the bidding process. Open bidding may be particularly appropriate when specific requirements are hard to rigidly define, or when the product and services of competing suppliers vary substantially.

In selected buying situations, a negotiated pricing process may be employed. Complex technical requirements or uncertain product specifications may lead buying organizations to center their evaluation, first, on the capabilities of competing industrial firms and then to negotiate the price and the form of the product/service offering. Negotiated pricing is especially appropriate for procurement decisions in both the commercial and governmental (as discussed in chapter 2) sectors of the industrial market.

Strategies for Competitive Bidding

Careful planning is fundamental to success in the competitive bidding environment. Such planning includes three important steps: (1) a precise definition of objectives; (2) development of a screening procedure for evaluating alternative bid opportunities; and (3) a method for assessing the probability of success of a particular bidding strategy.

Objectives. Before preparing a bid for any potential contract, the industrial firm must carefully define its objectives. This aids the firm in pursuing particular types of business, determining when to bid, and providing guidelines for what level to bid. These objectives may range on a continuum from profit maximization to company survival. Other objectives might focus on keeping the plant operating and the labor force intact or gaining entry into a new type of business. The marketer can also benefit by analyzing the objectives of those competitors who are likely bidding rivals.

Screening Bid Opportunities. Because developing bids is a costly and time-consuming process, the contracts to bid on should be chosen with care.

Potential contracts offer differing levels of profitability and converge on the technical expertise, past experience, and objectives of the industrial firms to different degrees. Thus, a screening procedure is required to isolate properly the contracts that offer the most promise to the bidder. Key components of such a procedure are illustrated in table 13.2.

Screening Procedure.[34] The use of such a screening procedure in evaluating alternative contracts has improved the bidding success of industrial marketers.[35] The procedure involves three steps. First, the firm identifies criteria that they deem important in evaluating contracts. While the number and nature of the criteria employed in the evaluation process vary by firm and industry, five common criteria (prebid factors) are illustrated in table 13.2. Observe that these prebid factors center on:

1. the impact of the contract on plant capacity;
2. the degree of experience the firm has had with similar projects;
3. follow-up bid opportunities;
4. expected competition;
5. delivery requirements.

Once identified, the prebid factors are assigned weights based on their relative importance to the firm (e.g., a weight of 25 out of the total of 100 is assigned to plant capacity). The third step involves evaluating individual bid opportunities. Here, each factor is evaluated and given a high (10), medium (5), or low (0) value. In table 13.2, the contract is evaluated favorably on all factors except follow-up bid opportunities. Summing the product of each factor's weight and rating provides a total score. The industrial marketer can employ this procedure in evaluating the merits of alternative potential contracts. The firm may wish to establish a minimum acceptable score that a contract must surpass before effort is invested in the preparation of a bid. Since the bid opportunity evaluated in table 13.2 yields a score above the cut-off point, a bid would be prepared.

Table 13.2 / Evaluation of a Bid Opportunity

Prebid Factors	Weight	×	Rating of High 10	Rating of Medium 5	Rating of Low 0	Score
Plant Capacity	25		10			250
Degree of Experience	20		10			200
Follow-up Bid Opportunities	15				0	0
Competition	25		10			250
Delivery Requirements	15		10			150
Total	100					850

Ideal Bid Score: 1000

Minimum Acceptable Score: 750

Probabilistic Bidding Models. Having isolated a project opportunity, the attention of the marketer now turns to estimating the probabilities of winning the contract at various prices. Assuming that the contract is awarded to the lowest bidder, the chances of the firm winning the contract decline as the bid price increases. How will competitors bid? At what bid price will the firm optimize its chances of winning and optimize the level of profit if it does win? Probabilistic bidding models assist the firm in dealing with such questions.[36] Research suggests that firms that utilize probabilistic bidding models are more successful in the competitive bidding process than those that do not.[37]

Such models often draw upon historical data and assume that competitors will behave in the future as they have in the past. Clearly, new competitors may emerge, or existing competitors may alter their bidding strategies. However, probabilistic bidding models provide the marketer with an objective procedure for evaluating the success probabilities and potential profits expected under different bidding scenarios. A key virtue of these formalized bidding approaches is that they motivate managers to assess carefully the costs, competition, and potential profit opportunities that encircle a particular work project. In addition, screening procedures allow the marketer to isolate those projects that are most consistent with the firm's objectives and capabilities.

The Role of Leasing in the Industrial Market[38]

Leasing is assuming increased importance in the industrial market. A lease is essentially a contract through which the asset owner (lessor) extends the right to use the asset to another party (lessee) in return for a periodic payment of rent over a specified period. The original cost value of industrial equipment on lease exceeded $100 billion in 1976, and may be as high as $150 billion in 1980. New leases account for roughly 20 percent of corporate capital expenditures, and leasing is growing at a rate of 10 to 15 percent annually.

Financial Leases vs. Operating Leases

Leases can be divided into two broad categories: financial (full-payout) leases and operating leases. Financial leases are noncancellable contracts that are usually long term and fully amortized over this term. Lease payments over the contract period equal or exceed the original purchase price of the item. For example, a food packaging machine might be purchased outright at a price of $21,000 or leased for five years with lease payments of $5,800 per year. The organization leasing the equipment is generally responsible for operating expenses, but the marketer/lessor may attach benefits (e.g., maintenance) if competitive pressures dictate. A purchase option is frequently a part of financial leases. This option may be exercised at the termination of the contract, and it is usually for the asset's fair market value at that time. Operating leases (sometimes called rental agreements), by contrast, are shorter-term, cancellable agreements which are not fully amortized. Since the purpose is to provide equipment which is only needed for short periods, a purchase option is usually not a feature of the contract. Operating lease rates are usually higher than financial lease rates because the marketer is assuming the operating costs as well as the risks of obsolescence. Particular attention will be given to financial leasing.

Lease vs. Purchase

As emphasized throughout the chapter, organizational buyers examine the cost/benefit tradeoffs of alternative offerings. Thus, organizational buyers, contemplating the purchase of capital equipment items, confront the "lease vs. purchase" decision. Paul Anderson and William Lazer note that "a manufacturer's product and service mix is augmented by the additional benefits, largely economic in nature, available to customers through leasing."[39] How do organizational customers evaluate the benefits and costs of a lease? Among the benefits and costs are:

Benefits	vs.	Costs
avoidance of cash purchase cost		cash outflow of lease payments
avoidance of those operating costs absorbed by lessor		foregone tax shields resulting from depreciation, interest, and operating expenses
tax shield provided by lease payments		sacrifice of asset's salvage value

Essentially, the decision should rest on the present value sum of the costs and benefits of the lease: that is, do the cash flow benefits of the lease exceed the cash flow costs?

At the same time, however, there is evidence to suggest that lessees may also enter into lease arrangements for reasons that cannot be reflected in the lease versus purchase cash flows. Surveys of lessee motivations consistently indicate that leasing is believed to provide various nonquantifiable benefits.[40] For example, lessees suggest that leasing preserves their credit capacity, minimizes equipment disposal problems, allows for the acquisition of equipment when other financing sources are not available, avoids the dilution of ownership or control that accompanies debt or equity financing, and protects against the risks of equipment obsolesence. Thus, it has been suggested that the ultimate decision to lease or purchase may depend on a balance between the quantifiable costs of leasing on the one hand and both the quantifiable and nonquantifiable benefits on the other.[41]

Industrial Lease Marketing: Strategic Implications

Evidence suggests that many large industrial customers, when confronting the lease versus purchase decision, employ financial techniques that fail to give appropriate weight to the potential economic benefits of leasing.[42] Anderson and Lazer contend that such a bias against leasing might best be overcome by creating a financial specialist position within the sales organization. This specialist would interface with financially oriented influencers within the buying center and provide the customer with a range of consulting services and financial information (e.g., tax and accounting information). Xerox Corporation, for example, caters to customers who express an interest in leasing through a marketing financial analyst known as a *consulting service representative*. In turn, customers who express an interest in outright purchase are served by another specialist—the *sold equipment representative*. Such specialization permits the marketer to respond to the particular needs and objectives of organizational customers. As emphasized throughout this volume, such services increase the value of the firm's total offering in the minds of organizational buyers and often provide the marketer with a differential advantage over competitors.

Successful lease marketing efforts require a careful assessment of the role of leasing in the overall marketing program. Thus, strategic leasing decisions cannot be isolated from product, pricing, and marketing communication decisions. A particularly delicate decision emerges in the development of pricing strategy. Here, a price *and* a lease rate must be established for the same product.

Pricing Strategy. Depending upon the firm's objectives, the marketer can establish the lease rate at a level which: (1) encourages leasing by customers; (2) encourages outright purchase; or (3) achieves balance between the lease rate and the sales rate. To illustrate, a marketer might offer favorable lease rates that encourage leasing in order to link buying organizations to the firm's product line or to reach new market segments that were previously inaccessible. Alternatively, the industrial marketer might wish to set relatively high lease rates in order to stimulate customers to purchase the capital items outright. Leasing can place a troublesome cash flow drain on the industrial firm. Thus, marketers might wish to improve their cash flow position by encouraging customers to buy rather than lease.

Regardless of the strategy followed, the price-setter must adopt a product line perspective. A change in the price or lease rate of one item may directly or indirectly influence the demand for other items. To illustrate, IBM cut the price of several small computer systems but left the leasing rates of these systems unchanged.[43] Such a strategy would encourage customers to purchase the equipment that they are currently leasing. Likewise, new customers would be more inclined to purchase rather than lease those systems. To stimulate demand for new items in the product line, the firm might offer attractive lease rates.

The marketer of industrial equipment requires an understanding of the benefits and costs of leasing from the customer's perspective. This knowledge provides the groundwork for defining the strategic role of leasing in the industrial marketing program.

Price Strategy Boomerang

IBM surprised the entire computer industry with the price strategy introduced for its new 4300 series computer in early 1979. The low pricing strategy surprised competitors, many of whom were hard pressed to compete on a price/performance basis. As market leader, IBM had traditionally set prices to provide a favorable "umbrella," profitable for all competitors. The new price strategy radically changed IBM's posture to that of a very aggressive competitor.

IBM, however, reassessed its pricing strategy and reversed itself in late 1979, raising prices by 5 to 7 percent on almost all products. Why the sudden shift? Many observers believe that IBM realized that it had made a mistake. First, by following the low price policy, the company was unnecessarily forfeiting close to one billion dollars in revenue as the demand for computers is generally price inelastic. Secondly, the firm was put into a cash flow bind as a result of customer expectations. Because customers expected low prices on future new models, many were currently leasing machines rather than buying them outright. Not only did IBM lose purchase revenues, it had to finance a larger lease and rental base than it had expected. Thus, the price strategy reversal will help correct the cash flow problem.

Source. "Why IBM Reversed Itself on Computer Pricing," *Business Week* (January 28, 1980), p. 84.

Summary

At the outset, the industrial marketer must define the specific role that pricing is to assume in the firm's overall marketing strategy. Assigning an "incorrect" price to a particular industrial product or service can trigger a chain of events that detrimentally influences the firm's market position, channel relationships, and pricing and personal selling strategies. Price is but one of the costs that procurement decision makers examine in the buying process. Thus, the marketer can profit by adopting a strong end-user focus which gives special attention to the manner in which buyers tradeoff the costs and benefits of the firm's product offerings vis-à-vis those of competitors.

Price-setting is a multidimensional rather than a one-dimensional decision. To establish a price, the manager must identify the firm's objectives and analyze the behavior of demand, costs, and competition. While gathering information on these variables is difficult and clouded with uncertainty, the industrial pricing decision must be approached in an active rather than a passive manner. Likewise, efforts to isolate demand, cost, or competitive patterns enable the manager to secure insights into market behavior and market opportunities that were neglected.

Competitive bidding, a unique feature of the industrial market, calls for a different strategy. Again, carefully defined objectives are the cornerstone of the industrial marketer's strategy. These objectives, combined with a carefully designed screening procedure, aid the firm in identifying those projects that converge on company capability. Probabilistic bidding models can be a useful managerial tool in determining the probability of winning and gauging expected profit outcomes.

Leasing, an area of rising importance in the marketing of industrial equipment, creates numerous strategy options for the industrial firm. Successful lease marketing requires a well-integrated marketing program that effectively conveys information on the benefits of leasing to potential organizational customers. The marketer can adjust the relationship between the price and lease rate of a good to encourage or discourage leasing and to meet changing company or market conditions.

Footnotes

[1]Benson P. Shapiro and Barbara B. Jackson, "Industrial Pricing to Meet Customer Needs," *Harvard Business Review* 56 (November–December 1978), p. 125.

[2]Ibid., pp. 119–27.

[3]Ibid.

[4]For an interesting discussion of supplier evaluation from a marketer's perspective, see C. David Wieters and Lonnie L. Ostrom, "Supplier Evaluation as a New Marketing Tool," *Industrial Marketing Management* 8 (1979), pp. 161–66.

[5]J. Patrick Kelly and James W. Coaker, "Can We Generalize about Choice Criteria for Industrial Purchasing Decisions?" in Kenneth L. Bernhardt (ed.), *Marketing: 1776–1976 and Beyond* (Chicago: American Marketing Association, 1976), pp. 330–33.

[6]Robert F. Lanzillotti, "Pricing Objectives in Large Companies," *American Economic Review* 48 (December 1958), pp. 921–40; see also, J. Fred Weston, "The Myths and Realities of Corporate Pricing," *Fortune* 85 (April 1972), p. 85.

[7]"Pricing Strategy in an Inflation Economy," *Business Week* (April 6, 1974), pp. 42–49.

[8]Shapiro and Jackson, "Industrial Pricing to Meet Customer Needs," pp. 123–24.

[9]Robert J. Brown, "A New Marketing Tool: Life Cycle Costing," *Industrial Marketing Management* 8 (April 1979), pp. 109–13.

[10]Shapiro and Jackson, "Industrial Pricing to Meet Customer Needs," pp. 119–27.

[11]Phillip D. White and Edward S. Cundiff, "Assessing the Quality of Industrial Products," *Journal of Marketing* 42 (January 1978), pp. 80–86.

[12]Alfred R. Oxenfeldt, "A Decision-Making Structure for Price Decisions," *Journal of Marketing* 37 (January 1973), p. 50.

[13]Reed Moyer and Robert J. Boewadt, "The Pricing of Industrial Goods," *Business Horizons* 14 (June 1971), pp. 27–34.

[14]Ibid., p. 28.

[15]Ibid., p. 30.

[16]Ibid., pp. 27–34.

[17]For example, see Bill R. Darden, "An Operational Approach to Product Pricing," *Journal of Marketing* 32 (April 1969), pp. 29–33.

[18]Kent B. Monroe, *Pricing: Making Profitable Decisions* (New York: McGraw-Hill Book Company, 1979), pp. 52–57.

[19]William J. Abernathy and Kenneth Wayne, "Limits of the Learning Curve," *Harvard Business Review* 52 (September–October 1974), pp. 109–19.

[20]Ibid., pp. 109–19; see also, Staff of the Boston Consulting Group, *Perspectives on Experience* (Boston: Boston Consulting Group, Inc., 1972).

[21]Derek F. Abell and John S. Hammond, *Strategic Market Planning: Problems and Analytical Approaches* (Englewood Cliffs, N.J.: Prentice-Hall, Inc., 1979), p. 112.

[22]Abernathy and Wayne, "Limits of the Learning Curve," pp. 109–19.

[23]Abell and Hammond, *Strategic Market Planning,* pp. 125–27.

[24]John G. Udell, *Successful Marketing Strategies* (Madison, Wisconsin: Mimir Publishers, Inc., 1972), p. 109.

[25]Joel Dean, "Pricing Policies for New Products," *Harvard Business Review* 54 (November–December 1976), p. 151.

[26]Ibid., p. 152.

[27]Monroe, *Pricing,* p. 143.

[28]Jeffrey A. Tannenbaum, "IBM Introduces New Processors for System 370," *Wall Street Journal* (January 31, 1979), p. 2.

[29]Monroe, *Pricing,* p. 153.

[30]For a comprehensive discussion of the Robinson/Patman Act, see Monroe, *Pricing,* pp. 249–67.

[31]Joseph P. Guiltinan, "Risk-Aversive Pricing Policies: Problems and Alternatives," *Journal of Marketing* 40 (January 1976), pp. 10–15.

[32]Stuart F. Heinritz and Paul U. Farrell, *Purchasing, Principles and Applications* (Englewood Cliffs, N. J.: Prentice-Hall, Inc., 1971), p. 206.

[33]J. H. Westing, I. V. Fine, and Gary J. Zenz, *Purchasing Management* (New York: John Wiley and Sons, Inc., 1976), p. 198.

[34]This method is adapted from Stephen Paranka, "Competitive Bidding Strategy," *Business Horizons* 14 (June 1971), pp. 39–43; see also, Stephen Paranka, "Question: To Bid or Not to Bid? Answer: Strategic Prebid Analysis," *Marketing News* (April 4, 1980), p. 16.

[35]For example, see "Evaluation System Boosts Job Shop's Bidding Average," *Steel* (September 21, 1964), p. 47.

[36]For a more complete discussion of probabilistic bidding models, see Douglas G. Brooks, "Bidding for the Sake of Follow-On Contracts," *Journal of Marketing* 42 (January 1978), pp. 35–38; see also, Murphy A. Sewall, "A Decision Calculus Model for Contract Bidding," *Journal of Marketing* 40 (October 1976), pp. 92–98; and Wayne J. Morse, "Probabilistic Bidding Models: A Synthesis," *Business Horizons* 16 (April 1975), pp. 66–74.

[37]Stephen Paranka, "The Pay-Off Concept in Competitive Bidding," *Business Horizons* 12 (August 1969), pp. 77–81.

[38]This section is largely based on Paul F. Anderson and William Lazer, "Industrial Lease Marketing," *Journal of Marketing* 42 (April 1978), pp. 71–79. For additional research in the lease marketing area, see Paul F. Anderson, *Financial Aspects of Industrial Leasing Decisions: Implications for Marketing* (Division of Research, Graduate School of Business Administration, Michigan State University, East Lansing, Mich., 1977).

[39]Anderson and Lazer, p. 72.

[40]Paul F. Anderson, "Industrial Equipment Leasing Offers Economic and Competitive Edge," *Marketing News* (April 4, 1980), p. 20, and Paul F. Anderson and Monroe M. Bird, "Marketing to the Industrial Lease Buyer," *Industrial Marketing Management* 9 (April 1980), pp. 111–16.

[41]Anderson and Bird, p. 115.

[42]Paul F. Anderson and John D. Martin, "Lease vs. Purchase Decisions: A Survey of Current Practice," *Financial Management* 6 (Spring 1977), pp. 41–47.

[43]"IBM Cuts Quotes for Buying Parts of Small Systems," *Wall Street Journal* (December 3, 1979), p. 5.

Discussion Questions

1. Explain why it is often necessary for the industrial marketer to develop a separate demand curve for different segments of the market. Wouldn't one total demand curve be better for making the industrial pricing decision? Explain.

2. The rising cost of labor has stimulated industrial marketers to develop machine tools that offer users the opportunity to reduce production costs. Programmable robots are frequently the center of attention at machine tool trade shows. Many machine tool manufacturers contend that the robot will assume increasing importance in the workplace of the 1980s because of the opportunities that they provide for cost-savings. To illustrate, the cost of labor (including fringe benefits) is over $14 per hour in the auto industry, while the cost per robot-hour is $4.80, including installations, maintenance, depreciation, and energy. Illustrate how the concept of life cycle costing could be employed by machine tool producers in marketing high-priced, but efficient, "robots."

3. The XYZ Manufacturing Corporation has experienced a rather large decline in sales for its component parts. Mary Vantage, vice president of marketing, feels that a 10 percent price cut may get things going again. What factors should Mary consider before reducing the prices of the components?

4. Define the *experience effect* (behavior of costs) and explain why it occurs. Next, explain how the experience effect relates to strategic pricing decisions.

5. An industrial marketing manager often has great difficulty in arriving at the optimum price level for a product. First, describe the factors that complicate the pricing decision for the industrial marketing manager. Second, outline the approach that you would follow in pricing an industrial product. Be as specific as possible.

6. Leasing is playing an increasingly important role in the marketing of capital equipment items. Describe the factors that the industrial marketer must consider in determining the relationship of the lease rate to the purchase price (e.g., low lease rate–high purchase price; high lease rate–low purchase price).

7. Explain how a change in the price of one item in a product line often contributes to the need for a change in price of other items in the product line.

8. Evaluate the competitive bidding strategy followed by a West Coast commercial air conditioning contractor: "To improve my chances of winning contracts, I bid on virtually every contract that comes up in our market area."

Chapter 14

Industrial Marketing Communications: Advertising and Sales Promotion

Advertising plays a special role in industrial marketing strategy by supporting and supplementing personal selling efforts. In contrast to consumer-goods marketing, a smaller share of the marketing budget is devoted to advertising in the industrial market. A well-tailored industrial advertising campaign can, however, contribute to the increased efficiency and effectiveness of the overall marketing strategy.

After reading this chapter, you will have an understanding of:

1. *the specific role of advertising in industrial marketing strategy*
2. *the key decisions that must be made in forming an industrial advertising program*
3. *the nature of industrial media options*
4. *methods for measuring industrial advertising effectiveness.*

Communication with existing and potential customers is vital to the success of industrial marketing strategy. Years of experience have taught marketing managers that not even the "best" products sell themselves: the benefits, problem solutions, and cost efficiencies of those products must be effectively communicated to *all* of the individuals who influence the purchase decision. As a result of the technical complexity of industrial products, the relatively small number of potential buyers, and the extensive negotiation process, the primary communication vehicle in industrial marketing is the salesperson. However, nonpersonal methods of communication, including advertising, catalogs, and trade shows, have a unique and often critical role to play in the communication process.

Consider the recent decision made by a manufacturer of automotive shock absorbers to purchase an autopart made of zinc rather than aluminum. The decision process involved 43 separate steps in which 30 different individuals were involved![1] Clearly, it is not possible for a salesperson to know that 30 individuals were involved, let alone effectively contact each one of them. However, it is possible to know that a variety of specialists will be involved in the decision and to create advertisements in selected industrial trade publications to reach these influencers. A very important role for industrial advertising is to communicate to those buying influences inaccessible to the salesperson. Industrial advertising and promotion, of course, serve many more functions in the communication strategy, and these will be highlighted later in the chapter.

The focus of this chapter is fourfold: (1) to provide a clear understanding of the role of advertising in the industrial marketing strategy; (2) to present a framework for structuring advertising decisions that integrates the decisions related to objectives, budgets, messages, media, and evaluation; (3) to develop an understanding of each of these key industrial advertising decision areas; and (4) to develop an evaluation of the various supplementary forms of promotion, including catalogs, trade shows, and trade advertising.

The Role of Advertising

Integrated Communication Programs

Advertising and sales promotion are rarely employed by themselves in the industrial setting, but are intertwined with the total communications strategy—particularly personal selling. Personal and nonpersonal forms of communication interact to provide a unified presentation to key buying influences. The important challenge for the industrial marketer is to develop the advertising and sales promotion strategy that effectively blends with personal selling efforts to reach the firm's sales and profit objectives. In addition, the advertising and sales promotion tools must be integrated; that is, a comprehensive program of the various media and sales promotion methods must be coordinated to achieve the desired results.

Nature of Organizational Buying Affects Industrial Advertising

To understand the role of advertising we must be cognizant of the forces that shape and influence organizational buying decisions. Industrial purchasing decisions are typically joint decisions. The complexities and intricacies of the buying center were well documented in chapter 4 and need not be reiterated here. Recall, however, that an industrial marketer must focus on the full range of individuals involved in the buying center for a particular purchase. Salespeople are not able to make contact with all potential purchase decision influencers. Studies of industrial buying have suggested that "the average salesperson does *not* reach six to seven out of every ten purchase decision influentials!"[2] Table 14.1 indicates the extensive nature of the problem of contacting relevant buying influencers. Note the variety of industrial situations in which salespeople are unable to reach key purchase decision makers.

The point is clear: industrial advertising fills the void to reach important buying influencers inaccessible to the industrial salesperson.[3] Carefully targeted advertising extends beyond the salesperson's reach and covers unidentified and often unknown buying influentials. In many cases, advertising may be the *only* means of communicating the existence of a product to the potential buyers. In addition to reaching buying influences, advertising also facilitates the recognition of the company's name and reputation, enhancing the salesperson's opportunity to create a sale.

Advertising: Enhancing Sales Effectiveness

Effective advertising has the potential to make personal selling efforts more productive. John Morrill examined nearly 100,000 interviews on 26 product

Table 14.1 / Contacting the Unidentified Buying Influentials

Century Electric Co.	Century evaluated its own buying process and found that 12 individuals are typically involved in a buying decision. On the average, only 2 are ever contacted by salespersons!
Yale and Town	Nine individuals are involved in a typical Yale and Town buying decision. However, analysis reveals that only an average of 1.3 individuals were contacted by salespersons!
Chilton Company	Chilton interviewed 4420 buying influencers (each of whom had "purchasing influence" in an average of 4.3 products) in eight major industries. Sixty-one percent of the respondents had not been called on by a salesperson in the past six months!
American Rubber Co.	An analysis of 903 prospects revealed that their salesperson knew only 169, or 19 percent. Thus, out of every five prospects, only one was known by the sales force.

Source. Adapted from Richard Manville, "Why Industrial Companies Must Advertise Their Products," *Industrial Marketing* 63 (October 1978), p. 47.

lines at 30,000 different buying locations to study the impact of industrial advertising on salesperson effectiveness.[4] Morrill concluded that dollar sales per salesperson call were significantly higher for calls made on customers who had been exposed to advertising, as compared to those who had not. In addition, buyers who were exposed to a supplier's advertisement rated the supplier's sales personnel substantially higher on product knowledge, service, and enthusiasm than those who were not exposed.[5] Importantly, a primary role of industrial advertising is to enhance the reputation of the supplier, thereby making buyers more receptive to the supplier's sales personnel. Industrial advertising also contributes to increased sales efficiency.

Advertising: Increased Sales Efficiency

The impact of advertising on the overall efficiency of the industrial marketing program is evidenced in two important ways. First, advertising may be the *only* communication method that can economically reach a broad array of buyers. Industrial suppliers frequently need to remind actual and potential buyers of their products or to make them aware of new products or services. Although these objectives could be partially accomplished through personal selling, the costs of reaching a vast group of buyers in this manner would be prohibitive. The average cost of an industrial sales call is approaching \$150.[6] An industrial operations executive at General Electric predicts that each of their sales calls will cost \$400 by the mid-1980s.[7] Advertising placed in appropriate media can reach hundreds of buying influences for only a few cents per contact.

Secondly, advertising appears to make all selling activities more effective; that is, there may be some economies of scale associated with industrial advertising. Gary Lilien and others reviewed a variety of research studies that attempted to evaluate the impact of industrial advertising expenditure levels on total marketing costs.[8] The general conclusion of most studies was that the larger the advertising budget of an industrial firm, the lower was the total marketing expenses as a percentage of sales. However, some studies have shown that economies to scale in advertising do not exist. Thus, the industrial marketer must be careful in always assuming that "more" advertising is better. In summary, advertising effectively interacts with all communication and selling activities, and it may result in higher levels of efficiency for the *entire* marketing expenditure.

Advertising: Creative Awareness

Buyers generally select a brand or supplier after moving through a series of steps in the buying process. However, from a communications standpoint, the process can be viewed as taking potential buyers sequentially from *unawareness* of a product or supplier to *awareness,* brand *preference, conviction* that the particular purchase will fulfill their requirements, and, ultimately, to actual *purchase*.[9] Industrial advertising often assumes the important function of creating awareness of the supplier and the supplier's products; it also may make some contribution to achieving preference for the product. As noted earlier, advertising performs this role in a very cost efficient manner.

A recent study highlights the impact of advertising on creating product awareness.[10] Buyers of machine tools were surveyed to ascertain the importance of five different communication channels in providing information about machine tool products and services. The five information channels included: (1) salespersons, (2) company catalogs, (3) advertising in industrial trade magazines, (4) trade shows, and (5) direct mail. The results of the study are depicted in table 14.2. Industrial advertising is the primary source of information to these buyers, suggesting the importance of advertising in providing product and company awareness.

The Limitations of Industrial Advertising

Understanding the contribution of industrial advertising to the total marketing effort also involves the recognition of what advertising cannot accomplish. To develop an effective communications program, the industrial marketing manager must blend all communication tools into an integrated program. Each tool must be utilized for the purposes for which it is most effective and efficient. Industrial advertising quite obviously has limitations, and it should not be applied beyond those limitations. Advertising cannot substitute for an effective personal selling effort; it must supplement, support, and complement that effort. In the same way, personal selling is constrained by the costs involved, and need not be applied to creating awareness and disseminating information—tasks quite capably performed by advertising.

Generally, advertising cannot create product "preference," as achieving this goal often requires demonstration, explanation, and specific operational testing. Similarly, the creation of "conviction" and "purchase" are tasks to be achieved by personal selling. Recognition of the supporting role of

Table 14.2 / The Importance of Information Sources to Industrial Buyers

Information Source	Rank	Mean Rating*	Percent Selected Most Important
Advertising in Industrial and Trade Magazines	1	2.10	37
Salesmen	2	2.35	27
Trade Shows	3	2.66	26
Company Catalogs	4	3.48	10
Direct Mail	5	4.49	0
			100%

*Where 1 = most important, through 5 = least important.

Source. Charles H. Patti, "Buyer Information Sources in the Capital Equipment Industry," *Industrial Marketing Management* 6 (1977), p. 261. Reprinted by permission.

advertising, one that relies on creating awareness, providing information, and uncovering important leads for salespeople, will lead the marketing manager to utilize advertising in its most efficient and effective manner.

Managing the Industrial Advertising Effort

The development of effective advertising involves careful consideration of the important elements that are essential ingredients of the advertising campaign. The advertising decision model portrayed in figure 14.1 shows the structural elements involved in the management of industrial advertising. This model will provide the necessary framework for understanding the advertising management process.

First, advertising is only one aspect of the entire marketing strategy and must be integrated with other components to achieve the goals of that strat-

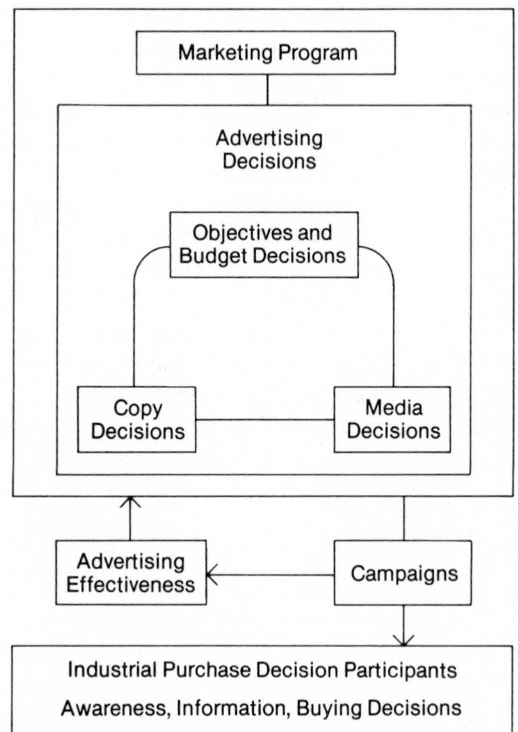

Figure 14.1 / An Advertising Decision Model

Source. Adapted from David A. Aaker and John G. Myers, *Advertising Management*, (Englewood Cliffs, N.J.: Prentice-Hall, Inc., 1975), p. 25. Reprinted by permission of Prentice-Hall, Inc.

egy. The first key element in the advertising decision process is the formulation of advertising objectives, which are derived from marketing goals. Delineation of advertising goals makes possible the determination of expenditure levels necessary to achieve those goals. Then, specific communication messages are formulated to achieve the target market behavior specified by the objectives. Equally important is the evaluation and selection of the media required to reach the desired audience. The result is an integrated advertising campaign focused on eliciting a specific attitude or behavior by the target group. A final, yet extremely critical, step in the process is the need to monitor and evaluate the effectiveness of the campaign. Also note that research information on the target segments plays an important role in the formulation of the entire campaign. Each component of the advertising decision model is examined below.

Advertising Objectives

The determination of advertising objectives must be the first step in designing an advertising strategy because the objectives will specify what advertising is to accomplish. Knowing what advertising must accomplish enables the manager to determine more accurately an advertising budget, and it also provides a yardstick against which advertising can be evaluated. Two key prerequisites to the specification of advertising goals are: (1) *an understanding that the advertising mission flows directly from the requirements of the overall marketing strategy.* That is, advertising is utilized to fulfill a marketing strategy objective, and the goal set for advertising must reflect the general aim and purpose of the entire strategy; then, (2) *the objectives of the advertising program are determined relative to the roles of advertising delineated earlier.* Advertising goals are constrained by what advertising can reasonably be expected to accomplish—creating awareness, providing information, influencing attitudes, and reminding buyers of company and product existence. The goals of advertising become meaningful only when advertising's function is considered in relation to a marketing problem and a specific sales objective.[11]

Specific Written Objectives. An advertising objective is a concise statement of the intended outcome of a particular advertising action. As such, advertising objectives need to be stated in unambiguous terms that relate to a specific outcome. The underlying purpose of advertising objectives is to establish a single working direction for everyone involved in creating, coordinating, and evaluating the advertising program.[12] In addition, correctly conceived objectives set meaningful standards against which the advertising effort can be evaluated. A specific objective might be stated:

> To develop the awareness among at least 25 percent of the chemical processing plant building and maintenance engineers of the use-benefit fact that our brand of industrial-maintenance paint stops metal corrosion.

In this case, the objective directs the manager to create a message related to the major product benefit, using media that will reach building and maintenance engineers. The objective also provides a way to measure accomplishment (awareness among 25 percent of the target audience).

In specifying advertising objectives, it must be realized that industrial advertising objectives frequently bear no direct relationship with specific dollar sales targets. Although dollar sales results would provide an absolute "hard" measure of advertising accomplishment, it is often impossible to directly link advertising to sales. Personal selling, price, product performance, and competitive actions have a more direct relationship to sales levels, and it is almost impossible to sort out the impact of advertising. Thus, advertising goals are typically stated in terms of "communication goals," that is, brand awareness, recognition, and buyer attitudes. These goals can be measured, and it is presumed that the achievement of them will indirectly relate to sales volume.

Target Audience. A final consideration in the determination of advertising objectives is the specification of target audiences. Because a primary role of advertising is to reach buying influences inaccessible to the salesperson, the industrial marketing manager needs to define the specific buying influence groups to be reached. Generally, each group of buying influencers is concerned with distinct product and service attributes and criteria, and the advertising must be focused on those salient dimensions. Thus, objectives need to specify who the intended audience is and its relevant decision criteria.

In summary, the specification of advertising objectives is required to plan an effective advertising campaign. Objectives provide an important road map to structure media and measure results.

Determining Advertising Expenditures

One of the most challenging aspects of industrial advertising management is the development of a rational method for allocating funds to the advertising task. Typically, industrial companies use a blend of intuition, judgment, experience, and, occasionally, some more advanced decision-oriented techniques for determining advertising budgets. Some of the more frequently applied techniques include rules of thumb and objective-task methods.

Rules of Thumb. Often, advertising is a relatively small part of the total marketing budget for industrial firms, and the value of using sophisticated methods for advertising budgeting is not great. In these cases, managers tend to follow simple rules of thumb (e.g., "allocate 1 percent of sales to advertising" or spend "what competition spends"). Unfortunately, percentage-of-sales decision rules are all too pervasive throughout industrial marketing, even in instances when advertising is an important expenditure item.

The fundamental problem with percentage-of-sales decision rules is that they "implicitly make advertising a consequence rather than a determinant of sales and profits and can easily give rise to disfunctional policies."[13] For example, percentage-of-sales decision rules suggest that the industrial advertiser reduce advertising when sales volume declines. Obviously, increased advertising may be the appropriate tool to halt the sales decline. Nevertheless, simple rules of thumb will continue to be applied in industrial budget decisions as a result of their ease of application and management familiarity with them.

Objective-Task Method. The task method for budgeting advertising expenditures is an attempt to relate advertising costs to the objective to be accomplished by advertising.[14] David Nylen succinctly states the dimensions of the task approach:

> While acknowledging that the ultimate objective of advertising is profitable sales, the task approach sees a series of intermediate objectives or profit-facilitating tasks assigned to advertising. The budgeting problem under the task approach becomes one of determining how much it will cost to accomplish each of the tasks assigned to advertising.[15]

Thus, the task method focuses on the communications effects of advertising, not the sales effects. The approach has particular relevance to the industrial market, since the function of industrial advertising is to create awareness and provide information.

The task method is applied by evaluating the tasks to be performed by advertising, analyzing the costs associated with each task performance, and summing up the total costs to arrive at a final budget. Specifically, the steps include:

1. Establish specific marketing objectives for the product in terms of factors such as sales volume, market share, and profit contribution, as well as target market segments.
2. Assess the communication functions that must be performed to realize the overall marketing objectives, and determine the role of advertising and other elements of the communications mix in performing these functions.
3. Define specific goals for advertising in terms of the levels of measurable communication response required to achieve marketing objectives.
4. Estimate the budget needed to accomplish advertising goals.[16]

The task method addresses the major problem area associated with rule of thumb methods—funds are applied to accomplish a specific goal so that advertising is a *determinant* of those results, not a consequence. Using the task approach, managers will allocate all the funds necessary to accomplish a specific objective, rather than allocating some arbitrary percentage of sales. However, there are problems associated with the task method. The most troubling problem relates to the fact that management must have some feeling for or knowledge about the relationship between expenditure level and the level of communication response. It is difficult, at best, to know exactly what is required to produce a certain level of awareness among industrial purchase influencers. Will 12 two-page insertions in *Iron Age* over the next six months create the desired recognition level or will 24 insertions over one year be necessary? These are troublesome questions to answer [17]

The ADVISOR Project: Guidelines of Industrial Advertising Budgets

The lack of specific guidelines to assist industrial advertisers in formulating advertising budgets stimulated an extensive research project to determine key industrial product and market factors that affect advertising expenditures. The ADVISOR project, formulated by Gary Lilien and John Little, resulted in a model that specifies the typical size and range of marketing budgets based on six key product and market characteristics.[18] The ADVISOR project is based on an analysis of 66 products manufactured by 12 different companies.

ADVISOR Results. Six factors were judged to be predominant in describing the impact of product-market-customer characteristics on advertising and marketing budgets.[19] Table 14.3 describes the six factors and their important

Table 14.3 / ADVISOR: Variables Affecting Advertising and Marketing Budgets

1. Life Cycle Stage	As the life cycle progresses, the ratio of marketing expenditures (advertising and personal selling) to sales (M/S) decreases. The advertising expense to sales ratio (A/S) behaves differently: early in the life cycle it is high; later it tends to be low.
2. Frequency of Purchase	Frequency of purchase does not affect the M/S ratio but does impact the ratio of advertising expense to marketing expense (A/M). The greater the purchase frequency, the higher is the A/M ratio. As a result, purchase frequency has a positive effect on the A/S ratio.
3. Product Quality, Uniqueness, and Identification with Company	Products with quality, uniqueness, and strong identification with company name have high A/M ratios. The conclusion is that these products have a "story to tell," and advertising is used to do it. More is spent on advertising, and the A/S ratio is larger, as well.
4. Market Share	The M/S ratio tends to decrease as market share increases. So too with A/S, as advertising expenditures as a percentage of sales decrease with higher market shares.
5. Concentration of Sales	As sales are concentrated with fewer large customers, the M/S ratio declines. The net effect on the A/S is small.
6. Growth of Customers	As the percentage increase in the *number* of customers grows, all three ratios—M/S, A/M, A/S—will increase.

Source. Gary L. Lilien and John D. C. Little, "The ADVISOR Project: A Study of Industrial Marketing Budgets," *Sloan Management Review* 16 (Spring 1976), pp. 24–25. Reprinted by permission.

impacts. The model developed in the ADVISOR project combines these effects to determine budget norms and ranges.

An interactive computer program can be used by an industrial advertiser to evaluate appropriate *budget norms*.[20] The program asks the user a series of questions related to the important product-market variables shown in table 14.3. The data are analyzed by the computer model and, based on the user's response to the product-market questions, produces budget and allocation guidelines. Industrial marketing managers may then adjust their budgets to conform to the guidelines prescribed by the ADVISOR model. ADVISOR does not tell the manager what to do; it only provides what the typical industrial firm would do under the prescribed conditions.[21]

Table 14.4 provides an illustration of the ADVISOR output. As the table indicates, the company's M/S ratio (marketing expenditures to sales ratio) is within guidelines. However, advertising expenditures are below the dollar guideline limit. The A/M ratio (advertising expense to marketing expense ratio) is acceptable, but it is in the lower range. So, although the overall marketing expenditures are within the industry guidelines, the proportion allocated to advertising is not up to the standards established by industry norms. In this case, the manager may desire to reallocate funds to the advertising function.

The ADVISOR project is a landmark effort to understand the advertising budget process and provide workable decision rules for allocating marketing expenditures. A refinement and extension of the original ADVISOR project, ADVISOR 2, is reported by Lilien.[22] In the ADVISOR 2 study, the data base was expanded to additional companies and product situations, and many of the model equations were refined. In effect, the results of ADVISOR 2 serve to confirm the consistency and validity of the earlier model approach. Also, a number of additional variables were found to be significant: customer growth rate is better represented by product plans and number of users; purchase frequency was found to be ambiguous and was deleted. In sum, the ADVISOR studies provide a valuable benchmark for determining industrial advertising budgets.

The budgeting process is an important step in assuring the efficiency and effectiveness of the advertising program. Underbudgeted advertising cam-

Table 14.4 / ADVISOR Program Output for a Sample Company

	Actual Expenditure	Advisor Norms	
		Center	Range
Advertising (thousands)	$105	$330	$120–$745
Advertising/Marketing Ratio	0.0323	0.0600	0–0.1100
Marketing/Sales Ratio	0.0680	0.1100	0.0600–0.1400

Source. Gary L. Lilien and John D. C. Little, "The ADVISOR Project: A Study of Industrial Marketing Budgets," *Sloan Management Review* 16 (Spring 1976), p. 30. Reprinted by permission.

paigns will have difficulty achieving their objectives; overbudgeting results in marketing inefficiencies and the use of funds in unproductive ventures. Managers must not blindly follow convenient rules of thumb in the budgetary process. Instead, they should evaluate the tasks required and their associated costs along with an understanding of industry norms. With clear objectives specified and budgetary allocations made, the next phase of the process is the design of effective advertising messages.

The Advertising Message

Creating effective advertising messages is indeed a challenging task for the industrial advertiser. Message development is a critical and complex task in industrial advertising because of the diverse representation and divergent perceptions of organizational members in the buying process. Highlighting a product attribute that is unimportant to a particular buying group not only is a waste of advertising dollars, but also results in a lost opportunity to facilitate a sale. Both the appeal and the manner in which that appeal is conveyed are vital to successful communication. Thus, the creation of industrial advertising messages involves an evaluation of the buying criteria salient to the target audience and an analysis of the language, format, and style of presenting that message. The objectives of the advertising strategy will dictate the type of message to be formulated. Critical aspects of the message creation process are explored below.

Perception. There are two important prerequisites for a successful advertising message.[23] First, an individual must be exposed to it and pay attention to it. Second, once the individual has noticed the message, he or she must interpret it in the way the advertiser intended. Each of these aspects represents some phase of the perceptional process—that is, how a message enters an individual's mind. Perceptual barriers often prevent a message from being perceived by a receiver. An industrial advertisement must be successful at stimulating the organizational decision maker's attention. Yet, even though the individual is "exposed" to an advertisement, there is no guarantee that the message will be processed. In other cases, the industrial buyer may read the entire copy, but interpret its meaning totally opposite from that intended by the advertiser.

The industrial advertiser must contend with two important elements of perception: *attention* and *interpretation*. Recall the discussion in chapter 4 that dealt with the selective processes involved with the way buyers process information. Buyers tend to screen out messages that are inconsistent with their attitudes, needs, and beliefs, and to interpret information in the light of those beliefs. Thus, unless advertising messages are carefully designed and targeted, the chances are good that those messages will be disregarded or interpreted improperly. A necessary prerequisite to creating effective advertising messages is to first examine how those messages will be interpreted by the receiver. Here, advertisers must put themselves in the position of the receivers to evaluate how the message will appear to them.

The Appeal: Benefits. An industrial buyer purchases benefits—a better way to accomplish some task, a less expensive way to produce a final product, the solution to a problem, faster delivery, and so on. Advertisers are prone to concentrate on a physical product—forgetting that the physical product is meaningless to an industrial buyer unless it solves some problem. A public warehousing company undertook an extensive analysis of the advertising strategy of the public warehousing industry. To their horror, they discovered that many companies, themselves included, were totally concentrating their advertising messages on the "product" provided by public warehouses. That is, almost every analyzed advertisement focused on public warehousing "product" characteristics: for example, "we offer 200,000 square feet of refrigerated space"; and "our company has 17 delivery trucks." In an effort to appeal more effectively to the concerns of warehouse users, the company developed a series of advertisements focusing on the benefits provided to warehouse users.

Figure 14.2 is an example of an advertisement designed for marketing and sales managers who are important influencers in the public warehousing decision. Note the central theme of the advertisement: using a public warehouse will make the marketing manager's customers happy. In addition, the message stresses that the burden of responsive distribution is borne by the warehousemen and not the customer. The benefit to the potential user is clear and unambiguous, while specific "product" features are hardly mentioned. In summary, then, the pivotal element of good message strategy is the "benefits provided" approach versus the "product feature" approach.

Understanding Buyer Motivations. Message strategy focuses on product benefits, but a perplexing problem emerges: which product benefits are important to each separate buying influence group? The industrial advertiser cannot assume that some standard set of "classical buying motives" applies in every purchase situation. Industrial advertisers must understand the key factors influencing the purchase of their products; research suggests that they often do not understand the buying motives of important market segments.[24]

Because industrial advertising messages must focus on the salient product dimensions and benefits perceived by buying decision participants, a methodology for determining those dimensions would be extremely useful to industrial advertisers. A very promising effort along these lines is the industrial marketing strategy response model developed by Jean-Marie Choffray and Gary Lilien.[25] Recall that the basic structure of the model was discussed in chapter 8, in connection with strategy development. Their model, along with the associated measurement methodology, is applicable for providing information on the advertising decision. An application of the model to industrial cooling system purchases revealed information relevant for developing advertising messages in that industry. For example, product attributes varied in importance for each of the six identified decision participants. In the purchase of cooling systems, production engineers were concerned with operating cost and energy savings, while heating and air con-

Fast Deliveries and Small Inventories make your Customers Happy . . .

. . . Distribution Centers Inc. can make it Happen for You!

Distribution Centers, Inc. is a specialist in distribution—our skill is operating warehouses for other companies. We operate in eight major markets, we've been doing it since 1904, and it's all we do. We also have the flexibility to open new warehouses in markets where you require distribution. Our goal is to give *your customers what they want — local product availability, quick response to their needs, and lower inventories.* That sure makes you look good!

The moment you sign a warehouse agreement with DCI, the burden of quick response to your customer's requirements is ours. No more headaches with rush orders, missed shipments and uncooperative transportation carriers. Our staff of distribution experts work out all the details of the distribution system from order processing to delivery scheduling. *The result is satisfaction — yours and your customers'.*

We would like to explain more to you about DCI. Our brochure, "Public Warehousing" fully explains all the details. Send the enclosed reply card today and we will be happy to forward the brochure by return mail.

® **Distribution Centers, Inc.**
...the flexibility people

General Office • 1310 Dublin Road. • Columbus, Ohio 43215 • (614) 486-0601

Figure 14.2 / An Industrial Advertisement Focused on Important User Benefits

Source. Reprinted courtesy of Distribution Centers, Inc.

ditioning consultants focused on noise level in the plant and first cost. Importantly, this type of data will be essential in creating effective advertising appeals for each type of decision participant.

In conclusion, the important guideposts for formulating industrial advertising messages involve the need to evaluate carefully the perceptual process, focus the appeal on product benefits, and understand the salient buying criteria employed by different types of decision participants. Once these tasks are completed, the industrial advertiser is better prepared to develop creatively effective advertising messages. Although the message is vital to advertising success, an equally important factor is the medium through which it is presented.

Industrial Advertising Media

Selection of the appropriate industrial advertising media focuses on the target audience—the particular group of purchase decision participants to be reached. Generally, industrial advertising media choice centers first on a decision to use *trade publications, direct mail,* or both. Within the trade publications arena, the advertiser must choose among an impressive number of options. Selection of particular publications also involves budgetary considerations—where are dollars best spent to generate the number of customer contacts desired? The discussion of the media decision will first focus on providing an understanding of business publications. Next, the media decision will be examined. Finally, the direct mail alternative will be investigated.

Business Publications. It is estimated that there are over 2000 business publications with circulation exceeding 50 million readers.[26] Each type of industry and professional specialization seems to have a trade publication which centers on their needs. For those specializing in distribution, *Handling and Shipping, Distribution Worldwide, Traffic Management,* and *Modern Materials Handling* are a few of the available publications. *Iron Age* and *Steel* are two publications aimed at individuals in the steel industry. Typically, business publications are divided into two classifications: *horizontal* or *vertical.* Horizontal publications are directed at a specific task, technology, or function in all industries employing them. Thus, *Advertising Age, Purchasing,* and *Handling and Shipping* are classified as horizontal "papers." Vertical publications, on the other hand, are directed at a specific industry and may be read by everyone from a foreman to the president. Vertical publications would include magazines such as *Glass Industry* or *Manufacturing Confectioner.* Figure 14.3 provides a short description and some examples of the major classifications of industrial trade publications.

The type of publication is an important determinant in media selection decisions. If an industrial marketer's product has application only within a few industries, then vertical publications targeted to those industries are a logical media choice. In cases where many industries are potential users,

General Business Publications

Usually such publications will take a strong management slant and will cut across industry lines. They should be classed as horizontal publications, therefore. Among the most prosperous are:

Fortune	*Barron's-National Business & Financial Weekly*
Business Week	*Wall Street Journal*
Forbes	*Nation's Business*
	Dun's Review

Specialized Business Publications

Numerous publications fall in this category, which actually embraces many publications listed under other headings. A number of these, like the general business magazines, have a decided management slant. Among these publications are:

Modern Franchising	*Journal of Accountancy*
Advertising Age	*Personnel Journal*
Modern Office Procedure	

Industrial Publications

Another large classification, industrial magazines, very often adds another group of interested readers, the engineers. Many of these publications assume that the readers, in addition to having a management interest, will also have a deep knowledge of technical subjects such as engineering, physical science, physics, and electronics. Included here may be:

Industry Week	*Plant Engineering*
The Iron Age	*Consulting Engineer*
Electronic News	*Automation*
Power	

Trade Magazines

Those in retail, merchandising, and mercantile activities are served by trade magazines aimed largely at retailers but also of interest to those who supply or service the retail trade. Found among the many publications in this class are:

Progressive Grocer	*Supermarket News*
Chain Store Age	*Office Products*
Hardware Retailer	*The College Store Journal*
Drug Topics	

Professional Publications

Aimed at doctors, dentists, architects, lawyers, or teachers, among others, these publications seem far removed in their editorial content from the world of business, but their advertisements seek business just as unmistakably as the advertisements appearing in other business publications. In this category are such publications as:

Journal of the American Medical Association	*Architectural Record*
Practical Lawyer	*American Bar Association Journal*
	Surgery

Institutional Publications

Serving those who are responsible for the running or management of hotels, restaurants, hospitals, and other institutions are the institutional publications. Some of the publications in this field:

Hotel and Motel Management	*Drive-In Fast Service*
Institutions Magazine	*The Nation's Schools*
Hospitals	*Resort Management*

Figure 14.3 / Types of Business Publications

Source. Phillip W. Burton and J. Robert Miller, *Advertising Fundamentals* (Columbus, Ohio: Grid Publishing, Inc., 1976), p. 346. Reprinted by permission.

but where well-defined functions are the principal buying influencers, a horizontal publication is effective.

Controlled circulation is another important aspect of industrial trade publications. Controlled circulation is free, as opposed to paid subscriptions, to a carefully selected list of people in a position to influence buying decisions. Potential users of controlled circulation publications will find this a valuable asset as subscribers must indicate their title and function, buying responsibilities, and other information. Thus, the advertiser can carefully evaluate each publication as to whether it includes the desired buying influencers. In fact, the main selling point of most trade publications is their selectivity and audience quality. Controlled circulation papers often require their subscribers to meet precise standards—functions performed, responsibilities, and so on. In this way, trade publications can report the exact makeup, in detail, of their customers.

Media Selection. Selection of a specific publication will hinge on how well the circulation matches the target group of purchase decision makers sought by the advertiser. Obviously, media choice is predicated on a complete understanding of the range of purchase decision participants and the industries where the product will be used. Once these important facts are determined, the target audience can be matched to the circulation statements of alternative business publications.

Advertising Cost. Circulation is an important criteria in the selection of publications, but circulation must be tempered by the costs involved. First, the total advertising budget must be allocated among the various advertising tools. Most studies indicate that the breakdown of expenditures among the types of advertising tools is approximately:[27]

Trade Publications	40 percent
Sales Promotion	25 percent
Direct Mail	25 percent
Trade Shows	10 percent

Of course, these percentage distributions will vary with company situations and the type of advertising mission. However, the 40 percent allocation does appear to be fairly consistent from company to company.

Allocation of the trade publication budget among various media will be made on the bases of their relative effectiveness and efficiency. A frequently used measure for allocation purposes is that of *cost per thousand.* The formula is:

$$\text{Cost per thousand} = \frac{\text{Cost per page}}{\text{Circulation in thousands}}$$

To compare two publications on their actual page rates would be misleading, because the publication with the lower circulation will usually be less expensive. Importantly, the cost/1000 calculation should be based on circulation to the target audience, not the total audience. Although some publications may appear high on a cost per thousand basis, they may in fact be very cost effective given the small amount of wasted circulation.

Some industrial firms are very sophisticated in their approach to media selection. The Timken Company has its own computerized media fact file, which includes information on 91 publications that reach industries desired by Timken.[28] Circulation by SIC code and job function for over 80 percent of the publications are kept on the computer; this enables media planners to determine, for example, the best circulation for the machine tool industry in the purchasing, design/engineering, administrative management, and production functions. Cost per thousand data are also maintained so that publications can be compared on this basis. To make comparisons effective, cost per thousand calculations are based on very specific targets—that is, "cost per thousand purchasing agents in SIC 3341."

Frequency and Scheduling. Additional components of the media selection decision center on the frequency and timing of advertisements. Many readership studies demonstrate that even the most successful business publication advertisements are seen by a fairly small percentage of people who read the magazine; therefore, one-time ads are generally ineffective. Because a number of exposures are required before a message "sinks in," and because the reading audience varies from month to month, a schedule of advertising insertions is required. One expert suggests that to build continuity and repetitive value, monthly publications require at least six insertions per year; weekly, 26 to 52 insertions, with a minimum of 13.[29]

Direct Mail Advertising. A frequent alternative to or complement of trade publication advertising is *direct mail.* Direct mail advertising involves delivery of an advertising message directly to selected individuals through the mail. The variety of possible mailing pieces is extensive, ranging from a sales letter introducing a new product to a lengthy brochure or even a product sample. Direct mail advertising can accomplish all of the major advertising functions discussed earlier, but it's real contribution is in delivering a message to a precisely defined prospect.

Although exhaustive lists of the specific uses of direct mail advertising have been suggested, most of the applications of direct mail are focused on categories which include:

1. corporate image promotion;
2. product and service promotion;
3. sales force support;
4. distribution channel communication;
5. special marketing problems.[30]

Promoting corporate image is frequently utilized by companies such as NCR, in which case the direct mail advertising may help to establish the reputation of technological leadership among key buying influences. On the other hand, product advertising by direct mail allows the advertiser to reach each of the buying influence groups with specific product information. Kaiser Aluminum targets booklets explaining aluminum's advantages to industrial buyers and specifiers, while a series of messages related to how to work with aluminum and a quantity/weight calculator are sent to machine operators and shop foremen.[31] In this way, Kaiser can tailor messages to the exact needs of each buying influence group. Direct mail also supports the salespersons' activities—providing new leads from returned direct mail inquiry cards, paving the way for a first sales call. In addition, direct mail can be utilized effectively to notify potential customers of the availability and location of the manufacturer's local distributors. Finally, direct mail is applicable to a host of special situations, such as identifying new customers and markets, meeting competitor claims, and promoting items that are not receiving the required sales support.

Direct mail is a viable advertising media when "potential buyers can be clearly identified and easily reached through the mail. It can be a wasteful medium if the prospect lists are so general in nature that it is difficult or impossible to find a common denominator among its prospects."[32] Importantly, a direct mail advertisement typically gains the full attention of the reader, and, therefore, it provides greater impact than a trade publication advertisement. Timing flexibility is also possible, as, for example, a new price schedule or new service innovation can be communicated to the buyer at any time. Finally, direct mail makes it easy for the potential buyer to respond—usually a reply postcard is included or the name, address, and phone number of the local salesperson or distributor is provided.

Most direct mail programs seek some type of response from the prospect. Often, the potential buyer is asked to return a reply card to receive additional information, such as a sample or a brochure explaining the benefits and applications of a product. The direct mail package may even contain an order form or ask the recipient to call the local company salesperson.

The critical ingredient of a direct mail advertising campaign is the *mailing list of buying influencers*. The selectivity of direct mail, although its primary advantage, also poses the greatest challenge. There are literally hundreds of mailing lists available to the industrial advertiser. Mailing lists for industrial advertising purposes may be secured from three primary sources: (1) circulation lists provided by trade publications; (2) lists provided by industrial directories; and (3) lists provided by mailing list houses (i.e., firms specifically engaged in renting industrial mailing lists). A catalog published by Standard Rate and Data Service provides an inventory and description of most of the available industrial mailing lists. In many cases, mailing lists using individual names of each executive are available. However, if the lists are even slightly out of date, a list by company and functional title would be utilized.

In conclusion, the selection of industrial advertising media involves a matching process—determining the linkage between various media and the desired target audience. Industrial advertising media, as opposed to many consumer media, generally provide specific details relative to their circulation. The industrial advertiser must carefully evaluate the specific purchase decision participants to which an advertising message will be directed, and then match these to the circulation records of the various media. The final decision on media choice will depend on the available budget, the cost per thousand of the media, and the media's circulation. A final step in the advertising management area is that of evaluating advertising performance.

Advertising Effectiveness

The industrial advertiser rarely expects new orders to result immediately from advertising, rather advertising is designed to create awareness, stimulate loyalty to the company, or create a favorable attitude toward the product. Even though advertising may play no direct role in precipitating a purchase decision, advertising programs must be held accountable for accomplishing some type of measurable results. Thus, the industrial advertiser requires a method for measuring the results of current advertising in order to improve future advertising programs. Likewise, the effectiveness of advertising expenditures can be evaluated against expenditures on other marketing strategy elements. Effective management practice dictates that expenditure and results be related.

Discussions of advertising effectiveness inevitably turn to the question: What should be measured? In answering this question, consideration must be given to the role of advertising in general and the specific objectives of a given advertising campaign. To judge advertising performance, the advertiser should turn toward the decision-making process that occurs between a customer viewing an advertisement and the resulting behavior. This process is conceptualized in figure 14.4.

Measuring Impacts on the Purchase Decision Process. Measuring advertising effectiveness involves an assessment of advertising's impact on what "intervenes" between the stimulus (advertising) and the resulting behavior (purchase decision).[35] The underlying rationale for such an approach is that advertising can affect awareness, knowledge, and related dimensions that more readily lend themselves to measurement. In essence, the advertiser attempts to gauge advertising's ability to move an individual through the purchase decision process. Understand, however, that this approach presumes that enhancement of any one phase of the decision process or the movement from one step to the next increases the ultimate probability of purchase. Considerable debate exists over the validity of this assumption.

As a general rule, the effectiveness of advertising diminishes as the buyer moves through the decision-making process. Figure 14.5 presents a generalized picture of the decreasing impact of advertising during the later stages

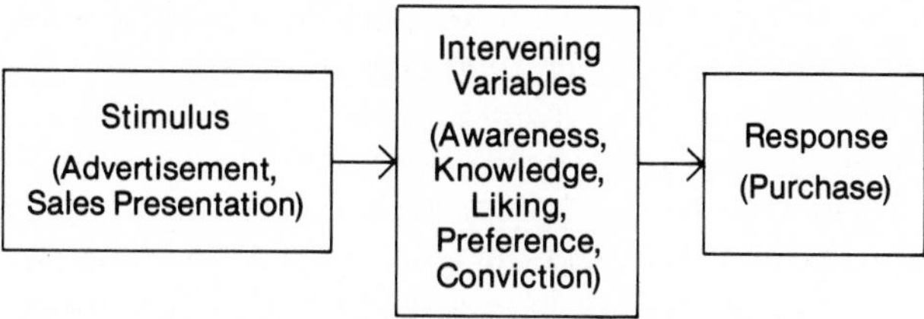

Figure 14.4 / The Communication Decision-Making Process

Source. Adapted from Robert J. Lavidge and Gary A. Steiner, "A Model for Predictive Measurements of Advertising Effectiveness," *Journal of Marketing* 25 (October 1961), pp. 59–62.

of the decision-making process. Such a conceptualization of industrial advertising serves to reinforce the importance of focusing the measurement of advertising effectiveness on factors like awareness and knowledge.

In summary, advertising effectiveness will be evaluated on the basis of achieving specified objectives—objectives formulated in terms of the elements of the buyer's decision process. In addition, the question of cost must be considered, meaning that advertising efforts will be judged, in the final analysis, on cost per level of achievement (e.g., dollars spent to achieve a certain level of awareness or recognition).

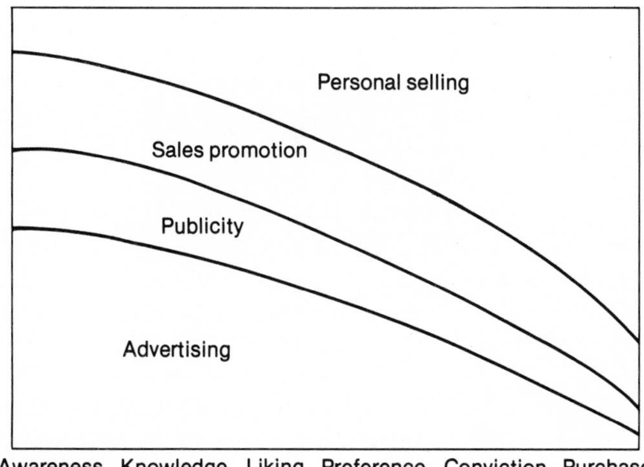

Figure 14.5 / Effectiveness of Different Communication Tools at Different Stages of the Decision-Making Process

Source. Adapted from Philip Kotler, *Marketing: Analysis, Planning and Control* (Englewood Cliffs, N.J.) Prentice-Hall, Inc., 1980, p. 491. Reprinted by permission of Prentice-Hall, Inc.

The Measurement Program. A good measurement program entails substantial advanced planning so that the right type of data will be gathered. Table 14.5 depicts the basic areas of advertising evaluation. Note that each area requires a planning aspect (pre-evaluation) and an evaluation aspect (post-evaluation). Thus, the manager must determine in advance what is to be measured, steps to be taken, and the techniques to be used. A comprehensive evaluation program will require a number of different measurements. Observe from table 14.5 that five primary areas for advertising evaluation are: (1) markets, (2) motives, (3) messages, (4) media, and (5) overall results.

The evaluation of industrial advertising is a demanding and complex task. However, it is an absolutely essential ingredient of an effective advertising program. Budgetary constraints are generally the limiting factors in specifying the extent of such programs. Usually outside professional research companies will be called on to develop field research studies. Most effectiveness measures will focus on the impact of advertising on moving a decision participant from awareness of the product/company to a position of readiness to buy. Thus, the specific type of evaluations required may include some of the following: knowledge, recognition, recall, awareness, prefer-

Table 14.5 / The Five Primary Areas for Advertising Evaluation

Area	Pre-Evaluation	Post-Evaluation
1. Markets	Identifying the market targets at which the advertising is aimed	Measuring extent to which advertising succeeded in reaching its market targets
2. Motives	Determining what causes people to buy (as preparatory step toward constructing advertising message)	Measuring motivating factors after the action (such as a purchase) occurred
3. Messages	Determining the best ways to construct and communicate messages	Measuring extent to which the message registered
4. Media	Determining the best combination of media to reach the market with the messages	Measuring extent to which various media succeeded in reaching the market with the message
5. Overall Results	Identifying the specific results that advertising is uniquely qualified to perform	Evaluating extent to which advertising accomplished its objectives as a basis for deciding what to continue, what to change, how much to spend

Source. Maurice I. Mandell, *Advertising* (Englewood Cliffs, N.J.: Prentice-Hall, Inc., 1974), p. 610. Reprinted by permission of Prentice-Hall, Inc.

ence, or motivation tests. Although the manager would like to measure sales impacts of advertising, such an ideal is unfortunately not often possible.

The focus of this chapter to this point has been on media advertising and the nature of the decision process in creating an effective campaign. However, there are additional promotional tools available to the industrial marketer that often play an important role in the broad industrial promotional program. The final section of the chapter will provide a brief look at some of these tools.

Supplementary Promotional Tools

Media advertising and direct mail advertising form the cornerstone of most industrial nonpersonal promotional programs. In terms of budgetary allocations, most industrial advertising funds are designated for trade publication and direct mail. A variety of additional promotional activities supplement the main thrust of advertising, and these include exhibits and trade shows, catalogs, and trade promotion.

Exhibits and Trade Shows

A multitude of industries annually stage a business show or exhibition to display new advances and technological developments in the industry. Generally, leading sellers are invited to present their products and services in booths that are visited by interested industry members. Quite obviously, a trade show exhibit offers the industrial marketer a unique opportunity to publicize a significant contribution to industry technology or to demonstrate products. Significant advantages that may accrue to the exhibitor include: (1) an effective selling message can be delivered to a relatively large and interested audience at one time (for example, over 30,000 people attend the annual Plant Engineering Show); (2) new products can be introduced to a mass audience; (3) potential customers can be uncovered, providing sales personnel with qualified leads; (4) general goodwill can be enhanced; and (5) often free publicity is generated for the company. Research suggests that the cost of reaching a prospect at a trade show is less than $40, while the cost of making an industrial sales call approaches $150.[34]

Specific Objectives Required. The challenging aspects of utilizing the trade show effectively involve deciding which trade shows to attend and how much of the promotional budget should be expended. One way to answer the first question is to evaluate the attendance at the trade show in light of the company's target audiences. Clearly, the firm will want to be represented at those shows frequented by its important customer segments. A useful service in this regard is the *Exposition Audit,* provided by Business Publication Audit of Circulation, Inc. The audit contains a headcount of the registered attendance at trade shows and a complete profile of each one's business, job title, and function.

The budgetary question is difficult to answer. Norman Hart provides an interesting insight on exhibitions, stating:

> It is strange to find that so little is known about the usefulness of exhibitions, that they are so often an expression of faith rather than fact, with such factors as size of stand and budget determined intuitively by some senior executive.[35]

Hart goes on to say that more money is probably wasted at exhibitions than in any other advertising medium. One reason seems to be the apparent need for competitors to outdo each other in creating the grandest displays. As with all other promotional vehicles, the planning and budgeting for trade shows must focus on specific objectives to be accomplished. Once these objectives are determined, a rational approach can be used to identify the tasks that must be accomplished and the levels of expenditure required.

Catalogs

A wide range of industrial firms produce items that are sold through industrial distributors. Because it is not possible to inventory all items, many manufacturers provide loose-leaf catalogs to their distributors, enabling the distributor to order from the catalog. In similar fashion, many suppliers of products that can be described by size, shape, or other features develop extensive catalogs describing their products and potential applications. The catalogs are then mailed to industrial buyers that conceivably would have a need for such products. Catalogs are a powerful promotional device because, if properly distributed, they will be on the shelves of every important potential buying firm in the industry.

Catalogs actually represent a form of direct marketing. They generally contain enough information on the products that they display for the reader to make a purchase. In effect, a good catalog is analogous to having a salesperson in the buyer's office at all times. In addition, the catalog will supplement the salesperson's efforts by providing information between sales calls. Some industrial marketers find that catalogs may in fact substitute for a salesperson or a rep in peripheral market areas.

Distribution of the catalog is an especially important consideration. If the supplier distributes the catalog, appropriate mailing lists must be developed. Catalog mailing lists need to be continually updated to keep abreast of the dynamics in the market. Important potential buyers may be missed if efforts are not made to add new companies to the list. An industrial marketer can delegate the catalog distribution function to a firm specializing in such activities. Distributing companies, such as Sweets, collect catalogs from a number of firms, bind them together, and distribute them to a variety of industrial users. Users find a compendium of catalogs a convenient device for reducing search time, and, as a result, the advertiser is assured of greater life and greater use of its section of the catalog file.[36]

Trade Advertising

Trade advertising refers to the promotional efforts of a supplier that are directed at middlemen in the distribution channel. Generally, the approach to trade advertising is different from the approach taken in customer/user advertising. The focus of advertising to customer/users is on communicating product benefits, but the focus of trade advertising centers on an appeal to middlemen profits and effectiveness. Trade promotion attempts to stress the profits associated with carrying the manufacturer's line. In addition, promotional pieces are made available to distributors and reps so they can associate their name with the manufacturer in a local advertising campaign. In still another application, suppliers often develop dealer aids, such as displays or sales kits, which are provided to middlemen to enhance their effectiveness. The quality of promotional support provided to distributors can be an important element in solidifying an effective channel relationship.

Summary

Advertising plays an essential role in the marketing strategy of industrial marketers. Because of the nature of the industrial buying process, personal selling assumes the primary role in creating sales, but advertising works to support and supplement personal selling efforts. In fact, advertising performs some tasks that personal selling simply cannot perform. Most important is the fact that advertising is able to reach buying influences that sales personnel are precluded from contacting. In other ways, advertising supports the personal selling effort by making the company and product known to potential buyers. The result is greater overall selling success. Effective advertising tends to make the entire marketing strategy more efficient, often lowering total marketing and selling costs. Finally, advertising can provide information and company/product awareness more efficiently than personal selling.

Managing the advertising program begins with the determination of advertising objectives. Usually, these focus upon communications goals—affecting some aspect of the decision process. Advertising objectives need to be written, and they should focus on a specific target audience. Once objectives are specified, the process of allocating funds to advertising can be accomplished. Although frequently applied, rules of thumb are not the ideal approach to specifying advertising budgets. The task method, along with industry guidelines established by the ADVISOR studies, provides more effective budgetary guidelines. Advertising messages are created with the understanding that the potential buyer's perceptual process will influence his or her receptivity to the message. The most effective appeal is one that focuses on product benefits that are salient to the relevant buying influencers.

Advertising media are selected on the basis of their circulation; that is, how well their audience matches the desired group of purchase decision influencers. Direct mail overcomes this problem by directing advertisements at precisely defined audiences. Finally, advertising effectiveness must be evaluated in light of the communication objectives established for the advertising campaign. Readership, recognition, awareness, attitudes, and intention-to-buy are typical measures of industrial advertising performance.

A variety of supplementary promotional tools are available to the industrial advertiser. Trade shows are an effective way to reach large audiences with a single presentation. Care must be taken in evaluating the appropriate allocation of funds to trade shows. Catalogs, on the other hand, may lead to direct sales if effectively developed and distributed. Trade advertising tends to focus on profitability considerations of the middleman and on devices to enhance middleman effectiveness. Finally, the industrial advertising agency is often a valuable asset in the creation and design of total campaigns.

Footnotes

[1]John Lamson, "The 'Top Dog' Theory Has Holes in It," *Media Decisions* 11 (November 1976), p. 88.

[2]Richard Manville, "Why Industrial Companies Must Advertise Their Products," *Industrial Marketing* 63 (October 1978), p. 47.

[3]A number of studies have documented the ability of advertising to reach industrial buying influences not accessible to the salesperson. Two of the most frequently cited are *The U.S. Steel/Harnischfeger Study: Industrial Advertising Effectively Reaches Buying Influences at Low Cost* (New York: American Business Press, 1969) and *The Evolution of a Purchase Study* (Bloomfield Hills, Michigan: Bromsom Publishing Co., 1967).

[4]John E. Morrill, "Industrial Advertising Pays Off," *Harvard Business Review* 48 (March–April 1970), pp. 4–14.

[5]Ibid., p. 6.

[6]Thayer C. Taylor, "Selling Costs Go through the Roof," *Sales & Marketing Management* 119 (February 26, 1979), p. 27; see also "Marketing Briefs—Average Cost of an Industrial Sales Call," *Marketing News* (April 8, 1980), p. 2.

[7]"As Sales Costs Rise, Management Expects More from Advertising," *Industrial Marketing* 64 (March 1979), p. 83.

[8]Gary L. Lilien, Alvin J. Silk, Jean-Marie Choffray, and Murlidhar Rao, "Industrial Advertising Effects and Budgeting Practices," *Journal of Marketing* 40 (January 1976), pp. 20–21.

[9]Robert J. Lavidge and Gary A. Steiner, "A Model for Predictive Measurement of Advertising Effectiveness," *Journal of Marketing* 25 (October 1961), pp. 59–61.

[10]Charles H. Patti, "Buyer Information Sources in the Capital Equipment Industry," *Industrial Marketing Management* 6 (1977), pp. 259–64; see also Alicia Donovan, "Awareness of Trade-Press Advertising," *Journal of Advertising Research* 19 (April 1979), pp. 33–35; and related research by Dominique M. Hanssens and Burton A. Weitz, "The Effectiveness of Industrial Print Advertisements Across Product Categories," *Journal of Marketing Research* 17 (August 1980), pp. 294–306.

[11]W. H. Grosse, *How Industrial Advertising and Sales Promotion Can Increase Marketing Power* (New York: American Management Association, Inc., 1973), p. 41.

[12]"Preplanning the Advertising Campaign," *Industrial Marketing* 59 (August 1974), p. 51.

[13]Lilien et al., "Industrial Advertising Effects and Budgeting Practices," p. 22.

[14]Russell H. Colley, *Defining Advertising Goals for Measuring Advertising Results* (New York: Association of National Advertisers, 1961). pp. 1–5.

[15]David W. Nylen, *Advertising: Planning, Implementation and Control* (Cincinnati: Southwestern Publishing Co., 1975), p. 230.

[16]Lilien et al., "Industrial Advertising Effects and Budgeting Practices," p. 22.

[17]Some industrial firms have developed quantitative models which relate advertising expenditures to profits or sales. For example, see David A. Aaker and John G. Myers, *Advertising Management* (Englewood Cliffs, N.J.: Prentice-Hall, Inc., 1975), chapter 3, pp. 51–81.

[18]Gary L. Lilien and John D. C. Little, "The ADVISOR Project: A Study of Industrial Marketing Budgets," *Sloan Management Review* 16 (Spring 1976), pp. 17–31.

[19]Ibid., p. 23.

[20]Ibid., p. 28.

[21]Ibid.

[22]Gary L. Lilien, "ADVISOR 2: Modeling the Marketing Mix for Industrial Products," *Management Science* 25 (February 1979), pp. 191–204.

[23]Aaker and Myers, *Advertising Management,* p. 270.

[24]Gordon McAleer, "Do Industrial Advertisers Understand What Influences Their Markets?" *Journal of Marketing* 38 (January 1974), pp. 15–23.

[25]Jean-Marie Choffray and Gary L. Lilien, "Assessing Response to Industrial Marketing Strategy," *Journal of Marketing* 42 (April 1978), p. 29

[26]Maurice I. Mandell, *Advertising* (Englewood Cliffs, N.J.: Prentice-Hall, Inc., 1968), p. 328.

[27]Lilien and Little report approximately the same distribution of budget dollars in their ADVISOR study. Various McGraw-Hill studies have shown similar results. See Phillip Burton and J. Robert Miller, *Advertising Fundamentals* (Columbus, Ohio: Grid Publishing, Inc., 1976), p. 364.

[28]"No Substitute for the Truth," *Media-Decisions* 12 (July 1977), p. 108.

[29]Burton and Miller, *Advertising Fundamentals,* p. 354.

[30]J. Taylor Sims and Herbert E. Brown, "Increasing the Role of Direct Mail Marketing in Industrial Marketing Strategy," *Industrial Marketing Management* 8 (November 1979), p. 294.

[31]Ibid., p. 295.

[32]Terry Quinn, "The Marketing Base for International Direct Marketing Programmes," in John Dillion (ed.), *Handbook of International Direct Marketing* (London: McGraw-Hill Book Company, 1976), p. 2.

[33]Aaker and Myers, *Advertising Management,* p. 89.

[34]Estimates based on studies by the Trade Show Bureau and McGraw-Hill, reported in "Trade Show Costs Holding Steady," *Marketing News* (December 15, 1978), p. 5.

[35]Norman Hart, *Industrial Advertising and Publicity* (New York: John Wiley and Sons, Inc., 1978), p. 56.

[36]Mandell, *Advertising* (2nd ed., 1974), p. 661.

Discussion Questions

1. While the bulk of the promotional budget of the industrial firm is allocated to personal selling, advertising can play an important role in industrial marketing strategy. Explain.

2. The Hamilton Compressor Company increased advertising expenditures 15 percent in the Chicago market last year and sales increased 4 percent. Upon seeing the results, Mr. White, the president, turns to you and asks: "Was that increase in advertising worth it?" Outline your reply. (Feel free to include questions that you would ask Mr. White.)

3. Breck Machine Tool would like you to develop a series of ads for a new industrial product. Upon request, Breck's marketing research department will provide you with any data they have concerning the new product and the market. Outline the approach that you would follow in *selecting media* and *developing messages* for the campaign. Specify the types of data that you would draw upon to improve the quality of your decisions.

4. Outline the approach that you would follow in evaluating the effectiveness and efficiency of an industrial firm's advertising function. They would like you to center on advertising budgeting practices and specific performance results.

5. Explain how a message presented in an industrial advertisement may be favorably evaluated by the production manager, unfavorably evaluated by the purchasing manager, and fail even to trigger the attention of the quality control engineer.

6. Given the rapid rise in the cost of making industrial sales calls, should the industrial marketer attempt to substitute direct mail advertising for personal selling whenever possible? Support your position.

7. What role does trade advertising perform in the industrial marketer's promotional program?

8. It is argued that industrial advertising is not expected to precipitate purchases directly. If industrial advertising does not persuade organizational buyers to buy brand A versus brand B, what does it do, and how can we measure its impact against expenditures on other marketing strategy elements?

Chapter 15 Industrial Marketing Communications: Personal Selling

Industrial marketing communications consist of two major components: advertising and personal selling. As explored in the last chapter, advertising and related sales promotion tools serve to supplement and reinforce personal selling efforts. Thus, personal selling constitutes the primary demand-stimulating force in the industrial marketer's promotional mix. It is through the sales force that the marketer links the firm's total product and service offering to the needs of organizational customers.

After reading this chapter, you will have an understanding of:

1. *the role of personal selling in industrial marketing strategy*
2. *the importance of examining industrial marketing management as a buyer-seller interaction process*
3. *the nature of the industrial sales management function*
4. *selected managerial tools that can be applied to major sales force decision areas.*

Personal selling often assumes a dominant role in industrial markets because the number of potential customers is relatively small (compared to consumer markets) and the dollar purchases are sufficiently large. The degree of importance of personal selling in the industrial firm's marketing mix is dependent upon many factors, such as the nature and composition of the market, the nature of the product line, and the company's objectives and financial capability. Recall from our discussion of industrial marketing channels that industrial marketers have many potential links to the market. Some may rely on manufacturer's representatives and distributors, while others rely exclusively on a direct sales force. Similarly, each firm must determine the relative importance of the various components of the promotional mix—advertising vs. sales promotion vs. personal selling.

Across all product categories, research indicates that industrial firms spend 12.9 percent of each sales dollar on marketing costs. Personal selling accounts for 6.3 percent of each dollar of sales; warehousing and delivery, 2.1 percent; and miscellaneous market costs, 2.9 percent. Industrial firms with sales less than one million dollars spend a higher percentage—17 percent—of each sales dollar on marketing costs.[1] Of course, these figures would vary, depending upon specific product and market conditions. They do point up, however, that significant resources are invested in personal selling in the industrial market. To maximize effectiveness and efficiency, the personal selling function must be carefully managed and integrated into the firm's marketing mix. This is especially true given the marked rise in the cost of making an industrial sales call. The cost of an average sales call is rapidly approaching \$150.[2] As noted in the last chapter, General Electric forecasts that the average costs associated with making one industrial sales call will approach \$400 by 1985.[3]

This chapter is divided into two major parts. First, an important conceptual perspective is delineated, and examines industrial marketing management as a buyer-seller interaction process. Substantial attention was devoted to organizational buying behavior earlier in the text (chapters 3 and 4). Key dimensions of that discussion will be highlighted and related to the personal selling process. The second part of the chapter turns to the important function of sales force management. Attention will be given to defining personal selling objectives, structuring the sales organization and sales force allocation, and the evaluation and control of sales force operations.

Foundations of Personal Selling: An Organizational Customer Focus

Personal selling provides the means through which industrial marketing strategy is executed. Once the marketer defines target segments in the organizational market on the basis of organizational characteristics (macro) or the characteristics of decision-making units (micro), the sales force is employed to meet the needs of these market segments. The salesperson augments the firm's total product offering and serves as a representative for the seller as well as for the buyer. The image, reputation, and need-satisfying capability of the seller is conveyed, to an important degree, by the sales force. By aiding procurement decision makers in defining requirements and matching the industrial firm's product/service offering to these requirements, the salesperson is offering much more than a physical product. Ideas, recommendations, technical assistance, experience, confidence, and friendship are provided to the buying organization. A large toy manufacturer, for example, evaluates industrial suppliers on the basis of product quality, delivery reliability, price, and *the value of ideas and suggestions provided by industrial sales personnel.* This buying organization, in fact, openly solicits and encourages ideas, and it periodically evaluates suppliers formally on the number and quality of these recommendations.

As a representative for the buyer, the salesperson will often articulate the specific needs of the organizational customer to research and development or production personnel in the industrial firm. Particular product specifications, delivery, or technical service needs are often negotiated and coordinated through the salesperson. Thus, the salesperson serves as an uncertainty absorption point, reducing conflict in the buyer-seller relationship.

Organizational Buying Behavior

Successful personal selling relies heavily upon a knowledge of the similarities and differences that exist among organizational customers and recognition of their unique requirements. Many industrial products have numerous applications and are used by organizational customers in many different ways. Likewise, organizational buyers have varying levels of experience in purchasing selected products and reflect a range of information requirements. A sensitivity to how buying organizations vary, coupled with a knowledge of organizational buying behavior, provides a cornerstone for successful personal selling outcomes. Thus, part two of this volume—*The Organizational Buying Process*—establishes a foundation for a discussion of the personal selling process and will be briefly recapped here.

A salesperson can benefit by examining a potential buying organization from several perspectives. First, how would the organization view this specific buying situation—new task, modified rebuy, or straight rebuy? As emphasized in chapter 3, each buying situation calls for a different personal selling strategy—the exact form depending on whether the marketer is an "in" or an "out" supplier. Second, attention centers on the forces that encircle the organizational buying process. These include environmental, organizational, group, and individual influences. Among the questions that will form the nature and direction of the personal selling task are:

1. *Environmental.* How are business conditions (e.g., growth, inflation) or political-legal trends (e.g., governmental regulation) affecting the industry within which this firm operates?

2. *Organizational.* Is the procurement function of this buying organization centralized or decentralized? To what extent does the procurement department utilize the computer in buying and in selecting and evaluating suppliers?
3. *Group.* Which organizational members will be included in the buying center, and what are their respective roles?
4. *Individual.* What selection criteria are most salient to each member of the buying center?

These questions establish the base for isolating the similarities and differences that exist among potential prospects. The salesperson can profit by examining purchasing requirements from the perspective of the customer. Knowledge of the special competitive challenges that the buying firm faces, how the proposed product/service offering will be applied, how it will influence the cost structure and performance of different departments—these are the insights that allow the marketer to develop sharply focused personal selling strategy. Empathy with the buyer provides the core of a successful and mutually beneficial buyer-seller relationship.

Buyer-Seller Interactions

At its most basic level, selling can be viewed as an exchange process in which two individuals trade items of value.[4] The buyer receives a physical product combined with attached services, as well as certain psychological assets. In turn, the seller receives financial, as well as psychological, benefits that issue from the relationship.

A Dyadic Exchange Model

Thomas Bonoma and Wesley Johnston assert that rich insights into industrial marketing can be secured by examining the smallest unit of analysis in marketing—the dyad.[5] Their exchange model of industrial marketing, which is based upon dyadic interactions (i.e., two parties, two firms), is presented in figure 15.1. There are five important dyadic relations depicted in the model. (Note that each is numbered in figure 15.1.)

1. *The sales representative-purchasing agent relationship.* Here, the seller exchanges information and assistance in solving a purchasing requirement for the reward of a specific sale given by the buyer. Friendship, trust, and cooperation can develop in buyer-seller interactions.
2. *The sales representative-selling firm relationship.* Here, the salesperson exerts sales effort in return for a salary and/or commission from the industrial marketer. Psychological income (e.g., recognition, praise) is often exchanged for loyalty.
3. *The purchasing agent-buying organization relationship.* The purchasing agent exchanges the talent at buying for a salary. Likewise, the pur-

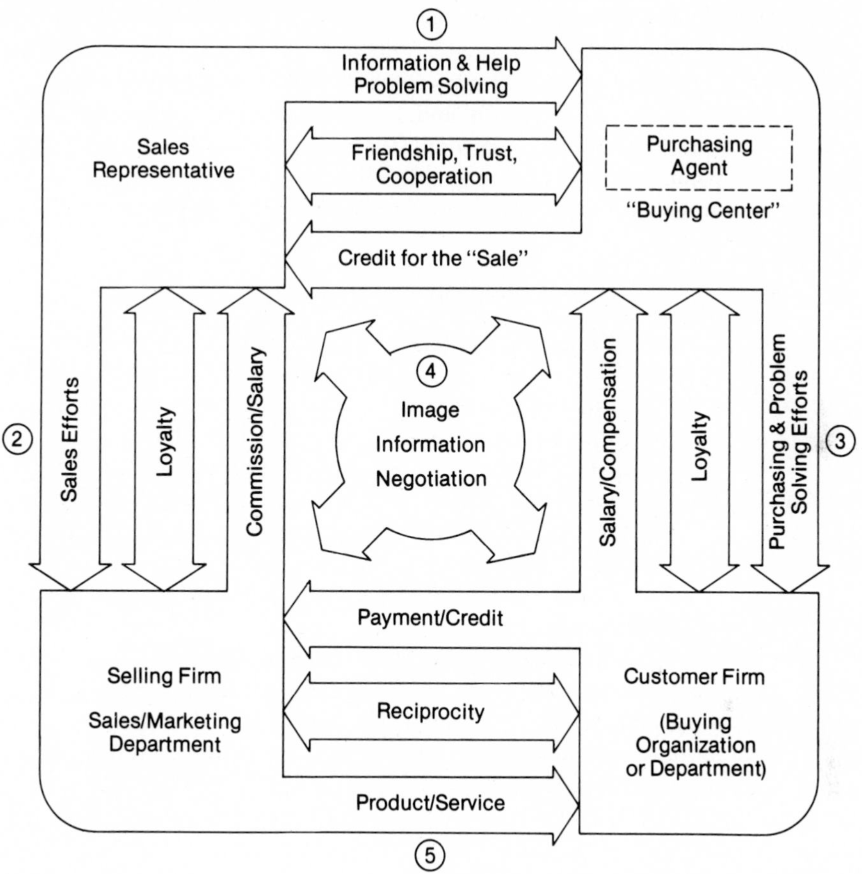

Figure 15.1 / Exchanges in Industrial Marketing and Purchasing Interactions

Source. Thomas V. Bonoma and Wesley J. Johnston, "The Social Psychology of Industrial Buying and Selling," *Industrial Marketing Management* 7 (1978), p. 216. Reprinted by permission.

chasing specialist may receive psychological income (e.g., organizational status) and display loyalty to the firm.

4. *The seller's view of the buying firm; the buyer's view of the selling firm.* The image that each party has for the other aids in establishing the boundaries of the purchasing interaction. The salesperson and the buyer each have plans, goals, and intentions that they hope to satisfy. While these are often negotiable, they serve as the starting point for the interaction process.
5. *The buying firm-selling firm exchange.* Here the product/service is given in return for money or credit. Reciprocal trade agreements (each buying from the other) are often an outgrowth of this exchange.

This exchange model points up the importance of determining not only what the seller is getting out of the transaction, but also what the buyer gets in return. To some degree, every transaction changes the selling firm and the salesperson, *and* the buying firm and key participants in the purchasing process. Bonoma and Johnston contend that "it is only when all these complex flows of influence are managed effectively that maximal marketing response will be generated, and maximal customer satisfaction will result."[6]

Buyer-Seller Interactions: Style and Content of Communication[7]

Important elements of buyer-seller relationships center on the content and style of communications. Jagdish Sheth theorizes that these elements strongly influence the quality of the interaction between buyer and seller. The *content of communication* refers to the substantive dimensions of the purpose that brought the two parties together. Included here are the recommending, offering, or negotiating of a set of product-specific utilities, and the expectations of the participants. Thus, content centers on the performance characteristics of a product or service as well as a bundle of other utilities (e.g., social, organizational, and emotional).

The *style of communication* constitutes the second dimension of the buyer-seller interaction process. This refers to the format, ritual, and mannerism that the buyer and the seller utilize in their interaction. One of three styles of communication can be adopted: (1) task-oriented, highly purposeful; (2) interaction-oriented, socializing or personalizing; or (3) self-oriented, preoccupation with self-interests.

Sheth hypothesizes that successful interaction will only occur when the buyer and the seller are compatible with respect to both content and style of communication. Observe in figure 15.2 that an ideal transaction requires compatibility on both style and content, and incompatibility on these two dimensions results in no transaction. The latter case may, in fact, lead to

	Compatible Style	Incompatible Style
Compatible Content	ideal transaction	inefficient transaction
Incompatible Content	inefficient transaction	no transaction

Figure 15.2 / Outcomes of Dyadic Interaction Processes: The Influence of Content and Style of Communication

Source. Adapted from Jagdish N. Sheth, "Buyer-Seller Interaction: A Conceptual Framework," in B. B. Anderson (ed.), *Advances in Consumer Research, Volume III* (Cincinnati, Ohio: Association for Consumer Research, 1976), p. 383. Used by permission of the Association for Consumer Research and the author.

negative side effects, such as distrust or unfavorable word-of-mouth concerning one another. When the content is compatible and the style is incompatible, the process might be terminated, or, if a sale results, negative feelings will remain concerning the manner in which each handled the transaction. Finally, if the incompatibility centers on content rather than style, the interaction process will either cease or negotiations will continue with each attempting to alter the other's product expectations.

This conceptual scheme raises important implications for sales force management. Knowledge of incongruity between the buyer and the seller with respect to style or content can signal problems for the marketer. If the incompatibility centers on content, adjustments may be needed in the firm's product/service offering, or an assessment may be warranted of the market segmentation rationale employed by the firm. The product may be inconsistent with the needs of the firm's defined market segments. By contrast, if the incompatibility concerns style-related problems in the interaction process, corrective actions might include modifying personal selling approaches or retraining the sales personnel. The firm also might consider changes in the recruiting and selection of sales personnel.

A research study of buyer-seller interactions concerning life insurance reinforces the importance of using the dyad as a basic unit of analysis in understanding buyer behavior. The findings indicated that there were greater attitudinal similarities between agents and sold prospects than between agents and unsold prospects. Further, the implication emerges that ". . . sales success in a dyadic encounter may be a function of the degree to which the prospect perceives the salesperson as fulfilling his attitudinal and behavioral expectations."[8]

The Industrial Salesperson: An Interorganizational Link[9]

To survive, the industrial firm must interact effectively with its environment. Industrial salespersons provide a means by which firms are linked to critical elements in their enterprise's relevant environment. For example, the salesperson serves as an important interorganizational link in the industrial firm's communication with its customers. This points up the importance of understanding the key boundary-spanning activities assumed by the industrial salesperson:

1. *Representing and transacting*. The salesperson represents the marketer but is charged with the task of balancing the needs of two organizations—the industrial firm and the customer's organization.
2. *Buffering*. The salesperson enhances environmental stability by attempting to smooth the irregularities between the production cycle of the marketer and the sales ordering cycle of customers.
3. *Information processing and monitoring*. The salesperson monitors important environmental conditions and transfers relevant and timely information back to organizational decision makers.

4. *Linking and coordinating.* The salesperson initiates and guides informal coordination effort between the industrial firm and a client firm or among the industrial firm, a middleman, and a client firm.

Recognition of the strategic importance of these boundary-spanning activities and the strains and conflicts that are inherent in these activities is fundamental to effective sales management.

Managing the Industrial Sales Force

Effective management of the industrial sales force is fundamental to the firm's success, because substantial resources are invested in this component of the communications mix, and because personal selling often plays a dominant role in industrial marketing strategy. Sales management centers on the planning, organizing, directing, and control of personal selling efforts. An overview of the sales force management decision process is provided in figure 15.3.[10]

Note that sales force decisions are tempered by overall marketing objectives and must be integrated with the other elements of the marketing mix. It is within this framework that personal selling objectives are developed. Forecasts of the expected sales response guide the firm both in determining the total selling effort required (sales force size) and in allocating the sales force to various organizational levels (such as sales territories). The techniques for estimating market potential and forecasting sales (discussed in part three—*Assessing Market Opportunities*) are particularly valuable to the sales manager in dealing with these decisions. Once these important decisions are made, sales management also involves the ongoing activities of sales planning, recruiting and selecting sales personnel, training, motivation, and supervision. Finally, sales operations must be evaluated and controlled to identify problem areas and to monitor the efficiency, effectiveness, and profitability of the firm's personal selling units.

Particular attention in this section will be devoted to four areas. First, the role of personal selling in the marketing program will be briefly delineated. Second, methods for organizing the sales force will be explored. Third, a sketch of the requirements for successful sales force administration will be highlighted. Fourth, attention will turn to models that can be employed in managing the industrial sales force.

Defining the Role of Personal Selling in the Industrial Marketing Program

A strong customer focus coupled with an understanding of organizational buying behavior and the communication process are fundamental to successful personal selling. The specific role that personal selling assumes in the marketing program varies by company and product/market conditions. The following scenarios show two different personal selling roles.

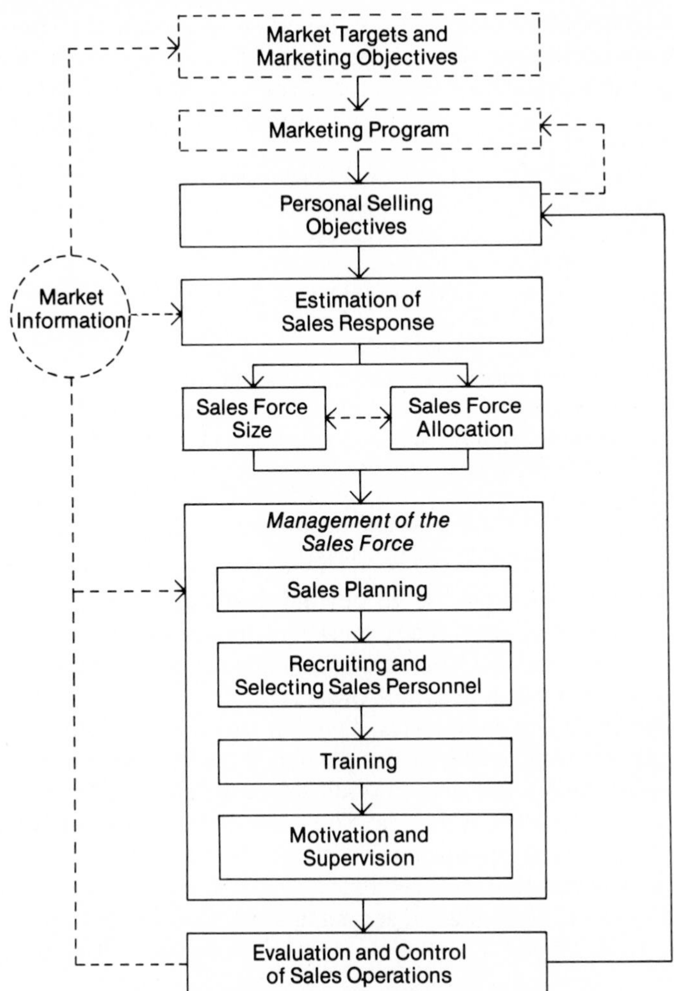

Figure 15.3 / Sales Force Management Decision Process

[1]*Source*. David W. Cravens, Gerald E. Hills, and Robert B. Woodruff, *Marketing Decision Making: Concepts and Strategy* (Homewood, Illinois: Richard D. Irwin, Inc., 1976), p. 674 and 735. Reprinted by permission. © 1976 by Richard D. Irwin, Inc.

Kim Kelly, a sales representative for Honeywell, Inc., had been competing with the sales personnel of four other firms for a large computer account. He made numerous sales calls to different individuals in the buying organization over a three-year period. In fact, for the last three months as the firm neared a decision, he had been working nearly full time on this account. This diligent selling effort and follow-up culminated in an order for an $8 million computer system on which Kim received an $80,000 commission.[11]

The prime personal selling function assumed by Kim was *demand-stimulation.* Although supported by advertising, sales promotion, and technical personnel, personal selling constitutes the dominant demand-stimulating force in the communications mix. This is often referred to as a *push strategy*.

Joe Smith is the sales representative for a major manufacturer of industrial accessory equipment. He travels several states calling on industrial distributors who are authorized dealers for his company's product line. These distributors sell the equipment to industrial users. Joe begins his day by stopping at a nearby distributor to solicit an order to replenish inventory levels. Joe checks the distributor's inventory, prepares an order, discusses it with the buyer, and gets it approved and signed. The order is placed in the outgoing mail.

After a 20 minute drive, Joe arrives at another distributor. He is informed that a shipment came in freight collect and should have been freight prepaid. Joe calls his traffic department and authorizes a credit memo for the amount of the shipping charges. With the problem resolved, Joe leaves.

On the third distributor call, Joe is informed that a recent bid was lost to a competitor. He gathers all the available information on the missed sale, writes a brief report, and mails it to his sales manager.[12]

The functions assumed by Joe go beyond demand-stimulation and center, instead, on channel assistance, market intelligence, and strengthening buyer-seller relationships. This more passive role for personal selling (as in Joe's case) is referred to as a *pull strategy*.

In contrasting the two strategies, a *push strategy* is more frequently found in industrial marketing. Often, sales personnel perform primarily a demand-stimulating function while also providing a range of services to the organizational customer. Some industrial firms will divide the sales force on the basis of a specific selling mission. To illustrate, Xerox employs "new business" selling teams that are dedicated to obtaining new accounts, while other selling teams specialize in servicing existing accounts.

Organizing the Personal Selling Effort

A strategic question confronting the industrial marketer is: How should the sales force be organized in order to meet the needs of important market segments and to achieve the firm's objectives? The appropriate form of the sales organization is dependent upon many factors, including the nature and length of the firm's product line, the role middlemen assume in the marketing program, the diversity of market segments served, the nature of buying behavior in each market segment, and the structure of competitive selling effort. Likewise, the size and financial strength of the industrial manufacturer often dictate, to an important degree, the feasibility of particular organizational forms. The industrial marketer can organize the sales force on three bases: (1) geographical, (2) product, or (3) market. Large industrial concerns that market diverse product lines may employ all three of these sales force configurations at different points throughout the organizational structure.

Geographical Organization. The most common form of sales organization found in the industrial market is geographical. Here, each salesperson is responsible for performing required selling tasks for all of the firm's products in a defined geographical area. By reducing the travel distance and travel time between customers, this method usually minimizes costs. Likewise, sales personnel have a clear understanding of the specific customers and prospects that fall within their area of responsibility.

The key disadvantage of the geographical sales organization is that each salesperson must possess the ability and knowledge to perform all of the selling tasks associated with all of the firm's products, and to perform these tasks for all customers in a particular territory. If the products lend themselves to rather diverse applications, this can be a very difficult task. A second disadvantage of this organizational scheme is that the salesperson has substantial flexibility in choosing which products and customers to emphasize. Sales personnel may have a tendency to emphasize those products and end-use applications with which they are most familiar. Of course, this problem might be remedied through training and capable first-line supervision. Since the salesperson plays a crucial role in operationalizing the firm's segmentation strategy, careful coordination and control is required to align personal selling effort with important marketing objectives.

Product Organization. A product-oriented sales organization is one in which salespersons specialize in relatively narrow components of the firm's total product line. This organizational scheme is especially appropriate when the product line is large and diverse or technically complex. Product specialization is appropriate when a high degree of application knowledge is required by the salesperson in order to meet customer needs. Furthermore, different products often elicit different patterns of buying behavior. Thus, the salesperson that concentrates on a particular product becomes more adept at identifying and communicating with members of the buying center.

A prime benefit of this approach is that it allows the sales force to develop a level of product knowledge that enhances the value of the firm's total offering to organizational customers. In addition to augmenting the firm's products, the product-oriented sales organization often facilitates the identification of new market segments.

A drawback of this organizational scheme concerns the cost of developing and deploying a specialized sales force. A product must have the potential for generating a level of sales and profit that justifies individual selling attention. Thus, a "critical mass" of demand is required to offset the costs of having two or more salespersons in a particular geographical area.

Market-Centered Organization. Rather than organizing the sales force by geographical area or product, the industrial marketer may find it beneficial to organize personal selling effort by customer type. To illustrate, the Xerox information system group, which markets copiers and duplicators, shifted from geographical selling to vertical selling by industry type.[13] By developing knowledge concerning the specific requirements of a particular industry or customer type, the salesperson is better prepared to identify and respond to buying influentials. Also, key market segments defined by the marketer become more accessible, thus providing the opportunity for differentiated personal selling strategies. The market segments must, of course, be sufficiently large to warrant specialized treatment.

Related Organizational Issues. Decisions concerning the appropriate structure of the sales organization cannot be made in a vacuum, but must be integrated with the broader organizational structure in a manner consistent with corporate strategy. Product management, research and development, manufacturing, distribution, and the sales force must be inextricably linked for marketing strategy to be successful. A structure is sought that directs the organization toward meeting the needs of organizational customers while at the same time preserving as much flexibility as possible to meet change in the future.[14]

Typical Job Titles

Top-level marketing management

Marketing vice president. Typically the top marketing executive in the company or division.

Sales vice president. Sometimes another title for marketing vice president but sometimes the top sales executive who will report to either the president or the marketing vice president.

Top-level line sales management

National sales manager. The top sales executive responsible for all sales force-related activities.

General sales manager. Another title for national sales manager.

Middle-level line sales management

National account sales manager. Usually responsible for a separate, high-quality sales force which calls on national accounts. Often the only person in the national account sales force and responsible for actual selling, but the accounts are so large that the position needs a relatively high-level manager.

Regional, divisional, or zone sales manager. These are titles for high-level field sales managers to whom other field sales managers report. Occasionally, the titles are used for first-level sales management jobs in which salespeople are managed.

Market sales manager. A sales manager responsible for salespeople calling on a specific group of accounts. Often this position has marketing responsibility in addition to sales management and perhaps sales responsibility. A company which specializes its sales force by market will have one market sales manager to head each separate sales force.

Product sales manager. The same as market sales manager except that the job is organized around a product line instead of a customer category. Both positions are more likely to occur in industrial companies than in consumer-goods companies. The product sales managers are usually more involved with product-oriented decisions than are market managers.

Lower-level line sales management

District or field sales manager. The first line sales manager to whom the salespeople report.

Upper-level sales positions

Account executive, key account salesperson, national account salesperson, major account salesperson. These people are responsible for selling to major accounts. In the consumer-goods field, the title sometimes involves chain stores, meaning usually the three large national general merchandise chains (Sears, Penney, Montgomery Ward), food chains, or mass merchandisers such as discount department stores.

Typical sales positions
Salesperson, field salesperson, territory manager, account representative, sales representative. All are typical titles for the salesperson responsible for selling and servicing a variety of accounts.

Staff sales management
These positions are usually functionally oriented and include titles such as manager of sales training, sales analyst, etc. The typical staff responsibilities include training, recruiting, and sales analysis. More general staff positions include the title assistant to the national sales manager. Assistant national sales managers may be either line or staff managers. Staff positions may occur at any level in the organization. Some companies with divisional sales forces, for example, have a job of corporate vice president of sales who has no line sales management responsibility. Other companies have regional or area sales vice presidents responsible for aiding salespeople from various divisions with major account sales. This is found, for example, in some weapons marketers where various product-oriented divisions call upon the same buying organization.

Note: The titles and descriptions above are generalities. Different industries and different companies in many cases use different titles for the same job and organize job content differently.

Source. Benson P. Shapiro, *Sales Program Management: Formulation and Implementation* (New York: McGraw-Hill Book Company, 1977), p. 7. Reprinted by permission.

Sales Administration

Successful administration of the sales force involves the following significant activities: recruiting and selecting salespersons, training, motivation and supervision, and evaluation and control of the sales force. The industrial firm can benefit by fostering an organizational climate that encourages the development of a sales force capable of meeting the needs of organizational customers and achieving important marketing objectives.

Recruiting and Selecting Salespersons. An important component of a total sales force management program concerns the recruiting and selection of sales personnel. Ben Enis and Lawrence Chonko contend that more emphasis is being placed on the recruiting process and on reducing salesperson turnover because:

> Today's salesperson must have many talents: knowledge of business, current affairs, and organizational politics; social graces to mingle with company presidents and workers on the shop floor; patience, persistence, etc.[15]

The recruiting process presents numerous tradeoffs for the industrial marketer. First, should experienced salespersons be sought or should inexperienced individuals be hired and trained by the company? The appropriate recruiting strategy is situation specific and varies with the size of the firm, the nature of the selling task, the firm's training capability, and the company's market experience. Smaller firms often reduce training costs by hiring experienced and more expensive salespersons. By contrast, large organizations, often possessing a more complete training function, may wish to hire less experienced personnel and support them with a carefully developed training program.

A second tradeoff that emerges in the recruiting process concerns the quantity versus quality question.[16] Often, sales managers are interested in screening as many recruits as possible in selecting new salespersons. Such an approach, however, can overload and damage the selection process, thus hampering the firm's ability to identify quality candidates. A poorly organized recruiting effort that lacks closure leaves candidates with a negative first impression. Recruiting, like selling, is an exchange process that takes place between two parties. A well-organized recruiting effort is needed to insure that candidates fitting the position requirements are given the proper level of attention in the screening process. Thus, established procedures must be developed to insure that inappropriate candidates are screened out at an early stage in the evaluation process, so that the pool of candidates is reduced to a manageable size.

The responsibility for recruiting and selecting salespersons may lie with the first level supervisor who often receives assistance from an immediate superior, or the personnel department or other executives at the headquarters level may have the responsibility. The latter group tends to be more involved when the sales force is viewed as the training ground for marketing or general managers. Ultimately, company policies, the size and organization of the sales force, and related issues determine the location of recruiting and selection activities.

Training. To prepare adequately new salespersons entering the industrial marketing environment, a carefully designed training program is required. Likewise, periodic training is required to sharpen the skills of experienced salespersons, especially when the firm operates in a rapidly changing product/market environment. Changes in industrial marketing strategy (e.g., new products, new market segments) require corresponding changes in the personal selling function. The salesperson requires a wealth of knowledge about the company, the product line, customer segments, and competition. As indicated earlier, the salesperson also needs an understanding of organizational buying behavior and effective communicative skills. These knowledge requirements establish the focus of industrial sales training programs.

Effective training builds the confidence and motivation of the salesperson, thereby increasing the probabilities of successful sales performance. In turn, training aids the industrial marketer by keeping the personal selling function aligned with marketing program objectives. For example, the sales force plays a significant role in putting the firm's basic segmentation strategy into operation. Furthermore, a successful training effort can reduce the costs associated with recruiting; many industrial firms have found that the salesperson turnover rate declines as improvements are made in training. Clearly, a salesperson who is inadequately prepared to meet the demands of selling tasks can quickly become discouraged, frustrated, and envious of friends who selected other career options. Much of this anxiety—which is especially prevalent in the early stages of many careers—can be removed by effective training and capable first-line supervision.

Supervision and Motivation. Capable supervision is needed to direct the activities of the sales force in a manner that is consistent with the company's policies and marketing objectives. Critical supervisory tasks for managing the sales force include continued training, counseling, assistance (e.g., time planning), and related activities which aid sales personnel in planning and executing their work. In addition, supervision involves developing sales performance standards, fulfilling company policy directives, and integrating the sales force with higher organizational levels.[17]

Motivation, which must be addressed from the perspective of the salesperson, can be viewed as the amount of effort that the salesperson "desires to expend on each of the activities or tasks associated with his job, such as calling on potential new accounts, planning sales presentations, and filling out reports."[18] A model that outlines the determinants of a salesperson's performance is presented in figure 15.4. Note that the model hypothesizes that job performance is a function of three factors: (1) the salesperson's level of motivation; (2) the salesperson's aptitude or ability; and (3) the salesperson's perceptions concerning how his or her role should be performed. Each of these three factors is influenced by personal variables (e.g., personality), organizational variables (e.g., training programs), and environmental variables (e.g., economic conditions). Sales managers can influence some of the personal and organizational variables through selection, training, and supervision policies, but environmental forces fall outside the control of management.

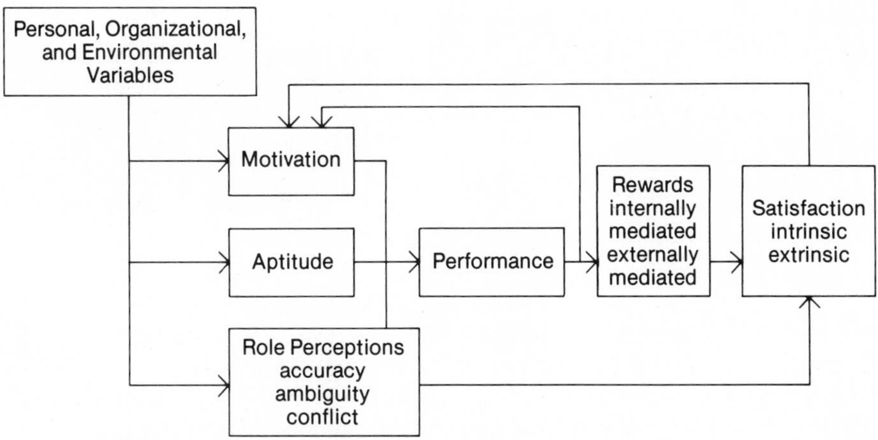

Figure 15.4 / Determinants of Salesperson's Performance

Source. Orville C. Walker, Jr., Gilbert A. Churchill, Jr., and Neil M. Ford, "Motivation and Performance in Industrial Selling: Present Knowledge and Needed Research," *Journal of Marketing Research* 14 (May 1977), p. 158. Reprinted from the *Journal of Marketing Research,* published by the American Marketing Association.

The salesperson's motivation to perform is theorized to be related strongly to the individual's perceptions of the types and amounts of rewards that will be obtained in return for various kinds of job performance, as well as to the value the salesperson places on these rewards. For a given level of performance, two types of rewards might be offered to a salesperson:

1. *internally mediated rewards,* those that the salesperson attains on a personal basis, such as feelings of accomplishment or self-worth;
2. *externally mediated rewards,* those controlled and offered by managers or customers, such as financial incentives, pay, or recognition.

The received rewards strongly influence the level of satisfaction that the salesperson feels concerning the job and the work environment. In addition, the level of satisfaction derived from a sales position is influenced by the individual's role perceptions. Job satisfaction is theorized to *decline* if the salesperson's perception of the role: (1) is *inaccurate* vis-à-vis the expectations of superiors; (2) is characterized by *conflicting* demands among role partners (company and customer) such that the salesperson cannot possibly resolve them; or (3) is surrounded by *uncertainty* due to a lack of information concerning the expectations and evaluation criteria of superiors and customers.[19]

Organizational Climate and Job Satisfaction.[20] Gilbert Churchill, Jr., Neil Ford, and Orville Walker, Jr., who contributed the model presented in figure 15.4, also provide empirical support for selected propositions that flow from the model. In examining the job satisfaction of a cross section of industrial salespersons, the authors found that role ambiguity and role conflict have a detrimental influence on job satisfaction. Salespersons who are uncertain about the expectations of role partners are likely to experience some anxiety and dissatisfaction. Likewise, the same feelings result when the salesperson feels that role partners (e.g., customer, superiors) are making demands that are incompatible and impossible to satisfy.

Women Contrasted to Men in the Industrial Sales Force

Paul Busch and Ronald Bush explore possible differences between women and men in the industrial sales force on several dimensions—job satisfaction, values, role clarity, performance, and propensity to leave. Concerning job satisfaction and the value importance of job components, women sales representatives are closely similar to men when the time on the job, number of jobs, age, and educational level are controlled. Some differences did, however, emerge.

"Promotion" was assigned greater importance by men while women valued "customers" and "co-workers" more highly than men. Female sales representatives were also found to have a lower degree of role clarity (the extent to which required job information is communicated and understood). The authors suggest that the reason for the lack of role clarity may result from: (1) women may be less willing to ask for help and ask questions; (2) available role models are lacking; and (3) women are often left out of fraternization. Female sales representatives likewise displayed less commitment to their job, as indicated by a propensity to leave index. Collectively, these results point to the need for sales managers to improve the role clarity, thereby reducing the problem of turnover, especially among women.

Overall, then, while the bulk of the measures used in the study yielded no significant differences between male and female sales representatives, the contemporary sales management function may need to adjust to the changing environment. Of course, as more women enter selling positions, an increasing number of training and supervisory personnel will be female. Thus, training and role clarity among female sales personnel is likely to improve.

Source. Paul Busch and Ronald Bush, "Women Contrasted to Men in the Industrial Salesforce: Job Satisfaction, Values, Role Clarity, Performance and Propensity to Leave," *Journal of Marketing Research* 15 (August 1978), pp. 438–48.

The research raises other important implications for sales management. First, salespersons tend to have a higher level of job satisfaction when: (1) they perceive that their first-line supervisor closely directs and monitors their activities; (2) management provides them with the level of assistance and support that is needed to meet unusual and nonroutine problems; and (3) they perceive themselves to have an active part in determining company policies and standards that affect them. Second, job satisfaction appears to be related more to the substance of the contact between sales managers and salespersons rather than the frequency of contact. Third, salespersons appear to be able to accept authority and direction from a number of different departments in the organization without a significant negative impact on job satisfaction. Interestingly, then, unity of command does not appear to be a necessary prerequisite for a high level of morale in the industrial sales force.

In addition to the organizational climate factors noted above, other research indicates that performance and individual differences in achievement motivation, self-esteem, and verbal intelligence may also affect job satisfaction. Richard Bagozzi notes:

> Salespeople tend to be more satisfied as they perform better, but the relationship is particularly sensitive to the level of motivation and positive self-image of the person. Although management may have no direct control over the performance achieved by salespeople, they can influence the level of motivation and self-esteem through effective incentive and sensitive supervisor-employee programs and thereby indirectly affect both performance and job satisfaction.[21]

Collectively, these findings provide rich insights for managing the industrial sales force. While some of the areas that influence job satisfaction and performance are beyond the control of sales managers, this line of research points up the importance of responsive training, supportive supervision, and clearly defined company policies that are congruent with the needs of the sales force.

Evaluation and Control. A significant and ongoing sales management responsibility concerns the evaluation and control of the industrial sales force at all levels—national, regional, and district. Here, attention centers on monitoring the effectiveness and efficiency of the personal selling function to determine if objectives are being attained. Also, this assessment allows the sales manager to identify problems, recommend corrective action, and keep the sales organization in tune with changing competitive and market conditions.

A key requirement in the evaluation and control of the sales force concerns the standards by which salespersons are evaluated. These standards provide the focus in comparing the actual performance of different salespersons or sales units (e.g., districts), as well as gauging the overall productivity of the national sales organization. Managerial experience and judgment are important in developing appropriate standards for the personal selling function. Depending upon the role that personal selling assumes in the firm's marketing program, performance standards can take many forms but are usually related to sales, profit contribution, or activity (e.g., number of new accounts developed, number of prospects contacted). Often, quotas are used for evaluation and motivation. As discussed in part three, quotas are often derived from the sales forecast and estimates of market potential. These quotas can be expressed in terms of dollar sales volume, product-line sales, new accounts developed, new account sales volume, sales volume by customer type, and number of prospecting calls. Care must be exercised in developing one or more standards for a sales unit.[22] The standards must be relevant to overall marketing objectives, and they must be developed to take into account the differences in the organization's sales territories. The number and aggressiveness of competitors, the level of market potential, and the workload can vary markedly between sales territories.

The control system that the industrial marketer employs can have an important impact on the behavioral patterns of sales personnel. Research suggests that there is a positive relationship between goal clarity and task performance.[23] Thus, the specific nature and importance of goals should be clearly defined for salespersons, and continued feedback should be provided concerning the extent to which they are achieving these goals. First-line supervisors play a vital role in providing salespersons with current performance standings vis-à-vis the pre-established goals. Likewise, supervisors can aid sales personnel in taking corrective action early in the performance cycle.

To enhance the salesperson's involvement in sales goals, a system of management by objectives (MBO) is frequently recommended. Here, the supervisor and the salesperson jointly identify common goals, define each other's major areas of responsibility in terms of expected results, and rely on these measures as a guide in executing the sales program and in evaluating performance. J. Taylor Sims contends that the MBO system is ideally suited to common problems of industrial sales force management.[24] Industrial sales personnel often operate with a minimal level of contact with supervisors, seek personal goals (feeling of accomplishment as well as financial goals), and possess individual strengths and weaknesses. An MBO system responds to the industrial selling environment by acknowledging the needs of the individual salesperson and by establishing specific, measurable, and achievable goals.

Models for Industrial Sales Force Management

The sales management function involves a range of challenging and complex tasks. To this point, our discussion has centered on the following managerial tasks: (1) recruiting and selection, (2) training, (3) motivation and supervision, and (4) evaluation and control. Poor decisions in one area can create a backlash of effects in other areas. One critical sales management task remains—allocating the sales force over customer units. Here, the objective is to find the most profitable way of forming sales territories, allocating salespersons to potential customers in those territories, and allocating the available time of the sales force among those customers. Selected models, which are applicable to the industrial marketing environment, have been developed to aid the sales manager with this phase of the decision process.

Territory Sales Response

What factors influence the level of sales that a salesperson might achieve in a particular territory? Eight classes of variables that influence territory sales are outlined in table 15.1. This list points up the complexity that the manager faces in attempting to estimate sales response functions. Such estimates are needed, however, to make meaningful sales allocation decisions.

Table 15.1 / Selected Determinants of Territory Sales Response

1. Environmental Factors (e.g., health of economy)
2. Competition (e.g., number of competitive salespersons)
3. Company Marketing Strategy and Tactics
4. Sales Force Organization, Policies, and Procedures
5. Field Sales Manager Characteristics
6. Salesperson Characteristics
7. Territory Characteristics (e.g., potential)
8. Individual Customer Factors

Source. Adrian B. Ryans and Charles B. Weinberg, "Territory Sales Response," *Journal of Marketing Research* 16 (November 1979), pp. 453–65.

Concerning specific territory characteristics, Adrian Ryans and Charles Weinberg present research that suggests three territory traits are worthy of particular attention in sales response studies: potential, concentration, and dispersion.[25] *Potential* (as discussed in chapter 6) is a measure of the total business opportunity for all sellers in a particular market. *Concentration* refers to the degree to which potential is available in the larger accounts in a particular territory. If potential is concentrated, the salesperson can cover a large proportion of the potential in a territory by calling on a few customer accounts. Finally, if the territory is geographically *dispersed,* sales might be expected to be lower due to the salesperson's greater travel requirements. Past research efforts often centered on *territory workload*—the number of accounts. Ryans and Weinberg present empirical results, coupled with a review of past research, which suggests that workload is of questionable value in estimating sales response. They note that ". . . from a managerial standpoint, the recurrent finding of an association between potential and sales results suggests that sales managers should stress territory potential when making sales force decisions."[26] Likewise, they recommend that future research might profitably center on the concentration of potential and geographical dispersion, as well as territory potential.

A Model for Allocating Sales Effort

Several models are available to support the decision maker in allocating sales effort.[27] To illustrate the workings of these models, one will be discussed—the PAIRS model (Purchase Attitudes and Interactive Response to Salesmen). Developed by A. Parasuraman and Ralph Day, this model draws upon the relevant features of earlier models and incorporates some new features.[28] Key components or building blocks of this model are discussed in sequence.

1. Customers in a territory who are similar in their response to selling effort are classified into mutually exclusive and collectively exhaustive groups of approximately equal potential.
2. Salesperson characteristics that management deems useful to the selling job are employed. Selling ability of a salesperson is dependent on characteristics such as education, knowledge of the company's products, and personal traits.
3. The impact of selling effort on a customer in any period is dependent upon the selling ability of sales personnel as well as on the number of sales calls made.
4. The planning horizon is divided into periods of time based on the average length of the purchase cycle or a similar criterion.
5. Variations in the time per sales call for different customers are included.
6. The expected total volume of sales from each type of customer is specified in terms of potential dollar revenue.

7. The model's output consists of an estimate of the sales revenue for each customer or customer group for each period in the planning horizon.

The model draws upon the experience and judgment of sales managers as well as salespersons. Sales managers participate in the development of a salesperson's *effectiveness index* by defining the selling skills viewed as important in dealing with the company's customers. Each salesperson is rated on each characteristic on a 0 (extremely poor) to 10 (excellent) scale. These skills or characteristics are then weighted for each customer category that the firm serves. This approach recognizes that different skills or qualities may be required to reach different market segments or customer types.

Sales personnel also participate in the implementation of the model. They provide three estimates of the potential sales revenues for each customer in each district—a most likely estimate, a pessimistic estimate, and an optimistic estimate. Likewise, sales personnel provide subjective estimates of the sales response at each of four different call levels for each customer. These are used in developing a sales response function for each customer.

An additional feature of the PAIRS model of significance is the inclusion of a carry-over effect of past sales effort to a current period. To gather the necessary data, sales personnel are asked this question: What share of the customer's business could we obtain next year if *no* sales calls were to be made on the customer after the current period?

This model illustrates the feasibility of examining salesperson-customer interaction in a particular territory. Note that the model does not replace the seasoned judgment of sales managers or the field experience of sales personnel, but instead relies heavily upon the experience and judgment of both for key judgmental inputs. Such an approach forces all parties involved to ask the right questions and think creatively about the factors that influence territory sales response.

Sales Management: A Systems Perspective

To reinforce the strategic role of the sales force in the industrial marketing communications mix, the chapter closes with a systems view of the marketing function. Note in figure 15.5 that the inputs of the marketing system include the firm's objectives; product, distribution, and pricing strategies; and the resources that are allocated in order to achieve company objectives in defined market segments. The industrial marketer communicates the existence of the firm's offerings to organizational market segments through two channels: (1) the sales force and (2) advertising and sales promotion. The last two chapters have explored each in detail. Both types of marketing communication require evaluation and control to insure maximum effectiveness and efficiency. Essential to a systems perspective is the measurement of output. The goal of marketing strategy is to achieve specific marketing results—for example, profit, return-on-investment, and market share.

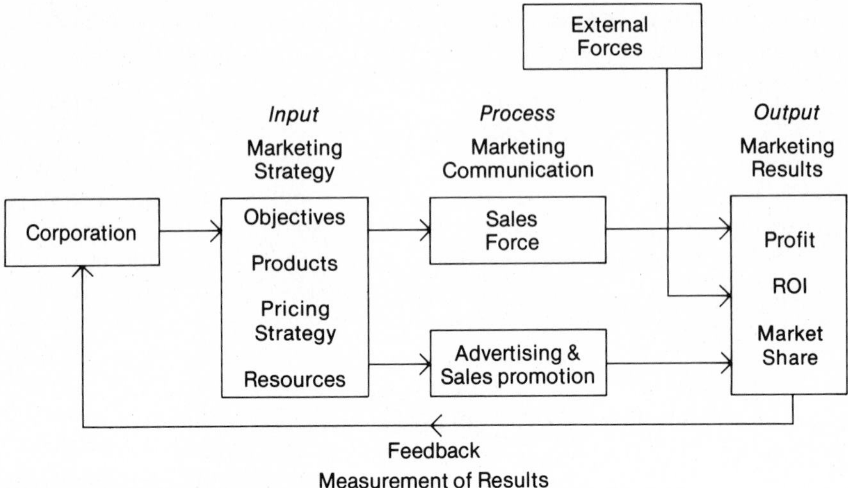

Figure 15.5 / The Sales Force as Part of the Corporation's Marketing System

Source. Reprinted by permission of the *Harvard Business Review*. Exhibit from "Manage Your Sales Force as a System," by Porter Henry (March–April 1975). Copyright © 1975 by the President and Fellows of Harvard College: all rights reserved.

Having completed our examination of each component of the marketing mix here in part four, attention now turns to the evaluation and control of overall industrial marketing strategy.

Summary

Personal selling is a significant demand-stimulating force in the industrial market. Given the rapidly escalating cost of making industrial sales calls and the massive amount of resources invested in personal selling, the industrial marketer must carefully manage this function. Knowledge of the needs of organizational customers as well as the rudiments of organizational buying behavior are fundamental to effective personal selling. Likewise, important insights into the personal selling process emerge when viewed as an exchange process. A satisfactory transaction is more likely to transpire when the buyer-seller relationship includes parties who are compatible concerning communication style and content.

Managing the industrial sales force is a multifaceted task. First, the marketer must clearly define the role that personal selling is to assume in overall marketing strategy. Second, an appropriate method of structuring the sales organization must be determined—geographical, product, market-centered, or some combination. Third, sales force administration is an ongoing process that includes recruiting and selection, training, supervision and motivation, and evaluation and control. A particularly challenging sales management task centers on the allocation of sales effort across products, customer types, and territories. Here, the industrial marketer can benefit by examining available management-oriented models that deal with this sales allocation problem.

Footnotes

[1]McGraw-Hill Research, reported in *Marketing News* 12 (October 20, 1978), p. 2.

[2]"Marketing Briefs—Average Cost of an Industrial Sales Call," *Marketing News* (April 8, 1980), p. 2.

[3]"As Sales Costs Rise, Management Expects More from Advertising," *Industrial Marketing* 64 (March 1979), p. 83.

[4]For example, see David T. Wilson, "Dyadic Interactions: Some Conceptualizations," pp. 31–48; and Thomas V. Bonoma, Richard Bagozzi, and Gerald Zaltman, "The Dyadic Paradigm with Specific Applications Toward Industrial Marketing," pp. 49–66; both included in Thomas V. Bonoma and Gerald Zaltman (eds.), *Organizational Buying Behavior* (Chicago: American Marketing Association, 1978).

[5]Thomas V. Bonoma and Wesley J. Johnston, "The Social Psychology of Industrial Buying and Selling," *Industrial Marketing Management* 7 (1978), pp. 213–24.

[6]Ibid., p. 224.

[7]This section is based largely on Jagdish N. Sheth, "Buyer-Seller Interaction: A Conceptual Framework," in B. B. Anderson (ed.), *Advances in Consumer Research, Volume III* (Cincinnati: Association for Consumer Research, 1976), pp. 382–86.

[8]Edward A. Riordan, Richard L. Oliver, and James H. Donnelly, Jr., "The Unsold Prospect: Dyadic and Attitudinal Determinants," *Journal of Marketing Research* 14 (November 1977), p. 536.

[9]This section is based on Robert E. Spekman, "Organizational Boundary Behavior: A Conceptual Framework for Investigating the Industrial Salesperson," in Richard P. Bagozzi (ed.), *Sales Management: New Developments from Behavioral and Decision Model Research* (Cambridge, Mass.: Marketing Science Institute, 1979), pp. 133–44.

[10]A comprehensive treatment of all aspects of sales management is beyond the scope of this volume. For a more extensive discussion, see Herbert W. Johnson, *Sales Management: Operations Administration Marketing* (Columbus, Ohio: Merrill Publishing Co., 1976); see also Richard P. Bagozzi (ed.), *Sales Management: New Developments.*

[11]"To Computer Salesmen, the 'Big-Ticker' Deal Is the One to Look For," *Wall Street Journal* (January 22, 1974), pp. 1, 35.

[12]Noel B. Zabriskie and John Browning, "Measuring Industrial Salespeople's Short-Term Productivity," *Industrial Marketing Management* 8 (April 1979), pp. 168–69.

[13]Mack Hanan, "Reorganize Your Company Around Its Markets," *Harvard Business Review* 52 (November–December 1974), pp. 63–75.

[14]For an interesting discussion of these strategic organizational design decisions, see V. H. Kirpalani and Mark MacPherson, "Organize Around End-Use Markets," *Industrial Marketing Management* 8 (1979), pp. 305–312.

[15]Ben M. Enis and Lawrence B. Chonko, "A Review of Personal Selling: Implications for Managers and Researchers," in Gerald Zaltman and Thomas V. Bonoma (eds.) *Review of Marketing 1978* (Chicago: American Marketing Association, 1978), p. 291.

[16]Benson P. Shapiro, *Sales Management: Formulation and Implementation* (New York: McGraw-Hill Book Company, Inc., 1977), p. 457.

[17]B. Charles Ames, "Building Marketing Strength into Industrial Selling," in Donald E. Vinson and Donald Sciglimpaglia (eds.), *The Environment of Industrial Marketing* (Columbus, Ohio: Grid, Inc., 1975), pp. 310–29.

[18]Orville C. Walker, Jr., Gilbert A. Churchill, Jr., and Neil M. Ford, "Motivation and Performance in Industrial Selling: Present Knowledge and Needed Research," *Journal of Marketing Research* 14 (May 1977), pp. 156–68.

[19]Ibid.

[20]This section is based on Gilbert A. Churchill, Jr., Neil M. Ford, and Orville C. Walker, Jr., "Organizational Climate and Job Satisfaction in the Salesforce," *Journal of Marketing Research* 13 (November 1976), pp. 323–32. For a related discussion, see Charles M. Futrell, "Measurement of Salespeople's Job Satisfaction: Convergent and Discriminant Validity of Corresponding INDSALES and Job Descriptive Index Scales." *Journal of Marketing Research* 16 (November 1979), pp. 594–97.

[21]Richard P. Bagozzi, "Performance and Satisfaction in an Industrial Sales Force: A Causal Modeling Approach," in Bagozzi (ed.), *Sales Management: New Developments,* pp. 70–91, See also, Bagozzi, "Performance and Satisfaction in an Industrial Sales Force: An Examination of Their Antecedents and Simultaneity," *Journal of Marketing* 44 (Spring 1980), pp. 65–77.

[22]For a more comprehensive discussion of sales quotas, see Shapiro, *Sales Program Management,* p. 308.

[23]Charles M. Futrell, John E. Swan, and John T. Todd, "Job Performance Related to Management Control Systems for Pharmaceutical Salesmen," *Journal of Marketing Research* 13 (February 1976), pp. 25–33.

[24]J. Taylor Sims, "Industrial Sales Management: A Case for MBO," *Industrial Marketing Management* 6 (1977), pp. 43–46; see also Donald W. Jackson, Jr., and Ramon J. Aldag, "Managing the Sales Force by Objectives," *MSU Business Topics* 22 (Spring 1974), pp. 53–59.

[25]Adrian B. Ryans and Charles B. Weinberg, "Territory Sales Response," *Journal of Marketing Research* 16 (November 1979), pp. 453–65.

[26]Ibid., p. 464.

[27]For example, see Leonard M. Lodish, "CALLPLAN: An Interactive Salesman's Call Planning System," *Management Science* 18 (December 1971), pp. 25–40; see also Lodish, "Sales Territory Alignment to Maximize Profit," *Journal of Marketing Research* 12 (February 1975), pp. 30–36; and James M. Comer, "The Computer, Personal Selling and Sales Management," *Journal of Marketing* 39 (July 1975), pp. 27–33.

[28]A. Parasuraman and Ralph L. Day, "A Management-Oriented Model for Allocating Sales Effort," *Journal of Marketing Research* 14 (February 1977), pp. 22–33.

Discussion Questions

1. In planning an industrial sales call on a particular organizational account, what specific information would you like concerning the buying center, purchasing requirements, and competition?

2. Explain how the style and content of communication may strongly influence the quality of interaction between buyer and seller.

3. Some industrial firms organize their sales force around products, while others emphasize a market-centered organizational scheme. What factors must be considered in selecting the most appropriate organizational arrangement for the sales force?

4. A successful sales training program can reduce the costs associated with recruiting. Explain.

5. An emerging body of research suggests that role ambiguity and role conflict have a detrimental impact on the job satisfaction of industrial salespersons. What steps can sales managers take to deal with these problems? What role might a management-by-objectives system play in these efforts?

6. To make effective and efficient sales force allocation decisions, the sales manager must examine key traits of sales territories. Describe how the sales manager can profit by examining the (a) potential, (b) concentration, and (c) dispersion of territories.

7. Describe the role that sales managers assume in operationalizing the PAIRS model (Purchase Attitudes and Interactive Response to Salespersons). Explain how such decision support models can be applied in improving the quality of sales force allocation decisions.

8. What benefits can be derived by examining the industrial marketing communications mix from a systems perspective?

Part V

Evaluating Industrial Marketing Strategy and Performance

Chapter **16**

Controlling Industrial Marketing Strategies

Two industrial marketing managers who face identical market conditions and possess equal amounts of resources to invest in marketing strategy could conceivably generate dramatically different performance results. Why? One manager carefully monitors and controls the performance of industrial marketing strategy, while the other does not. The astute marketer evaluates the profitability of alternative segments and examines the effectiveness and efficiency of the individual components of the marketing mix. This evaluation and control process permits the manager to isolate problems and opportunities and alter the course of marketing strategy as market or competitive conditions dictate.

After reading this chapter, you will have an understanding of:

1. *the function and significance of marketing control in industrial marketing management*
2. *the central components of the control process*
3. *specific methods that can be used in evaluating marketing strategy performance*
4. *the nature and function of marketing research in the industrial marketing environment.*

The process of managing a firm's marketing strategy is very similar to the job of coaching a football team. The excitement and challenge rests in the formulation of strategy. Shall we focus on running or passing? What weaknesses of the opposition can we exploit? What variation on our standard plays shall be implemented? True coaching talent addresses such questions in preparing game strategy. So too, the industrial marketer experiences the excitement of creatively applying managerial talent in developing unique marketing strategies that not only center on customer requirements but capitalize on competitive weaknesses. And indeed, the most visible and stimulating aspects of coaching and managing are evidenced in the strategy area.

However, effective strategy formulation is only half of the coaching and management process; the basic structure of effective strategy lies in the other half of the process—control. A truly great coach devotes significant energies to evaluating the team's performance in last week's game as a prerequisite for setting next week's strategy. Did our strategy work? Why? Where did it break down? Answers to these and other questions will suggest changes in personnel, specific tactics, or the design of certain plays. Similarly, much of the success of a good marketing strategy rests with the less visible, and sometimes more mundane, techniques and programs for evaluating marketing performance. The other half of strategy planning is the *system of marketing control;* that is, the procedures by which the firm checks actual performance against planned performance. Here, the profitability of specific products, customer segments, and territories is evaluated. Likewise, the effectiveness and efficiency of individual elements of the marketing strategy are analyzed.

The marketing control process is necessary and extremely important in measuring performance in the most recent period. But it is even more critical in a forward-looking sense. Information generated by the marketing control system is an essential element in revising existing marketing strategies, in formulating new strategies, and in allocating funds to specific programs. The requirements for an effective control system are strict—data must be gathered on the appropriate performance measures on a continuous basis. Thus, the roots of an effective marketing strategy lie in careful development and implementation of a control system.

This chapter will provide a clear comprehension of the rudiments of a marketing control system. First, a framework that includes the essential elements of the control process will be developed. Next, the types of performance measurement required by an effective control system will be examined. Finally, the essential aspects of industrial marketing research that are associated with marketing control systems will be reviewed.

Marketing Strategy: Allocating Resources

The purpose of any marketing strategy is to yield the best possible results to the company in terms of specified objectives. In this sense, resources are allocated to the marketing effort in general and to individual strategy elements in particular to achieve the prescribed objectives. To guide the allocation of funds to marketing efforts, profit contribution, market share percentage, number of new customers, and level of expenses and sales are typical performance criteria. Regardless of the criteria employed by the marketer, four interrelated evaluations are required to determine the specific marketing strategy configuration:

1. Determination of the total amount of funds to spend on the marketing program during the relevant planning period. This represents the marketing budget to be used to accomplish marketing objectives.
2. Allocation of dollars to the various controllable factors of the marketing mix. For example, what portion of resources is to be spent on advertising and personal selling?
3. Decisions on how to allocate dollars within each element of the marketing strategy to facilitate the best use of resources to achieve marketing objectives. For example, what advertising media should be selected? How shall sales personnel be deployed among customers and prospects?[1]
4. Allocation of dollars to market segments, products, and geographic areas. Each market segment may require a different amount of effort as a result of competitive intensity or the amount of market potential available.

The link between market strategy formulation and the firm's marketing control system is highlighted by these four decision areas. First, results in the most recent operating period will indicate how successful past marketing efforts were in obtaining desired objectives. Second, performance below or above what was expected will signal where funds should be reallocated for future periods. For example, if the firm expected to earn a 20 percent market share in the OEM market and actually realized only a 12 percent share, a change in strategy may be required. Analysis of performance information provided by the control system might indicate that sales personnel in the OEM market were reaching only 45 percent of the potential buyers. In this case, additional funds could be allocated for expanding the sales force or the advertising budget to communicate to a larger proportion of buying influences.

In summary, all decision elements of market strategy must be effectively integrated to achieve desired impacts on target segments. Marketing managers must weigh the interactions among the strategy elements and allocate resources among the elements to create effective and efficient marketing strategies. In order to develop successful strategies, a system to monitor past performance in terms of strengths and weaknesses is an absolute necessity. The important dimensions of such a control system are discussed below.

The Marketing Control Process

Marketing control is a process whereby management generates information on marketing performance. Two major forms of control can be identified: (1) the control over efficient allocation of marketing effort, and (2) the control that involves a comparison of planned and actual performance.[2] In the first case, the industrial marketer may utilize past profitability data for selected products or markets as a standard against which to evaluate future marketing expenditures. The second form of control alerts management to any differences between planned and actual performance and also reveals the reasons for performance discrepancies. The challenge to management in either case is to develop an information system that will provide timely and meaningful data.

Control Means Information

The essence of control is information; in fact, a control system is nothing more than an organized body of information which allows management to evaluate how the firm has done and where future opportunities may lie. Philip Kotler suggests that the main components of a marketing information system (MIS) include:[3]

1. Internal Accounting System
2. Marketing Intelligence System
3. Marketing Research System
4. Marketing Management-Science System

The internal accounting system provides sales, expense, and other accounting data for use in analyzing performance. The focus of the marketing intelligence system is on the environment—that is, information regarding economic, industry, and competitive conditions. The purpose of the marketing research system is to obtain information to solve specific problems or to evaluate particular market opportunities. The marketing management-science system is oriented to the development of quantitative models to describe and predict market behavior and performance. The industrial marketing control system utilizes the information provided by all components of the marketing information system. In fact, the control system should specify the nature and sophistication of the MIS system, and it will always be constrained by the extent and scope of the MIS.

The rudiments of the MIS have already been discussed in previous chapters of the text. The environment of industrial marketing and the important information relative to it were described in chapter 2 and chapter 5 (dealing with the SIC system). A major portion of industrial marketing research, which focused on market potential and sales forecasting, was developed in chapters 6 and 7. In turn, a number of models—specifically related to organizational buying, pricing, advertising, and distribution—were presented in preceding chapters. Thus, the remainder of this chapter will focus on the *use* of information in controlling the industrial marketing process. Here, particular attention will be given to describing accounting systems necessary to the control process. Likewise, industrial marketing research, a component of the marketing information system, will be examined.

Control at Different Levels

The control process specified above is universal in that it can be applied to any level of marketing analysis. For example, industrial marketers frequently must evaluate whether their general product/market strategies are appropriate and effective. However, an equally important aspect of control is whether the individual elements in the marketing strategy are effectively integrated for a given market. Further, management needs to evaluate resource allocation within a particular element; for example, the effectiveness of direct selling versus the effectiveness of using industrial distributors. The control system should be equally applicable to any of these situations. The four primary levels of marketing control are delineated in table 16.1. The role and purpose of each is examined below.

Table 16.1 / Levels of Marketing Control

Type of Control	Primary Responsibility	Purpose of Control	Tools
I. *Strategic Control*	Top management	To examine whether the company is pursuing its best opportunities with respect to markets, products, and channels	Marketing audit
II. *Annual Plan Control*	Top management, middle management	To examine whether the planned results are being achieved	Sales analysis Market-share analysis Sales-to-expense ratios Other ratios Attitude tracking
II. *Strategic Component Control*	Middle management	To examine how well resources have been utilized in each element of the marketing strategy	Expense ratios Advertising effectiveness measures Market potential Contribution margin analysis
IV. *Profitability Control*	Marketing controller	To examine where the company is making and losing money	Profitability by: product territory, market segment, trade channel, order size

Source. Adapted from: Philip Kotler, *Marketing Management, Analysis Planning and Control,* 4th ed. (Englewood Cliffs, N.J.: Prentice-Hall, Inc., 1980), p. 629. Reprinted by permission of Prentice-Hall, Inc.

Strategic Control. Strategic control involves a comprehensive evaluation of whether the firm is headed in the appropriate direction with its marketing strategies. Because the industrial environment is subject to rapid change, existing product-market situations may lose their potential while new product-market match-ups provide important opportunities. Thus, management must continually monitor market situations in an effort to detect the need for a basic shift in general strategy. Philip Kotler suggests that the firm periodically conduct a *marketing audit*.[4] The marketing audit is a comprehensive, periodic, and systematic evaluation of the firm's marketing operation that specifically analyzes the market environment and the firm's internal marketing activities. An analysis of the environment would include such elements as assessing company image, customer characteristics, competitive activities, regulatory constraints, and economic trends. Evaluation of this information will suggest areas of potential for which the firm may be able to adapt its strategy.

As an example of environmental analysis, Hunkar Labs, a supplier of electrical programmers, analyzed the container market in the late 1960s. The analysis suggested that disposable plastic bottles were the wave of the future in the container industry. As a result, Hunkar focused its efforts on developing electrical programmers that could be utilized to control the flow of plastic into a bottle mold. Because the programmers significantly reduce the quantity of plastic required for a container, Hunkar approached major companies that used significant quantities of plastic containers and convinced them to request their plastic container suppliers to utilize the electrical programmers. The results of the environmental assessment and its strategic implications directed the company into a highly profitable market venture, as container manufacturers were quick to accept the new programmers.

An internal evaluation of the marketing system carefully scrutinizes marketing objectives, organization, and implementation. In this way, management may be able to spot situations where existing products could be applied to the new markets revealed in the environmental analysis or new products developed for existing markets. The marketing audit, if applied on a periodic and systematic basis, is a valuable technique for evaluating the general direction of marketing strategies.[5]

Annual Plan Control. The key aspect of annual plan control is to determine how effective the total marketing program was in achieving prescribed objectives. The objectives specified in the plan should become the performance standards against which actual results are compared. Typically, sales volume, profits, and market share are the important performance standards for many industrial marketers. *Sales analysis* is an attempt to determine what factors caused actual sales to vary from the planned level of sales. Expected sales may not be realized because of price reductions, inadequate volume, or both. A sales analysis would separate the impact of these variables so that corrective actions could be taken. *Market share analysis* focuses on how the firm is doing relative to competition. For example, a machine tool manufacturer may experience a 10 percent sales gain which, on the surface, appears favorable. However, if total machine tool industry sales are up 25 percent, an analysis of market share would pinpoint that the firm has not fared well relative to competitors. Finally, *expense-to-sales ratios* provide an analysis of the efficiency of marketing operations. In this regard, management is concerned with over- or under-spending in a particular area. Frequently, industry standards or past company ratios are used for standards of comparison. Total marketing expenses and expenses of each strategic marketing element are evaluated in relation to sales. Recall the discussion in chapter 14 on advertising expenditures which provided a range of advertising expense-to-sales ratios for industrial firms. These figures provide management with a basis for evaluating the company's performance in regard to expenditures.

James Hulbert and Norman Toy suggest a comprehensive framework for integrating the above measures into a marketing control system.[6] The basic approach is to identify the factors that caused a variance of actual product profitability from planned profitability. The data shown in table 16.2 are the sample data used in their analysis. The objective is to isolate the reasons for the differences between planned and actual results (the *variances* displayed in column three), specifically the profit contribution variance.

In this case, management seeks to understand why actual profit contribution was $100,000 less than planned profits. A detailed analysis of the data showed that although the total market sales were larger than expected (50 million vs. 40 million units), the firm failed to achieve its targeted market share. In addition, the firm was unable to maintain the price policy it sought to achieve. An interpretation of the results suggests that management needs to review the forecasting programs, as the market size was underestimated

Table 16.2 / Operating Results for a Sample Product

Item	Planned	Actual	Variance
Revenues			
Sales (units)	20,000,000	22,000,000	+2,000,000
Price per unit ($)	0.50	0.4773	−0.0227
Total Market (units)	40,000,000	50,000,000	−10,000,000
Share of Market	50%	44%	−6%
Revenues ($)	10,000,000	10,500,000	+500,000
Variable costs ($.30 unit) ($)	6,000,000	6,600,000	−600,000
Profit Contribution ($)	4,000,000	3,900,000	−100,000

Source. Adapted from James M. Hulbert and Norman E. Toy, "A Strategic Framework for Marketing Control," *Journal of Marketing* 41 (April 1977), p. 13.

by 25 percent (40 million vs. 50 million). To the extent that marketing strategy allocations are predicated on estimated market size, the firm may have failed to allocate sufficient effort to this market. Thus, unfavorable profit variances resulted. Importantly, though, the variances do point to some real weaknesses in the forecasting process. The market share analysis indicates that the firm did not proportionately share in the market growth with its competitors. Thus, the entire marketing strategy must be reevaluated. The unfavorable results attributed to the variation of planned and actual price per unit indicate that pricing policies (reductions, discounts) had to be adjusted in order to expand industry and company sales. Management apparently underestimated the magnitude of price reductions necessary to expand volume. Clearly, this type of *annual plan control* provides valuable insights to where the plan faltered and suggests the type of remedial action that should be taken in the future.

Strategic Component Control. Some of the measures suggested under annual plan control can be used in evaluating the performance of individual mar-

Table 16.3 / Illustrative Measures for Strategic Component Control

Product
- Sales by market segments
- Sales relative to potential
- Sales growth rates
- Market share
- Contribution margin
- Percentage of total profits
- Return on investment

Distribution
- Sales, expenses, and contribution by channel type
- Sales and contribution margin by middlemen type and individual middlemen
- Sales relative to market potential by channel, middlemen type, and specific middlemen
- Expense to sales ratio by channel, etc.
- Order cycle performance by channel, etc.
- Logistics cost by logistics activity by channel

Communication
- Advertising effectiveness by type of media
- Actual audience/target audience ratio
- Cost per contact
- Number of calls, inquiries, and information requests by type of media
- Dollar sales per sales call
- Sales per territory relative to potential
- Selling expenses to sales ratios
- New accounts per time period

Pricing
- Price changes relative to sales volume
- Discount structure related to sales volume
- Bid strategy related to new contracts
- Margin structure related to marketing expenses
- General price policy related to sales volume
- Margins related to channel member performance

keting strategy elements (e.g., pricing). However, the focus of control for strategy elements is the evaluation of the efficiency and effectiveness of each component of the marketing strategy. A good control system will provide data on which to evaluate the efficiency of resources used for a given element of marketing strategy on a continuing basis. Table 16.3 provides a representative sample of the types of data required to monitor carefully each element of marketing strategy. The specific performance measures and standards will vary by company and situation. Importantly, the goals and objectives delineated in the marketing plan will provide the general framework of performance standards for each strategic component.

Important measures in the control process are market and sales potential. Recall the extensive discussion in chapter 6 which dealt with the techniques and procedures for calculating market potential. Because potential represents the *opportunity to sell,* it provides an excellent bench mark against which to measure performance.

The use of potential to evaluate strategic element performance places severe demands on the industrial marketer's information system. Nevertheless, the results are often well worth the effort as performance comparisons to market and sales potential facilitate the manager's ability to uncover strategic weaknesses. Consider the data shown in table 16.4. On the surface, salesperson *A* appears to be both more efficient and effective. Note that *A*'s sales exceeded the historical trend forecast while expenses were relatively low in relation to sales volume. Not only did salesperson *B* fail to achieve the forecast level of sales, but *B*'s expense ratio is high. However, further analysis is required in order to evaluate effectively performance.

Table 16.5 adds another dimension to the analysis—sales potential. Suppose that the firm developed sales potential figures for the first time during 1979, and these are used as one performance standard. The results in table 16.5 provide a keen insight to the "real" performance achieved by each salesperson. Moreover, the analysis of sales performance relative to potential pinpoints a number of problems and weaknesses. First, salesperson *A*'s performance is relatively poor given the business available, while salesperson *B* is coming much closer to realizing the total available sales. Second, A's relatively low expense to sales ratio may be explained by poor sales performance—*A* may be "skimming" the large accounts and ignoring much of the business that requires significant developmental effort. Salesperson

**Table 16.4 / Sales Performance—
Percentage of Forecast and Expense/Sales Rates**

	1979 Sales Volume	1979 Sales Forecast Historical Trend	Percentage of Forecast	Expense/ Sales Ratio
Salesperson A	$500,000	480,000	104%	0.084
Salesperson B	300,000	330,000	91%	0.14

Table 16.5 / Sales Performance vs. Sales Potential

	1979 Sales Volume	Estimated Sales Potential 1979	Actual to Potential Sales Ratio
Salesperson A	$500,000	$1,200,000	42%
Salesperson B	300,000	350,000	86%

B, by contrast, is putting in the effort to maximize sales possibilities. Finally, the analysis of potential reveals that the forecasting system may be suspect. Forecasting on the basis of historical sales volume tends to compound the error of ignoring potential; thus, poor sales performance relative to potential is encouraged by estimating sales on the basis of what was achieved in the past.

Similar analysis of performance relative to potential can be made for distribution channels, channel members, and products. The information gleaned from these analyses are sometimes combined with profitability control, the last area of a comprehensive control system.

Profitability Control. The essence of profitability control is to provide management with information that describes where the firm is making or losing money in terms of the important *segments* of its business. A *segment* refers to the unit of analysis utilized by management for control purposes, that is, customer segments, product lines, territories, and channel structures. The analysis of performance by segment of the business is a critical one. The information provided by the control system can be utilized by management to allocate resources to each segment based on the profit potentials associated with each. Suppose an industrial firm focuses its efforts on three customer segments: machine tools, aircraft parts, and electronics manufacturers. The annual planning process will require that the marketing budget be allocated among the three segments. To accomplish such an allocation, reference will be made to the profit contribution associated with each segment and the expected potential. The task of profitability control, then, is to provide a methodology for associating marketing costs and revenues to specific segments of the business.

Relating sales revenues and marketing costs to market segments improves decision making and control with respect to the industrial marketer's objectives. More specifically:

> For both strategic and tactical decisions, marketing managers may profit by knowing the impact of the marketing mix upon the target segment at which marketing efforts are aimed. If the programs are to be responsive to environmental change, a monitoring system is needed to locate problems and guide adjustments in marketing decisions. Tracing the profitability of segments permits improved pricing, selling, advertising, channel and product management decisions. The success of marketing policies and programs may be appraised by a dollar and cents measure of profitability by segment.[7]

Profitability control, a necessary prerequisite to strategy planning and implementation, has rather stringent information requirements. To be effective, the firm will need an accounting-marketing information system to facilitate the financial analysis of marketing performance.

To meet the control needs of marketing managers, the accounting system must be able to first associate costs with the various marketing functions, and then attach these "functional" costs to the important segments utilized in analyzing marketing performance.[8] Thus, as a particular cost is incurred—say warehouse salaries—the cost will be coded as to the function to which it applies and then to the appropriate segments for which it is incurred. In the case of warehouse salaries, the distribution function will be debited with the expense. If the warehouse salaries can be related to the handling of specific products and for specific customer segments, the proportion of expense applicable to each product and customer segment will be coded as such. In similar fashion, each sale to customers by product will be coded in the data base as applicable to these segments. The final result is a data base that allows management to evaluate each segment of the business on the basis of applicable cost and revenues.

Frank Mossman and his colleagues refer to this type of system as a *modular data base*.[9] That is, by coding costs and revenues as to function and segment, *cost modules* will be created which allow management to regroup cost and revenues for the type of analysis that is required. Cost modules can be regrouped in three ways.

1. Costs can be grouped into functions under common responsibilities (i.e., all costs associated with physical distribution), allowing a comparison of estimated and actual costs by function.
2. Cost modules can be assigned to marketing segments, and then added to manufacturing costs of products. The total costs are then deducted from revenue to analyze profitability of the segment.
3. Finally, cost modules can be totaled to arrive at expense groupings utilized for typical external reporting purposes.[10]

Clearly, cost modules cannot universally be applied to all marketing segments. Advertising expenses cannot logically be applied to specific customers because there is no rationale for determining the proper amount of expense to associate with each customer. However, advertising expenses can be associated with products or territories, depending on the nature of the media.

In summary, profitability control requires a marketing-accounting system that codes expenses, as they are incurred, to the relevant functions and marketing segments. The result is a data base composed of cost modules that can be easily manipulated to determine profit performance by marketing segments—customers, products, and territories. A final consideration is how the cost and revenue data can be combined most effectively to provide a measure of profit performance.

To evaluate effectively the performance of marketing segments, management must determine the contribution to profit associated with each segment. Note that the important concept is *contribution to profit* rather than net profit. The reason for this distinction is that to arrive at a net profit figure, certain cost elements that are fixed or uncontrollable by the marketing manager must be deducted from revenues. For example, administrative and overhead costs do not vary with the level of marketing effort in the short run, and thus no attempt should be made to arbitrarily allocate such expenses to a given marketing segment. Thus, certain fixed costs assigned to an unprofitable territory would not be eliminated by an elimination of service to that territory. In addition, these costs are generally not controllable by the marketing manager. Net profit figures simply involve too many arbitrary allocations of fixed and noncontrollable costs to make them suitable for control and performance evaluation purposes.

A more useful and valid measure of performance is controllable profit contribution, that is, revenue associated with a marketing segment (product sales, sales to a particular customer group) minus the costs that can be directly attributed to that marketing segment. It is here that the modular data base plays a significant role: by coding all expenses as they are incurred to the relevant marketing segment, many key marketing expenses can be directly related to the segment in question.

Under a contribution margin approach, not all costs are allocated to marketing segments, but instead only *controllable costs* are related to the segment in question. Controllable costs are those costs that originate in a particular department (marketing) and over which the manager has some influence.[11] For example, the expenditure of $1,500 for a two-page, six-issue advertisement in *Plastics World* is a controllable cost for the marketing department. However, the expense could not be assigned to customer segments as there is no meaningful base for allocating the cost between the various market segments. On the other hand, the advertising expense could be assigned to products, as the advertising is focused on one specific product. Certain expenses, like a plant manager's salary or plant labor costs are not controllable by marketing nor could they be related to specific products, customers, or territories.

The net result of contribution margin analysis is the *segment margin statement*. An example of the segment margin statement is displayed in table 16.6. Each of the measures of segment performance permits a different type of analysis. The *segment contribution margin* represents the contribution to profits of the segment based on the revenue generated and the controllable costs for that segment. The goal in this case is to maximize revenue with respect to the controllable costs. The *segment controllable margin* includes a subtraction of those costs controllable by the manager, but ones which do not vary directly with the level of sales. For example, if the salespersons who sell to OEM accounts are paid on a straight salary basis, the sales expense does not vary with the level of sales, but if OEM accounts were dropped the expense would disappear. The *controllable margin* represents the net impact (positive or negative) of the segment on the

Table 16.6. / Segment Margin Statement

Revenue	$800,000
Less: Production and marketing costs directly attributable to the segment	300,000
Segment Contribution Margin	500,000
Less: Nonvariable costs which were incurred specifically for the segment	180,000
Segment Controllable Margin	320,000
Less: A charge for the use of assets utilized by the segment, but whose benefits apply over many future periods	80,000
Net Segment Margin	$240,000

Source. Adapted from Frank H. Mossman, Paul M. Fischer, and W. J. E. Crissy, "New Approaches to Analyzing Marketing Profitability," *Journal of Marketing* 38 (April 1974), p. 46. Reprinted from the *Journal of Marketing*, published by the American Marketing Association.

firm's operation during the period. If a longer-term view of the segment is desired, the net segment margin is determined by subtracting current costs associated with long-term assets. Net segment margin is not as useful as the other measures for decision-making purposes because it requires some form of cost allocation.

Contribution margin data developed from the modular data base are essential in evaluating the profit impact of products, territories, channels, and types of customers. The contribution margin statements can be used for budgeting, performance analysis, short-run decision making, pricing, and evaluating alternatives—for example, whether to keep a territory or to drop it, whether to use a distributor or a direct channel.[12] Because costs are developed first by functional areas and then by segments, the resulting information system can be utilized to evaluate the efficiency and effectiveness of various marketing functions—for example, personal selling, distribution, and advertising.

In summary, profitability control focuses on evaluating the performance of various marketing segments. The key ingredient to a successful system is the marketing-accounting data base that provides the appropriate information to develop segmented contribution statements. The controllable contribution margin is the primary segmental performance measure as it relates controllable costs to segment revenues. A final area for consideration in the control process is the means by which all relevant marketing information is provided to the industrial firm. Thus, our final section will briefly investigate the nature of industrial marketing research.

Industrial Marketing Research

The planning and control of industrial marketing strategy requires a vast array of information—sales, expenses, market share, profits, competitive actions, and environmental data. Prior chapters have described a number of analytical tools and techniques to be used for making decisions within various marketing strategy components. To this point, this chapter has specified much of the internal marketing-accounting data required to evaluate performance. A final component of the marketing information system is the development of marketing information through marketing research techniques.

Industrial marketing research is a very broad area, and is defined as "the systematic gathering, recording, and analyzing of information and opportunities relating to the marketing of industrial goods and services."[13] Industrial marketing research typically includes such diverse activities as sales and market potential analysis, sales forecasting, secondary data collection, market surveys, experiments, and observational studies. Importantly, formalized marketing research is often the means by which much of the data used in planning and control is generated. What are the distinguishing characteristics of industrial marketing research?

Industrial Market Research Is Different

Marketing research techniques and procedures involve certain basic elements that apply regardless of the setting in which they are employed. That is, the research study must be planned, a data gathering instrument designed, and a sampling plan designed. Likewise, the data must be gathered, processed, analyzed, and presented in a final report. However, the environment of the industrial market and the nature of organizational buying tend to make industrial marketing research somewhat unique when compared to consumer-goods research. Some of the more relevant differences include:[14]

1. Greater reliance on exploratory studies, secondary data, and expert judgment data in industrial research. Because of demand concentration, market information tends to be concentrated among a few knowledgeable people. Surveys of knowledgeable individuals are useful when time and cost constrain large sample designs. The wealth of government and trade association data reported by SIC categories provides a valuable data base for many industrial decisions, thus indicating the key role of secondary data gathering.
2. Industrial marketing research tends to place more emphasis on surveys as opposed to experimental and observational primary data methods. The nature of the industrial buying process suggests that experimental and observational studies are not as effective in industrial markets as they are in consumer-goods markets.
3. Personal interviewing receives heavy emphasis in the industrial marketing research process. Usually, specific respondents can be identified in the industrial market (although sometimes difficult to reach) and the target population is smaller and more concentrated. Thus, specific individuals in the buying center can be singled out for in-depth interviews.
4. A key role of industrial marketing research is the determination of market

size and potential, as opposed to consumer research, which seems to focus more attention on psychological market segmentation.

5. Survey research projects in industrial marketing frequently encounter different problems than those met in consumer research and, as a consequence, the survey process is often quite different. Figure 16.1 displays a comparison of the survey research process in industrial and consumer marketing research. Note the difficulties associated with respondent accessibility and cooperation on the industrial side. These are important considerations given the prevalence of personal interviewing in industrial research.

Consumer vs. industrial marketing research: What are the differences?

	Consumer	Industrial
Universe/ population	Large. Dependent on category under investigation but usually unlimited. 72.5 million U.S. households and 215 million persons.	Small. Fairly limited in total population and even more so if within a defined industry or SIC category.
Respondent accessibility	Fairly easy. Can interview at home, on the telephone, or using mail techniques.	Difficult. Usually only during working hours at plant, office, or on the road. Respondent is usually preoccupied with other priorities.
Respondent cooperation	Over the years has become more and more difficult, yet millions of consumers have never been interviewed.	A major concern. Due to the small population, the industrial respondent is being over-researched. The purchaser and decision makers in an industrial firm are the buyers of a variety of products and services from office supplies to heavy equipment.
Sample size	Can usually be drawn as large as required for statistical confidence since the population is in the hundreds of millions.	Usually much smaller than consumer sample, yet the statistical confidence is equal due to the relationship of the sample to the total population.
Respondent definitions	Usually fairly simple. Those aware of a category or brand, users of a category or brand, demographic criteria, etc., etc. The ultimate purchaser is also a user for most consumer products and services.	Somewhat more difficult. The user and the purchasing decision maker in most cases are not the same. Factory workers who use heavy equipment, secretaries who use typewriters, etc., are the users and, no doubt, best able to evaluate these products and services. However, they tend not to be the ultimate purchasers and in many cases do not have any influence on the decision making process.
Interviewers	Can usually be easily trained. They are also consumers and tend to be somewhat familiar with the area under investigation for most categories.	Difficult to find good executive interviewers. At least a working knowledge of the product class or subject being surveyed is essential. Preferably more than just a working knowledge.
Study costs	Key dictators of cost are sample size and incidence. Lower incidence usage categories (for example, users of soft-moist dog food, powdered breakfast beverages, etc.) or demographic or behavioral screening criteria (attend a movie at least once a month, over 65 years of age, and do not have direct deposit of social security payments, etc.) can up costs considerably.	Relative to consumer research, the critical element resulting in significantly higher per-interview costs are: the lower incidence levels, the difficulties in locating the "right" respondent (that is, the purchase decision maker), and securing cooperation (time and concentration of effort) for the interview itself.

Figure 16.1 / Comparing the Survey Research Process

Source. Martin Katz, "Use Same Theory, Skills for Consumer, Industrial Marketing Research," *The Marketing News* (January 12, 1979), p. 16. Reprinted by permission of the American Marketing Association.

Marketing research in the industrial setting places emphasis on developing relevant secondary data for application to market potential estimation. Primary data is more often developed through personal interviewing techniques, and efforts must be carefully developed to secure interviewee accessibility and cooperation.

A final note of importance on industrial marketing research is the increasing emphasis placed on systematic research aimed at delineating the organizational buying process. Significant advances have been made in this area over the past ten years, and refined marketing research techniques and approaches will be required in the future to enable the industrial firm to more fully comprehend the buying decision center in target customer industries.

The Tasks of Industrial Marketing Research

The industrial marketing research department performs numerous tasks of importance in developing and controlling the marketing program. A survey by the American Marketing Association reports on the responsibilities of marketing research departments of industrial firms. The results of the survey indicate that industrial research efforts are focused on: estimating potential, market share analysis, sales analysis, forecasting, and competitive product studies.[15] Many of these procedures and techniques were discussed at length in part three of this volume. Clearly, an effective marketing research department is a valuable asset to the industrial firm. The data resulting from the performance of these research tasks provide the foundation on which effective marketing strategies are built.

Research Methods

The industrial market researcher utilizes two types of data to solve marketing problems: (1) secondary data and (2) primary data. Secondary data, data which has previously been collected and published (e.g., *Annual Survey of Manufacturers, Census of Business*), was discussed at length in chapter 5. Primary data, on the other hand, refers to data that is not presently available but must be collected to analyze a specific current problem. Although industrial marketers rely heavily on secondary data, primary data collection may often be required to gain firsthand knowledge of customer attitudes, motivations, and buying intentions. For all types of marketing research, the basic methods for gathering primary data include:

1. *Surveys*—questioning people believed to possess the information desired.
2. *Observation*—viewing people and behavior and recording the information without asking questions.
3. *Experimentation*—setting up a controlled situation in which the outcome of some test is evaluated. One or more factors is varied in order to measure cause-and-effect relationships.

Surveys are the most frequently applied research method in industrial marketing research.[16] The widespread application of survey research in industrial marketing results from the ability of this method to provide the type of information sought by industrial marketers.

Applications of Survey Research

Survey techniques are effective for gathering primary data of the following types:[17]

1. awareness and knowledge
2. attitudes and opinions
3. intentions
4. motivations
5. demographic characteristics
6. behavior

As this list suggests, the survey technique's central focus is oriented to developing an understanding of the buying behavior of present and potential industrial customers. The information gleaned from a survey of buying behavior then becomes a key input to the formulation of marketing strategy. Figure 16.2 provides a rich example of the nature and use of survey data in industrial marketing. Although the situation in Figure 16.2 is hypothetical, it does demonstrate the versatility of the survey method in generating a broad range of primary data that would be unattainable from secondary sources. As the example indicates, survey data can be pivotal in evaluating performance and providing input on which to adjust future market strategies. Let us now consider the different methods of applying survey research.

Survey Methods in Industrial Marketing

A way to view the survey approach is to consider how contact will be made with the sample of respondents. Three methods of contact prevail in industrial marketing: (1) personal interview, (2) telephone, and (3) mail.

Personal Interviews. Because industrial research is often focused on relatively small samples and much of the information involves in-depth questioning and probing, personal interviewing tends to be the dominant survey approach. Generally, the greater the complexity of the information sought, the more effective personal interviewing is. When technical data, graphs, and illustrations are required, personal interviews are the only choice.

Importantly, personal interviewing is usually quite effective in producing high response rates to the survey. The high response rate results from the ability of the interviewer to locate the correct respondent and secure his or her attention. In addition, a greater quantity of information can generally be elicited through personal interviews. Personal interviewing is obviously the most expensive and time-consuming form of survey research, and the expense may limit its application.

Figure 16.2 / Explaining Market Share Performance

Suppose an evaluation of desk-top copier sales reveals that market share for Xerox varies widely between the three primary market segments: commercial, industrial, and government. A survey among a sample from each segment can be utilized to explain the variance in performance.

First, each sample group would be queried on their general *awareness* and *knowledge* of Xerox desk copiers as well as competitive offerings in this product line. The goal here would be to ascertain whether market share performance is related to the job Xerox has done in communicating to the three market segments. A second phase of the survey would relate to assessing the decision-maker's *attitude* toward Xerox and its competitors in terms of company image, product characteristics and service performance. Thus, although the segments may each be aware of Xerox, negative attitudes toward the firm or its product and service performance might explain the difference in sales penetration in the three segments.

A key feature of the survey in this case would be to develop a clear picture of the underlying *motivations* associated with the purchase of desk-top copiers. Part of the survey would be structured to elicit a ranking of key product and service attributes that different members of the buying center use in making a supplier choice. In this case, the survey might be able to show that Xerox has not focused their sales program on key product attributes that are important to the low-market share segments.

Most surveys include a section on *demographics,* that is, company characteristics (size, nature of business, location) and decision-maker characteristics (title, experience, job function, age). Evaluation of the demographic data relative to sales penetration may suggest important relationships between company and decision-maker characteristics and market share.

A final section of the survey may focus on *intention,* that is, an estimation of future buying plans for desk-top copiers. Although valid estimates of specific brand intentions would be difficult to obtain, the survey may be able to assess future product category expenditures. In this way a rough estimate of potential could be developed.

Source. Adapted from William E. Cox, *Industrial Marketing Research* (New York: John Wiley and Sons Inc., 1979), p. 242.

Telephone Surveys. Telephone interviewing has found application in industrial marketing research, particularly for such purposes as evaluating advertising recall, assessing corporate image, and measuring company and brand awareness. If prior contact has been made with respondents and a shared vocabulary of technical terms is present, telephone surveys are a cost-effective way to obtain primary information. For telephone surveys to be effective, the researcher must be able to identify and reach the correct respondent. In terms of time, telephone interviews are clearly the fastest method for gathering information. The major drawbacks to telephone interviews are the limitation on the amount and kind of information that can be gathered and the inability to control and detect interviewer bias. In addition, telephone interviewers often have difficulty in gaining access to the respondent, as secretaries are quite adept at screening calls to their superiors.

Nevertheless, some firms find that telephone surveys can be effective in cases where advice or opinions are required to make a particular decision rapidly. In this case, a broad group of firms can be maintained from which a sample can be drawn quickly.

Mail Surveys. Mail surveys are also restricted in terms of the amount and complexity of information that can be gathered. The quality and quantity of data resulting from a mail survey depend on the respondent's interest in the topic and the degree of difficulty in answering the questions. The most severe problem associated with industrial mail surveys is nonresponse, particularly among large firms.[18] The nonresponse problem has two facets: (1) the original respondent simply fails to return the survey, or (2) the survey is returned by someone other than the original respondent. The latter form of nonresponse is often difficult to detect, thus reducing the validity and reliability of the survey. Generally, response rates to industrial mail surveys tend to be lower than those to consumer surveys.[19] This is a continuing problem and one that industrial market researchers must address.

Mail surveys take more time to construct and administer than telephone surveys, but are not as demanding as personal interviews. Because of the impersonal nature of the contact and the complexity of the subject matter, the wording and structure of the questionnaire are extremely critical in the success of a mail survey. In addition, to secure meaningful response rates, follow-up mailings are frequently required. As one might expect, however, mail surveys are generally the least expensive survey method in industrial marketing research.

In summary, table 16.7 provides a comparison among the three survey techniques on the basis of six important criteria. The inherent tradeoffs among the three survey research methods were highlighted above. These tradeoffs must be evaluated in light of the type of information sought, available time and research funds, and the levels of validity and reliability required. Only then can the apropriate method be selected.

Organizing for Research

The research function can be administered in a variety of ways—centralized, decentralized, or performed by specialized industrial market research companies. To have maximum impact, research findings must be effectively integrated into the decision-making process, and the organizational placement of the research function will have a definite effect on whether this goal is accomplished. The decision on how to organize the marketing research function requires consideration of several delicate organizational issues. Generally, marketing research should

1. be free from the influence of those whom its work affects;
2. have a location which is conducive to maximum operational efficiency;
3. have the wholehearted support of the executive to whom it reports.[20]

Table 16.7 / A Comparison of Industrial Survey Methods

Approach	Criteria					
	Cost	Time	Information Quality	Information Quantity	Nonresponse Problem	Interviewer Bias
Personal Interview	Highest cost per respondent	Most time consuming	Can elicit in-depth, complex information	Extensive	Few problems, as a result of face-to-face contact	Hard to detect and control
Telephone	Second highest cost	Least time consuming	Complex information if prior contact established	Limited	Difficult to insure that contact is made with correct respondent	Hard to detect and control
Mail	Least cost	Moderate	Moderately complex information	Moderate depends on respondent interest and effort required	Difficult to control who responds and how many will respond	Can be controlled by rigorous pretesting

Source. Adapted from William E. Cox, Jr., *Industrial Marketing Research*, (New York: John Wiley and Sons, 1979) pp. 246–51.

Two-Tier Research Staff. Large industrial firms often have a centralized marketing research unit at the corporate level and smaller scale marketing research units located at the divisional levels. The central research unit usually includes a full-time staff whose major function is to gather broad-gauge data on the economy and the industry, and to conduct studies for product line alternatives, new product opportunities, and acquisitions. The centralized research staff may significantly contribute to the development of marketing plans and strategy. The general rule is that the central staff focuses on research activities affecting more than one group or division—preparing economic forecasts, planning support, and researching management science and information systems.[21] The research conducted by the divisional or operating unit research staff usually centers on divisional performance areas such as product sales rates, advertising effectiveness, and market share studies.

Management Support. Regardless of how the industrial marketing research function is organized, the unit requires the support of top management. Because of the importance of this support, it is suggested that the central research department report to a high level executive or even to the president. This ensures that: (1) marketing research information will be properly utilized in the decision-making process; and (2) the marketing research function will be given a fair hearing during the corporate budgeting process. The contribution of marketing research can be realized to its fullest when top management recognizes the role this function plays in supporting the development and control of industrial marketing strategy.

Utilizing "Outside" Research Specialists. Many types of industrial marketing research require specialized skills not possessed by the firm in its own research department. Special studies on organizational buying behavior, company image evaluations, or strategic adjustments required by environmental conditions are examples of projects that may require outside assistance. Here the industrial marketer can draw upon the services of "outside" research specialists. The range of alternatives is wide—from free advice provided by advertising agencies to very expensive special-purpose studies conducted by management consultants or market research specialists. Some consulting and marketing organizations specialize in the industrial field.[22] The purpose and scope of the needed research coupled with the research funds available determine which of the alternative forms of outside assistance is most appropriate for a particular project.

To recap, industrial marketing research provides the data necessary to evaluate performance and plan future marketing strategies. The research process focuses on different techniques and tools than those frequently employed in the consumer-goods market. However, sound research methods are equally necessary in both environments. The organization of the marketing research function will depend on the size, nature, and role of research in the industrial firm. However, for research to be effective, top management must understand and adhere to the tenet that research plays a vital role in the industrial marketing process.

Summary

A key aspect of market strategy determination is the allocation of resources to each strategy element and the application of marketing efforts to market segments. The marketing control system is the process that the industrial firm uses to generate information on which to make these decisions. Moreover, the marketing control system provides the means by which current performance can be evaluated and steps can be taken to correct any deficiencies. An effective control system will include four distinct components. *Strategic control,* which is operationalized through the marketing audit, provides evaluative information on the present and future course of the firm's basic product-market mission. *Annual plan control* compares annual results to planned results in an effort to provide input for future planning. *Strategic component control* focuses on the effectiveness of each element in the marketing strategy. Finally, *profitability control* seeks to evaluate profitability by market segment. Much of the data developed for control purposes is gathered and analyzed by the marketing research department in the industrial firm.

Looking Back

Figure 16.3 synthesizes the central components of industrial marketing management and serves to highlight the material presented in this volume. Part one introduced the major classes of customers that constitute the organizational market—commercial enterprises, governmental units, and institutions. The buying behavior of these important organizational consumers provided the focus of part two. Particular attention was devoted to the myriad forces that encircle organizational decision makers and decision influencers. Part three turned to a discussion of tools for assessing industrial market opportunities. Here, techniques for measuring market potential, identifying industrial market segments, forecasting sales and developing

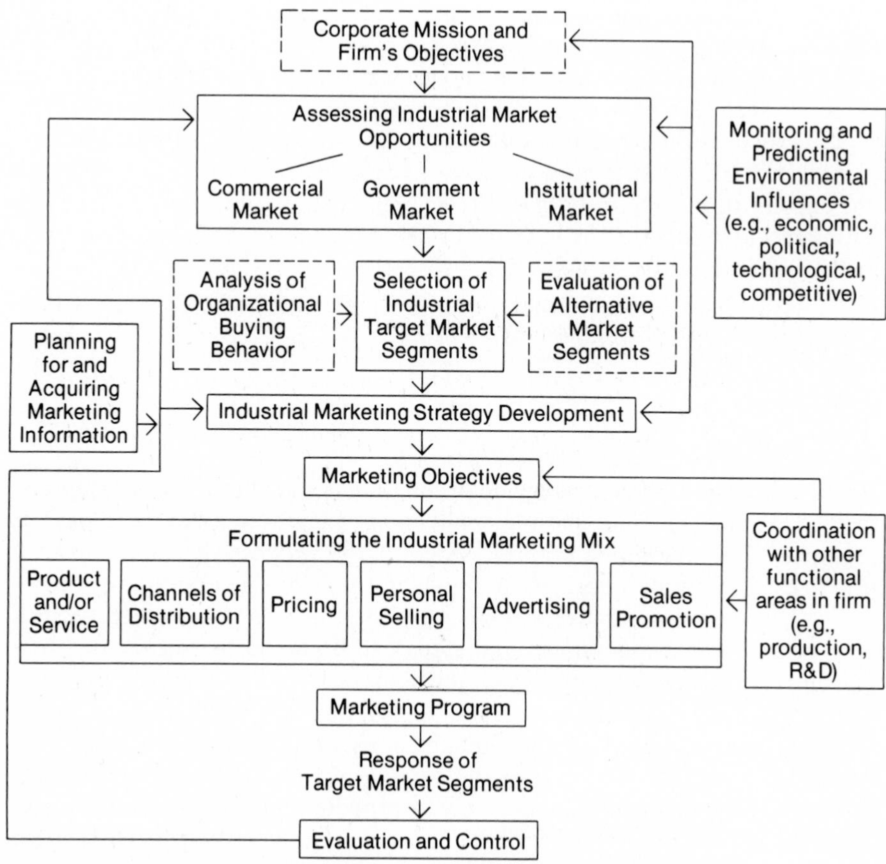

Figure 16.3 / A Framework for Industrial Marketing Management

Source. Adapted from David W. Cravens, Gerald E. Hills, and Robert B. Woodruff, *Marketing Decision Making: Concepts and Strategy* (Homewood, Illinois: Richard D. Irwin, Inc., 1976), p. 20.

marketing strategy were explored. Each component of the marketing mix was analyzed from an industrial marketing perspective in part four.

Once industrial marketing strategy is formulated, the manager must evaluate the response of target market segments to insure that the discrepancy between planned and actual results is minimized. This chapter, part five, explored the critical dimensions of the marketing control process. This process centers on the final loop in the model presented in figure 16.3—planning for and acquiring marketing information. Such information forms the core of the firm's management information system; it is derived internally through the marketing-accounting system and externally through the marketing research function. The evaluation and control process enables the marketer to reassess industrial market opportunities and make needed adjustments in industrial marketing strategy.

Footnotes

[1]David W. Cravens, Gerald E. Hills, and Robert B. Woodruff, *Marketing Decision Making: Concepts and Strategy* (Homewood, Illinois: Richard D. Irwin, 1976), p. 417.

[2]V. H. Kirpalani and Stanley S. Shapiro, "Financial Dimensions of Marketing Management," *Journal of Marketing* 37 (July 1973), p. 47.

[3]Philip Kotler, *Marketing Management: Analysis, Planning, and Control,* 4th ed.; (Englewood Cliffs, N.J.: Prentice-Hall, Inc., 1980), p. 603.

[4]Philip Kotler, *Marketing Management: Analysis, Planning and Control,* 3rd ed. (Englewood Cliffs, N.J.: Prentice-Hall, Inc., 1976), p. 447.

[5]For example, see Philip Kotler, William Gregor, and William Rogers, "The Marketing Audit Comes of Age," *Sloan Management Review* 18 (Winter 1977), pp. 25–43; Urban T. Kuechle, "A. O. Smith Audits to Sharpen Marketing Teams," *Industrial Marketing* 53 (December 1968), pp. 35–38; Frank Rotheman, "Intensive Competitive Marketing," *Journal of Marketing* 28 (July 1964), pp. 10–17.

[6]James M. Hulbert and Norman E. Toy, "A Strategic Framework for Marketing Control," *Journal of Marketing* 41 (April 1977), pp. 12–19.

[7]Leland L. Beik and Stephen L. Buzby, "Profitability Analysis by Market Segments," *Journal of Marketing* 37 (July 1973), p. 49.

[8]Frank H. Mossman, Paul M. Fischer, and W. J. E. Crissy, "New Approaches to Analyzing Marketing Profitability," *Journal of Marketing* 38 (April 1974), p. 44.

[9]Ibid.

[10]Ibid.

[11]Patrick M. Dunne and Harry I. Wolk, "Marketing Cost Analysis: A Modularized Contribution Approach," *Journal of Marketing* 41 (July 1977), p. 84.

[12]Ibid., p. 85.

[13]Wiliam E. Cox, *Industrial Marketing Research* (New York: John Wiley and Sons, Inc., 1979), p. 3.

[14]The first four items are based on William E. Cox, Jr., and Luis V. Dominguiz, "The Key Issues and Procedures of Industrial Marketing Research," *Industrial Marketing Management* 8 (January 1979), pp. 81–93.

[15]*1973 Survey of Marketing Research* (Chicago: American Marketing Association, 1973), pp. 28–30.

[16]Cox, *Industrial Marketing Research,* p. 81.

[17]Ibid., p. 242.

[18]T. L. Renschling and M. J. Etzel, "The Disappearing Data Source," *Business Horizons* 16 (April 1963), p. 17.

[19]Cox, *Industrial Marketing Research,* p. 250.

[20]*Marketing, Business and Commercial Research in Industry,* Studies in Business Policy, No. 27 (New York: National Industrial Conference Board, 1955), p. 7, as reported in H. Robert Dodge, *Industrial Marketing* (New York: McGraw-Hill Book Company, 1970), p. 117.

[21]William P. Hall, "Marketing Research for Industrial Products," *Industrial Marketing Management* 4 (1975) p. 211.

[22]For example, see William Hall, "Marketing Research," p. 211.

Discussion Questions

1. Last December, Lisa Schmitt, vice president of marketing at Bock Machine Tool, identified four market segments that her firm would attempt to penetrate in the next year. As the year comes to an end, Lisa would like to evaluate the firm's performance in each of these market segments. Of course, Lisa turns to you for assistance. First, what information would you seek from the firm's marketing information system to perform the analysis? Second, how would you know if the firm's performance in a particular market segment was good or bad?

2. Susan Breck, president of Breck Chemical Corporation, added three new products to the firm's line two years ago (Products A, B, C). These products were designed to serve the needs of five SIC groups. Each of the products has a separate advertising budget, although they are sold by the same salesperson. Susan requests your assistance in determining what type of information the firm should be gathering to monitor and control the performance of these products. Outline your reply.

3. Assume that the information you requested in question 2 has been gathered for you. How would you determine whether advertising or personal selling funds should be shifted from one product to another (e.g., A to C)?

4. Hamilton Tucker, president of Tucker Manufacturing Company, is concerned about the "seat-of-the-pants" approach used by managers in allocating the marketing budget. He cites the Midwest and Eastern regions as examples. The firm increased its demand stimulating expenditures (e.g., advertising, personal selling) in the Midwest region by 20 percent and sales climbed only 6 percent last year. In contrast, demand stimulating expenditures were cut by 17 percent and sales dropped by 22 percent in the East. Hamilton would like you to assist the Midwest and Eastern regional managers in allocating their funds next year. Carefully outline the approach that you would follow in completing this task.

5. Delineate the central components of the marketing control process. Describe the role of the control system in formal marketing planning.

6. Distinguish between *contribution to profit* and *net profit.*

7. Compare and contrast marketing research in the industrial versus the consumer-goods sector.

8. The marketing research function can be centralized at the corporate level or decentralized at the divisional level. Likewise, the marketing research function can be found in the research and development area or may be fully integrated into the marketing department. What factors must be considered in positioning the marketing research function in the corporate structure of the industrial firm?

Case Planning Guide

Page	Case Title	Relevant Chapters 1	2	3	4	5	6	7	8	9	10	11	12	13	14	15	16
391	Caloway Box Company	●	●				●		●		●					●	
395	A.T.&T.				●	●			●							●	
398	Duralake Plastics, Inc.		●			●	●			●							
404	Airbus Industrie					●	●		●	●							
405	The Xerox Store				●	●				●	●	●					
407	Modern Plastics (A)							●	●	●							
416	Transairways, Inc.	●				●			●					●	●		
422	Hyde-Phillip Chemical Co.										●	●			●	●	
426	Transcon Parts												●				
431	The Ajax Pump Company										●	●	●				●
434	Westinghouse Canada Limited													●		●	
444	APP Company								●					●			
447	Virginia Chemicals Advertising														●		
450	Lectron Corporation			●		●	●	●	●		●				●	●	●

Part VI Cases

Caloway Box Company*

The Folding Box Industry

Folding paper boxes are manufactured by die-cutting paper board on equipment similar to a printing press. The board itself, typically runs between 0.016 to 0.030 inches in thickness. Depending upon the requirements of the purchaser, the die-cut paper board may be either treated with glue along certain edges or cut with corner locks which allow the purchaser to set up the box without gluing it.

Compared to other packaging items, the folding paper box is relatively inexpensive. One distinct advantage, which it has over competing containers, is the fact that it can be shipped and stored in its flat position thus lowering the cost of handling and transportation.

The firm purchasing the box converts it to its set-up position either by hand or by using automatic equipment. In very large-volume use situations, such as the breakfast food and detergent industries, the folding box may be set up on sophisticated, high-speed equipment. In relatively low-volume situations, such as manufacturers of small hardware items, it may be set-up manually.

---

*This case was prepared by Professor William P. Dommermuth of Southern Illinois University.

There are a wide diversity of end uses for folding boxes: including foods, cosmetics, sporting goods, medicinals, toys, tobacco, soap, bakery items, candy, and textiles. In terms of dollar volume, the food category represents the greatest part of the market, accounting for slightly over 50 percent of the usage. In terms of value per ton of shipments, the cosmetic, medicinal, hardware, toy, and sporting goods fields are highest and are thought by some analysts to represent the fastest growing end uses.

Approximately 460 companies in the United States produce folding boxes. The sizes of these firms vary greatly. It has been estimated that the top eight companies hold over one-third of the dollar volume for the total industry. In general, these very big firms concentrate upon large orders. At the opposite end of the field are many small producers, such as Caloway, who serve lower volume accounts. As reported by the Department of Commerce, the dollar value of shipments for the period of 1960–1974 was as follows (in millions of dollars):

1960	$ 893
1963	912
1965	950
1967	1109
1970	1225
1971	1250
1972	1330†
1973	1400†
1974	1460†

†Estimated

In terms of "value added," the industry average approximates 50 per cent of the selling price. As a rough rule of thumb, in estimating the price of a folding carton, one can double the cost of the raw materials used, mainly the paper board. However, this relationship varies with the size of order, quality of materials, and intricacy of design.

Folding carton plants are oriented toward operation on a local or regional basis. Being in or near large-usage areas not only reduces shipping costs but enables firms to respond quickly to changes in customer demand and to supply maximum service. Service and flexibility are considered highly important for successful operation in this field.

In addition to die-cutting paper board into the required shape and providing gluing surfaces where necessary, the folding carton firm generally prints the box as well. Frequently, graphic design work is required in connection with such printing.

Background of the Caloway Box Company

The Caloway Box Company was founded in 1960 by Harold Callahan and Charles Wayman. Each man had had about 10 years of experience as a salesman for box-making firms in the Los Angeles, Calif. region (company name and location are disguised). For some time they had considered the possibility of establishing their own company to manufacture and sell folding boxes. In order to do so, they estimated that they would require an initial capitalization of roughly $50,000.

To acquire sufficient funds to begin operations, they worked out a loan arrangement with Mr. Richard Foster, who was the owner of two very successful automobile agencies in the area.

By 1963, Callahan and Wayman had fully repaid the loan. While Mr. Foster had never taken an active part in the operation of the firm, he had been designated as vice president for finance and a director of the corporation. Mr. Callahan served as president and Mr. Wayman as executive vice president. This arrangement was continued after repayment of the loan.

Mr. Foster's role had always been largely of an advisory nature on matters of general business practice. While he had no direct experience in the box industry, he had extensive industrial experience in other areas, stretching over some 35 years. In addition, the office staff at one of Mr. Foster's automobile agencies handled all clerical and bookkeeping activities for Caloway.

Mr. Callahan and Mr. Wayman held an informal luncheon meeting with Mr. Foster each Friday. At that time they discussed the general progress of the company and also turned over the necessary information for Mr. Foster's staff to handle invoicing, payment of bills, and general bookkeeping procedures. For these services, as well as for his services as director and advisor, Mr. Foster received $3,000 per year. The arrangement permitted Caloway to operate with no secretarial or clerical staff.

Caloway employed approximately 15 people, including the two co-owners. Of the 15, only the principals, Harold Callahan and Charles Wayman, were directly engaged in sales and customer contact work. Because of the small size of the organization, Callahan and Wayman were also deeply involved in all other aspects of the firm's operations. One man, Jack Grant, was employed as an assistant reporting to both of the owners. He concerned himself mainly with purchasing and shipping. The company employed a chief pressman, who was responsible for all production activities and who reported to Mr. Wayman. All of the remaining employees were engaged in production.

Sales History of the Company

During its first year of operation, Caloway acquired 19 customers, primarily through previous contacts which Mr. Callahan and Mr. Wayman had made during their years as box salesmen. By 1970, the number of customers had reached 102. Dollar sales volume rose from approximately $125,000 in 1961 to about $650,000 in 1973. The growth rate was heaviest in the first few years of operation but continued at approximately 10 percent per year after

1966. Caloway concentrated upon customers in the Los Angeles, Calif. area, with a few customers as far away as San Diego, Calif. In terms of size, the company's accounts varied from $80,000 per year to very small firms doing less than $500 a year with Caloway. The average run of boxes for current customers was around 20,000 units. Gross profit was about 30 percent.

Promotional Policies

Caloway is relatively inactive in terms of seeking new business through any planned promotional program. The company runs a display advertisement in the yellow pages of the telephone directory and maintains contact with four paper jobbers who refer customers to Caloway on a commission basis. On the average, the company estimates that it gains about two new accounts from the telephone directory listing and from 10 to 12 new accounts from the jobbers each year. In addition, new accounts are acquired through referrals by current customers. Occasionally, Mr. Wayman makes unsolicited calls on potential customers, but such activity rarely runs to more than three calls per year.

Essentially, most prospects initiate contact with the company after seeing the yellow page listing or through referral by a paper jobber or present customer. Upon determining the customer's needs, Mr. Wayman, who handles most of the new accounts, prepares a sample box and submits an estimate on the cost. No charge is made for preparation of the sample or for cost estimates. Roughly 50 percent of the prospects, for whom samples are prepared, become customers of the firm. The usual procedure for the company is to produce only upon receiving an order rather than attempting to anticipate customer requirements. Even though Caloway has not been especially active in seeking new accounts, the growth rate of the company has been consistent, and both Mr. Callahan and Mr. Wayman feel that provision of excellent customer service is at the heart of their success. By remaining relatively small, Caloway has been able to stay close to its customers and to remain flexible in its ability to meet their needs. For example, while the company maintains little or no advance inventory, it is able to rearrange production to meet rush orders whenever necessary.

Company officials regard their competition as coming mainly from about 10 other firms in the area whose sales are under $1 million a year. In general, larger firms are not interested in the low volume accounts handled by Caloway. By the same token, Caloway feels itself unable to compete on very large orders. In several cases, the company handles small portions of the folding carton business for firms who purchase much larger quantities from other suppliers.

The company's equipment includes three two-color printing presses, three single-color presses, four die-cutting machines, and a machine for glue application.

Expansion Possibilities

In the spring of 1974, Caloway was considering moving from its present location, where it occupied about 15,000 square feet, to a building in which it would occupy approximately 20,000 square feet. Given its present equipment, the company could handle an annual volume of $800,000 to $900,000. If the plant is moved to this new location, it would be possible to add additional equipment and to increase output potential substantially.

Callahan and Wayman were also considering the possibility of adding a full-time salesperson. They felt that a good person could be found if they could guarantee earnings of at least $18,000 per year, based on a commission of 5 percent of sales. They estimated that a competent, new person might take about two years to reach a sales level of $360,000. Having a full-time salesperson would place an added workload on Mr. Wayman, since he would be required to have samples prepared and to make job estimates for the increased number of potential customers such a salesperson could be expected to produce. While about half of Caloway's present prospects become customers, the ratio might be much lower should the firm turn to active solicitation of new business.

When they discussed the possibility of expansion with Mr. Foster, he indicated his feeling that, based on the past success of the company, he felt it deserved strong consideration. If necessary, he was prepared to loan the company up to $150,000 for expansion purposes. He also suggested that it might be wise to consider increased promotional activity either in place of or in addition to the hiring of a salesperson.

A.T.&T.*

Until very recently, A.T.&T. was regarded as the antithesis of a marketing-oriented company. Protected as a regulated monopoly, the firm traditionally "waited for its customers to call" rather than taking an aggressive marketing approach. Over the past decade, technological advances, a relaxation of government regulation, and key judicial decisions all rendered many of A.T.&T.'s markets unprotected. Complex communications equipment for business and private transmission lines are two of the important markets where A.T.&T. no longer enjoys a monopoly. The response by A.T.&T. has been to transform the corporation from "a dedicated monopolist, intent on preserving its privileges, into a vigorous marketing company, responsive to customers and capable of thriving on unfettered competition."

---

*Adapted from Bro Uttal, "Selling Is No Longer Mickey Mouse at A.T.&T.," *Fortune* 98 (July 17, 1978), pp. 98–104. Reprinted by permission of *Fortune*.

Gearing Up for Marketing

To become a "marketing company," the firm doubled their marketing expenditures to $2.1 billion from 1973 to 1978. In that same period, over 1500 managers a year from the operating companies have passed through special courses in marketing. Management and staff personnel have been actively recruited from top-ranking companies.

To develop a true marketing orientation, many analysts feel that A.T.&T. must make some fundamental changes in strategy. One change is in the area of pricing—in the past the firm has charged all customers similar prices for basic services, regardless of the cost of supplying the service. Secondly, because federal regulators rewarded the company on the basis of its investment in plant, the company had never developed a system to measure the relative profitability of its many businesses. Such data is mandatory if a firm desires to adjust its product mix to customer needs by selling what is profitable and avoiding what is not. Finally, the firm must adjust the service motivation "bred in the bones of telephone people over the course of 100 years" to a competitive motivation based on the market.

The Business Market

Significant opportunities exist for A.T.&T. and the entire communications industry in the business market. The market is primarily composed of two distinct segments: interconnect devices, such as switchboards that connect to the Bell System; and private transmission lines leased to larger users. A.T.&T. dominates both markets, but increasingly heavy competition severely dampens the outlook for both.

Competition in the interconnect market has grown as a result of an FCC decision which will eliminate A.T.&T. restrictions on non-Bell equipment. Another FCC action in the private transmission line area will have similar effects in this market. Perhaps the strongest competition facing A.T.&T. is in the data-processing industry. I.B.M. and many other computer manufacturers have developed products which already compete with A.T.&T.'s best Teletype machine. Digitally based private switchboards, which are really nothing more than minicomputers, are being successfully developed and marketed by I.B.M. and other computer terminal manufacturers. In addition, use of the computer by business for the purpose of controlling communication expenditures is expected to substantially reduce what business spends on actual *transmission*—a key part of A.T.&T.'s business.

The A.T.&T. Response

The final phase of the A.T.&T. strategy was to set up a system to anticipate customer needs. Thus, market managers now segment business customers into more than 50 industry classifications and then study each segment to determine how communications affect profit and loss. The goal is to increase customer expenditures with the Bell System by finding ways customers can use communications to increase their own profits. As a result of these studies, new products are suggested, at which time a product manager takes over to translate the research findings into new product offerings. The product manager evaluates the expected demand and profitability and if the product proves out, oversees its development. Once the product is installed, the product manager and a team of specialists—repair, maintenance, and accounting—keep track of its costs and ultimate profitability. By 1978 the new system had not developed any entirely new products. However, the system had only been in existence for two years, which probably is not sufficient time to gauge its effectiveness.

Sales Force Adjustments

A.T.&T. believes that the critical ingredient to the new marketing system is the Bell System sales force, which is organized strictly along industry lines. Account executives are assigned to various markets carefully segmented according to their S.I.C. code, and are held responsible for all customers in that specific industry. The account executive is expected to become the communications "problem solver" for customers in a particular segment: that is, to build customer trust, understand customer decision making, and become involved in the customer's business planning. The goal is to enhance the ability to anticipate the customer's needs and ultimately garner increased expenditures on Bell System services.

A.T.&T.'s brand of "systems selling" also includes some other important refinements in management orientation. Line marketing executives must treat their operating costs not as expenses to be minimized, but as investments that will enhance revenue and future new business. Evaluation of the managers likewise is altered so that each manager is gauged on revenue generated *and* how much was spent to earn that revenue.

The major obstacles to implementing the new program are focused on training, customer orientations, and operating company acceptance. First, many operating companies (local Bell System telephone companies) have been reluctant to adopt the new sales and marketing system. Many still cling to old ways, where a customer had an array of Bell System sales personnel calling on them. Some feel that training is a more severe problem, because substantial technical training will be required in order to fully implement the "systems selling" concept. Further, simply retraining existing sales people may not be sufficient. One Bell customer complained, "some of the Bell people have been yanked out of mechanical and clerical positions and given a few weeks of training, and they don't even know what a WATS line is."

Finally, the Bell System sales force will have to change the way customers think. Many corporate communications managers still focus on cost control rather than looking at communications services as a way to improve their own firm's profits. As one executive stated, "communications managers won't accept higher communications bills unless there is a lot of sophisticated cost/effectiveness analysis to justify them." The director of communications for a $9 billion corporation says, "A.T.&T. salesmen wanted to study our inventory control so they could develop a proposal. But they lack the expertise and sophistication. Why, we have very high-priced inventory-control specialists who've been working on the problem for 40 years. The guy who goes to school on the subject for only six weeks has nothing to teach that man. It's *our* guys who end up doing the teaching!"

Duralake Plastics, Inc.*

Duralake Plastics, Inc., is a large producer of plastics which are sold to industrial concerns for use in making their consumer products. Duralake's productive output is measured in millions of pounds per year, and its customers are located throughout the world.

Duralake has a large research and development laboratory called the Technical Center. The Technical Center pursues both basic and applied research in an attempt to discover and develop new compounds with potentially useful characteristics. In the late 1960's a polymer was discovered by the Technical Center that had some promising properties. With a proper mix of chemical compounds and a suitable catalyst, a highly reactive, low weight polymer could be prepared. The chemical properties of this new polymer were judged by the Technical Center research staff to be of potential value as an intermediate product to other products. Therefore, although the polymer was not typical of Duralake's other products, it was decided to pursue the development of the product. The compound was named Malake, and it was patented by Duralake.

Based upon the characteristics of Malake, it was felt that the product might find use in three areas: the detergent market as a builder, the textile industry as a sizing agent, and the glass industry as a coupling agent. Since Duralake did not produce detergents, textiles, or glass, this developmental research was done in cooperation with firms that did produce those products. At this stage of the product's development, the chemical properties of the product were quite variable. Many variations were developed by the Technical Center either on their own initiative or in response to a participating firm's request.

In order to support the laboratory work and market development, it was necessary to provide a sufficient supply of Malake. Duralake thus developed a manufacturing process which provided enough Malake to meet these developmental needs. The production of Malake was done by the Technical Center in a pilot plant operation using commercially available raw materials.

By the early 1970s it had been concluded that Malake, although a tech-

---

*This case was prepared by Professor Jay H. Coats, of West Virginia University, and Thomas Coyner. Reprinted by permission.

nical success, was not cost competitive in either the detergent or textile industries. Developmental work in those areas was halted. Two other firms cooperating with Duralake did proceed to develop proprietary applications of Malake in their production processes. A large chemical firm found that, even with the relatively high price, Malake had significant advantages in a particular type of cleaning compound. In the other case a major glass manufacturer developed a patented manufacturing process based upon Malake. Both of these companies encouraged Duralake to finalize the chemical-property design of Malake and place it in commercial production since such action would be of great benefit to these two firms in their respective marketplaces.

Therefore, under external pressure for production of the product and normal internal pressure to recover developmental costs, Duralake decided to proceed with market introduction of Malake. However, production and commercialization of Malake created some problems for the firm.

Production and Commercialization of Malake

The primary products of Duralake were high volume plastic materials. Malake, being a liquid polymer, was quite different from Duralake's normal products, and its manufacture required production equipment that the firm did not have. There was no doubt that the sales volume forecasted for the foreseeable future would not justify Duralake's investment in the specialized production equipment. The two existing customers demanding Malake represented a very low volume demand. Potential market demand in addition to these two firms was questionable. However, the pricing of Malake did promise a profitable product. More importantly, the two firms which would purchase Malake were important customers for other Duralake products, and Duralake felt some pressure and obligation to meet all of the product demands of these customers.

Since existing production facilities were not available within the Duralake organization, the product commercialization plan that was developed included two elements not typical of the firm's normal operations. First, the product would be manufactured by an outside firm under a custom manufacturing arrangement. A custom manufacturer, called a toller, is a production firm that manufactures a product to the client's specifications. The arrangements are similar to arrangements for private brand production of hard goods for national retailers such as Sears, Roebuck and Company, Inc. The use of a toller by Duralake would allow the firm to meet the current low volume demand for Malake without investing in productive facilities. The revenue generated from the sale of Malake could be used to support continued market development. If the market was developed to sufficient volume to justify the investment by Duralake in production facilities, manufacturing would ultimately be continued internally rather than through the tolling arrangement. Second, the market development of the product was assigned to a single individual within the marketing department. This would allow overhead to be held to a minimum and at the same time provide the careful, controlled direction necessary if the plan was to succeed.

The use of custom manufacturing is unusual in the chemical industry, but is quite popular with other types of industry. For example, in the consumer and industrial cleaner markets, most large firms look to small, independent compounders to provide test market quantities of product. In some cases the custom manufacturer is used to provide a continuous supply of the product in difficult-to-reach market segments. The custom manufacturing arrangement is usually an extremely profitable and flexible relationship for both firms involved. It also involves some potential dangers for both firms. Under customer manufacturing, the larger client firm (the buyer) has the advantage of medium-scale production capability at reasonable cost without the need for capital expenditure. Therefore, the risk of new product introduction is substantially reduced. The client firm, however, retains liability for the product produced by the toller and is also ethically, if not legally, responsible for the safety and good manufacturing practice of the toller. The custom manufacturer, on the other hand, can realize increased plant utilization which will decrease its operating costs and improve its profits. The toller does have certain responsibilities. It is required by the client firm to produce the correct quality product in the proper volume within a given time. The toller is also normally held responsible to provide the product based upon a specified manufacturing process provided by the client. Legal Agreements prevent the toller's selling the product to other than the client firm.

In firms that use custom manufacturing extensively, the relationship between the client and the toller is the responsibility of an identifiable group of the client's employees. This liaison group has three fundamental responsibilities. First, it is charged with providing the manufacturer with the technical and informational support necessary to produce the product. Second, this group is responsible for minimizing the liability of the client firm in connection with both the product and the toller. Third, the group is responsible also for the security of trade secrets which may be transferred to the toller. These responsibilities are discharged by the development, coordination and transfer to the custom manufacturer of a manufacturing "package." This "package" would normally include raw materials specifications, product formula and specifications, and safety information on both raw materials and the final product.

Duralake proceeded to establish a liaison group composed of personnel from the marketing and technical departments. A workable relationship was established with a custom manufacturer which met the quality and cost requirements of the firm, and Malake was commercialized with initial sales to the two cooperating firms in the chemical and glass industries.

Because of the attractive chemical characteristics of Malake, Duralake felt that there was a large range of possible applications for this product. The potential of a great demand bode well for Malake's future, but the wide range of possible applications made it financially impossible for Duralake's

Technical Center to pursue the necessary technical developmental work. It was decided that a new marketing approach would be used instead. Space advertisements were placed in chemical trade magazines giving technical information about Malake but without specifying applications. The response was very encouraging and literature was followed-up with samples of the product as requested.

As a matter of convenience, samples were normally shipped from the Technical Center rather than from the toller's plant. Large drums of the product were shipped by the toller to the Technical Center where laboratory technicians repackaged the product into sample-sized quantities. Late in 1974 a laboratory technician noticed an unusual condition in one of the drums.

An Unexpected By-Product

The drum in question had a crystallized material on the steel lid. Since the product could not crystallize under reasonable conditions, an investigation was begun to determine the nature of the substance. It was concluded that the substance was probably a by-product of catalyst decomposition. Samples of the crystallized substance and the product itself were sent to the catalyst supplier for further analysis. The report was that the crystals were in fact a by-product of the catalyst and that low levels were present in all of the product. The by-product was identified by the catalyst manufacturer as a highly dangerous toxic compound.

Upon receiving this information Duralake immediately took four actions. First, both existing customers purchasing Malake were notified of the presence and characteristics of the toxic material. They were also provided with recommendations as to how the product could be handled safely. Second, the custom manufacturer was provided with the same information. Third, the Technical Center began a project to find a suitable substitute to replace the offending catalyst. Fourth, an outside consulting firm was contracted to do a toxicological analysis of the product to determine its possible hazard to ultimate consumers.

As a consequence of the toxicity problem, the chemical firm determined that they could no longer use Malake in their cleaning compound. They reformulated their product to exclude Malake, and those sales were lost to Duralake. The glass manufacturer performed an industrial hygiene survey of their facilities using Malake and concluded that the toxic by-product did not present a problem for them and they continued to purchase the product. The Technical Center's effort to replace the catalyst was very successful in the laboratory, but the alternative catalyst could not be made to perform satisfactorily in large-scale production operations. The consulting firm reported that their analysis indicated that Malake was one thousand times less toxic than the crystalized substance. The product was not toxic, they reported, by the standards of the Occupational Safety and Health Administration.

Production of Malake was continued throughout 1975 and 1976 in order to meet the needs of the purchasing customer. Even with the low volume and tolling arrangement, Malake remained a very profitable product.

In January of 1977, as a result of internal organizational changes, a new manager was assigned responsibility for the marketing of Malake. During the transfer of responsibility, the new manager developed several concerns about the handling of the toxicity problem with Malake.

A review of the history of the toxicity situation uncovered many related problems. The glass manufacturer, for example, had been notified of the toxicity problem (in 1974) only by a telephone call. Without any written record of Duralake's having informed the glass company, Duralake's liability concerning any legal action caused by the toxicity could not be defined.

It was further discovered that Duralake's internal product control procedures had been unintentionally bypassed by the custom manufacturing operation. The normal control procedure required that every product be internally reviewed every year to insure that all formulas, specifications, safety information sheets, and manufacturing processes complied with all federal and state regulations on safety and pollution control. In the case of Malake these responsibilities were supposed to have been assumed by the liaison group formed to oversee the custom manufacturing arrangement. In early 1977 it was determined that many of the internal control procedures for Malake were never implemented or else, in some cases, review forms were signed in a perfunctory manner after a brief or nonexistent review.

It was also determined that only the two original customers for Malake were told of the toxicity problem. No information on the safety or toxicity of the product had been given to any of the hundreds of firms which had been sent samples of the material.

Action by Duralake

The status of Duralake's relationship with the toller was also questionable. No contractual agreement had ever been made between the two firms. The product was ordered and produced on the basis of a simple purchase order system. The lack of a contractual agreement raised the question of legal liability concerning the toller's treatment of toxic by-products removed from Malake as it was being manufactured. The by-product is removed with a solvent which the toller then uses as a cooling agent in his plant before it is discharged into his normal waste treatment system. Additionally, the toller did not, nor was he required to, test the products for the level of toxic contaminant. The new manager of the Malake product developed a program to minimize the liability of the firm while providing for the adequate protection of both customers and the custom manufacturer. The basic premise was that any product could be sold as long as it was properly represented to the customers, the manufacturer, and the firm. However, the manager went one step further: the overriding objective of the manager was to insure that not only minimal but complete safety and health information was provided to all who were involved with the project. This was a significant decision since it meant that the firm was committed to complete disclosure of the problem to the customer, those who had received samples, and to the custom manufacturer. Clearly, the concern was for principle, not profit. The first action to be taken was to set up a central clearing point for information to insure that accurate and consistent information was disseminated. Next, the corporate legal department was notified of the many problems involved and it was requested to provide a recommendation as to the quality of all historical actions and to propose a course of future action. Based upon their recommendation and under the guidance of the manager, an action plan was developed to resolve the toxicity question. The plan was made up of three sections. The first involved the immediate, proper representation of the products and problems, both internally and externally, while corrective action was being taken. This was done by renotification of the customer of the present status, placing all sample and literature requests on a "hold" status, and notifying all customers or potential customers who had received significant quantities of the product about the problem. The manufacturer was also notified of the potential disposal problem associated with the toxic by-product. Action was also taken to insure that all internal controls (formulas, manufacturing, package, etc.) were consistent with the product being produced.

The second and third sections of the action plan were contingency plans based upon the continued use of either the offending or the alternate catalyst system. These plans involved revision of the product literature, development of internal procedures to insure that both literature and samples were accompanied by correct safety information, etc. Based upon the work to be completed it was anticipated that all problems would be resolved by June 1, 1977.

The firm's legal department made three interesting recommendations. First, it decided that it was in the best interest of the firm to continue to manufacture outside without a contract. Their opinion was that common business law was sufficient to protect both parties regardless of the toxicity and waste disposal problems. They also decided that Duralake was only required to inform the manufacturer that his waste disposal system was probably insufficient and that Duralake was not required to provide an adequate disposal method. Finally, after a review of all information, the legal department concluded that the alternate catalyst should not be used under any conditions. This was based on the fact that this catalyst, as received, was potentially explosive. The firm would be liable for any accident regardless of negligence or circumstances. The risk of using the toxic material was substantially less, and the legal liability could be controlled by proper documentation.

Airbus Industrie*

In December 1970, Airbus Industrie was incorporated in France as a form of unlimited partnership. The firm itself is only a marketing and coordinating body: Production is carried out by a group of partner companies, which are at the same time subcontractors. Airbus Industrie manufactures the A300 European Airbus. The A300 is a wide-body, twin engine, 250-passenger, short- to medium-range jet airplane. The plane was originally designed in the mid-1960s, and the prototype A300 made its maiden flight in October 1972. Air France put its first airbus into service in May 1974.

The World Commercial-Aircraft Market

The world's airlines have typically bought American-made jetliners. During the late sixties and early seventies the U.S. "Big Three"—Boeing, McDonnell-Douglas, and Lockheed—together accounted for over 90 percent of the world market for jet airliners. International sales of European airliners have been disappointing—the last ones to achieve any measure of sales were the French Caravelle and the British BAC One-Eleven, and their success occurred in the early 1960s.

The Airbus Plan

The long-range plan for Airbus Industrie involves three major components. First, the firm decided to produce an airplane that was wide-bodied, yet suitable for short- to medium-range flights on a fuel-efficient basis. The A300 is the only two-engine wide-bodied jet, with the result that it enjoys substantial fuel economy. Recent results have shown the A300 to have the lowest costs per-seat-mile of any commercial aircraft flying on shorter routes. The general idea is to provide an aircraft that is designed as a "no-nonsense" way of carrying a lot of passengers over short to medium distances. The A300 is designed to be reliable rather than radical and incorporates the best proven technology. President Bernard Lathietre espouses the firm's basic philosophy: The key to marketing the Airbus is to "tailor the aircraft to the market rather than to existing technology and national prestige."

Some industry experts question the two-engine configuration. In the first place, U.S. airlines tend to think that a wide-body jet automatically means three or even four engines. Second, three or four engines is a fuel-efficient arrangement on long flights, such as nonstop coast-to-coast junkets. Third, superstition had something to do with putting three or four engines on planes intended for shorter distances: It was thought to be risky to send several hundred passengers up in a wide-body plane powered by only two jet engines.

---

*Adapted from Robert Ball, "Who's That Chasing After Boeing?" *FORTUNE* (April 2, 1980), pp. 138–44. Used by permission of *FORTUNE*.

Penetrating World Markets

The second aspect of the firm's plan is to saturate the European market to the maximum possible extent; make an inroad in "the silk route," that is, the Far East airline route; and, finally, to crack the U.S. market. The key to success in the strategy is to overcome one major selling problem—"showing customers that after-the-sale service would be up to the standards offered by American competitors." The U.S. market could be penetrated, the company feels, if Airbus could overcome the loyalty of U.S. airlines to U.S. aircraft manufacturers. Patriotism and negative U.S. government views concerning the procurement of foreign aircraft by U.S. airlines are anticipated to be major stumbling blocks.

An Expanding Product Line

Finally, Airbus envisions a Boeing-style family of aircraft (e.g., Boeing 707, 727, 737, 747, 757, 767) in the very long run. Currently, the firm is developing the A310, a smaller version of the A300, which will seat 200 passengers. The plane is designed for efficiency at distances up to 1500 nautical miles—a range that includes three-quarters of all airline routes. In addition, longer- and shorter-range versions of the A300, as well as all-cargo and convertible cargo models are planned. A project under current consideration is stretching the A300 to accommodate 300 passengers, which would put it in the same league as the Lockheed L-1011 and the Douglas DC-10.

A final entry considered for the "family" of planes is a 150-seat, single-aisle aircraft. A problem here is that long production runs of the Boeing 737 and the McDonnell-Douglas DC9 have made it possible to offer improved versions of them at bargain-basement prices. The challenge is to develop a plane that provides such sensational operating economy that it offsets a high initial price.

The long-term goal of the Airbus plan is to capture a 30 percent share of the world aircraft market.

The Xerox Store*

A very difficult segment of the office equipment market to reach efficiently is the extensive group of small businesses. In total, the segment is rather large—about 10 million customers (4 million small businesses with less than 20 employees and 6 million offices in the home). The unit sales volume would not support nor would it justify the expense of a direct sales force. However, Xerox Corporation wants to become a major force in this growing

---

*Adapted from "What Xerox Sees in Retail Stores," *Business Week* (April 21, 1980), pp. 130–31; "Xerox Formally Opens Dallas Retail Store, First of Planned Chain," *Wall Street Journal* (April 10, 1980), p. 11; and "In the News: New Chain," *FORTUNE* 101 (May 5, 1980), p. 48.

market for office equipment for small businesses. As a consequence, Xerox embarked on a radically different marketing strategy to capture this segment in April 1980. Their approach is to market office equipment through retail stores that cater to small business needs.

The Xerox Plan

Seven retail stores are scheduled to open in 1980, with an additional 150 to be completed by 1981. The goal is to become "the supermarket for office supplies," with the intended result being to capture the largest share of the low-end copier business. Robert Reiser, President of the firm's Retail Market Division, suggests that the impetus for the radical departure in marketing methods is the fact that "there is no way we could reach that marketplace with our own direct sales force and do it cost-effectively."

Xerox will merchandise a wide line of office products produced by other manufacturers. Included in the line is a coated-paper copier from Develop Dr. Eisberrin & Co. in West Germany, a personal computer from Apple Computer Corp., a line of calculators from Hewlett-Packard Co., dictation machines from Matusushita Electric Co., Centronix data printers and Remington Rand typewriters. In addition, the stores will carry Xerox word processors, its facsimile units and the low-priced end of its plain copier line.

Besides expanding their customer base, Xerox plans to dramatically increase copier sales, as copier sales are projected to account for half of all store sales. A side benefit to the expansion of low-priced copier sales is that additional sales may be generated from customers who trade up as their own volume and copying needs expand.

The Service Advantage

A potential problem associated with the retailing of sophisticated products like computers and copiers to small businesses is the after-sale product servicing. Xerox feels that they will avoid any problems in this regard because no new national servicing network will have to be developed: The firm's 11,000 field representatives will also service the new customers. As a result of the readily available service network, the firm expects to realize 5 to 10 percent higher profits than they do by selling through a direct sales force.

The Name Plus Convenience

Industry observers feel that the well-known Xerox name will be a significant factor in drawing small business customers to the store. Because of the breadth of product line, the chances will be good to sell something once a prospective customer has been attracted to the store.

The retail approach to servicing business customers is unique to the industry and Xerox, at least at the outset, will be the only copier company providing such service. It is expected that one-stop shopping for the office needs of a small businessperson will provide a significant convenience appeal. However, the company expects strong competitive reaction over the longer term. Digital Equipment Corp. already maintains 21 stores and is considering expansion. IBM currently sells some of its products through retail outlets in foreign markets.

The firm's final concern is developing the "right" success formula. Such things as store design, store location, advertising support, and follow-up service are being evaluated in an attempt to come up with the most effective combination for reaching this sector of the market—now and in the years ahead. Xerox President David T. Kearns states, "Things will shift through the 1980s. It may be best to do things differently in different cities. I wouldn't rule out anything."

Modern Plastics*

Institutional Sales Manager Jim Clayton had spent most of Monday morning planning for the rest of the month. It was early July and Jim knew that an extremely busy time was coming with the preparation of the following year's sales plan.

Since starting his current job less than a month ago, Jim had been involved in learning the requirements of the job and making his initial territory visits. Now that he was getting settled, Jim was trying to plan his activities according to priorities. The need for planning had been instilled in him during his college days. As a result of his three years field sales experience and development of time management skills, he felt prepared for the challenge of the sales manager's job.

While sitting at his desk, Jim recalled a conversation that he had a week ago with Bill Hanson, the former manager who had been promoted to another division. Bill told him that the sales forecast (annual and monthly) for plastic trash bags in the Southeast region would be due soon as an initial step toward developing the sales plan for next year. Bill had laughed as he told him, "Boy, you ought to have a ball doing the forecast being a rookie sales manager!"

When Jim had asked what Bill meant, he explained by saying that the forecast was often "winged" because the headquarters in Chicago already knew what they wanted and would change the forecast to meet their figures, particularly if the forecast was for an increase of less than 10 percent. The experienced sales manager could throw numbers together in a short time that would pass as a serious forecast and ultimately be adjusted to fit the plans of headquarters. However, he felt an inexperienced manager would have a difficult time "winging" a credible forecast.

---

*This case was prepared by Thomas Ingram, Danny Bellenger, and Kenneth Bernhardt, Georgia State University. © 1977 by Danny N. Bellenger and Kenneth L. Bernhardt. Reprinted by permission.

Bill had also told Jim that the other alternative meant gathering mountains of data and putting together a forecast that could be sold to the various levels of Modern Plastics management. This alternative would prove to be time consuming and could still be changed anywhere along the chain of command before final approval.

Clayton started reviewing pricing and sales volume history (see Exhibit 1). He also looked at the key account performance for the past two and a half years (see Exhibit 2). During the past month Clayton had visited many of the key accounts, and on the average they had indicated that their purchases from Modern would probably increase about 15–20 percent in the coming year.

Schedule for Preparing the Forecast

Jim had received a memo recently from Robert Baxter, the regional marketing manager, detailing the plans for completing the 1978 forecast. The key dates in the memo began in only three weeks:

August 1	Presentation of forecast to regional marketing manager
August 10	Joint presentation with marketing manager to regional general manager
September 1	Regional general manager presents forecast to division vice president
September 1–30	Review of forecast by staff of division vice president
October 1	Review forecast with corporate staff
October 1–15	Revision as necessary
October 15	Final forecast forwarded to division vice president from regional general manager

Company Background

The Plastics Division of Modern Chemical Company was founded in 1965 when Modern Chemical purchased Cordco, a small plastics manufacturer with national sales of $15,000,000. At that time, the key products of the Plastics Division were sandwich bags, plastic tablecloths, trash cans, and plastic-coated clothesline.

Since 1965, the Plastics Division has grown to a sales level exceeding $200 million with five regional profit centers covering the United States. Each regional center has manufacturing facilities and a regional sales force. There are three product groups in each region:

1. Food Packaging	PVC meat film, plastic bags for various food products
2. Institutional	Plastic trash bags and disposable tableware (plates, bowls, etc.)
3. Industrial	Case overwrap film, heavy duty fertilizer packaging bags, plastic film for use in pallet overwrap systems

Each product group is supervised jointly by a product manager and a district sales manager, both of whom report to the regional marketing manager. The

Exhibit 1. / Plastic Trash Bags
Sales and Pricing History 1975–1977

	Pricing Dollars per Case			Sales Volume in Cases			Sales Volume in Dollars		
	1975	1976	1977	1975	1976	1977	1975	1976	1977
January	$6.88	$ 7.70	$15.40	33,000	46,500	36,500	$ 227,000	$ 358,000	$ 562,000
February	6.82	7.70	14.30	32,500	52,500	23,000	221,500	404,000	329,000
March	6.90	8.39	13.48	32,000	42,000	22,000	221,000	353,000	296,500
April	6.88	10.18	12.24	45,500	42,500	46,500	313,000	432,500	569,000
May	6.85	12.38	11.58	49,000	41,500	45,500	335,500	514,000	527,000
June	6.85	12.65	10.31	47,500	47,000	42,000	325,500	594,500	433,000
July	7.42	13.48	9.90[E]	40,000	43,500	47,500[E]	297,000	586,500	470,000[E]
August	6.90	13.48	10.18[E]	48,500	63,500	43,500[E]	334,500	856,000	443,000[E]
September	7.70	14.30	10.31[E]	43,000	49,000	47,500[E]	331,000	700,500	489,500[E]
October	7.56	15.12	10.31[E]	52,500	50,000	51,000[E]	397,000	756,000	526,000[E]
November	7.15	15.68	10.72[E]	62,000	61,500	47,500[E]	443,500	964,500	509,000[E]
December	7.42	15.43	10.59[E]	49,000	29,000	51,000[E]	363,500	447,500	540,000[E]
Total	$7.13	$12.25	$11.30	534,500	568,500	503,500	$3,810,000	$6,967,000	$5,694,000

[E]July–December 1977 figures are forecast of Sales Manager J. A. Clayton. Other data comes from historical sales information.

Exhibit 2. / 1977 Key Account Sales History (in cases)

Customer	1975	1976	First 6 Mos. 1977	1975 Monthly Avg.	1976 Monthly Avg.	First Half 1977 Monthly Avg.	First Qtr. 1977 Monthly Avg.
Transco Paper Company	125774	134217	44970	10481	11185	7495	5823
Callaway Paper	44509	46049	12114	3709	3837	2019	472
Florida Janitorial Supply	34746	36609	20076	2896	3051	3346	2359
Jefferson	30698	34692	25044	2558	2891	4174	1919
Cobb Paper	13259	23343	6414	1105	1945	1069	611
Miami Paper	10779	22287	10938	900	1857	1823	745
Milne Surgical Company	23399	21930	—	1950	1828	—	—
Graham	8792	15331	1691	733	1278	281	267
Crawford Paper	7776	14132	6102	648	1178	1017	1322
John Steele	8634	13277	6663	720	1106	1110	1517
Henderson Paper	9185	8850	2574	765	738	429	275
Durant Surgical	—	7766	4356	—	647	726	953
Master Paper	4221	5634	600	352	470	100	—
D.T.A.	—	—	2895	—	—	482	—
Crane Paper	4520	5524	3400	377	460	566	565
Janitorial Service	3292	5361	2722	274	447	453	117
Georgia Paper	5466	5053	2917	456	421	486	297
Paper Supplies, Inc.	5117	5119	1509	426	427	251	97
Southern Supply	1649	3932	531	137	328	88	78
Horizon Hospital Supply	4181	4101	618	348	342	103	206
Total Cases	346007	413217	156134	28835	34436	26018	17623

sales representatives report directly to the district sales manager but also work closely with the product manager on matters concerning pricing and product specifications.

The five regional general managers report to Mr. J. R. Hughes, vice-president of the Plastics Division. Mr. Hughes is located in Chicago. Although Modern Chemical is owned by a multinational paper company, the Plastics Division has been able to operate in a virtually independent manner since its establishment in 1965. The reasons for this include:

1. Limited knowledge of the plastics industry on the part of the paper company management.
2. Excellent growth by the Plastics Division has been possible without management supervision from the paper company.
3. Profitability of the Plastics Division has consistently been higher than that of other divisions of the chemical company.

The Institutional Trash Bag Market

The institutional trash bag is a polyethyelene bag used to collect and transfer refuse to its final disposition point. There are different sizes and colors available to fit the various uses of the bag. For example, a small bag for desk wastebaskets is available as well as a heavier bag for large containers such as a 55 gallon drum. There are 25 sizes in the Modern line with 13 of those sizes being available in three colors—white, buff, and clear. Customers typically buy several different items on an order to cover all their needs.

The institutional trash bag is a separate product from the consumer grade trash bag which is typically sold to homeowners through retail outlets. The institutional trash bag is sold primarily through paper wholesalers, hospital supply companies, and janitorial supply companies to a variety of end users. Since trash bags are used on such a wide scale, the list of end users could include almost any business or institution. The segments include hospitals, hotels, schools, office buildings, transportation facilities, and restaurants.

Based on historical data and a current survey of key wholesalers and end users in the Southeast, the annual market of institutional trash bags in the region was estimated to be 55 million pounds. Translated into cases, the market potential was close to 2 million cases. During the past five years, the market for trash bags has grown at an average rate of 89 percent per year. Now a mature product, future market growth is expected to parallel overall growth in the economy. The 1978 real growth in GNP is forecast to be 4.5 percent.

General Market Conditions

The current market is characterized by a distressing trend. The market is in a position of oversupply with approximately 20 manufacturers competing for the business in the Southeast. Prices have been on the decline for several months, but are expected to level out during the last six months of the year.

This problem arose after a record year in 1976 for Modern Plastics. During 1976, supply was very tight due to raw material shortages. Unlike many of its competitors, Modern had only minor problems securing adequate raw material supplies. As a result, the competitors were few in 1976, and all who remained in business were prosperous. By early 1977 raw materials were plentiful and prices began to drop as new competitors tried to buy their way into the market. During the first quarter of 1977 Modern Plastics learned the hard way that a competitive price was a necessity in the current market. Volume fell off drastically in February and March as customers shifted orders to new suppliers when Modern chose to maintain a slightly higher than market price on trash bags.

With the market becoming extremely price competitive and profits declining, the overall quality has dropped to a point of minimum standard. Most suppliers now make a bag "barely good enough to get the job done." It was believed that this quality level is acceptable to most buyers who do not demand high quality for this type of product.

Modern Plastics vs. Competition

A recent study of Modern vs. competition had been conducted by an outside consultant to see how well Modern measured up in several key areas. Each area was weighted according to its importance in the purchase decision, and Modern was compared to its key competitors in each area and on an overall basis. The key factors and their weights are shown below:

	Weight
1. Pricing	0.50
2. Quality	0.15
3. Breadth of Line	0.10
4. Sales Coverage	0.10
5. Packaging	0.05
6. Service	0.10
Total	1.00

As shown in Exhibit 3, Modern compared favorably with its key competitors on an overall basis. None of the other suppliers were as strong as Modern in breadth of line nor did any competitor offer as good sales coverage as that provided by Modern. Clayton knew that sales coverage would be even better next year since the Florida and North Carolina territories had grown enough to add two salespeople to the current eight in the institutional group by January 1, 1978.

Pricing, quality, and packaging seemed to be neither an advantage nor a disadvantage. However, service was a problem area. The main cause for

Exhibit 3. / Competitive Factors Ratings by Competitor*

Weight	Factor	Modern	National Film	Bonanza	Southeastern	PBI	BAGCO	Southwest Bag	Florida Plastics	East Coast Bag Co.
0.50	Price	2	3	2	2	2	2	2	2	3
0.15	Quality	3	2	3	4	3	2	3	3	4
0.10	Breadth	1	2	2	3	3	3	3	3	3
0.10	Sales Coverage	1	3	3	3	4	3	3	4	3
0.05	Packaging	3	3	2	3	3	1	3	3	3
0.10	Service	4	3	3	2	2	2	3	4	3

*Overall Weighted Ranking***

1. BAGCO	2.15	6. Southeastern	2.55
2. Modern	2.20	7. Florida Plastics	2.60
3. Bonanza	2.25	8. National Film	2.65
4. Southwest Bag (Tie)	2.50	9. East Coast Bag	3.15
5. PBI (Tie)	2.50		

*Ratings on a 1 to 5 scale with 1 being the best rating and 5 the worst.
**The weighted ranking is the sum of each rank times its weight. The lower the number, the better the overall rating.

this, Clayton was told, was temporary out of stock situations which occurred occasionally, primarily due to the wide variety of trash bags offered by Modern.

During the past two years, Modern Plastics had maintained its market share at approximately 27 percent of the market. Some new competitors had entered the market since 1975 while others had left the market (see Exhibit 4). The previous district sales manager, Bill Hanson, had left Clayton some comments regarding the major competitors. These are reproduced in Exhibit 5.

Developing the Sales Forecast

After a careful study of trade journals, government statistics, and surveys conducted by Modern marketing research personnel, projections for growth potential were formulated by segment and are shown in Exhibit 6. This data was compiled by Bill Hanson just before he had been promoted.

Jim looked back at Baxter's memo giving the time schedule for the forecast and knew he had to get started. As he left the office at 7:15 he wrote himself a large note and pinned it on his wall—"Get started on the sales forecast!"

Exhibit 4. / Market Share by Supplier 1975 and 1976

Supplier	% of Market 1975	% of Market 1976
National Film	11	12
Bertram	16	0*
Bonanza	11	12
Southeastern	5	6
Bay	9	0*
Johnson Graham	8	0*
PBI	2	5
Lewis	2	0*
BAGCO	—	6
Southwest Bag	—	2
Florida Plastics	—	4
East Coast Bag Co.	—	4
Miscellaneous & Unknown	8	22
Modern	28	27
	100	100

*Out of business in 1976.

Source. This information was developed from a field survey conducted by Modern Plastics.

Exhibit 5. / Characteristics of Competitors

National Film	Broadest product line in the industry. Quality a definite advantage. Good service. Sales coverage adequate, but not an advantage. Not as aggressive as most suppliers on price. Strong competitor.
Bonanza	Well-established, tough competitor. Very aggressive on pricing. Good packaging, quality okay.
Southeastern	Extremely price competitive in Southern Florida. Dominates Miami market. Limited product line. Not a threat outside of Florida.
PBI	Extremely aggressive on price. Have made inroads into Transco Paper Company during 1977. Good service but poor sales coverage.
BAGCO	New competitor in 1977. Very impressive with a high quality product, excellent service, and strong sales coverage. A real threat, particularly in Florida.
Southwest Bag	A factor in Louisiana and Mississippi. Their strategy is simple—an acceptable product at a rock bottom price.
Florida Plastics	Active when market is at a profitable level with price cutting. When market declines to a low profit range, Florida manufactures other types of plastic packaging and stays out of the trash bag market. Poor reputation as a reliable supplier, but can still "spot-sell" at low prices.
East Coast Bag	Most of their business is from a state bid which began in January 1976 for a two-year period. Not much of a threat to Modern's business in the Southeast, as most of their volume is north of Washington D.C.

Exhibit 6. / 1978 Real Growth Projections by Segment

Total Industry	+5.0%
Commercial	+5.4%
Restaurant	+6.8%
Hotel/Motel	+2.0%
Transportation	+1.9%
Office Users	+5.0%
Other	+4.2%
Noncommercial	+4.1%
Hospitals	+3.9%
Nursing Homes	+4.8%
Colleges/Universities	+2.4%
Schools	+7.8%
Employee Feeding	+4.3%
Other	+3.9%

Source. Developed from several trade journals

TransAirways, Inc.:

Air Freight Marketing Strategy*

Bill Brown turned from his desk and looked out the window of his twenty-third-floor office in the TransAmerica Building and saw a tri-jet 727 climb steeply out of San Francisco International and bank away toward the East Coast. It was Wednesday afternoon (in September 1976) and the vice president in charge of freight operations at TransAirways knew he should begin to organize his thoughts for next year's freight marketing plan. He had scheduled a meeting for Friday morning with his staff of planners and had invited the financial people from TransAirways to attend. And next Monday afternoon he and Bob Pursell, the Marketing Administration Director at TA, would present the freight marketing plan for 1977 to Mr. George B. Johnson, who was TransAirways Senior Vice President for Planning and Marketing. Although freight sales had been steadily increasing for the last several years, TransAirways had shown no improvement in market share in its air cargo operations and would, it appeared, show a significant operating loss in its freight operations for this current year. To make matters worse, a decision was due in six weeks on the initial financial commitment required to begin production of new aircraft that were scheduled for delivery in 1978 according to TransAirways' present forecast. Bill knew that whatever plan he brought to the meeting Monday had better provide the answers to put the freight operations back on course.

William C. Brown graduated *cum laude* from Columbia University in 1952 and had worked in marketing and market analysis positions at two other airlines before coming to TransAirways in 1961. In his nine years with the company, he had worked exclusively in the area of air cargo, responsible for Eastern Operations from 1965 to 1970 (which included the New York, JFK; Chicago, ORD; and Dallas, DAL freight operations), and accepting responsibility for the entire company freight operation in 1971, nearly six years ago.

TransAirways, History and Status

TransAirways, Incorporated, was started in 1930 by Bradley J. Barkley and T. Phillip Kruger, two ex-World War I fighter aces who had amassed a small fortune in an expanding air mail service in the early Thirties. With the passage of the Air Commerce Act of 1926, air transportation was made a reality, and TransAirways began a domestic passenger service along the West Coast with three airplanes. Although the largest portion of their traffic was between the cities of Seattle, San Francisco, and Los Angeles, their route structure in the mid-thirties included seven cities. Air traffic grew at

---

*This case was prepared by Professors Edwin C. Hackleman and Subhash C. Jain of the University of Connecticut. © 1977 by the School of Business Administration, University of Connecticut. Reprinted by permission.

enormous rates between 1934 and 1937, and by the end of 1937, TransAirways had accumulated a total of 25 aircraft and was beginning to offer a promising service in air cargo transport aboard its passenger airliners. Managing to retain nominal growth rates over the war years, TransAirways enjoyed substantial growth in the late forties by early investment in the longer range and more comfortable Douglas DC-6 and DC-7 and the Lockheed Constellation. This represented a period of substantial growth and earnings and a period of financing through equity funding. With the introduction of jets in 1958, heavy financial commitments and traffic declines led to five years of poor performance, with the company seeing its first year of net loss in 1960. But as traffic revived in the mid-sixties, TransAirways again shared good growth and profits with revenue passenger miles (RPM), increasing by an average of 11 percent per year, and revenue ton miles (RTM) of cargo increasing an average of 14 percent per year. In 1968, TA decided to complement its passenger-cargo service with all-cargo freighter service utilizing Boeing 707 and Douglas DC-8 stretched aircraft. Still increasing demand for air freight service continued through the late sixties along with strong demand for passenger service. In the first quarter of 1971, TransAirways accepted delivery of its first wide-bodied jet, a Boeing 747. By January of 1976, TA expected to have a total of 20 wide-bodied aircraft (B747 and DC-10) scheduled and operational. 1975 had represented a year of unpredictable changes in the availability and costs of fuel as well as a year of serious decline in passenger traffic that coincided with the depressed United States and world economies. Although freight sales had managed to increase substantially over this period, freight operations produced net losses. The expectations for the future were uncertain although the general trend of optimism over an improved economy seemed to indicate that the airline industry might also recover. In terms of future commitments, TA was to take delivery of 10 new aircraft in 1976, most of which were to replace aging smaller aircraft. It also had orders for the purchase of aircraft for 1977 and 1978. Initial payments for the aircraft to be delivered in 1977 had already been made and a financial commitment for the 1978 aircraft would have to be made in a month and a half. The 1978 orders included options toward purchase of a 747F aircraft, a wide-bodied freighter developed specifically for all air cargo transportation.

The Air Freight Industry

As early as the late sixties, U.S. scheduled air cargo traffic represented well over a billion dollars in gross revenues to scheduled airlines. But despite substantial growth in recent years, the air cargo business remains a secondary, though quite significant, segment of the entire domestic air transport operation. Worldwide, air cargo traffic for the ICAO carriers (International Commerical Airline Operators) represents over 15 percent of their total revenues. Air freight is carried both in the belly pits of passenger planes (called combination service) and in freighter planes which carry only air cargo and no passengers. The "combination carriers" operate both freighter and combination planes (for example, TransAirways) but the all-cargo carriers operate only freighter aircraft. Although other categories represent significant portions of the total traffic, the most important area appears to be in scheduled combination domestic passenger-cargo freight operations. Growth patterns for both combination carriers and the all-cargo carriers are averaging around 20 percent for the past several years although dropping off most recently into the mid-teens.

The air freight industry consists of more than just aircraft and airlines, however. Since the objective of all air cargo traffic is to move goods quickly and efficiently, the coordination of surface and air systems is vital to profitable operation. It is evident that the nucleus air carrier is subject to many restrictions within the framework of the air freight industry in its entirety. Virtually every air freight shipment requires surface transportation at two or more points in its distribution cycle. Government regulation at the federal level through the Civil Aeronautics Board (CAB) controls the structure of routes and fares as well as providing safety and operating restrictions. And local governments, through airport and municipal authorities, impose restrictions on environmental qualities including arrival and departure times, thus providing even less flexibility in the carrier's ability to control industry functions.

Air cargo and air freight growth rates appear to be most closely relatable to real GNP, the price of air freight and a service index representing the level of service quality. One model predicts that a 1 percent change in GNP will result in a 2.8 percent increase in air freight traffic and that a 1 percent decline in air freight prices will increase traffic by 1.5 percent.[1] So air freight traffic appears to be both income and price elastic. Three classifications of goods have been used to describe products that travel by air: emergency traffic, routine perishable, and routine surface divertible. *Emergency traffic* is time essential, unplanned in advance, and the price is of little importance, whereas the penalty for failure to deliver may be significant. Such items as emergency medical shipments of vaccine and antivenom and repair parts for critical machinery would fall into this category. *Routine perishable* is still time essential, but is planned in advance. Examples of this category might include cut flowers and fresh fruit or, perhaps, some magazines. *Routine surface divertible* products are planned for shipment ahead of time, but speed and time are somewhat less important and cost factors (rather than the demand factors) are significantly more important. This system usually competes through cost with a combination surface-transportation field-warehouse system for items with low density and high value per pound. Items that would be described as routine surface divertible could include precious metals, expensive machined parts, clothing and furs.

---

[1]Irving Saginor and David B. Richards, *Forecast of Scheduled Domestic Air Cargo for the 50 States,* 1971–1975, CAB, Washington, 1971.

Although the classifications seem quite distinct theoretically, airlines have had much difficulty in determining what percentages of goods that pass through their freight system fall into the various categories, much less give much thought to forecasting future estimates. Yet it is obviously imperative that a marketing strategy for a given carrier must rest fundamentally upon which of these three areas (or which combination of areas) is to receive attention.

The areas of flight equipment (aircraft), containerization, and terminal technology should not be underestimated in developing a freight system forecast. But each area represents a wide range of variability in terms of possible costs and returns. Most airline industry experts believe that the success or failure of an airline in the air cargo industry will depend not so much on the selection of optimal technologies but rather on the implementation of perceptive management strategy.

Market and Market Position

In 1974, TransAirways was the fourth largest domestic trunk air carrier in the United States in terms of total revenues. TA was third nationally in terms of air freight revenues behind Skyway and U.S. Air Lines. Freight traffic tripled over the past ten years. The comparison of financial statistics for TransAirways and its two closest competitors is presented in Exhibit 1 for 1976. Of the three carriers, TransAirways was the only one estimated to project a loss for the year, although Skyway and U.S.'s profit levels are quite meager.

Exhibit 1. / Financial Statistics—
Passenger plus Cargo 1976 Estimated—$M

Airline (Carrier)	Operating Revenue	Operating Expense	Operating Profit	Net Profit
Skyway	1200	1100	100	30
U.S.	1100	1050	50	10
TransAir	1000	990	10	(1)

TransAirways served 21 major U.S. cities, including Chicago and New York in the eastern portion of the country, but maintained the major concentration of their services along routes that linked the Southwest and the West. The company's base of operations and headquarters were in San Francisco, and their maintenance and overhaul facility and engine repair center was adjacent to Los Angeles International Airport (LAX). The airline offered freight and passenger service between all of its regular terminal points, although the majority of its freight operations occurred between points of the seven major largest cities on its route structure. Although studies in 1971 had shown that there was no significant difference among the costs or revenues among the seven major city routes or among the smaller routes, the profitability of the large city routes had been shown to be about 2 percent higher than that of the smaller city routes. Yet analysis of market potentials for the cities on TransAirways' system indicated that the large city routes were relatively saturated and could improve profits only through improved market share capture, while the smaller city routes offered a better potential for an expanding market. The most recently available competitive comparison among TA and its prime competitors is presented as Exhibit 2.

TransAirway's position in terms of general market share also seemed to be in a deteriorating situation. Exhibit 3 shows the recent trends of market share development for each of the three large air freight handlers in their own respective markets. (It should be noted that, since the airline industry

Exhibit 2. / 1975 Capacity and Competitive Positions—TransAirway's Seven Major City Pairs

	SKYWAY				U.S.				TRANSAIR			
	Flts		ATM		Flts		ATM		Flts		ATM	
Routes	#	%	#	%	#	%	#	%	#	%	#	%
LAX-SFO	42	40	4575	40	33	21	2396	21	30	19	1832	16
LAX-JFK	22	31	2290	32	22	31	2289	32	12	17	1249	18
SFO-ORD	16	26	1263	28		NR			24	39	1416	32
LAX-DAL		NR			5	24	551	23	5	24	683	28
SEA-SFO	11	26	976	28		NR			21	49	1394	40
SFO-DAL	12	27	889	28	11	24	815	25	17	38	1055	33
LAX-DEN		NR			10	21	205	23	11	23	1007	53

Key:
LAX—Los Angeles
JFK—New York
DAL—Dallas
DEN—Denver
SFO—San Francisco
ORD—Chicago
SEA—Seattle
Flts—Flights ATM—Available Ton Miles NR—No Route between city pair

Exhibit 3. / Market Shares of Airlines in Total Respective Air Freight Markets

	Year						
Airline	1970	1971	1972	1973	1974	1975	1976
Skyway	28%	27%	29%	31%	31%	32%	32%
U.S.	28	26	28	27	27	28	28
Transair	25	27	24	21	21	21	20

is highly regulated by the CAB, information dealing with all aspects of a carrier's status must be filed with this authority on a regular basis for all carriers. Thus financial and operating statistics for each airline are consistently drawn and available from the public record.)

Advertising

Since Jim Evans had taken over control of the freight operations, a major effort had been launched to emphasize advertising as a means of increasing market share. A market research program had been conducted in 1974, at the cost of $15,000, in the four largest volume city pairs which indicated that the market in these areas dealt in goods shipped by air, 80 percent of which fell into the routine perishable category. The other city pairs had not been surveyed and the value of freight shipment for the remaining 20 percent of goods in the surveyed market had not been established. Based upon the study, however, an advertising campaign carrying the following themes had been used for the past two years:

- Fast system of delivery
- Door-to-door service
- High quality control

In 1976, an advertising campaign had been outlined which was to attempt market penetration into the surface divertible market that probably constituted a good portion of the remaining 20 percent of air-shipped goods. The theme of this program was to concentrate on the comparison between the costs and advantages of air freight shipment as opposed to those of ground transportation-based distribution and remote warehouse complex. But funds for this new promotion were curtailed as profits turned to losses in the third quarter of 1976.

Strategy

From the company statistics, it was obvious to Bill Brown that the company's freight operations did not suffer from lack of capacity at the present time but rather from a decrease in profitability, resulting from a loss in market share and increased operating expenses. In fact, freight load factors for all aircraft were much lower than expected, and this was especially true in the case of the wide-bodied jets whose performance, for this reason and because of greater-than-anticipated introduction costs for the new aircraft, did not seem to exhibit any indications of their inherent economy of scale. Some revision of Brown's freight marketing plan could possibly improve market share and load factors. With this improvement and a generally expected overall improvement in the national economy, profitability might again become favorable, possibly to the point of justifying extensions of orders for more new narrow and wide-bodied freighter aircraft for the late 1970s. How should he proceed?

Hyde-Phillip Chemical Company

Alternative Forms of Sales Representation*

Michael Claxton, a recent marketing graduate of a well-known college, has been assigned the task of evaluating Hyde-Phillip Chemical Company's methods of selling the firm's products. Hyde-Phillip currently utilizes a mix of company salespersons, merchant wholesalers and agent wholesalers to present its products to present and potential users. While this combination of selling forces is somewhat unusual it reflects the orientation of management over time as to the relative values of alternative forms of sales representation. Claxton's challenge is to review the data that has been gathered on the three types of sales efforts, determine if additional information is needed, and make recommendations as to what changes, if any, should be made in the firm's approach to sales representation.

Information on the Company

Hyde-Phillip was formed in the early 1960s through the merger of Hyde Industrial Chemicals and Phillip Laboratories. Both firms had a broad range of experience in the development and production of certain types of chemicals and related supplies for a variety of industrial users. While the two firms had a few overlapping product lines, each brought to the merger some exclusive product offerings. The resulting combination of the two firms yielded a new organization capable of marketing a complete line of chemicals for industrial use.

Prior to the merger, Hyde Industrial Chemicals had utilized a group of industrial distributors (merchant wholesalers) to market its products. Phillip Laboratories, on the other hand, had several manufacturers' agents (agent wholesalers) who sold its product offering. The new firm, after the merger, retained some of the industrial distributors and some of the manufacturing agents and then began to develop its own sales force.

Today, Hyde-Phillip serves 30 sales territories in states east of the Mississippi through its own sales force of 50 individuals (six women and 44 men), nine industrial distributors, and nine manufacturers' agents. The 50 salespeople are about evenly allocated across 12 of the sales territories. Each of the industrial distributors and manufacturers' agents has exclusive selling rights in one of the 18 remaining sales territories. Individual distributors and agents have from five to 30 people working for them and many represent other noncompeting manufacturers. The 30 sales territories were originally established to represent areas of approximately equal sales potential for Hyde-Phillip's products.

Many types of sales support are made available to each sales territory by the company. Individual managers of the territories have the option of using

*From W. Wayne Talarzyk, *Cases for Analysis in Marketing* (Hinsdale, IL: The Dryden Press, 1977), pp. 70–74. © 1977 by The Dryden Press. Reprinted by permission.

or not using each type of sales support. Sales support items currently available include: (1) a variety of descriptive brochures to supplement the information given in the firm's product catalog, (2) study programs with cassette tapes to enable sales representatives to be more familiar with the firm's products and current market situations and developments, (3) a program to provide generous product samples to potential customers for test purposes, and (4) direct-mail programs aimed at prospective customers to solicit inquiries for descriptive materials and product samples.

Data on Sales Territories

As a first step in beginning his analysis, Claxton asked his assistant to compile the available information on each of the 30 sales territories. This information is presented in coded form in Exhibit 1.

In terms of level of sales, nine territories have annual sales in excess of $2 million, 15 have sales between $1 and $2 million, and six have sales less than $1 million. As already indicated, in 12 of the territories the firm is represented by its own sales force, and industrial distributors and manufacturers' agents each represent the company in nine territories.

Based on estimates provided by the sales support department, 12 of the territories make extensive use of the available sales support programs, 12 are moderate users, and six are light users. Each of the firm's sales territories is also divided into one of three geographic divisions: Northern, Southern, or Eastern. As indicated in Exhibit 1, each of these geographic locations includes 10 sales territories.

Initial Analysis

Using the information in Exhibit 1, Claxton constructed the cross tabulation of sales versus type of representation as shown in Exhibit 2. He first set up the cross tabulation using raw numbers and then calculated the conditional probabilities for each row and column.

As seen in part B of Exhibit 2, 30.0 percent of Hyde-Phillip's territories with sales over $2 million were ones served by industrial distributors. Only 11.1 percent of the largest sales territories were represented by manufacturers' agents and 33.3 percent were served by the company sales force. Stated differently, as shown in part C of Exhibit 2, 25 percent of territories served by the company's sales force had sales over $2 million, while 55.6 percent of the industrial distributors and 11.1 percent of the manufacturers' agents served territories with sales over $2 million.

Claxton's initial reaction was that the firm should consider replacing part of its own sales force and the manufacturers' agents with more industrial distributors. He was concerned, however, with what other variables should be taken into account to more fully analyze and evaluate Hyde-Phillip's current approach to sales representation.

Exhibit 1. / Available Data on Sales Territories

Territory Number	Level of Sales	Type of Representation	Use of Sales Support	Geographic Location
1	2	1	2	3
2	3	1	3	3
3	2	2	1	1
4	1	1	1	1
5	2	3	1	1
6	2	1	2	1
7	3	3	2	3
8	1	2	1	1
9	2	1	2	2
10	2	1	2	3
11	1	2	1	1
12	1	1	1	2
13	2	2	2	2
14	2	3	2	1
15	1	1	2	3
16	2	3	2	2
17	2	1	3	1
18	1	2	1	2
19	2	3	2	2
20	3	1	3	2
21	1	3	1	3
22	2	2	1	3
23	3	3	1	1
24	3	1	3	2
25	3	2	3	1
26	1	2	1	2
27	2	1	2	2
28	1	2	1	3
29	2	3	3	3
30	2	3	2	3

Codes:
Level of sales: 1 = over $2 million; 2 = $1–2 million; 3 = under $1 million.
Type of representation: 1 = company sales force; 2 = industrial distributor; 3 = manufacturers' agent.
Use of sales support: 1 = extensive user; 2 = moderate user; 3 = light user.
Geographic location: 1 = Northern; 2 = Southern; 3 = Eastern.

Exhibit 2. / Cross Tabulation of Level of Sales versus Type of Representation

			Company Sales force (1)	Industrial Distrib-utor (2)	Manu-facturers' Agent (3)	Totals	
	Over $2 million	(1)	3	5	1	9	
Level of Sales	$1–2 million	(2)	6	3	6	15	A
	Under $1 million	(3)	3	1	2	6	
		Totals	12	9	9		

			Company Sales force (1)	Industrial Distrib-utor (2)	Manu-facturers' Agent (3)		
	Over $2 million	(1)	33.3	55.6	11.1	100.0	
Level of Sales	$1–2 million	(2)	40.0	20.0	40.0	100.0	B
	Under $1 million	(3)	50.0	16.7	33.3	100.0	
		Totals	40.0	30.0	30.0	100.0	

			Company Sales force (1)	Industrial Distrib-utor (2)	Manu-facturers' Agent (3)		
	Over $2 million	(1)	25.0	55.6	11.1	30.0	
Level of Sales	$1–2 million	(2)	50.0	33.3	66.7	50.0	C
	Under $1 million	(3)	25.0	11.1	22.2	20.0	
		Totals	100.0	100.0	100.0		

Code: A = raw numbers.
B = row conditional probabilities
C = column conditional probabilities.

Transcon Parts*

Interoffice
Memorandum

To: Mr. Leo Sarns, Distribution Manager

From: George Kall, Warehouse Manager, Aurora

Subject: Parts Delivery

Date: January 12, 1977

Ref: P.O. Nos. 11-76-328C
11-76-012C
11-76-921C

Routing: TX

I must call to your attention that to date the back-ordered items on these P.O.s have not been received as follows:

21 NE 040	3 gross
2100-0125-0050	7 dozen
19 NTE 080	4 gross

Customers are jumping up and down. Please advise immediately re current status by return TX.

Mr. Sarns hesitated outside Norman Jane's office while he mulled the contents of the memo. He could predict Mr. Jane's reaction to it, but there seemed to be no alternative but to bring the matter before his boss, who was vice president of marketing and customer service.

"Come in, Leo what's on your mind today?"

"Hi, Norm. Another one just came in on the Telex, this time from Aurora, Illinois. Here, take a look at it. I have checked with shipping and those backorders were shipped on December 20 out of our Anaheim plant. The fleet manager has traced two of them, which were misrouted to Mobile. He can't pin down the other one. . . I've tried, Norm. I guess we all have. Two of those customers are Cone Brothers and Kennecott Copper. I guess you know that heads will roll if we lose either one of them."

"Yeah, Leo, I know. How many complaints like this are we getting?"

"This makes the eleventh since the first of the year."

---

*This case was prepared by Professors W. B. Ayars and H. F. Rudd of California State College, Bakersfield. Reprinted by permission.

"Wow. Say, I have an appointment in 15 minutes with John Seamon, why don't you join me? I want to bring this thing up, and I need you to help me on the details."

The Company

Mr. Seamon was actually not very surprised that this matter was brought to his attention. In fact, he had foreseen such an eventuality years before he became president of Transcon Parts.

He had joined the company in 1942, shortly after it had formed in response to government demand for tank tracks, sprockets, axles, and pins during World War II. The company had done very well until 1946, as it had just one customer who quickly bought all it could produce.

After the war, the company had switched over to making replacement tractor and loader parts and attachments. While the production operation required relatively little modification, the company had soon found itself serving many diverse markets, and the distribution function had taken on a whole new and constantly changing complexion.

By 1965 the original plant in Joliet, Illinois, had been supplemented with plants in Anaheim, California; Pittsburgh, Pennsylvania; Mobile, Alabama, and Portland, Oregon. In addition, the company operated a total of 18 storage and distribution warehouses in large cities in Arizona, Utah, Colorado, Texas (2), Oklahoma, Kansas, Iowa, Louisiana, Tennessee, Ohio (3), Georgia, Florida (2), New Jersey, and Massachusetts.

Each plant and warehouse provided full multistate service to customers either through their own facilities or through dealers, distributors, manufacturers' representatives, or jobbing contractors in every state of the Union.

Iron and steel was purchased from steel mills for motor vehicle transportation to the plants. Each plant had distinctly different production patterns. That is, one plant might do rough castings and finished tracks, where another would finish rough castings and produce rough forgings. Still another plant reclaimed and converted used track. Thus, one plant was dependent to some extent for its raw materials upon the output of another plant.

Additions to the product mix included rollers, shafts, lifting devices, bushings, seals, and lugs. By 1972, Mr. Seamon had the impression that the augmented product lines were generally in line with customer expectations.

Mr. Seamon knew that Transcon's price structure was slightly above that of the competition, but his decision has been made at the request of the sales force. In this way they could argue that the company provided superior service in exchange for premium prices. Most customer purchasing agents had seemed to be more interested in service than they were in shaving the prices.

This strategy had been effective over the years as the company grew larger. However, now that it was a nationwide operation there was some question regarding the company's continuing ability to meet expected levels of service.

The permanent fleet at present includes 15 tractors and 35 trailers. Six tractors and 15 trailers are stationed at Joliet, while four tractors and nine trailers are stationed in Anaheim, with the same in Pittsburgh and the remainder in Mobile. All vehicles are dispatched by the fleet manager's office in Joliet.

An individual truck might typically be routed as follows: Loaded at Joliet with track and finished castings, it would proceed toward Pittsburgh, stopping en route for partial unloadings at warehouses in Ohio and for on-site deliveries to contractors in Michigan, Indiana, Kentucky, and West Virginia. At Pittsburgh the vehicle may reload with stock destined for dealers, wholesalers, and contractors in New York, Vermont, New Hampshire, Maine, Connecticut, and Rhode Island. The vehicle may return via Pittsburgh with imported goods loaded in Boston and Hoboken, New Jersey, partially unloading en route in states as far south as Virginia. Some of this lading may be destined for finishing in Anaheim; therefore, additional loadings will take place at Pittsburgh and Joliet, and the truck will be routed westward in a similar manner.

The Industry

Mr. Seamon knew that customer service always had been of paramount importance in this business. Customers depended on quality of steel and workmanship in casting, forging, milling, grinding, and fabrication to be sure, but they were even more concerned about on-time deliveries and minimizing loss, damage, and misroutings.

On the other hand, competition keeps the company's net margin to 25–30 percent. This constraint requires that warehouse stock turn an average of four times per year. Just a few years ago, when inflation was not as serious as it has recently become, three times a year was sufficient.

Top Management Meets

Mr. Seamon greeted Mr. Jane and Mr. Sarns as they walked into his office. He studied the memo and ventured an opinion.

"Gentlemen, it looks like we have outgrown private carriage as our best method of distribution. Let's explore the other feasible alternatives. What is our competition using?"

Mr. Sarns responded.

"Well, Topper Corp. operates east of the Mississippi, as you know. They have been using common carriers and UPS blue label* for four years that I know of. Apparently, they have found this to be satisfactory. Then there is Trans-United.

---

*This is United Parcel Service combined with air freight.

They are nationwide, and they recently switched over from private carriage to a contract surface carrier. I imagine that they supplement this with air freight. It is too early to say just how well this arrangement is working out. There is also the Abel Speeder Corp. which has been a West Coast firm and appears to be going nationwide. They have been using common carriers and bus package express. Now Earthworm Tractor uses rail freight in combination with regular air cargo service nationwide, but they're not into replacement parts like we are."

Mr. Jane was next to comment.

"That's a good rundown on the competition, Leo, but I don't see that it helps us very much. How can we get a good handle on the types of services which these carriers can provide for us, and how good are they?"

"Well, an interstate common motor carrier may tell you seven days delivery time from pick up anywhere in the country. But you don't know when he will pick up and how often the lading must be interlined.** Therefore, you really cannot tell when your lading will arrive at destination. In practice, intrastate hauls can arrive two days after pickup, which is pretty good. In any case, they will not haul without a full load.

"Contract carriers vary quite a lot. If you can get one to make regularly scheduled runs between our plants and maybe warehouses, you can depend on his delivery dates. On the other hand, you may not have much lading for a particular run, but you will need to pay him in full for the run anyhow. In such a case he may fill up with other shipper's stuff or he may not. You must share this risk with him, and his terms will reflect this. Regarding on-site contractor deliveries, I don't know. I imagine that this is negotiable, perhaps on a cost-plus basis.

"Rail freight is similar to common motor carriers, but you never do have much of an idea when it will get there. Heavy loads are cheaper, but you have to haul it to the rail head. You also have to load it onto a spotted rail car to the carrier's specifications.

"Bus and air freight both require packages no longer than six feet, and each shipment must be no heavier than 100 pounds in two or more cartons. Bus will take three days from the West Coast to, say, St. Louis and five days to Boston. Air freight will get it there in one to two days portal to portal, but it'll cost you.

"Now you wanted to know how good these carriers are. Here are the results of a recent survey done by *Purchasing* magazine. (See Exhibit 1). Looks like the Postal Service is not competitive, but the rest of the data may help us."

Mr. Seamon replied.

"Thank you, Leo. It looks like we have something to work with here. Norm, I'd like you to come up with a recommendation. Keep in mind that it may still be possible to revamp our private carriage to handle the job, although I realize that you have already tried several different arrangements. At any rate, we'll have to move on this so our company image will not go straight down the tubes. Let's have a preliminary recommendation by next Wednesday. Thank you, gentlemen, and good day."

Back in his office, Mr. Jane cancelled his Saturday morning golf date and

---

**Interlining means unloading from a truck belonging to a carrier who does not have I.C.C. authority to haul farther, and loading onto one that does. Each interline requires an extra 1–2 days.

Exhibit 1. / Survey by the Editors of *Purchasing* Magazine, May–June, 1976: How Buyers Rate Carriers

Buyers surveyed were asked to rate carriers for each factor on a scale from 1 to 10, where 10 indicates best possible performance and 1, the worst possible.

	Strongest points (7.0 or higher)		Weakest points (5.0 or lower)			
Air	Reliability of service	Reasonable rates	Assistance, advice, other aid	Careful handling	Claims handling	Overall performance
United Parcel Service (air)	8.0	7.8	6.9	7.6	6.4	7.5
Air Express	7.1	5.4	7.0	7.3	5.8	7.0
Air freight forwarder	7.5	6.1	7.6	7.2	6.4	6.6
Air Taxi/Commuter	7.7	5.7	7.0	7.3	5.9	6.6
Regular air service	7.0	5.8	6.7	6.7	5.8	6.6
Air Parcel Post	5.5	5.8	5.1	4.5	4.2	5.0
Surface						
United Parcel Service (surface)	8.3	8.3	6.9	7.6	6.4	7.9
Bus package express	7.6	7.7	6.3	7.1	6.1	6.9
Water carriers (inland & intercoastal)	6.6	6.6	6.4	6.6	6.4	6.7
Motor carrier (trucks)	7.0	6.3	7.4	6.3	5.6	6.6
Water carriers (ocean)	6.5	6.8	6.4	6.6	5.4	6.4
Rail freight forwarder (carloading companies)	5.9	6.0	7.0	6.3	5.2	6.1
Rail	4.9	6.0	6.3	5.2	5.2	5.3
Parcel Post	4.3	5.5	4.5	4.0	4.2	4.2

glanced through a sheaf of memos which were similar to the one that brought Leo Sarns into his office. It now occurred to him that during the past few months the number of phone calls which he had received from dissatisfied customers had increased dramatically. Also, most of them dealt with promised delivery dates not kept. Apparently, customers still liked the quality of Transcon products, but this was of little consolation when they were not getting them when and where they needed them.

The Ajax Pump Company*

The Ajax Pump Company is the number two supplier of small pumps and valves to industrial replacement markets. The company's early (1940s and 1950s) success was built on the basis of local availability of virtually all replacement pumps and valves. In response to that market need, Ajax developed a strong distributor network, backed up by 23 small field warehouses under the direct control of the local marketing managers.

Two plants, one in New York and one in Chicago, ship to the field warehouses direct through small plant warehouses. Warehouse replenishment orders are generated by warehouse clerks who maintain a manual system. Clerks record sales and shipments received and therefore determine actual inventory levels on a continuous basis. Orders for replenishing the inventory are placed when a predetermined level of on-hand inventory is reached. Order entry is accomplished in the field, utilizing a manual system. Manual order records are mailed to headquarters for billing and accumulation of sales statistics.

Several important market trends developed in the 1960s:

1. Ajax's distributors, since being caught in the first modern credit crunch (1966), have become much less willing to hold adequate inventory. They carry most of the line but now rely more heavily on the Ajax field warehouse for backup stock and all fringe items.
2. The company's marketing department has successfully developed national service contracts with major industrial concerns to be administered on a direct basis. These accounts are served from the regional warehouses, and their demand is more difficult to predict than the demand generated through the local distributors.
3. The product line has proliferated: In 1960, the line amounted to 1575 separate items or stock-keeping units; today's product offering amounts to 5320 separate items.
4. Manufacturing completed a three-year program to reconfigure the production facilities and integrate foundry and aluminum die casting capabilities. While costs are lower, economic run sizes are now substantially larger and flexibility has been reduced from before when most components were purchased outside.

---

*This case was prepared by James D. Blaser, director, Cleveland Consulting Associates. Reprinted by permission.

Table 1. / Ajax Pump Company: Summary Financial Statements, 1976

Profit and Loss Statement

	Thousands
Sales	$75,000
Cost of Goods	42,220
Gross Profit	$32,780
Distribution Costs	$12,760
Selling and Administrative	5,750
Depreciation	9,000
Interest	2,520
Income Taxes	1,250
Net Income	$ 1,500

Balance Sheet

Assets		Liabilities and Capital	
Cash	$ 400	Current Liabilities	$ 5,600
Receivables	8,000	Long Term Debt	26,500
Inventories	20,000		
Manufacturing Facilities[1]	38,200	Total Debt	$32,100
Distribution Facilities[1]	12,900		
Other	500	Shareholder Equity	$47,900
Total	$80,000	Total	$80,000

[1]Net of accumulated depreciation

During the chaotic 1973–1975 economic period, Ajax was thrown into a loss position for the first time in 36 years. Inventories skyrocketed and, coupled with funding requirements associated with the manufacturing program, forced the company to borrow funds up to the limit of its financial ability. Market conditions have stabilized but inventory remains too high by traditional standards. In spite of high inventories, Ajax's customer service level is below customer expectations and industry standards. In fact, marketing has gone on record that Ajax has lost market share because of poor service.

A new distribution manager has been hired and been given responsibility for the warehouses, finished goods inventory control, order processing, and traffic. His first job is to develop a plan to restore Ajax's distribution position, for presentation to top management for approval within the next three months.

The new distribution manager has been through an improvement effort like the one required at Ajax before and, after becoming thoroughly familiar

Table 2. / Key Financial Relationships and Ratios (Dollars in Thousands)

Incremental Pretax Profit Contribution:

	Total % of sales	Variable % of sales	% of Sales
Reported gross margin			43.7%
Other variable costs:			
Distribution	17%	38%	– 6.5
Selling and administrative	8	15	– 1.2
Contribution Margin			36.0%

Finished Goods Inventory Turns:

Cost of goods	$42,220	2.6
Average f.g. inventory	16,000	

with the situation, has developed a shopping list of major projects and programs he would like to evaluate and hopefully implement:

1. Evaluate a consolidated distribution network with five to seven new modern distribution centers to take the place of the present 23 warehouses.
2. Design a new order entry/inventory control/billing system that would automatically update inventory records and have extensive order and stock inquiry capabilities.
3. Develop a shipment consolidation program to accumulate a greater share of outbound shipments into truckloads.
4. Evaluate the possibility of pulling back the fringe items into a master warehouse and provide rapid-response national service for those items using premium transportation.

Over lunch one day, the distribution manager bounced these ideas off the president and vice president of marketing. The president was very interested but reminded the distribution manager that these appeared to be major long-term projects, requiring considerable analysis and capital to implement. He reiterated his wish that the distribution improvement plan include detailed financial evaluations and justification.

In view of his objective to restore a sound financial position, the president asked that less capital intense improvements be looked at first. The vice president of marketing added that Ajax's major competitors were delivering orders within a three-day turnaround time and achieving a reported 92 percent initial order fill level. As a result, the company was losing sales and market share every day.

With those facts in mind, the distribution manager set about developing an approach to evaluating his options and developing the improvement plan.

Table 3. / Key Distribution Data

Analysis of Distribution Costs:

	Thousands	Percent of Sales
Inbound transportation	$ 3,150	4.2%
Outbound transportation	2,100	2.8
Warehouse operating costs		
–fixed	3,345	4.5
–variable	1,380	1.8
Order entry/billing system	1,100	1.5
Packaging	535	0.7
Logistics administration	100	0.1
Traffic, receiving, and shipping	600	0.8
Taxes, obsolescence, and insurances	450	0.6
Total	$12,760	17.0%

Shipment Profile:

	Truckload	LTL	Other
Inbound replenishment	73%	27%	0%
Outbound	3	96	1

	Dollars	Pounds
Average Shipment Size:	$700	800

Order Cycle Time:

	Average	95% Confidence
Order mail in	2	4
Internal processing	4	10
Outbound shipment	1	3
Total	7	17

Customer Service Level: –% of items filled	83%

Westinghouse Canada Limited*

On November 19, 1973, Mr. J. B. Johnson, president of Westinghouse Canada Limited, issued a memo to the senior management of the company in which he suggested that Westinghouse apply a price escalation factor to many of the company's quotations. Mr. Johnson indicated that he was anxious to adopt a price-quotation policy that would:

*This case was prepared by Professor Adrian B. Ryans of Stanford University.

1. Provide a policy umbrella for all Westinghouse Canada Limited division marketing managers to make the best pricing decisions under the present and foreseen conditions of rapidly rising costs and probable scarcity of materials and components.
2. Be effective in counteracting profit erosion from these causes.
3. Incorporate some flexibility for unusual situations.

In the memo he suggested a tentative policy that had been developed in consultation with some of the senior marketing and division managers. The purpose of the memo was to acquaint a wide range of the company's management with the rising costs the company was facing and to encourage discussion among management and with key customers so that an appropriate price escalation policy could be developed.

The Company

Westinghouse Canada Limited was a major manufacturer of a wide range of electrical and electronic products with its head office located in Hamilton, Ontario, and plants scattered across Canada. The 1972 sales of the company were $281,451,000 and income after taxes was $3,370,000. About 75 percent of the outstanding common shares of Westinghouse Canada Limited were beneficially owned by Westinghouse Electric Corporation of Pittsburgh, Pennsylvania. The company was divided into three major product groups: Power Systems, Consumer Products, and Construction and Industrial groups.

The Power Systems Group included divisions that produced steam and gas turbines, high voltage direct-current apparatus, industrial brakes, power transformers, distribution transformers, capacitors, and atomic fuel and reactor components.

The Consumer Products Group included divisions that produced major appliances, such as refrigerators, ranges, laundry equipment, room air conditioners and dehumidifiers, a wide range of portable appliances, small radios, and a number of lamp products.

The divisions in the Construction and Industrial Group produced electric motors, industrial switchgear and control products, heaters, instruments, relays, dry type transformers, electrical heating products, electronic products, commercial and institutional air conditioning products, and elevators and escalators.

Sales and income by group for 1972 are shown in Exhibit 1.

History of Price Escalation at Westinghouse

After World War II it had been common in the heavy electrical business for companies to have escalation clauses in their price quotations. Westinghouse had in some early postwar years received a significant proportion of its revenue from price escalator clauses since some costs had risen quite rapidly. At that time in the United States, price at time of shipment (PTS) quotations were quite common in the heavy electrical business, but PTS had never been accepted in this business in Canada.

After the Korean War inflation was reduced and foreign competition became a more significant factor in the Canadian market. Some customers, particularly some utilities, began to request a choice between firm and escalated prices on quotations. Gradually electrical equipment suppliers reverted to firm prices for most quotations, although customers did not exert any major direct pressure for them to do this.

However, even though price escalation clauses had disappeared from most contracts, there were still a few orders for very long delivery (three years and longer) that had price escalation clauses. This policy continued through the 1960s and early 1970s. Typically, these contracts involved major items of equipment valued in the hundreds of thousands or millions of dollars. The price escalation factor was typically based on an appropriate Statistics Canada materials index, such as the Primary Metal Industries Selling Price Index.

The 1973 Situation

During the late 1950s and early 1960s the cost of most of the raw materials used by the electrical industry increased very slightly, and some, such as plastics, copper, and aluminum actually decreased in price. Selling price indexes for some of the raw material used by the industry are shown in Exhibit 2. In this same period, prices for most types of electrical equipment were very weak, and manufacturers often found it difficult to raise prices even as costs rose.

Costs of raw materials increased gradually in the early 1970s. However, it was not until early in 1973 that the rate of increase accelerated sharply, and it was slightly later, the summer and fall of 1973, before manufacturers were able to raise prices. At that time price increases made by Westinghouse or its competitors in a number of product categories were found to stick. By the fall of 1973 it became apparent to the head office management at Westinghouse that most product divisions were experiencing an abnormal rise in a large number of raw material costs. In comparison with year earlier prices, November 1973 copper prices were up 30 percent, insulating oil was up 17 percent, steel castings were up over 30 percent, sheet steel was up 10 percent, and aluminum was up 26 percent. These were all materials used in a wide range of Westinghouse products. In the summer and fall of 1973 suppliers of plastics, insulating materials, castings, and fasteners had also changed their price policy to PTS from firm price at time of order. Similarly, fuel oil had changed to PTS from annual fixed price contract. There were also indications that suppliers of capital equipment were tightening up their terms.

While there was considerable variation from product to product, wages and salary costs accounted on average for about 50 percent of the cost of Westinghouse's finished products. Even these costs were not as predictable as they had been historically—in the fall of 1973, the company had paid its employees a special increase above what its labor contracts required in order to help offset the unexpected rise in the cost of living.

It was against this background that Mr. Johnson issued his memo. The tentative policy he suggested in his memo which was to be used for discussion purposes was:

1. Apply escalation to all domestic negotiations where;
   a. Delivery is more than one year *and* order value exceeds $50,000.
   b. Extended delivery, beyond normal interval, is required by the customer regardless of the value.
2. Apply to Utility and Industrial customers only.
3. Present format and procedure for escalation is usable (see Exhibit 3).

In his memo Mr. Johnson suggested a two-week time frame for the price escalation decision. He also indicated that there were a number of potential problems that would need to be resolved. Among the ones he noted were:

1. This is a major change in the way of doing business. If not followed by competition, customers will have to add something to our bid. This may be more than the actual escalation or what would be added for a firm price.
2. What exceptions will be taken? Should certain customers who are extremely resistant to price escalation, such as contractors, OEM's, and Hydro Quebec, be excluded from the policy?
3. The actual administration of the plan—should escalation be applied to actual or promised delivery date?
4. For successful implementation, the plan must have sales management commitment and support.

Mr. Johnson's memo was discussed in a meeting of Westinghouse's top management on November 20. After a considerable amount of discussion, Mr. West, the vice president of marketing, recommended to the group:

1. Firm prices for shipments up to six months from date of quotation.
2. An escalation clause based on Statistics Canada indexes (which would have to be selected) for shipments beyond six months.

At the close of the meeting Mr. Johnson asked the operating vice presidents at the meeting to review his comments and Mr. West's tentative recommendations with their divisional managers and to report back their comments and recommendations to Mr. West and him.

The Distribution Apparatus Division

On December 4, 1973, Mr. Bob Hughes, marketing manager for the Distribution Apparatus Division (one of the divisions in the Power System Group) was requested by the division manager to respond to the request of the head office for an immediate review of the suggested price escalation policy and to develop a policy that would be tailored to the division's products and markets.

Mr. Hughes had become aware about a month earlier that costs for metal products the division purchased were rising at abnormal rates. He was still wondering how he should factor this deteriorating cost situation into his price quotations when the head office request arrived.

The main product of the Distribution Apparatus Division in London, Ontario, was distribution transformers, which constituted about two-thirds of the division's dollar volume. The market for distribution transformers was an extremely competitive one with Westinghouse competing with Canadian General Electric, Ferranti-Packard, Pioneer Electric, Reliance Electric, and four smaller companies. In recent years Westinghouse had had the largest market share, but in 1973 the top position in the market had been taken over by Canadian General Electric, when Westinghouse had been unable to satisfy the demand for transformers due to the lack of sufficient production capacity in the London plant. Canadian bookings for all manufacturers combined for distribution transformers had been $36M in 1972. By December 1973, it was clear that 1973 bookings would be about $54M and 1974 bookings were again expected to increase by at least an additional 50 percent. In response to this rapid growth in bookings the normal four month backlog at the London plant of Westinghouse had increased by November 1973 to about ten months.

The market for distribution transformers in Canada was extremely concentrated with three purchasers, Ontario Hydro, Hydro Quebec, and B. C. Hydro, accounting for over 60 percent of the dollar volume. The situation varied considerably even in the three main provinces. In Ontario, besides Ontario Hydro, about 350 municipal utilities, who purchased power wholesale from Ontario Hydro and retailed it, also purchased distribution transformers. In Quebec and British Columbia, on the other hand, there were very few municipal utilities so that the provincial power authority accounted for practically all the sales. The City of Sherbrooke in Quebec and West Kootenay Light and Power in British Columbia were the two main exceptions. Large companies such as Alcan at Arvida, Quebec, purchased some transformers for their own internal use. The markets in the other provinces were in general somewhat more fragmented; for example, in Alberta four utilities accounted for most of the market. Any particular order or quotation request from a provincial or a municipal utility might involve 20 different items or sizes, including both transformers and the other items sold by the distribution apparatus division.

Mr. Hughes was concerned about how his major customers would react to any price escalation clauses. Ontario Hydro had always allowed price escalation clauses to be written into its contracts, but this practice had not been used in recent years for distribution transformers. Hydro Quebec, on the other hand, had never accepted a non-firm Westinghouse price and was known to be firmly opposed to escalation clauses of any kind. B. C. Hydro was also expected to be resistant to price escalation clauses but was not likely to be as adamant as Hydro Quebec.

Mr. Hughes was also concerned about the acceptability of Statistics Canada indexes as a basis for escalating prices to his customers. He felt that public utilities, which are ultimately responsible to commissions which contain politicians, would strongly resist accepting contracts where the amount of the price increase was unknown.

Mr. Hughes had been asked to make his recommendations and comments on price escalation by December 6, so that his views could be used by division and corporate management in developing the final policy.

The Corporate Marketing Viewpoint

Mr. Bill Smith, manager of marketing services for Westinghouse Canada Limited, had been intimately involved with the deteriorating cost situation since it had begun to develop. As reaction to Mr. Johnson's memo and Mr. West's recommendations began to come in, he wondered what plan of action he should recommend.

He was aware from early reactions to the price escalation proposal that, while the Power Systems Group was generally receptive to some form of price escalation, the marketing managers in the Construction and Industrial Group didn't want price escalation. The contractors who represented a large customer group for the latter division were firmly opposed to any form of price escalation. Mr. Smith felt their position was understandable since many of these contractors were bidding on fixed price contracts, and price escalation would make it very difficult to estimate their costs on a project that might not be completed for two or three years. On the other hand, he was aware that on November 1, 1973, Crane Canada Limited had announced that effective immediately it would no longer offer price protection on its china and steel plumbing fixtures. Any products that were not shipped within 90 days of a new price going into effect would be billed at the then current price. Many of Crane's customers were also customers of the Commercial and Industrial Group, and it was clear that these contractors were very upset at Crane's move.

Mr. Smith was unsure how to reconcile the conflicting views in the company, so there would be a more homogeneous perception of the price situation and how Westinghouse should react to it. Mr. Smith also felt there was a need for consistency in any price escalation policy across divisions and product groups since it was quite common for one customer to deal with several divisions and several different Westinghouse salespersons. He felt that the probability of a successful implementation of a pricing policy would be higher if it were applied with uniformity to most of the company's products. Mr. Smith was also aware that the volume of orders dealt with by the different divisions varied widely, from a few orders per week in one division to several hundred per week in other divisions.

In late November, Mr. Smith had received a memo from the manager of marketing planning, Mr. Collins, containing his comments on the Westinghouse price escalation policy, including a discussion of possible price indexes. The memo is contained in Exhibit 4. As he reviewed Mr. Collins's comments and the latest graphs of industrial selling price indexes (Exhibit 2), he wondered what course of action he should recommend to Mr. West and Mr. Johnson.

Exhibit 1. / Westinghouse Canada Limited—1972 Sales and Income by Product Group

	1972			
Group	Sales ($000)		Income ($000)	
Power Systems	56,940		2,022	
Consumer Products	104,560		5,970	
Construction and Industrial	136,995		4,145	
Total		296,495		12,137
Less Intergroup sales	15,044			
Total Sales		281,451		
Common Costs			3,724	
Interest			2,178	
Income Taxes			2,865	
Total Company-level costs				8,767
Net Income				3,370

Exhibit 2. / Average Annual Industrial Selling Price Indexes (1961 = 100)

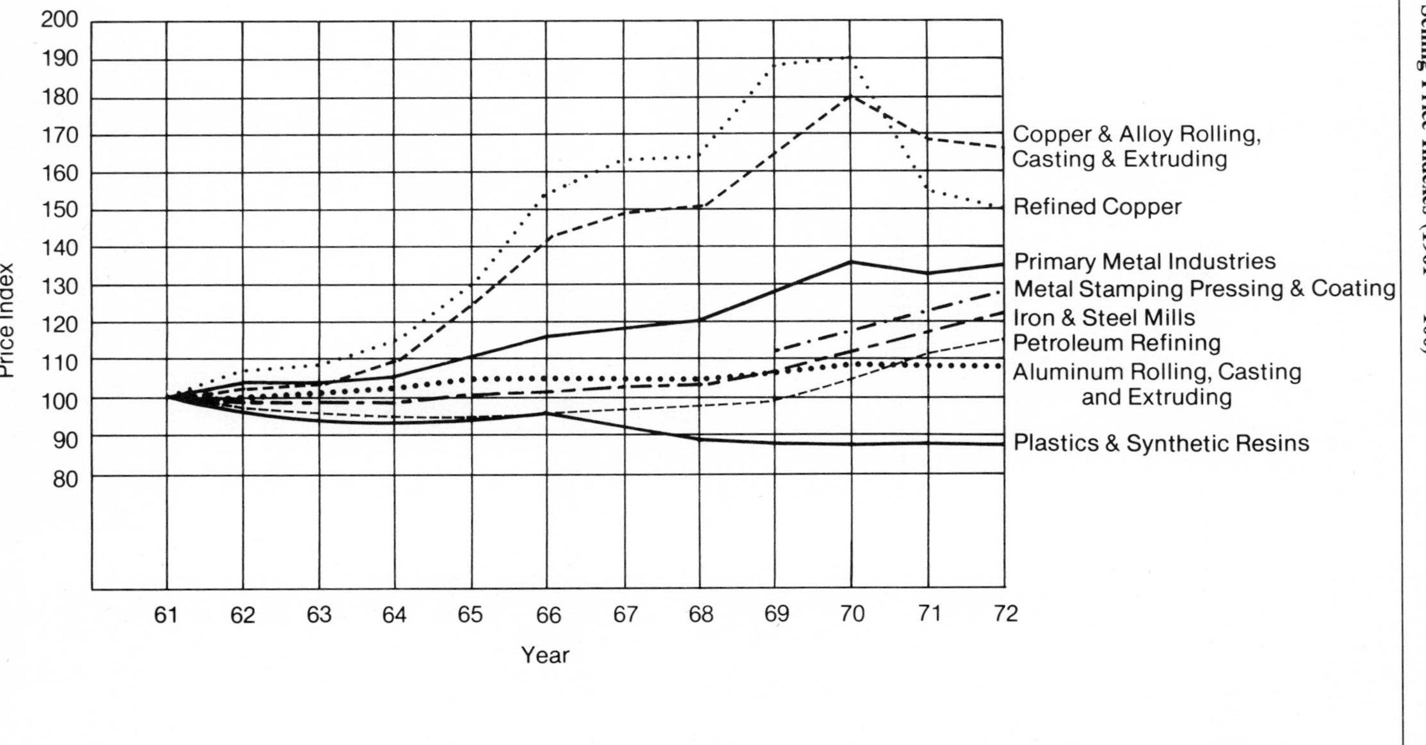

Exhibit 3. / Westinghouse's Format and Procedure for Price Adjustment—Attached to November 19, 1973 Memo From Mr. Johnson

PRICE ADJUSTMENT PROVISION

The contract price set out elsewhere is:

□ (a) firm for shipments made until .... .After this date the contract price will be adjusted for variations in labor and material costs using the following methods.

OR

□ (b) subject to adjustment for variations in labor and material costs from the date of this proposal using the following methods.

Labor

The labor portion of the contract shall be considered to be 50% of the contract price (excluding sales taxes and erection). This portion of the price will be revised to reflect the changes in "Average Hourly Earnings in the Electrical Industrial Equipment Industry" (DBS Catalogue 72-003) between the index for the month stated above and the average of the indices during the three months immediately preceding shipment.

Material

The materials portion of the contract shall be considered to be 40% of the contract price (excluding sales taxes and erection). This portion of the price will be revised to reflect the changes in the index for ....
....
....
....
....
....
....
....
.... (DBS Catalogue 62-002) between the index for the month stated above and the average of the indices during the six months immediately preceding shipment.

Erection

Where erection is included in the total contract price, this portion of the price is considered to be $ .... and will be revised to reflect the changes in.....
....
....
....
between the month of .... and the date of completion of erection.

Purchaser Reference ....Company Reference ....Page ....
Form 1124-5 Rev. 8-71

Exhibit 4. / Comments on WCL Escalation Policy

Statistics Canada Price Index Characteristics

1. Industry Selling Price Indexes reflect prices to Canadian producers for Canadian goods, but do not include imports, taxes, middlemen markups, or transportation.
2. Theoretically the Wholesale Price Indexes do include some imports, markups, and transportation but not taxes and therefore should reflect our costs more accurately. However, Statistics Canada do not recommend their use for escalation primarily because the sample from which they are derived is too small for confidence, and there is very little content of the above adders.

3. Statistics Canada is developing Input-Output Price Indexes to replace and increase the accuracy of GWIs, but these are "a couple of years away." In the meantime, they strongly recommend the use of ISPIs for escalation purposes, with the provision to change over when IOIs are available.
4. The 30 Industrial Materials Index is no good for us since only four of the components are applicable, and they are unweighted. Most are agricultural, mining, and forest products.
5. The ISPI indexes are suspected to reflect list or book prices in some cases rather than transaction prices, and therefore their movement will be damped and lag behind the market movements.
6. ISPI indexes for several segments of our industry are given by Electrical Products Industries Indexes. However, they do not reflect our costs and lag our cost movements so are no good for escalation.
7. ISPI indexes for goods we buy are the best available at present, but there is no single index to reflect our purchasing mix. Furthermore, the mix varies widely between divisions.
8. No index of average hourly earnings is available for the electrical products or electrical industrial equipment industries, but average hourly earnings is available for both Canada and Ontario. Electrical products only is available for Quebec and none for other provinces. Indexes can be derived from these earnings.

Recommendations

1. Survey the divisions to determine:
   a. Material vs. labor content
   b. Major components and weights of material purchases
2. Analyze responses and group divisions into those with similar patterns; 3 or 4 groups maximum.
3. Select ISPI indexes to reflect the major purchases of each group, including copper, aluminium, iron and steel, plastics, paper, petroleum, etc. Select aggregate rather than specific indexes where possible. (See** recommendations on attached table.)
4. Combine the key indexes for each group by purchasing weights.
5. For labor, use National Average Hourly Earnings for Electrical Industrial Equipment in Dollars and derive an index from the change in earnings.
6. Develop an escalation form on which the appropriate indexes and the method of weighting can be clearly defined and easily calculated.

Problems

1. Obtaining purchasing mix from division.
2. Selecting key indexes for division groups and combining them realistically.
3. Convincing customers of need for escalation.
4. Convincing customers that the index selection and weights are appropriate for a particular contract.
5. Combining more than one escalation clause in a mixed apparatus contract.
6. Possible different escalation clauses for alternate bids; e.g., copper or aluminium in bus duct or transformers.
7. Risk of loss during decline of volatile indexes; e.g., copper.
8. Provision for changeover to Input-Output indexes when available in "a couple of years."
9. Purchased services not covered.
10. Detailed Statistics Canada indexes are not published for up to six months, but are available by phone two to four months earlier. The most recently published index is preliminary and is frequently revised by up to a point the following month.
11. For WCL protection it would be preferable to base escalation on indexes developed in house from current purchasing experience. However, this would be difficult to administer and impossible to sell to customers.

APP Company*

APP is a large manufacturer of paper products, and corrugating medium is one of its major products. The company sells its corrugating medium both at home and abroad. For both of these markets, the company had consistently followed a full cost pricing policy (a cost-plus-mark-up-pricing). In late 1971, APP was faced with a pricing decision: How much should it bid on the 1972 contract for supplying 5,500 tons per season corrugating medium to an important foreign customer, SMFC. This customer was the largest fiber container maker in that part of the world. This contract represented approximately 50 percent of the local market. APP was the winner of the contract in each of the previous three years since SMFC was organized.

In late 1971, world trade was generally prosperous, and the real Gross Domestic Product in that part of the world jumped 8 percent and was forecast to increase by 10 percent the following year. This was a major foreign market of APP. For a long time, APP encountered very little competition there. But the market in 1971 changed. First, the world economic powers had recently abandoned the fixed exchange rates in favor of a floating exchange rate system, thus affecting the terms of trade. Second, the competitors, principally Japanese and Finnish, had shown a more aggressive attitude than ever before. For example, the Japanese raised their price by only 4 percent in spite of exchange rate adjustments of 6 percent or more against Japanese yen. Moreover, they expanded their capacity by 142,000 tons per day in 1971. So, apparently, APP was encountering a new competitive environment in that market.

The demand for corrugating medium is a derived demand. It is derived from the demand for fiber containers, which in turn is derived from the demand for other products. The demand for corrugating medium is therefore predominantly influenced by general economic activity.

On the other hand, the cost of corrugating medium is a small fraction of the total cost of a fiber container. The cost of a fiber container is, in turn, but a small fraction of the value or cost of the commodities in the container. Thus, the price of corrugating medium constitutes only a minute fraction of the cost or value of the goods in the container. Furthermore, fiber containers have only very imperfect substitutes, most of which are of much higher prices. All of these would indicate that the industry demand for corrugating medium is very price inelastic within a wide range of prices.

The company's management considered that its corrugating medium market at home indeed fit the above analysis, because the company was the largest in the industry at home, accounting for almost 70 percent of the industry's capacity and sales. Also, the home market was protected from outside competition by a high tariff. The management was confident that the company could maintain its prominence at home as long as its prices did not go well above the protected level.

---

*This case was prepared by Professor Franklin Ho of California State Polytechnic University, Pomona. Reprinted by permission.

In the past, the same analysis was applicable to the company's markets abroad. The company's corrugating medium markets abroad were concentrated in areas where the nation had special preferential trade agreements. Through experience, traditional ties, and preferential treaties, the company was able to secure those markets virtually as its home market.

But significant changes had taken place in the early 1970s. Traditional ties had been weakened. Powerful new competitors had emerged. At the same time, the cost of freight and production was expected to increase by 8 percent of the export prices for APP. Now the bidding price of the SMFC contract would determine the prevailing prices for that particular market. The APP local staff urged the management to forego the cost-plus-mark-up-pricing to meet the new competition in submitting the bid. In support of their position, they presented the following analysis:

The major competition of APP's corrugating medium in that part of the world came from the Japanese suppliers. The Finnish producers were only a minor factor. The local manufacturer, the United Pulp and Paper Corporation, being newly organized, produced insufficient quantities of inferior products so as to be a very inconsequential competitor, for at least the next five years.

The Japanese producers had the ability to obtain low freight rates for exports and had the capability of adjusting their medium export prices on a wide range, probably ± 10 percent without affecting their total production or profits. Although APP's freight and production costs are expected to increase in 1972, the Japanese suppliers will likely absorb any such increases and maintain their prices at previous levels.

The market in that part of the world could be divided into two segments: the contract and the noncontract markets. The contract market consisted of a buyer and a seller signing an exclusive one-year contract. There was only one buyer there doing this. With the noncontract market the buyers entered no exclusive agreement with sellers. They bought on the open market. These buyers (several small producers of fiber containers) were expected to purchase approximately 5,500 tons of corrugating medium in 1972. The price in the noncontract market was customarily 2.5 percent higher than in the contract market. There was little likelihood that this price spread would change in the foreseeable future. Thus, the contract market price automatically determined the noncontract market price.

The contract price in 1971 was $132.50 per ton. The noncontract market price was then $135. To be more specific, the 1971 prices in the noncontract market at the locality were as follows:

Suppliers	Prices Adjusted to Yield
APP	$135.00
Japanese	134.00
Finnish	123.50

As stated earlier, the Japanese suppliers increased their prices by 4 percent as a result of exchange rate adjustments in late 1971, and it would be unlikely that they would raise their prices again in 1972. If so, a rise of 3 percent of APP prices would bring APP prices at par with the Japanese suppliers'—all at $138.50 per ton on an adjusted-by-yield basis. In that event, APP probably would not lose any market share, even if the Finnish suppliers did not change their prices.

But a rise of more than 3 percent on the part of APP, assuming no further increase by the Japanese and no action by the Finnish, would probably cause the APP market share in the noncontract segment to drop from 70 percent to 30 percent or less. Furthermore, APP might also risk losing the 100 percent contract market segment by such a move.

The price elasticities of the company's corrugating medium at that particular market could be inferred, then, if the above conjecture were correct. With a further assumption of constant marginal cost and unit cost within the output range under consideration, a table could be constructed to show that the rational decision in that situation was to bid the contract at only 3 percent higher than the 1971 price, even though the cost of production and freight would be expected to increase by 8 percent. The staff presented the following tables to show their best estimates:

A. Contract Segment

If Price Rise %	Price $/Ton	Mkt. Share %	Tonnage	Gross Margin $/Ton	Gross Profit $
3	136	100	5,500	13.00	71,500
5	138	100	5,500	15.00	82,500
8	143	0	0	20.00	0

B. Noncontract Segment

If price Rise %	Price $/Ton	Mkt. Share %	Tonnage	Gross Margin $/Ton	Gross Profit $
3	138.5	70	3,850	15.5	59,675
5	141	30	1,980	18	29,700
8	145	5	275	22	6,050

C. Total Market (Both segments combined)

If Price Rise %	Mkt. Share %	Tonnage	Gross Profit $
3	85	9,350	131,175
5	65	7,480	112,200
8	2.5	275	6,050

On the basis of these estimates, the staff recommended a bid of 3 percent increase. This recommendation was forwarded to the management of the company. After a serious consideration of the situation, top management decided to submit a bid of 5 percent increase. SMFC awarded the contract to APP. But the noncontract market segment suffered a greater loss of sales than the staff anticipated. APP's tonnage sold in that market segment dropped to about 40 percent of the normal level. Why? While APP's prices went up by about 5 percent, the Finnish and Japanese competitors held firm at their previous prices. As a matter of fact, the Japanese suppliers even softened the previous exchange rate adjustment increase for a few months.

Virginia Chemicals Advertising*

Background

Headquartered in Portsmouth, Va., Virginia Chemicals, Inc., has had an annual net sales growth pattern as follows:

Year	Net Sales (million)	% Change from Previous Year
1970	32	4
1971	36	12
1972	44	22
1973	51	16
1974	69	35

The major portion of the company's sales is derived from the sale of bulk and packaged industrial chemicals for various processing industries, such as agriculture, food preservation, pharmaceutical, photographic, pulp and paper, textiles, and refrigeration. Mechanical equipment and parts related to refrigeration systems are also manufactured by the company. None of the company's products are sold in the mass-consumer markets. Virginia Chemicals, Inc., has facilities throughout the U.S. and Canada.

Advertising

Space advertising for the company is limited to industry trade publications. (Exhibit 1 shows a media scheduling plan for the industrial chemicals segment of company business.) With regard to media selection and scheduling, advertising manager Gene Abrams states that in 90 percent of the cases he follows the recommendations of the company's advertising agency, Vansant

*This case was prepared by Professors A. C. Ruppel and C. Allan Foster of the University of Virginia.

and Dugdale of Baltimore. He views media selection as a decision involving the agency's recommendation and common sense.

Abrams "inherited" Vansant and Dugdale when he joined the company as ad manager seven years ago. Virginia Chemicals has not actively sought out help from any other agency. Abrams feels that the relationship with the agency is good, pointing out that campaigns worked up for the company are rarely rejected. In most cases the agency provides at least three different campaigns for presentation in response to an ad work-up request. As noted previously, the company follows agency recommendations in 90 percent of the cases. They feel that if you are going to pay the agency to come up with appropriate recommendations, then those recommendations should be followed.

In late August or early September, Abrams meets with the vice president–director of marketing, who possesses input from his various product managers as to their products' current status, future market potential, and advertising needs. Also present is a representative from Vansant and Dugdale. For a couple of days the three merely kick ideas around concerning various advertising strategies and possibilities. Abrams refers to these meetings as "hopes, dreams, and ambitions" sessions. Shortly after these meetings, the advertising agency sends back to Abrams a call report outlining what the agency sees as relevant and where advertising emphasis should be. After carefully reviewing these reports Abrams goes to Baltimore where he sits down with the agency to tell them where they have missed the mark in coming up with salient and useful advertising strategies. Abrams feels that these exchanges of communication should ultimately accomplish two things:

1. Succinctly state the goals of advertising in the order of their importance;
2. Determine the amount of money needed to reach sales goals.

Ad manager Abrams feels that these sessions have been beneficial. The agency has been able to come up with good advertisements because specific needs and reasons for advertising in a certain area have been carefully predelineated.

Advertising Budget

On the question of how much to spend on advertising, Abrams relies heavily on experience and what he thinks he can justify to management. There are no set fixed rules for budget preparation. He states that the budget, by necessity, is somewhat nebulous.

Though it is not practiced at Virginia Chemicals, Abrams feels that the most intelligent and efficient way to determine an advertising budget is on a percentage of net sales-billed basis: His rationale is that this procedure ties advertising directly to overall operation plans and gives a fix on advertising levels and allocations. Exhibit 2 provides a breakdown of the current budget. Approximately $150,000 is spent on national advertisement production costs and space purchases.

Exhibit 1. / Industrial Chemicals—1975 Advertising Program

Month	J	F	M	A	M	J	J	A	S	O	N	D
American Dyestuff Reporter		•		•		•		•		•		•
Chemical Week	•	•	•	•	•	•	• — •	•	•	•	•	•
Chemical Marketing Reporter	• • • •	• • • •	• • • • •	• • • •	• • • •	• • • • •	• • • •	• • • •	• • • • •	• • • •	• • • •	• • • • •
Water and Sewage Works			•	•	•	•	•	•				
Journal American Water Works Assn.			•	•	•	•	•	•				
Pulp and Paper	•	•	•	•	•	• — •	•	•	•	•	•	•
TAPPI	•	•	•	•	•	•	•	•	•	•	•	•
Textile World	1976 •	•	•	•	•	•	•	•	•	•	•	•
Paper Age	•	•	•	•								
Paper Trade Journal	•											

Exhibit 2. / Advertising Expenditure Breakdown

Item	% of Total Advertising Expenditures
Ad Space-National	41%
Salaries	15
Sales Promotion	15
Annual Report	12
Ad Production Costs	9
Conventions	5
Travel and Entertainment	1
Price List Printing	1
Other Printing	1
TOTAL	100%

Lectron Corporation*

The Lectron Corporation was founded in the early 1970s by William Patton, with the objective of developing new electrical products for industrial and commercial markets. Prior to founding Lectron, Mr. Patton was the executive vice president of a leading electrical products manufacturing company and had 20 years successful experience in the electrical products industry.

After two years of extensive research and development at a cost of approximately $300,000, the Lectron control was developed. Although the product was being marketed primarily as a motor control, the general design of this unit is suitable for many electrical switching applications, including temperature controls, lighting controls, and as a motor control. During the development stage, sales were minimal and usually to selected industries for special applications which served to prove the product under normal operating conditions.

Recently Mr. Patton shifted his emphasis from development and field testing to consideration of how best to market the product with limited funds. The product by all estimates fits a market need, is technically sound, priced competitively, and has superior performance characteristics, yet is far from reaching its full market potential, estimated to be in the millions of dollars. As a result, a great deal of discussion and planning is being done to identify the type of marketing program that would lead to increased sales growth and the "take off" stage in the product life cycle.

Product

The Lectron motor control was a completely solid-state device; that is, it was totally electronic and had no mechanical moving parts. Its design was well tested and used only top quality components, such as those manufactured by RCA and Westinghouse. It met appropriate National Electrical Manufacturers Association standards and was the first such device approved for switching applications by Underwriter's Laboratory, a safety and circuit certification company. Underwriter's approvals are accepted and often required by state and industry safety departments and insurance companies.

The primary function of the Lectron control was to provide a "soft start," i.e., to reduce the heavy current inrush and starting torque of an electric motor. By avoiding the high initial current flow and torque, the following benefits occurred:

1. Reduced starting power requirements.
2. Reduced line voltage drop during motor starts.
3. Reduced possible damage to the motor and equipment that it drives.
4. Reduced thermal and electrical stress on motor and electrical circuits.

---

*This case prepared by Professor David McConaughy of the University of Southern California. Reprinted by permission.

The Lectron control was more trouble-free, provided smoother operation, was quieter, operated in a wider range of environments, and was less expensive than alternative ''soft-start'' equipment. Because of its solid state design, the Lectron control did not cause electromagnetic interference that was common with mechanical types of switching and thus reduced ''electromagnetic pollution,'' which was of growing concern to the FCC. Exhibits 1 and 2 show the product, and an example of the literature which lists some of the relevant data and benefits. Exhibit 3 gives the background on a highly successful application on a Coast Guard cutter which created a great deal of interest in the marine industry and received widespread publication in new product and new application sections of trade publications.

Competition

At the time, there was no direct competition, and the Lectron control was the only effective solid state product on the market. This probably would change in the future, as many solid state control circuits were being developed and published by component manufacturers and the Institute of Electrical Engineers. However, Mr. Patton does hold several comprehensive patents on the Lectron circuit. Electromechanical starters that provided a similar function produced by GE, Westinghouse, Allen-Bradley, and other firms were, of course, competition because they were an accepted method of ''soft-start'' control. Of these, the principal control being used was the auto-transformer. While this device limited initial power surge, it made a jerky shift to each power level as the current was increased. This jerky movement had a high burn-out risk compared to the Lectron control, which was smooth throughout the entire starting cycle. Other ''soft-start'' controls were the part winding starter, which may require a specially designed (thus costly) motor, and the primary resistor starter, which mechanically switched an electrical resistor bank in series with the motor as it was started. Exhibit 4 gives a brief comparison among the costs and features of the various starting devices. Exhibit 10 describes these different devices.

Market Potential

The exact market potential for the Lectron control was unknown because it could be used in a large number of industrial equipment and electrical control applications. The total market for motor and related controls of all types was in excess of $1 billion a year with the relevant control market perhaps as large as $800 million a year.

To aid in market planning, Mr. Patton collected available market data and developed a list of potential industrial applications where he felt that the Lectron control offered distinct advantages. Exhibit 5 lists the value of shipments of switchgear and control apparatus, Exhibit 6 lists the shipment of selected industries where the Lectron control could be used, and Exhibit 7 is a list of possible applications.

While the demand and shipments for industrial equipment were clearly derived from capital investment plans of industry, even in those years when such spending declined, the demand for labor-saving devices and motors rarely declined. Thus, Mr. Patton thought that general economic conditions should not affect the need for the Lectron control very much. On the other hand, developing a marketing program to sell to an industry that was having rapid growth, such as the pump and compressor industry (due to energy-related capital expansion and the growth of food processing), mining, and pulp and paper mills, might produce built-in growth once the Lectron control was adopted.

The customers that Lectron were currently selling to seemed unrelated by product or industry, and usually purchased the Lectron control for very limited and unusual applications where no other starter would work. Two major crane manufacturing companies were in the process of testing the Lectron control, and Mr. Patton hoped to sell 2,000 to 3,000 units in this market. Several brewing and bottling companies had successfully tested the Lectron device to control pumping operations and had expressed great enthusiasm for the product, although no formal commitments from either of these markets had yet been forthcoming. At a volume of 2,000 units the manufacturing margin was estimated to be about 75 percent.

In addition to his own efforts, Mr. Patton used six sales representatives in the major industrial areas of the country. Most orders, however, ended up being placed directly with the company as a result of several press releases describing the Lectron control, or as a result of Mr. Patton's work with selected customers. Orders were typically for one or only a few controls and were shipped by United Parcel Service after being built to order by the small production department.

Marketing Strategy

After five years of directing his attention to problems of product development and manufacturing, Mr. Patton became increasingly aware of the need for a comprehensive marketing plan if Lectron was to reach its full business potential. He was not sure that his sales representatives were effective in developing new markets, although his sales cost was only 8 percent of sales with this approach. Company-employed salespersons would be more committed to sell the product, except they were expensive, and Mr. Patton was not sure which companies and market areas to direct them to. Exhibit 8 lists some typical sales costs he had collected, but he recognized that selling costs were higher in major metropolitan areas, such as New York, Chicago, and San Francisco, where costs were 40 to 60 percent higher than average. In the smaller cities of the Southeast, such as Greenville, near the textile industry, costs were 15 to 20 percent below average.

Mr. Patton also developed a list of possible trade publications where Lectron advertising might be placed. Before he did any advertising, he wondered if he should get wholesale distribution so that customers could get local service and delivery of the product. He was not strongly in favor of distribution through wholesalers, as his earlier experience with electrical wholesalers led him to the conclusion that: (1) wholesalers didn't make an effort to push the product; (2) wholesalers carry too many other products; and (3) wholesalers really lacked the technical knowledge to understand potential applications. It seemed to him that some form of personal selling would be required, and if this were done properly, perhaps he might not have to advertise until he could better afford it, as the costs for advertising in many trade publications seemed quite high. Exhibit 9 lists the publications Mr. Patton was considering.

Mr. Patton had identified three possible marketing strategies he felt had some promise for success:

1. Sell product concept to electrical design engineers and OEM equipment manufacturers and encourage them to specify the Lectron Control or include it with their products or at least recommend it to their customers.
2. Sell control services by selling the control, including wiring and connecting equipment, to end users of equipment or possibly to OEM equipment manufacturers.
3. Sell control to manufacturing and maintenance buyers to solve a specific application problem or to reduce maintenance costs and breakage.

Other possible market considerations were selling to government agencies, such as the Coast Guard, or other manufacturers of controls even though there seemed to be little interest among the major manufacturers. Also, he wondered if he might be more successful if he sold the complete control package including possibly the motor rather than just the control alone.

As Mr. Patton cleared a space on his desk he wondered to himself if Thomas Edison and other pioneers in the electrical industry had gone through this process.

He then carefully began considering how to choose an appropriate marketing strategy that would hasten the success of the Lectron control.

Exhibit 1. / The Lectron Control

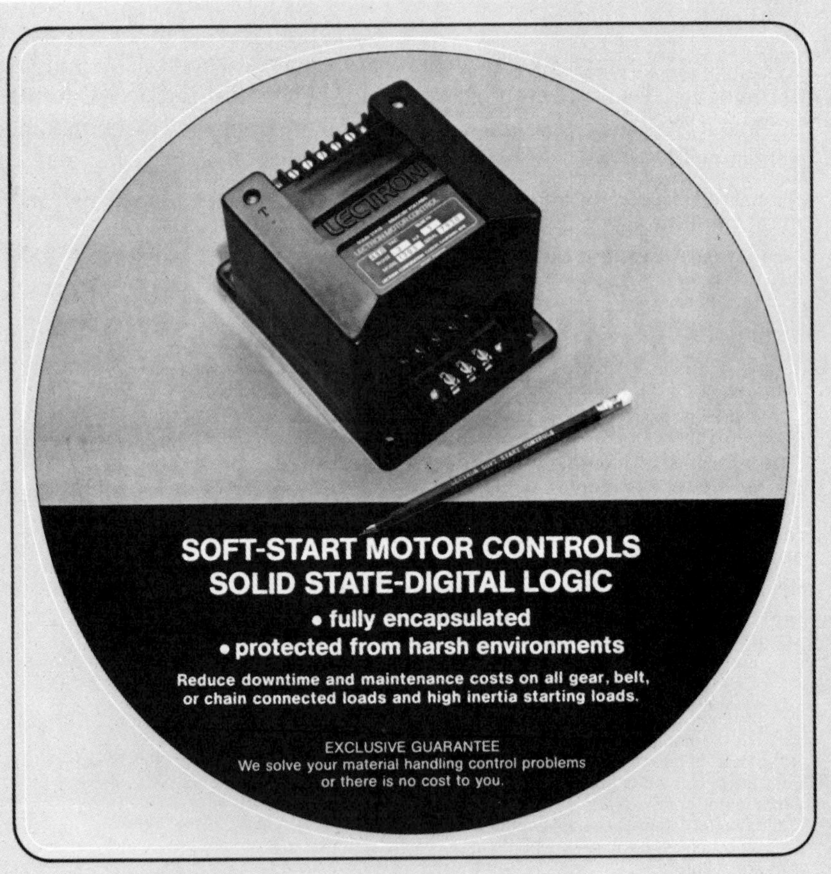

Exhibit 2. / The Lectron Control: Features and Applications

Lectron Soft-Start Controls

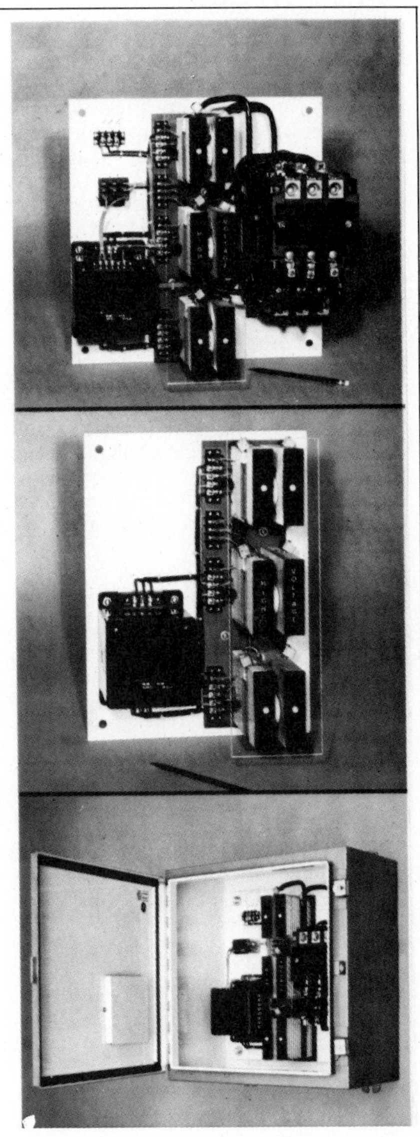

General Description:

Lectron soft-start controls are general-purpose devices for remote, automatic, or manual starting of three phase squirrel cage induction motors.

Starting characteristics, both torque and acceleration, are readily adjustable by access to simple adjustment screws through the top of the control module.

Switching options include low voltage, three wire momentary start/stop, 110 low voltage on/off or by contactor for reversing or dual speed operation.

The low voltage digital logic design, encompassing state of the art technology, insures perfect balance, reliability, long life, and easy interface with other control systems.

Applications:

- □Conveyor lines, both high-speed and heavy duty.
- □Bridge cranes and monorail systems.
- □Stackers, balancers, unloaders, etc.
- □Centrifugal blowers and pumps.
- □Other high-inertia starting loads.
- □Any belt, gear, or chain connected load.

Features:

- Adjustable starting torque—limits inrush and mechanical shock.
- □Adjustable rate of acceleration—1 to 30 seconds— standard (other by request).
- □Noiseless, maintenance-free operation.
- Fully encapsulated affected by difficult environmental conditions.
- Eliminates switching transients common to electromechanical devices—the prime cause of motor failure.
- Smooth, stepless transition from start to full-on.
- □Compact size—lightweight.
- □Guaranteed performance.

Exhibit 3. / Case History: Solid State, Reduced Voltage Motor Controls Give the Coast Guard a Low Cost Cure for Electronic Failure

Environment:

Coast Guard Cutter Point Carrew, operating out of the Eleventh Coast Guard District.

Problem:

The addition of electrical and electronic equipment on ocean going vessels, generally, and small craft, particularly, has taxed the generator and distribution system beyond its capacity to supply constant voltage. The condition becomes critical on start up of three-phase induction motors.

The voltage drop on normal starting of a three horsepower motor reduced line voltage below the tolerance of electronic equipment such as Radar, thus creating a potential hazard and, at best, an interruption in communications.

Test Duration:

Device installed June 14, 1972 and is still operating as of this date, November 24, 1972.

Solution:

Repeated tests using the LECTRON MOTOR CONTROL showed no visible effect on the Radar performance. There was no detectable radio interferance on AM and FM receivers. The test installation was considered 100% satisfactory and seems an attractive cure for electronic failure caused by voltage fluctuations that exist on many cutters and boats. It appears more cost effective than the alternatives of individual voltage regulators and rewiring to provide a separate, quiet ship's distribution system.

Comparative Cost:

	Autotransformer Reduced Voltage Starter	Lectron Solid-State Control
Material Cost (Note)	$1,100	$265
Installation Cost	$100 (est)	$20
Weight	80 lbs (est)	3.5 lbs
Volume	7060 cu in.	64 cu in.
Moving Parts	17	0

Note: The Autotransformer consisted of a total replacement of existing controls, whereas, the Lectron device was a retro-fit unit installed within and compatible with the existing system.

Comparative Performance:

	Before Installation	After Installation
Bus Volts (steady state)	450 Volts	450 Volts
Bus Volts–max drop	20 Volts	5 Volts
Current Starting Surge	28 Amps	8 Amps
Current–Steady State	4.3 Amps	4.3 Amps

The material contained herein was furnished by the United States Coast Guard, Eleventh Coast Guard District. It should not be considered as Coast Guard approval nor a recommendation of the Lectron Solid State Motor Control.

Exhibit 4. / Comparison Among Features and Prices for Selected 10-Horsepower Motor Starters

Type of Control	Type of Start	Size	Weight	List Price	Comments
Magnetic Starter	On-Off Only	12″×7″×6″	15 lbs.	$ 162	Switches full power only.
Primary Resistor	Stepped-Smooth	29″×18″×10″	120 lbs.	$ 839	Low efficiency.
Autotransformer	Stepped-Smooth	35″×24″×12″	450 lbs.	$1139	Most widely used reduced voltage starter.
Part Winding	Stepped-Smooth	21″×14″×7″	100 lbs.	$ 448	Requires special motor with winding taps.
Star-Delta	One-Step Start	35″×35″×12″	210 lbs.	$ 695	Three-phase motors only.
Lectron	Continuous-Smooth	12″×10″×5¾″	15 lbs.	$ 875	Solid state—no moving parts.

Source: Company records.

Exhibit 5. / Value of Shipments of Selected Switchgear and Control Apparatus 1974

SIC	Product	Number of Producing Companies	Shipments (Mil$)	Growth 1973–74
3613 701	Magnetic Control Circuit Relays	56	$256.5	9.3%
3613 704	Starter Accessories, Inc., Overload Relays	25	17.2	3.6%
3622 012	A.C. Full Voltage Starters 600 Volts or Less	42	182.9	27.4%
3622 013	A.C. Contactors 600 Volts or Less	30	37.5	-6.0%
3622 011	A.C. Reduced Voltage Controls	19	25.2	NA
3622 015	Synchronous Motor Starters	6	NA	NA
3622 016	Motor Control Centers	55	145.1	54.0%
3622 018	Starters and Contractors for Motors over 600 Volts	21	37.3	33.2%
3622 081	Rheostats and Resistors	17	20.1	39.6%
3622 097	All Other General Industry Devices	48	268.1	28.5%
3622 045	Marine and Navy Auxiliary Controls and Accessories	18	27.0	.4%
3622 048	Metal Mill, Crane and Hoist Controls, Constant and Adjustable Voltage	30	66.3	11.6%
3622 049	Definite Purpose Contractors and Starters for Refrigeration and Air Conditioning	9	23.5	NA

Source. U.S. Department of Commerce

Exhibit 6. / Selected Industry Data

Industry Category	SIC	1975 Shipments (Mil$)	Establishments	Average Annual Growth Rate 1967–75: Shipments	Average Annual Growth Rate 1967–75: Exports	Major Producing Areas
Pumps and Compressors	3561 3563	$4,700	643	10.8%	15.6%	North Central Northeast
Material Handling Equipment	3534 3535 3536 3537	$3,720	1,250	5.7%	17.9%	Middle Atlantic North Central Western
Mining Machinery	3532	$1,550	240	14.5%	16.4%	Pennsylvania West Virginia Ohio
Oil Machinery	3533	$3,250	314	20.6%	28.6%	Texas Oklahoma California Louisiana
Food Products Machinery	3551	$1,745	675	10.8%	16.1%	North Central California New York
Textile Machinery	3552	$ 845	578	1.8%	12.7%	Northeast Southeast
Switchgear	3613	$2,760	898	5.0%	NA	NA
Motors and Generators	3621	$3,125	775	4.0%	NA	NA
Industrial Controls	3622	$2,093	1,173	6.0%	NA	NA
Shipbuilding	3731	$4,710	455	8.6%	NA	Great Lakes East, West, and Gulf Coasts

Source. U.S. Department of Commerce

Exhibit 7. / Potential Applications

Blowers
Centrifugal
Constant Pressure

Brick Plants
Augers
Conveyors
Dry Pans
Pug Mills

By-Product Coke Plants
Door Machines
Leveler Rams
Pusher Bars
Valve Reversing Machines

Cement Mills
Conveyors
Crushers
Dryers—Rotary
Elevators
Grinders, Pulverizers
Kilns

Coal Mines
Car Hauls
Conveyors
Cutters
Fans
Hoists—Slope
Hoists—Vertical
Jigs
Picking Tables
Rotary Car Dumpers
Shaker Screens

Compressors
Constant Speed
Varying Speed
 Centrifugal
 Plunger Type

Cranes—General Purpose
Hoist
Bridge or Trolley—Sleeve Bearing
Bridge or Trolley—Roller Bearing

Concrete Mixers

Flour Mills
Line Shafting

Food Plants
Butter Churns
Dough Mixers

Hoists
Mine Hoists—Slope
Mine Hoists—Vertical
Contactors Hoist
Winch

Larry Car

Lift Bridges

Machine Tools
Bending Rolls
Boring Mills
Bull Dozers
Drills
Gear Cutters
Grinders
Hobbing Machines
Lathes
Milling Machines
Presses
Punches
Saws
Shapers

Exhibit continued on following page.

Exhibit 7. / Potential Applications ***(Continued)***

Material Handling
Coal and Ore Bridges:
- Holding
- Closing
- Trolley
- Bridge

Metal Mining
Ball, Rod, or Tube Mills
Car Dumpers—Rotary
Converters—Copper
Conveyors
Crushers
Tilting Furnace

Paper Mills
Beaters
Calendars

Pipe Working
Cutting and Threading
Expanding and Flanging

Power Plants
Clinker Grinders
Coal Crushers
Conveyors—Belt
Conveyors—Screw
Pulverized Fuel Feeders
Pulverizers, Ball Type
Pulverizers, Centrifugal Type
Stokers

Pumps
Centrifugal
Plunger

Rubber Mills
Calendars
Crackers
Mixing Mills
Washers

Steel Mills
Accumulators
Casting Machines—Pig
Charging Machines
- Bridge
- Peel Revolving
- Trolley

Coiling Machines
Conveyors
Converters—Metal
Cranes
- Hoist
- Bridge and Trolleys, Sleeve Bearing
- Bridge Trolleys, Roller Bearing

Crushers
Furnace Doors
Gas Valves
Gas Washers
Hot Metal Mixers
Ingot Buggy
Kick Off
Levelers
Manipulator Fingers
Pickling Machine
Pliers—Slab
Racks
Reelers
Saws—Hot or Cold
Screw Downs
Shears
Shuffle Bars
Side Guards
Sizing Rolls
Slab Buggy
Soaking Pit Covers
Straighteners
Tables
- Approach
- Roll
- Shear Approach
- Lift
- Main Roll
- Transfer
- Tilting Furnaces
- Wiring Stranding Machines

Exhibit 7. / Potential Applications *(Continued)*

Textiles	*Wood Working Plants*
Weaving	Boring Machines
Knitting	Lathe
Throwing	Mortiser
Winding	Moulder
Tufting	Planers
	Power Trimmer and Mitre
	Sanders
	Saws
	Shapers
	Shingle Machines

Exhibit 8. / Productivity and Costs for Selected Types of Salespersons

		Metropolitan Area		Suburban Area	
Type of Salesperson	Average Direct Cost	Calls/ Year	Cost/ Call	Calls/ Year	Cost/ Call
Account Representative—calls on already established customers; selling is low key with minimal pressure to develop new business.	$23,500	1,195	$20	598	$39
Detail Salesperson—performs promotional activities and introduces new products; actual sale is ultimately made through a wholesaler.	$20,500	1,912	$11	1,195	$17
Sales Engineer—sells products where technical know-how and technical aspects are important to sale; experience in identifying and solving customers' problems is required.	$29,750	1,030	$29	665	$45
Industrial Products Salesperson—sells a tangible product to industrial or commercial purchasers; a high degree of technical knowledge is not required.	$25,000	1,673	$15	956	$26
Intangibles/Service Salesperson—must be able to sell effectively intangible benefits such as design services or application concepts.	$24,250	2,153	$11	1,195	$20

Source. Sales and Marketing magazine, February 9, 1976

Exhibit 9. / Cost and Circulation Data on Selected Trade Publications

Magazine	Circulation	Cost of B & W Page	Comments
Automaton	90,223	$2,280	Production engineering emphasis; trade show issues.
Control Engineering	70,627	$1,925	Instrumentation and automatic control emphasis.
Design News	123,189	$2,760	Design engineer's idea magazine.
Electrical Apparatus	15,031	$ 750	Magazine of electromechanical operation and maintenance, edited for the after-market.
Electrical Contractor	40,004	$1,350	Electrical construction and maintenance industry.
Electrical Construction and Maintenance	70,521	$2,295	
Electrical Equipment	75,060	$3,053	Edited for electrical and electromechanical engineers who research, design, and install electrical or electromechanical products.
Electrified Industry	32,600	$1,110	Edited for electrically responsible engineers; covers automation, electric controls, material handling, and electrical maintenance.
Electrical Wholesaling	16,114	$1,350	Controlled circulation to electrical distributors; sourcebook of electrical wholesaling, marketing, and selling.
Factory	91,086	$2,590	General interest manufacturing magazine.
Food Processing	56,031	$1,420	New product reports, case histories; covers processing equipment, material handling, etc.
Industrial Equipment News	142,735	$7,915	What's new in equipment, parts, and materials; covers literature and catalogs that are available.
Industrial Maintenance and Plant Operation	105,581	$3,390	News tabloid magazine for those responsible for maintenance and operation of industrial plants.
Machine Design	127,419	$2,554	
Marine Engineering/ Log	22,490	$ 800	Covers new developments in marine engineering and naval construction.
Materials Handling Engineering	76,733	$2,090	Technical magazine for material handling, packaging, and shipping specialists.
New Equipment Digest	139,120	$2,340	Covers equipment, materials, processes, and design literature and catalogs.

Exhibit 9. / Cost and Circulation Data on Selected Trade Publications (*Continued*)

Pit and Quarry	22,242	$1,085	Directed to management who specify and buy equipment, supplies, and services for mining, quarrying, and processing non-metallic minerals.
Purchasing	74,498	$2,385	News magazine for industrial buyers.

Source. Standard Rate and Data Service, June 24, 1976

Exhibit 10. / Starting Devices: Product Description

Auto-Transformer Control

Auto-transformer-type starters are the most widely used reduced voltage starter because of their efficiency and flexibility. All power taken from the line, except transformer losses, is transmitted to the motor to accelerate the load. Taps on the transformer allow adjustment of the starting torque and inrush to meet the requirements of most applications. The following characteristics are produced by the three voltage taps:

Tap	Starting Torque % Locked Torque	Line Inrush % Locked Ampere
50%	25%	28%
65%	42%	45%
80%	64%	67%

Part Winding Controls

Part winding starting provides convenient economical one-step acceleration at reduced current where the power company specifies a maximum, or limits the increments of current drawn from the line. These starters can be used with standard dual-voltage motors on the lower voltage and with special part-winding motors designed for any voltage. When used with standard dual-voltage motors, it should be established that the torque produced by the first half-winding will accelerate the load sufficiently so as not to produce a second undesirable inrush when the second half-winding is connected to the line. Most motors will produce a starting torque equal to between 1/2 to 2/3 of NEMA standard values with half of the winding energized and draw about 2/3 of normal line current inrush.

Primary Resistor

Primary resistor-type starters, sometimes known as "cushion-type" starters, will reduce the motor torque and starting inrush current to produce a smooth, cushioned acceleration with closed transition. Although not as efficient as other methods of reduced voltage starting, primary resistor-type starters are ideally suited to applications such as conveyors, textile machines, or other delicate machinery where reduction of starting torque is of prime consideration. Starters through size 5 will limit inrush to approximately 80% of lock rotor current and starting torque to approximately 64% of locked torque. Larger sizes are custom designed to the application.

Star-Delta Control

Star-Delta-type starters have been applied extensively to industrial air conditioning installations because they are particularly applicable to starting motors driving high inertia loads with resulting long acceleration times. They are not, however, limited to this application. When six or twelve lead delta-connected motors are started star-connected, approximately 58% of full line voltage is applied to each winding and the motor develops 33% of normal locked rotor current from the line. When the motor has accelerated, it is reconnected for normal delta operation.

Subject Index

Name Index